AF750725

Munich Studies on Innovation and Competition

Volume 3

Series Editors
Josef Drexl, Germany
Reto M. Hilty, Germany

More information about this series at
http://www.springer.com/series/13275

Anna Friederike Busch

Protection of Traditional Cultural Expressions in Latin America

A Legal and Anthropological Study

Springer

Anna Friederike Busch
Berlin
Germany

ISSN 2199-7462 ISSN 2199-7470 (electronic)
Munich Studies on Innovation and Competition
ISBN 978-3-662-46769-5 ISBN 978-3-662-46770-1 (eBook)
DOI 10.1007/978-3-662-46770-1

Library of Congress Control Number: 2015939267

Springer Heidelberg New York Dordrecht London
© Springer-Verlag Berlin Heidelberg 2015
This work is subject to copyright. All rights are reserved by the Publisher, whether the whole or part of the material is concerned, specifically the rights of translation, reprinting, reuse of illustrations, recitation, broadcasting, reproduction on microfilms or in any other physical way, and transmission or information storage and retrieval, electronic adaptation, computer software, or by similar or dissimilar methodology now known or hereafter developed.
The use of general descriptive names, registered names, trademarks, service marks, etc. in this publication does not imply, even in the absence of a specific statement, that such names are exempt from the relevant protective laws and regulations and therefore free for general use.
The publisher, the authors and the editors are safe to assume that the advice and information in this book are believed to be true and accurate at the date of publication. Neither the publisher nor the authors or the editors give a warranty, express or implied, with respect to the material contained herein or for any errors or omissions that may have been made.

Printed on acid-free paper

Springer-Verlag GmbH Berlin Heidelberg is part of Springer Science+Business Media (www.springer.com)

"Nothing is more thrilling or beautiful than the flight of Morpho butterflies,
filling the dark trails of tropical forests with scintillating blue flashes from their iridescent wings. . . .
I have sat for many pleasant hours with the Kayapó watching
the kilometers-long strings of 'were-ngrãngrã' . . . and their ribbons of colour as they hover, drink and flutter on the sandy beaches and river banks. . .
. . .it is predictable that insects would play an important role in cultural knowledge, material culture and belief systems of Amerinds."
Darrell Addison Posey, in: D.A. Posey and K. Plenderleith (Eds.), 2004, Indigenous Knowledge and Ethics. A Darrell Posey Reader, Routledge New York and London

".... and . . . you cannot step twice into the same stream."
Heraclitus (as quoted by Plato, Carylus, in 402, a).

Preface

This thesis was written at the Max Planck Institute for Innovation and Competition and the Faculty of Law of the Ludwig Maximilians University of Munich. Part of research was done through field research in Panama, Ecuador, Brazil and Argentina.

The work contributes to interdisciplinary research at the interface of law and anthropology, in the area of intellectual property (IP) rights and customary law.

I would like to thank, first of all, my supervisor Prof. Dr. Josef Drexl, LL.M. (Berkeley), Director of the Max Planck Institute for Innovation and Competition, and my second referee Prof. Dr. Dr. h.c. Wolfgang Fikentscher, LL.M. (Michigan), for their outstanding support and supervision of this thesis, highly valuable advice and inspiring discussions.

I would also like to thank Sibylle Schlatter, my academic advisor, for her exceptional support and personal engagement, Adj Professor (Franklin Pierce Center for IP, Uni of NH) Dr. Silke von Lewinski, for highly valuable discussions and for inviting me to the XIII. Session of the IGC on Intellectual Property and Genetic Resources, Traditional Knowledge and Folklore of WIPO, Prof. Marie-Claire Foblets, Director of the Max Planck Institute for Social Anthropology and Prof. Dr. Dr. h.c. Annette Kur, Dr. des. Anna Meiser for the valuable input, and the Max Planck Institute for Innovation and Competition for the scholarship and financial support of the international research.

I can't thank enough the Latin American contributors to this work, who supported my research on the ground and shared their practical experiences, including Yahelis Arenas, Aresio Valiente López, Atencio López Martinez, Luis Touaris—one of the most impressive encounters of my life, Luz Celeste Ríos de Davis, Rodrigo de la Cruz, Egberto Tabo Chipunavi, Valentín Muíba, Jenny Muñoz, Karin Grau-Kuntz, Marcos Alves de Souza, Juliana Santilli, José Carlos Levinho, Ana Cristina Bandeira Lins, Daniel Mundurukú, Fernanda Kaingang, Luciano Cuervo M., Fernando Zapata, Alberto Usieto-Blanco.

Finally, and above all, I want to thank my family.

Berlin, Germany
2014

Anna Friederike Busch

Contents

Chapter I. Introduction

On April 24, 1973, the president of the Andean country of Bolivia approached the then Director General of UNESCO, asking him in a now historic memorandum to investigate "whether an international instrument protecting folklore could be elaborated."[1] That was only shortly after Simon and Garfunkel had released their version of "El Condor Pasa" in 1970, which became a world hit based upon, or even a copy of, a traditional Andean folk song.

Around 30 years later, in 2003, another case in an Andean country, this time Colombia, created a furore: the unauthorized use of a traditional design of isolated indigenous peoples of the Colombian Amazon region in an international fashion show in Bogotá.[2] Still, neither a national nor an international system of appropriate protection stood at hand—and this is still the case.

As reaction to the Bolivian president's approach of UNESCO back in the 1970s, the idea was to attach a Protocol on the preservation, commercialization, and dissemination of folklore to either an international convention on copyright[3] or the Universal Convention on Human Rights.[4] The issue appeared to be "quite complex", as Lucas-Schlötter tells, and a UNESCO expert committee suggested examining the whole topic following two paths: a multidisciplinary approach

[1] Lipszyc (1993) 96.

[2] The design of the Nukak Makuk people was used by the John Estrada Foundation. According to investigations by *El Tiempo*, the designer committed himself to donate 7% of the total sales of his collection in favor of the Nukak Makuk peoples. However, it was never mentioned or manifested that this design belonged to the Nukak Makuk as collective intellectual property and a prior informed consent to the use of the design was never obtained, *El Tiempo* reported. The Nukak Makuk indigenous people are semi-nomads and live in voluntary isolation and maybe never learned that someone is economically benefiting from their cultural richness. *See* El Tiempo, "Nukak Fashion", March 17, 2003, cited from CHIRAPAQ/Rivera Zea (2007) 90 note 20. This is at the same time one of the very few cases of TCEs infringement reported from Latin America.

[3] Lipszyc (1993) 96 and Unterguggenberger (1999) 176.

[4] Lucas-Schlötter (2008) 446 note 532.

© Springer-Verlag Berlin Heidelberg 2015

A.F. Busch, *Protection of Traditional Cultural Expressions in Latin America*,
Munich Studies on Innovation and Competition 3, DOI 10.1007/978-3-662-46770-1_1

conducted by UNESCO on the one hand and an intellectual property approach assisted by WIPO on the other.[5]

This was the beginning of intense international discussions on an appropriate way of protecting what is now called "traditional cultural expressions", TCEs. Since then scientists and practitioners have published contributions treating the topic from different perspectives. In the Latin American ambit, a supranational organization—the Andean Community—has worked out elements for a possible future legislation, and one country—Panama—has found its own sui generis legislative solution meanwhile. Others are still discussing. The WIPO Intergovernmental Committee (IGC) on Intellectual Property and Genetic Resources, Traditional Knowledge and Folklore had its first meeting in 2001, and the process of seeking an adequate protection of *inter alia* TCEs or "expressions of folklore" continues with growing intensity and interest, and finds itself at a crucial stage these days.

When it comes to the question of whether at all, and if so, how to protect these TCEs—especially against the background of a search for an adequate protection of TCEs at the international level—Latin America can provide many examples and helpful insights. Why and what is so special about Latin America in this regard?

(1) Latin America was the cradle of the international movement towards an adequate protection of TCEs, as mentioned above.
(2) The continent is still one of the places of the greatest biological and socio-cultural diversity in the world today and hosts a rich cultural heritage, including TCEs.
(3) Similarly, the legal situations regarding TCEs in the different countries are diverse, and thus allow differentiated observation, description, and comparison.
(4) A general tendency can be noted towards a higher estimation of the traditional culture and towards legal acknowledgement of the different socio-cultural patterns, mainly the importance of the phenomenon of collectivity in general, as well as TCEs as legally relevant categories in particular.[6]
(5) Within the framework of factual and legal diversity of the continent, there are some countries that have indeed established concrete legal solutions on protecting TCEs.

Section 1. Aim, Focus, and Background of the Study

The aim of this study is to provide insights, draw consequences, and formulate concrete recommendations.

It focuses on general, Latin-America-wide aspects of the topic on the one hand, and gives specific insights into situations of selected countries on the other. The

[5] *Id.*

[6] On this *see* at Chapter II Section 3.A. and Chapter III Section 3.A. below.

connecting bridge is the exposition of international, regional, and national legal frameworks and examples of dealing with TCEs. Thereby, one important principle of international private law is considered: to classify the content of legal solutions in the field in question and qualitatively compare them, instead of sticking to certain national legal conceptions or divisions into legal areas. Thus, framing constitutional aspects are considered as well as intellectual property legislation; and cultural law, contractual solutions, case law, and customary law are included as well.

The review of the current international discussions and publications has shown that, so far, a great emphasis lies on either general political and social observations and statements, or on highly technical details of legal regulations concerning the issue, the latter mainly originating from the area of traditional knowledge and biodiversity. The Peruvian Law on Traditional Knowledge and Biodiversity, for example, as well as the 2002 WIPO Model Law for the Pacific, are acknowledged as being technically advanced but lacking successful results with regard to their practical implementation and positive perception by the indigenous peoples concerned.[7] In the scientific sphere where TCEs play a role, evaluations of legislations have been made mainly from a theoretical point of view,[8] which, especially in developing countries, leads to a very different perception than the situation in reality.[9]

At the international level, as a key issue, "a past failure of dialogue and mutual incomprehension" had been diagnosed, and the intergovernmental process at WIPO has attempted to take "steps to ensure that the voices of indigenous and local communities" would be "central to the work" of the IGC.[10] Regardless of such noble goals, the way the topic is mainly discussed in the scientific legal area, and how "representatives" of "indigenous peoples" have been involved at the international and Latin American national levels, shows that this attempt is far from a successful aim. It is still a key issue and challenge in the question of whether and how to adequately protect TCEs.[11]

To a certain degree, this study will show that parts of the dilemma of mutual incomprehension and unadaptable models of legal protection will remain unsolved. Nonetheless, some important steps can be made forward—involving both sides moving toward each other. Thus, instead of designing another technically well-elaborated proposal for a legal instrument, the problem will be treated here from a broader perspective. In addition to the legal examination of existing and potential future regimes from a law-on-paper perspective, the focus of this study is placed on enabling a more successful intercultural dialog in the legislative process and

[7] On the discussion in Peru *see* Bucher (2008) 182 *et seq.*

[8] On TCEs and the indigenous legislation in Chile, for example, *see* Lucas-Schlötter (2008) 444.

[9] For general studies on the indigenous legislation on paper and in reality *see* Heise (2000).

[10] Taubman and Leistner (2008) 33 *et seq.*

[11] On indigenous voices in Brazil *see* Busch (2010) 215–221 and, on the situation of the Peruvian legislative process of establishing Law *see* Bucher (2008) 182 *et seq.*

beyond, as well as a better understanding of the anthropological situation and the effectiveness of measures in reality.

The aspect of considering law and reality is of special relevance in the Latin American area of TCEs. Although generalizations always imply inaccuracies, political experts have observed that maybe the "biggest internal contradiction" of the region is that normatively, Latin America seems to be a part of the "far West." But regarding implementation, in its political, social and economic structures, the situation in the great majority Latin American countries reveals "vast segments of underdevelopment."[12] More precisely, the specific area of traditional or indigenous rights is dominated by "an ambivalent and bitter-sweet sensation:"[13] Demands on *inter alia* cultural rights have attained a certain international legitimacy by having been introduced in different international agendas, but they lack a more practical approach and implementation in the local realities, especially concerning the relationship between indigenous communities and states, Barié argues.[14] The "true test" of a (new) right would therefore be whether it has an impact on the every day life of the indigenous peoples or local communities.[15] In this manner, the country rated perhaps *the* Latin American country on the "best" path towards the establishment of favorable legal conditions of life for the indigenous population, Colombia, is at the same time the place where legal implementation, at least in indigenous territories, finds itself in rather poor if not "desolate" condition, Semper argues.[16] In view of these findings, one aim of this study is also to consider the situation of the law, namely, existing or potential legal instruments on TCEs in reality.

Prioritizing this latter aspect over the elaboration of another proposal of a legal instrument in theory also reflects the fact that an adoption, not to mention the implementation of a regional or other national sui generis regime, is currently unlikely. Probably producing a paper tiger would have even more predictable results, as the paper itself could literally be a "killer" of the traditional cultures e.g. in the Amazon region. From an office-desk perspective in a developed country this might seem quite a stretch. But in the every-day reality of indigenous communities in the Amazon region, this apparently poor connection is a very close and

[12] *See* Mols (2009) 67, for the political situation in general.

[13] Barié (2008) 33.

[14] *Id.*

[15] Natalia Álvarez Molinero "Pueblos Indígenas, comunidad internacional y derechos humanos en la era de la globalización" (2004) 64, cited from Barié (2008) 33.

[16] Besides the "special nature of the indigenous rights," *Semper* sees the main reason for the lack of implementation of indigenous rights in the *de facto* "state of war" between governmental security forces, paramilitary units and rebels in the Colombian countryside and especially in indigenous territories, "where extralegal executions, murdering, kidnapping, forced recruitments, and expulsions take place". Improving this situation would not require the establishment of further specific legal instruments, but "simply" a demilitarization of indigenous territories – a task that the Colombian state is currently not capable of fulfilling, argues Semper (2008) 154.

bitterly felt one, as deforestation and other environmental exploitation directly impact the "objects" and "subjects of protection" and thus the vitality of TCEs.[17]

To disregard such interdependences would be to fall short of the mark. Identifying, considering, and evaluating small elements that form relevant connections is essential for understanding the topic in its full dimension and for analyzing adequate solutions.

Notwithstanding the attempt to follow a broad approach, some restrictions have to be made in order to pursue the main aim and focus explained above. Thus, the protection of languages is a peculiar topic requiring the consideration of distinct particularities and will therefore not be a subject of this thesis.[18] Suffice it to indicate here that languages form an essential part of traditional or any other culture, they are an essential part of preserving cultural diversity,[19] and the American continent is said to have the highest concentration of linguistic families in the world.[20] Closely related to the issue of traditional languages is that of education, i.e. the mode and content of education, the question of rights to bilingual education, and teaching of traditional culture. This will also not be dealt with in detail here. Interesting to note is, however, that the sui generis regime in Panama has included provisions on the topic, which will be displayed shortly in the national context.[21] TCE-related education has also been considered as a subject in personal interviews and fieldwork missions, as it is one of the most important factors for passing along traditional cultural expressions to the coming generations, and thus keeping TCEs alive.

Section 2. Concrete Research Questions

Against the background of this broader aim, a number of concrete research questions can be formulated. These research questions are of a descriptive character on the one hand and an analytical, comparative, and evaluating nature on the other. Specifically, they are:

---

[17] Personal communication with Jenny Muñoz of the Asháninka Indians living in the Peruvian Amazon Region on June 10, 2008.

[18] For an overview of the topic of languages and intellectual property rights *see* the example of Mexico: http://www.digerpi.gob.pa/pls/portal/docs/PAGE/NOTICIAS/CONGRESO_DERECHO_COLECTIVO/GEORGANNE%20WELLER-MÉXICO.PDF. Noteworthy is the case of the Chilean Mapuche Indians opposing the decision of Microsoft "to launch its Windows software package in Mapuzugun, a Mapuche tongue spoken by around 400,000 indigenous Chileans, mostly in the south of the country," *see* http://www.williams.edu/go/native/mapuchelang.htm, and the announcement of Microsoft at http://www.microsoft.com/chile/mapuzugun/, last visited January 20, 2011.

[19] *See, e.g.*, Article 5 of the 2001 Universal Declaration on Cultural Diversity of UNESCO.

[20] http://www.digerpi.gob.pa/pls/portal/docs/PAGE/NOTICIAS/CONGRESO_DERECHO_COLECTIVO/GEORGANNE%20WELLER-MÉXICO.PDF.

[21] *See* at Chapter IV Section 1.C.X. below.

(1) What is understood by TCEs in the Latin American region, what is the subject matter, and who are the bearers involved?
(2) How are TCEs legally protected in the Latin American region and which alternative ways are discussed?
(3) In particular, how are the core issues dealt with, namely: use of terminology, customary law, indigenous cosmovision, ways of negotiating, and dispute resolution?
(4) How can the existing protection be evaluated legally and factually ("law on paper"—"law in reality"), including the points of view of peoples concerned?
(5) Could a regional agreement on sui generis protection, similar to the WIPO Pacific Model Law, be a solution within the Latin American ambit?
(6) What kind of insights, perceptions, and lessons learned can be gleaned, and what recommendations formulated, which could be of use for the current discussions and negotiations at the national, regional, and international levels?

Section 3. Methods Applied

To approach these issues, the following methods and theoretical foundations have been applied:

A. Classic Juridical Methods

In line with the historical and personal background of the author of this thesis, namely, the German judicial field, the methodological starting point is influenced by great German legal methodologists like Josef Esser, Karl Larenz, and Claus-Wilhelm Canaris. This primary approach implies a classic juridical research of the literature and the method of interpretation of laws.[22] As there exist few regulations on the topic of TCEs in Latin America so far, and all the more discussions on a future system of protection of TCEs, methods aiming at the preparation of legislative processes are of special relevance. This also requires the consideration of methods of sociology of law for fact-finding and for comprehending the factual setting,[23] as well as methods of comparative law, as suggested by the classic preparation-of-law method.[24]

[22] Larenz and Canaris (1995).
[23] Ryffel (1974) 163.
[24] Larenz and Canaris (1995).

B. The Proper Perspective: Modes of Thought and the Emic Approach

The topic of the study is strongly characterized by inter-culturality in a double sense. This regards the Latin American legal culture and mentality on the one hand, and "indigenous" ones on the other. Therefore, first, different "modes of thought" are involved that need to be identified, and second, the issue of legal reality in both its dimensions has come to be of special relevance, as demonstrated above.

The concept of different cultural "modes of thought" and their legal extensions has been developed by Wolfgang Fikentscher.[25] He defines a mode of thought in anthropology as "a mind-set that connects human data perception with mentally reflected behavior in a culture-shaping way that is predominantly covert."[26] In its legal extension, it is a precondition for understanding and treating a legal phenomenon, here TCEs, according to the culture-specific way of thinking of the people involved, here particularly the bearers of TCEs. Similarly, sociology of law observed a necessity of leaving aside the conditionings and limits of one's own mode of thought. There, it was described as a pre-conditioning or even bias of the evaluating and judging person in prejudices stemming from his social environment, origin, and education, which determine his observations, categorizations, and judgings.[27] According to legal scholars, overcoming this bias is only possible by means of a steady, life-long process of self-monitoring, an essential aspect required of any researcher (or judge).[28]

More concretely, the consideration and interrelation of different modes of thought without "weighting"[29] may be achieved—as far as possible—by the application of the "synepeia analysis" or "synepeics."[30] This four-step-approach developed by Wolfgang Fikentscher calls for "consequential reasoning in any given mode of thought."[31] It requires, first, a "consequential thinking within a given culture," second, the discovering of the other as "the beginning of dual thinking," third, a comparison of modes of thought for defining "common denominators on a meta-level," or corresponding equivalents, and, finally, creating different responsibilities and policies similar to "applied anthropology."[32] The division of modes of thought is often related to the distinction between *emic* and *etic* categories. The

[25] Fikentscher (2004 II).

[26] *Id.* 21.

[27] Ryffel (1974) 350 *et seq*. Similarly, in developing the concept of the modes of thought as a basis for the emic–etic distinction, *Fikentscher* (2004 II) 16 admits that "[n]eedless to say . . . this means being incomplete, exposed to errors and over-generalizations, and fully aware of the tentative nature of the enterprise".

[28] Larenz and Canaris (1995) 33.

[29] On this *see* Fikentscher (2004 II) 11 *et seq*.

[30] Fikentscher (2009) 235.

[31] *Id.*

[32] Synepeics I–IV; for details hereon *see id.* 236–246.

emic–etic distinction in its linguistic dimension was coined by Kenneth Pike, and then "adopted to distinguish the inside (emic) and the outside (etic) views of a social science phenomenon, such as culture."[33] In the specific area of fieldwork in anthropological research on native peoples, "'[e]mic' interpretations reflect cognitive and linguistic categories of the natives, whereas 'etic' interpretations are those that have been developed by the researcher for purposes of analysis."[34]

This distinction is faced by two challenges of major relevance for this study. First, the definition of the *emic* perspective in a rather abstract legal ambit of TCEs with a focus on indigenous TCEs provoked the question of what "indigenous perspective" really means. The use of the expression "the indigenous peoples" by lawyers accustomed to generalizations and abstractions on the one hand, and that of "nosotros los pueblos indígenas" ("we, the indigenous peoples") by indigenous persons, on the other hand, has been extended and picked up by academics and representatives of states and of international organs as well as by indigenous organizations.[35] However, neither from a legal nor from a factual point of view does there exist such a category or uniformity.[36] Especially anthropologists underline the danger of generalizations and the use of the terminology "indigenous perspective" in the discussions on protecting TCEs. Similarly, on the mode of thought often opposed to such (alleged) "indigenous one", Fikentscher remarks that "(t)he popular view holds that there is usually a 'Western' way of looking at a problem, as well as . . . a 'developing country' way. That these approaches are too simplistic need not be demonstrated."

Second, the differentiation between *emic* and *etic* categories in practice faces difficulties even in individual situations. After 12 years of studies on the Kayapó Indians in Brazil, Darell Posey remarked on the linguistic emic–etic distinction: "It would be nice if such distinctions clearly existed. . . . I have learned and relearned that dialogue between researcher and informant obscures these categories. This is only natural, since individuals from two different cultures inevitably think and speak with different cognitive 'realities'."[37] The usefulness of this distinction is under debate in social science in general.[38] Nonetheless, it raises awareness for the need of rational and emotional sensitivity for comprehending and dealing with the phenomena of different modes of thought. For purposes of research on normative or legal phenomena, a correlational analysis might be of additional use, considering

[33] *Id.* 228.

[34] Posey and Plenderleith (2004) 56 say the reason for the distinction was "an attempt to separate cultural interpretations by the investigator from explanations by the natives".

[35] Natalia Álvarez Molinero "Pueblos Indígenas, comunidad internacional y derechos humanos en la era de la globalización" 65, (2004), cited from Barié (2008) 33.

[36] Fikentscher (2004 II) 10.

[37] Posey and Plenderleith (2004) 56.

[38] Fikentscher (2009) 228.

and correlating three different matrices for the subject, the object, and the legal relationship between the subject and object.[39]

C. Key Aspect: Preconception

Similar to the afore-mentioned awareness of the intercultural particularities, one key aspect in the legal dimension of the topic is preconception, the *Vorverständnis* we all possess and bring to bear on any topic we attempt to comprehend.[40] In general, this preconception is essential for and relates to the whole "issue of law."[41] According to Esser, it embraces all factors like idiom, context of transmission, human behavior, situation of interests, and living conditions as "private aspects" on the one hand, as well as socio-political and macroeconomic interests as general aspects.[42] The method of building one's preconception would consist in a lengthy learning process, or processes.[43] According to Esser, it involves the knowledge obtained during one's education, as well as multiple professional and non-professional experiences with social matters of fact and nexuses, by means of sense perception, including reflected and unreflected understanding.[44] The importance of this preconception is probably *the* essential precondition for adequate comprehension of legal issues, as Canaris argues.[45]

D. Individual Approach

Finally, scrupulous methodology is indispensable, but in contrast to the simple application of existing methods, the finding of new ones and the creative imagination of the researcher behind this task make up the tang of any research, Gadamer says.[46]

Guided by this incitement, additionally, a specially developed method was applied in preparing and conducting this study. It is characterized by communication and visualization apart from applying the classic legal methods of abstraction and analysis, and goes beyond research and study conducted from the desktop.

[39] This approach was developed by Leopold Pospíšil; for further details and references *see id.* 231.

[40] This term was introduced into hermeneutics by Hans Gadamer. *See* Esser (1972) 12. On the term and concept in general *see* Esser, "Vorverständnis und Methodenwahl" (1972).

[41] Die "Sache Recht" in German, *see* Larenz and Canaris 1995) 30 *et seq.*

[42] Esser (1972) 10, and Larenz and Canaris (1995) 30 *et seq.*, especially 31.

[43] Esser (1972) 10.

[44] *Id.*10 and Larenz and Canaris (1995) 25 *et seq.*, 30 *et seq.*

[45] *Id.* 30 *et seq.*

[46] Gadamer (1965) 513.

It embraces the following inspiring sources, paths, and recognitions:

(1) "Design-thinking"[47] as a new interdisciplinary method for solving complex problems, which can also improve the basic understanding of the complex inter-relation between multi-polar interests, actors, and entities as in the field of TCEs.
(2) A growing interdisciplinary approach between law, economy, and psychology. The field of behavioral economics is developing further the idea of the *homo economicus*, which makes it clear that all three aspects are of importance when developing and implementing legal instruments.[48] For a legal protection of TCEs, that means that economic and psychological factors should be considered, hard law and soft law.
(3) "Nudges" in modern terms[49] or, similarly, motive generation, in older terms[50]: They should be given due consideration, as they (may) stimulate the individual to voluntarily implement and follow the legal rule as well as to upheld the vitality of TCEs on the factual side.
(4) The emerging tendency towards more sociological and anthropological approaches to jurisprudence: One of the "most characteristic features of twentieth-century jurisprudence has been the development of sociological approaches to law,"[51] and "the most characteristic feature of jurisprudence in the new century could be the development of anthropological jurisprudence and the anthropology of law."[52]
(5) Within this tendency, the new, rather universal than ultra-relativistic movement in anthropology: This new understanding and approach is rather one based upon a search for universal similarities than for differences, in contrast to the (ultra) relativistic tendency in the past years.[53] It supports the aim of elaborating an adequate protection of TCEs by bridging the gaps, overcoming discrimination, promoting mutual cultural understanding, and considering anthropological aspects where possible.
(6) Regional approaches: Especially in Latin America, there is a strong tendency of an interdisciplinary approach in dealing with TCEs.[54]

---

[47] Plattner, Meinel and Weinberg (2009).

[48] On the interface of the liberalized neo-behaviorism and intentional psychology relevant for the legal ambit *see* already Ryffel (1974) 301.

[49] Thaler and Sunstein (2009).

[50] Ryffel (1974) 305 *et seq*

[51] Freeman (1994) 509.

[52] Hinz, "Jurisprudence and Anthropology", in: Hinz, "The Shade of New Leaves: Governance in Traditional Authority – A Southern African Perspective" 458–469, 458 (2006).

[53] On those universalities *see* Antweiler (2009).

[54] For such practical approaches for instance in Brazil *see* Chapter IV below Section 2.D. II. 3. b. aa. and D. V. For one of many sources in theory *see* Ministério da Cultura – Secretaria de Identidade e da Diversidade Cultural (2006) 162 *et seq.* The principles documented there expressly state that "transdisciplinarity" is considered as "fundamental" for the comprehension of

(7) Developing hybrid fields of sciences: Particularly in the hybrid area of ethnobiology, methodological barriers have been identified and overcome in favor of a more fruitful outcome of the research. There, "[o]ne of the greatest barriers to interdisciplinary scientific investigation is the differential time frames used by social and natural scientists."[55] This difference is quite similar to the one between social and judicial scientists. Like the hybrid field of ethnobiology researching traditional knowledge, a hybrid field of anthropological jurisprudence dealing with TCEs is more able to show that the cognitive analysis of semantic fields is equally important as the collecting of legal provisions or data.

(8) Overcoming methodological oppositions existing even *within* one area: During the past decades, sociology was dominated by a controversy, even dichotomy, between an empiric-analytical approach on the one hand, and a comprehending-reconstructing method on the other.[56] While the latter, critical-reflecting approach indeed goes further,[57] the methods do not have to be regarded as opposing but can be applied in a complementary manner, especially in sociology of law[58] and this particular ambit of TCEs.

(9) An increasing recognition of customary law or a lex-loci approach in TCEs in particular, supported by WIPO,[59] and the experience of the "past failure of dialogue and mutual incomprehension" at the international level[60]: An *emic* approach is followed as far as possible, and voices of bearers of TCEs are heard and reproduced.

(10) The recent view in Native spirituality, which argues that the only theory is a "genuine concern to 'get it right' through methodologies that work best" for the individual author[61]: Similarly, in the ambit of the core issue of indigenous worldviews, the very nature of the issue is multidisciplinary, and "non-reducible to either a single methodology or a single hermeneutics." Thus, here as well the "genuine concern to 'get it right'"[62] by following the individual approach works best.

---

and dealings with popular cultures, including TCEs, and at the same time the establishment of adequate principles and instruments for the legal relationship between creators, maintainers and users of such culture.

[55] Posey and Plenderleith (2004) 59: While biologists consider a short period for gathering data as enough, anthropologist take years "to delve into native perceptions of natural resources" and beyond.

[56] This opposition is known as the "Positivismus-Streit", the positivism dispute, and it dominates the whole field of social sciences, Ryffel wrote in the 1970s, *see* Ryffel (1974) 181.

[57] For a detailed analysis *see id.* 189–201 (1974).

[58] On the term *see id.* 167 note 62 (1974), referring to Julius Stone and N. S. Timasheff.

[59] WIPO (2006).

[60] Taubman and Leistner (2008) 33 *et seq.*

[61] Irwin, (2000) 1–8, 2, 7.

[62] *Id.*

(11) The recent understanding that precisely this approach is a process that "requires much more of the observer than a theoretical language of analysis. The issue is . . . communication."[63]
(12) Studies on the importance of soft skills in law: Considering and purposely employing soft skills like common sense, compassion, and deception are relevant and effective elements for the understanding and development of law, especially when there is the need to bridge distinctions in legal cultures.[64] Similarly, as Posey puts it in a more general way: "For mutual interpretation to occur, sharing of 'realities' must also occur."[65]
(13) Finally, not only in jurisprudence, but also in the designing of future laws, to consider experiences of other, comparable legal solutions on paper and the law in reality.[66]

Section 4. Concrete Research Activities and Procedures

Consequentially, the research also included (i) the exchange of experiences and discussions in the form of conferences and meetings of scientists, practitioners, and bearers concerned, as well as (ii) research trips in order to personally approach entities and individuals dedicated to the topic including E-mail or telephone conversations.

As regards the first aspect, input has been given by discussions and presentations held by others or as a reaction to those of the author herself, at various conferences, meetings, sessions, and promotion activities, among them the following ones (see Table 1).

The second category of research activities was guided by two main aims: to provide for, first, a survey on the current situation and (future) intentions on the protection of TCEs in Latin American countries, and, second, a deeper insight into the legislations, realities, practices, and discussions at one or two national levels.

The investigation included online search and communication, but focused mainly on personal interviews in face-to-face situations.

The main challenge in preparing the personal interviews in 2008 for the following fieldwork was the task of identifying appropriate contact persons, a time-consuming and precarious challenge, as—with the exception of the Panamanian Department of Collective Rights and Folkloristic Expressions in charge of

[63] *Id.*

[64] These three attitudes have been subjects of research in the ambit of the evolution of law by Gruter and Masters, *see* Gruter and Masters, (1998) 91 *et. seq.*

[65] Posey and Plenderleith (2004) 56.

[66] Hirakuri (2003) 30 *et seq.*

Table 1 Conferences et al.

ALAI (Association littéraire et artistique internationale) Study Days on Copyright, Cultural Diversity, and Globalization	Dubrovnik, Croatia, September 2008
XIII. Session of the IGC on Intellectual Property, Genetic Resources, Traditional Knowledge, and Folklore of WIPO	Geneva, Switzerland, October 2008
"Concurso de Mascará de Diablo Congo de Colón," promotional activity of an Afro-Panamanian traditional culture, organized by the Panamanian Department of Collective Rights and Folkloristic Expressions in charge of implementing the Panamanian sui generis regime on the protection of TCEs with the kind permission of Yahelys Arenas, official at the respective Department	Portobelo, Panama, February 2009
International Meeting of COICA ("Coordinadora de las Organizaciones Indígenas de la Cuenca Amazónica," "Coordinator of the Indigenous Organizations of the Amazonian River Basin." For details on COICA *see* at Chapter II Section 4.C.I. below.) ("Evento Climático") with the kind permission of Egberto Tabo Chipunavi, then General Coordinator of COICA (2005–2009) and Valentín Muíba, Technical Coordinator of the Directive Council of COICA	Quito, Ecuador, March 2009
Strategic Workshop of the Latin American Group on Plural Legal Systems ("Taller estratégico del Grupo Latinoamericano por Sistemas Jurídicos Plurales") of the Konrad Adenauer Foundation, which the author was allowed to attend with the kind permission of the Uruguayan and Ecuadorian Office of the Konrad Adenauer Foundation	Quito, Ecuador, March 2009
X International Congress on Intellectual Property of ASPI on "Amazon: Diversity and Integration in Intellectual Property"	São Paolo, Brazil, June 2009
AIPPI International Forum regarding case studies on the protection of traditional knowledge and genetic resources in Latin America	Buenos Aires, Argentina, October 2009

implementing the Panamanian sui generis regime on the protection of TCEs—no clear competences are discernable and specific institutions rarely identifiable, online data was difficult to obtain, and requests by e-mails produced far less resonance than the personal interview afterwards. These results reflect many aspects characterizing the topic of TCEs in Latin America, mainly the plurality of institutions and actors involved, the little coordination and interaction between them, just recently arising activity in documenting, digitizing, and localizing on internet experiences and activities in the field, and, finally, the impossibility to portray exhaustively the entire scenario.

Similar difficulties have also been described in detail by a recommendable study focusing on the situation in Brazil.[67] However, once the contact was established, the author here experienced a great openness, will to cooperate, and support, from the

[67] Arantes (for WIPO) (2009 I), 14 on the study *see also* at Chapter II Section 5.D.I.1 and Chapter IV Section 2.D.II.3.b.bb below.

vast majority of the individuals involved, be it officials of public institutions, indigenous organizations, educational institutions, or private individuals dedicated to the topic or involved as bearers of TCEs. Experiences, information, and available documentation were shared voluntarily and freely, further recommendations made, and existing contacts activated.

In this context, the author wants to take this opportunity to express her heartfelt thanks to all persons met during the research activities and fieldwork, whose contributions to enriching this study are of uncalculable value.

The type of institutions as well as reference and contact persons can be divided at a very general level into

(1) Public institutions like administrative bodies and government agencies
(2) Non-governmental organizations, both national and international
(3) Private persons, mainly bearers of TCEs and researchers of different disciplines including law, politics, and anthropology.

The institutions can be divided again according to their tasks and competences, into the following categorizations:

(1) Institutions dealing with Intellectual Property Law
(2) Institutions dealing with intangible cultural heritage or patrimony
(3) Museums and cultural institutions
(4) Indigenous, local, and other communities as bearers of TCEs
(5) Representatives and organizations of bearers of TCEs
(6) Research institutions
(7) Development agencies
(8) Users and commercializers of TCEs

The personal research activities on the ground took place in Argentina, Brazil, Ecuador, Panama, and other discussions at meetings in Coratia, Germany, and Switzerland. In concrete, the following institutions and contact partners stemming from the different countries as indicated below have been approached in the below disposed manner (see Table 2).

As regards the content of the interviews, first, a concrete and detailed questionnaire was prepared, inspired by the Draft WIPO Questionnaire for community, national, and consultation on options for effective systems for the protection of TCEs/Expressions of Folklore.[68] However, in the first interviews and conversations, especially with bearers and custodians of TCEs, but also with anthropologists, policy makers, and officials dealing with the topic in practice, it became clear very quickly that the issue was rather to establish a forum for trust, confidence, and mutual comprehension in order to share experiences, communicate needs,

[68] *See* Annex to WIPO/GRTKF/IC/7/INF/4.

Table 2 Research activities and discussions

Country	Institution	Contact person	Means of communication
Argentina	Dirección Nacional del Derecho de Autor/National Copyright Directorate	Graciela Peireti	Telephone conversation
	Fondo Nacional de las Artes (Secretaría de Cultura—Presidencia de la Nación)/ National Arts Fund (Secretariat of Culture)	Gerardo Bobbio	Telephone conversation
	Instituto Nacional de la Propiedad Industrial/ National Institute of Industrial Property	Alberto Usieto-Blanco	Personal communication
	Sociedad Argentina de Compositores y Escritores (SADAIC)/Argentinean Society of Composers and Writers	Staff Member	Telephone conversation
	Universidad de Buenos Aires/University of Buenos Aires	Delia Lipszyc, Professor of Law and President of the National Group of the Association Littéraire et Artistique Internationale (ALAI)	Personal communication in Dubrovnik
		Carlos A. Villalba, Vicepresidente del Instituto Interamericano de Derecho de Autor (IIDA)/Vice President of the Interamerican Copyright Institute	Personal communication in Dubrovnik and E-mail correspondence
		Monica Witthaus, Attorney-at-Law and Lecturer in Traditional Knowledge	Personal communication
Brazil	Associação Brasileira da Propriedade Intelectual (ABPI)/Brazilian Intellectual Property Association	Karin Grau-Kuntz	Email correspondence and telephone conversation
	Conselho Indigenista Missionário (CIMI)/Indigenous Missionary Council	Staff Member	E-mail correspondence
	Coordenação-Geral de Direito Autoral (CGDA)/ General Coordination of Copyright (Ministry of Culture)	Marcos Alves de Souza, Head of General Coordination	Personal communication and E-mail correspondence
	Coordenação Geral de Artesanato (CGART) da FUNAI/General Direction of Handicrafts of FUNAI	Pedro Mortale, General Director	Personal communication

(continued)

Table 2 (continued)

Country	Institution	Contact person	Means of communication
	Coordenação de Defesa dos Direitos Indígenas da FUNAI (CGDDI)/General Coordination of the Defence of Indigenous Rights of FUNAI	Paolo Pankararu, Hugo Meireles Heringer	Personal communication
	Coordenação das Organizações Indígenas da Amazônia Brasileira (COIAB)/Coordination of Indigenous Organizations of the Brazilian Amazon	Francisco Avelino Batista, Representative/President	Personal communication
	Fundação Nacional de Artes (FUNARTE)/National Foundation for the Arts (Ministry of Culture)	Officials	Personal communication
	Fundação Nacional do Índio (FUNAI)/National Foundation for Indigenous Peoples (part of the Ministry of Justice)	Staff Members according to special entity	Personal communication
	Fundação Biblioteca Nacional (FBN)/National Library Foundation (Ministry of Culture)	Officials of the Escritório de Direitos Autorais (EDA)/ Copyright Office	Personal communication
	Gesellschaft für Technische Zusammenarbeit (GTZ)/ Society for Technical Cooperation	Luciana Rocha, Consultant, Brasilia Office	Personal communication
	Museu do Índio/Museum of the Indian, Rio de Janeiro (part of FUNAI and the Ministry of Justice)	José Carlos Levinho, Director of the Museum	Personal communication
	Ministério da Cultura/Ministry of Culture	Staff Members according to specific entity	Personal communication
	Ministério Público Federal/ Ministry of Public; especially the 6. Chamber of Coordination and Revision, competent for indigenous and minority issues	Ana Cristina Bandeira Lins, Procuradora da República/ Federal Prosecutor, and Carla Daniela Leite Negócio, Coordenadora Jurídica/Legal Coordinator [of 6. Chamber]	Personal communication and E-mail correspondence
	Instituto Indigena Brasileiro para Propriedade Intelectual (INBRAPI)/Brazilian Indigenous Institute for Intellectual Property	Daniel Mundurukú, President of INBRAPI, Philosopher, and Author, of the *Mundurukú* tribe, and Fernanda Kaingang, Executive Director or INBRAPI,	Personal communication with both

(continued)

Table 2 (continued)

Country	Institution	Contact person	Means of communication
		and lawyer, of the *Kaingang* tribe	
	Instituto Nacional da Propiedade Industrial (INPI)/National Institute of Industrial Property (part of the Ministry of Development and Foreign Trade)	Lucia Regina Fernandes, Official for Geographic Indications	Personal communication
	Instituto do Patrimônio Histórico e Artístico Nacional (IPHAN)/Institute of the National Historic and Artistic Patrimony; Departamento de Patrimônio Imaterial (DPI)/ Department of Immaterial Patrimony	Ana Gita de Oliveira	Personal communication
	Instituto das Tradições Indígenas, Institute of Indigenous Traditions	Eurico L. Sena Baniwa	Personal communication
	Instituto Socioambiental (ISA)/Socioenvironmental Institute	Fernando Mathias	E-mail correspondence and personal research
	Secretaria da Identidade e da Diversidade Cultural/ Secretariat for Cultural Identity and Diversity (Ministry of Culture)	Marcelo Manzatti	Personal communication
	Universidade de Brasilia (UnB)/University of Brasília, Department of Anthropology; hosting also the Associação Brasileira de Antropología (ABA)/ Brazilian Association of Anthropology	Marcela Stockler Coelho de Souza, Professor of Anthropology, and Luis R. Cardoso de Oliveira, Professor of Anthropology	Personal communication with both
		Juliana Santilli, Legal Advisor and Promoter of Justice (Promotora de Justiça) for the Ministry of Public	Personal communication
		Denis Borges Barbosa, Lawyer and Legal Author	Personal communication
Chile	General Directorate of International Economic Affairs (Ministry of Foreign Affairs)	Luciano Cuervo M., Economic Advisor of the Intellectual Property Department and other	Personal communication in Geneva

(continued)

Table 2 (continued)

Country	Institution	Contact person	Means of communication
		Members of the Delegation of Chile attending the XIII. Session of the IGC on Intellectual Property and Genetic Resources, Traditional Knowledge and Folklore of WIPO	
Colombia	Dirección Nacional del Derecho de Autor (DNDA)/ National Copyright Directorate	Fernando Zapata, Director	Personal communication in Dubrovnik and E-mail correspondence
Ecuador	Confederación de Nacionalidades Indígenas del Ecuador (CONAIE)/ Confederation of the Indigenous Nationalities of Ecuador	Miguel Guatemal, Vice President; Fausto R. Vargas, Director of Education, Science and Technology, and Kichwa Indian	Personal communication
	Consejo de Desarrollo de las Nacionalidades y Pueblos del Ecuador (CONDENPE)/Council for the Development of the [Indigenous] Nationalities and Peoples of Ecuador	Andrés Andrango, Anita Paziguan, and Analucía Tasiguano	Personal communication
	Consejo Consultivo de Pueblos Indígenas de la Comunidad Andina/Consultive Council of Indigenous Peoples of the Andean Community	Andrés Andrango	Personal communication
	Coordinadora de las Organizaciones Indígenas de la Cuenca Amazónica (COICA)/Coordinator of the Indigenous Organizations of the Amazon Basin	Egberto Tabo Ch., General Coordinator (2005–2009); José V. Muíba G., Technical Coordinator	Personal communication
	FLACSO University (Facultad Latinoamericana de Ciencia Sociales/ Latinamerican Faculty of Social Sciences)	Fernando García Serrano, Professor and Researcher in Juridical and Political Anthropology; Anita Krainer, Professor and Researcher in Intercultural Studies, Indigenous Issues, and Philosophy; Teodoro Bustamante, Program Coordinator of Socioenvironmental Studies	Personal communication

(continued)

Table 2 (continued)

Country	Institution	Contact person	Means of communication
	Fundación Konrad Adenauer/Konrad Andenauer Foundation	Jaqueline Coronel	E-mail correspondence
	Ministerio de Cultura/Ministry of Culture	Humberto Muenala, Office for Indigenous Peoples	Personal communication
	Instituto Ecuatoriano de la Propiedad Intelectual (IEPI)/Ecuadorian Institute of Intellectual Property	Rodrigo de la Cruz, Principal Expert in Traditional Knowledge, indigenous lawyer, and consultant to WIPO	Personal communication
	Instituto Iberoamericano del Patrimonio Natural y Cultural (IPANC)/Ibero-American Institute for the Natural and Cultural Patrimony	Patricio Sandoval	Personal communication
	Universidad Andina/ Andean University	Eulalia Flor Recalde, Academic Coordinator, Rights of Indigenous Peoples, and Diana Atemaint, Indigenous Professor and Ex-Deputy	Personal communication, Telephone conversation
		Ampan Karankes, Indigenous Leader	Telephone conversation
		Mama Rosario Pichamba, Indigenous Shaman	Personal communication
		Philip Gondecki, Ethnologist, researching conflicts and dispute settlements among indigenous peoples, mainly *Quichua* and *Huaoraní*	Personal communication
		Anna Meiser, M.A., Ethnologist and Researcher at the Ludwig Maximilian University, Munich, researching among the *Shuar* and *Achuar*	Personal communication in Munich and E-mail correspondence
Mexico	Comisión Nacional para el Desarrollo de los Pueblos Indígenas (CDI)/National Commission for the Development of the Indigenous Peoples	Gabriela Nava Domínguez, Área de Asuntos Internacionales/Area of International Issues, and other Members of the Delegation of Mesico attending the XIII. Session of the IGC on Intellectual Property and Genetic Resources,	Personal communication in Geneva

(continued)

Table 2 (continued)

Country	Institution	Contact person	Means of communication
		Traditional Knowledge and Folklore of WIPO	
		Gabriel Larrea Richerand, Legal Advisor and Professor of Law, expert in the legal area of cultural diversity	Personal communication in Dubrovnik and E-mail correspondence
		Luis C. Schmidt, Lawyer and Mexican expert in TCEs/Folklore	Personal communication in Geneva
		Creators of Traditional Indigenous Carpets and Textiles in Oaxaca	Personal communication
Panama	Congreso General Kuna Comarca Kuna Yala/General Kuna Congress	Bolívar López C., Sub-Secretario del Congreso General Kuna/Sub-Secretary of the General Kuna Kongress and other Staff Members	Personal communication
	Dirección del Derecho de Autor/National Copyright Office (Ministry of Education)	Marcos Polano, Director	Personal communication
	Dirección General de Artesanías Nacionales (DGAN)/Directorate General for National Handicrafts (Ministry of Commerce and Industries)	Staff Members	Personal communication
	Dirección General del Registro de la Propiedad Industrial (DIGERPI)/Directorate General of the Industrial Property Registry (Ministry of Commerce and Industries)	Jean Joseph Mathieu, Head of Department	E-mail correspondence
	Dirección General de Aduana/Directorate General for Customs, Departamento de Propiedad Intelectual/Department of Intellectual Property	Luz Celeste Ríos de Davis, General Director	Personal communication
	Dirección Nacional de Educación Intercultural Bilingüe/National Directorate of Bilingual and Intercultural Education (Ministry of Education)	Evangelista Lucas, Director	Personal communication

(continued)

Table 2 (continued)

Country	Institution	Contact person	Means of communication
	Dirección Nacional de Educación de Jóvenes y Adultos/National Directorate of Youth and Adult Education (Ministry of Education)	Prof. Guillermo Smith Lange, Director, former Director of Intercultural Bilingual Education	Personal communication
	Departamento de Derechos Colectivos y Expresiones Folklóricas/Department of Collective Rights and Folkloric Expressions (part of DIGERPI and the Ministry of Commerce and Industries)	Yahelys Arenas (main contact person), Iris Arila, and Rosina Lasso (Head of Department)	Personal communication and E-mail correspondence
	Ministerio de Comercio e Indústrias (MICI)/Ministry of Commerce and Industries	Staff Members according to specific entity	Personal communication
	Ministerio de Educación/ Ministry of Education	Staff Members according to selected entity	Personal communication
	Oficina de Contacto de la UNESCO/National Contact Office of UNESCO	Aristides Burgos, Funcionario/Official	Personal communication
	Instituto Nacional de Cultura (INAC)/National Cultural Institute; Departamento de Folklore/ Department of Folklore	Edmundo de la Cruz, Head of Department	Personal communication
	Impulso Panamá—Projecto de Desarrollo Indígena (PRODEI)/Impulse Panama—Project for the Development of Indigenous Peoples (Ministry of Commerce and Industries, MICI)	Kathia Arjona, Maria Teresa Muñoz	Personal communication and E-mail correspondence
		Enrique Montezuma, Ex-Deputy, and Legislator of Law No. 20 of 2000, Ngäbe Indian, and Administrator/Official at the National Directorate for Bilingual and Intercultural Education (Ministry of Education)	Personal communication
		Jony Rojas, Promoter of Law No. 20 of 2000 in the indigenous territory of Kuna Yala	Telephone conversation

(continued)

Table 2 (continued)

Country	Institution	Contact person	Means of communication
		Luis Touar, General Cacique Dagar Kunyala (Traditional Authority of the Kuna Indians in Eastern Panama), with the kind translation by Flaviano Iglesias, *Kuna* Indian	Personal communication
		Atencio López Martinez, Lawyer and *Kuna* Indian	Personal communication
		Aresio Valiente López, Lawyer, *Kuna* Indian, and consultant on the draft of the Panamanian sui generis regime	Personal communication and E-mail correspondence
	Art galleries and shops dealing in *molas* and other TCEs in Casco Viejo, Panama City	Rosina Ynzewga, Owner of Karavan Gallery, and other traders as well as indigenous women producing the *molas* (Kuna Indians)	Personal communication
	Mercado Nacional de Artesanía/National Handicraft Market, Panama Viejo	Creators and sellers of TCEs	Personal communication
		Indigenous inhabitants of the Comarca Kuna Yala/ Indigenous Territory of *Kuna Yala*	Personal communication
Peru		Jenny Muñoz, Indigenous Leader of the *Asháninka* Indians, currently Alcalde del Distrito de Rio Negro/ Mayor of the Rio Negro District	Personal communication in Munich
	Centro de Cultural Indígenas del Perú (CHIRAPAQ)/Centre of Peruvian Indigenous Cultures	Tarcila Rivera Zea, Presidenta del Consejo Directivo/President of the Directive Council	Personal communication in Geneva

expectations, and challenges. Beside, the different conversation partners had expertise in very distinctive areas, so that some questions made more sense than others in the individual case. Concrete legal questions had to be reformulated and adapted to each situation, openness developed towards interrelated aspects of other disciplines as well as political, socio-economic, and cultural significance and circumstances. Thus, rather than standardized, but little helpful questionnaires, key issues were taken as a basis for the individual interview and conversation, always adapting the details and focus to the particular conversation partner.

Themes for consultation were

(i) the institutional or individual position on the current protection of TCEs on paper and in practice in the respective country and beyond, including legal, socio-cultural, political, anthropological, or economic aspects,
(ii) needs and expectations from the bearers' point of view,
(iii) experiences with either the sui generis system (as in Panama) or the intellectual property system, cultural rights, land rights, customary law, the jurisdictional system, and alternative approaches related to the topic,
(iv) experience with or personal perspectives on the intercultural dialog, spiritual basis, and cooperation of bearers of TCEs on the one hand, and public institutions or NGOs on the other hand,
(v) experience in promoting TCEs by documenting, digitizing, and harnessing them for information and dissemination activities, trade, and development as well as in TCE-related education
(vi) expectations regarding the national situation of the topic in the future, and
(vii) recommendations for an improvement of the current national situation, and for a more appropriate protection of TCEs at the regional or international level, including legal and factual approaches.

Section 5. Conception and Content of the Study

Based upon the sum of these experiences, the study in its Chapter II addresses elementary aspects and core issues of the topic of protecting TCEs, namely

(1) important questions of legal terminology and definitions,
(2) reasons and challenges for a legal protection of TCEs, the setting of historic, socio-cultural, and economic influences and the current actors involved,
(3) underlying indigenous philosophies and intercultural dialogues as bases for such protection (and in contrast to Western world views),
(4) various aspects of customary law concerning TCEs, and
(5) the relationship between TCEs and indigenous land rights.

These aspects are crucial for the topic of TCEs, and have not been considered adequately enough at either Latin American national levels or the international one.

The subsequent Chapter III of the study contains a general survey of the legal situation considering both classic legal instruments including the international and regional framework, constitutional and ordinary provisions, and alternative methods of protection by means of protocols or contracts; moreover, aspects of case law, as well as practical examples of applied legal means of protection in Latin American countries and examples of factual "protection" by documenting, digitizing, and promoting TCEs.

Naturally, a Latin America-wide survey can only address more general aspects and certain selected examples. Therefore, more specific, deeply interesting insights into national situations on the legal protection of TCEs will be given then on selected countries in Chapter IV. The selected countries are Panama and Brazil.

Panama has been chosen because it is one of the very few countries in the world that have established a sui generis regime, starting from an intellectual-property as well as a customary-law perspective, inspired in part by the work of WIPO. Ten years after the Law was established, the first practical experiences with it allow us to formulate summaries and pinpoint the lessons learned for adequate ways of protecting TCEs in the region and beyond.

Brazil, in contrast, has not established specific sui generis instruments on a protection of TCEs (yet), but rather follows a cultural-law approach that encompasses TCEs among other things, and that is inspired by the work of UNESCO. At the same time, it has gathered various interesting and interdisciplinary experiences in closely related areas, like indigenous legislations and policies, a former paying public domain, current discussions on a reform of the copyright law, a sui generis protection of traditional knowledge on biodiversity and genetic resources, and in documenting, digitizing, and promoting TCEs and popular culture. These experiences and current official discussions on all three—an establishment of a system protecting TCEs, a reform of the copyright, and of the general indigenous legislation—are one of the three main reasons for selecting Brazil for a deeper study of the national situation. The second reason is that it possesses the highest degree of socio-cultural diversity in the Latin American region, although its indigenous population is relatively small. This high socio-cultural diversity is a factor that is typical, crucial, and challenging for the whole issue of protecting TCEs. Thirdly, due to its size, Brazil displays a quite different situation from the one in Panama, for example, and plays an important and at the same time critical role in the international ambit of negotiating a protection of TCEs, which—as will be seen—is also determined by national particularities.

Naturally, other Latin American countries are also of particular interest. Guatemala, for instance, follows an interesting cultural-law approach, too, and has even strongly inspired the Panamanian sui generis regime by having created legal solutions in 1947 already, and it is one of the countries with the largest indigenous population. Besides, Colombia, for example, has the distinction of being the Latin American country that has managed best to overcome the formerly common regressive concepts of eradication, assimilation, conversion, and state dictation since the 1990s and established convincing legal conditions for the indigenous population, as Semper argues.[69] With regard to TCEs in particular, however, Colombia has neither implemented any kind of legal protection so far nor does it intend to do so in the near future.[70] In Ecuador, the Ecuadorian Institute for Intellectual Property has elaborated a very detailed and highly advanced draft on a sui generis regime on TCEs and traditional knowledge—which, at this stage,

---

[69] Semper (2008) 141.

[70] Personal and e-mail communication with Fernando Zapata Lopez, General Director of the National Copyright Directorate of Colombia, in October, 2008 and February, 2009.

however, is unlikely to become reality. Ecuador, Guatemala, Colombia, and other Latin American countries will serve as references with regard to general aspects and special ones as well as case law throughout the study, but not as entire chapters of their own.

Finally, in view of the over-arching aim of this study, namely to contribute to the national, regional, and international discussion on an adequate protection of TCEs, to enrich and promote the intercultural dialog by research and observations of exemplifying situations in Latin America, the study finishes with a summarizing survey, concluding recommendations, and an outlook on the future of the topic in Chapter V.

Chapter II. Elementary Aspects of Protecting TCEs

Section 1. Terminology and Scope of Analysis

A. Terminology

I. The Term "Traditional Cultural Expressions"

In accordance with current WIPO terminology and the wording of Article 31 of the UN Declaration on the Rights of Indigenous Peoples,[1] this study uses the term "traditional cultural expressions" (TCEs).

Apart from other substantive arguments, which also define the scope of analysis,[2] the main reasons for using this term are:

- The aim of elaborating a study which might be of use for a further international treatment of TCEs, and
- the simple lack of terminological conformity in Latin America.

Aside from the "umbrella" work elaborated and the terminology used at the international level of WIPO, in Latin America, there is no uniform use of terminology so far, neither at the national levels nor at the regional one. Most of the

---

[1] Article 31 grants the indigenous peoples the "right to maintain, control, protect and develop their cultural heritage, traditional knowledge and *traditional cultural expressions*". Emphasis added by the author. Article 31 then continues: "1. (...) as well as the manifestations of their sciences, technologies and cultures, including human and genetic resources, seeds, medicines, knowledge of the properties of fauna and flora, oral traditions, literatures, designs, sports and traditional games and visual and performing arts. They also have the right to maintain, control, protect and develop their intellectual property over such cultural heritage, traditional knowledge, and traditional cultural expressions. 2. In conjunction with indigenous peoples, States shall take effective measures to recognize and protect the exercise of these rights." For details *see* at Chapter III Section 1. A.I. below.

[2] *See* the arguments against the use of "folklore" and "expressions of folklore," as well as "traditional knowledge" and "cultural heritage," below.

© Springer-Verlag Berlin Heidelberg 2015

A.F. Busch, *Protection of Traditional Cultural Expressions in Latin America*,
Munich Studies on Innovation and Competition 3, DOI 10.1007/978-3-662-46770-1_2

countries that are actively involved in the discussions on further protection of TCEs adopt or approximate the internationally used terms such as those used by WIPO. They do so either in the broader understanding of the term "traditional knowledge"[3] or as regards concrete "TCEs".

The Andean Community, for example, uses the working term "collective and integral traditional knowledge," which explicitly includes *cultural expressions* like "pieces of art, designs and paintings," "artistic and literary creations, legends, myths, ceramics, handicrafts."[4] In Brazil, e.g., the General Coordination of Copyright within the Brazilian Ministry of Culture has adopted the term "TCEs" and formulated a definition of TCEs explicitly "in conformity with" the international discussions at WIPO.[5]

II. "TCEs" Instead of "Folklore"

Some years ago, the term "folklore" was still accepted as the term most often used at the international level and in academic writing.[6] It had been in use for decades, despite its discriminative connotation.[7] This usage no longer reflects reality. An international consensus was reached by decision-making delegates within the WIPO working group (relevant governmental authorities) on "traditional cultural expressions": "As the term 'folklore' is viewed pejoratively in certain cultures, regions and countries while on the other hand the term 'expressions of folklore' has been used in earlier international processes and is used in many national laws, the terms 'expressions of folklore' and 'traditional cultural expressions' are used interchangeably and as synonyms in the WIPO questionnaire."[8]

"Traditional cultural expressions" is also the term used by the most recent international instrument in the area of indigenous rights, the UN Declaration on the Rights of Indigenous Peoples.[9]

From an "emic" point of view, from within the world of Latin American indigenous peoples, the term folklore has been regarded critically, too, for example in the intercultural educational context. According to that understanding, the term folklore is problematic because folklore stands in implicit contrast to the authentic culture, or, more precisely, to an authentic, equal intercultural approach to the indigenous culture. This "appropriate" approach is based upon an interest in mutual

[3] On the use of the terms "traditional knowledge" and "TCEs" by WIPO, *see* at Section 1.C.I. below.

[4] Andean Community (2005) 24, translation by the author.

[5] Ministry of Culture – Coordenação-Geral de Direito Autoral (2007) 1, translation by the author.

[6] *See, e.g.*, Lucas-Schlötter (2008) 339–506.

[7] *See, e.g.*, Markowski (2004) 135 note 22.

[8] Annex WIPO/GRTKF/IC/7/INF/4.

[9] Article 31, *see* at fn. 70 above in Chapter I. For details on the Declaration with regard to the protection of TCEs in Latin America *see* at Chapter III Section 1.A. below.

understanding, while "folklore" implies a simplified observation from an outside, etic realm with no interest in sharing the cultural reality and background of the object of study. "During the decade of the eighties and early nineties, the treatment of interculturality in education often was done from a *folkloric* point of view. During the last few years, the concept of interculturality has been enriched, in the inclusion of indigenous wisdoms, through the incorporation of the social, living and affective dimension of the interculturality process and of the importance that has been given to the knowledge of the 'other', understanding it in multiple levels, and not only concerning ethnical characteristics."[10]

Moreover, indigenous communities often understand "folklore" as the kind of culture that they perform or "sell," while simple "culture" or "cultural expression" is used when they refer to the culture within their own context or for their own use. This is for example the case among the *Shuar* and *Achuar* communities in Ecuador.[11]

To a certain extent, such a distinction is also made in the Panamanian *sui generis* law, the Special Intellectual Property Regime Governing the Collective Rights of Indigenous Peoples for the Protection and Defence of their Cultural Identity and their Traditional Knowledge of Panama, 2000.[12] Although at first glance, the law tries to embrace as many objects with relation to the indigenous culture as possible,[13] "*folkloric* performances of dances" are excepted from the core protection according to Article 15, namely the use of the "collective intellectual property rights and traditional knowledge of the indigenous peoples" according to the specific rules of use of each indigenous community.[14] The background of and reason for this exclusion from the protection was that this "folkloric" way of presenting dances was regarded "to be outside of the traditional context" (i.e. sacral)[15]—different from the traditional cultural expressions and knowledge of the indigenous peoples.

Nonetheless, it is worth mentioning that, when examining TCEs and folklore in Latin America, one finds the term "folklore" or "folclore" in the (vast) majority of national legislations. Definitions of folklore can be found e.g. in Articles 21 *et seq.* and 58 lit b) of the Bolivian Copyright Law, in Article 187, Nr. 2, of the Colombian Copyright Law, and in Articles 2 Nr. 12, 5 lit l), and 6 lit. e) of the Peruvian Copyright Law. These definitions, especially in the Bolivian and Peruvian

---

[10] COICA (2005) 76; translation by COICA at http://www.coica.org.ec/ingles/aia_book/index.html, emphasis added by the author.

[11] Personal communication with ethnologist Anna Meiser on January 8, 2009, who has been doing anthropological research in Shuar and Achuar communities in Ecuador for over 5 years now.

[12] For details on this legislation *see* at Chapter IV Section 1.B. *et seq.* below. Translation by WIPO. *See, e.g.*, WIPO (2010) Annex 20.

[13] For the limitations *see* at Chapter IV Section 1.C.II.2.d. below.

[14] Articles 15 and 16 of the Panamanian Law No. 20 of 2000; for details hereon *see* at Chapter IV Section 1.C. below.

[15] Personal communication with Aresio Valiente López, Kuna Indian, lawyer, and consultant in the process of drafting the law, on February 11, 2010 in Panama City.

Copyright Law, correspond to the (former) common understanding of folklore used in the area of possible legal protection.[16]

III. "Expressions of Folklore"

In the context of Latin American copyright, it is important to consider the distinctive Spanish term "expresiones del folklore," expressions of folklore. This term appears in many copyright legislations of Latin American countries like Paraguay, Barbados, Ecuador, Peru, and Cuba, and has a more limited meaning than the term "folklore": apart from demonstrating traditional cultural elements, these expressions of folklore have to fulfil the copyright category of a "work."[17]

Mostly, these expressions are qualified as part of the category of derived works or as part of the public domain, e.g. in Bolivia, Colombia, the Dominican Republic, and Peru.[18]

These "expressions of folklore" therefore do not have the same meaning as those contained in the 1982 WIPO/UNESCO Model Provisions for National Laws on the Protection of Expressions of Folklore Against Illicit Exploitation and other Prejudicial Actions. The Model Provisions cover only "artistic" heritage:

> "This means that, among other things, traditional beliefs, scientific views [e.g. traditional cosmogony] or merely practical traditions as such, separated from possible traditional artistic forms of their expression, do not fall within the scope of the proposed definition of 'expressions of folklore.' On the other hand, 'artistic' heritage is understood in the widest sense of the term and covers any traditional heritage appealing to our aesthetic sense. Verbal expressions, musical expressions, expressions by action and tangible expressions may all consist of characteristic elements of the traditional artistic heritage and qualify as protected expressions of folklore."[19]

Thus, there are two main differences between "expressions of folklore" referred to in the WIPO Model Provisions and the ones contained in the Latin American copyright legislations mentioned above:

- First, when these latter expressions of folklore receive protection analogous to the copyright protection, only literary or artistic manifestations are covered, corresponding to the literary or artistic works as objects of copyright.
- Second, these expressions have to fulfill the general requirements of copyright: a kind of "expression" in contrast to a mere idea, and the "originality" of this expression.[20]

[16] Unterguggenberger (1999) 108.

[17] Antequera Parilli (2007) 511.

[18] *Id.* 510 (2007).

[19] WIPO (2001) 43.

[20] Antequera Parilli (2007) 513 *et seq.*

While WIPO tried to standardize and thereby simplify the use of terminology by equating the terms "TCEs" and "expressions of folklore," the Latin American countries themselves were the last to break up this synonymous understanding: In one of the discussions on the working version of substantive provisions on a protection of TCEs, the Mexican and Venezuelan delegations suggested including the conjunction "and" instead of "or" between the two terms.[21] Against the just displayed backdrop of Latin American copyright legislations, this could be interpreted as reflecting the countries' different perception of the content of the two terms used at WIPO level. At least, it indicates that the concepts of how to use the prevalent terminology in the area of TCEs are still not uniform, requiring thus a closer and more differentiated look.

To confuse the situation of divergent usage even more, it is worth mentioning that the sui generis regime of Panama, besides e.g. "traditional expression of the indigenous peoples,"[22] "traditional artistic expressions," and "traditional knowledge . . . on their creations,"[23] uses the term "expresionses folclóricas"[24]—folkloric expressions. According to the wording of the Law, these "folkloric expressions" are considered as part of the "traditional expressions of the indigenous peoples"[25]—while part of them, namely folkloric dances, receive a legal treatment different from that of other traditional cultural manifestations, as mentioned above.

It should not be concealed either, however, that the (frozen) Draft Agreement on the Free Trade Area of the Americas, involving 34 national states of the broader American region, including the United States of America and Canada, uses the term "expressions of folklore."[26] This draft is currently not under development, though.[27]

It becomes clear once more that neither at the regional nor at WIPO level, does there exist a uniform understanding or use of the terms "TCEs" and "expressions of folkore" within the different Latin American countries so far.

Due to the different meaning of "expressions of folkore" within the copyright protection at some national levels of Latin American countries, this study focuses

[21] WIPO (2010) Annex 11.

[22] Article 2 of the Panamanian Law No. 20 of 2000; for details on the Law *see* at Chapter IV Section 1.C. below.

[23] Article 1 of the Law.

[24] Article 2 of the Law.

[25] "Las . . . expresiones folclóricas . . . y cualquier otra forma de expresión tradicional de los pueblos indígenas . . .", Article 2 of the Law.

[26] Chapter XX Intellectual Property Rights, Subsection B.2.c. Copyright and Related Rights, Article 1. Definitions of the Draft Agreement, FTAA – Free Trade Area of the Americas, FTAA.TNC/w/133/Rev. 3 (November 21, 2003), available at www.ftaa-alca.org/ftaadraft03/ChapterXX_e.asp, last visited November 2, 2010. Although the targeted deadline of the agreement was set for 2005, the last meeting held at Mar del Plata, Argentina, in November 2005, did not lead to the signing of an FTAA agreement, and negotiations have not actively developed since. *See* http://www.ftaa-alca.org/alca_e.asp.

[27] For details on the draft *see* at Chapter III Section 2.A.I.1.d. below.

on the broader term of "TCEs," which is also used by WIPO—so far[28]—as a synonym of the "expressions of folklore" in *lato sensu*.

IV. "Traditional" and "Indigenous"

The term '*traditional* cultural expressions' involves two elements:

(i) The objects and
(ii) The subjects of the topic or of (potential) legal protection.

As regards the objects of such protection, the term "traditional" conveys rather substantive than terminological points for clarification, which are dealt with in the context of traditional and dynamic aspects below.

With regard to the possible subjects or holders of rights, the term "traditional" refers to a broader scope than "autochthonous" or "indigenous." The decision of WIPO to use the term "traditional knowledge" or "traditional cultural expressions" in contrast to "indigenous" ones was made so as not to limit the discussions and concept of protection *a priori* to autochthonous or aboriginal communities[29]—at least on paper.[30]

In Latin America, there exists no similar decision at the regional level, and at the national levels, this aspect of use of terminology is, again, heterogeneous,—and reflects the heterogeneity involved in the question of potential bearers of TCEs.

The sui generis law established in Panama only covers "indigenous peoples," apart from the inclusion of some special provisions on small local handicraft producers.[31] The establishment of a parallel legislation for *local communities* was initiated, but the project has been stopped again.[32] Similarly, the elements for a sui generis protection of TCEs of the Andean Community combine the terms traditional and indigenous—and, in the end, cover only indigenous peoples: the relevant document is titled "Elements for the Protection of the Collective and Integral *Traditional* Knowledge of the *Indigenous* Peoples."[33] In Brazil, however, in accordance with the WIPO approach, the definition used by the General Coordination of Copyright refers to the traditional cultural heritage maintained by any "community."[34] The legislative project on the protection of TCEs in Ecuador, in turn, uses

[28] *See*, however, the new, diverging discussions just mentioned: WIPO (2010) Annex 11.

[29] WIPO (2001) 23.

[30] The debates in practice would nonetheless be limited to expressions of autochthonous peoples, argues Ramsauer (2005) 42, note 166.

[31] Article 23 of the Panamanian Law No. 20 of 2000, and, on the reasons for the inclusion of these groups, *see* at Chapter IV Section 1.C.V.3. below.

[32] Personal communication with Luz Celeste Ríos de Davis, General Director of the General Direction of the Industrial Property Registry (DIGERPI), on February 18, 2009, in Panama City.

[33] Andean Community (2005) Elementos para la protección sui generis. Emphasis added by the author.

[34] Ministry of Culture – Coordenaçåo-Geral de Direito Autoral (2007) 2.

the term "collective traditional knowledge" (including cultural expressions) of "the indigenous peoples and nationalities ("nacionalidades"), the Montubio peoples, Afro-Ecuadorian peoples and peasant ("campesinos") communities."[35]

The parallel situation, regarding certain traditional *knowledge* in *stricto sensu*, is characterized by a similarly diverse picture. For example, in Peru, the Law on the Protection of Indigenous Peoples' Collective Knowledge Associated with Biological Resources No. 27811, the "first national law of its kind in the world,"[36] only covers "indigenous" peoples,[37] while Costa Rica and the Andean Community in similar areas have included "local communities,"[38] whereas Brazil has included even "Quilombolas," special Afro-Brazilian communities, in its legislation on traditional knowledge related to biodiversity and genetic resources.[39] The concepts of "traditional" and "indigenous" become even more unclear or impossible to differentiate when looking at Articles 2 and 3 of the just mentioned Peruvian Law: there, the law stipulates that "indigenous" can be used and understood as a synonym of "traditional," among other terms.[40]

This variety in the terminology reflects the difficulty in:

- First, defining and characterizing the subjects and objects of potential rights, and,
- Second, elaborating general statements on the region of Latin America.

Additionally, when considering and researching the term "indigenous", another aspect of terminology becomes relevant, a Latin American particularity: the use of and distinction between the Spanish and Portuguese terms "índio" and "indígena" or even other terms like e.g. "silvícola". These particularities will be addressed in the context of definitions and content.[41] As regards the use of English terminology in the present study, the terms "traditional" and "indigenous" are used.

In sum, as regards the terms "traditional" and "indigenous," most of the discussions on an adequate protection of TCEs in Latin America use the term "traditional," in order not to exclude other bearers and potential right holders of TCEs *a*

---

[35] "Conocimientos Tradicionales Colectivos de las Nacionalidades y Pueblos Indígenas, Pueblo Montubio, Pueblo Afroecuatoriano y comunidades campesinas", *see* de la Cruz I. (2008 II) 43.

[36] Ruiz, Lapeña and Clark (2004) 758.

[37] Its title makes that clear already: "Regime for the Protection of Indigenous Peoples' Collective Knowledge Associated with Biological Resources." For more details hereon *see* Pacón (2004) 175 *et seq.* and Ruiz, Lapeña and Clark (2004) 755–798.

[38] Article 4, para. II, Article 7, No. 9, Article 10, Nos. 4 and 6, of the Costa Rican Law No. 7788 on Biodiversity (*Ley de Biodiversidad*), for more details hereon *see* Bucher (2008) 251 *et seq.*; Article 1 of Decision 391 of the Andean Community; on the Decision *see* at Chapter III Section 2.B.II.3. below.

[39] Article 7, para III, of the Provisional Act No. 2186-16; on this *see* at Chapter IV Section 2.D.I. below.

[40] Articles 2 and 3 of the Peruvian Law No. 27811. *See* also Ruiz, Lapeña and Clark (2004) 777.

[41] *See* at Section 1.B.II.1.a. below.

priori (similar to the practice at WIPO), although the main focus lies on the *indigenous* population or communities.

This is also the approach to be followed in the present study.

B. Definitions

I. Definitions and Content of "TCEs" as Objects of Protection

1. Official (Working) Definitions and Understandings of TCEs

a. General Aspects

The picture of definitions and understandings of what TCEs are or embrace is not very clear—in the Latin American region as well as within the different countries.

The only existing specific legislation on TCEs, the Panamanian sui generis law, does not contain a legal definition of TCEs. Nonetheless, the Decree regulating the Law contains, "for the effects of this Decree," a definition of "traditional knowledge" including TCEs, defining it as

> collective knowledge of an indigenous people based in centuries-old, and up to millennia-old, traditions which are at the same time tangible and intangible expressions comprising indigenous peoples' sciences, technologies, cultural manifestations, including the genetic resources, medicine, seeds, knowledge on the characteristics of flora and fauna, the oral traditions, designs, visual and representative arts.[42]

This definition, however, does not correspond to the scope of traditional knowledge governed by the Law itself, as will be demonstrated later on,[43] and is therefore of only limited value for defining the content and scope covered by the term and topic of TCEs dealt with in this study.

The legislative project in Ecuador comprises "traditional knowledge, innovations, and practices," defined as

> all collective knowledge, wisdoms, innovations, and ancestral practices which the indigenous peoples and nationalities, the Montubio peoples, Afro-Ecuadorian peoples and ancestral communities posses, and which are transmitted from generation to generation habitually in an oral manner. They are characterized by their antiquity as well as their actuality. That means that it is dynamic knowledge in a constant process of innovation and adaptation to new realities, based in the cosmovision of the communities.[44]

---

[42] Article 2 No. 3 of the Panamanian Decree 12 of 2001.

[43] On this problem *see* at Chapter IV Section 1.C.II.2.d.aa. below.

[44] Preliminary Title – Definitions of the "Proyecto de Ley: Protección de los Conocimientos Colectivos, los Saberes Ancestrales y las Expresiones Culturales Tradicionales de las Nacionalidades y Pueblos Indígenas, Pueblo Montucio, Afroecuatoriano, y de las Comunas y Comunidades Ancestrales del Ecuador" of February 2009. The author expresses her deepest gratitude to Rodrigo de la Cruz of the IEPI for sharing the draft document in March 2009 in Quito.

The subject matter of protection of the Draft explicitly covers "tangible forms of traditional cultural expressions like: traditional clothing, all types of works of art such as drawings, designs, paintings, sculptures, carpets, ... handicraft; architectural works of all kinds; and, music and working instruments ...."[45] It also covers "intangible forms" of TCEs like "myths or legends, symbols, dances, traditional games, traditional songs and phonographic interpretations, indigenous names and ritual ceremonies, disregarding whether they are or are not fixed in electromagnetic carriers."[46]

The definition, which the Brazilian General Coordination of Copyright has chosen as a basis for the discussion on a legislative project on the protection of TCEs in Brazil, is based upon the WIPO definition.[47] It reads: "TCEs, or expressions of folklore, are understood as expressions of traditional knowledge, which means productions consisting of elements which are characteristic of the cultural traditional patrimony, developed and maintained by a community, peoples in one country or by individuals reflecting the traditional cultural expectations of this community or peoples."[48] Then, the General Coordination gives examples of what "TCEs include"—similar to the illustrative enumeration of most typical kinds of TCEs/expressions of folklore contained in the Model Provisions. According to the forms of expression, they can be subdivided into four groups:

(i) "Verbal expressions" (expressions by words), "like folk tales, folk poetry, riddles etc";
(ii) "Musical expressions" (expressions by musical sounds), "like folk songs and/or traditional songs and traditional instrumental music";
(iii) "Expressions by action of the human body" (expressions by action) "like folkloric and/or traditional dances, plays and traditional rituals";
(iv) "Expressions incorporated in material objects or tangible expressions like paintings, drawings, designs, sculptures, ceramics, terracotta, woodwork, jewellery, basket weaving, needlework, carpets, costumes, textiles, musical instruments and architectural forms."[49]

A regional definition, embracing potential state parties even beyond Latin American countries, namely the United States of America and Canada, is contained

---

[45] Article 2, lit. g) of the Ecuadorian Legislative Project of February 2009.

[46] Article 2, lit. h) of the Ecuadorian Legislative Project of February 2009.

[47] This definition used by WIPO Secretariat is based on the one in the 1982 WIPO–UNESCO Model Provisions. *See* http://www.wipo.int/tk/en/glossary/index.html and http://www.wipo.int/tk/en/glossary/#tce, last visited July 5, 2010.

[48] Ministry of Culture – Coordenaçåo-Geral de Direito Autoral (2007) 2. According to the WIPO Model Provisions, "expressions of folklore" are understood as productions consisting of characteristic elements of the traditional artistic heritage developed and maintained by a community in the country or by individuals reflecting the traditional artistic expectations of such a community, Section 2 of the Model Provisions.

[49] *Id.* (2007) 2. For comparison *see* Section 2 of the Model Provisions. WIPO (2001) 22.

in the Draft Agreement on a Free Trade Area of the Americas.[50] Although the draft is unlikely to become reality in the forseeable future,[51] and the definition is termed "expressions of folklore," it is worth mentioning for illustration purposes. Expressions of folklore are defined in the Draft Agreement as "(p)roductions using elements characteristic of the traditional cultural patrimony, consisting of all literary and artistic works created in the national territory by unknown or unidentified authors presumed to be nationals or members of their ethnic communities, and that are transmitted from generation to generation and reflect the traditional artistic or literary perspective of a community."[52] As said before, this definition as well as the Draft itself has neither reached a consensus yet, nor happened to have any practical application.

When defining the content of TCEs, there are, among others, three points of special interest or, more precisely, (apparent) dichotomies and areas of tension, which characterize the whole topic of protecting TCEs. At first stage, they relate to the content of the term TCEs in its juridical dimension and regard the following three areas: the apparent dichotomy or field of conflict of

- tangible versus intangible
- collective versus individual, and,
- traditional versus modified, or evolved expressions.

b. Intangible and Tangible Expressions

Although starting from an intellectual property point of view, the conception of TCEs dealt with here is not limited to intangible expressions, but encompasses the intangible and tangible ones. This is, on the one hand, due to the holistic perspective of indigenous peoples themselves, and on the other, in accordance with existing Latin American legislations and the work of WIPO.

According to the sui generis regime in Panama, e.g., handicrafts as tangible goods are part of the expression of cultural identity of traditional communities, and are thus TCEs.[53] This is also the path WIPO takes. Although one could question whether "expressions incorporated in a material object" only cover the relevant expression and not the material object itself, WIPO argues on handicrafts in particular that "handicrafts are an intertwined, symbiotic combination of ideas and of expressions. They are useful objects (at least, so they were originally), which conform to popular esthetic values. Like the other elements of TK, they stem from traditions and express those same traditions: they are linked to a certain

[50] Chapter XX Intellectual Property Rights, Draft Agreement, FTAA – Free Trade Area of the Americas, FTAA.TNC/w/133/Rev. 3 (November 21, 2003), available at www.ftaa-alca.org/ftaadraft03/ChapterXX_e.asp, last visited November 2, 2010.

[51] For current developments *see* the official homepage http://www.ftaa-alca.org/alca_e.asp, last visited November 2, 2010.

[52] Article 1 Subsection B.2.c. Copyright and Related Rights of the FTAA Draft Agreement. For details on the Draft and the FTAA *see* at Chapter III Section 2.A.I.1.d. below.

[53] Articles 2, 4, and 5 of Law No. 20; for details *see* at Chapter IV Section 1.C.II. below.

community and serve as an element of its identification." Therefore, WIPO argues, they "constitute one category of TK" in the broader sense.[54]

The Ecuadorian Legislative Project also covers both tangible and intangible TCEs as subject matter of protection, as seen above.[55]

The "holistic" approach followed by most of the indigenous peoples themselves by definition also argues in favor of the incorporation of intangible and tangible goods.[56]

c. Collective and Individual Expressions

Although one of the main characteristics of TCEs is regarded to be their collective ownership, there exist not only collective but also individual expressions, especially in an emic understanding. As this study widely tries to consider an emic approach,[57] a Latin American indigenous perspective will be considered first on whether individual expressions also are or should be covered by the term TCEs.

Latin American indigenous peoples have formulated their understanding of the different types of TCEs and traditional knowledge in *lato sensu*. According to the indigenous organization of the Amazon Indians, COICA,[58] there are also TCEs consisting of individual expressions, or rooted in individual knowledge holders, called "ancestral wisdom," while others are rooted in "collective knowledge." The distinction is described as follows:

"Ancestral wisdoms" are "wisdoms linked to highly specialized knowledge, which require the subjects that acquire them to have determined conditions and traits. Wisdoms link the real world of the forest with the spiritual world of the forest itself. Due to this, people who can access these wisdoms must demonstrate, either through ritual ceremonies and very strong demands, their spiritual and physical strength. Specialized wisdoms cannot be transmitted to a person who is not capable of making long-term diets; of going to the forest in absolute solitude to inhabit it; of taking sacred plants and reaching the vision."[59] This type of highly specialized knowledge, rituals, and expressions is "almost secret for most people. To this

---

[54] WIPO Secretariat (2005) 4.

[55] Article 2, lit. g) and h), of the Ecuadorian Legislative Project of February 2009 ("Proyecto de Ley: Protección de los Conocimientos Colectivos, los Saberes Ancestrales y las Expresiones Culturales Tradicionales de las Nacionalidades y Pueblos Indígenas, Pueblo Montucio, Afroecuatoriano, y de las Comunas y Comunidades Ancestrales del Ecuador" of February 2009.) The author expresses her deepest gratitude to Rodrigo de la Cruz of the IEPI for sharing the draft document in March 2009 in Quito.

[56] COICA (2005) 62, translation by COICA at http://www.coica.org.ec/ingles/aia_book/index.html. On this *see* at Section 4.G. below.

[57] On the term and approach *see* at Chapter I Section 3.B. above.

[58] "Coordinadora de las Organizaciones Indígenas de la Cuenca Amazónica"; for details on COICA *see* at Section 4.C.I. below.

[59] COICA (2005) 58, translation by COICA at http://www.coica.org.ec/ingles/aia_book/index.html.

knowledge, only some members of our communities had access, which is considered of much importance; however, they did not transmit them to all of us but to certain wise people of the new generations, which complied with certain personal and social requisites."[60]

"Collective knowledge," in contrast, is understood as "the knowledge to which men and women have had access ... through the education that the adult generations developed for new generations." It embraces "all the information that helped our existence to confront concrete" situations of "human needs," such as "hunting, fishing, recollection, agriculture, handicrafts, metallurgy, raising children, physical and spiritual health, leisure activities, music, dance, painting, the preparation of food and its conservation, dressing, parties, human reproduction."[61]

Both categories thereby cover what before has been termed "TCEs", or, in other words, "TCEs" are regarded as part of "collective knowledge" and "ancestral wisdoms." The distinction between the latter categories rather refers to the aspect of collective and individual responsibility or creation regarding TCEs and traditional knowledge in *lato sensu*.

One example of a TCE created and also used only by one part of the community is the Panamanian *mola*: it has always been, and is today, created and worn by the female part of the *Kuna* population, the Kuna women.[62] Officially, in the relevant legal instrument, it is even called "women's art."[63] It is legally categorized, however, as "traditional knowledge, which belongs to the indigenous people of the Kuna, and is therefore collective property and not the property of certain individuals who form a part of the people. It has been transmitted from generation to generation, and therefore, it is the intellectual property of the Kuna people."[64]

Without going into further details on the questions of concrete right holders and possible dispute resolution in the tribe, which will be part of a further examination below,[65] it becomes clear that even according to an emic perspective of Latin American indigenous peoples, the question of the creator of a TCE or holder of the related knowledge, on the one hand, and that of the "holder of rights,"[66] on the other, might be considered as different questions, to be answered distinctively.

---

[60] *Id.* 58, translation by COICA at http://www.coica.org.ec/ingles/aia_book/index.html.

[61] *Id.*

[62] For history and context of the *mola see* Valiente López (2006) 38–50, and at Chapter IV Section 1.B. below.

[63] "Arte de la mujer", Article 3 of the Rules of Use of the Collective Right "Mola Kuna Panama." On this *see* at Chapter IV Section 1.D.II.3.a. below.

[64] Article 1 of the Rules of Use of the Collective Right "Mola Kuna Panama"; on this *see* at Chapter IV Section 1.D.II. below.

[65] *See* at Section 5.D.VI. and Chapter IV Section 1.D.II.3.e. below.

[66] This is also the case if these perspectives and conceptions are not expressed in such technical terms. On the aspect of language *see* at Chapter IV Section 1.D.II.3.a. below.

d. Traditional, Dynamic, and Revitalized Aspects

It is still not determined clearly, in the Latin American region and discussions as well as beyond, what exactly the term "traditional" refers to.

In Brazilian literature on TCEs for example, one reads: "The creations of a '*silvícola*,' or indigenous spirit, include the music, legends and tales, handicrafts and dances, truly composing the indigenous cultural tradition and the one of their ancestors .... As one knows, this cultural tradition goes back to the times of the discovery of America by Christopher Columbus in 1492, a time in which the very existence of copyright was unheard of."[67]

Does "traditional" imply that the objects treated as TCEs have to have a connection to the pre-Colombian time? If so, what kind of connection must that be? Should alterations or even innovation be excluded or included, in that case? Should revitalized practices likewise be embraced?

aa. Emic Perspectives

Considering an emic point of view, the Kuna Indians in Panama—one of the few countries in the world which have already established a sui generis regime on TCEs—regard their TCEs as dynamic expressions. They have even managed to include this perspective in the national system of legal protection of TCEs, as regards a particular Kunan handicraft, the *mola*.[68] According to the regulation of use set up by the Kuna Indians themselves, "innovations" also are a part of this particular TCE: "The innovations which have been obtained with the Mola" are "proof that the knowledge of the Kuna peoples is not static." Rather, the knowledge, and the *molas,* are still "in constant evolution."[69]

The dynamic aspect of traditions is also emphasized by the Xingu Indians in Brazil, in an abstract sense but also a very concrete one: the Kuikuro, part of the Indians living in the Xingu region, for example, depict tradition as "a movement." The concrete meaning of this movement covers the understanding of traditions as "a movement of bodies, words, sounds and rhythms." The underlying concept is called "ügühütu" and is wide-ranging: "it may be translated as 'custom', 'way of being' or 'way of doing.'" And none of these ways, these traditions like "ways of painting, dancing, singing, speech-making, receiving guests, and welcoming and feeding spirits," are static; they are "on the move."[70]

---

[67] De Hollanda Sheldrick (2009) 69. She discusses this aspect of TCEs in the context of works that have never been protected by copyright as long as they have existed.

[68] For details hereon *see* at Chapter IV Section 1.D.II.3.f. below.

[69] Article 4 of the Rules of Use of the Collective Right "Mola Kuna Panama". *See* at Chapter IV Section 1.D.II.3.f. below.

[70] "The Xinguano way of being-and-doing is vividly linked to a ritual, a moment in which all the meanings of tisakisü and ügühütu come together through intense action: a way of painting, dancing, singing, speech-making, receiving guests, and welcoming and feeding spirits," Fausto and Franchetto (2008) 9, translation by the author. Texts and illustrations are by the Karib masters of the Alto Xingu.

Even from the broader perspective of the international representation of the Amazon Indians, there is clearly emphasis on revitalized elements of TCEs as subject matter of protection.[71]

bb. Anthropological and Sociological Perspectives

From an anthropological and sociological perspective, "traditions" rarely have a "real" continuity with the past. Instead, rituals or tangible cultural artifacts tend to be responses to novel situations. Creating such responses constitutes a universal human behavior in any culture or society. Sometimes, but not always, such new creations are an essential precondition for the survival of a society or community, as new circumstances sometimes require and provoke adaptation, assimilation, and acculturation.[72]

Hobsbawm, in his now classic anthropological study, introduced and elaborated the phenomenon of the "invention of tradition". This phenomenon is socio-culturally "normal behaviour," Hobsbawm argues,[73] typical for all kinds of societies and communities: Western and Eastern, modern and traditional ones. Such "invented traditions" are understood as

> a set of practices, normally governed by overtly or tacitly accepted rules and of a ritual or symbolic nature, which seek to inculcate certain values and norms of behaviour by repetition, which automatically implies continuity with the past. In fact, where possible, they normally attempt to establish continuity with a suitable historic past. … [T]he peculiarity of 'invented' traditions is that the continuity with it is largely fictitious. In short, they are *responses to novel situations* which take the form of reference to old situations, or which establish their own past by quasi-obligatory repetition.[74]

The term "invented traditions" not only covers adaptations and new uses of old traditions for new purposes, but also the re-use of ancient elements in new contexts, as well as "extinct" traditions, when revived, Hobsbawm argues.[75]

Thus, such only apparent continuities of traditions might not only be socio-culturally "normal behavior," but also a social and consequently juridical criterion hardly separable or distinguishable from the category of tradition and TCEs. According to Hobsbawm, there is probably no society that has not seen the

---

[71] COICA (2005) 62, translation by COICA at http://www.coica.org.ec/ingles/aia_book/index.html, on this *see* at Section 4.G. below.

[72] On the terms and concepts of assimilation, acculturation, culture change, culture loss, and culture transfer *see* Fikentscher (2009) Chapter 5.

[73] Hobsbawm (1983) 1 *seq.*

[74] *Id.* According to their distinctive functions, such "invented traditions" can be subdivided into three types: (i) the "invented traditions" establishing or symbolizing social cohesion and collective identities, (ii) those establishing or legitimizing institutions and social hierarchies, and (iii) those socializing peoples into particular social contexts. *See* Hobsbawm (1983) 9.

[75] Hobsbawm (1983) 5–8.

"invention" of tradition. Still, invented traditions might occur more frequently at times of rapid social transformation when "old" traditions would disappear. Hobsbawm therefore expected an especially large number of "new" traditions to be invented over the past two centuries, in both "traditional" and "modern" societies.[76]

With regard to handicrafts, the reality of their dynamic character has also been observed in famous Latin American literature.[77]

cc. Practical Perspectives

Sometimes, the pure desire within an indigenous community of maintaining a tradition and ensuring its continuity incites the use and maybe even adaptation of new elements and ways of transmission, conceivably even new technologies. If we accept this push for renewal as an inherent part of a culture, we must call into question a narrow understanding of "traditional" cultural expression: The Brazilian project and exhibition "Tisakisü" reveals exactly this phenomenon and this challenge. The Kuikuro community of the region of the Upper Xingu, worried about "the continuity of their tradition in a context of rapid change," solicited the project of linguistic and cultural documentation, which is precisely dedicated to "the challenge of transmitting" the knowledge of an "entire musical universe,"[78] to be transmitted to new generations, "along with everything associated with it: mythic narratives, ritual routines, modes of execution, interpretations."[79] This project, "as well as revealing the beauty of tradition," also indicates "the challenges of the present and the new tools being used to confront them. How to keep a tradition alive during a period of intense change? This is the question the Kuikuro ask themselves and have tried to answer in close collaboration with the exhibition's curators."[80] Sometimes, there is also help needed from outside the community. If "tradition" is or should be characterized by a "transmission from generation to generation," and at the same time help from outside the community is needed for such a

[76] *Id.* 4 *et seq.*

[77] The great Latin American poet Octavio Paz has described it like this: "Handicrafts do not seek to last millenia, nor are they possessed by the haste of dying soon. They go by with the days: they flow with us. They wear out slowly, they do not seek death, nor do they deny it: they accept it. Handicrafts are the heartbeats of the human time. They are useful objects and yet they are also beautiful; objects that last; and yet objects that also wear out and resignate to wear out; objects that are not unique as an artwork and which can be replaced by similar objects – but never identical. Handicrafts teach us how to die and thus they teach us how to live," Octavio Paz, "Los Privilégios de la Vista," translation by WIPO Secretariat (2005) 5.

[78] The documentation embraces around "90 hours of vocal songs and instrumental pieces, without repetition, to be transmitted intergenerationally." *See* Carlos Fausto and Bruna Franchetto in: Fausto and Franchetto (2008) 11.

[79] *Id.*

[80] *Id.*

transmission, the question arises of whether this aspect should be of juridical relevance, i.e. how "traditional" the concrete TCE still is.[81]

dd. Legal Consequences

In this manner, from a legal perspective, the essential question is the following: Should these evolved, dynamic appearances of traditions also fall under the scope of TCEs?

The examples above make clear that, if TCEs in their terminology and content should be understood and treated according to the understanding and concepts of the bearers and potential right holders, it is essential to consider concepts of culture and the underlying world views from an emic perspective—as far as possible.[82]

Besides, if the protection of TCEs is understood as politically following a socio-economic approach, aiming at the upholding of cultural diversity, and not as a museum-like preservation of the past, then even such "new" adopted phenomena should be part of TCEs as objects of protection.

Similarly, with relation to the disputed aspect of "revitalization" of TCEs, a parallel can be drawn to the 2007 UN Declaration on the Rights of Indigenous Peoples. Its Article 13, para 1, explicitly includes "the right to revitalise, use, develop and transmit to future generations their ... philosophies."[83]

More particularly, the Ecuadorian Legislative Project on Traditional Collective Knowledge and TCEs explicitly defines traditional knowledge, practices, and expressions as "dynamic," and "in a constant process of innovation and adaptation to new realities, based in the cosmovision of the communities."[84]

II. Definition and Content of the Subjects or Holders of Rights

In the majority of Latin American countries, holders of TCEs and (potential) right holders are indigenous, Afro-, and peasant groups, and some other local communities. As regards the indigenous communities, there never existed one people of

[81] José Carlos Levinho, Director of the Indian Museum in Rio de Janeiro, said the project of the Tiokirü was only possible due to "a deep engagement between a group of people united by a common aim, the record of a dialogue bringing together anthropologists and Indians, indigenous filmmakers and linguists, indigenous researchers and film directors, master singers and ethnomusicologists, in the name of a shared adventure in defence of a unique culture." *See* Levinho in *id.* 10.

[82] For examples of world views *see* at Section 4.B. below. On the emic approach and its challenges *see* at Chapter I Section 3.B. above.

[83] On the Declaration and TCEs in general *see* at Chapter III Section 1.A. below. The Declaration is available at: http://www.un.org/esa/socdev/unpfii/documents/DRIPS_en.pdf, last visited March 11, 2010.

[84] Preliminary Title – Definitions of the "Proyecto de Ley: Protección de los Conocimientos Colectivos, los Saberes Ancestrales y las Expresiones Culturales Tradicionales de las Nacionalidades y Pueblos Indígenas, Pueblo Montucio, Afroecuatoriano, y de las Comunas y Comunidades Ancestrales del Ecuador" of February 2009. The author expresses her deepest gratefulness to Rodrigo de la Cruz of the IEPI for sharing the draft document in March 2009 in Quito.

"indios," as Kayser emphasises, but rather various, very distinctive indigenous tribes in Latin America. Still, those lumped together under this designation have—at some point—undergone a similar, oppressing and discriminatory socio-cultural treatment in the various countries. Also, they mainly underlie a common regime of international norms and legal instruments.

All these groups stated above will be treated jointly in the present context—while regarding other groups, even those of African descent, the situation is different.

1. Definition and Content of "Indigenous Peoples" and "Indigenous Communities"

As indicated above, in most of the discussions on an adequate protection of TCEs in Latin America, similar to the practice at WIPO, the term "traditional" is used in order not to exclude other bearers and potential right holders of TCEs *a priori*, although the main focus lies on the *indigenous* population or communities. At the same time, however, this main focus on the more specific term and subject of indigenous peoples as potential holders of rights in TCEs does not really simplify the topic, as the term "indigenous peoples" itself entails problems of definition.

a. Terminology: "Índio" and "Indígena"

A Latin American particularity with need of clarification regards the use of and distinction between "indígena" and "índio," in the Spanish-speaking as well as Portuguese-speaking countries.

"Índio" as designating the native people of the region goes back to Christopher Columbus' mistaken belief of having landed in India, and thus constitutes a historical error. It had, and from some perspectives, it still has a negative connotation of being wild, uncivilized, dirty and lazy.[85] This history notwithstanding, the term "índio" has been used in the context of self-nomination and is thus regarded as rehabilitated, for example in Brazil.[86] On the one hand, it is used by most of the indigenous peoples in describing themselves, and, on the other hand, it is found in most of the current Brazilian legislation dealing with the topic, and the meaning is the same as "indígena."[87] Until 2003, the terms "silvícola/s" (savage), "aborígene," "indígena," and "índios" were used interchangeably in the Brazilian legislation. "Silvícola" has been replaced by "índio" or "índios" only recently.[88] Today, the

---

[85] Personal communication with Eurico L. Sena Baniwa of the *Instituto das Tradições Indígenas*, Institute for Indigenous Traditions, on June 23, 2009 in São Paolo, and Busch (2010) 220. For details hereon *see* at Chapter IV Section 2.D.II. below.

[86] Kayser (2005) 46.

[87] *Id.* 45 *seq.* The reference of De Hollanda Sheldrick to the term "silvícolas" in Article 6 of the Civil Code stems from 2001 (although published in 2009, the article was concluded in May 2001 already) *see* De Hollanda Sheldrick (2009) 61 note 7.

[88] De Hollanda Sheldrick (2009) 61.

Constitution, Civil Code, and Indian Statute mostly use "índio" and "indígena", the latter term especially as an adjective.[89]

Lately, however, in the same country, indigenous peoples have raised the demand for a coherent, official use of the term "povos indígenas" in Portuguese, "indigenous peoples" in English, in accordance with the UN Declaration on the Rights of Indigenous Peoples,[90] especially in the context of the discussions on adequate protection of TCEs.[91]

b. Legal Definitions of "Indigenous Peoples"

As regards the content of the term "indigenous", neither at the regional level, nor in the majority of the domestic laws in Latin America, does there exist a uniform definition of "indigenous peoples." At the broader international level, the central instrument regarding the legal aspects of indigenous peoples, the UN Declaration on the Rights of Indigenous Peoples of 2007,[92] does not contain a definition either.

In the special area of TCEs, the sui generis regime of Panama uses the term "pueblo indígena" or "pueblos indígenas," but does not contain a definition. A definition might not even be needed in Panama, as there exists a consensus on the specifications of the seven indigenous peoples inhabiting the country.[93]

In the similar area of traditional knowledge in *lato sensu*, some legal definitions can be found, e.g. in the Peruvian Law on the Protection of Indigenous Peoples' Collective Knowledge Associated with Biological Resources No. 27811.[94] According to Article 2 of the Law, indigenous peoples are those who have original rights that predate the first Constitution of Peru and who maintain their own culture, territory, and self-identity. Somewhat astonishingly, the law also instructs that the term "indigenous" can be understood as and used synonymously with, among other words, "aboriginal," "native," "ethnic," "ancestral," or even "traditional."[95]

In general, the biggest difference between the modes of defining or determining the category of "indigenous" lies between a subjective approach on the one hand, and an objective one on the other—in Latin America and elsewhere. The subjective approach is based on the self-definition of the peoples concerned. The objective one

---

[89] *See, e.g.*, "direitos indígenas" (Art. 109), "direitos e interesses das populaces indígenas" (Art. 129), "culturas indígenas" (Art. 215, para. 2), "terras indígenas" (Art. 231, para. 3). In contrast, "índio" or "índios" is used in Artt. 20 XI, 231, 232 of the 1988 Brazilian Constitution and (since 2003) in Art. 6 of the Civil Code. Kayser disregards the widespread use of "indígena." *See* Kayser (2005) 45.

[90] For details on the Declaration in the context of TCEs *see* at Chapter III Section 1.A. below.

[91] Speech and personal comments of Fernanda Kaingang, Indigenous lawyer from the Kaingang tribe, at the ASPI International Congress on Intellectual Property June 21–23, 2009, in São Paolo, Brazil. On the speech and further aspects *see* also Busch (2010) 215–221.

[92] For TCE-relevant aspects *see* at Chapter III Section 1.A. below.

[93] *See* at Chapter IV Section 1.A. below.

[94] Ruiz, Lapeña and Clark (2004) 758.

[95] Articles 2 and 3 of the Peruvian Law No. 27811, translation by *id.* 777.

can either be based upon objective criteria or upon the official act of the state's vesting in someone the status of "Indian," and thus dubbing the person a "status Indian."

As regards the "status Indian", many Latin American legislations define this status of an indigenous person *de lege*, while e.g. in Colombia, in contrast, such a legislative regulation does not exist.[96] In practice, from an indigenous point of view, this *lack* of legislative regulation and thus public "dominance" is considered rather positive: due to this lack, the indigenous peoples can maintain a certain free space for self-identification and self-definition, Semper argues.[97]

The Brazilian Indian Statute lays down a legal definition of "índio" or "silvícola" "for the purposes of this law," reading: "Any individual of pre-Colombian origin or descent who identifies himself and is identified by others as belonging to an ethnic group whose cultural characteristics distinguish him from the national society."[98] Thus, two objective and one subjective criteria must be fulfilled: Objectively, pre-Colombian origin, and the existence of an ethnic group which is distinctive from the national society due to cultural characteristics; and subjectively, self-identification as belonging to this group is required. Other authors define "subjective" as in relation to the person, and thus regard the "two criteria" of self-identification and identification by others as subjective criteria.[99]

c. Self-Definition: Reflections on the Subjective Approach

Legally categorizing "indigenous peoples" by means of self-definition is often regarded as the most appropriate method from indigenous perspectives in the area of TCEs as well, especially against the background of indigenous demands for the right of self-determination.

It is somewhat problematic, however. "(O)ften, ethnicity is used strategically in order to have access to resources (like land)," anthropologists observed in the area of indigenous self-determination and territories in Colombia.[100] Distinguished scholars have put it even more drastically: "More often than not, ethnic nationalism – an appeal for a separate ethnitic identity within a given culture – occurs among indigenous groups who *use their first-on-the-scene status as an ideological weapon as well as a claim to territory*. This is certainly true in the case of American Indians. . . ."[101] This criticism of strategically using ethnicity is a comment often heard in Brazil, too, parallel to the increasing grant and

---

[96] Semper (2008) 149.

[97] *Id.* (2008) 149.

[98] Article 3, para 1, of the Indian Statute, Estatuto do Índio, Law No. 6001 of December 19, 1973. For further TCE-related issues of the Statute *see* at Chapter IV Section 2.B.III. below.

[99] Kayser (2005) 47.

[100] Kloosterman (1997) 14.

[101] Peterson Royce (1982) 48. Emphasis added by the author.

implementation of specific rights for indigenous peoples after the 1988 constitution and especially in the last 10 years.[102]

Anthropologists call such phenomena of claiming a certain ethnic status and using it for political aims "panethnic movements," which, in contrast to the mere co-existence of indigenous peoples without strategically organized dynamics,[103] are regarded as "advantageous" in relation to demands for specific rights.[104]

Such a phenomenon could also be observed in Panama when the different indigenous tribes were "fighting" for the grant of collective intellectual rights of indigenous peoples. The movement was initiated by one tribe or people, the Kuna Indians, and then organized within a newly created, inter-tribal indigenous organization, COONAPIP, *Coordinadora Nacional De Los Pueblos Indígenas De Panama.*[105] After the successful implementation of the rights, Law No. 20 of 2000 in Panama, the panethnic movement and thus the organization lost its "common aim," energy, and activity.[106]

In sum, this phenomenon makes it clear that purely subjective criteria would not be sufficient for an appropriate determination of what constitutes "indigenous."

d. Race: An Appropriate Objective Factor for Defining "Indigenous"?

One objective factor could be a person's race. However, societies like the countries in Latin America "have been marked by a centuries-old tradition of miscegenation, a tradition which has inevitably blurred the distinction between the Indian and non-Indian sectors of society along racial lines."[107] It is thus "extremely difficult to apply precise criteria to the identification of indigenous groups," particularly purely racial ones. "It is therefore widely accepted today that the concept of Indian is . . . not primarily a racial," but a "cultural" one.[108] This is also the result of the most

---

[102] Research trip made by the author from March to April 2009.

[103] Like countries in the Asian region – so far, *see* Peterson Royce (1982) 48.

[104] In such "panethnic movements," American Indians "share the symbols of a common origin and the same relationship to the land. These can, under certain circumstances, overcome tribal differences," *Id.* 48–49, 48 (1982)

[105] It was founded in 1991. For further details *see* http://www.cicaregional.org/leer.php/570046, last visited November 20, 2010.

[106] Result of the personal fieldwork mission to Panama in February 2009. The author tried to arrange an interview with representatives of the organization, but no contact could be made, as none of the indicated contact data were valid anymore. The author was then informed that the organisation was not "active" at that stage, that after the implementation of Law No. 20, no common activities had been performed anymore, and that another organization, called *Mundo Dugbis,* had taken over. Personal communication with Aresio Valiente López, Kuna Indian and lawyer, in February 2009 in Panama City.

[107] Grote (1999) 497 note 2.

[108] *Id.*

accepted definition in sociology, formulated by the great sociologist Max Weber, stating that "it does not matter whether an objective blood relationship exists."[109]

e. The Socio-Cultural Concept of "Indigenous Peoples" and "Ethnic Identity"

Weber defined ethnic groups as "those human groups that entertain a subjective belief in their common descent because of similarities of physical type or of customs or both, or because of memories of colonization and migration; this belief must be important for group formation."[110]

This concept also embraces objective as well as subjective criteria. These socio-cultural criteria can serve as elements determining the factor that should be relevant for an adequate protection of TCEs from a legal point of view: the need for protection.

f. The "Need for Protection" as Crucial Element: Some Reflections

The legal-political concept of indigenous peoples that is relevant for the protection of TCEs, being the need for protection, derives from the cultural circumstances.[111] This could be determined according to the criteria set up by the socio-cultural concept of Max Weber just mentioned, as well as by the still most relevant source for the development of rights on indigenous peoples at the international level, the UN System, the Cobo Report.

Although Ecuadorian UN Special Rapporteur Martínez Cobo has also laid down a definition,[112] the term "indigenous peoples" in the context of TCEs is rather a denomination of a type.[113] It consists of mainly four aspects,[114] of which not every

---

[109] Weber (1922 (1978)) 389. In order to adequately regulate the social reality by legal provisions in national laws or international treaties, it is held to be of essential importance in legal science to consider expertise in other sciences like sociology. Such consideration of the social situation to be governed by the law and the interdisciplinary study including the application of aspects of sociology, among other fields, is essential for the interpretation of the law, and even more important in the phase of designing new laws or provisions, as also Larenz and Canaris argue (1999) 12 and 57.

[110] Weber (1922 (1978)) 389.

[111] Ramsauer (2005) 10 *et seq.*

[112] Cobo (1986) para. 379: "Indigenous communities, peoples and nations are those which, having a historical continuity with pre-invasion and pre-colonial societies that developed on their territories, consider themselves distinct from other sectors of the societies now prevailing in those territories, or parts of them. They form at present non-dominant sectors of society and are determined to preserve, develop and transmit to future generations their ancestral territories, and their ethnic identity, as the basis of their continued existence as peoples, in accordance with their own cultural patterns, social institutions and legal systems".

[113] This term goes back to the logic "ideal type" developed by Max Weber. Types and series of types are acknowledged as part of the classic juridical methods. *See* Larenz and Canaris (1999) 461 *et seq.*

[114] These four criteria are the same as in Article 1 of the ILO Convention Nr. 169 and Article 4 of the World Bank Operational Directive 4.20. *see also* Ramsauer (2005) 8.

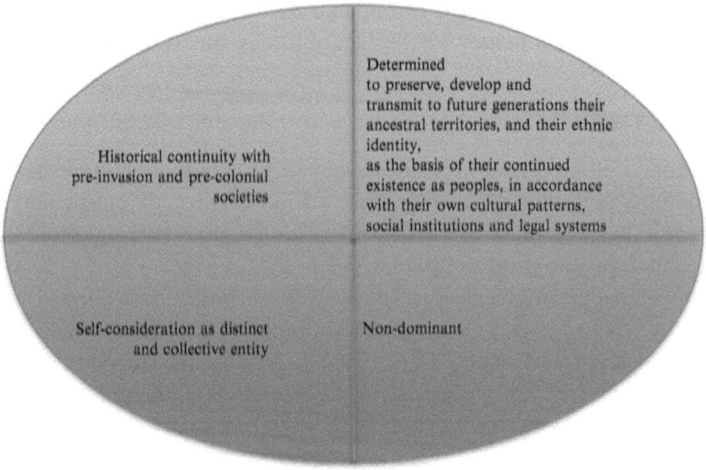

Fig. 1 Cobo definition of indigenous peoples

one must be fulfilled, but rather regarded in their inter-connection.[115] It could be illustrated like this (see Fig. 1).

g. Critical Remarks on the Cobo and Weber Criteria as Regards the Protection of TCEs

While these criteria are still the most common ones used in the area of indigenous rights as well as in the particular discussions on the protection of TCEs, from a broader, inter-disciplinary perspective, some critical remarks are necessary to consider.

The classic definition of "indigenous peoples" by Cobo also puts emphasis on the ethnic identity of the Indian people. In anthropology and sociology, however, this concept has been studied and criticized for decades now. Wolfgang Fikentscher pursued an identification of ethnic groups according to cultural distinctions based upon a categorization by mode of thought.[116] Max Weber, although having tried to formulate a definition of ethnic groups, remarked that "the whole conception of ethnic groups is so complex and so vague that it might be good to abandon it altogether."[117]

Particularly as regards indigenous peoples, it has been criticized that a form of "essentialism" has been employed to define indigenous identity, by trying to describe the ethnic identification "in terms of a set of essences,"[118] acting on the conviction that indigenous peoples or groups in general "have one or more defining

[115] Cobo (1986) para. 379, and Ramsauer (2005) 10 *et seq.*

[116] Fikentscher (2009) Chapter 15.

[117] Weber (1922 (1978)) 389.

[118] Les Field (1999), cited from Levi and Dean (2003) 13.

traits particular to all members of that group."[119] A contrasting, constructivist view argues that indigenous, indeed, "all identities are in effect fictive, their properties and origins traceable, mutable and vulnerable to deconstruction," and thus "'imagined' in and over historical time."[120]

According to anthropologist Ronald Cohen, ethnicity is rather "a *series* of nesting dichotomizations of inclusiveness and exclusiveness," and ethnic boundaries are rather determined by political needs and circumstances.[121]

The boundaries as well as visible and invisible characteristics of an ethnicity are products of the interaction with other groups.[122] "Mutuality is the most important single feature of ethnic identity. Ethnic boundaries are created and dissolved; ethnic groups lie dormant and then burst into activity; symbols of ethnic identity are constantly recreated; hierarchies of ethnic groups shift in response to system-wide changes."[123]

This is also the reason why the criterion of "historical continuity" is critical. Of what nature must this continuity be? What should the continuity consist of? With regard to Latin American indigenous identity, anthropologists have observed that "(s)ometimes one thinks that certain customs stem from the past, while in reality, they stem from outside of the ethnic group, or, inclusively, have been completely invented."[124] This latter phenomenon has been termed "invention of tradition," as mentioned above.[125]

While the Panamanian sui generis regime indeed refers to "centuries-old and up to millenia-old traditions" of the indigenous peoples,[126] and the Brazilian cultural legislation also preferred the criterion of "historical continuity" instead of "authenticity," for example,[127] the problem is, on the one hand, that often, communities or ethnic groups in general claim cultural or historic continuities over time, while many ethnic diacritics which imply "continuity with the past" are "responses to novel situations which take the form of reference to old situations, or which establish their own past by quasi-obligatory repetition" and are thus of relatively recent invention.[128]

On the other hand, a required domination of the past is dangerous, and rather disadvantageous for indigenous peoples, as it denies them a meaningful present. "Indigenous peoples are trapped in a sort of 'freeze-frame,' their cultures regarded

---

[119] *Id.* 14.

[120] Les Field (1999), cited from *id.* 13 (2003).

[121] Cohen (1978) 386 *seq.* says "ethnicity ... can be narrowed or broadened in boundary terms in relation to the specific needs of political mobilization."

[122] Peterson Royce (1982) 6.

[123] Peterson Royce (1982) 48.

[124] Kloosterman (1997) 15.

[125] For the definition and understanding of "invented tradition" according to Hobsbawm *see* above and Hobsbawm (1983) 1 *seq.*

[126] Art. 2, No. 3, of Decree 12 of 2001 to the Panamanian Law No. 20 of 2000.

[127] Art. 1, para. 2, of the Brazilian Decree 3551 of 2000, *see* at Chapter IV Section 2.C.II. below.

[128] Hobsbawm (1983) 1 *seq.*

if not as static, then at least as not progressive,"[129] for which reason the criteria of historical continuity is critical.

Another important element or "useful reference point" in determining the holders of rights according to the Cobo criteria is the different world view, namely "the diametrical opposition between the impersonality and rationally ordered 'modern' worldview of the scientific world, and the 'traditional' world view which is personal and steeped in concepts of magic and religion," "the body of ideas and values that give shape to this view of the world (cosmovisión, imago mundi, Weltanschauung)."[130]

In practice, this is, admittedly, a very difficult point of reference, as it, first, requires a substantive examination on the ground, and does not allow a general assertion, and, second, underlies constant, day-to-day change. Cobo himself admits that "the passage of time and the accumulation of experiences are also important factors altering cultures which evolve with time, in part to adapt to changing circumstances, even in isolation."[131] Notwithstanding these difficulties, the different world views are still an important aspect especially in the area of TCEs, and therefore they will be considered more carefully against the Latin American background below.[132]

Finally, within this "traditional world view" as a reference point for the determination of "indigenous peoples" and consequently holders of rights in TCEs, one of the most essential aspects, also according to Cobo, is the connection to "ancestral territories." More precisely, he characterized it as the "special and profoundly spiritual relationship of indigenous peoples with Mother Earth as basic to their existence and to all their beliefs, customs, traditions and culture" in contrast to a mere "possession or a means of production."[133] This crucial aspect will therefore also be considered more carefully in the Latin American context below.[134]

As a reference point for the determination of indigenous peoples as holders of rights on TCEs, this aspect is also difficult to handle in practice. Besides, it is ridiculous and somewhat contradictory to require a special relationship with the Earth or territory to meet the requirement for the legal protection, while at the same time the simple existence of the territory is challenged more and more every day: "The expropriation, erosion, pillage, improper use and abuse of, and the damage inflicted on, indigenous lands are tantamount to destroying the cultural and spiritual legacy of indigenous populations. Forcing them to hand over such land is tantamount to allowing them to be exterminated. In a word it is ethnocide."[135]

It is remarkable that Cobo made these observations in the mid-1980s, and more than 20 years have passed in which the destruction and exploitation of land has

[129] Levi and Dean (2003) 14.
[130] Cobo (1986) Vol. III 255.
[131] *Id.* (1986) Vol. III 183 *et seq.*
[132] *See* at Section 4. below.
[133] Cobo (1986) Vol. IV 4.
[134] *See* at Section 6. below.
[135] Cobo (1986) Vol. IV 4.

increased immensely, on the one hand, and the legal situation regarding land rights has—especially on paper—improved, on the other hand, for example in Brazil.[136]

Similarly, considering social relations and organization as vital to maintaining a group's identity over time and linking the integrity of such relations and organization to indigenous rights[137] is part of the dilemma of indigenous rights.

The reifications and the demands regarding particular practices "in order to define and bound themselves as different from the wider society" are "products of legal systems"[138] rather than social facts taken up or interpreted by legal categories.

In the end, the term *indigenous* remains a convenient conceptual construct in the legal need for categorization, while at the same time it should be borne in mind that it "occludes the heterogeneity and divisions among the people it refers to."[139]

2. Other Bearers of TCEs in Latin America

Aside from indigenous peoples, there exist other particular communities or groups affected by the topic of TCEs in the various Latin American countries.

In some Latin American countries, there even exists particular legislation dealing with collective rights of such other communities, mainly negro and Afro-communities. In Ecuador, for example, in 2006, a special law on such rights was established, even dealing with traditional knowledge and cultural rights.[140]

On TCEs in particular, the legislative project in Ecuador refers to the "collective traditional knowledge" (including cultural expressions) of "the indigenous peoples and nationalities ("nacionalidades"), the Montubio peoples, Afro-Ecuadorian

---

[136] Kayser (2005) 53, 295 *seq.* and 529 *seq.* A much more frightening fact is that "ethnocide" as a real, purposely provoked action, is still the indigenous reality in Latin American countries, e.g. Ecuador.

[137] Levi and Dean (2003) 14.

[138] Olivia Harris, "Introduction: Inside and Outside the Law" (1996) 1, cited from *id.* (2003) 14.

[139] *Id.* (2003) 13, remarking also that the construct is convenient for "distilling and representing complex, and in many regards contradictory, social and historical processes" – which is however part of the juridical dilemma of having to answer to the need of generalization and abstract rules for a heterogeneous reality.

[140] Art. 3 of the Law "Ley de los Derechos Colectivos de los Pueblos Negros o Afroecuatorianos", No. 2006–46, provides that "(e)l Estado promoverá, fomentará y garantizará la vigencia y respeto a las distintas expresiones culturales y artísticas de los pueblos negros o afroecuatorianos." This – at first sight – progressive approach is then, however, limited again: "Al mismo tiempo garantizará su plena participación en la sociedad ecuatoriana, en el marco de la interculturalidad." Art. 4 para. 2 manifests that "(t)odas las manifestaciones culturales afroecuatorianas, constituyen parte del acervo cultural de la nación."

On "collective intellectual property rights," Art. 17 stipulates that "(e)l Estado y sus instituciones reconocerán la propiedad intelectual colectiva de los conocimientos, técnicas y prácticas de las comunidades afroecuatorianas en el campo de la medicina tradicional, seguridad y soberanía alimentaria, de acuerdo con la normativa nacional, comunitaria y los convenios y tratados internacionales en materia de propiedad intelectual y biodiversidad."

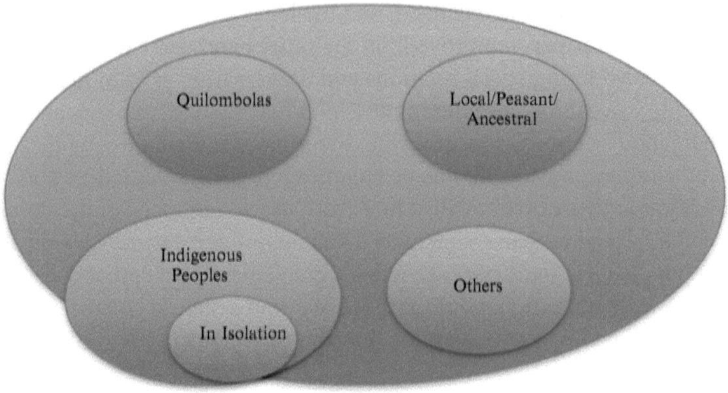

Fig. 2 Bearers of TCEs in Latin Americas

peoples and peasant ("campesinos") communities."[141] The discussions in Brazil on TCEs also embrace local communities and "Quilombolas," the special Afro-Brazilian communities, which are at least covered by the existing special legislation on traditional knowledge related to biodiversity.[142] The delegation of Mexico requested in recent negotiations at WIPO the inclusion of the expression "indigenous peoples and communities *and traditional and other cultural communities.*"[143] These examples indicate that even at the regional level in Latin American, the term and scope of potential bearers and holders of rights in TCEs vary. These differences obviously face challenges when a uniform legal treatment is to be reached.[144]

In sum, the situation of the different bearers of TCEs and potential rights in Latin America could be illustrated as follows (see Fig. 2).

On indigenous peoples in voluntary isolation *see* below Section 3.B.I.2., on *quilombolas see* Chapter IV Section 2.A.I. below.

C. Scope of Analysis

This thesis tries to consider an emic and thus a holistic approach as far as possible. The topic "protection of TCEs in Latin America" at the same time sets the principal focus on "traditional cultural expressions." This implies that the main scope of analysis excludes other related subjects, which are often interrelated,

[141] IEPI (February 2009): "Conocimientos Tradicionales Colectivos de las Nacionalidades y Pueblos Indígenas, Pueblo Montubio, Pueblo Afroecuatoriano y comunidades campesinas." The author expresses her deepest gratefulness to Rodrigo de la Cruz of the IEPI for sharing the draft document in March 2009 in Quito. *See also* de la Cruz (2008 II) 43.

[142] *See* above and Article 7, para III, of the Provisional Act No. 2186-16. For more details *see* at Chapter IV Section 2.D.I. below.

[143] WIPO (2010) Annex *e.g.* 12, 19, 26.

[144] For possible solutions *see* at Chapter V Section 3 (9) and Chapter III Section 2.A.I.1.d. below.

however, and thus difficult to separate. For example, the knowledge of the coloring extract called *bixa*, which is rooted in the biodiversity of the Amazon region, is a precondition for—and thus part of—a special TCE of body-painting art in Brazil.[145] Legally, this knowledge and TCE should therefore be treated jointly.

The main areas of distinction of TCEs according to the international discussions influencing also the Latin American situation are those of traditional knowledge on the one hand (below I.), and of cultural heritage on the other hand (below II.).

I. TCEs and Traditional or Indigenous Knowledge

According to the holistic view of many communities mentioned above, traditional knowledge and TCEs are closely related, even integral, aspects of respect for and protection of their cultural and intellectual heritage.

Even Western authors argue, within the Latin American ambit that no differentiation should be made between the terms, as "traditional knowledge embraces also the areas of music, storytelling of an ethnic community, dances and handicraft."[146]

The Group of Latin American and Caribbean Countries at WIPO differentiates between "traditional knowledge in the broad sense" and "in the strict sense" rather than between traditional knowledge and TCEs. They define TCEs as traditional knowledge in a broader sense: "traditional knowledge (including folklore)."[147] However, when going into details, "folklore" and handicrafts are examined separately, at the factual as well as at the legal level.[148]

This is the dilemma that appears when examining the details, especially against the backdrop of the Western intellectual property system.

As mentioned before, the Decree regulating the Panamanian sui-generis law No. 20 also contains a particular definition "for the effects of this Decree" of "traditional knowledge" including TCEs.[149] This definition is problematic insofar as the Law does not include medical and associated knowledge, and the Decree thus goes beyond the legal scope of protection of the Law.[150] Nonetheless, it makes clear that the scope of traditional knowledge is not understood as a contrasting or dichotomous term in relation to TCEs, but rather as broader, all-embracing term, including TCEs.

However, in certain circumstances, the term "traditional knowledge" is meant differently, not necessarily in contrast to TCEs, but definitely excluding them. This

[145] Bucher (2008) 245.

[146] Markowski (2004) 134.

[147] Group of Countries of Latin America and the Caribbean (GRULAC) (2001) Annex II, 1.

[148] Group of Countries of Latin America and the Caribbean (GRULAC) (2001) Annex I, 6 *seq.*

[149] Article 2, No. 3, of the Panamanian Decree No. 12 of 2001: "[C]ollective knowledge of an indigenous people based in/founded in centenary and up to millenary traditions which at the same time are tangible and intangible expressions which comprise their sciences, technologies, cultural manifestations, including the genetic resources, medicine, seeds, knowledge on the characteristics of flora and fauna, the oral traditions, designs, visual and representative arts."

[150] On this problem *see* at Chapter IV Section 1.C.II.2.d.aa. below.

is, for instance, the case of the collective traditional knowledge of indigenous peoples "associated with biological resources" regulated by the Peruvian Law No. 27811.[151] Still, the differentiation is not as clear or accepted as it might appear from the wording at first glance: Precisely in this case of Peru, there are authors arguing in favor of an inclusion of TCEs or at least analogous application of the provisions for cases on TCEs—at least as regards "expressions of culture and folklore that are inherently linked to such biological resources."[152] Admitting that the law "only refers to collective knowledge as that which addresses 'properties, uses, and characteristics of . . . biological diversity'" (Article 2), the authors argue that

> this separation of TK into separate forms in order to give the various classes of TK differing levels of legal treatment and protection, albeit complying with a common understanding, may well come to be considered as artificial, unrealistic, and impossible. Studies show that spiritual and practical elements of TK are intertwined and difficult to compartmentalize: they are embedded in a community's way of life and deeply interconnected with each other. These circumstances clearly call for a holistic approach. Indeed, it is this holistic quality of TK that intensifies the difficulty of designing a regime of protection that responds comprehensively to such characteristics.[153]

From an emic point of view, a broader approach was desired:

> Different communities objected to the narrow scope of the second proposal of Law 27811, which was linked exclusively to the relation of TK to biological resources. Many of those communities consulted argued that the regime's scope should extend to protect their customs, sacred icons, handicrafts, ceramics, and any knowledge associated with their spirituality, which is also susceptible to commercialization by third parties.[154]

This broader approach was also the one chosen by WIPO for the purposes of the fact-finding missions carried out in 1998–1999. The WIPO Secretariat used a similar "all-encompassing and working concept of 'traditional knowledge,'" including "tradition-based[155] literary, artistic or scientific works; performances; inventions; scientific discoveries; designs; marks, names and symbols; undisclosed information; and all other tradition-based innovations and creations resulting from intellectual activity in the industrial, scientific, literary or artistic fields."[156] The

---

[151] Articles 2, 3, and 10 of Law No. 27811. "Collective knowledge" here is defined as "accumulated and trans-generational knowledge evolved from indigenous peoples and communities, and related to biological diversity's properties, uses, and characteristics." *See also* Ruiz, Lapeña and Clark, Rev. (2004) 777 note 88.

[152] Ruiz, Lapeña and Clark, Rev. (2004) 780. Bucher (2008) 185, states that Ruiz, Lapeña, Clark argued that Law No. 27811 did "*not make a clear statement* on whether only technical knowledge associated to biodiversity or also folklore with such a background is capable of protection." Emphasis added by the author.

[153] Ruiz, Lapeña and Clark (2004) 780.

[154] *Ibid.*

[155] "'Tradition-based' refers to knowledge systems, creations, innovations and cultural expressions which: have generally been transmitted from generation to generation; are generally regarded as pertaining to a particular people or its territory; and, are constantly evolving in response to a changing environment." WIPO (2001) 25.

[156] *Id.*

categories of this "traditional knowledge" in *lato sensu* could cover technical, agricultural and medical knowledge among other on the one hand, and also "'traditional cultural expressions' ('expressions of folklore') in the form of music, dance, song, handicrafts, designs, stories and artwork; elements of languages, such as names, geographical indications and symbols; and, movable cultural properties" on the other hand.[157] Excluded from this description of traditional knowledge would be "items not resulting from intellectual activity in the industrial, scientific, literary or artistic fields, such as human remains, languages in general", and other similar elements of "heritage" in the broad sense.[158]

This is, however, only one of the two senses in which WIPO uses the term "traditional knowledge." The second one, in terms of its actual chronological use within the IGC, and currently applied, is a narrower one, "traditional knowledge" in *stricto sensu*, referring

> to the content or substance of knowledge that is the result of intellectual activity and insight in a traditional context, and includes the know-how, skills, innovations, practices and learning that form part of traditional knowledge systems, and knowledge that is embodied in the traditional lifestyle of a community or people, or is contained in codified knowledge systems passed between generations. It is not limited to any specific technical field, and may include agricultural, environmental and medicinal knowledge, and knowledge associated with genetic resources.[159]

In consequence of this differentiation, WIPO has also set up two distinct sets of provisions, one dealing with TCEs (or expressions of folklore) and the other with traditional knowledge as such.[160]

Also, in Latin America, differing legislations exist already. In Costa Rica, Peru, or Brazil legislation on traditional knowledge is restricted to certain areas of traditional knowledge, mainly on biodiversity or genetic heritage, and thus requires a special treatment. Besides this legislative differentiation, which will also be relevant for future legal instruments, traditional knowledge associated with genetic resources and that involving technical know-how raise different policy issues, are relevant to other aspects in the intellectual property system, namely, patent law embracing the particular aspect of obligatory documentation,[161] and involve distinct sets of interest groups. These differences necessitate the consideration of too many particularities that are not applicable to cultural or copyright materials, and should therefore not be dealt with in the scope of this study. For the area of Latin

---

[157] *Id.*

[158] *Id.*

[159] WIPO Doc "Traditional Knowledge – Operational Terms and Definitions", WIPO/GRTKF/IC/3/9 (2002). On further details of theses aspects *see* also Wendland (2002 I) 492 *seq.*

[160] *See* http://www.wipo.int/tk/en/consultations/draft_provisions/draft_provisions.html, last visited December 27, 2010.

[161] Obligatory documentation of technical traditional knowledge might be necessary in order to defeat claims of novelty and inventive step for patent-examination purposes. On the other hand, the copyright system does not allow for the imposition of any formalities – in contrast to industrial-property law prescribing prior examination.

America, there exist some publications particularly focussing on the issue of traditional knowledge related to biodiversity and genetic resources.[162]

However, considering emic approaches, linkages seen from the indigenous perspective should be borne in mind. As, according to the holistic view, any kind of knowledge and cultural expression is regarded as part of the community social life, rather than as an asset to be distinguished according to different subject matters of the intellectual-property system, at least those parts of traditional knowledge that relate to techniques employed in the creation of e.g. handicrafts should be covered by TCEs and are thus treated here.[163]

II. TCEs and Cultural Heritage or Cultural Patrimony

Similar to the international situation that existed between WIPO and UNESCO at the time when discussions about protecting TCEs were starting, there now seems to exist a need, at least from a Western legal point of view, to distinguish TCEs from—especially intangible—cultural heritage and cultural patrimony.

In general, such a differentiation has been described as one of the "age-old dilemmas, such as the very definition of 'culture,'"[164] and in international legal literature, much has been written on possible differentiations.[165]

In Panama, the country hosting the first and so far only sui generis protection of TCEs, no "official" definition of intangible cultural heritage has been found yet, although UNESCO had stipulated that it must develop one.[166]

Many Latin American countries have established cultural legislation, among them Guatemala, Peru, and Brazil. Here, the situation of Brazil will be examined further,[167] as there exists a Decree on the protection of the Brazilian immaterial cultural patrimony that explicitly embraces TCEs.

The term "cultural patrimony" in general is defined by the Brazilian Constitution as "goods of material and immaterial nature, individually or as a whole, which bear

---

[162] *See, e.g.*, Bucher (2008).

[163] Similarly, WIPO underlines that despite their formal separation, the two sets of draft provisions are "complementary and closely coordinated in order to answer to the rather holistic perspective of indigenous communities. Taken together, they do form a holistic approach to protection. The draft objectives and principles acknowledge those diverse choices and facilitate a holistic approach." *See* http://www.wipo.int/tk/en/consultations/draft_provisions/draft_provisions.html, last visited December 27, 2010.

[164] Maffi (2000) 32 *et seq.*

[165] For the meaning of culture in the anthropological context *see, e.g.*, the definition in the classic US-American work on cultural anthropology by Edward B. Tylor, Primitive Culture, 1 (1871). With regard to TCEs, *see* Wendland, who criticizes that with regard to intangible cultural heritage and TCEs, the "use of "intangible" may weaken the assessed worth of the folklore and traditional cultures it describes." Wendland (2002) 490 *et seq.* On "heritage" *see id.* 494.

[166] Personal Communication with Aristides Burgos, National Consultant of the Contact Office of UNESCO in Panama, on February 13, 2009 in Panama City.

[167] *See* at Chapter IV Section 2. below.

reference to the identity, activity, and memory of the different groups that form a part of the Brazilian society, including:

(i) Forms of expression,
(ii) Ways of creating, making and living,
(iii) Scientific, artistic and technological creations,
(iv) Works, objects, documents, buildings and other spaces dedicated to artistic-cultural expressions,
(v) Urban complexes and sites of historic, natural, artistic, archaeological, paleontological, ecologic and scientific value."[168]

For the Decree on the immaterial cultural patrimony, various expressions were discussed as defining best the sum of these cultural goods constituting the "immaterial patrimony of Brazil," mainly "intangible patrimony," "immaterial patrimony," "traditional and popular culture," "oral patrimony"—all equally problematic and simplifying from a conceptual point of view.[169]

Two points of criticism are of particular interest for the topic of TCEs:

- the attributes "immaterial" and "intangible," and
- the terms "traditional" and "popular" culture.

"Immaterial" and "intangible" had been criticized as disregarding the result of the expression and the material conditions of its existence, as Sant' Anna tells: They would not reflect the whole complexity of the object that they pretended to define.[170] This line of criticism is quite similar to the demand of indigenous peoples, i.e. the Latin American organization COICA, for an adequate protection of TCEs, which in their view would not be limited to the intellectual, immaterial, intangible part of their culture, but be in line with their own holistic understanding, embrace the whole process, expression, and object within the relevant context.

The second critique of the term "traditional (and popular) culture" also reflects a crucial point in the discussion on an adequate protection of TCEs, although it literally corresponds to the term commonly used, "*traditional cultural* expressions"—and this is exactly the crux as regards TCEs. That means: As the term facilitates the exclusion of contemporary expressions, it was held to be inadequate for the goal of embracing a nationwide cultural patrimony.[171] With regard to TCEs, this issue correlates to the question of whether only "traditional," originally transmitted expressions should be covered or also contemporary variations of such expressions created by the community itself should be admitted, as discussed above.

[168] Article 216 of the Brazilian Constitution. Another term of relevance is even closer to TCEs: "expressions of popular, indigenous and afro-Brazilian cultures and other groups participating in the national civilisation process" – which are not defined more specifically though, *see* Article 215 of the Brazilian Constitution. On all of this *see* at Chapter IV Section 2.B.I. below.

[169] Sant' Anna (2006 II) 15, 16, translation by the author.

[170] *Id.* 15, 17.

[171] *Id.*

In Brazil, in the end, the term "goods of immaterial nature which constitute the Brazilian cultural patrimony" was chosen, and the "Brazilian cultural patrimony" was defined as including those intangible goods "with a historical continuity" and "national relevance for the memory, identity and formation of the Brazilian society."[172]

According to Sant' Anna, doubts arose that the expressions "immaterial patrimony" and "cultural good of immaterial nature" might generate or even reinforce a false dichotomy between those vital cultural goods and the so-called material patrimony. However, it was found that this distinction was both legally correct and necessary to delimit the sum of all cultural goods, which, although intrinsically connected to a material culture, are not officially recognized as national patrimony.[173]

In terms of its legal relationship to TCEs, this definition of the immaterial cultural patrimony constitutes no dichotomy. It includes and at the same time excludes TCEs: They are covered by the term if and *only if* they bear "reference to the identity, activity, and memory of the different groups that form part of the Brazilian society."

Similarly, in this study, the focus lies on TCEs, and considers cultural heritage or cultural patrimony only as far as TCEs, in their scope as defined above, are concerned.

Finally, for a broader perspective, the different terms and categories touching on the objects of cultural heritage, TCEs, traditional knowledge, and cultural patrimony against the Latin American background as disposed above, may be illustrated like this (see Fig. 3).

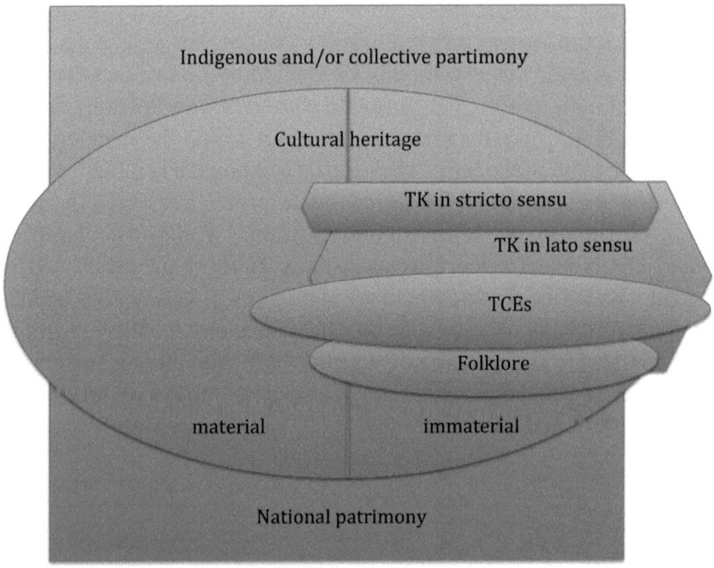

Fig. 3 TCEs, cultural patrimony, cultural heritage et al

[172] Art. 1 of Decree No. 3551 of 2000, translation by the author, *see* at Chapter IV Section 2.C.II.2. below.

[173] Sant' Anna (2006 II) 15, 17.

Section 2. Doubts, Concerns, Criticism: After All These Years—Why Protect TCEs at All?

Defining the terminology and the scope of analysis of this study has revealed that simply determining the topic and questions relating to it is difficult enough already. It is even more difficult to comprehend these "realities" as (potential) subject matter of concrete legal protection.

Against this background, during the research for this thesis, the question of why to protect TCEs at all came up time and again, especially after each new experience on the ground. There are indeed good reasons to argue against such protecting TCEs. Some of these reasons have been raised for as many years as the claim in favour of it has endured—around 30 years now. Opposition is mainly general, especially—but not exclusively—brought forward by industrialized countries.

Other reasons, concrete arguments, have arisen out of the every-day experience of trying to advance the protection of TCEs in Latin American countries themselves.

These concerns are also the reason why even some Latin American countries strongly oppose an adoption of legislative measures to protect TCEs, as does Colombia, for example.[174] This fact, that there are different political approaches towards the topic, by the way, leads to a very heterogeneous picture of the status quo of protection of TCEs in Latin America, as will be seen below.

Facing the task of contributing to the discussions on adequate protection of TCEs, it is worthwhile to display the main doubts, and criticism, especially arising out of the daily experiences.

A. Reasons Against Protection of TCEs

Arguments against protection are or could be the following ones:

(1) The protection of TCEs mainly aims at ensuring the survival of the traditional culture in which the expression is rooted. Seen through the lens of "Cultural Darwinism," such protection, however, would be an artificial construct and contravene the natural dynamics in the history of cultures. According to the concept of "Cultural Darwinism," as Mader explains, there have always been cultures disappearing and new ones arising, and even strong or high cultures, like the Roman Empire, disappear.[175] Thus, the protection of TCEs would in

[174] There are no legislative projects, nor the political intention to initiate such projects, so far in Colombia; electronic communication with Fernando Zapata Lopez, General Director of the National Copyright Direction of Colombia, in February, 2009.

[175] Mader (no year) Chapter 5.1.2.

the end constitute an artificial maintenance of a "dying" culture, which does not make sense within the context of cultural evolution.

(2) The very members of the relevant community or society, especially within the younger generation, sometimes do not even want to keep up their traditions (actively). This is also one of the main challenges discovered in projects on TCEs in Brazil, for example.[176] In such cases, the survival of the culture cannot be ensured practically through legal instruments alone.

(3) Even if the indigenous community wanted to keep up its traditional culture, effective measures would rather have to be taken at the factual (practical and personal) level. Respect for and appreciation of traditional cultures are of much greater importance for keeping TCEs alive than are legal provisions.

(4) Even if legal provisions were set up by a national state hosting traditional communities, these could not lead to an appropriate solution. Rules or even decisions made by national authorities could never reach the same level of legitimation as those set up by the relevant communities themselves. Such instruments or measures would rather lead to counter-productive effects of weakening the social structure, identity, and inner strength of the community, and thus contravene the most important aims of protecting TCEs.

(5) The spiritual level involved in TCEs makes up one of the biggest and most important differences to usual products to be purchased on the market. This level, however, is not protected in the Western system either. Holy sacraments of the Christian church, for example, have to be protected via the religious community itself. There is no reason why stronger protection should be granted to spiritual elements of a traditional community than to an officially recognized religious community.

B. Reasons in Favor of Protection of TCEs

Aside from the challenging or even critical aspects mentioned above, there are many good reasons for advancing the protection of TCEs, also and especially in Latin American countries.

(1) Incentives for and protection of cultural creations aiming at their survival have been set up in other societies, too. One of these instruments is copyright.[177]

(2) The fact that copyright is not able to provide adequate protection of TCEs is mainly[178] due to its different underlying philosophy, based upon the

176 IPHAN (2008) 107.

177 Ramsauer (2005) 174.

178 There are several reasons why copyright and other classic IP-rights do not fit for the protection of TCEs, for example that a traditional expression is handed over from generation to generation and therefore does not fulfil the requirement of a creative act. For a complete overview of the (disputed) issue *see* Nordmann (2001) 90 *seq*.

individualism of the eighteenth century in Europe.[179] This philosophy and the resulting legal argumentation of natural rights, however, is not necessarily to be regarded as the one and only leading concept or even "superior" view, to the exclusion of divergent perspectives in designing a protection of the different cultural expressions, particularly with regard to the form of ownership.[180] Quite the contrary, as Frech philosopher Morin argues: even Western societies might benefit from a better knowledge and general credence of alternative world-views, as for example the Andean world visions.[181] In this manner, Latin American legislations have already acknowledged a *collective* intellectual property right, as well as different indigenous collectives as right holders with regard to property in general, the latter for decades now.[182]

(3) These days, new creations and cultural expressions arise quickly and are exchanged rapidly through different channels of communicative media. Against this background, traditions as fundaments of and elements within the different societies are likely and worthy to be regarded as important values to be protected legally as well, although they lack an act of creation covered by copyright.

(4) Similarly, TCEs contribute to cultural diversity, which is being "discovered" as a high value in these times.[183]

(5) Due to the close connection to environmental issues at a concrete as well as at a general level, and due to economic aspects regarding the communities,[184] protection of TCEs can even serve as an instrument for implementing environmental and developing policies.[185]

(6) An adequate protection of TCEs could simply follow the general function of legal instruments: pacification. Social conflicts have been noted that affect the stability and development of the indigenous peoples or the Latin American Nations,[186] even as regards the legal level, in particular an adequate

---

[179] *See* Ramsauer (2005) 63, referring to John Locke, Second Treatise on Government (1698), §§25–51. For the actuality of this perception *see, e.g.*, a fundamental decision of the German High Court: BGH GRUR 1955, 492, 496.

[180] Critical on this argumentation ("Naturrechtsbegründung") Ohly (2003) 548.

[181] Andean Community (2009), last visited December 29, 2010.

[182] *See, e.g.*, Article 124 of the Venezuelan Constitution on the collective intellectual property rights and Article 40 of the 1973 Brazilian Indian Statute on right holders.

[183] *See* the UNESCO policy and Conventions below Chapter III Section 1.B. and COICA (2005) 77, translation by COICA at http://www.coica.org.ec/ingles/aia_book/index.html.

[184] On these connections *see* at Section 3.B. below.

[185] *See, e.g.*, the planting project of the Panamanian Department of Collective Rights and Folkloric Expressions within DIGERPI, *see* at Chapter IV Section 1.G.II.2.a. below and Article 58 of the Brazilian Indian Statute as an example for legally promoting TCEs as developing measure, at Chapter IV Section 2.D.IV. below.

[186] A famous example of a serious social conflict on TCEs is the organized crime dealing with *tsantsas*, shrunken heads, in Ecuador and Peru; personal communication with N.N., who wants to stay anonymous.

consideration of customary rules and their interaction with national laws and legal standards.[187]

(7) There exists a need for protection because of the special sensitivity of TCEs: besides the challenge to uphold communal social structures as a precondition for maintenance of TCEs, there are multiple forms of general threats as well as concrete infringements of TCEs.[188]

C. Conclusion and Consequences

Some of the arguments against protecting TCEs at all indeed reflect serious difficulties regarding the topic. However, the arguments should not completely hinder the advancement of protection for TCEs, as there are even better arguments in favor of protection, and there is still a realistic chance left to implement such protection. Following this path of trying to protect TCEs, in spite of all these opposing arguments, does not mean following a path of easy success. The arguments to the contrary can and should rather serve as indicators for challenges on the way and as appeals to all persons involved in the issue.

Section 3. Understanding the Latin American Setting: Political, Social, and Economic Background of the Topic of TCEs in Latin America

A. Political Setting

Despite all the particularities in the different national countries in Latin America, one can say that, especially in the first decades, the policy of the twentieth century on the indigenous population was characterized by an "integrationist" or "assimilationist approach".[189] This policy might be illustrated best by the statement of the Mexican President Lazaro Cárdenas, made at the first Inter-American Indigenist Congress in Patzcuaro in 1940: "Our 'indigenismo' does not Indianize Mexico, but Mexicanizes the Indian."[190] Diversity of cultures was regarded as an obstacle and permanent threat to the sovereignty of the young nation-states. Therefore, the

[187] For the fact that contradictions between customary law and positive law of Latin American States provoke social conflicts affecting the stability and development of the countries, *see* Stavenhagen and Iturralde (1990) 15. On the topic of customary law and TCEs *see* at Section 5. below.

[188] For the various threats and infractions to TCEs *see* at Section 3.C. below.

[189] For a broader picture of the different policies on the indigenous population in Latin America, namely Mexico, Guatemala, Ecuador, Peru, and Bolivia, *see* Meentzen (2007).

[190] Cited from Albó (2004) 21.

education of indigenous peoples had the "sole function" of "integration and assimilation," which later turned into marginalization.[191]

Only in the 1970s, this policy started to change slowly. One of the factors introducing this change was a new conception in anthropology, as Kayser argues, based upon the theory of cultural relativity, established and promoted strongly by Claude Lévi-Strauss.[192] Brazil was one of the first countries that in its 1988 Constitution officially abolished its integrationist policy, as Kayser tells. According to him, that was also an important signal for other Latin American countries, leading to the further development of a policy and the constitutional granting of explicit, subjective rights, acknowledging the multi-ethnicity and pluri-culturality in the different Latin American countries.[193]

Today, the political current seems to generally—although slowly—move in more progressive, advanced, pro-indigenous directions—while, then again, it is changing quickly towards more economy-driven, equalizing forces. For example, only a few years ago, the "Regional Study in the Andean Countries" argued that in Ecuador, it was

> clear that indigenous peoples are the ones who must assume control of their own institutions, ways of life, economic development, and strengthen their cultural identities, while ensuring that their knowledge, innovations and traditional practices are respected, preserved and maintained, and that their broader application is promoted, with the approval and participation of the owners of traditional knowledge, and the recognition by the authorities of the competence which indigenous peoples have in the effective control of traditional knowledge through their own customs or customary law.[194]

While the Ecuadorian Institute for Intellectual Property (IEPI)[195] indeed elaborated a proposal for a sui-generis protection of TCEs and traditional knowledge, realities, i.e. politics under the leadership of Rafael Correa have been moving in the opposite direction: The newly created administrative entity of "Citizenship" aims at an equalization of all Ecuadorian citizens and thus denies special rights to certain minorities.[196]

Another common strategy of weakening the public organizations and political representations of the indigenous population is to repeatedly reform or re-allocate them in varying parts of the ministerial structure, like the National Indigenous

[191] Panamanian Ministry of Education on Intercultural Bilingual Education, cited from Valiente López (2006) 48.

[192] Kayser (2005) 243.

[193] *Id.* 259. On the constitutional aspects in general *see* at Chapter III Section 3. below.

[194] de la Cruz (2006) 9.

[195] Instituto Ecuatoriano de la Propiedad Intelectual (IEPI).

[196] "Consejo de Participación Ciudadana y Control Social". *See* Articles 207 *et seq.* of the 2008 Constitution of Ecuador, and personal communication on the political situation in Ecuador with Professor Fernando García Serrano, longtime professor and researcher for the Anthropology Department at FLACSO University (Facultad Latinoamericana de Ciencia Sociales) in Quito, Ecuador, in March 2009, in Quito.

Foundation, FUNAI, in Brazil, which had been allocated within different ministries.[197]

Similarly, the picture of the constitutions and constitutional reforms is a relatively quickly changing one.[198]

B. Environmental, Economic, and Socio-Cultural Influences

Looking at the social and economic context of any legal protection of TCEs is essential for

(i) The *design* of such protection, as regards the political aim as well as the factual background and content of the legal provisions and additional measures, and
(ii) its subsequent implementation.

Essential factors are social contexts and the economic situation, especially when representatives of industrialized countries with little experience in developing countries are negotiating the issue at the international level.

I. Socio-Environmental Aspects

1. General Aspects

According to official studies conducted by the United Nations Environment Program (UNEP), Latin America and the Caribbean is the region with the greatest biological diversity on the planet, hosting almost one half of the world's tropical forests, 50 % of the world's total amphibians, and over 40 % of its birds.[199] Six of its countries are considered mega-diverse: Brazil, Colombia, Ecuador, Mexico, Peru, and Venezuela.[200] Latin America and the Caribbean are said to hold more than 30 % of all the planet's available freshwater and some 40 % of its total renewable water resources.[201] The sub-region of the Andes holds "90 per cent of the world's tropical glaciers, producing 10 per cent of the planet's freshwater."[202]

---

[197] Today, FUNAI is part of the Brazilian Ministry of Justice. *See* http://www.funai.gov.br/, last visited August 2, 2010.

[198] On the political situation and developments with regard to TCEs *see* at Section 3.A. below. On the constitutional aspects *see* at Chapter III Section 3. below.

[199] UNEP – United Nations Environment Program, "State of Biodiversity in Latin America and the Caribbean", 1 (2010).

[200] *See* http://www.unep.org/geo/geo4/media/fact_sheets/Fact_Sheet_11_LAC.pdf, last visited November 2, 2010.

[201] UNEP – United Nations Environment Program (2010) 2 *seq.*

[202] *Id.* 3.

At the same time, the region faces major environmental challenges. According to UNEP, it has the highest deforestation rate in the world now, with considerably impact on the region's environment, socio-cultural structures, and economies.[203] Besides, infrastructure, particularly roads, represents an important factor in increasing deforestation rates, mainly in Central and South America. Roads open the way for agriculture to expand, but also for illegal logging—as "a rule, deforestation takes place less than 30 kilometers away from an official road", UNEP found out.[204]

The hugest infrastructure program in Latin American history has just been accomplished: the construction of a road between Manaus, Brazil, and Manta, Ecuador, crossing the whole, previously undivided Amazon rainforest—a development that will cause unforseeable and irreversable changes for the whole region.

In addition, oil spills and elevated oil pollution from refineries are a serious problem off the coast of Brazil, in the Greater Caribbean, the Gulf of Mexico, and also the Ecuadorian "Oriente."[205]

According to UNEP, the greatest risks to biodiversity in the Latin American region, however, "stem from the change of land use, with the consequent reduction, fragmentation and even loss of habitats." In this respect, the most important driving force of change of land use and habitat loss has been "the significant expansion of commercial agriculture for exportation" of e.g. soy, bio-fuels, and flowers, that is responsible for "close to one half of the deforestation in the region."[206]

Although, as initially indicated, Latin America is one of the world's most water-abundant regions, the resource is "distributed very unequally and subject to multiple pressures, including increasing pollution, degradation of watersheds and the depletion and unsustainable use of aquifers as a result of population growth, climate change, social and economic development and societies' increasing interference in the hydrological cycle."[207]

Moreover, most Andean Glaciers are expected to melt over the coming 10–20 years, probably causing many vulnerable communities throughout the sub-region to suffer from water shortage, UNEP says.[208] To implement an integrated (trans-boundary) water resource management process, according to UNEP, the national legislations and regional co-operations had to take due account of three essential elements:

- participation,
- transparency, and
- accountability.[209]

---

[203] *Id.* 2.

[204] *Id.* 5.

[205] *See* http://www.unep.org/geo/geo4/media/fact_sheets/Fact_Sheet_11_LAC.pdf, last visited November 2, 2010.

[206] UNEP (2010) 2 *seq.*

[207] *Id.*

[208] *Id.* 3.

[209] *Id.* 6.

2. Consequences of Socio-Environmental Aspects for the Topic of TCEs

An illustrative example for having provoked a documented alteration of indigenous customary law is the quest for water.[210] Impacts such as this are likely to lead also to a change of indigenous economic-philosophical principles (away from abundance to scarcity) and social patterns, directly leading to alterations of cultural "traditions."[211]

It becomes clear that the issue of TCEs cannot be understood without first comprehending the environmental circumstances and living conditions of the holders of TCEs.

Apart from the lasting discrimination, the biggest threats to indigenous peoples (and TCEs) seem to be environmental devastation and poverty. In general, the region has a limited political, institutional, and technological framework to deal with environmental impacts.

The fieldwork experience especially has revealed that two distinctions can be made which are of relevance for the different particularities of protecting TCEs:

- The distinction between indigenous communities that still have resources left and those that do not, and
- The communities in exchange with the national society and those in voluntary isolation.

Both aspects are often, but not necessarily, linked to each other. First of all, it is essential to distinguish between (1) communities that still have natural resources left (currently the Paríjaro in Peru for instance), and (2) those that do not.[212] The latter have one overwhelming aim of first priority: food security.

For the issue of protecting TCEs, the lack of natural resources has five main consequences:

(1) As de la Cruz observes, scarcity of resources leads to a disequilibrium of goods and needs, and finally to a dysfunction of the principle of reciprocity that has ruled the community's social life for centuries.[213] The monetary system of the Western world takes over. For example, a typical drink, *masato*, has always been offered as a gift, for free, as an expression of sharing goods and life in the communal *fiestas* of the Asháninkas in Peru. A couple of years ago, it was offered for sale for the first time.[214] Consequently, the economic value of TCEs gains more and more importance.

(2) Scarcity of resources and the subsequent urgent need of alimentary supply provokes egoism and individualism, and leads to decimation and finally the

[210] *See* at Section 5.B.III.2.d. below.

[211] *See ibid.* and at Section 1.B.I.1.d. above.

[212] Personal communication with J.M. of the Asháninka Indians of Peru on June 10, 2008.

[213] de la Cruz (2006) 29.

[214] Personal communication with J.M. of the Asháninka Indians of Peru on June 10, 2008.

breaking down of essential customary rules, like the collective character of land, resources and rights.

(3) Expressions of traditional culture as means to strengthen the collective identity are not realized as such anymore, as the collective identity is vanishing and the elders, rich in traditional knowledge concerning cultural expressions, are not held in high estimation anymore—as they are regarded to be useless facing the challenges of material modernization. Traditional practices are regarded as meaningless. Cultural diversity thus diminishes.

(4) If (or although) TCEs are still appreciated—at least for their economic value—in reality they are considered merely as a supplement to the question of alimentary supply because TCEs offer only a marginal source of income. Therefore, only little effort is made to maintain TCEs. Other occupations are more acute for the "indigenous individual" (e.g., breeding of small animals).

(5) As in those difficult circumstances the community has gained the experience that women are more responsible and reliable in fulfilling tasks and providing for the family, the traditional allocation of responsibilities, social tasks, and finally knowledge is often not operative anymore. To better fulfill the social tasks and strengthen their forces, the women tend to cooperate and found associations which take over functions and allocate responsibilities according to personal engagement rather than traditional structures.

In general, even in rather remote areas like the Ecuadorian rainforest, a strong commercialization has taken place, simply because economic integration follows even simple structures of social integration into the national state, e.g. by means of the educational system and taxes. Thus, the Shuar and Achuar Indians in the Ecuadorian rainforest, like the less isolated groups, also need to participate in the monetary system to enable their kids to participate in school.[215]

Second, the situation of "voluntarily isolated" peoples is different and should be treated differently from others. This is due to both the decision of those communities, which should be respected, and the different level of vulnerability they generally face.

The indigenous head organization "Coordinator of the Indigenous Organizations of the Amazonian River Basin" (COICA)[216] describes the situation as follows:

> Within the Amazon Basin, there are approximately 80 peoples in a natural-state situation. 53 peoples are known in Brazil, 20 in Peru and 3 in Ecuador. Many of these peoples occupy frontier zones (Ecuador-Peru, Peru-Brazil). The level of vulnerability that they confront tends to increase as a result of the pressure over their territorial spaces by the great oil and wood firms and construction enterprises who have an interest on building highways. Although some important measures have been taken for their protection, such as the

[215] Personal communication with ethnologist Anna Meiser on January 8, 2009, who has done ethnological research on the Shuar and Achuar communities for more than five years.

[216] COICA stands for "Coordinadora de las Organizaciones Indígenas de la Cuenca Amazónica." COICA represents those indigenous communities who are organized in the nine different member organizations from the nine countries containing part of the Amazon region. COICA will be presented in detail below, *see* at Section 4.C.I. below.

intangible lands in Ecuador, or the Reserves of the Nahua Kugapakori State in Peru, these dispositions have not prevented conflicts from developing both between our peoples as well as mainly with invaders. Such as is the case of the massacre of the Taromenane peoples in Ecuador, motivated by wood industry; conflicts between the Isolated Peoples with the Asháninka in Ucayali, as a product also of the territorial occupation of wood firms. Or the concession for the hydrocarbon exploitation, the Camisea Project in the heart of the reserved territory, in Peru. This is a country in which all the officially recognized territories in favor of natural state peoples, without exception, currently find themselves invaded by wood and oil firms, religious groups and sects, researchers, film companies – who have an unfortunate compliance, be it due their actions or by their omissions –, and from State entities.[217]

Nonetheless, the apparently negative impact of the oil industry can also have positive effects in some cases. According to Feser, it was due to worldwide protests against planned oil drilling in the Ecuadorian Yasuní National Park, that the Ecuadorian State declared the respective part of the National Park indigenous territory in favor of the Huaraní Indians—and according to Ecuadorian law, in indigenous territories, oil exploitation is legally allowed.[218] This act of granting land rights can be a great opportunity for the Huaraní tribe. Naturally, it constitutes an exception in the Latin American reality so far, and does not hinder the environmental and potential socio-cultural consequences of oil exploitation in the region.

Consequences of the special situation of indigenous peoples in voluntary isolation for TCEs in particular constitute special needs, to be addressed by corresponding measures. For example, the Interethnic Association for the Development of the Peruvian Rainforest (AIDESEP),[219] focuses, among others, on creating a specific strategy for the defense of voluntarily isolated peoples. It has developed a Voluntarily Isolated Indigenous Peoples Program including a proposal for a special regime on isolated indigenous peoples and legal stability for their territories. AIDESEP has implemented special procedures for the withdrawal of external agents that have invaded the territories of these peoples.[220]

More specifically, the Ecuadorian Institute for Intellectual Property (IEPI) elaborated a proposal for a sui-generis protection of TCEs and traditional knowledge with particular provisions on voluntarily isolated indigenous peoples. Article 9 of the Draft stipulates that

the collective knowledge, ancestral wisdom and know-how, and traditional cultural expressions of the indigenous peoples in voluntary isolation are unlimited in time, inalienable, and

[217] COICA (2005) 38 *seq.*, translation by COICA at http://www.coica.org.ec/ingles/aia_book/index.html, last visited January 10, 2011.

[218] For details hereon *see* Feser (2008) 177 *et seq.*

[219] AIDESEP, the Asociación Interétnica de Desarrollo de la Selva Peruana, is a national indigenous organization struggling for the rights of the indigenous people of the Peruvian Amazon region, *see* http://www.aidesep.org.pe, last visited January 10, 2011.

[220] However, COICA says "there isn't yet a level of coordination amongst member organizations for a common treatment in defence of voluntarily isolated peoples located in frontier zones." *See* COICA (2005) 39, translation by COICA at http://www.coica.org.ec/ingles/aia_book/index.html, last visited January 10, 2011.

> non-transferable, and are not subject to utilization for either scientific or commercial aims. The State establishes appropriate guarantees for the intangibility of these peoples and watches over the respect for their rights.[221]

II. Socio-Cultural Aspects

1. Demographic Situation

The socio-demographic data of indigenous populations vary enormously in the different Latin American countries from less then 1 % to over 50 % of the whole population.[222] According to Stavenhagen, the indigenous population of Argentina consists of 398,000 peoples, which makes up 1.5 % of the whole population; Colombia, 547,000 or 2.2 %; Ecuador, 3,340,000 or 40 %; Guatemala, 4,200,000 or 59 %; Mexico, 12,000,000 or 18 %; Nicaragua, 152,000 or 5 %; Panama, 126,000 or 6 %; Paraguay, 76,000 or 2.3 %; Peru, 10,200,000 or 55 %; and Venezuela, 331,000 or 2 %.[223]

These numbers (whether absolutely precise or not) impressively demonstrate the heterogeneity of the indigenous populations both in relative and absolute terms within the different Latin American countries.

2. Socio-Cultural Interaction with the "National Society"

a. Some Historical Aspects, Including the Role of the Church

The Church, Christian belief in its missionary extension, played an important role in colonized Latin America. This fact is important to know with regard to TCEs, in particular when determining "traditional" as well as "indigenous," including the "different world view" and spirituality, and the related scope of protection.

In most of the Latin American countries, the official policy of European colonizers was to "civilize" the "savages" and to convert pagans to the Christian faith.

In Panama, this policy endured until the twentieth century, and the first laws issued after the country became independent implemented exactly this aim by involving an active role of the Catholic Church.[224] In Brazil, it had been the legitimization for Portuguese expansion and slavery as laid down in various papal

---

[221] IEPI (February 2009). The author expresses her deepest gratitude to Rodrigo de la Cruz of the IEPI for sharing the draft document in March 2009 in Quito.

[222] Facts are difficult to obtain, the census in the different countries based upon diverging criteria, *see* at Section 1.B.II.1. above.

[223] *See* Stavenhagen (1992) 8. The numbers were calculated for the report of Rodolfo Stavenhagen for the Inter-American Commission of Human Rights of the Organization of American States (OAS) and are only partially based upon official collections of data and date back to 1991.

[224] Panamanian Law 59 of December 31, 1908, "Ley de Civilización de los Indígenas." *See* Valiente López (2006) 48.

bulls.[225] At the beginning, during the first five decades after the "discovery" of the South American continent, the ostensible aim of Christianization had in fact been used for the appropriation of land and goods, Kayser argues.[226] Then, when the new political aim became the settlement of the colonies, the official "main reason" for the settlement was to convert the native people to the Portuguese "Holy Catholic faith", Kayser tells.[227]

Before being converted by Portuguese Jesuits, some indigenous tribes lived in a community house called *maloca*. It was used by around 50–200 persons, as a working, sleeping, and eating place and for ceremonies.[228] The egalitarian character of the *malocas* enabled the conservation of indigenous customs and resistance to such cultural change as the Portuguese wished to introduce, as Kayser says, and therefore, the *malocas* were prohibited in the wake of the Christianization of Brazil and replaced by re-organized nuclear families or *aldeias* (villages).[229]

Interestingly, today, the biggest regional organization of indigenous peoples of the whole Amazon region has chosen the name *Maloca* for its philosophy, policy, and guiding principles, thus embracing the main aim of the new indigenous way symbolically to "return to the *maloca*."[230]

As regards TCEs in particular, an oppression of the indigenous culture and social structures took place in the colonial era. One of the most important aims of the Jesuits was, according to Kayser, to abolish traditions and customs, like the practice of unchristian rituals and celebrations and indigenous songs and chants, which were replaced by Catholic ones, and to abolish the special positions of the *caciques*, the indigenous leaders.[231] In most of the cases, a mixture of the different cultures and religions occurred, so that they are hardly separable anymore.

In this respect, it is also remarkable that Christianization was one of the initiating factors in the discontinuance of the nudity of indigenous tribes in Latin America.[232] Against this background the question arises: how "traditional" are the traditional indigenous textiles called *molas* of the Kuna Indians in Panama in fact? Is

---

[225] Kayser (2005) 139.

[226] According to Kayser, the appropriation was legitimized again by a papal bull, the *Dum diversus et Divino Amore Communiti* of June 18, 1452, by Nikolaus V. The decree was initially directed at the appropriation of goods of Moslems, and other non-believers, in the days of Turkish expansion across Europe. Other decrees on the appropriation of land in Latin America followed. For details *see id.* 139 *et seq.*

[227] As Kayser shows, this aim was expressed in the guiding principles for settlement contained in the *Regimento de Tomé de Sousa* of December 17, 1548, set up by the Portuguese King *Dom João III.*. *See id.* 141.

[228] For example, the way of life of the Tupi Indians in Brazil was characterized by those houses, before they were converted by the Portuguese Jesuits. *See id.* 143.

[229] *Id.* 144 *seq.*

[230] On this *see* at Section 4.C.II. below.

[231] Kayser (2005) 145.

[232] *Id.* 145 (2005).

"traditional" the right term to use in this context? This question on TCEs has been addressed above.[233]

Also in the Spanish-reigned part of the continent, according to Elliot, the Spanish monarchy, acting as a "supreme mediating institution," on the one hand went along with the fact of two distinct societies existing in the colonies, the Spanish and the Indian one. On the other hand, cultural and especially religious assimilation was pursued, Elliot. This policy was even implemented legally, by means of the legal construction called *encomienda*.[234] In its beginnings, this system was intended to provide the colonizers with easy access to Indian tribute and labour. As a "consideration" in return, the *encomenderos*, the large landowners, had to ensure, among other things, the assimilation of the Indians to the Spanish culture and their Christianization.[235]

As regards the diverse relationship between the Church and indigenous communities today, in some regions the role of the Christian entities has converted into supportive institutions with regard to all question of indigenous daily life, including legal aid. In Brazil for example, this is the Conselho Indigenista Missionário (CIMI), created in 1972 by the National Confederation of the Bishops of Brazil (CNBB) and self-defined as "an organization that supports the struggle of the indigenous peoples in Brazil." CIMI plays an important role in overcoming social, cultural, and legal problems of indigenous tribes, while it focuses on land rights and issues, "because land is central for the well-being and survival of Brazils indigenous population."[236] Interestingly enough, CIMI regards dialogue with the indigenous cultures as the base of the its work, as learning about these cultures "is important in order to be able to respect these cultures."[237] At the same time, CIMI regards this dialogue as a mutual exchange, as it "believes that the indigenous people can inspire the world of today, review the meaning, the history, and social, political and economic practices within this world."[238]

For implementing this credo in practice, CIMI requests that the people who are working for the organization "live together with the indigenous peoples on every moment, especially during the fight for their rights." With regard to TCEs in

---

[233] *See* at Sections 1.A.IV. and B.I.1.d. above.

[234] The *encomienda* was introduced by the first royal governor of Hispaniola, Nicolás de Ovando, *see* Elliot (1984) 149, 163. On details hereon and its connection to the topic of indigenous customary law *see* at Section 5.E.II.1. below.

[235] *Id.* 149, 163.

[236] *See* www.cimi.org.br/, for the English version http://www.cimi.org.br/?system=news&eid=336, last visited January 10, 2011.

[237] *See* ibid.

[238] *See* ibid.

concrete, CIMI refers to the respect for "indigenous diversity in its ethnic-cultural . . . plurality and the value of the traditional knowledge."[239]

b. Level of Cultural Integration into the National Society

Today, the different levels of assimilation of indigenous peoples are as diverse as the peoples themselves. In order to systematize this heterogeneity, there exist different models of classification of the indigenous communities in Latin America. One model is of special interest in the legal context, as it is also the one adopted (in a slightly simplified version) for defining the legal categories of indigenous peoples in the 1973 Brazilian Indian Statute, to be dealt with in details below.[240] This typology was developed by Darcy Ribeiro and differentiates the following four groups:

(i) "Isolated groups"
(ii) "Groups with occasional contact to the national society"
(iii) "Groups with constant contact to the national society"
(iv) "Groups integrated into the national society".[241]

This differentiation follows the understanding of distinct social realities. Based upon this anthropological perception, the need for a distinct legal treatment was realized and codified in the Indian Statute. With regard to TCEs, it can be of value for comprehending the essentiality of a flexible treatment. This is a factor of differentiation additional to the aspect of the different social and economic reality caused by environmental impacts and living conditions as indicated above.[242]

c. Indigenous Voices and Perspectives

The importance of the socio-cultural setting for the topic of protecting TCEs, in particular the social structures as a precondition for maintenance of TCEs, has also been underlined by indigenous peoples themselves: "If our different social patterns are not recognized, we cannot distinguish and guarantee our rights as such." "(O)ur

[239] This point of view is part of the basic principles defining the work of CIMI. In general, these are, as CIMI says: "1. Respect for indigenous diversity in its ethnic-cultural and historical plurality and the value of the traditional knowledge of indigenous peoples; 2. The indigenous people as prime actors and Cimi as an ally in the fight to guarantee their historical rights; 3. The choice for the indigenous cause, and the commitment with it, within a broader perspective of building a society based on democracy, justice, solidarity, multi-ethnicities and multi-cultures." *See* http://www.cimi.org.br/?system=news&eid=336, last visited January 10, 2011.

[240] Categories (iii) and (iv) are pooled. In view of the reformed indigenous policy laid down in the 1988 Brazilian Constitution, this legal classification is critical. *See* at Chapter IV Section 2.B.III. below, and Kayser (2005) 66.

[241] For further details on the characteristics of these categories *see id.* 65.

[242] *See* the distinction according to the presence of natural resources at Section 3.B.I.1.b. above.

cultural diversity ... has served as trenches that have disabled ... our destruction."[243]

Especially with the migration to urban areas, the peoples' "main principles" get lost, and they "become baits and fall easily to the traps of economic power and individualism. With these traps, we've become suicide agents of our own social and cultural systems. The shame of being what we are generates changes in ourselves, as persons."[244]

Moreover, the economic setting has been rated an important factor for the traditional culture as well:

> We have a greater dependence on manufactured products; dependence on external resources for all kind of community activities, and without a doubt, the weakening of our sustainable patterns. ... Almost every one of us in the Amazon produce something for the market economy and negotiate directly with it, be it through the sale of our products or of external ones. This market economy has broken the reciprocity system – production, distribution and consumption – and has altered the use of natural resources and the social mobility mechanisms, and specially changed eating patterns.[245]

Natural resources and

> our own daily life ... have become now a currency. The natural resources have started scaling up sales, and our daily lives are exploited as entertainment for 'solidary' tourists. In this way, we open our communities to commercial activities such as eco tourism, whose most drastic result has been the abandonment of our daily tasks of continuance, to become labor for the entertainment market.[246]

Finally, the previously addressed aspect of the influence of the Church has also been observed as crucial for the maintenance of the traditional culture. It led to the assessment of ancestral wisdoms "as diabolic". Terms like "witches" and "demons" were used "mainly by the clergy and by Western church shepherds to refer to our wisemen." This was regarded as one reason why indigenous youths distance themselves from traditional wisdoms, making it "each time more difficult for wisemen to transmit their ancestral knowledge" and cultural expressions.[247]

III. Economic Aspects

As regards the economic realities surrounding the particular topic of TCEs, statistics on the one hand, and a look at the reality "outside" or "on the ground" on the other hand, are useful illustrators. As this study focuses on the legal context, only

---

[243] COICA (2005) 71, translation by COICA at http://www.coica.org.ec/ingles/aia_book/index.html, last visited January 10, 2011.

[244] *Id.* 26, translation according to COICA, *see* fn. above.

[245] *Id.* 27, 59, translation according to COICA, *see* fn. above.

[246] COICA (2005) 27, translation by COICA at http://www.coica.org.ec/ingles/aia_book/index.html.

[247] *Id.* 59.

Table 1 Quality-of-life indicators for selected areas in Mexico according to Eisenstadt [Eisenstadt (no year) 25]

Area	Illiterates (15 years and older)	Population without electricity	Population without drainage or toilet	Population with dirt floor
All Mexico	18	10	20	32
Indigenous localities	31	21	73	54
All Chiapas	23	12	19	41
Santiago Ixtayutla, Oaxaca	55	57	18	82
San Nicolas, Nuevo León	2	0	0	0

Source of Data as cited by Eisenstadt: Serrano Carreto, ed. (2002), Instituto Nacional para el Federalismo y el Desarrollo Municipal (2003)

two examples will be given for a first impression. In general, the living conditions among the indigenous population in Latin America are very poor. What is remarkable from a Western-industrialized point of view are not only the numbers, but also the indicators providing information about the specific living conditions and socio-economic circumstances of the holders and producers of TCEs (see Table 1).

"Indigenous localities" are understood as localities "where more than 40 percent of the population speaks indigenous languages. This group represents nearly 8 million people (some 8 per cent of Mexico's total population)."[248]

Santiago Ixtayutla and San Nicolas had been chosen as examples by Eisenstadt because they—obviously—illustrate the difference between indigenous and non-indigenous living-conditions quite well, Eisenstadt argues. In Santiago Ixtayutla, "65 percent of the residents were linguistically indigenous, and 85 percent of these indigenous language speakers are monolingual (most speak Mixteco)", and it constitutes the "18th poorest" municipality of Mexico's total 2,440 ones.[249] San Nicolas, in contrast, is a suburb of Mexico's northern industrial center Monterrey and "perhaps the most affluent municipality in Mexico", where the indigenous population "is negligible."[250]

According to Panamanian national data, as Valiente López shows, 21.2 % of the whole national population, in contrast to 95.4 % of the indigenous population, live in "general poverty" in Panama, and 18.8 % of the national population, in contrast

[248] *Ibid.*

[249] *Ibid.*

[250] *Ibid.*

to 84.4 % of the indigenous population, live in "extreme poverty."[251] The average annual income of the Panamanian population is said to be about 2,850.00 Panamanian dollars—while that of the indigenous population is said to be about 712.00 Panamanian dollars, thus an amount four times less than the national average.[252]

IV. Legal Regulation of TCEs in the Broader Sense and the Socio-Economic Situation

In Latin American legal instruments, there are legal provisions explicitly addressing the economic situation of indigenous peoples in relation to TCEs like handicrafts. Thus, Article 53 of the Brazilian Indian Statue stipulates that the "handicraft art and rural industry shall be promoted in order to elevate the living standard of the Indians, adequately adapting it to modern technical conditions."[253]

The position of this provision within the law also gives an interesting insight about the comprehension of indigenous culture in general and of handicraft in particular. Article 53 is located in Section V entitled "On education, culture and health," which contains other provisions dealing among other things with the respect for the cultural patrimony, artistic values, and forms of expressions (Article 47) on the one hand, and socio-economic issues on the other, like the facilitating of appropriate vocational training (Article 52), the right to enjoy the same resources/ instruments of the national health system (Article 54), and the application of rules on social insurance (Article 55).

From this observation one can see that there is a much closer connection of the different socio-cultural and economic issues surrounding the particular question of treatment and protection of TCEs than it would seem when it is reduced to a topic of intellectual property law. The technical realm to which the discussion of protection of TCEs is allocated at WIPO tends to place the focus on intellectual property aspects,[254] as WIPO's sphere of competence is limited to the area of intellectual property. Experience with specific national laws and the practical treatment of indigenous or other particular communities, however, reveals that the different socio-cultural and economic issues are much more closely interrelated than has been indicated in the literature, and it is these issues that must be considered when one intends to address the topic of adequately protecting TCEs.

---

[251] Valiente López (2006) 46 with further references.

[252] *Ibid.*

[253] Article 53 of the 1973 Brazilian Indian Statute, translation by the author.

[254] *See e.g.* von Lewinski (2007) 207–231.

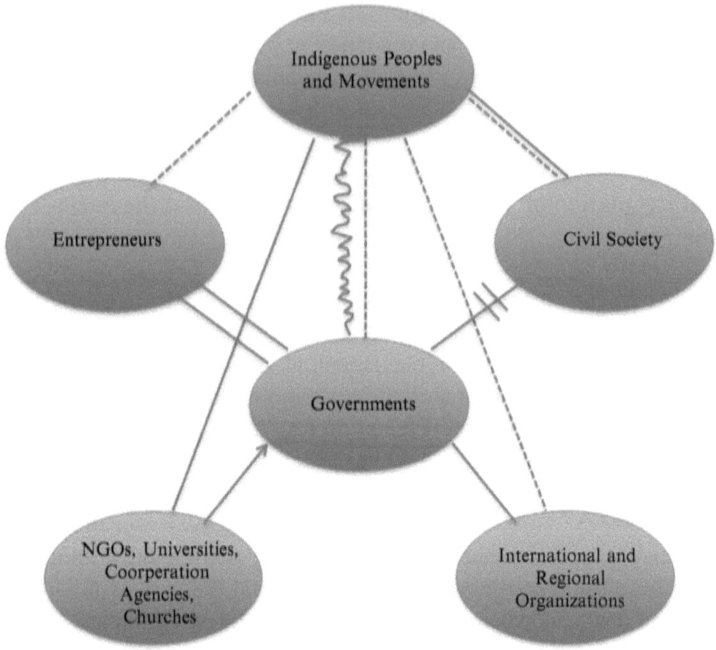

Fig. 4 Actors involved according to Barié (2008) 37 and Fisher (2000), as cited by Barié. *Key*: —: Close relationship; ---: Week relationship; ═: Alliance; →: Dominance/power; ∿: Conflict; ‡: Defective relationship; ⬬: Actors and conflicting parties. The size of the spheres indicating the actors vary according to their power in the particular topics concerned

C. The Different Actors and Interests Involved in Latin America

A visual impression of the different actors involved in the arena of indigenous issues might look like this (see Fig. 4).[255]

The particular current phenomena of "cognopiracy" and "folklorization" of TCEs, as de la Cruz calls it, describing the unauthorized use or exploitation of indigenous and other traditional crafts and cultural expressions, covers similar different actors. Latin American indigenous experts refer to the following external players as directly involved in "the game" on traditional knowledge and TCEs[256]:

- The "design industry", with an interest in "tribal designs and paintings of indigenous peoples"

[255] Graph according to Barié (2008) 37, which, in turn, was inspired by Fisher (2000), see Barié, *ibid.*

[256] de la Cruz I. (2006) 37.

- The "cultural industry", including "photographic, film, literary, and record industries"
- "Ethnic tourism", as regards the interest in "ceremonies", "traditional practices", or the respective TCEs
- The "plant-breeding industry",[257] e.g. when traditional "plant-breeding practices" are a precondition for obtaining the material to create certain TCEs.[258]

The interests in using TCEs vary in accordance with the diversity of the actors involved. Correspondingly, when elaborating an adequate legal protection the interests of these different parties and persons concerned have to be, first, considered and second, balanced appropriately.

Section 4. Latin American Indian Philosophy and Worldviews as Bases, Content, and Context of TCEs

A. Introductory Remarks

What do the terms Indian philosophy and worldviews stand for? Why should they, or any kind of philosophy, matter here at all? These question are to be answered first, before then discussing and defining appropriate methods of substantially approaching the topic. Subsequently, four examples of indigenous philosophies at the local as well as supra-local levels will be presented (see below at B. and C.)—the core of this chapter. Then, these examples will then be analyzed and compared to, first, each other, and second, other, mainly Western world views, philosophical and legal understandings in this area, with the aim of identifying universalities as a means of bridging inter- and supra-cultural gaps in the topic of TCEs (see below at D.).

In view of the existing differences between Native spiritualities in theory and in practice, some remarks on challenges for the research in this area and current realities are added (see below at E.). Then, references to some of the presented indigenous spiritual concepts contained in Latin American legislations will be displayed, in order to illustrate the practical legal relevance of the topic (see below at F.). The chapter concludes in drawing legal and practical consequences for the protection of TCEs in Latin America and beyond (see below at G.).

---

[257] *Id.* 37, 38 (2006).

[258] *See, e.g.*, the discussions on raw material as precondition for maintaining TCEs in Panama, at Chapter IV Section 2.G.II.2.a. below.

I. Terminology

"Philosophy" in this study does not refer to a Western scientific *terminus technicus*. Nor does it, in contrast, correspond to the Western understanding of "religion" as a post-enlightenment concept, which is rooted in dichotomous categories like "sacred" and "profane". Such a distinction has been experienced as "an artificial and non helpful locus for understanding the primary foundations of Native spirituality."[259] This experience affirms the assumption of the great Bronislaw Malinowski as early as in 1925 of a universal humanitarian understanding of science and metaphysics, as in either "pre- or postliterate societies, all peoples operate within the domain of the Sacred and the Profane, within the areas of magic and religion, and of science."[260]

Similarly—as regards the conclusion, though not the underlying argumentation[261]—the great anthropologist Claude Lévi-Strauss once said that what would matter in the future, more than anthropology, would be philology, a "history of ideas," or *philosophy*.[262]

Whether following Malinowski's idea of universal similarities in knowledge and belief systems[263] or the view of a new "philosophy of particularism" made up of the transformation of anthropology as predicted by Lévi-Strauss, the philosophical approach here is understood from a humanitarian, even *emic* perspective, as "native spirituality." This might best be defined as "that connectedness to core values and deep beliefs" which, in their traditional or revitalized form,[264] constitute "a persuasive quality of life that develops out of an authentic participation in values and real-life practices meant to connect members of a community with the deepest foundations of personal affirmation and identity."[265]

II. Why Should (Indigenous) Philosophy Matter at All?

Confronted with the dogma or current trend that philosophy is of little practical value in the areas of law, especially in their international dimension, one may

259 Irwin (2000) 3.

260 Malinowski (1925), "Magic, Science and Religion", summarizing citation by Nader (1996) 260.

261 Lévi-Strauss argued that the repertoire of cultural differences was and would be depleted due to the omnipresent influence of the Western culture and society, FAZ (2008).

262 *Id.*

263 This tendency of researching similarities rather than sticking to the perception of a(n ultra-) relativism in cultural anthropology is also dominating in the current anthropological science, *see, e.g.*, Antweiler (2009).

264 On divergences between idealistic and realistic descriptions of spiritual systems and practical realities, *see* at Section 5.E. below.

265 Irwin (2000) 3.

reasonably ask: Why is a look at Latin American indigenous philosophies valuable for the topic of TCEs, is it even worthwhile at all? It is, for several reasons:

(1) The probably most important English anthropologist, Jack Goody, remarked: The "most significant elements of any human culture" include not only "what we habitually think of as customary behaviour but also such items as ideas of space and time, generalized goals and aspirations, in short the *Weltanschauung* of every social group. In Durkheim's works, these categories of the understanding are 'priceless instruments of thought which the human groups have laboriously forged through the centuries and where they have accumulated the best of their intellectual capital.'"[266]
(2) In this manner, Latin American indigenous philosophy, i.e. spirituality, is the basis and source of the majority of TCEs, for which reason an understanding of TCEs as a subject matter of protection requires the comprehension of the underlying *Weltanschauung*. Irrespective of the specific kind of protection, the starting point for an appropriate protection of TCEs is the respective mode of thought, and foremost, the philosophy of the respective culture or, according to Fikentscher, cluster of cultures.[267]
(3) More generally, only when we understand the basic principles contained in the values and spiritual guidelines for life of the communities, do we have a chance to appropriately understand the functioning of and threats to their culture and the conceptions of TCE protection that derive from that culture.[268] The "principle of inter-related cultures towards a knowledge-based dialogue is essential"[269] in the topic, and such knowledge of a culture is enabled by knowledge of its philosophical superstructure and behavioral principles.
(4) Legally, indigenous spiritual concepts have been acknowledged by Latin American Constitutions as legal or political aims, values, principles, and even rules of behavior for the whole respective nation.[270]
(5) In the area of TCEs, when following a "tort-law approach,"[271] or the "principle of locality,"[272] or of *lex loci*,[273] Latin American indigenous philosophies function as modes of thought[274] not only for a comprehension, but for the legal determination of the subject matter according to the respective indigenous cultural understanding.

---

[266] Goody and Watt (1968) 28.

[267] "Kulturbündel," as Fikentscher calls it. *See* Fikentscher (2005) 7.

[268] Similarly, on the example of African Philosophy with regard to collective intellectual property rights ("Geistiges Gemeineigentum"), *id*. On the argument regarding Latin American indigenous concepts: de la Cruz I. (2006) 38.

[269] *Id*.

[270] On this *see* at Section 5.F. below.

[271] On this and in general *see* Fikentscher (2005) 6.

[272] Daes (2000).

[273] Taubman and Leistner (2008) 66.

[274] This term was developed by Fikentscher (1995) 21.

(6) Similarly, if one applies customary law as a consequence of said "tort-law approach," of the "principle of locality"[275] or of *lex loci*,[276] knowledge of the Latin American indigenous worldview is an essential precondition for any appropriate consideration of customary law. This is because many rules of behavior, traditional rights and obligations, as well as customs are emissions, or even expressions, of the indigenous worldview.[277]

(7) Even in Western societies, metaphysics as sources of values in a "legal society" and the awareness thereof have been understood as necessities or even "imperatives" in law.[278] As this is the case within Western societies, it is even more true of fields with a great diversity of legal cultures.

(8) Comparing indigenous philosophical and ideological points of view with non-indigenous ones facilitates a realistic prognosis of success or failure of national and international negotiations on the adequate protection of TCEs: in the Western legal hemisphere as well, it is widely acknowledged that "where fundamentally contrary ideological positions oppose each other, rational legal discussions reach their limits,"[279] because there exists "no law without values or ethics".[280] Consequently, legal negotiations on legal protection of TCEs would be predestined to fail if the philosophical and ideological positions of the parties involved were fundamentally opposed. The essential question here is therefore whether "Western" world visions and indigenous ones—here, from Latin America—are utterly opposed or whether existing gaps might be bridged. To be able to conduct such a comparison, it is necessary to know about the content of at least some Latin American indigenous philosophies.

(9) It is not yet clear or discussed officially that economic, as opposed to moral, values have taken over as the elementary preconditions for the success of legal negotiations on protecting TCEs. Even if one were convinced of the dominance of "economics over ideologies,"[281] understanding indigenous philosophies of today and their way of transmission can serve as a positive input to the negotiations and as an essential condition for the successful implementation of any future legislation on TCEs. Such an insight reflects and reveals certain

---

[275] Daes (2000).

[276] Taubman and Leistner (2008) 66.

[277] For example, the Native American Graves Protection and Repatriation Act (NAGPRA) aims at protection and especially restoration of human bones, sacred objects, and the cultural heritage of the native peoples of the United States. Moran (1998) 111, note 456, observes: "Ironically, among the Navajo, one of the largest Native American groups, leaders believe that their cultural property, including sacred objects and human remains, became linked to evil spirits because of the misappropriation and that it was not in Navajo interest to have such cultural property returned to them." For further details *see* at Section 5.A.III.2. (15) below.

[278] Rüthers (2009) 30 *et seq.*

[279] Thesis No. 8 of Rüthers (1986) 20 (translation by the author).

[280] Thesis No. 7 of *ibid.* 19 (translation by the author).

[281] Different voices were raised in this vein in non-official conversations with the author at the XIII Session of the Intergovernmental Committee on in Geneva in October 2008.

obstacles or—to put it in positive terms—challenges, which at the same time characterize the stony path towards a concrete and binding consensus on what is "appropriate protection" of TCEs.[282]

(10) Article 13 of the relatively new UN Declaration on the Rights of Indigenous Peoples demands the consideration of indigenous worldviews, stating that: "1. Indigenous peoples have the right to revitalize, use, develop and transmit to future generations their . . . oral traditions, philosophies . . .. 2. States shall take effective measures to ensure that this right is protected and also to ensure that indigenous peoples can understand and be understood in political, legal and administrative proceedings, where necessary through the provision of interpretation or by other appropriate means."[283]

(11) Not only states, but also Western or non-indigenous industries and persons should "get ready to better understand and to exercise respect for different world-views," as highly appreciated Western scholars have called for, in order to reach long-lasting solutions.[284] This is especially true for practical measures and "soft law" like ethical codes in addition to legal and semi-legal initiatives, but likewise for the implementation of the latter: Understanding indigenous worldviews is a precondition for respect and for the successful implementation of legal measures.

(12) Finally, insights into indigenous philosophies are not only "should dos" but "want to dos": they can enrich and expand Western points of view while also reconciling the different philosophies with each other within the current national and international negotiations. "At a time when the Western myth of total superiority is shrinking," Western scholars and practitioners have themselves broached "the need to chart a more inclusive paradigm"[285] of "science," religion, and metaphysical superstructures. "Rapid globalization renders the search for a more balanced, indeed more scientific, treatment of disparate knowledge systems inevitable"[286]—a more inclusive treatment than the simple contrasting of notions like "science," "superstition" and "practices of the occult" or of dichotomous categories like "science/religion, rational/ magical, universal/particular, theoretical/practical."[287] Western ways of life are becoming more open to alternative worldviews. Distinguished Laura Nader even argues that "in human-plant interaction, indigenous people carry a knowledge from which Western scholars have much to gain."[288] In

---

[282] On these consequences *see* at Section 5.I. below.

[283] On the Declaration and TCEs in general *see* at Chapter III Section 1.A. below. The Declaration is available at http://www.un.org/esa/socdev/unpfii/documents/DRIPS_en.pdf, last visited March 11, 2010.

[284] von Lewinski (2008) 528.

[285] Nader (1996) xiv.

[286] Nader (1996) 6 *seq*.

[287] *Id*. 2.

[288] *Id*. 8.

particular, indigenous world visions of the Andean and Amazon regions have even been rated as a valuable point of orientation in our globalized world.[289] Irwin describes a similar tendency: "Native religious and spiritual traditions are no longer simply 'objects of analysis' or mute data lacking either voice or rights in the process of becoming known." Contemporarily, there is "a developing self-reflection on the part of researchers and respondents that what we are all engaged in is ... the negotiation of cultural understanding *among* responsible members of alternative communities whose concerns overlap to a degree that evokes insights and mutual learning in the process."[290]

This is also what the author has experienced through her research on the ground and interaction with indigenous peoples.

III. How to Approach It?—Aspects of an Intercultural Dialogue

When trying to understand the different concepts of thought, the philosophical and spiritual superstructure, it is essential to bear in mind that nearly none of the words used here originates from the mode of thoughts and expression of the source of the philosophy under discussion. From this finding one can deduce methodological and practical consequences.

1. General Direction in Native American Studies

A consequential direction observed in the area of Native spirituality in general is that there is "a tentativeness to such a process that requires much more of the observer than a theoretical language of analysis," which is "clearly the direction of future thematic writings.... The issue is not analysis but communication."[291] As there is "no authoritative perspective in the interpretation of specific religious worldviews and practices" and the very nature of these studies is "multidisciplinary" and "non-reducible to either a single methodology or a single hermeneutics," the only "theory" is a "genuine concern to 'get it right'" through "methodologies that work best" for the individual author.[292]

---

[289] For the region of the Andean Community, *see* the French Philosopher Edgar Morin in CAN http://www.comunidadandina.org/ingles/press/press/np27-8-09.htm, last visited December 2, 2010, for details hereon *see* at Chapter III Section 2.B.V. below. With regard to the Amazon region, Darrel Posey wrote: "Traditional peoples can teach us how to give greater value to the living resources of Amazonia," Posey (2004) 63.

[290] Irwin, "Introduction", in: Irwin, "Native American Spirituality – A Critical Reader" 2 (2000).

[291] *Id.* 2 (2000).

[292] *Id.* 7 (2000).

2. Voices Raised in the Legal Environment

Reducing this treatise exclusively to "communication" would appear a bit too absolute, or at least extraordinarily challenging, considering its aim of drawing concrete legal conclusions and designing suggestions. However, first, such tension between social and legal science is nothing new.

Second, even Western legal scholars specializing in the area of intellectual property law have admitted that one crucial point in the field of protecting traditional knowledge and cultural expressions was "a past failure of dialogue and mutual incomprehension."[293] The reason for that was seen in the fact that "two distinct policy domains – concerning the law and policy of IP, and concerning a cluster of inter-related indigenous and environmental issues – had hitherto largely been considered discrete and isolated from one another, often assumed to be at odds in terms of values."[294] This is rated as a "past failure of communication."[295] Against the backdrop of said "counter-position of opposed value systems", as Taubman and Leistner call it, the approach and aim here is to analyze and compare the bases of these positions and thereby enhance mutual comprehension.

It is worth noting that the same book cited above—without further argumentation—maintains that "(t)his book follows the terminology of Western legal systems and refers to 'indigenous and traditional resources'.... The notion of intellectual property as it is understood in Western legal systems ... is generally not shared by indigenous peoples and is not referred to when indigenous communities talk about their intellectual property and heritage."[296] Ironically, this fact reflects exactly the dilemma which is then criticized later on, and the question arises: How can a dialogue and mutual comprehension then come about if "we" (Western scholars) simply declare that the expressions we use are not understood as such by the other party, but that—without further explanation, only by stating that fact—we intend to keep using them?

At the same time, the challenge is clear: how *can* we communicate if we do not speak the other's language, or—even if we try to learn the language or employ an interpreter—how can we comprehend each other accurately if we do not find any kind of equivalent or correlation in the other's toolbox of thoughts and words? During my fieldwork in Panama, one situation I witnessed kept me reflecting for hours, which led to engaged discussions with non-indigenous Panamanian nationals working in the area of TCEs, and which perfectly illustrates an attitude that plays a large role in the issue of mutual comprehension: I had just had an intense conversation with an highly impressive wiseman and general *Cacique* (traditional authority) of the Dagar Kunyala, Luis Touar, who only speaks the native language of his Kuna community, enabled by the kind translation of another Kuna Indian from a

---

[293] Taubman and Leistner (2008) 67.

[294] *Id.*

[295] *Id.*

[296] Stoll and von Hahn (2008) 20.

different Kuna community, who thus spoke a slightly different native language. After this conversation, this modest "big man" thanked me for having communicated with him, offering his sincerest apologies for not being able to speak my language or any of my languages. But wasn't this apology rather due from my side, being someone who is interested in his culture and cultural expressions, and yet incapable of speaking his language?[297]

In view of the approximately 180 different native languages spoken only in Brazil,[298] the practical dilemma and limits become obvious.

Moreover, Margaret Gruter, expert and pioneer in the relations between biology, human social behavior, and the law, has observed that "cultural 'modes of thought' – and their legal extensions – diverge more deeply than is often assumed. Paradoxically, however, this variability requires that we find some trans-cultural perspective from which we can understand otherwise alien modes of thought without attempting to reduce them to our own."[299] To implement such a superior point of view in practice requires the application of soft skills of non verbal communication like empathy or compassion and common sense[300]—which are the basis of "common emotional and behavioral predispositions, which have been called the 'sense of justice.'"[301]

Thus, it is not only the "pointed methodological question about how the issues should be addressed and framed, whose perspective should be dominant – drawing an analytical tool from linguistic anthropology, the contrast is essentially between the 'emic' or 'etic' approaches, the subjective worldview of the insider and community member, or the purportedly objective external perspective of the analyst or observer."[302] It is indeed one step more, namely, the practical question or, better: challenge of finding "some trans-cultural perspective," as Gruter calls it. This involves also the application of the broader concept of legal sociology in general, according to which "sociology" in this dimension refers to "all branches of the science of empirical knowledge,"[303] and, more specifically, the soft skills for identifying and addressing common emotional and behavioral predispositions in the concrete research activities.

Probably only when truly and personally sitting in front of a "TCE holder" who has never yet been comprehensively in touch with any other language, mode of thought, and mental concepts like Spanish or English ones, can the meaning of these words be comprehended fully. Nonetheless, it is absolutely worth trying to

[297] Personal communication with Luis Touar, General *Cacique* Dagar Kunyala (Traditional Authority of the Kuna Indians in Eastern Panama), with the kind translation by Flaviano Iglesias on February 13, 2009 in Panama City.

[298] On this *see* at Chapter IV Section 2.A.I. below.

[299] Gruter and Masters (1998) 91.

[300] *Id.* 93.

[301] *Id.*

[302] Taubman and Leistner (2008) 67.

[303] Rehbinder (1998) 202.

work toward the realization that a minimum of not only similar legal concepts, but simply of basic idioms and thought concepts must be identified and agreed upon for a mutual exchange in a complex area like this one.

3. Perspective of Latin American Indigenous Peoples Themselves

Latin American indigenous peoples themselves have brought forward "the principle of interculturality" in the dialogue about the different forms of knowledge and wisdom as one important principle to be observed in the area of traditional knowledge and TCEs.[304]

That includes, among other things, a respectful non-discriminative appearance and behavior in intercultural interaction. The Wajãpi Indians, for example, still tell of difficulties in communication and intercultural understanding, as they "encounter daily discrimination", being the "targets of taunting by passersby who laugh" or "imitate Indian dances by tapping their hands to their mouths as seen in some movies."[305] Similarly, other tribes in Brazil still find themselves faced with a general perception of the "lazy, dirty, stupid Indian," since especially the Brazilian entertainment industry maintains these stereotypes.[306] Another substantial reason for appearing to be lazy in the perception of non-indigenous peoples is the lack of inter-cultural knowledge on the different concept of time dominating among most of the indigenous communities, its spiritual background, and implementation in the daily life.[307]

Moreover, indigenous communities themselves observe comprehension difficulties, even when they have excellent command of Portuguese, the national language, as they perceive difficulties in translating their own concepts and meanings, reflected in their language.[308]

[304] de la Cruz I. (2008 I) 208.

[305] Arantes (2009) 24.

[306] Personal communication with Eurico L. Sena Baniwa of the *Instituto das Tradições Indígenas*, Institute for Indigenous Traditions, on June 23, 2009 in São Paolo, and Busch (2010) 220. For details hereon *see* at Chapter IV Section 2.D.II. below.

[307] Personal communication with Daniel Mundurukú, philosopher, member of the Mundurukú tribe, and Director of the Brazilian Indigenous Institute for Intellectual Property, Instituto Indigena Brasileiro para Propriedade Intelectual (INBRAPI), on June 23, 2009 in São Paolo. For details hereon *see* at Section 4.B.III.2. below.

[308] Arantes found out: "we have difficulties translating our language. So we use the language of the whites and are unable to make a correct translation", Arantes (for WIPO), "Documenting and Disseminating Traditional Knowledge and Cultural Expressions in Brazil – Volume 1 – Survey" 24 (2009).

4. Consequences of This Dialogue: Language and Translation

This latter aspect mentioned by the Wajãpi Indians reveals one essential particularity of such intercultural dialogue and communication: language—direct and indirect, verbal and nonverbal expressions.

In sociology—mainly Max Weber with regard to positive law[309]—and in anthropology, language, linguistics, and literacy, or non-literacy, have been subject to studies and research for decades already,[310] with a focus on the socio-cultural as well as legal differences between literary and non-literary society, especially in the work of Jack Goody.[311]

In the legal ambit, however, this aspect has received almost no attention so far, too little, considering how essential it is to the topic of protecting TCEs. Besides the intercultural character, to be addressed later on, one other elementary aspect is the particularities of oral traditions, which includes the famous *Weltanschauung* according to Durkheim, as well as customary law, to be dealt with below.[312] The relative continuity and transmission of the worldvisions is primarily ensured by language.[313]

In non literate societies, language is developed

> in intimate association with the experience of the community, and it is learned [and transmitted] by the individual in face-to-face contact with the other members. What continues to be of social relevance is stored in the memory while the rest is usually forgotten: and language – primarily vocabulary – is the effective medium of this crucial process of social digestion and elimination which may be regarded as analogous to the homeostatic organization of the human body by means of which it attempts to maintain its present condition of life.[314]

Thereby, the "intrinsic nation of oral communication has a considerable effect upon both the content and the transmission of the cultural repertoire." First of all, "it makes for a directness of relationship between symbol and referent."[315] This relation was also underscored by the Greek philosopher Plato.[316] Secondly, "the meaning of each word is ratified in a succession of concrete situations, accompanied by vocal inflections and physical gestures, all of which combine to particularize both its specific denotation and its accepted connotative usages. This process of

---

309 Weber (1976).

310 *See* only "Sociological Aspects of the Relation between Language and Culture" by Lewis S. Feuer, "Language, Thought, and Culture" by Paul Henle, "Structural Analysis in Linguistics and Anthropology" by Claude Lévi-Strauss, all in: Manners and Kaplan (1968).

311 Goody and Watt (1968) 27–68.

312 *See* at Section 5. below.

313 On other ways of transmitting elements of cultural heritage, *see id.* 27–68, especially 31 *et seq.*

314 *Id.* 30 *et seq.*

315 *Ibid.*

316 Phaedrus (no year) at 275d–e, available at http://www.perseus.tufts.edu, last visited December 6, 2010. On this and references to both contemporary Western lawyers and customary law *see* at Section 5.B.IV.2. below.

direct semantic ratification, of course, operates cumulatively; and as a result the totality of symbol-referent relationships is more immediately experienced by the individual in an exclusively oral culture, and is thus more deeply socialized."[317]

In written communication and publications, naturally written, more precisely, literate expressions are the exclusive instruments at hand. This complicates the appropriate transmission of the content and meaning of the *Weltanschauung*, and cultural repertoire in general, and limits the process of transmission and direct semantic ratification as part of the culture itself.

Moreover, nearly all of the words used here are originally *not* expressed in English. Thus, translation is another key element. The crucial thing about translation is that most of the words change their meaning in line with the different cultural and religious backdrop of the target language, as languages are always stamped by the way of life of the society in which they are used or at home. In Latin America, this is first of all the translation into a Catholic-colored vocabulary of the Spanish or Portuguese language. One example of such a change of meaning is the word "confession" as used by the Asarios and Kogi Indians in the Andean highlands of Colombia.[318] According to their primary understanding, "confession" rather implies reflecting on what has brought one to the point where one is standing, concentrating "on the things that matter," "adopting a public stance of responsibility and awareness"[319]—in contrast to its Catholic connotation.

Of course, this phenomenon of "semantic shift" or meaning change through borrowing, as Goody and Watt discussed, appears in any process of translation all over the world. However, it is stronger, the broader the gaps between the different cultural and religious backgrounds of either language are, e.g. in the context of indigenous traditions. For instance, the non material dimension of the Kogi is not only their "spiritual world," but could also be called "the world of essence" or "the cosmic mind."[320] With regard to legal and indigenous aspects, another remarkable example is one from the Iroquois Indians in North America: Their word for "law" at the same time means "peace" (and, by the way, also "good")—so according to this understanding, law should not only fulfil the function of bringing and securing peace, but the existence of law *is* peace.[321]

Further complications are:

- The rich use of metaphors in indigenous languages in the ambit of philosophies or world views, or even in the every-day-life communication when such concepts and ideas are implied,
- The double or triple meaning of many words, and
- The character of some single words as full story-tellers.

---

[317] Goody and Watt (1968) 28 *et seq.*

[318] On these tribes *see* at Section 4.B.I.1. below.

[319] Gil (2006) 24.

[320] *Ibid.*

[321] Mohawk (Irokesen) (1992) 42.

An example of such story-telling words is the Kogi expression *Sentura Gwiawimundua*. According to Gil, each word tells a different story, and even each syllable of both words tells its own, chronologically ordered one. Altogether, the expression explains "The Roots of Being," of which *Sentura* narrates the part about the "absolute beginning of things" and *Gwiawimundua* the "spiritual earth" or ideas of the material world to be organized by a "male, active creative energy", as Gil explains.[322] As every single syllable tells its own story within this big one, separating the individual sounds of *Sen-tu-ra Gwi-a-wi-mun-dua*, as Gil says, leaded to (at least) eight different actions, plots, places, spiritual "protagonists," and concepts of thoughts or beliefs.[323]

Certainly, translating "God" out of a Christian context or the "categorical imperative" of Immanuel Kant out of its own philosophical conception laid down in German would also require difficult explanations. Thus, it is also a question of the subject of the discussion or presentation to be translated—and the familiarity of the translator with the source language and relevant context. But neither the topic of protecting TCEs nor their spiritual superstition constitute simple areas of conversation, and lawyers dealing with them are rarely familiar with the various Latin American indigenous languages involved.

What becomes clear is that "translating" such concepts, story-words, and metaphors requires literally painting pictures and telling stories on the basis of complex expressions created and used by societies with completely different mental and spiritual patterns. This aspect of course complicates and decelerates the process of communication, intercultural exchange, and negotiations. However, at the same time it becomes clear that without any knowledge of the different spiritual superstructure on which the concept of minds and modes of thought are based, a mutual understanding—even if ostensibly using the same words (e.g. in English)—will hardly be possible.

With regard to a presumably Western-stamped background of the reader, especially one who is used to clear and precise technical terms in the area of law, the study will now focus on (re-)structuring the main points of the philosophies that are relevant to the topic of TCEs in the broad sense.

[322] Called *serankua*. *See* Gil (2006) 24.

[323] *Ibid.* Just to give an idea of the richness and complexity of one single syllable, here is an example of the first syllable: *Sen* stands for "the original darkness," as Gil explains, which existed before the universe was born. Contrary to the idea of "black holes", it does not constitute a big vacancy but the essence of everything, Gil says: It is the "realm of ideas," the idea of spirit, soul, thought, life, and movement, and because ideas are mainly words, *sen* also represents the idea of language. Finally, according to Gil, as it constitutes the place of origin, it is also understood as the place of law, *see ibid.*

B. Examples of Philosophies of Certain Tribes

The examples given here are, first, those from certain tribes (immediately following), and second, constitute collected common guiding philosophical principles of many indigenous peoples (below at III.). They have also been selected to present variation in terms of geographical and environmental impact: The first two examples stem from the region of the Andean highlands, the third one as well as the regional compilation from the tropical Amazon Basin.

I. Colombia: Law of Sé, Philosophy of the Kogi and Asarios

An interesting, far-reaching example of a Latin American indigenous philosophy is that of the Kogi and Asarios from Colombia.

1. The Kogi and the Asarios: Some Facts

The Kogi and the Asarios are indigenous tribes living in a remote area in the Colombian mountain of the Andes, the Sierra Nevada de Santa Marta. According to Gil (translation by Ereira), they still (try to) continue to "preserve and protect" their "traditional life, practices, and way of understanding".[324] Nonetheless, like many other indigenous groups, the Kogi and Asarios have been touched by increasing Western pressures, Gil says. To strengthen and represent their interest in resisting these influences, their *Mamas*, or priests, founded the local indigenous group *Gonavindua Tairona* in 1987.[325]

2. The Law of Sé: "Linking the Spiritual and Material"[326]

The following outline of general elements of the Kogi philosophy is based upon a speech by the spokesman of the *Gonawindua Tairona* group, Ramón Gil, held at a big gathering of tribal elders in the Sierra Nevada and translated by Alan Ereira.[327]

Considering the points made in the introduction, the elements have been (re-) structured, ordered and titled here in the habit of a Western-formed author, while trying to still uphold the sound of the *Mama*.

---

[324] Gil (2006) 21.

[325] *Ibid.*

[326] *Id.* 25.

[327] *Id.* 21–27.

a. The Order of the World

According to the Kogis' and Asarios' philosophy, as Gil says, the world is divided into a material and a non material part. The material world is embedded in the non material one, in particular in the cosmos of "memory and possibility," past and future.[328] These latter elements are symbolized by a plain cloth in the Kogi genesis. According to this genesis told by Gil, the active creative energy (*Serankua*) laddered, separated the aforementioned cloth—representing memory and possibility, past and future,—and in that originated space lying in between, the idea of the world, of everything existing in the world appeared. Thus, "making the present was making the world;" both expressions are understood to be synonymous.[329]

The idea of the material world was then organized according to the original spiritual law, the law of *Sé*.[330] The rock, as the structure, the column of the world "to give it consistency and strength", was created first, as Gil explains.[331] It also represents the "mental constitution", which fixes "natural law" as an infinite, unlimited universal law.[332] The "active, creative, male energy" (*Serankua*) then crossed a thought and lifted it "to make the center".[333] A peak above and one below appeared, and they worked as "the motor of the world", representing life and death, mirroring the living world in the underworld, as Gil says. At all four corners guardians were installed making the material world "circularly turning and constantly revitalising life".[334] But this spiritual world just became and constantly becomes the material one, when the feminine energy (fertility) appeared,[335] and, in the conjunction of the "masculine and feminine", "positive and negative", turned the spiritual into a material world.[336] This would be the explosive moment of coming into existence, the Kogis believe, and because of this explosive energy, the tense between "memory and possibility," past and future "quivering on the edge of collapse," a law on the order of the world "must function", Gil explains.[337]

b. The Reason of Our Existence

There is a reason why we are here. According to the Kogis, all species were given a specific function and a tribute to pay. Humans have the ability to live the life of the

[328] *Id.* 24.
[329] *Id.* 25.
[330] *Ibid.*, on the Law of *Sé see* below points 3 and 4.
[331] *Ibid.*
[332] *Ibid.*
[333] *Id.* 26.
[334] *Ibid.*
[335] It is called *seynekun*, *id.* 25.
[336] *Id.* 26.
[337] *Id.* 25.

mind "in the realm of ideas" as well as "of the body",[338] i.e. the material and non material world, Gil explains.

The non material world is "the source of infinite possibilities".[339] A "disruption of the delicate relationship between what is and what might be could change the material world in unimaginable ways" and is therefore "inherently dangerous".[340] The material world is "understood to be ordered, organised, and a stable balance of living and dying".[341]

As humans are able to live both worlds, they and their societies are the "necessary guardians" at the gates between the world of ideas and the material world, Gil argues. Thus, according to the Kogis, the reason why we exist is to sustain the (material) world, to fulfil our "responsibility to interpret" and implement the natural, original law.[342]

c. The "Law"

According to Gil, this natural or original law just mentioned is the law of *Sé*. *Sé* is the overwhelming spiritual principle of existence and the cradle of all that exists, Gil says. Even more than that, it organizes everything "to create harmony". *Sé*—or "the spiritual parents"—was the one who gave each species a specific function and tribute to pay in the single, interconnected whole. Likewise, the law of *Sé* establishes material being and legislates everything in harmony. When the law is not implemented, as Gil says, *Sé*—being the ultimate power over all birth and death—can destroy this world and create another, because *Sé* would contain endless spiritual possibilities which have not been materialized yet.[343]

d. Consequential Axioms

From *Sé,* several axioms are derived:

- the "concept of order",
- the "concept of matter",
- the "concept of time", and
- the "concept of gender".[344]

According to Gil, the concept of order is regarded to be "the first step in creation", the idea of "setting things out."[345] The concept of matter is the next

[338] *Id.* 23.
[339] *Ibid.*
[340] *Ibid.*
[341] *Id.* 22.
[342] *Id.* 26.
[343] *Id.* 24.
[344] *Id.* 25.
[345] *Ibid.*

step in creation, "the notion that there can be a physical, material world". It is the "idea of matter".[346] The concept of time is a bit more complex. According to Gil, matter itself can only exist in the present, and creating the idea of making the material world is synonymous for creating the idea of making the present as a totality, which embraces the past, future and present.[347] Nevertheless, for the material world to exist, "there must be a concept of the past", because the world is not continually re-created. The present has rather "an ancestry, that gives it form and defines it".[348] Finally, there is the concept of gender, of "mother" and "father" in the spiritual as well as material world. All the living things on this earth "are born through a combination of masculine and feminine energy".[349] Therefore, according to the Kogi, the world is charged with a basic generative force, charged with "sexual energy". As a consequence, "love and fertility", "life and mortality" cannot be separated but would fully depend upon each other.[350] The axioms of *Sé* help to understand the balance between these elements.

e. Consequential Rules of Behavior, or: How to Sustain the World

As a consequence of the understanding that the material world makes up only one part of the bigger picture, i.e. of the endless and enduring spiritual world and possibilities, the "first logical rule of right action" is "to act thoughtfully".[351]

The "second logical rule of right action" is "to ask permission to use what we need"[352]: Due to the different type of energies, "deliberate human interaction with the world" (like agriculture, killing animals, construction work, etc.) would "inevitably have consequences which cannot be readily anticipated".[353] According to Gil, the only way in which such interaction can "be done safely" is by "involving the unseen creative power, the nonmaterial intelligence that shaped the world, as a partner in what is to be done".[354] As a logical consequence, this involves "making offerings and sacrifices".[355]

Following the logic of *Sé*, there are even some concrete rules on right behavior, i.e.[356]:

---

[346] *Ibid.*

[347] *Id.* 25.

[348] *Id.* 21.

[349] *Id.* 22.

[350] *Ibid.*

[351] *Id.* 23.

[352] *Ibid.*

[353] *Ibid.*

[354] *Ibid.*

[355] *Ibid.*

[356] For the comparison and analysis with special regard to such rules, *see* at Sections 5.D.III. and E. below.

Not to plunder the water without permission;
Not to build housing without making a spiritual payment;
Not to make a road without making a spiritual payment;
Not to eat or drink without making a spiritual payment;
Not to breathe the air without making a spiritual payment;
Not to accept the light without making a spiritual payment;
Not to plunder the earth without paying tribute.[357]

"Spiritual payment" thereby involves an act of seriousness, responsibility, awareness of "confession,"[358] as Gil says, a connection with the "creative power that transcends" and includes all time.[359]

f. Reason for Existence and Original Meaning of TCEs

As a consequence, all cultural expressions constitute a manifestation of a certain concept of life, of the laws of nature, of the law of *Sé*, at least from a theoretical point of view. Indeed, many of the spiritual payments, tributes, asking for permission, and the ways of expressing them are ultimately traditional cultural expressions.[360]

g. Diversity and Its Value

Diversity in and variety of life are intentionally created phenomena, Gil argues. They are a precondition for all different living entities to "fulfill a certain task" and to "pay their tribute to the functioning" of it all.[361] Diversity and variety are therefore essential for survival and revitalization in the big circle.

When we learn how to "take care of the diverse elements, different living entities, and alimentary supplies" by fulfilling the law of *Sé* in spirit, i.e. making spiritual payments, then the "material world becomes revitalized".[362] In turn, if we do not, or if we follow a path towards monocultures in a broad sense, the circle of revitalization might be interrupted.

---

[357] *Id.* 24.

[358] Gil (2006) 24: "confession" in this context means "a process of concentration on the things that matter" and "adopting a public stance of responsibility".

[359] Gil (2006) 24.

[360] *Id.* 21.

[361] *Id.* 25.

[362] *Ibid.*

h. Special Guardians

Beside from the ability and responsibility of all humans to respect and enact the law of *Sé*, there are some people who are even "more capable" of doing so, Gil explains: the *Mamas*, or priests, as the Kogis call them.[363] The essential connection between the material and immaterial world, mortality and immortality, is the generative energy: fertility. Fertility is "axiomatic to the existence of the material world", as fundamental as death.[364] Life "comes into the material world and goes out of it" through the eternally "opening and closing doors" between the limited material and the unlimited non material world.[365] As these two worlds are not fully compatible, fertility at the same time would open "the door to chaos and disorder".[366] To manage the interface and to try "to hold the dangerous balance between the material and the transcendent," between life and death, some intermediaries were needed. These intermediaries are the *Mamas*, Gil says,—without them, fertility itself could destroy the world.[367]

Moreover, according to Gil, there is another reason for the need of such *Mamas*: The elementary logic saying that "every living thing" is involved in the process of fertility and thus has its own "predetermined place and specific behavior patterns allowing it to live and reproduce without endangering everything else," would not hold true when it comes to human beings.[368] We would rather seem to shape our own lives, as Gil says,—while however still remaining part of the mortal material world. This is the other reason why we would need the work of the priests, handling the interface between the material and non material, "consciously engaging the cosmic mind in a partnership with human activities".[369]

Thus, the reason for conserving the knowledge and practices of the *Mamas* would be to fulfill the human's task of organizing and maintaining the material world.[370]

i. Current Situation

According to Gil, even if the exercise of these offerings and sacrifices has decreased, or their spiritual meaning has even been completely lost on the way, the "very existence", the "ongoing presence of fertility" in the material world mean that the link between the supernatural and the natural was still unbroken. Thus, the intermediaries and their rites would also still be of relevance. According to the

[363] *Id.* 23.
[364] *Ibid.*
[365] *Ibid.*
[366] *Ibid.*
[367] *Ibid.*
[368] *Id.* 24.
[369] *Id.*
[370] *Id.* 27.

Mamas, the path of adapting the Western way of life is rather dangerous, as many people of the Western societies, called the "Younger Brothers of humanity," appear to them as "rapacious and dangerous children incapable of concentration and analysis," without sufficient respect for the things beyond their "own individual greed."[371]

II. Ecuador: Vision of the Peoples in the Cuenca del Imbakucha

1. Region of the Cuenca del Imbakucha and Its Peoples

The Cuenca del Imbakucha—Lago San Pablo in Ecuador is part of the Mojanda Cajas Plateaus, high mountain ecosystems located between 3,200 and 4,500 m above sea level in the north of the Andes chain, stretching across northern Peru, Ecuador, Colombia, and Venezuela.[372] The Cuenca del Imbakucha itself is situated in the province of Imbabura, and includes three lagoons and a high concentration of biological and cultural diversity.[373] Within this area live some 22 communities of the Otavalo peoples and 16 communities of the Kichwas Kayampi peoples,[374] making up around 25,000 people who are all organized in different forms of local organizations like communities, associations, cooperatives, a water board, and unions of communities.[375]

2. Aspects of the World View

With regard to the topic of protecting TCEs, the following aspects of the world view of the second example of indigenous peoples in the Andean Region, the Otavalo and Kichwa peoples, are of interest.

[371] *Id.* 21.

[372] Centro de Estudios Pluriculturales (CEPCU, Center for Multicultural Studies) in *Otavalo*, *see* http://www.cepcu.org.ec/index.php?option=com_content&task=view&id=32&Itemid=57, last visited January 14, 2010.

[373] *Ibid.*

[374] These data stem from the CEPCU, *see* http://www.cepcu.org.ec/index.php?option=com_content&task=view&id=32&Itemid=57, last visited January 14, 2010, which refers to the National Institute for Statistics and Census, *see* http://www.inec.gov.ec/web/guest/inicio, last visited January 14, 2010. Other data indicate about 17 indigenous peoples of *Otavalo* and *Kayambi* (also a slightly different spelling) in total, de la Cruz I. (2006) 30. The area also hosts about 17% of a "mestizo" (mixed or half-indigenous) population but the study here only refers to the 36 indigenous communities. Most of the indigenous peoples are bilingual (*Kichwa* and Spanish), according to CEPCU.

[375] http://www.cepcu.org.ec/index.php?option=com_content&task=view&id=32&Itemid=57, last visited January 14, 2010 and de la Cruz I. (2006) 30.

a. Order of the World

According to the Otavalo and Kichwa peoples, there exist four different worlds:

- the *kay pacha*, the world "in which we live",
- the *uku pacha*, the world "outside",
- the *hawa pacha*, the "world above, containing the clouds, rain, wind, moon, and sun", and
- the *kay shuk pacha*, which is the world "beyond, containing dreams, the unknown, and the sphere where the future of indigenous peoples is interpreted".[376]

All four different worlds must be respected, especially the worlds outside and above. All worlds together are understood as the indigenous territory, the *Pacha Mama*.[377]

b. Aim and Way of Life

The aim and at the same time the ideal way of life is the *sumak kausay*, the "Good Living".[378] According to de la Cruz, this essential idea and its rationale can be traced back to one statement: "We are Sons of Mother Earth and therefore we want to live well."[379] This is at the same time the central focus of the community effort that has been made within the relationship between the indigenous communities and the Mojanda plateaus. Consequently, the efforts to maintain and recover traditional knowledge and traditional cultural practices were made, and thus the latter was able to survive, because the indigenous peoples consider themselves to be sons of *Pacha Mama*, as de la Cruz says.[380]

c. Symbiosis and Interrelation

According to the Otavalo and Kichwa peoples, all elements of *Pacha Mama* are united in a symbiotic relationship between mankind and nature. In visualising this relationship, water—being an obvious, natural resource in the area of the Mojanda plateaus and at the same time the essential element for human survival—is understood as "the life blood of *Pacha Mama*" and must therefore be taken care of as the highest priority—in a material and spiritual manner, as de la Cruz explains.[381] Thus, within this world and territory, natural resources and biodiversity are interrelated with traditional knowledge and cultural expressions.

---

[376] *Id.* 30 *et seq.*

[377] *Id.* 31.

[378] *Id.*

[379] In the most common local indigenous language, Kichwa, it is: "Pachamamapak Churimi Kanchik, Chaimanta Sumak Kausayta Munanchik", cited from *id.* 31.

[380] *Id.* 30 *et seq.*

[381] *Id.* 31 *et seq.* (2006).

d. Most Important Principle of Behavior

One of these practices is at the same time one of the most important ancestral principles of behaviour, as de la Cruz argues, the *randi – randi*.[382] It means "giving and giving," and refers to man's giving to nature and vice versa, as "nature and the plateaus constitute life and indigenous man is part of that life."[383] In practice it means that because the "Mojanda plateaus provide many resources for local people, mainly water," man must also pay a tribute of a spiritual or non-spiritual nature when using this water and other natural resources, as de la Cruz explains.[384] This very traditional request is ancestrally called the *wakcha karay*.[385]

III. Brazil: The *Maracá*, Philosophy of the Mundurukú Peoples

The following example stems from the tropical Amazon region. It not only makes visible some elements of a Brazilian indigenous philosophy, but also a way of interaction of third parties with indigenous communities that is common today.

1. The Mundurukú

The Mundurukú (or Mundurucú) is an indigenous tribe with an estimated population of around 10,000 people living quite isolated along the Tapajós river in the state of Pará in Brazil.[386] The language they speak is Tupí. Originally, the Mundurukú were an aggressive, war-like tribe, feared by neighboring people.[387] Their culture is based upon an oral tradition and—at least to a certain extent—this culture is still alive so far, meaning that the community does not have a common code or any official written paper on either their "law" or their philosophy.

There do exist books on the Mundurukú way of life displaying some aspects of this philosophy. These were written by a member of the tribe, Daniel Mundurukú. He also speaks and writes Portuguese, and studied at a public Brazilian University. With his background, he functions as a kind of "bridge" between the different worlds of the tribe and of life as a regular citizen in Brazil's present-day society, enabling a dialogue despite the existing idiomatic, cultural and territorial gaps while at the same time embodying the fate of a transforming traditional way of life. In this sense, this man's personal situation perfectly reflects the one generally characterizing the topic of protecting TCEs.[388]

---

[382] *Id.* 32.

[383] *Ibid.*

[384] *Ibid.*

[385] *Ibid.*

[386] http://www.britannica.com/EBchecked/topic/397471/Munduruku, last visited December 2, 2010.

[387] *Ibid.*

[388] For more details on this aspect, *see* at Section 4.G.II.3. below.

2. Aspects of the Philosophy

The following outline of traditional aspects of Mundurukú philosophy is based on a personal talk with and a presentation by Daniel Mundurukú, given in a forum discussing the protection of TCEs and traditional knowledge in Brazil.[389] As an important introductory remark, Daniel Mundurukú emphasized that he could only speak on his own behalf, on the basis of his personal experience and modes of thought learned when growing up in a Mundurukú community. He did not want to be (mis-)understood as a philosophical or political representative of all the Mundurukús, because according to the still existing traditional structures of the tribe, he was no such representative. As true and honest as it is, this aspect also reflects general obstacles or at least great challenges within the discussions on an adequate protection of TCEs—which will be dealt with later.[390]

Particular aspects of the philosophy are as follows[391]:

a. Name and Symbol

The philosophy is called *maracá*, which is both a symbol and the name of the spiritual superstructure. *Maracá* is Portuguese for "rattle," and has a double meaning, describing the material and immaterial good, a thing and its spiritual content, as D. Mundurukú explains. In the broader sense, it also stands for the reflection on oneself and on nature. This reflection, as well as the combination of material and immaterial goods in one expression, are guiding elements of the philosophical superstructure of the Mundurukú as regards TCEs and their possible protection.[392]

b. Sense of Existence

The overwhelming sense of our existence is that man is born to live the aim of life. The aim of life is to be useful and valuable, to overcome egoism in a broader sense. According to the understanding of the Mundurukú, this latter aspect collides fundamentally with the Christian belief of the sense of man's subduing the earth and having dominion over every little thing that moves upon it, as is laid down in the first chapter of the Old Testament in the Bible.[393]

---

[389] "Amazon: Diversity and Integration in the Intellectual Property," International Congress on Intellectual Property ASPI 2009, June 21–23, 2009, São Paulo. On the Congress in general and the speech of Daniel Mundurukú in particular, *see* Busch (2010) 215–221.

[390] *See* at Section 4.G.II.3. below.

[391] As mentioned above (*see* at Sections 4.A.III.4. and B.I.2.), these points have been selected with regard to the topic of protecting TCEs and are structured in a Western-influenced mode.

[392] Speech of Daniel Mundurukú in São Paolo on June 23, 2009, *see also* Busch (2010) 215–221.

[393] *Ibid.*

c. Way of Life

According to D. Mundurukú, a way to overcome egoism, and thus a kind of "liberator," is traditional knowledge. Traditional knowledge is regarded to be holistic, which means that according to the cosmovision body, mind, soul, and everything is one. Consequently, knowing nature means knowing yourself—it would be quite the contrary to impose thoughts on others and how they are or should be. The "way of life" instead means being attentive.[394]

d. Understanding of Traditional Knowledge

Knowing nature as one important aspect of this way of life at the same time implies that knowledge is in the thing, not in the human. As a consequence, according to the Mundurukús' understanding, knowledge cannot belong to anyone, not be the property of an individual. At the least, it has to be used in favor of mankind as a whole, and ultimately in favor of our biosphere.[395]

e. Concept of Time

Traditional knowledge and life in general are circular. Notwithstanding that daily life includes the facts of yesterday and tomorrow, philosophically there exists only one time: the present. This is because the present is at the same time the future of the past, and the past of the future. In contrast, the occidental conception of future can rather only be a speculation. As there is a different spiritual conception of time, there is also a different factual concept of time in work and negotiations.[396]

f. Value of Generations

As life is circular, the different generations are all equal and all of great importance. The elder can teach the young the traditional way and knowledge learned in their lives, and the results are different expressions of tradition, which are highly esteemed.[397]

g. Perception of New Elements

Daily percipience as the basis of traditional knowledge and traditional cultural expressions is a dynamic process. While taking over the old ways, each generation at the same time shall be aware of actual changes in the environment. Consequently,

---

[394] *Ibid.*

[395] *Ibid.*

[396] For general intercultural aspects of the dimension of time in disputing processes *see* Nader and Todd Jr. (1978) 24 *et seq.*

[397] Speech of Daniel Mundurukú in São Paolo on June 23, 2009, *see also* Busch (2010) 215–221.

they also incorporate new elements. Transformation and adjustments within "the time" are part of the "traditional" way of life.[398]

h. Understanding of Culture

From all these foregoing points follows an integral, all-encompassing conception of culture.

C. Example of a Philosophy Taken Up by an International Indigenous Organization: Maloca by COICA

All three examples just disposed contain similarities—expressed in a more or less traditional way—as well as elements relevant to the protection of TCEs. Before turning to a comprehensive analysis of these worldviews, it is worth looking at one last example, this time of philosophical elements already compiled by a large indigenous organization.

To some extent, indigenous tribes and peoples in Latin America and all over the world have gathered together to improve their interaction with bigger political powers like national states. Part of clarifying their position and points of view—as far as they exist or common ones have been developed—is to make visible and understandable their philosophical foundations, the main reasons for their "being different" and fighting for greater participation in the political processes that touch on their lives. An example of these principles in Latin America is the compilation set up by the COICA, probably the biggest and most important Latin American indigenous organization.[399]

It is interesting to note a slight transformation in the nature of these philosophical elements: observing that they are influenced by (international) "Western" politics, we come to realize that they thus rather constitute guidelines than a "pure" philosophical superstructure.

I. Facts on COICA

COICA stands for the "Coordinator of the Indigenous Organizations of the Amazon Basin."[400] Today it is an international indigenous organization with a private-rights legal status.[401] It was founded in 1984 as a reaction to the Amazon Cooperation

[398] *Ibid.*

[399] On the latest aspects of challenging realities within the organization, *see* at Section 5.D.II. below.

[400] "Coordinadora de las Organizaciones Indígenas de la Cuenca Amazónica."

[401] *See* http://www.coica.org.ec, last visited January 10, 2011.

Treaty set up in 1978 by the nine national states possessing territory in the Amazon Basin.[402] Similarly, COICA unites nine indigenous organizations coming from the nine countries that share the Amazon basin.[403] Against this background, COICA defines its purpose as to defend indigenous ideals and the Amazon as a "free and peaceful space."[404] Concrete objectives are *inter alia* to enable and improve the interaction and coordination of indigenous peoples and their organizations in the Amazon region, to fight for or defend territorial claims, respect for human rights, and self-determination, and to instill or renew the appreciation of the own indigenous culture.

According to the facts indicated by COICA, the Amazon region constitutes 40 % of the territory of the whole of South America. Of this area, the indigenous peoples of the Amazon inhabit a geographical area of approximately 10,268,471 km^2, and constitute a total population of 2,779,478 divided into about 390 peoples found throughout this region.[405]

Seen from a formal perspective, COICA "represents" those indigenous communities who are organized in the nine different member organizations. These organizations tend to be the biggest organizations existing at the national levels, in particular the AIDESEP[406] in Peru; the APA[407] in Guyana; the CIDOB[408] in Bolivia; the COIAB[409] in Brazil; the CONFENAE[410] in Ecuador; the FOAG[411] in French Guyana; the CONIVE[412] in Venezuela; the OIS[413] in Suriname; and the OPIAC[414] in Colombia.

---

[402] *See id.*

[403] *See id.*

[404] COICA (2005) 10, translation by COICA at http://www.coica.org.ec/ingles/aia_book/index.html, last visited January 10, 2011.

[405] *Id.*

[406] The Inter-Ethnic Association of Development of the Peruvian Jungle. *See* http://www.aidesep.org.pe/, last visited January 10, 2010.

[407] Association of Amerindian Peoples of Guyana, *see* http://www.sdnp.org.gy/apa/, last visited January 10, 2010.

[408] Confederation of Indigenous Peoples of Bolivia, *see* http://www.cidob-bo.org/, last visited January 10, 2010.

[409] Coordinator of Indigenous Organizations of the Brazilian Amazon/Coordenação das Organizações Indígenas da Amazônia Brasileira, *see* http://www.coiab.com.br/, last visited January 10, 2010.

[410] Confederation of Nationalities of the Ecuadorian Amazon, http://www.confeniae.org.ec/, last visited January 10, 2010.

[411] Federation of Native Organizations of the French Guyana.

[412] Indian National Council of Venezuela, *see* http://www.conive.org/, last visited January 10, 2010.

[413] Indigenous Organization of Surinam, *see* http://www.ois-sr.org/, last visited January 10, 2010.

[414] Organization of Indigenous Peoples of the Colombian Amazon, *see* http://www.opiac.org.co/, last visited January 10, 2010.

In 2002, COICA became (theoretically) a consultative entity of the Working Group on the Rights of Indigenous Peoples of the Andean Community,[415] and in 2003, it gained the Consultative Status at the Economic and Social Council (ECOSOC) of the United Nations Organization and, in 2004, of the Organization of American States (OAS).

In general and until lately,[416] COICA has been deemed a "most capable interlocutor."[417]

II. Philosophical Elements Compiled by COICA

As one of COICA's many objectives is to promote the cultural re-valorisation and claims of its members,[418] COICA has compiled a catalog of common values and philosophical elements of the member communities. They are regarded as fundamental tools for the maintenance and the improvement of the "indigenous living conditions and welfare".[419] On the basis of these elements, COICA has set up the "Amazon Indigenous Agenda" as its action strategy or political concept. It aims at the process of returning to the *Maloca*, which COICA's members have acquired "through the interaction with other cultures" and from their aspiration, as they say.[420]

1. General Aspects

Maloca stands for the "encounter space between the spiritual and the material, where human beings and spirits intertwine."[421] It is the philosophy of the *sacha runa*, the "man of the jungle" and embraces both, the material and immaterial, like the Amazon and the peoples that inhabit it.[422] It is understood as omnipresent and

---

[415] Article 4, lit. b), of Decision 524, available at http://www.comunidadandina.org/ingles/normativa/D524e.htm, last visited December 7, 2010, which however was never implemented and later substituted by Decision 674, available at http://www.comunidadandina.org/ingles/normativa/D674e.htm, last visited December 7, 2010. The consultative entity which COICA "remained" part of was then called "Consultative Council of the Andean Community Indigenous Peoples", for details *see* at Chapter III Section 2.B.IV. below.

[416] On recent challenging realities within the organization *see* at Section 5.D.II. below.

[417] Wörrle (2009) 234.

[418] COICA (2005) 9, translation by COICA at http://www.coica.org.ec/ingles/aia_book/index.html.

[419] *Id.* 12.

[420] *Id.* "Malocas" were called the communitarian houses of indigenous tribes, for the Tupi Indians in Brazil *see* at Section 3.B.II.2. above and Kayser (2005) 143.

[421] COICA (2005) 28, translation by COICA at http://www.coica.org.ec/ingles/aia_book/index.html.

[422] *Id.*

incorporated in every human being, a "basic element of nature and the Universe".[423]

In its political (or maybe even idealistic) dimension, the "Return to the *Maloca*" means to be open for a "balanced" exchange, to combine elements of the occidental and the native world without abandoning one's own values and socio-cultural practices, COICA says.[424] In particular, it would not mean "being opposed to research and discovery of new alternatives for the preservation of humanity", nor to development in general. But any such research should include respect for different ways of living, socio-cultural diversity, wisdoms, and—finally, the existence of indigenous peoples, COICA argues.[425]

2. Determining Factors of Life

According to COICA, what determines the Amazon indigenous peoples' existence is the "equilibrium and the symbiosis" between the material and spiritual realms inspired by *sacha runa yachai*, the "wisdom of the man of the jungle", consisting of three great principles or codes.[426]

3. The Three Great Principles of Wisdom

These three codes of the "wisdom of the man of the jungle" are, as COICA explains:

- First, the *suma kausay*—"the life in plenitude", which would be "integral, healthy in its spiritual, physical, ethical, moral, and intellectual aspects". These facts would be the ones allowing the "present and future generations to exist."[427]
- Second, the *tukuy pacha*, a principle that refers to the sum of knowledge, wisdom, and apprenticeship. It would deal "with the time needed to understand, comprehend, and learn the things that belong to us as well as those of strangers. It allows us to see within the darkness, to listen within noise, and to speak when there is no voice," as COICA says.[428]
- Third, there is the *musuk allpa*, which means to respect not only the new earth, but also the "sacred relationship with *pachamama*, integrating the present world, the one outside, and the one above".[429]

---

[423] *Id.* 13, 28 (2005), translation by COICA at http://www.coica.org.ec/ingles/aia_book/index.html.

[424] *Id.* 13, translation by COICA at http://www.coica.org.ec/ingles/aia_book/index.html.

[425] *Id.*

[426] *Id.* 28, translation by COICA at http://www.coica.org.ec/ingles/aia_book/index.html.

[427] *See id.* 13 et seq., translation according to COICA, *see* fn. above.

[428] *See id.* 28, 72, translation according to COICA, *see* fn. above.

[429] *See ibid.* It is understood as everything which includes the *Ukupacha*, the *Jawapacha* and the *Kaypacha, see ibid.*, expressions similar to the ones used by the peoples from the Cuenca del Imbakucha. *See* at Section 4.B.II. above.

The key element of these principles is renovation, COICA says. The jungle as a set of things is "born, grows, expands, gets sick, reproduces itself, dies, and renews itself"—a permanent cycle, so that land could always be renewed.[430] This would apply to anything.

4. Guidance for Reproduction of Mankind

From these three great codes, further values and rules of behavior derive according to COICA, *inter alia*: respect for diversity, ethics, reciprocity, and acknowledgement of shared responsibility.[431] These principles are understood as a "universal guidance" towards a life "led by spiritual strength, providing an access to material goods," through which all human beings can "reproduce themselves in a healthy and long-lasting way", as COICA says.[432]

5. Conception of Time

According to the understanding of COICA, time is circular. It is the circular time of the "great return", "where the future is always behind, the upcoming, the present and the past in front of us, with the teachings and individual lessons of the process of immemorial life."[433]

6. Collectivity

Due to this understanding of time, *Maloca* means being not "an individual but rather a collective person, living in a circular time of the great return."[434] Thus, collectivity is not only understood as a single instance in opposition to present individualism, but as an all-encompassing, "intergenerational awareness related to mankind".[435]

---

[430] COICA (2005) 72, translation by COICA at http://www.coica.org.ec/ingles/aia_book/index.html.

[431] *Id.* 15, translation according to COICA, *see* fn. above.

[432] *Ibid.*

[433] *Id.* 28, translation according to COICA, *see* fn. above.

[434] *Ibid.*

[435] *Ibid.*

7. The Principle of Shared Responsibility and Benefit

As a consequence, one essential principle is the "shared responsibility". According to COICA, "shared responsibility" constitutes a crucial term "that connects present and future generations," representing the conscience of generations, which embraced humans' relationships with their ancestors and "commits us to deliver [them] to future generations."[436] Responsibility regarding the Amazon, COICA argues, this means that the Amazon is worthy of having its "own life" throughout all generations that might come. According to the *Maloca*, it is a must—and a challenge—for the indigenous peoples of the Amazon to keep defending their existence and that of the Amazon itself, guaranteeing that it remains a "free and peaceful place".[437]

"Shared responsibility" means, as COICA says, that responsibility is a collective one, involving "all individuals and their sum as the collective", which at the same time provides for a collective benefit. In metaphorical terms used by COICA that means: the oxygen coming "from the Amazons' veins is life for all lives."[438]

8. The Principle of "Real" Sustainability

Such "shared responsibility" is also understood as an intergenerational one, requiring a "serious understanding" and implementation of sustainability. Human sustainability implies a "collective practice" and the "exercise of the rights of present and future generations", COICA says.[439] It implies managing natural resources, guarding socio-biodiversity, and the necessary knowledge involved, COICA says.

The Amazon peoples had been "such guardians over hundreds of years". However, the concept clashed with the ways of thinking and acting in the current capitalist development model, COICA says.[440] "Sustainable" development projects by other parts of the world's society and activities of economic exploitation based on a different, non-reciprocal market economy was promoting the disappearance of guarding peoples, COICA argues.[441] Their elimination, however, COICA says, was also the "elimination of socio-cultural patterns", including knowledge on sustainable use of plants, animals and natural resources[442]—and TCEs.[443]

---

[436] *Id.* 70, translation according to COICA, *see* fn. above.

[437] *Ibid.*

[438] *Id.* 15, translation by COICA at http://www.coica.org.ec/ingles/aia_book/index.html.

[439] *Id.* 22, translation according to COICA, *see* fn. above.

[440] *Ibid.*

[441] *Ibid.*

[442] *Id.* 71, translation according to COICA, *see* fn. above.

[443] On this *see also* No. 12 right below.

9. Respect for Ethics and Reciprocity

COICA views the Amazon as a physical and symbolic place, as an "inspiration and a great example of self-development and reciprocity".[444]

The "Western" market economy had perceived the huge green basin as a "demographic vacuum," the "lungs" of the world, or the "world's shop," and thereby altered the native peoples' own use of natural resources, their social mobility mechanisms, and especially their eating patterns, COICA argues.

In contrast, the *Maloca* is based on a system of reciprocity, i.e. "production, distribution, and consumption", COICA says.[445] It implies teachings which equilibrate "the quality in the simplicity," which was part of the balanced, healthy existence "of our ancestors."[446] According to COICA's understanding, production and consumption are axes that articulate within the social organization process, which are used to strengthen the exchange networks of the members of the group. In this manner, "each family nucleus" in each community would represent "a small unit of production and consumption".[447]

10. Respect for Diversity

According to COICA, diversity is a precondition of existence. Specifically, cultural diversity serves, in the words of Amazon Indians, "as trenches that have disabled, and are still protecting us from, our destruction."[448] The spirituality, cultures, and gods maintained the indigenous peoples firm for building a human world. Therefore, the diversity of the different cultures in the world had to be respected. Without formal recognition of the different social patterns, COICA argues, the indigenous peoples of the Amazon region were not able to distinguish and assume their rights as such.[449]

11. "Wisemen" and Their Functions

Despite the collective being the bearer of the common memory and wisdom, COICA argues, there are few people who have special characteristics and tasks within every community in order to uphold this common memory and to take care of special practices and spiritual knowledge.[450] That was or in some cases still is a

---

[444] *Id.* 70, translation by COICA at http://www.coica.org.ec/ingles/aia_book/index.html.

[445] *Id.*

[446] *Id.*

[447] *Id.* 27, translation according to COICA, *see* fn. above.

[448] *Id.* 71, translation by COICA at http://www.coica.org.ec/ingles/aia_book/index.html.

[449] *Id.*

[450] *Id.* 59. On the use of the different terms and their particular meaning according to the COICA *see* at Section 1.B.I.1.e. above.

"small elite of wise people," elders, "possessors of wisdoms and very joyful people", "depositories of our collective memory," people who have been chosen for the task of transmitting the wisdom and memory from generation to generation.[451] As the ancestral wisdom has little by little been lost during the last years, COICA warns that now more than ever "we must support all efforts to continue with the wisdom chain or to fix it wherever it has been broken."[452]

12. Traditional Practices and Cultural Expressions

The (millenary) wisdom is regarded to be "registered in rocks, pottery, in myths, songs, in the management of beings of the material and spiritual universe".[453] This is because *Maloca*, the living in a circular time with collective memories, also entails "cherishing and protecting" the ancestral wisdoms, technologies, and sacred places and maintaining harmonious relationships with the environment, COICA says.[454]

The traditional sciences are wisdoms experienced and extracted from the teachings of the objects of art by ancestors, COICA says. "It is through these forms of teachings that we sustain our lifestyles, our journey and historic background. They are life practices that generate life and gain strength in each birth of a being, be it human or not."[455]

Therefore, COICA regards indigenous knowledge and TCEs not as part of the public domain, but as parts of a "collective cultural and intellectual property", which should be protected under the communities' common rights.[456] The "collective information" and expressions are the "fruit of our experiments and generational labor" and spiritual superstructure, COICA argues.[457] For this reason, it should not be treated and used as "goods of private consumption and earnings of a few," COICA says. The use of the collective intangible goods and expressions only made sense "if it is in function of a collectivity."[458] This means also that any unauthorized use or improper appropriation of these cultural goods is understood as "usurpation."[459]

---

[451] *Id.* 59, translation by COICA at http://www.coica.org.ec/ingles/aia_book/index.html. According to COICA, in Asháninka, they are called *Sheripiari*; in Shipibo, *Onanya*; in Yine, *Kahonxi*; in Shuar, *Uwishin*, *see* COICA (2005) 59.

[452] *Id*, translation by COICA at http://www.coica.org.ec/ingles/aia_book/index.html.

[453] *Id.* 70.

[454] *Id.* 28, translation according to COICA, *see* fn. above.

[455] *Id.*

[456] *Id.* 71 *et seq.*

[457] *Ibid.*

[458] *Ibid.*

[459] *Ibid.*

D. Analysis of These Philosophies

Which similarities within these different philosophies can be found (below I.)? Are there similarities to other Native worldviews (below II.) and/or to Non-Native ones (below III.)?

The following analysis aims at improving the junction between the Native spiritual superstructure and a legal protection of TCEs and bridging the gap of a too isolated consideration of "two distinct policy domains – concerning the law and policy of IP, and concerning a cluster of inter-related indigenous and environmental issues.".[460]

This "analysis" is not meant to contradict Lee Irwin's experience that dealing with Native spirituality "is not analysis but communication."[461] It is rather to use the foregoing communication and a following comparison for further understandings. Also, the focus here does not exclusively lay on Native spirituality, but on its use for probing an adequate protection of TCEs. More particularly, the aim is to enhance "one's ability to understand and employ the others discipline's tools and structures, not least with a view to probing their appropriateness for mastering the challenges" of an appropriate protection of TCEs in the future.[462]

I. Commonalities Within the Different Examples

All examples stress an interdependence of all things in the cosmos, in which the abstract and tangible are indivisible. They all put forth a circular perception of life, prenatal and post-mortal *stadia*. As a result, they imply similar concepts of time, space, and interconnection, and their guiding principle for right behavior is respect for the big picture, the "whole" in an immaterial and material dimension. Thus, maintaining life and the living environment and its fertility for the current and the coming generations is essential. The key to successfully doing so lies in "living" respect for nature and respecting the law of equilibrium, balance in every step one takes. Standards for action should be oriented towards the benefit of mankind rather than towards pure individual interests.

On this basis, the environment is able to provide for all needs, and thus property is also understood as a consequence of the concept of abundance rather than

---

[460] These had, "due to a failure of communication . . . hitherto largely been considered discrete and isolated from one another, often assumed to be at odds in terms of values," *see* Taubman and Leistner (2008) 67.

[461] *See* at Section 4.A.III.1. above.

[462] Such aim has been viewed as essential for a similar problem of linking expertise in different legal disciplines, namely those of the law on intellectual property and private international law, *see* Drexl and Kur, "Preface" in: Drexl, J. and A. Kur, (eds.), "Intellectual Property and Private International Law", Oxford, vii–viii, vii (2005).

scarcity. "Property" is managed and controlled by a definable group of custodians that cuts across different societal sectors.

II. Similarities to Other Indigenous Philosophies

Some of these essential aspects are elements that also appear in indigenous superstructures other than those from Latin America. The idea that "all life is circular" and subject to continuous change; that "everything is related;" the values and ritual acts of sharing and "reciprocity;" the idea of the "Four Worlds and Four Doors" are also essential principles of the spirituality and driving motions of TCEs of the Odawa Indians in the Great Lakes region of North America, for example.[463]

III. Similarities and Differences in Western and Other Philosophies, Religions, World Views, and Sciences

"Western" is understood here not as a pure geographical term, but as differentiation to "indigenous" in terms of content. Thus the two can even characterize conditions within the same Latin American countries, as the overwhelming majority of the politically and economically leading sector of the Latin American societies is strongly influenced by "Western" values regarding both, philosophies as well as every-day life phenomena, such as education, entertainment, and social behavior.[464]

In view of the strong (ultra-)relativistic tendencies in anthropological as well as other intercultural sciences or topics in sciences in the past decades, numerous publications supporting well-known distinctions between indigenous and Western world views could be cited—which would not add value to the task of elaborating an appropriate protection of TCEs though. In the following, only the main differences between the spiritual and religious beliefs will be highlighted (below 1.), and then general (below 2.) and particular legal similarities (below 3.) elaborated.

1. Main Differences

The main differences between "Western" world visions and the indigenous ones presented above might be seen in

(1) in the relationship between man and nature,

[463] Pflüg, "Pimadaziwin - Contemporary Rituals in Odawa Community", in: Irwin, "Native American Spirituality – A Critical Reader" 121–144, 123 *seq.*, 138 (2000).

[464] Mols, "Lateinamerikas internationale Zukunft. Der Subkontinent zwischen 'Dependencia' und Globalisierung", in: Scheuzger and Fleer (eds.), "Die Moderne in Lateinamerika – Zentren und Peripherien des Wandels" 51–69, 54 (2009).

(2) the philosophy of individualism, and
(3) the (ethical) principles of economy.

Although the indigenous concept of *abundancia* "involves the idea that the environment will provide for all needs,"[465] and this idea can also be found in the Christian faith, even as an explicit expression, *abundance*, in Psalm 36,[466] nonetheless, it is rather the directive "replenish the earth, and subdue it: and have dominion over . . . every living thing that moveth upon the earth"[467] which dominates the behavior, understanding of property, and legal rules of most of the societies that have a Christian background.

2. General Universalities

At the same time, several similarities can be found between the native philosophy and Christian belief: The laws of right behavior following from the logic of *Sé* and the Ten Commandments, for example, correspond to a large extent: both include commandments such as not to covet, not to want to kill, not to steal, not to tell lies or be false in thought.

Very similar to the indigenous cosmovision is also the idea of harmony of heaven, earth, and mankind in the old Chinese philosophy as transmitted in Tao Te Ching by Lao Tsu (also spelled Laozi).[468] The conception of a circular time, the circle of life, and the relative existence of humans is also the basis of the Buddhist perspective.[469] A similarity can also be observed among the terms and conceptions of (the Law of) *Sé*, the *Zen* and *Chi*. The idea of duality, be it yin and yang in the Chinese or Taoist philosophy, or female and male energy in general, and the aim of connecting of the dual elements in the world, is also a common idea in these worldviews.[470] External and internal balance as described by the Kogi is also a concept dealt with in psychology by Carl Jung as well as in Buddhist spirituality.[471] Abundance is also a concept followed in Buddhism, which can only be reached if the individual aims at prosperity or benefit for mankind and not exclusively for the individual.[472]

---

[465] Lettington and Manek, "Indigenous Knowledge Rights: Recognizing Alternative Worldviews", 24.4 (2001).

[466] "How precious is your steadfast love, O God! All people may take refuge in the shadow of your wings. They feast on the abundance of your house, and you give them drink from the river of your delights. For with you is the fountain of life."

[467] Genesis 1: 28: "God said unto them [male and female], Be fruitful, and multiply, and replenish the earth, and subdue it: and have dominion over the fish of the sea, and over the fowl of the air, and over every living thing that moveth upon the earth."

[468] Lao Tsu, "Tao Te Ching" (1997).

[469] The Wheel of Life, *see* Ian A. Baker in Shrestha (2006 I) 30 and in Shrestha (2006 II) 58.

[470] *See* Shrestha (2006 I) 28.

[471] Ian A. Baker in Shrestha (2006 II) 52.

[472] Ian A. Baker in: *id.* 48.

Similarly, in African philosophy, the basis is the understanding of the changing whole,[473] from which ethical principles of behaviour follow, namely human activity, the creative drive, humanity, and altruism.[474] Quite similar is also the way of comprehending the interconnectedness of all things, by fully recognizing the inseparability of all existence, by means of applying basic human qualities like compassion and empathy.[475] Compassion, in turn, has also been studied and "discovered" by Western anthropological scholar Margaret Gruter as one basis of "common emotional and behavioral predispositions, which have been called the 'sense of justice.'"[476]

Other contemporary philosophers, anthropologists, lawyers and other interdisciplinary researchers of this and the last century have also moved in a similar direction. As regards the attitude of keeping the balance, the Western humanist and doctor Albert Schweitzer observed critically that while it might be true that all beings kill, man would be the only one of them that takes more than he needs, and from this observation he developed his theory on "reverence for life."[477] This is quite similar to the awareness of the Kogi and the Asarios that deliberate human interaction in the world inevitably has consequences that could not be readily anticipated, and therefore these actions had to be done safely, involving a momentum of seriousness, responsibility, and connection with the creative power that transcended all times, as the Kogis say.[478]

Other elementary concepts relayed above, which are common to several different world philosophies, are "future generations" and "mankind," put forward as parameters for action and fundamental principles. According to the philosopher Hans Jonas, an imperative responding to the new type of human action and addressed to the new type of agency that operates it, might run:

"Act so that the effects of your action are compatible with the permanence of genuine human life." Or, negatively: "Act so that the effects of your action are not destructive of the future possibility of such life;" or simply: "Do not compromise the conditions for an indefinite continuation of humanity on earth;" or: "In your present choices, include the future wholeness of Man among the objects of your will."[479]

Some years later, in 1987, this philosophical imperative was also elaborated and formulated as the key principle of economic behavior and development policy: under the telling title "Our Common Future," the international Brundtland

---

[473] "(S)ich wandelnde Ganzheit," *see* Fikentscher (2005) 9.

[474] *Id.* 9.

[475] Compassion is represented by *avalokitshvara* or *chenrezig* in Indian and Tibetan Buddhism, *kuan shih yin* in China, *kanzeon* in Japan, *quan'am* in Vietnam, *kanin* in Bali, as Ian A. Baker says, *see* Baker in Shrestha (2006 II) 50 and in Shrestha (2006 I) 22 and 22.

[476] Gruter and Masters (1998) 93.

[477] Schweitzer (1966) 20.

[478] On the laws of right behavior following from the Law of *Sé see* at Section 4.B.I.2. above.

[479] Jonas (1979) 11.

Commission developed the principle for which it coined the term "sustainable development."[480]

In anthropology today, there exists a tendency to move away from the (ultra-) relativistic approach of the last decades towards a more universal one, a path that reveals several universalities among most of the societies of the world, in anthropological as well as other interdisciplinary sciences.[481] Even positive impacts of interaction with traditional Latin American communities have been underscored by various researchers: Darell Posey, for one, argues that "(t)raditional peoples can teach us how to give greater value to the living resources of Amazonia."[482]

Recently, at a brainstorming session of the Andean Community in August, 2009, in Lima, the contemporary French sociologist and philosopher Edgar Morin emphasized "the need to incorporate into the Western conception of the world, which severed the communication between man and nature," other conceptions that would restore that relationship and (re-)balance the two players.[483] With regard to the future of Andean integration, Morin stressed the importance of revitalizing the indigenous Andean roots, which prioritize the relationship between man and nature, and he "recommended persevering in this undertaking, despite any difficulties that could arise."[484]

The advantage of a multigenerational perspective was emphasized even in the fields of applied architecture, urban planning, and development sciences: in "current attempts at sustainable development in the region" of the Brazilian Amazon, there were valuable principles and practices based upon a "careful, multigenerational resource creation and management," which constituted lessons worth learning from the local, traditional communities.[485]

3. Similarities in Philosophical Aspects of Law, Particularly Intellectual Property

Finally, current tendencies in law—naturally in their own technical terms and concepts—pay due consideration to various aspects of the afore-mentioned spiritual principles.

---

[480] Brundtland Commission (1987).

[481] Antweiler (2009).

[482] "[B]ut only if their diversity of cultures survives." Posey (2004) 63.

[483] Andean Community (2009).

[484] *Ibid.*

[485] *See* Heckenberger et al. (2008) 1217: "(T)he pre-Columbian societies of the Upper Xingu river basin in Brazilian Amazonia lived in an urban landscape of distributed towns, villages, and hamlets organized by a road network that connected settlements arranged in a grid like pattern. The inhabitants created a highly productive and heterogeneous cultural landscape through careful, multigenerational resource creation and management. These arrangements may provide lessons for current attempts at sustainable development in the region…".

a. Sustainability

First of all, the principle of sustainability has been codified: In the 1992 Rio Declaration, the international community of states committed itself to "sustainable development" as coined by the international Brundtland Commission, namely to the "key principle of considering ecological, economic, and socio-cultural aspects in any development policy".[486]

Herein, particularly the role of traditional communities and their traditional lifestyles has been juridically recognized; they "became a key element of this concept [of sustainable development], as they were understood to exemplify ways for securing human needs while preserving the environment."[487] Principle 22 of the 1992 Rio Declaration acknowledges this "vital role in environmental management," and calls upon the member states to "recognize and duly support their identity, culture and interest" in view of the major aim of "sustainable development."[488]

b. Reciprocity

Likewise, the principle of reciprocity has not only been acknowledged as an elementary principle in Western law in general,[489] but also in international copyright law in particular, for many decades now.[490] The specific shape of the content of that principle varies, of course, and depends upon diverging factors, values, and time.[491] Nonetheless, the idea of reciprocity of rights and duties, of exchange, mutuality, and reciprocal treatment, is shared universally among the diverse worldviews in question. The famous German legal scholar, philosopher, and sociologist of the late nineteenth century, Otto von Gierke, stated that any kind of right is a "relation between human wills, not between an isolated singular will and an object lacking a will of its own."[492] Where human and human face each other, "dominance without duties is excluded"[493]—thus, no rights can exist without responsibilities.

---

[486] Brundtland Commission (1987).

[487] Stoll and von Hahn (2008) 31.

[488] Article 22 reads fully: "Indigenous people and their communities and other local communities have a vital role in environmental management and development because of their knowledge and traditional practices. States should recognize and duly support their identity, culture and interests and enable their effective participation in the achievement of sustainable development."

[489] Becker, "Reciprocity" (1990); and *see* at Section 5.D.VII. below.

[490] *See, e.g.*, Boytha (1968).

[491] *See, e.g.*, the different categories of reciprocity on the one hand and the concept of complementarity (or the principle of *do-ut-des* in law) on the other, developed by Alvin Gouldner. According to Gouldner, only the case of a right of ego implying a duty of ego, or, in other words, each party having rights *and* duties, corresponds to the concrete concept of reciprocity: Gouldner (1960)161–178.

[492] Gierke (1943, orig. 1889) 14 as well as Hann (1998) 4, 6.

[493] *Ibid.*

c. Property

The afore mentioned statement indicates that, finally, "property" from a Western perspective always has been and still is subject to debate. It is true that "one particular cluster" of forms of property relations, which "have come and gone as long as human societies have existed, . . . has achieved world dominance in the last two centuries[: t]he rigorous specification of private property rights."[494] However, "the actual preeminence of private property and of the liberal paradigm of which it forms a central element has never been as complete as either its proponents or its critics like to claim. To a large extent it is a myth."[495]

Some similarities to the spiritual concepts and the resultant understanding of ownership in the examples of indigenous philosophies listed above can be found in Western concepts of property: first, in the intergenerational conception, second, in its social dimension, and third, in its conception as a collective good, and, finally, in the particular area of intellectual property law.

The intergenerational conception of property, namely its transmission from one generation to the next within the family is the common and basic understanding of inheritance law—which varies in its particular characteristics, of course.[496]

The social dimension of Western concepts of property has been disputed for centuries now. The famous nineteenth-century German lawyer Rudolph von Jhering, one of the main original advocates of an individualistic concept of property, later developed the rather contrary theory of social property, the "gesellschaftliche Eigentumstheorie."[497] The "idea of property" could not bring about anything contradicting the "idea of society," for which reason any kind of private property was socially bound with respect to the society, he argued.[498] Similarly, Otto von Gierke underscored that any human being is an individual and at the same time a social being, which is why the law would have to consider both aspects at any time.[499] The social dimension and obligation that rights entail, particularly property rights, was codified at the constitutional level in Germany years after this discussion took place.[500]

Notwithstanding the criticism by Gierke and Jhering, the German Civil Code followed and follows a rather individualistic concept of property. Today, in the context of the "dominant Western liberal paradigm" in general, the dichotomy between individual and communal has "acquired particular salience," Chris Hann argues.[501] Yet this "does not mean that these are the best terms with which to

---

494 Hann (1998) 1.

495 *Id.* 2.

496 On social change of the conception and its intimate connection to state policies *see id.* 1–47, 4 (1998).

497 Jhering, "Der Zweck im Recht", 526 *seq.* cited from Pahud (2000) 10.

498 Jhering, "Der Zweck im Recht", 523, 532 cited from *id.* 10.

499 Gierke (1943, orig. 1889) 4.

500 *See* Art. 153, para. 3 German Weimarer Reichsverfassung and Art. 14(2) German Constitution.

501 Hann (1998) 7.

capture the actual realities of modern Western societies, and many anthropologists have urged caution in the application of this dichotomy to other forms of society."[502] This is especially true in view of a universality that can be observed in all societies, namely that "[a]ll societies have property relations that transcend their individual members, i.e. they imply some sort of integrated collectivity."[503]

Collective goods are acknowledged in the Western system of law, too, even different categories thereof like pure public goods, club public goods, and free goods,[504] so that a concept of collective ownership of TCEs that follows an *emic* understanding could easily be integrated into the Western system of collective goods.[505]

Finally, as regards copyright law in particular, the famous British statesman and historian Thomas B. Macaulay argued in 1841 already in the context of copyright that "property is the creature of the law, and . . . the law which creates property can be defended only on this ground, that is a law *beneficial to mankind*."[506] From a similar perspective, though in the area of patent law establishing property monopolies, recent authors have questioned the narrow, Western understanding of "innovation," respectively the criterion of intellectual effort.[507]

E. Illusion Versus Reality: Some Remarks on Actual Tendencies in Practice

The comparison has revealed that in theory, there exist common understandings on universalities. These are e.g. the inter-relatedness between human socio-economic and environmental development and consideration of an inter-generational perspective. Nonetheless, this result does rarely reflect the dominant view. In practice, it is even less implemented, at least in Western lifestyles. The latter aspect in turn, has an impact on the traditional spiritual bases and beliefs of indigenous peoples.

As early as in 1955, in view of his experiences in the Brazilian native communities, Claude Lévi-Strauss realized that "[t]he paradox is irresoluble: the less one culture communicates with another, the less likely they are to be corrupted, one by the other; but, on the other hand, the less likely it is, in such conditions, that the respective emissaries of these cultures will be able to seize the richness and significance of their diversity."[508]

---

[502] *Ibid.*

[503] *Id.* 6.

[504] *See* the clear graph on collective goods and further explanations in: Fikentscher (2004 I) 192.

[505] *See* Fikentscher (2005) 10.

[506] Macaulay (1997) 246. Emphasis added by the author.

[507] Hassemer (2009) 153–167 and Busch (2010) 221.

[508] This paradox and dilemma, Lévi-Strauss argued further, had led to the miserable reality and fact, that "humanity has taken to monoculture," Lévi-Strauss, "Tristes Tropiques" (translated by John Russell) 45 (1961).

At the same time, the discrepancy increases between a rather traditional or romanticized theory of indigenous spiritualities and practice, between illusion and reality. Reasons for that can be found in both, internal and external influences. Lévi-Strauss underscored the importance of the role of the anthropological researcher in this regard. Anthropological reports would bear the risk to "preserve the illusion of something that no longer exists, but yet must be assumed to exist if we are to escape from the appalling indictment that has been piling up against us through twenty thousand years of history."[509] Still today, such risk exists, especially the case in customary rules,[510] but also as regards their spiritual bases and philosophies dealt with here.

With regard to external influences on the spiritual values and conservation efforts of indigenous communities, there exist interesting data from a recent empirical study, particularly on the communities in the Cuenca del Imbakucha.[511] The study gives a prime example of said impact by certain intensity of touristic interference, provided by the comparison of two communities of this region, Cotacachi and Otavalo. Both communities hold mountain landscapes of the Imbakucha watershed sacred, the study says. In Otavalo, a well-known market town, mass tourism became more and more popular, whereas the community of Cotacachi had "opted for ecotourism as an alternative".[512] The collected data suggest that "as mass tourism becomes more popular in Otavalo, spiritual values are being lost. In contrast, in Cotacachi, which has opted for ecotourism. . ., spiritual values are being preserved."[513]

Similarly, as regards the economic shift in the community of Otavalo in relation to their TCEs, mainly special traditional textiles, a strong tendency of shift from "primitive communism" to a "flourishing capitalism" can be noted.[514]

---

[509] *Id.* 39 (1961).

[510] On this *see* at Section 5.B.III.2.d. below.

[511] *See* at Section 4.B.II. above.

[512] Carter, "Achieving Holistic Sacred Sites Conservation for Indigenous Communities in Ecuador", Fall 2008 Perspectives 4 (2008).

[513] According to L. Carter, all interviewees agreed that a stronger influence of environmental ideals could and should be instilled into the livelihoods of indigenous communities in order to conserve sacred sites. To achieve these ideals, Carter recommended implementing "Robert Wild's holistic Sacred Site Conservation, which is based on principles of the World Conservation Union. These principles should allow the indigenous communities, especially those like Otavalo, to preserve their ancestral beliefs and values, while also providing economic benefits through ecotourism." As regards the empirical method of the study, the relevant data were collected "through 30 interviews with people who knew Cotacachi and Otavalo well," Carter, "Achieving Holistic Sacred Sites Conservation for Indigenous Communities in Ecuador", Fall 2008 Perspectives 4 (2008).

[514] Personal communication with the Indian Humberto Muenala, Ecuadorian Ministry of Culture, and with Patricio Sandoval, Instituto Iberoamericano del Patrimonio Natural y Cultural (IPANC), the Ibero-American Institute for the Natural and Cultural Patrimony, in March, 2009, in Quito, Ecuador.

With regard to the ancestral exchange system in general, indigenous peoples themselves admit that one of the great challenges is "not to give in to the temptation of the traps of money," as today, the traditional non-monetary exchange system is practiced only in traditional fairs in very remote areas in the mountains, Rivera-Zea says.[515] Exceptions might exist with regard to varieties of seeds, as they were still regarded as "fruits and gifts from mother earth", notwithstanding any human effort in raising them.[516]

Thus, if COICA argues that each family nucleus in each community represents a small unit of production and consumption,[517] this theoretical concept is difficult to implement, if the families do not live together anymore, as some of their members have emigrated to urban areas.

Moreover, indigenous peoples admit that the traditional philosophy of a collective life based on shared resources has been confounded by the progress of roads enabling new settlement in indigenous territory and exploitation of vital resources.[518] While roads may be the most visible menace, there are other internal and external realities painting a picture of life that diverges from the traditional philosophical one. "Guardians" of the communities are seduced by relatively enormous offers of international companies, sell land and resources and often do not return the money to the community, but spend it for individual purposes.[519] Sometimes, where intergenerational conflicts arise, the "wisemen" are hardly respected anymore.[520]

In certain regions of Panama, the author experienced a bleak picture: As a consequence of the strong "Western" influence, more and more indigenous people adopt an individualistic way of thinking and loose the dominance of the native language through which the philosophical superstructure had once been expressed. As a consequence of the interdependence with dominant "Western" ways of life and material needs, construction of streets, airports and the use of motorboats are enhanced to facilitate an industry of tourism—even if it is called "eco-tourism." Sometimes, "rituals" appear to have turned into usual parties rather than as traditional expressions of spiritual maintenance.

At a higher organizational level, COICA, the "most capable interlocutor" is said to have suffered a profound internal division in the last several years, a process that culminated in the establishment of two parallel advisory boards fighting against each other, as authors have stated.[521] The apparently unanimous representation of

---

[515] Rivera-Zea (2006) 1.

[516] *Ibid.*

[517] *See* at Section 4.C.II.4. above and COICA (2005) 7, translation by COICA at http://www.coica.org.ec/ingles/aia_book/index.html.

[518] Rivera-Zea (2006) 3. The latest and weightiest example of such a road is probably, as stated before, the first swath cut through the Amazon in its million years of history: the new connection under construction between Manaus (Brazil) and Manta (Ecuador).

[519] Personal communication with A.M. and J.M.

[520] On practical experiences in this regard, *see* the issue of representation according to customary law at Section 5.D.II. below.

[521] Wörrle (2009) 234.

emic views on collective values and goods might in fact be quite disputed internally. Closely connected to this aspect is the question of representation in customary law, which is dealt with below.[522]

Finally, the loss of spiritual values in people's real lives on the one hand, however, goes along with the re-introduction or revitalizing of such values and practices on the other. Ironically, it is sometimes even "Western people" who re-introduce the vitality of the "traditional" philosophy and connected rituals—i.e. TCEs—into native life by teaching indigenous people the manifestations that Western researchers have "recovered" through books, etc. and reintroduced into the contemporary community life. One example thereof is a "tea ceremony" formerly practiced by the Shuar Indians in the Ecuadorian rainforest that was reintroduced by a Swiss ethnologist (albeit with limited success).[523]

F. Legal References to These Concepts in Latin America in General

Notwithstanding these challenges and discrepancies in practice, the philosophical superstructure might still provide useful guidelines for a more successful and appropriate protection of TCEs.

Some of these "rules" have even been laid down as legal principles in national Constitutions. The two most recent Constitutions of Latin America, the 2008 Constitution of Ecuador, and the 2009 Constitution of Bolivia, take up many of these aspects. The texts of the Constitutions even use the expressions in the native language followed by a Spanish translation.

The farthest-reaching statute in this regard is the 2009 Constitution of Bolivia. Under the title "Principles, Values, and Aims of the State," it establishes that the state "assumes and promotes as ethic-moral principles of the plural society:" "*ama qhilla, ama llulla, ama suwa*" (don't be idle, don't lie, don't steal), "*suma qamaña*" (live well), "*ñandereko*" (harmonic life), "*teko kavi*" (good life), "*ivi maraei*" (earth without evil ("tierra sin mal")), and "*qhapaj ñan*" (noble way and life).[524] Even the former, 1988 Constitution of Ecuador, for example, stipulated that "[a]ll citizens have the following duties and responsibilities, without prejudice to others provided for in this Constitution and the law," for instance "*[a]ma quillu, ama llullu, ama shua:* Not to be idle, not to lie, not to steal."[525]

---

[522] *See* at Section 5.D.II. below.

[523] Personal communication with ethnologist Anna Meiser on January 8, 2009, who has been doing anthropological research in the indigenous communities of the Shuar and Achuar in Ecuador for over 5 years now.

[524] Article 8, para. 1, of the 2009 Constitution of Bolivia.

[525] Article 97 Nos. 8 and 20 of the former, 1988 Constitution of Ecuador. It has been replaced by the new one of 2008, *see* at Chapter III Section 3.A. below.

The principle of *sumak kawsay*, of "Good Living," which is rooted in the spirituality of the peoples of the Cuenca del Imbakucha and also taken up by COICA (spelled *sumak kausay*), as seen above, is not only included in the preamble of the 2008 Constitution of Ecuador, but also as a legal principle to be considered particularly in the implementation of a national law dealing with a special "integral planning" for the Amazon provinces.[526]

The preamble of the 2008 Constitution of Ecuador refers to many aspects mentioned by the Kogi and Asarios, the peoples of the Cuenca del Imbakucha, and Daniel Mundurukú, and also taken up by COICA, namely the native roots and spirituality, the close relationship with and spiritual concept of nature, the value of wisdom, the aim of good living, diversity, equilibrium and collectivity:

> We, the sovereign people of Ecuador, recognizing our millenary roots wrought by women and men of distinct peoples, celebrating the nature, the *Pacha Mama*, of which we are part and which is vital for our existence, invoking the name of God and recognizing our diverse forms of religion and spirituality, appealing to the wisdom of all cultures which enrich us as society, as inheritors of the social fights for liberation from all forms of domination and colonialism, and with a profound commitment to the present and the future, resolve to construct a new form of citizens' co-existence, in diversity and harmony with nature, to reach the good living, the *sumak kawsay*, a society which respects, in all dimensions, the dignity of the persons and collectives.[527]

Similarly, the Preamble of the 2009 Constitution of Bolivia postulates "[a] state ... where the search for the *good living* dominates ... with the strength of our *Pachamama* and thanks to God."

These and further aspects are incorporated into the 2009 Constitution of Bolivia as constitutional "Values of the State" to be supported by the State of Bolivia, namely, reciprocity, respect, complementarity, harmony, equilibrium, common wellbeing.[528] "Essential Aims and Functions" of the state are, among others, to guarantee the equal dignity of the peoples, nations and communities and to cultivate

---

[526] Article 250 of the 2008 Constitution of Ecuador: "El territorio de las provincias amazónicas forma parte de un ecosistema necesario para el equilibrio ambiental del planeta. Este territorio constituirá una circunscripción territorial especial para la que existirá una planificación integral recogida en una ley que incluirá aspectos sociales, económicos, ambientales y culturales, con un ordenamiento territorial que garantice la conservación y protección de sus ecosistemas y el principio del *sumak kawsay*," emphasis added by the author.

[527] "Preámbulo. NOSOTRAS Y NOSOTROS, el pueblo soberano del Ecuador RECONOCIENDO nuestras raíces milenarias, forjadas por mujeres y hombres de distintos pueblos, CELEBRANDO a la naturaleza, la Pacha Mama, de la que somos parte y que es vital para nuestra existencia, INVOCANDO el nombre de Dios y reconociendo nuestras diversas formas de religiosidad y espiritualidad, APELANDO a la sabiduría de todas las culturas que nos enriquecen como sociedad, COMO HEREDEROS de las luchas sociales de liberación frente a todas las formas de dominación y colonialismo, y con un profundo compromiso con el presente y el futuro, Decidimos construir Una nueva forma de convivencia ciudadana, en diversidad y armonía con la naturaleza, para alcanzar el buen vivir, el sumak kawsay; Una sociedad que respeta, en todas sus dimensiones, la dignidad de las personas y las colectividades...". *See* the preamble of the 2008 Constitution of Ecuador.

[528] Article 8, para. 2, of the 2009 Constitution of Bolivia.

mutual respect and intra-cultural, intercultural and pluri-lingual dialogue.[529] Further goals are: to promote and guarantee a responsible and planned use of natural resources, and to boost industrialization as well as the conservation of the environment, for the wellbeing of the current and future generations.[530]

G. Consequences for the Protection of TCEs

As just seen, principles of the native philosophies presented at the outset have been integrated as political and also legal principles in Latin American Constitutions.[531] Thus, they can and do have a legal impact indeed. Within this general framing, there are also principles or at least inspirations offered by these philosophies that can aid in the adequate legal protection of TCEs in particular.

Similarly, estimated Western scholars argue that "'IP Protection' in its essential form is not a stand-alone solution; ... the question remains, however, what overarching principles and legal mechanisms should in principle and can in practice be established at the fully international level."[532]

Such "legal mechanisms" could be various ones, to be dealt with in more detail below, in the context of considering customary rules as concrete implementation of the philosophies. Here, it will only be mentioned that no matter whether one follows a sui generis approach that includes *emic* perspectives (e.g. through the application of indigenous "customary" law or consideration of cultural particularities) or the path of tort law and international private law,[533] in both cases the inner perspective and the worldview of the bearers of TCEs is relevant. Even if neither of these two mechanisms were to be applied, the worldviews could serve as a source of orientation for values that are relevant for the legal order, i.e. as blanket clauses or as facts, similar to the famous Australian case *Bulun Bulun*.[534]

"Overarching principles" can be deduced from the analysis of the philosophies introduced here. In particular, principles for the *content* of the legal protection of TCEs but also for the *process* of dealing with TCEs can be defined. Apart from the above analysis of the different philosophies and consequences drawn by this study, there are consequences and positions formulated by Latin American indigenous

---

[529] Article 9, No. 2, of the 2009 Constitution of Bolivia.

[530] Article 9, No. 6, of the 2009 Constitution of Bolivia.

[531] To summarize: "the principle of *sumak kawsay*", in Article 250 of the 2008 Constitution of Ecuador; "nature, *Pacha Mama*," "the wisdom of all cultures which enrich us as a society," "to reach the *good living*, the *sumak kawsay*", in the Preamble of the 2008 Constitution of Ecuador; and "the search for the *good living*", "with the strength of our *Pachamama* and thanks to God", in the Preamble of the 2009 Constitution of Bolivia (emphasises added by the author); and on various principles contained in Article 8 of the Bolivian Constitution *see* at Section 5.F. below.

[532] Taubman and Leistner (2008) 179.

[533] On this *see* at Section 5.E. below.

[534] On this *see ibid.*

peoples themselves. The political "Amazon Indigenous Agenda" of COICA itself, which intended to show the "Return to the Maloca," for instance, includes concrete proposals of elements to be taken into consideration within an "alternative ancestral wisdom and collective rights protection system," which would include TCEs.

Analytical consequences will be summarized from all three examples of the different local indigenous philosophies disposed above as well as from the spiritual "Return to the Maloca" including related consequences drawn by COICA. Further, more far-reaching proposals of COICA will be attached. The principles and consequences are divided into those relating to the content of the protection of TCEs on the one hand (immediately following), and to the process of elaborating a solution on the other (below at II.).

I. Consequences Regarding the Content of a Possible Legal Protection of TCEs

1. Object of Protection

All philosophical superstructures displayed above are based upon a holistic view, characterized by an all-encompassing understanding of interdependence. Most of the TCEs which are expressed in a still traditional way and within their conventional surroundings are (somehow) rooted in these philosophies. Therefore, the object or subject matter of protection should be TCEs understood in the broadest possible sense. No separation should be made between the different expressions. In particular, there should be no distinction made between the material and immaterial good, nor an apparently "emic" distinction between different functions which any expressions might fulfill, nor such distinction according to the function of the person conducting or performing an expression. Practical problems, especially if the protection were adapted to or included in the area of intellectual property rights, will be addressed below, considering the example of Panama.[535]

Similarly, one element that COICA regards as essential for the protection of TCEs is "to acknowledge that ... the innovation is a cumulative process that includes all the manifestations of their creativity."[536]

2. No Static System

According to the philosophies and approaches dealt with above, TCEs as well as customary rules are understood as under ongoing development. Especially where the non-literate tradition is still reality, or has been revitalized, the social function of

[535] *See* at Chapter IV Section 1.G. below.

[536] All foregoing elements stem from COICA (2005) 62, translation by COICA at http://www.coica.org.ec/ingles/aia_book/index.html.

memory and of forgetting the elements of the cultural tradition is the "homeostatic organization of the cultural tradition,"[537] another reason why even revitalized and dynamic elements should be embraced.[538]

3. Holder of Rights

The philosophies displayed above, as well as the revitalization of those philosophies, embrace the fundamental principle of collective ownership—at least in theory. Nonetheless, there exists a distinction between different type of goods, rights, and responsibilities, as in the case of "ancestral wisdom and practices" as understood by COICA.[539] Primarily, when the communal life still functions, each community should have the right to determine the balance between individual and collective rights in its own way. There might also exist practical difficulties when it comes to the implementation of a principle of collective ownership—as will be seen in the case of the existing sui generis protection in Panama.[540] Still, especially when regarding the relationship to external, non-indigenous people, the general principle should be that of collective ownership. As seen before, collective goods are also found in Western systems of law,[541] so that such a concept of collective ownership of TCEs according to an *emic* understanding could be integrated into the Western system of collective goods without technical difficulty.[542] Finally, in the case of only acknowledging individualistic rights in TCEs, the exercise of such a right could be and—according to the above philosophies—should be strongly dependent upon the aspect of use for the good of the collectivity, idealistically, of mankind. Such limitations also exist in Western sociology, philosophy, and systems of law, as highlighted above.[543]

Also according to the COICA elements, there are two points of relevance, first, "to acknowledge the collective character of their knowledge, innovations and traditional practices," and, second, "to guarantee that they [the indigenous peoples] are the ones that take the decisions on the previous based consent principle [principle of prior informed consent]. A sui generis way must regulate that this consent be granted in a collective way by a community according to their own common practices."[544]

---

[537] Goody and Watt (1968) 30.

[538] On the discussion of these aspects *see* at Section 1.B.I.1.d. above and at Section 5.B.III.2.d. below.

[539] On this *see* at Section 1.B.I.1.e. above.

[540] On experiences from Panama *see* at Chapter IV Section 1.D.II.3.a. below.

[541] Even different categories thereof, like pure public goods, club public goods and free goods. *See* at Section 4.D.III.3. above and Fikentscher (2004 I) 192.

[542] *See* Fikentscher (2005) 10.

[543] *See* at Section 4.D.III.3. above.

[544] COICA (2005) 62, translation by COICA at http://www.coica.org.ec/ingles/aia_book/index.html.

4. Representatives

The implementation of collective rights requires a way of representing the collectivity. In line with the Latin American philosophies displayed here, it could be the "wisemen," shaman, or leaders according to traditional representation systems as mentioned by Daniel Mundurukú.[545] Following the tendency of further (political) organization of indigenous peoples like COICA, as presented above, there could also be indigenous organizations representing the collective owners, particularly when it comes to supra-local involvements. Further details and practical aspects of the question of representation will be dealt with below in the context of customary law.[546]

COICA itself expressed, as one essential element of protection, the need "to respect and guarantee their own institutions and organizations, including their original languages."[547]

According to studies on traditional knowledge in the Andean Region, it has been argued that the "recovery and revaluation of traditional authorities and their specific forms of organization are the best strategy for protecting traditional knowledge against misuse by third parties."[548] In contrast, in none of the analyzed cases has a need been identified for traditional knowledge to be protected or developed by means of the parameters set by intellectual property rights.[549]

5. Conception and Impact of Protection and Peoples' Own Principles

The philosophies are linked with axioms and rules of behavior, and they are based on interaction, namely with the environment. This practical aspect of spirituality—in contrast to rather theoretical philosophies in the Western tradition—is also reflected by the element of "good living." Therefore, at least in theory, the legal possibility of implementing the rules among themselves as well as with respect to outsiders is regarded as essential, in other words: the recognition of customary law, or, indigenous jurisdiction.[550]

[545] This is also the case of the *Congreso General Kuna* in Panama. On this – and on difficulties that appear in practice – *see* at Chapter IV Section 1.D.II.3.b. below.

[546] *See* at Section 5.D.II. below.

[547] COICA (2005) 62, translation by COICA at http://www.coica.org.ec/ingles/aia_book/index.html.

[548] de la Cruz I. (2006) 36.

[549] *id.* This might vary, of course, and is in such an absolute form not the view of this author, *see* at Chapter V Section 3. below.

[550] *See* at Section 5. below.

In this manner, COICA expresses an element going even further, namely the right "to acknowledge indigenous self-determination rights, including the right to decide on the use of their knowledge."[551]

6. Essential Link to Territory

Similar to the aspect of "living the spiritual concepts," the spiritual conception of and relation to *pacha mama* or, as also spelled *pachamama,* the earth, can be identified as essential from the above-mentioned philosophies. Therefore, COICA regards it as an elementary aspect of a protection of TCEs and traditional knowledge, namely "to guarantee the legal security of [indigenous] lands and territories."[552]

7. Important Principles

Essential elements for an appropriate use and method of protection of TCEs are the principles of reciprocity and sustainability, as follows for instance from the ancestral practice of *randi-randi* ("giving and giving") in relation to nature, but also as regards the "continuous exchange of goods and services between persons", constituting a "compulsory social mechanism" called reciprocity, or *ayni*.[553] Besides, the principles of balance and duality are also of value for legal relations: the "principle of balance" requires that balance has to be maintained with "(i) the other members of the community, (ii) *pachamama*, and (iii) the sacred world." Thus, as a legal consequence, capacities, needs, and efforts must be "subject to the criteria of proportionality."[554] From the spiritual "principle of duality" follows for the legal ambit that "situations, rights, and obligations are generated in favor of two or more parties" and their implementation is "necessary as a complement in order to achieve harmony."[555]

---

[551] COICA (2005) 62, translation by COICA at http://www.coica.org.ec/ingles/aia_book/index.html.

[552] *Id.* 62, translation by COICA at http://www.coica.org.ec/ingles/aia_book/index.html.

[553] Principles known from the Peru case study: the La Papa Park in the region of Cuzco. *See* de la Cruz I. (2006) 29.

[554] *See* the Peru case study: the La Papa Park in the region of Cuzco, *id.* 29 (2006). The principle of balance may also be called *chaninchay*, *pashminakuy* and *tupachiy, see id.*

[555] *Id.*

8. Further Consequences and Elements

There are further elements of protection expressed by indigenous peoples themselves, especially in the area of traditional knowledge. According to COICA, these are

(i) rules which encourage and support the exchange of their knowledge, innovations, and traditional practices between themselves;
(ii) a "veto right," i.e., the right to oppose to any research which would disregard the respect for and recognition of the indigenous rights;
(iii) provisions which ensure that any transaction aiming at destroying or discrediting the integrity of the indigenous knowledge, innovations, and practices is void;
(iv) elaborating and legally implementing strategies to "thwart plans" which "adversely affect" their knowledge, innovations, and practical traditions, especially when third parties implement mega-projects in their territories;
(v) ensuring that the common use of biological and other resources relating to traditional knowledge remains free, especially when a system for the protection of collective property rights is designed.[556]

Some of these points coincide with the consequences just drawn before, while others might appear very far-reaching and unrealistic from a Western point of view. Notwithstanding such critique, it becomes quite clear that two elements are essential for COICA and deserve further attention in this study. This is even more important as these two aspects have been included, but—as argued by participating experts—not understood well enough in international negotiations.[557] These two points are the acknowledgement of indigenous "customary" law and the connection between TCEs and land rights, to be dealt with in details below.

II. Consequences Regarding the Process of Dealing with the Topic of Protecting TCEs

As just seen, there are principles relating to the content of the law. But also useful consequences can be drawn in relation to the way towards establishing a legal protection of TCEs, i.e., the process of intercultural communication, negotiating, and preparing an adequate system of protection—especially in view of the "past failure of dialogue and mutual incomprehension."[558]

[556] COICA (2005) 62, translation by COICA at http://www.coica.org.ec/ingles/aia_book/index.html.

[557] *See* de la Cruz I. (2006) 5.

[558] Taubman and Leistner (2008) 67.

1. Similarities in Philosophical Superstructure

Despite all differences regarding the spiritual worldview, the foregoing analysis, in particular the comparison with Western and other philosophies has shown that there do exist intercultural similarities. Actually, the bigger difference lies within the economic system followed in the different societies, which however has a strong impact on the international legal framework and—through the increasing influence of international relations—on the indigenous communities. The philosophical and ethical principles that constitute the original form of guidance for legal systems, however, encompass the elements that bridge the cultures.

2. Mutual Enrichment

COICA believes that the ideal approach would be to combine ancestral wisdom with occidental knowledge. Similarly, Western, politically engaged philosophers have stated that the "occidental society" could and should learn from the ancestral wisdom and balanced way of life.[559] Thus, against the background of these broader elements, visions, and possibilities, gaps in negotiating an adequate protection of TCEs could (and should) be bridged by focusing on a long-term mutual enrichment—which is a personal, every-day challenge in practice, of course.

3. Intermediaries Are Rarely Traditional Representatives

By the way in which the indigenous philosophies have been communicated, one understands that in the process of dealing with TCEs and their protection, the intermediaries we can talk to are most often not the traditional representatives of the indigenous communities, as for instance in the case of Daniel *Munduruku*. It might be uncertain whether there is an official, legitimized, and/or respected representative at all. There are also further challenges to be dealt with in the context of customary representation.[560]

4. Rarely One Common "Indigenous" Position

Similarly to the difficulty in determining legitimized representatives—and as a consequence thereof,—there rarely exists "one common position" on the indigenous side. Although similar theoretical points of action have been set up by COICA, in every-day life the indigenous communities in Latin America face quite varied realities. The differences between the tribes appear to be a lot bigger than those

[559] Andean Community (2009), last visited January 25, 2010.

[560] *See* on customary law at Section 5. below.

between different Western societies.[561] Especially when considering particular field studies, it is difficult to address the question of whether there is a common position of "the tribe" or even "the indigenous peoples," or instead—most likely—an indefinite bundle of personal views (like that of Daniel Munduruků). For the sake of practicality in international negotiations on an adequate protection of TCEs, positions like that of COICA or other international indigenous organizations might be considered—while taking into account that the situation in a concrete case regarding a particular community might be different.

5. Particularities of an Intercultural Dialogue and Disputing Process

Within the dialogue on the protection of TCEs, it is quite helpful to remain aware of its intercultural character, and that there are different modes of thought involved,[562] including different concepts of words, ways of communicating, conceptions of interaction, of (collective) decision-making, and of time. Considering these different cultural conceptions of interaction and of time is also essential within the settlement of conflicts, as cross-culturally, disputes are "social processes embedded in social relations" and the "dimension of time is the essence of process."[563] Especially particularities of non-literate societies in the use of language and other forms of communication are to be considered, like the importance (and, in the international negotiations, mostly lack) of the relationship between symbol and referent, vocal inflections, and physical gestures, and also the constant change of the meaning of the words according to the "social process of memory and forgetting."[564] This aspect will be treated more deeply below.[565]

6. Role of Indigenous Peoples Themselves

The effectiveness of a system of protecting TCEs also depends upon the engagement, respective will, and activity of the indigenous peoples themselves in preserving the vitality of their traditional philosophy as the basis of TCEs and TCEs as expressions of such philosophy. Two main aspects are mentioned by representatives themselves: First, in order to successfully preserve their philosophy, culture,

---

561 This is not only due to the socio-historic development, in different clans, rather than in bigger national societies, but depends also upon distinct levels of integration into the "Western/national society" as well as upon the integrity of the environment and natural supplies having strong impacts on the way of life of the communities and on their position towards an adequate protection of TCEs.

562 On this term *see* Fikentscher (1995) 21.

563 Nader and Todd, Jr. (1978) 16, 24. For the different functions and cultural understandings of time in the disputing process, *see* Nader and Todd, Jr. (1978) 24 *et seq.*

564 On these aspects *see* at Section 4.A.III.4. above and Goody and Watt (1968) 28 *et seq.*

565 *See* at Section 5.B.IV.2. below.

knowledge, and resources, they must create mechanisms to transmit their values and appreciation of their culture to future generations, and, second, they must not be seduced by the monetary system contradicting the traditional philosophy, and sell out their own "treasures."[566] This, at the end, is a question of education and constant personal formation. "Nudges" implemented by state policies might facilitate such behavior.

Section 5. Indigenous Customary Law: Experiences from Latin America

A. *Understanding "Customary Law"*

I. Status Quo: Introduction

Customary law in the area of TCEs is "a very complex subject and still not very clear for many international negotiators", as Latin American experts have observed at the international level, especially regarding nature, scope, role, and jurisdiction.[567] Western scholars argue that precise customary rules would lay down the conditions for the production and the performance of TCEs and could give answers to nearly any aspect of their protection TCEs, including beneficiaries, formalities, sanctions, and the management of rights,[568] while a description of the concrete contents and applications of such rules is lacking.

What makes customary law on TCEs so complicated to deal with, in Latin America and worldwide? If it is so difficult to deal with, should it be considered at all? What might help in improving its understanding and handling?

The experience gained and observations made in the research on customary law on TCEs in Latin America during this study have brought to light several challenges inherent in the topic, and from time to time during the research the question came up of whether customary law should be considered or even applied at all. The main challenges will be highlighted in an introductory overview (below II.), and arguments against and in favor of applying customary law will be discussed subsequently (below III.)

To concretize the subject of research, and for the further treatment of customary law on TCEs, the term itself, its definition, and its key characterizing elements deserve a closer look (below B.). Then, historical and anthropological observations on customary law in Latin America will be displayed (below C). To gain a deeper

[566] Rivera-Zea (2006) 3.

[567] de la Cruz I. (2006) 5.

[568] Lucas-Schlötter, "Folklore", in: von Lewinski, "Indigenous Heritage and Intellectual Property – Genetic Resources, Traditional Knowledge and Folklore" 339–506, 414 (2007). For details and the problem of "inventing" customary law *see* at Section 5.B.IV.1. below.

insight into the substance of the topic, concrete examples on the different aspects of protecting TCEs are provided (below D.). When considering customary law, the crucial question then is how to technically enable the application of customary rules (below E.) and how to secure this protection at the international level (below F.). The chapter ends with a short conclusion and outlook (below G.).

II. Challenges

The main challenges of considering customary law in the framework of protecting TCEs in Latin America, but also beyond, are the following ones:

(1) As early as 1927, Robert Lowie pointed out challenges and difficulties in bringing together law and anthropology on the one hand, as well as "Western" legal concepts and tribal law on the other: "Primitive customary law does not present the rigid formalism of codified law. It would assuredly be the acme of artificiality to pigeonhole the rules of inheritance in a North American aboriginal community according to the standards of English jurisprudence."[569] Although in North America the codification of indigenous customary law has become quite popular,[570] Lowie's observation is still true for most of the indigenous communities in Latin America.[571]

(2) Customary law—at least in its original form—not only lacks "the rigid formalism of codified law,"[572] but often, it consists rather of *processes* than of *substantive rules*. According to mostly anthropological research, often, processes, in particular dispute settlements, decide on the legal problem—like the use or misuse of TCEs—rather than substantive rules. This is the case in particular communities in Latin America like the Shuar and Achuar Indians in Ecuador,[573] and has been observed in the customary treatment of the TCE *mola* of the Kuna Indians in Panama,[574] and indeed it is true of anthropological theory in general: The "prime concern" in the field of anthropology of law is rather the study of processes, in particular of dispute settlement, "which seems to be ... the most useful and productive focus."[575] This is also due to

[569] Robert Lowie, "Anthropology and Law", in: Ogburn and Goldenweiser (eds.), "The Social Sciences and their Interrelations", (Cambridge 1927), cited from Nader (1969) 2.

[570] For *e.g.* the Codes and perception of the codification of "customary rules" of the Pueblo Indians, *see* Cooter and Fikentscher (2008) 54.

[571] An exception is e.g. the Fundamental Law *(Ley Fundamental de la Comarca Kuna Yala)*, which is the general code of "customary law" established by parts of the *Kuna* Indians in Panama, on this *see* at Chapter IV Section 1.D.II. below.

[572] Robert Lowie, "Anthropology and Law", in: Ogburn and Goldenweiser (eds.), "The Social Sciences and their Interrelations", (Cambridge 1927), cited from Nader (1969) 2.

[573] *See* at Section 5.B.I.1. below and personal communication with ethnologist Meiser on January 8, 2009.

[574] On details *see* at Chapter IV Section 1.D. below.

[575] Gulliver (1969) 13.

the fact that "dispute settlement does not occur in a social vacuum, insulated from the continuous stream of interaction that makes up ongoing social life."[576] Consequently, first, social relationships can be even more important, meaning that they have a greater impact on the outcome of the dispute settlement than the matter in dispute, i.e. the subject matter as well as substantive "law" itself. Second, "the settlement in effect defines, or redefines, statuses, rights, and obligations, both for the disputants themselves and for other peoples."[577] Thus, when examining customary law as a means of protecting TCEs, it would be insufficient or even misleading to solely search for substantive "rules" on the use or in case of misuse of TCEs. But "it must be an examination within the full socio-cultural context of the dispute cases"—much more than is necessary for the understanding of codified law in Western legal cultures (at least on paper).[578]

(3) Similarly, the "original" customary law does not constitute a distinct and autonomous sphere separable from the society—in contrast to the law in complex societies, i.e. those societies with a state authority. The members of indigenous communities themselves often do not distinguish a specific juridical ambit from the conjunction of customs and norms of social behaviour or social control. For external observers, it is difficult to trace the limits of the *juridical* in these societies—for which reason the anthropological science has dealt relatively little with the topic and juridical science practically ignores it, as Stavenhagen argued.[579]

(4) Communication problems exist between the two collaborating disciplines of law and anthropology, which often lead to an inadequate use of categories. Experienced Brazilian anthropologist Manuela Carneiro da Cunha observed: "The knowledge of law of the majority of the anthropologists is at least precarious," and the lawyers commit the fundamental error of inferring a "reification" in the term "customary law."[580]

(5) Linguistic and other intercultural communication problems exist on the ground: Due to the different worldviews, socio-cultural ways of life and "modes of thought,"[581] the research on customary law is characterized by quite challenging and large-scale communication processes. This regards on the one hand the communication in general, in its time, intercultural, and particular personal dimension.[582] On the other hand, this is especially true of legal terms and conceptions, for example the understanding of the "owner" according to a Wajãpi perspective.[583] Depending upon the grade of

[576] *Id.* 16.

[577] *Id.*

[578] *Id.* 13.

[579] Stavenhagen (1990) 30.

[580] Carneiro da Cunha (1990) 299 *seq.*

[581] *See* Fikentscher (1995) 21.

[582] On this, *see* at Section 4.G.II.5. above.

[583] On this the understanding of the Wajãpi indigenous peoples in Brazil *see* at Section 5.D.I.1. below.

acculturation of the indigenous community or person, the comprehension of the spiritual belief can be imperative for the third party in order to understand the customary law.[584] In any case, good empathetic and humanistic skills are essential. Experienced anthropologists themselves admit that "it is no easy matter to record fully a sufficiently large number of adequate cases; there are linguistic problems and many severe practical difficulties."[585]

(6) A quick and frequent alteration of customary law: The rules change with time and according to circumstances.[586] In "modern" times, there is the even bigger challenge of a very rapid change of environmental impacts, social structures, and customary law, even in many Latin American tribal communities, which makes it difficult to define and to grasp, especially from a Western-trained view. This fact of alteration also reveals the necessity to comprehend "traditional" or "customary" rules as something dynamic, rather than "old" or static.

(7) Aside from the poor knowledge about tribal law, there has also been relatively little interest noted in its content so far, especially as regards TCEs, in Latin America and elsewhere. One reason for that might be that tribal law was historically regarded as inferior. This perception of inferiority was rooted, on the one hand, in the lack of formalism mentioned above—and formalism was a prized element in the Western view. On the other hand it was grounded in the general discrimination against indigenous tribes and cultures. Moreover, the difficulties in finding out substantive rules might have been another reason. In 1969 already, Nader remarked that "it is of interest to note a continued interest in the 'pigeonhole problem,'" as Lowie called it (see above), "and the general lack of interest [of researchers] in substantive law."[587] This situation is changing slowly now.

(8) Dealing with TCEs has not been a main area of research on or consideration of customary law so far: The interest in substantive law that existed did not cover rules on TCEs, but focused on the four main problems or fields of legal theory, which were: (1) family law, (2) property, (3) associations, and (4) the state—where "property" rather referred to material than immaterial property.[588] Even today it is still the case that most of the results of anthropological investigation deal with these aspects of "law." Likewise, *lawyers* dealing with questions of customary law rather did so in "more important", i.e. pressing, and obvious questions of family and criminal law or communal land rights—in Latin

---

[584] *See* the examination of different indigenous world views at Section 4. above.

[585] Gulliver (1969) 13.

[586] Stavenhagen (1990) 43.

[587] Nader (1969) 2. On the "pigeonhole problem" *see* Robert Lowie, "Anthropology and Law", in: Ogburn and Goldenweiser (eds.), "The Social Sciences and their Interrelations", (Cambridge 1927), cited from Nader (1969) 2.

[588] Robert Lowie, "Anthropology and Law", in: Ogburn and Goldenweiser (eds.), "The Social Sciences and their Interrelations", (Cambridge 1927), cited from Nader (1969) 2.

America[589] and elsewhere.[590] The same picture is revealed by Latin American legislation: the Constitution in Brazil considers the application of tribal law mainly in the area of penal law.[591] Also, distinguished Latin American scholars have demarked three main areas of customary law, namely (1) land rights, (2) persecution of torts, and (3) proceedings dealing with administration of justice.[592] Similarly, current discussions on customary law in the continent of Latin America deal with the specific topics of (1) administration of justice, (2) models of coexistence of different types of laws, and (3) criminal law.[593] Other ambits have been recognized as "existing", but it has been held that "only empiric and casuistic investigation could bring the corresponding specific analysis".[594]

(9) The issue of protecting TCEs addressed from a Western point of view involves the topic of intellectual property rights. This latter area of law still appears to be relatively new and complex, even more in connection with differently, i.e. less structured and subdivided customary laws. Lack of experience and expertise on both sides, indigenous and non-indigenous, regarding the law and anthropology on the one hand, and specific expertise in intellectual property rights on the other, has been identified by international and Latin American entities as great problems in approaching customary law in the area of TCEs.[595]

(10) Although the *importance* of considering customary law with regard to the topic of TCEs has been realized, this does not mean that its *application* has been acknowledged: despite anthropological and legal challenges, the recognition of customary law in general, and on TCEs in particular, is a highly political and politically disputed topic in Latin America.[596] The political dimension saw much discussion in the 1980s and 1990s, when for example the government of Chile opined that the acknowledgement of a "special legislation for determined sectors of the population" violated the "principle

---

[589] *See, e.g.*, the topics dealt with in Huber, Martínez, Lachenal and Ariza (2008).

[590] This is the case even in North America, where these studies were the most advanced ones so far. *See* the early beginnings like Malinowski's "Crime and Custom in Savage Society" (1926) or the latest field study of Robert D. Cooter and Wolfgang Fikentscher, which contains only a very short reference to TCEs: Cooter and Fikentscher (2008) 51.

[591] Article 231 of the Brazilian Constitution and Article 57 of the Brazilian Indian Statute.

[592] "1) El derecho a la tierra", "2) La persecución de delitos", and "3) Procedimientos de administración de justicia", *see* Stavenhagen (1990) 39–42.

[593] Barié (2003) 50 *et seq.*

[594] Stavenhagen (1990) 42.

[595] Ministério da Cultura - Coordenação-Geral de Direito Autoral (2007) 3 and de la Cruz I. (2006) 5.

[596] Strategic Workshop of the Latin American Group on Plural Legal Systems ("Taller estratégico del Grupo Latinoamericano por Sistemas Jurídicos Plurales") of the Foundation Konrad Adenauer, held on March 11–14, 2009, in Quito, Ecuador, which the author was allowed to attend with the kind permission of the Uruguayan and Ecuadorian Office of the Konrad Adenauer Foundation.

of equality before law."[597] Mexican scholars held that the local recognition of political organizations and representations according to indigenous customary law would, "without doubts, be a step backwards in the political evolution of the nation," counterproductive to the "integration into the nationality" and would "violate the ideals postulated in the Constitution."[598] While in some Latin American countries the constitutional recognition of collective land rights of indigenous peoples dates back to a very early time,[599] the question of giving validity to customary law in other countries, especially with connection to claims of self-determination, has a highly political dimension, which has been described as "true (downright) paranoia about the idea of multi-ethnicity" and "an aversion to recognize customary law."[600]

Thus, against the backdrop of these challenges, it is not surprising that research on such a particular area of customary law within the protection of TCEs is still at its inception, research by both, anthropologists and lawyers, as well as in the beginning of its political and legal acknowledgement in Latin America.[601]

III. In View of the Great Difficulties: Should Customary Law on TCEs Be Considered at All?

In view of the status quo just demonstrated, it is not astonishing that the issue of considering and acknowledging customary law at all is still highly disputed. On the one hand, the importance of—in whatever manner—recognizing customary law within the field of TCEs has been underscored, at the international as well as the Latin American level: The WIPO Intergovernmental Committee on Intellectual Property and Genetic Resources, Traditional Knowledge, and Folklore (IGC) has included in its agenda the treatment of customary law as one of the basic elements for the protection of TCEs.[602]

On the other hand, there are legal, as well as anthropological and political arguments that contest against protection, particularly, but not exclusively, as concerns the Latin American situation.

---

[597] Stavenhagen (1990) 45 *et seq.*, note 9.

[598] Gonzalo Aguirre Beltrán, cited from *id.* 45 note 9 (1990).

[599] As early as 1917, the Mexican Constitution conceded the right of collective property of communal or tribal lands (so-called *ejidos*), Article 27 of the 1917 Constitution of Mexico, available at http://www.diputados.gob.mx/LeyesBiblio/ref/dof/CPEUM_orig_05feb1917_ima.pdf, last visited on December 6, 2010. For details *see* at Section 6. below.

[600] Carneiro da Cunha (1990) 303 *seq.*

[601] This is different from the situation in Australia, and partly also in New Zealand, which is reflected by a well-developed case law in Australia, *see, e.g.*, Janke (for WIPO), "Minding Culture: Case Studies on Intellectual Property and Traditional Cultural Expressions" Study No. 1 (2002).

[602] WIPO, "Draft Document: Customary Law & the Intellectual Property System in the Protection of Traditional Cultural Expressions and Traditional Knowledge: Issues Paper – Version 3.0" (2006).

1. Cons

(1) At the international level, concerns have been mentioned about a lack of legal certainty.[603]

(2) If there is legal uncertainty, the application of customary law could have a negative impact on the economic value of traditional cultural expressions, as potential users could be deterred by the lack of legal certainty.[604] This aspect is of relevance only, of course, if (future) protection of TCEs should also be of economic value for the traditional communities—as e.g. the sui generis regime in Panama.

(3) According to some indigenous voices themselves in Latin America, customary law is not more than "a myth"[605] nowadays, as customary rules as such do not exist anymore. Therefore, first, the application is practically difficult, and, second, the "invention" of customary law,[606] or even its misuse,[607] might be a consequence.

(4) Even if there were rules, i.e. re-vitalized or newly elaborated ones, the attribute of "customary" is questioned, as in many Latin American indigenous realities, the alleged "basis" of the customary rules, the cosmovision, is practiced only very rarely.[608]

(5) Similarly, the role of customary law in providing adequate solutions for the treatment of TCEs and as a successful dispute resolution instrument may be "overly romanticized."[609] In Latin American reality, under the rule of customary law, even *internal* disputes are not solved, or even arise anew. This is true for the area of TCEs and elsewhere,[610] mainly as regards gender issues and (inter-)generational conflicts.[611]

---

[603] von Lewinski, "Adequate protection of folklore – a work in progress", in: Torremans (ed.), Copyright Law – A Handbook of Contemporary Research 207–231, 220 (2007). Lucas-Schlötter, "Folklore", in: von Lewinski, "Indigenous Heritage and Intellectual Property – Genetic Resources, Traditional Knowledge and Folklore" 339–506, 419 (2008).

[604] A solution to that could be the fixation of customary rules, for the case of Panama *see* at Chapter IV Section 1.D. below.

[605] *See* the voices on "usos y costumbres" caught by Eisenstadt (no year) 3.

[606] On the problem of "inventing" customary rules as a parallel to the invention of traditions according to Hobsbawm *see* at Section 5.B.IV.1. below. On "inventing tradition" in the topic of TCEs *see* at Section 1.B.I.1.f. above and in general Hobsbawm (1983) 1 *et seq.*

[607] For example, in the area of *usos y costumbres* in questions of representation and election processes, the application of customary rules was also used as "a means for controlling parties," and "to keep other parties out." Eisenstadt (no year) 15.

[608] On this, *see* at Section 4.E. above.

[609] Likewise for the case of *usos y costumbres* in questions of representation and election processes Eisenstadt (no year) 12.

[610] *E.g.* applying customary rules to local election processes; for concrete data on such, *see* "Oaxaca's and Mexico's Post-Electoral Conflicts 1989–2004" and the statistics in Eisenstadt (no year) 22.

[611] *See, e.g.*, the cases from Panama at Chapter IV Section 1.E.II. below.

(6) Due to growing external impacts on the traditional lifestyle, especially environmental impacts and the monetarization of the rural economies, in combination with the already weak fundament of the socio-cultural setting in the indigenous reality, rapid changes, together with a fast disappearance of "customary law" in practice is very likely.[612]
(7) Economic aid might be better suited to achieve the aim of upholding or supporting traditional rules and cultures in practice.[613]
(8) As years of practical experience in Latin America have shown, applying customary law sometimes is not desired by parts of the indigenous peoples themselves, e.g. by indigenous women.[614]
(9) The application might not only be undesired but could discriminate against other minorities from a national or international legal perspective.[615]
(10) The application of customary law might even contradict human-rights standards.[616]
(11) Political concerns have been raised, as the acknowledgement of customary law with relevance to TCEs brings with it a larger acknowledgement of indigenous autonomy or special rights for minorities, an effect that is not desired in some Latin American political concepts.[617]

---

[612] "Monetarization of Mexico's rural economy and globalization – more generally – seem to mitigate against the perpetuation of ... [customary rules] in the long term." Eisenstadt (no year) 16.

[613] As Eisenstadt argues, contributing to the families' and the communal living standard might in practice be more effective through externally earned monetary salaries than by upholding the customary rule of subsistence and free labor exchanges, like e.g. *cargos* (a "set of public positions" all citizens/men are "expected to fulfill") and *tequios* (various communal works, "such as the paving of roads") in rural Mexico, *see id.* 10–13.

[614] On this aspect, especially as regards the questions of holdership of rights, use of TCEs, and representation according to "customary law," *see* at Section 5.D.I.2. below. Such experiences have been made frequently in the year-long processes of cooperation and development projects of the German technical development agency, GTZ (Gesellschaft für Technische Zusammenarbeit) in different Latin American countries, e.g. the experiences gained from the project "Strengthening indigenous organisations in Latin America" supported by the GTZ (project No. 2006.2037.7) and personal communication with staff members in Germany and Brazil.

[615] This could imply a discrimination against women for example. Discrimination could also be provoked by the area of and preconditions for the application, e.g. when the application is connected to land rights, as is the case in Venezuela, *see* at Section 5.E. below. In such cases, "non-residents" or other, non-indigenous communities could be discriminated against. To illustrate the first example of discrimination against women, the following case from Mexico might be of interest: In the traditional leader-selection practices of *usos y costumbres* in Mexico, some 22 percent of the initial 413 *usos y costumbres* municipalities allow no participation by women whatsoever. For more concrete data *see* Eisenstadt (no year) 11 and the statistic there on page 23 (no year).

[616] On these problems *see* at Section 5.D.I.2. below.

[617] This can be noted in current tendencies of the government of President Rafael Correa in Ecuador, for example, which puts emphasis on a new strength of one, equal "citizenship", and includes the establishment of a new administrative public "power" in charge of implementing the idea of the *"ciudadanía,"* or citizenship, and at the same time the reform of several administrative

(12) Finally, one of the most important arguments is that applying customary law might have the opposite effect from what is desired by the protection of TCEs. The integration of customary law into a "Western" legal instrument for protecting TCEs might accelerate a transformation of customary law, and, as a consequence, of the social structure and culture of the communities. Today, the overwhelming majority of customary laws in Latin America still does not constitute a distinct and autonomous sphere separable from the society—in contrast to the law in complex societies, i.e. those with a state authority, in which one can speak of two ambits like law *and* society, instead of law *in the* society. Anthropologists have observed that in tribal societies, the legal is immersed in the social structure. There, neither a specific administrative body nor the professional specialists in charge of elaborating and/or applying the law—what Max Weber described as a special staff, a "Stab von Menschen," later called "Rechtsstab" by Rehbinder[618]—exist.[619] Depending upon how it is done, the application and instrumentalization of customary law for the protection of TCEs might change exactly these characteristics, and thus be counterproductive in terms of what the protection of TCEs was intended to achieve. This phenomenon would even be stronger in cases in which customary rules do not exist on the questions of how to protect TCEs and would have to be "developed."[620]

2. Pros

(1) Despite these difficulties, the consideration of customary law within the topic of TCEs is a key factor in the search for an adequate protection of TCEs. Above all, Latin American experts emphasize that the study and consideration of customary law is a "fundamental element for a better understanding of the indigenous cultures of the Latin American continent," as customary law is an integral part of the social and cultural structure of a community.[621] Besides, the following reasons argue in favour of an application of customary law.

entities and public institutions like the CONDENPE, Council for the Development of the [Indigenous] Nationalities and Peoples in Ecuador (Consejo de Desarrollo de las Nacionalidades y Pueblos del Ecuador, *see* http://www.codenpe.gov.ec/, last visited December 6,2010) and the IEPI, the Ecuadorian Institute for Intellectual Property, personal communication with Andrés Andrango, Anita Paziguan and Analucía Tasiguano of CONDENPE and staff members of IEPI in March, 2009, in Quito, Ecuador.

[618] Weber, "Wirtschaft und Gesellschaft" 17 (1976) or "staff of people" in the English translation, *see* Weber, "Economy and Society" (Guenther Roth and Claus Wittich, eds.) 34 ((1922) 1978) and Rehbinder, "Die Begründung der Rechtssoziologie durch Eugen Ehrlich" 109 (1967).

[619] Stavenhagen (1990) 30.

[620] Similarly, the Pueblo Indians stated that Indian (customary) law on the protection of TCEs was "in preparation;" Cooter and Fikentscher, "American Indian Law Codes: Pragmatic Law and Tribal Identity", 56 American Journal of Comparative Law 29–74, 54 (2008), *see* also the discussion at Section 5.B.IV.2.c. below.

[621] Stavenhagen (1990) 27.

(2) Legal uncertainty cannot be fully avoided. When establishing fixed rules, customary or otherwise, one would have to admit too many exceptions to adequately respond to the fact and nature of a widely diverse indigenous reality, rendering many fixed rules senseless anyway.[622] Moreover, in practice, the margin of remaining uncertainties can be reduced considerably by putting some effort into finding a legitimate representative, for example, and in talking to the collective, experienced Latin American authors argue.[623]
(3) Whether the economic value of TCEs should play a more important role, especially if the traditional, socio-cultural setting would have to be sacrificed by imposing Western legislative systems, should be the decision of each community. Moreover, against the backdrop of Latin American history and politics, the official act of recognizing and legalizing customary law may give indigenous customs and traditions "the dignity they deserve"[624] and thereby "elevate" indigenous peoples and "give them cultural and social resources which may be leveraged to improve their socio-economic positions."[625]
(4) Change through constant adaptation and transformation constitute the very nature of customary law, particularly because it is (usually) not codified. As customary law is widely influenced by the specific situation of subordination under a dominant, national, formerly colonial law, its transformation and modification are, likewise, influenced by its relation to the dominant, positive, national law, as Starr and Collier have found out. According to them, these modifications can thus be regarded as an attempt of the subordinated societies to adapt and reinterpret the positive national laws in accordance with their own structures, values, interests, and necessities. State law and customary law cannot be regarded as opposing and completely separated, but as interdependent, existing in a dynamic and sometimes contradicting process, as a juridical and legal change in situations of legal pluralism.[626] The validity of indigenous customary law constitutes "one of the indispensable elements for the preservation and reproduction of the indigenous cultures" of the Latin American continent.[627]
(5) In this manner, the application of customary law can support the aim of keeping cultural diversity alive. As TCEs are part of the living heritage and culture of special communities, the vitality and further existence of the expressions are best ensured within their native socio-cultural environment,

[622] Baptista and Valle, "Os povos indígenas frente ao direito autoral e de imagem" 24 (2004).

[623] *Id.* 25 (2004).

[624] Personal communication with Aresio Valiente López, Kuna Indian, lawyer and consultant on the draft of the Panamanian Sui generis Regime, on February 11, 2009, in Panama City, and Eisenstadt (no year) 3.

[625] *Id.* 6.

[626] Starr and Collier, "Historical Studies of Legal Change", 28 Current Anthropology 367–372 (1987).

[627] Stavenhagen (1990) 27.

and thus by giving effect to these communities' own legal treatment of these creations. Latin American experts argue that customary law is "a key element" for the protection of TCEs, as it "is precisely the nature of this system . . . that has made it possible" for traditional knowledge and TCEs "to be continuously adapted and improved for generations."[628] The indigenous peoples of major ethnic vitality in Latin America are "those in which their own customary law subsists."[629] Together with the language, law (customary or not) constitutes a basic element of the ethnic identity of a people, nation, or community.[630] The disappearance of customary law would contribute to the assimilation and "ethnocide" of the indigenous peoples.[631] Especially in areas where the influence of the global economic system leads to a disappearance of customary rules, legally recognizing customary law could serve as a supportive statement and thereby advance the further maintenance of the diverse legal systems.[632] Legal and cultural diversity is not only desired in the light of the 2005 UNESCO Convention on the Protection and Promotion of the Diversity of Cultural Expressions, and, in Latin America, by indigenous peoples themselves,[633] but might also be "refreshing" in "this age of cultural homogenization."[634]

(6) Realities—like a poor status quo of customary rules—should be considered when designing a sui generis protection to such extent that no ineffective or unrealistic rules are set up. Apart from that, however, the very nature of making laws consists in balancing different interests, in laying down justice, and is based on David Hume's dichotomy of the "is" and the "ought," which means that no simple deduction should be made from the "is" to the "ought," as the latter is "entirely different from" the former.[635]

(7) The application of customary rules might even reinforce the practice of other indigenous traditions.[636]

---

628 de la Cruz I. (2006) 24 *et seq.*

629 Stavenhagen (1990) 28.

630 *Id.* 27.

631 *Id.* 36.

632 The "pressures against maintaining the cultural homogeneity and uniqueness" could offer "a compelling reason to strive all the more diligently to preserve their histories and traditions, even if in adapted forms;" *see* Eisenstadt (no year) 16.

633 They state that any examination and application of customary rules "must be aimed at protecting the ethnic and cultural diversity of indigenous peoples and local communities, for the purpose of guaranteeing their physical and cultural survival;" de la Cruz I. (2006) 4.

634 Eisenstadt (no year) 6.

635 The idea of the imperative distinction between the "is and is not" and the "ought and ought not" goes back to the philosophy of Hume, "A Treatise of Human Nature – Being an Attempt to introduce the experimental Method of Reasoning into Moral Subjects" Book III, Part 1, (I) (first published in 1739). Immanuel Kant and Hans Kelsen further developed this concept in the area of 18th to 20th-century European philosophy and law.

636 As afore-mentioned, the application of customary law to local election processes reinforced the implementation of a customary system of co-habitation rules: "*Usos y costumbres* reinforces other Oaxaca traditions such as the system of *cargos* and the *tequio;*" *see* Eisenstadt (no year) 10.

(8) Historical experiences in Latin America show similar effects: The way to best enable the survival and preservation of the indigenous cultural heritage has always been to uphold indigenous autonomy, either intentionally[637] or unintentionally.[638] Globalization and the internationalization of culture might set up new challenges and a bigger bundle of external threats than were faced in the colonial situation of the sixteenth century and onwards. Nonetheless, the question of (cultural) survival within a very different philosophical and economic power is to some extent similar.

(9) This historic form of a dual-republic system bears similarity to current legal principles of private international law, like the "principle of locality," "akin to the principle of lex loci."[639] According to these principles, if a case in dispute has connections to more than one national legal system, the determination of the applicable law shall be made according to formal considerations of justice: formally, that law shall be applied to the case, which has the "closest connection" to the factual setting in dispute.[640]

(10) While there might exist experiences of newly arisen conflicts under the rule of customary law, there is also evidence for customary law as a means of diminishing social conflicts in Latin America.[641]

---

[637] As was the case *e.g.* in Guatemala, where the colonial power Spain created a *República de los Indios*, "a communal village or region where indigenous peoples could live and follow many of their cultural traditions while remaining under the Crown's jurisdiction." Due to this policy (the so-called dual-republic system), the Guatemalan Indians were able to preserve their cultural heritage, and they currently form a majority of that state's population. Ironically, they are currently facing more aggravated problems than other indigenous minorities. Torres argues that this is due to two reasons, first, "their inability to articulate their needs effectively as a group because they are numerous and scattered throughout the country." Second, "the uniqueness of the Indians' situation is obscured even though their needs have a different context and require different policies," because "many of these problems – lack of education, unemployment, absence of adequate housing – are shared by all inhabitants of the country." Torres, "The Rights of Indigenous Populations: The Emerging International Norm", 16 Yale Journal of International Law 127, 130, 131 note 20 (1991).

[638] That is the case of the Miskito Indians in Nicaragua. They have never been conquered by the Spanish, but continued living in a state of *de facto* autonomy which was then acknowledged as *de jure* by the Treaty of Managua in 1860. The Miskitos thus were able to preserve their traditions – until the Sandinista attempted to incorporate them into Nicaragua's social and economic life in 1979, *id.* 127, 131, 132 (1991).

[639] Taubman and Leistner (2008) 66.

[640] "Prinzip der engsten Verbindung" in German private international law or conflict of laws; in England, "the most real connection;" in the USA, "the most significant relationship," *see* Kropholler, "Internationales Privatrecht" 25 *et seq.* (2006).

[641] "In the Mexican context, recognition of *usos y costumbres* was also viewed as a means of diminishing social conflict;" *see* Eisenstadt (no year) 6.

(11) Sometimes, what appears to be a discrimination against other minorities, e.g. women, is even accepted voluntarily by exactly these groups when it is of strategic value and can be used purposely for their own benefit.[642]

(12) In Latin America, it has been noted that not (only) a future application of customary law, but rather the lack of acknowledgement of customary law in many situations provoked the violation of human rights of indigenous peoples.[643] Unsolved conflicts between customary law in practice and the positive national law (had) led to situations of social conflict, which did not contribute to the stability and development of the indigenous peoples or Latin American nations in their conjunction. The acknowledgement of a legal and juridical pluralism by the state thus would contribute an indispensable element for a better defense of the human rights of indigenous peoples and social stability.[644]

(13) No state, no legal order can be founded and preserved durably without a minimum of common, necessarily metaphysically founded values.[645] Such a minimum is a precondition for the peaceful coexistence of different metaphysically grounded positions in a plural polity. At the same time, however, such coexistence cannot be reached by denying actually existent diverging positions. In this positive manner, recognizing customary law might also be a means of (untechnical) "integration" of the indigenous population without denying their own particularities,[646] while this recognition would necessarily be limited by the minimum of common values.

(14) While it is true that the application of customary law might partially lead to undesired effects within the socio-cultural structure of indigenous communities, the introduction of foreign legal concepts like intellectual property structures and valuations are likely to lead to an even faster disappearance of the social structures that enable the cultural expressions to be protected, or at least covered, by the legal concept. However the details of these impacts might look like in a community *in concreto,* one thing is for sure: "Modifications of the laws," whether introduced by an individual or a group, do provoke "subsequent changes in the social structure" of a community or a village, as Leopold Pospíšil found out in field studies as early as the 1950s.[647] While

---

[642] According to Eisenstadt, "*usos y costumbres* clearly discriminates against women…, but these groups may also be somewhat strategic in their decisions about whether to contest" the application of the customary rules, and the process of local leader-selection as a whole. For instance, the women insisted on their right to vote at the 1998 assembly, and after having won their battle, they withdrew from public participation in the 2001 and 2004 local elections – arguing that they had decided "not to go to the assembly now because things have quieted down…. But if things get difficult again," they "will be back;" *see id.* 16.

[643] Stavenhagen and Iturralde (1990) 15.

[644] Stavenhagen (1990) 43.

[645] *See* thesis No. 52 of Rüthers (1984) 52, and, referring to the legal system in the sense of a political order ("Staatsform"): Leibholz (1933) 9.

[646] Eisenstadt (no year) 6.

[647] Pospíšil (1969) 209.

processes of fission appear in any segmentary society and thus can be rated as normal, unexciting, necessary, and not worth considering in the topic of protecting TCEs, structural changes in the social relations and culture of a community due to modifications of the law are extraordinary[648] and are of even greater impact in the sensitive field of traditional culture, which at least in its traditional aspect depends upon a certain continued existence of the social structures of a community.

(15) Considering customary rules can also serve to avoid legal contradictions in national laws or teleological uselessness of certain provisions, in other words, to ensure that this law, having been established with the best intentions for the indigenous population, is rendered useless. An example is the Native American Graves Protection and Repatriation Act (NAGPRA), not from Latin America, but the United States of America. It aims at the protection and especially restoration of human bones, sacred objects, and the cultural heritage of the native peoples of the United States.[649] "Ironically, among the Navajo, one of the largest Native American groups, leaders believe that their cultural property, including sacred objects and human remains, became linked to evil spirits because of the misappropriation and that it was not in Navajo interest to have such cultural property returned to them."[650] This example, by the way, also reveals the connection between spirituality and customary law and underlines the importance of being familiar with indigenous spiritual systems when drafting law on indigenous topics.[651]

(16) Potential conflicts with human rights or other national laws should not hinder the application of customary law at all, but rather be solved at the level of conflict of laws, e.g. by existing legal mechanisms like conflict-of-laws rules or the institution of the "ordre public."[652]

(17) Considering customary law is also of value for the rest of the society in a nation that harbors indigenous populations (and beyond): Recognizing different legal systems and cultures empowers societies to define and strengthen their own norms and identity,[653] as they "learn more about others and thus also learn more about themselves."[654]

---

648 *Id.* 209 (1969).

649 § 3001 (9): "Native Americans means of, or relating to, a tribe, people, or culture that is indigenous to the United States."

650 Moran, "Intellectual Property Law Protection for Traditional and Sacred 'Folklife Expressions' – Will Remedies Become Available to Cultural Authors and Communities?" 6 U. Balt. Intell. Prop. J., 109–116, 111 note 456 (1998).

651 On this *see* at Section 4.G. above.

652 *E.g.* Article 21 of the Rome I Regulation (European Regulation No. 593/2008), and Article 26 of the Rome II Regulation (European Regulation No. 864/2007).

653 Irwin, "Introduction", in: Irwin, "Native American Spirituality - A Critical Reader" 1–8 (2000).

654 Eisenstadt (no year) 6.

(18) Finally, it should be mentioned that considering customary law is also the tack that Latin American authors follow, although the overwhelming majority of Latin American countries has not acknowledged or implemented the application of customary law in the area of TCEs so far.[655] This supportive view is also the direction taken by the IGC at WIPO, as initially mentioned.[656]

Following these arguments in favor of a consideration of customary law, the next question arising is: what is to be looked for when thus considering "customary law" and doing research on it in the area of TCEs? What is meant by the term "customary law", and what does it encompass in theory and in practice?

B. Definitions and Characteristics of Customary Law in Latin America

I. General Remarks and Working Term

1. Fieldwork Experience

When members of the Shuar and Achuar Indians in the Ecuadorian Rainforest, Kaingang Indians in the Brazilian Amazon, Kuna Indians from the Panamanian–Colombian rainforest, or Asháninka Indians of Peru were asked about their "customary law" on TCEs, they rarely regarded themselves as possessing a "customary law" at all. They rather confirmed that they had certain rules settling their every-day life, set up by the community in frequent meetings of the community or by the leader or elder of the village and that were flexible and open to amendments depending on each situation that called for a decision or dispute resolution, possibly also for disputes on TCEs.[657] This result is true of many indigenous communities, especially those with little interaction with the Western "way of life."[658] It also

[655] For the situation in Brazil *see, e.g.*, Baptista and Valle, "Os povos indígenas frente ao direito autoral e de imagem" 11 (2004).

[656] The ICG has characterized the consideration of customary law as one of the basic elements for the protection of TCEs, *see* WIPO, "Draft Document: Customary Law & the Intellectual Property System in the Protection of Traditional Cultural Expressions and Traditional Knowledge: Issues Paper - Version 3.0" 3, 5 (2006).

[657] Personal communication with Fernanda Kaingang, Indigenous lawyer from the Kaingang tribe on June 23, 2009, in São Paolo, Brazil; personal communication with Luis Touar, General Cacique Dagar Kunyala (Traditional Authority of the Kuna Indians in Eastern Panama), with kind translation by Flaviano Iglesias on February 13, 2009 in Panama City; personal communication with Jenny Muñoz of the Asháninka Indians of Peru on June 10, 2008; and personal communication with ethnologist Meiser on January 8, 2009, about her research on the Shuar and Achuar indigenous communities in the Ecuadorian Amazon in 2008.

[658] "The members of indigenous communities themselves often do not distinguish a specific juridical ambit from the conjunction of customs and norms of social behaviour or social control," *see* Stavenhagen (1990) 30.

underlines the initial finding that according to Stavenhagen, by its very nature, the overwhelming majority of customary laws in Latin America (still) do not constitute a distinct and autonomous sphere separable from the society, since usually, there exists neither a specific administrative body nor a staff of professional specialists in charge of elaborating and/or applying the law or a technical language (like Max Weber's "Rechtsstab"[659]).[660]

2. Classic Western Understanding and Resultant Risks

In contrast, in the Western legal ambit, "customary law" ("Gewohnheitsrecht") is understood in a concrete way: it is mainly defined by its general preconditions of *consuetude longitudine* and *opinio iuris*.[661]

From such a "Western" juridical perspective, the term "customary law" might be misleading in the research on the ground. This phenomenon has already been affirmed by the experience gained during fieldwork, e.g. with the Shuar and Achuar in Ecuador and the Kuna *Cacique* in Panama.[662] Also, from a Latin American anthropological point of view, the reference to "custom," or "costumbre" in Spanish, has been regarded as infelicitous for various reasons.[663] In the same vein, Latin American indigenous legal experts have expressed that "[c]aution should be exercised in the use of terms such as 'customary,'" as it could lead to the "ambiguous perception that these laws are customs, as qualified by positive law," and thus generate an "inaccurate perception of the term 'customary law.'"[664]

3. Alternative Legal and Anthropological Terms

Leading lawyers and anthropologists have in their theoretical work argued in favor of alternatively using the term "Indian law" or "tribal law."[665] In Latin American

---

[659] On details *see* at Section 5.A.I.1.(12) above and Weber, "Wirtschaft und Gesellschaft" 17 (1976) or "staff of people" in the English translation, *see* Weber, "Economy and Society" (Guenther Roth and Claus Wittich, eds.) 34 ((1922) 1978) and Rehbinder, "Die Begründung der Rechtssoziologie durch Eugen Ehrlich" 109 (1967).

[660] Stavenhagen (1990) 30.

[661] For German Law *see* Larenz and Canaris, "Methodenlehre der Rechtswissenschaft" 176 *seq.*, and 258 *seq.* (1999).

[662] Personal communication with ethnologist Meiser on January 8, 2009, and personal communication with Luis Touar, General Cacique Dagar Kunyala (Traditional Authority of the *Kuna* Indians in Eastern Panama), with the kind translation by Flaviano Iglesias on February 13, 2009 in Panama City.

[663] Stavenhagen (1990) 29 *et seq.*

[664] de la Cruz I. (2006) 40.

[665] Cooter and Fikentscher, "American Indian Law Codes: Pragmatic Law and Tribal Identity", 56 American Journal of Comparative Law 29–74, 53 (2008).

scientific research on customary law, the Spanish term "derecho consuetudinario" is used, while there are also scholars who prefer terms like "costumbre jurídia," "costumbre legal," or "sistema jurídico alternativo,"[666] or "[Peoples'] Own Law or Indigenous Law, including both customary rights and positive law standards."[667]

Anthropological researchers, in contrast, prefer to talk of "juridical processes" rather than of an ostensible body of "customary law," because they understand and underscore that customary law consists rather of processes of dispute resolution than of a fixed body of substantive rules that—as Collier expressed it—are only waiting for their "discoverer," as imagined by most of the legal scholars.[668]

Formerly, starting in the 1930s, the expression "social structure" was used, for example by Radcliffe-Brown, which term however was criticized by later anthropologists as implying a substantive, permanent, and finite content, a "universe of mechanic and imperative rules, without ambiguities and contradictions"—while, in contrast, the concept of "society" itself, after Emile Durkheim, namely the criteria of the autopoetic production of a society, was understood as "a process of permanent elaboration."[669]

As a consequence of this criticism and observation that the rules are "social, steadily renovated products," contemporary anthropologists of Latin American origin have argued that not "specific rules" but "the authority to elaborate them" should be understood by and maybe even termed as customary law.[670]

4. Terms Used in Latin American Legislations

In Latin American constitutions and laws, different expressions are used. The Brazilian Constitution and the Brazilian Indian Statute, for example, refer to "social organization, customs, . . . and traditions,"[671] to "uses, customs and traditions of the indigenous communities and their effects in family relations, inheritance rules, property regime and acts and business transactions between the Indians"[672] and the application of "penal or disciplinary sanctions" according to their "own institutions."[673]

---

[666] Stavenhagen (1990) 29.

[667] de la Cruz I. (2006) 40.

[668] Collier, "Legal Processes", 4 Annual Review of Anthropology 121–144 (1987).

[669] Carneiro da Cunha (1990) 300 *seq.*

[670] *Id.* 299–313, 302 (1990).

[671] Article 231 of the 1988 Brazilian Constitution.

[672] Article 6 of the 1973 Brazilian Indian Statute.

[673] Article 57 of the 1973 Brazilian Indian Statute.

5. Conclusion

Notwithstanding these discussions, in the area of TCEs, the term "customary law" is still predominant. It is to be expected that other denominations will not really change the substantial problems either, at least at first glance. Thus, this study will continue to use "customary law" as its working term, while at the same time it intends to underscore and reiterate the terminological challenges and inadequacies shown above.

Probably more important than the question of the term applied, the content and characteristics of customary law remain to be clarified. Against the backdrop of the scenario of different legal cultures and ambits and linguistic challenges—should this clarification be done, or should we at least attempt to approach it, by means of a legal definition?

II. Definition of Customary Law: Is It Needed at All?

1. Arguments Against an Attempted Definition

Distinguished anthropologists of the twentieth century working in the area of different legal cultures and their differing legal systems have argued *against* a definition, already as regards the term "law." Gulliver exposed the dilemma, which exists especially in the constellation of customary law, in the 1960s:

On the one hand one could, *not un*reasonably, argue that "law", "a Western term and concept, should be defined by Western criteria." This view, however, leads to at least two difficulties: "first, that there are many non-Western societies in which 'law', thus defined, is then absent; and second, that alternative institutions and processes in non-Western societies have their comparable counterparts in Western societies, both within and without the legal system."[674]

On the other hand, "definitions have been widened – or perhaps, diluted – in attempts to include the varieties of non-Western phenomena, until the term has come to mean less and less." Such terms "are useful only if they are not rigidly defined but are left as loose labels of general areas of interest"—similar to "political system" or "religion." As regards "religion" and "political system," it has operationally been agreed to leave the definition aside. The "real problems and the interesting ones leading to further understanding, are not, and probably never have been, concerned with definitions and classifications," Gulliver argues. Thus, it should be "possible to ignore some of the older, and bitterly contested," and "increasingly fruitless . . . controversies" revolving around a definition of "law."[675]

---

[674] Gulliver (1969) 12.

[675] *Id.* 12.

2. Other Views

A classic Latin American book on indigenous customary law in the region has explicitly left the problem open: the different works (mostly anthropological ones) in the book in sum "neither presume an agreement on a definition of the field of knowledge that has generically been denominated *indigenous customary law*, nor on the limits of its application or sphere of operation."[676]

This was, however, a first "modest step"[677] only, and, hardly surprisingly, it is not the predominant perception among legal scholars today, especially those trained in the classic area of the continental-European "Begriffsjurisprudenz." At the same time, even in this continental-European legal ambit, it is admitted that any (abstract) term, legal or not, can only be understood through its context—a phenomenon or, more specifically, a process of understanding that Wittgenstein called the language game, or Sprachspiel."[678] Therefore, when aiming at the consideration of customary law as legal rules for an adequate protection of TCEs, certain legal perceptions or at least characteristics are needed.[679]

III. Approaching an Appropriate Definition or Characterizing Elements in the Area of TCEs

1. Definitions

Western scholars dealing with the topic of TCEs or folklore have proposed a definition characterizing customary law as "being the totality of non-codified practices of an ethnic community."[680] In many cases this definition will be suitable against the backdrop of the actual indigenous realities in Latin America—in contrast to those in the United States, for example.[681] Still, the current research has shown, that important examples would be excluded (like the customary law of the Panamanian Kuna Indians),[682] and more and more codification is taking place. Also, at the legal level, the definition would only partially fit: There do also exist positive laws defining customs and their legal impact, as well as registers especially set up for the "registration" of customary rules, i.e. compilations of the unwritten

[676] Stavenhagen and Iturralde (1990) 23.

[677] *Id.* 18.

[678] *See* Larenz and Canaris (1999) 25 *seq*, also on Wittgenstein ("Philosophische Untersuchungen" Teil I, Nr. 30) in the juridical context, i.e. on the idea that the meaning of a word is not contained in itself, but results from its specific use in a certain "Sprachspiel": To correctly interpret and apply a definition, one has to know what kind of role in language the words shall play.

[679] The need in this context is also admitted by lawyers with an indigenous background: "an approximation must be made towards a definition of customary law;" de la Cruz I. (2006) 23.

[680] *See, e.g.*, Lucas-Schlötter (2007) 413.

[681] The situation is different in the United States of America, with the Pueblo Indians for example.

[682] On this *see* at Chapter IV Section 1.D. below.

codes.[683] Those literally fixed customs and rules would thus be excluded by the initial definition, although they are the very part of the customary understanding and precepts regulating the indigenous community life. Besides, especially the term "practices" would probably have to face critique, such as—in Gullivers' words—being "widened – or perhaps, diluted –" and meaning "less and less."[684]

Another, more specific definition was proposed at the 2006 workshop on the Role of Customary Law in Regulations for Access to Genetic Resources, Distribution and Protection of Traditional Knowledge in Quito. According to this proposal, customary law is "a series of standards, uses, and customs that are passed on from generation to generation and exercised by authorities and institutions specific to indigenous peoples in their territories, and which constitute legal systems recognized, accepted and respected by a group and which incorporate the legal pluralism of countries with an indigenous population."[685]

The Executive Decree of the Panamanian sui generis system on protection of TCEs defines the customary rules on the use of the TCEs of each indigenous community as such rules "specifying the common characteristics of the traditional knowledge and objects capable of being registered as intellectual property. They represent the support of the tradition of the Collective Right and its application in the indigenous communities."[686]

What becomes clear from these definitions and reflections is that the simple or simplified idea of customary law as being the sum total of non-written rules, previous to and distinct from the positive national law, cannot be upheld anymore. There are some fundamental characteristics and discussions worth pointing out in the context of customary law and TCEs that are essential for interpretation and practical application of any definition as well as of the customary rules themselves.

2. Characteristics

In the sociology of law, it was not until Llewellyn, in his 1941 study on "The Cheyenne Way" who postulated the perception of a specific distinct system of law (customary law) within the national society.[687] Since then, the question of what concretely is customary law and what it is not has been hotly disputed, especially among lawyers, legal sociologists and anthropologists. It is not within the focus of

[683] Which is the case *e.g.* in Venezuela, de la Cruz I. (2006) 11.

[684] *See* the parallel points of critique by Gulliver (1969) 12.

[685] The workshop took place in January, 2006. *See* de la Cruz I. (2006) 24.

[686] Article 2 Nr. 12 of the Decree No. 12. This article establishes definitions to be applied "for the effects of this Decree." Thus, the definitions have a limited scope of application. On this *see* at Chapter IV Section 1.C.II.2.d. below.

[687] Llewellyn and Hoebel, "The Cheyenne Way. Conflict and Case Law in the Primitive Jurisprudence" 28 (1941).

this study to enter into these discussions, but some points are worth mentioning for the topic of customary law and TCEs.

The "fundamental problem" among lawyers, contemporary Latin American anthropologists have argued, is the "reification" or objectification contained in the use the lawyers make of the notion of customary law.[688] But in view of the facts and realities, at least in Brazil, the implication cannot stand up to opposition, as, according to Carneiro da Cunha, customary law is *not*

(i) a delimited, finite *corpus* of traditional content
(ii) antecedent to the states and therefore autonomous in its relation to the relevant state
(iii) of a similar nature to positive law, which enables the state to explicitly incorporate the relevant rules when political conditions allow it.[689]

What, then, characterizes customary law? Some important interpreting criteria and characteristics are listed below. Though important, most of them are neither unambiguous nor consistent, much less undisputed, but ambiguous, contradictory, and subject to discussions.

a. No State Authority

What characterizes customary law is precisely that it constitutes a sum of customs that are recognized and shared by a collective (community, people, tribe, ethnic or religious group, etc.), in contrast to written laws which emanate from a constituted political authority, and whose application is in the hands of this authority, generally the state. The fundamental difference, according to the Mexican expert Rodolfo Stavenhagen, thus is that "the positive law is linked to state power, while the customary law belongs to societies which lack the state, or simply operates without reference to the state."[690]

Nonetheless, within the indigenous societies, there are other points of reference, namely, traditional authorities. Similarly, there has been a call to recognize "the authority [of the minority groups] to elaborate" customary rules.[691]

b. No Specific, Highly Specialized, and Separable Sphere

From this first observation results a second fundamental characteristic and distinction from state law, which has been addressed shortly within the arguments against the consideration of customary law above: In complex societies (with a state), the law constitutes a specific and distinct sphere, separable from the rest of the culture and society—so that one can talk of law *and* society as two areas that in a certain

688 Carneiro da Cunha (1990) 300.
689 *Id.*
690 Stavenhagen (1990) 29 *seq.*
691 Carneiro da Cunha (1990) 302.

way are related but autonomous.[692] According to Stavenhagen, lawyers prefer the concept of "law and society" instead of "law in the society,"[693] as they attribute the law an autonomous sphere contrasting to the society.[694] The law has its own norms and language, like the professional specialists. It can—as a whole *corpus*—be transferred from one society to another, a phenomenon known as the reception of law.[695] The specialists can deal with the law with little or even no reference to the social or cultural context, and this is precisely what characterizes the majority of juridical contracts. In contrast, customary law in tribal or less complex societies does not constitute a different or autonomous sphere, separated from the society. Rather, the legal is part of the social structure, and usually, there is no administrative body, no professional specialists, no "Rechtsstab," as Max Weber called it, in charge of elaborating and/or applying the law, as mentioned above.[696] The society's own members often do not distinguish a specific legal sphere different from customs and norms of behavior and social control, Stavenhagen argues. As a consequence, for external observers it can be difficult to trace the limits of the law in these societies.[697]

c. Subordination

Another important characteristic is the subordinate status of customary law under a dominant, national law. Formerly, the latter was the colonial law, while the situation of subordination and dominance still remains today, though now the dominant system is a national, socio-economically dominant law.[698] Also, from a political-anthropological point of view, it has been stated that (Latin American) "[s] tates characterized as postcolonial may in fact still exercise neo-colonial forms of control."[699]

d. Constant Modification and Transformation

Change and constant transformation are inherent characteristics of customary law, particularly because it is—or until recently was—not codified.

---

[692] Stavenhagen (1990) 30.

[693] Anthropologists prefer the term "law in the society," as they do not recognize an autonomous sphere of the law.

[694] Stavenhagen (1990) 43 note 1.

[695] *Id.* 30 *seq.*

[696] *See* at Section 5.A.I.1. (12) above and Weber ((1922) 1978) 34, German version: Weber (1976) 17, *see* further Rehbinder (1967) 109.

[697] Stavenhagen (1990) 30.

[698] *Id.* 33.

[699] Levi and Dean (2003) 11.

Besides the general sociological understanding that the autopoetic production of the society is "a process of permanent elaboration,"[700] which can be reflected by non-codified customary law, the change within the system is mainly due to two factors: the customary law adapts in response to factual external changes, particularly environmental ones, as well as according to changes within the dominant national law. As just mentioned above, customary law is widely influenced by its specific subordinate status under a dominant, national, formerly colonial law. Within this relationship, as Starr and Collier have found out, subordinated societies have to adapt and reinterpret the positive national laws in accordance with their own structures, values, interests, and necessities, and thereby transform or modify their "customary law."[701]

Moreover, customary law reflects socio-cultural patterns in a much more direct way than codified state law does. Dynamics in customary law can thus be understood as a reflection of the dynamics in indigenous culture. As "custom is not a thing", but a "path",[702] customary law is likewise a path. This characteristic provokes conflicts that are also relevant for the question of protecting TCEs through customary law in Latin America, especially regarding the issue of representation.[703] However, these conflicts are discussed, the validity of indigenous customary law constitutes "one of the indispensable elements for the preservation and reproduction of the indigenous cultures" of the Latin American continent.[704]

Practical examples in Latin American customary law also support this view: While 25 years ago, according to de la Cruz, indigenous communities in the Mojanda Cajas plateaus in Ecuador had a natural water supply of 12 L/s, nowadays, it consists of only 3 L/s, with a steady increase in the population needing greater resources at the same time.[705] In view of these altered living conditions, ancestral knowledge and rules for applying certain standards and resource management have to be adapted accordingly, and sometimes even be recovered, before an alteration is possible.

Although it is not easy to detect the concrete result of a certain change, it is indeed possible to make out a certain direction of change: this is, among other aspects, the tendency towards the modernization of the economy and of the way of life that tends to accompany the transformations in a community's customs. To reveal more fundamental aspects of the legal dynamics and juridical practices in the indigenous regions, especially as regards possible impacts on TCEs, deeper explorations are necessary and would be extremely helpful.[706]

---

[700] Carneiro da Cunha (1990) 301.

[701] Starr and Collier (1987) 367.

[702] Carneiro da Cunha (1991) 276–294.

[703] On this *see* at Section 5.D.II. below.

[704] Stavenhagen (1990) 27.

[705] de la Cruz I. (2006) 30.

[706] Sierra (no year) 23.

IV. Special Problems and Points for Discussion

1. "Inventing" Customary Law?

As a consequence of admitting the dynamic nature of customary law, and analogous to the phenomenon of the "invention of traditions," which goes back to Hobsbawm,[707] there also exists a phenomenon that could be called the "invention of customary rules."

This regards two aspects:

(i) Inventing in the sense of remembering–directed towards the past, and
(ii) Inventing in the sense of newly creating—directed towards the future.

While the first situation corresponds to the phenomenon of invented traditions as examined by Hobsbawm, the second situation might be illustrated by the following practical example: In Mexico, customary law, in the term of *usos y costumbres*, "practices and customs," can be applied in election procedures at the local level. That means that municipal leaders are selected through "customary law rather than secret votes and ballot boxes."[708]

While elections seem to be a rather political issue at first glance, the selection of leaders at the local level is closely related to the question of "representation" of a community according to customary law in TCE matters.

Customary law in the case of the local elections is applicable either in those communities that have developed community assemblies or other collective forms of selecting local authorities, or in such communities that "by their own decision" opt for such a system.[709] This latter mechanism of giving effect to "customary law" in the local election processes "by choice" does not require any existence of relevant traditions at all, neither as continuous practices nor as revitalized rules. Consequently, there is the factual *and legal* possibility of "inventing" customs and practices. This possibility has been made use of in indigenous Mexico, for example in Oaxaca and Chiapas: In the highland region of central Chiapas, for example, anthropologists have documented the "updating" of traditional municipal configurations in 16 different indigenous municipalities.[710]

The example shows that it is difficult or maybe impossible to draw the line between *recovery* and *invention* on the one hand, as regards the fundaments of the past, and also between *change*, alteration, adaptation, or development (which is part

[707] *See* Hobsbawm (1983) 1 *et seq*. On "inventing tradition" in the topic of TCEs *see* at Section 1. B.I.1.f. above.

[708] Eisenstadt (no year) 1.

[709] Translation of the Mexican Electoral Law into English inspired by *id.* 15.

[710] Burguete Cal y Mayor, Araceli, "Ayuntamientos indígenas de facto en el Chiapas postzapatista (1994–2004): una tipología", paper presented at the XXI meeting of the Latin American Studies Association, October 9, 2004 (Las Vegas), cited from *id.* 15 (no year).

of the very nature of customary law, as shown above) and *invention* on the other hand, as regards facing challenges of the future.

Especially in the area of traditional knowledge and TCEs, experts in Latin America have argued in favor of giving indigenous communities time and patience for developing the necessary negotiating capacity[711]—and this could include the aspect of developing customary law.

Having the legal choice to opt for the application of customary law through elaborating (or inventing) this customary law seems to be disputable from a legal point of view.

While constant readjustments in customary law, especially in non-literate communities, are part of its intrinsic nature, the legal application and consideration of customary law, however, should be limited in cases of misuse of these legally acknowledged possibilities. For the purpose of applying customary law to the protection of TCEs, the limit to such misuses could be established for cases in which the connection with the particular fundament of the recovered or maintained indigenous world view and the actual socio-cultural conception is completely lacking.

A legal parameter for determining the limit in the individual case could be the principle of "good faith" or the German legal concept of "Treu und Glauben."[712]

2. Non-codified Law?

Another crucial aspect that has a great impact on both the definition of customary law and the concept of protecting TCEs as a whole is whether—or not—customary law *should be* or even *may* be written down. This embraces two fundamental questions:

(1) Should the traditionally oral character of the customary law be a precondition for being acknowledged as customary law as such, in other words, may codified laws be qualified as "customary law" at all?
(2) Or, conversely, should or must—in the name of (Western) legal certainty—customary law be written down in order to be acknowledged as legal rules or methods of protecting TCEs?

a. No Codification Because of Dynamic Character

Latin American scholars have argued against the codification of customary law, as this "would have the disadvantage of depriving it precisely of its dynamic and

---

[711] As Wörrle argues, the dilemma of protecting traditional knowledge and TCEs is due to a structural rather than legal problem, and to get out of it, first of all, "a lot of patience" will be required, in order to give the (Ecuadorian) indigenous peoples the chance to develop sufficient negotiation power: Wörrle (2008) 238.

[712] *See* Sec. 242 of the German Civil Code.

flexible nature, which constitutes the utility for the indigenous peoples."[713] Moreover, codification "would lead to [the customary law's] extinction, and [customary law] would become a positive right" (probably meaning positive law). Non-codification, in contrast, would give the law "greater flexibility and adaptability to different circumstances, thereby ensuring its continuity and legitimacy."[714]

One sure thing is that some type of dynamic element is necessary, as the defining nature of customary rules is their ability to be adapted to changing circumstances in the life of the community, as discussed above.[715]

b. No Codification Because of Probable Impact on Traditional Structures and Rules Themselves

Results of research on the ground have revealed, first, situations in which "*codified law* for the protection of works of art is *in preparation*, but . . . the subject matter is difficult and expert advice short."[716] Or, second, customary rules having been drafted and written down by "indigenous lawyers" instead of, for example, being (orally) expressed by traditional authorities or leaders of the community—in the case of a TCE of the Panamanian Kuna Indians, for instance.[717]

These observations lead to the questions: Who in fact defines the concrete form and content of customary law? Traditional authorities, elders? (Indigenous) lawyers? The relevant public entities?

Traditional leaders, possibly elders, whose words, terms, and modes of thought[718] are fundamentally different and hard to translate when discussing or negotiating the subject of TCEs with non-indigenous parties, national institutions, or lawyers with Western legal training.[719] Is it really these elders who define the concrete content, which can be read afterwards as customary rules of use divided into chapters and articles? And what if it is felt that "experts" are needed, as expressed by the observation that "the subject matter is difficult and expert advice short"?[720] And what is the role and impact in practice of even public institutions like the DIGERPI in Panama, when assisting the indigenous communities in writing

---

[713] Stavenhagen (1990) 43.

[714] de la Cruz I. (2006) 40.

[715] *See* at Section 5.B.III.2.d. above.

[716] Cooter and Fikentscher (2008) 54. Emphasis added by the author.

[717] Personal communication with Aresio Valiente López, *Kuna* Indian, lawyer and legal representative of the *Kuna* Indians in issues regarding the use of the *Kuna* TCE *Mola* and the "Rules of Use of the Collective Right 'Mola *Kuna* Panama'" on February 11, 2009 in Panama City. On details of this topic *see* at Chapter IV Section 1.D. below.

[718] On this term *see* Fikentscher (1995) 21.

[719] Personal communication with the elder and traditional authority Luis Touar, General *Cacique* Dagar Kunyala, translation by Flaviano Iglesias in February 2009 in Panama City on the traditional use of a special TCE of his community, the Kunan hammock.

[720] Cooter and Fikentscher (2008) 54, emphasis added by the author.

down their customary rules and when "approving and registering" them?[721] Maybe they "only" write down the Western-influenced formal parts, or maybe they answer the need of communities to be supported by drafting the rules. If adapting or developing customary rules to this relatively new situation of "protecting TCEs" requires capacity-building measures for the indigenous communities, the support and pre-drafting of rules by a public entity like DIGERPI could be regarded as just a means of such capacity building—or does it influence the traditional structures and competences of decision-making and rule-making to such a great extent that the outcome of such rules can no longer be regarded as "customary law"?

c. No Codification Because of Limited Power and Legislative Competence

The question of whether and how codification of customary rules influences traditional community structures and competences leads to another question, namely, whether any kind of "legislative competence" on the part of the communities for not only developing, but also codifying such law is first, necessary, and second, existent within the communities.

As mentioned, distinguished anthropological and legal scholars Robert D. Cooter and Wolfgang Fikentscher came to the result that usually, in more than eight reservations in which the question was raised, they "heard that *codified law* for the protection of works of art is *in preparation*, but that the subject matter is difficult and expert advice short."[722] In view of the Latin American situation, this result raises further questions: first, whether the development of codified law—even if set up by indigenous peoples themselves—may still be regarded as "customary law", and, second, whether it—in the most extreme dimension—might even constitute a substitution of the work usually done by the (democratically legitimized) legislature?

Apart from the characterization of "custom" dealt with before, the last question in particular refers to another aspect to be considered here: Do potential preconditions or limits set by the national law have to be observed? What consequences does this have on the codification of customary law?

The legal relationship between tribal and federal legislative powers in the United States of America, where the example cited above stems from, is characterized by a "dependent sovereignty" in favor of tribal sovereignty.[723] In Latin American countries, however, the question of developing tribal codes would give rise to concerns. Most of the federal or national legal frameworks in Latin American countries do not generally entitle indigenous communities to issue tribal codes.[724]

[721] *See* Article 15 of the Panamanian Law No. 20 of 2000. DIGERPI is the entity within the Ministry of Commerce and Industries in charge of the implementation of the sui generis Law in Panama. On all of this *see* at Chapter IV Section 1.C.IV. below.

[722] Cooter and Fikentscher (2008) 54, emphasis added by the author.

[723] For historical and legal details on the "dependent sovereignty," *see* Fikentscher (2008) Chapter 14 IV.

[724] Few countries acknowledge indigenous competence to follow or advance their own customary laws on certain issues and under certain circumstances, like within a demarcated indigenous territory in Venezuela, *see* de la Cruz I. (2006) 9 *seq*.

The topic of self-determination, autonomy, and preservation of national sovereignty and authority are politically highly controversial. Traditionally, in the last century, Latin American countries in general have demonstrated a phenomenon which Carneiro da Cunha called a "true paranoia about the idea of multi-ethnicity" and "an aversion to recognize customary law"—which may be rooted in the historical fact that the states had to constitute themselves politically before they had clear national identities and understood state and nation to be completely overlapping concepts.[725] While multi-ethnicity is recognized at least on paper in some states now, even as recently as 2009, in a "Strategic Workshop of the Latin American Group on Pluralistic Legal Systems," the topic of acknowledging customary law and corresponding indigenous competences was highly disputed.[726] The Panamanian state, for example, does not acknowledge all codified customary laws or articles therein, namely, those of the Fundamental Law of the Comarca Kuna Yala.[727]

Although codification of customary law is not such a highly developed topic in Latin America as in the United States, the example of the codification of the Kuna Law in Panama, as well as the registration system of the Panamanian sui generis regime in general, might be indicators for an emerging tendency towards more codification in Latin America, raising precisely the legal and political question of "legislative competence" of indigenous communities.

d. Codification in Other Legal Cultures: Arguments from Comparative Law

The whole question of codifying customary law in the topic of TCEs is strongly influenced by the Western legal culture—at a national as well as an international level. As demonstrated above, part of the changes in customary law result from reactions to the "dominant" national law and legal culture of the dominant society.[728] Likewise, Panamanian indigenous peoples drafting the sui generis regime of Panama felt that they had to include a requirement of registration and publication of their customary rules in order to ensure an effective rights enforcement against non indigenous peoples.[729] Especially the continental-European legal culture, which is also the basis of the dominant Latin American legal cultures due to Spanish and

[725] As mentioned at the beginning of this chapter, *see* Carneiro da Cunha (1990) 303 *seq.*

[726] "Taller estratégico del Grupo Latinoamericano por Sistemas Jurídicos Plurales" of the Konrad Adenauer Foundation, held on March 11–14, 2009, in Quito, Ecuador, which the author was allowed to attend with the kind permission of the Uruguayan and Ecuadorian Office of the Konrad Adenauer Foundation.

[727] *See* http://www.digerpi.gob.pa/pls/portal/docs/PAGE/NOTICIAS/CONGRESO_DERECHO_COLECTIVO/HERACLIO%20HERRERA%2C%20PANAMÁ-*KUNA*.PDF, last visited November 12, 2010; on this *see* also at Chapter IV Section 1.D.I. below.

[728] Starr and Collier (1987) 367 and Stavenhagen (1990) 33. *See also* at Section 5.B.III.2.c. above.

[729] Personal communication with Aresio Valiente, indigenous lawyer and one of the consultants of the deputies, on February 11, 2009, in Panama City.

Portuguese colonialization, are characterized by the concept of codification. In these legal cultures, is it possible that reverse tendencies are found, too?

From a comparative-law perspective, it is interesting to have a look at a decision issued by the German Federal Constitutional Court, the *Bundesverfassungsgericht*.[730] Although it treats an aspect of a very different area of law, the area of labor law, the particular aspect is of interest here: the question of the necessity of codifying law, considering socio-cultural realities.

As a consequence of a structural change affecting the whole *legal order* ("Wandlung im Gefüge der gesamten Rechtsordnung", a phenomenon similar to the change in the *situation* of the norm ("Wandel der Normsituation")),[731] the German Federal Constitutional Court denied the application of the principle of codification[732] to labor law on grounds that—due to the development in social law that had taken place since the establishment of the German Civil Code (BGB)—labor law had been extracted from private law.[733]

The conclusions that can be drawn from this decision with relevance to the question dealt with here of whether or not to codify customary law in the area of TCEs are:

(iv) Needs and practices in the social reality (here: the non-codification) can be considered in the process of designing law without breaking Hume's principle of the dichotomy of "is" and "ought."[734]
(v) Even in Western legal areas in which the principle of codification prevails, exceptions in favor of non-codification or, more generally, orality, are acknowledged—without breaking the principle of "legal certainty."[735]
(vi) On the other hand, allowing a "change of social circumstances" to be considered could in the case of increasing codifications of customary law lead to the recognition of written codes as "customary law."

A broader perspective, including other global scenarios and other legal cultures in the area of traditional knowledge, shows that oral traditions are recognized even in patent law, for example in India: oral or other informal knowledge systems, like the traditions of *sruti* (hearing) and *smriti* (remembering), are present and legally acknowledged on the Indian sub-continent.[736]

---

[730] 7 BverfGE 342, 350.

[731] This is a change at the factual level, i.e. when factual circumstances or conventions change in comparison to the situation existing when the codification took place; Larenz and Canaris (1999) 170 *seq*.

[732] *e.g.* contained in the Artt. 3, 55, 218 of the German Act introducing the Civil Code (EGBGB).

[733] 7 BverfGE 342, 350. *See also* Larenz and Canaris (1999) 173 note 82.

[734] Hume (1739) Book III, Part 1, (I).

[735] As displayed before, legal uncertainty is one of the major arguments against the application of oral customary law in the area of TCEs.

[736] For many others and further references *see* Taubman and Leistner (2008) 125.

e. Interdisciplinary Perspective: Orality as Inferior Approach?

Aside from the critique of legal uncertainty, orality as a concept of intellectual and social interaction is often also criticized or at least considered as inferior in the currently predominating part of the "global society." It is very true that literacy is essential for most interactions in this world. But is an oral tradition really to be regarded as inferior? In the classical antique intellectual tradition, orality is highly esteemed. Plato said of *written* words:

> you might think they spoke as if they had intelligence, but if you question them, wishing to know about their sayings, they always say only one and the same thing. And every word, when once it is written, is bandied about, alike among those who understand and those who have no interest in it, and it knows not to whom to speak or not to speak; when ill-treated or unjustly reviled it always needs its father to help it; for it has no power to protect or help itself.[737]

Similarly, in the modern legal tradition of Germany, Gadamer comprehends the understanding of a written text as analogous to the mutual comprehension in a spoken conversation. The text gives language to a thing, and it talks only to that particular listener who understands its language and the thing it is talking about to a great enough extent to find access to what the text tells him. The connecting basis or instrument is the language itself and the context of "tradition" of the language, the context in which it is transmitted or passed along (*Überlieferungszusammenhang*).[738]

f. Non-literacy as Support of the Vitality of Customary Law

It is exactly this oral "tradition" or *Überlieferungszusammenhang* that is key for the validity and vitality of customary law within the indigenous community.

While Max Weber already emphasized the importance of writing for a society in the area of positive law, more recently, English anthropologist Jack Goody developed tremendously useful insights on the impacts of literacy and its diffusion—which do not necessarily go hand in hand.[739] Goody observed crucial differences between literate and non-literate societies,[740] and correspondingly, written and oral law follow different logical operations and have different social uses. In Brazil, researchers (later) discovered that it had been a key element in constructing the laces of personal dependency that maintained the colonial system to conceal the customary law of the slaves in the nineteenth century.[741]

---

737 Phaedrus (no year) 275d–e, available at http://www.perseus.tufts.edu, last visited December 6, 2010.

738 Gadamer (1965) 391, and *see* Larenz and Canaris (1999) 30. On juridical hermeneutics in the area of the law in reality in general *see* Röhl (1974) 109 *seq.*

739 Carneiro da Cunha (1990) 303, 313.

740 Goody and Watt (1968) 30.

741 *See* Carneiro da Cunha, "Sobre os silencios da lei: lei costumeira e positiva nas alforrias de escravos no Brasil do seculo XIX" (1983) cited from Carneiro da Cunha (1990) 303.

For the area of orally practiced customary law in the area of TCEs, this means that externally enforced change from a non-literate to a literate legal system in a traditional society would bring about major changes for the customary law and the whole cultural heritage of the society. Similar to the ways of transmitting cultural heritage in general, the ways of transmitting customary law are changed by the widespread adoption of "any easy and effective means of written communication."[742] The transmission in non-literate societies depends upon particular forms of communication,[743] and has a considerable effect on the content of customs and customary law. As mentioned in the context of transmitting philosophy, the individual memory of each generation mediates the traditions, and the social function of memory and forgetting is regarded as "the final stage of what may be called the homeostatic organization of the cultural tradition in non-literate society."[744]

Orality or non-codification is thus a fundamental means for maintaining the vitality and knowledge of customary law within the society or community where it is practiced.

g. Orality as Advantage in "Getting the Rules Right"

As a further consequence of the particularities of communication in non-literate societies, but also of the intercultural aspect, oral communication on customary law has another advantage: it enables a more comprehensive explanation to outsiders. In the field of Native American studies, and specifically Native American spirituality, which is closely linked to customs and customary rules in their original form, the aim of "getting it right" has been given highest priority. A precise understanding of such rules, or the most appropriate intercultural understanding of results, in this field of research, is seen as more important than which method is used to achieve these results. This commitment to correct understanding underscores that it is a process "that requires much more of the observer than a theoretical language of analysis. The issue is [. . .] communication."[745]

Communication with an indigenous person having little contact or exchange with the rest of the national society, or having little or even no knowledge of a language other than indigenous ones, clearly reveals the difficulty: putting the conversation or words into a written text does not only raise great challenges, but also bears the great risk of changing the very content of the words by adapting them to a written, legally "workable" text. If questioned, the text would not be able to give answers beyond the literal appearance, and could only be understood by the particular listener familiar with the context of "tradition"—the convention—of the language. Few non-indigenous persons are likely to know the native language, and

[742] Goody and Watt (1968) 31.

[743] On these particularities *see* at Section 4.A.III.4. above.

[744] *Id.* 30 (1968).

[745] The only "theory" is a "genuine concern to 'get it right' through methodologies that work best" for the individual author: Irwin (2000) 2, 7.

translation even adds the risk of changing the content, as shown in the chapter on understanding indigenous world views.[746] A written, juridical document in a non-native language would probably limit the original perception and cut it off from its spiritual basis and holistic approach, which—if still existent in practice—is part of the very nature of customary law.

For illustration, a good example is the concept of the "owner" according to the perspective of the Brazilian Wajãpi, which is to be dealt with in more detail below.[747] Major difficulties in understanding as well as in maintaining the continuity of the Wajãpi form of "possession" do not (only) lie in the rule of a prior informed consent, but in managing the deeper cultural issues, among other things, the fact that the form of "possession" depends upon the "continuous and creative practice of this symbolic language as regulated by local custom, which includes the observance of cultural interdictions."[748] The practice of this symbolic language, however, can only be maintained in continuous (oral) communication within the community, and cultural interdictions can only be observed in the interaction, thus communication, with the concrete outsider.

h. Summary

In sum, the following arguments can be brought forward *against* the codification of customary law:

(1) Its dynamic nature in general,
(2) practical examples of the real need of adaptations, readjustments, and thus the retention of the dynamic character,
(3) the impact on the whole socio-cultural habit of non-literate societies and, as a consequence of the lack or alteration of the oral transmission, fundamental impacts on the content of the tradition and customary law itself,
(4) the risk of misunderstandings, as no "mode of thought"[749] or meanings of the context can be questioned and then explained by the text,
(5) the risk of limiting customary rules to a purely legal content, disregarding the broader spiritual belief, e.g. in the case of the "owner,"[750]
(6) the risk of "inventing" "a rule" in the moment of fixation, and
(7) potential conflicts with constitutional or political concepts like the separation of power in case of codification.

Nonetheless, without codification, the risk of wrongfully "inventing" customary law exists at any time. This, however, can be dealt with at the "material" level of juridically examining the concrete case, e.g., by means of "good faith."[751]

[746] *See* at Section 4.A.III.4. above.

[747] *See* at Section 5.D.I.1. below.

[748] Arantes (2009 I) 38.

[749] On this term *see* Fikentscher (1995) 21.

[750] *See* at Section 5.D.I. below.

[751] *See* also at Section 5.B.IV.1. above.

Arguments *in favor* of at least allowing a codification or fixation are:

(1) In the view of a growing complexity of legal issues, like the adequate treatment of TCEs, writing down rules that have been particularly adapted to this situation might be a good means of responding to this complexity.
(2) The result might constitute a better protection of TCEs for the indigenous peoples themselves.
(3) The degree of legal certainty is higher indeed—at least on paper, and might be desired by some indigenous communities who want to get in touch with persons interested in their TCEs.

In conclusion, the orality of customary rules should be no imperative precondition for the qualification as customary law. Orality would be preferable, but fixation or even codification should be accepted—within the constitutional legal frameworks.

C. Historical and Anthropological Observations on Customary Law in Latin America

The foregoing reflections on the characteristics of customary law might be helpful for determining a set of "rules" as customary law as well as identifying their content and applicability in the concrete case.

The question that then follows is what the process or content of such customary law could look like.

I. Historical Developments of Studies on Customary Law in Latin America

Interestingly, first observations of indigenous laws in Latin America were made at a very early stage, in the nineteenth century. These were, however, only very few approaches.[752] Customary law as an area of research appeared in Latin America only in the late 1980s and early 1990s. As a result of the (first) International Seminar on Indigenous Customary Law in Latin America,[753] it was deemed

[752] *See. e.g.* the descriptions of indigenous systems of law in 1832 of Carl Friedrich Philipp von Martius, "O estado do direito entre os autóctones do Brasil", Editora Itatiaia, São Paolo, 1982, cited from Kayser (2005) 144, note 229. The rules were not written down due to the lack of alphabets.

[753] Seminario Internacional sobre Derecho Consuetudinario Indígena en América Latina. It took place in July 1988 in Lima, Peru, *see* Stavenhagen and Iturralde (1990) 15.

"surprising" that the issue of customary law of the indigenous populations had received "so little attention" in Latin America so far.[754]

The Latin American, more precisely Ecuadorian, Special Rapporteur of the UN, José Martínez Cobo, as early as 1983 pointed out the importance of considering customary law, and gave the following advice:

> Given the coexistence of a national legal order and other customary legal orders which govern the lives of indigenous populations, it is recommended that:
>
> (i) Indigenous legal orders should be respected, and the existence of a pluralistic legal system, without any unjustified pre-eminence on the part of the national legal system, should be accepted;
> (ii) The criteria of individual rights and geographical-demographical considerations should be accepted for the application of existing legal systems, according to circumstances;
> (iii) The limits of legal pluralism should be defined, the cultural areas into which the national legal order must not intrude should be demarcated and those aspects which must inevitably be governed by the national legal order, to the extent that they relate to the force or values and rights internationally considered at present as fundamental and essential to contemporary life in society, should also be identified;
> (iv) The use of the national legal order by indigenous populations should be facilitated, as well as the prompt administration of justice in conditions of equality, for the protection of their rights and freedoms and without prejudice to observance of their own legal procedures. To this end, the principles of the national legal order should be publicized, appropriate legal assistance provided and economic and procedural measures adopted to ensure the real, rather than the merely formal, nature of the right to such use.[755]

In Latin America, until the late 1980s, the national legislations did not contemplate the recognition of indigenous customary law or, even less, the right of self-determination of indigenous peoples. Only then did constitutional changes take place in some Latin American countries, and legislative initiatives were taken, recognizing indigenous rights as a specific area of collective human rights, including indigenous customary law in some cases.[756] However, in the beginning of the 1990s, it was still held that the issue of indigenous customary law in Latin America had not been treated systematically so far, that "practically everything remained to be done,"[757] and a lot more research and "profound studies of the topic" were needed.[758]

[754] Stavenhagen and Iturralde say: "A pesar de los amplios conocimientos científicos acumulados sobre los pueblos indígenas del continente, resultaba sorprendente la poca atención que había recibido hasta la fecha el tema del derecho consuetudinario de estas poblaciones", *id.* 15.

[755] Cobo (1983) para 488.

[756] Stavenhagen and Iturralde (1990) 18.

[757] *Ibid.*

[758] *Id.* 24.

II. Current Status of Research on Customary Law on TCEs in Latin America

Lately, a lot more studies and publications have been conducted and released, in an interdisciplinary approach, especially by anthropologists.[759] With very few exceptions, these works mostly treat more theoretical questions and general debates on the consideration of customary law. Within this research, the three to four main fields of interest in customary law are still (1) land rights, (2) persecution of torts, and (3) proceedings of administration of justice[760]; or, according to another author, (1) administration of justice, (2) models of coexistence of different types of laws, and (3) criminal law.[761] From a more general anthropological perspective, the ranking of most popular topics has been (1) family law, (2) property, (3) associations, and (4) the state—where "property" refers to material rather than immaterial property.[762] A similar picture is painted by Latin American legislations. The Brazilian Constitution, for example, considers the application of tribal law mainly in the area of penal law.[763] Another point of especially intense political discussions has been the (wide) area of "legal pluralism" in general.[764]

In this study, however, customary law will be treated with special focus on TCEs.

On this question of applying customary law in the specific topic of TCEs, i.e. how TCEs are treated according to customary law, unfortunately, very little research exists so far, especially in Latin America, but also elsewhere. Even distinguished Latin American authors like the Mexican Rodolfo Stavenhagen provide few substantive examples in their classic publications on indigenous and customary law.[765]

Even if precise and faithful field research exists, the results thereof are of little value regarding any substantial content on the customary treatment of TCEs as legally protected interests. With very few exceptions,[766] this is also the result of the contributions on customary law that WIPO has collected so far, as well as of specific fieldwork and fact-finding missions.

Even "indigenous peoples" themselves, possessing knowledge, education, and experience in legal questions on traditional knowledge and TCEs, tend to refer to

---

[759] *See, e.g.*, Ochoa García (2002).

[760] "1) El derecho a la tierra", "2) La persecución de delitos", and, "3) Procedimientos de administración de justicia", *see* Stavenhagen (1990) 39–42.

[761] Barié (2003) 50 *seq.*

[762] Robert Lowie, "Anthropology and Law", in: Ogburn and Goldenweiser (eds.), "The Social Sciences and their Interrelations", (Cambridge 1927), cited from Nader (1969) 2.

[763] Article 231 of the Brazilian Constitution and Article 57 of the Brazilian Indian Statute; on this and further details *see* at Chapter IV Section 2.B. below.

[764] On the topic of legal pluralism in Latin America *see, e.g.*, Huber, Martínez, Lachenal and Ariza (2008).

[765] *See* Stavenhagen (1988) as well as Stavenhagen (1990) 27–46.

[766] *See, e.g.*, Arantes (2009 I) 24 *et seq.* and at D. below.

general aspects of spiritual values rather than concrete customary rules when dealing with the issue. The WIPO Regional Study in the Andean Countries, "Customary Law in the Protection of Traditional Knowledge," for example, refers to general principles such as reciprocity, duality, and balance, rather than to specific "customary rules," when addressing substantive questions on the legal treatment of TCEs.[767]

One reason for this dearth of detail might be the fact that customary law often consists rather of *processes* than of *substantive rules*, which means that decisions on legal problems—like the use or misuse of TCEs—are reached by means of a process, like a dispute settlement, rather than by applying a substantive rule.[768]

Another reason for the lack of specific examples might be the "dilemma" of approaching in legal terms the topic of TCEs: on the one hand, the few experts in this area, so far, tend to have a Western-influenced education and perspective. Moreover, in Latin America specifically, the overwhelming majority of the "indigenous population" consists of so-called *mestizos,* with a socio-culturally "mixed" background, rather than "traditional indigenous peoples," thus the old customary rules are slowly vanishing (giving truth to the verdict that "customary law is not more than 'a myth' nowadays").[769] On the other hand, those "traditional" indigenous peoples who do still "remain" either still follow a social or procedural, rather than a legal or substantive, approach, or they are rarely "experienced" in the topic from a Western point of view.

In this manner, also experienced anthropological and legal scholars like Robert D. Cooter and Wolfgang Fikentscher, who conducted field work in Indian reservations in the United States of America, an area that is much easier to access and thus has been the subject of much more intense research than the remote areas of the Latin American Amazon region, for example, found that "protecting traditional knowledge and artistic expression in arts and crafts" constitutes an area "rarely covered" in tribal codes.[770] Although this issue was regarded to be important to many Indians, and federal or national legislations worldwide were considered to be inadequate insofar, the application or adaptation of customary rules or their further development towards (intellectual) property rights—even understood as an *emic* term—had not been pursued seriously. In more than eight reservations in which the question was raised, Cooter and Fikentscher noted: "we heard that codified [tribal] law for the protection of works of art is in preparation, but that the subject matter is difficult and expert advice short." This situation held true "even for tribes that are famous for their works of art."[771]

---

[767] *See* mainly the chapter "Traditional knowledge protection through customary law: case studies" in de la Cruz I. (2006) 26 *seq.*

[768] This is the case in particular communities in Latin America like those of the Shuar and Achuar Indians in Ecuador, it has been observed in the customary treatment of the TCE *mola* of the Kuna Indians in Panama, and it is true of anthropological theory in general, Personal communication with ethnologist Meiser on January 8, 2009 and Gulliver (1969) 13.

[769] *See* the voices on *usos y costumbres* recorded by Eisenstadt (no year) 3.

[770] Cooter and Fikentscher (2008) 53.

[771] *Id.* 54 (2008).

I found similar answers among the Asháninka in Peru, the Shuar in Ecuador, and the Kaingang and Mundurukú in Brazil indicating the complexity of the subject. If they had heard about the topic at all, the tribal members exclusively referred to indigenous fellows specialized in national legal studies, irrespective of whether this person was from the same community, or even ethnicity, or not.[772] Or they referred to the broader, large-scale social context.

Likewise, the research on court decisions and cases dealing with customary law and TCEs did not provide more profound insights.[773] There are two reasons for that: On the one hand, as De Obaldia argues, the legal culture of indigenous communities in settling disputes is such that they have a long tradition of defending and exercising their rights by "their own hand" and traditionally do not solve their problems through the national judiciary.[774] On the other hand, public entities also prefer to settle such disputes at the administrative level, avoiding bringing the case to the regular courts, as little adequate or helpful outcome is expected even by the employees of the state themselves.[775]

Even at the high level of expertise and resources found within WIPO, exclusively cases from areas other than Latin American countries are reported there.[776]

Nonetheless, it was possible to gain some interesting insights. On this occasion, it should be remembered that even at a local level, research based upon interviews and communication is only able to reflect individual voices and only very rarely one "common understanding." Contradictions are an intrinsic part of the research and the topic as such. This is also due to the very nature of the traditional way of dealing with legal issues as social issues: if a kind of social behavior perceived as

[772] Personal communication with Fernanda Kaingang, Indigenous lawyer from the Brazilian Kaingang tribe, and Daniel Mundurukú, philosopher of the Brazilian Mundurukú tribe, on June 23, 2009 in São Paolo, Brazil; personal communication with Rodrigo de la Cruz, Indigenous lawyer, staff member of the IEPI and consultant to WIPO, in March 2009, in Quito, Ecuador; personal phone call with traditional indigenous leader Ampan Karankes, who just referred to Rodrigo de la Cruz; personal communication with ethnologist Meiser on January 8, 2009, and personal communication with Luis Touar, General Cacique Dagar Kunyala (Traditional Authority of the *Kuna* Indians in Eastern Panama), with the kind translation by Flaviano Iglesias on February 13, 2009 in Panamá City.

[773] The Brazilian Ministry of Public was so kind as to make available the records of all cases that could be of some relevance for the topic of TCEs, namely, the cases 2006.50.04.000458-0 6001 - ACAO CIVIL PUBLICA; ACP - ES - 2006.50.04.000458.0 - contra Aracruz Celulose; 2003.42.00.001505-0; 2007.72.08.000014-0. On these cases *see* at Chapter IV Section 2.C.V. below.

[774] For the example of Panamanian Indians *see* De Obaldia (2005) 375.

[775] Personal communication with Ana Cristina Bandeira Lins, *Procuradora da República* in the Ministry of the Public (Ministerio Público), which is similar to a public prosecutor or district attorney, on June 23, 2009, in São Paolo, Brazil. *See* also Busch (2010) 220 *seq.* For details on the situation in Brazil, *see* at Chapter IV Section 2. below.

[776] Most of the reported cases are from Australia and Canada. *See* WIPO (2006).

misbehavior appears, this misbehavior is discussed at the communal level and "creates" the case and the rules, sanctions, etc.[777]

D. Examples and Status Quo of Research in Latin America

Examples from Latin America partly can help to shed some light on the topic of customary law on TCEs, and partly, the examples simply confirm this nebulousness in the status quo of the topic.

The following section presents results from research in literature on existing fieldwork experience on customary law, but mainly interviews conducted by the author with representatives and members of different indigenous peoples and of COICA. The topic of the interviews, though varying depending on the interview partner, included conceptions of, or opinions on ownership (below I.), tribal representation (below II.), management of rights and benefits (below III.), registries and databases (below IV.), sanctions, remedies, and exercise of rights (below V.), dispute settlement (below VI.), and obligations (below VII.). The structure chosen here does not reflect the way in which indigenous peoples themselves talked about or displayed their own perceptions and rules, but is directed towards a better understanding, and thus applicability, of customary law.

Especially in the fieldwork, prepared and detailed questionnaires inspired by the ones elaborated by WIPO, appeared to be almost completely useless.[778] Therefore, the collection of examples here can also only be considered a "patchwork," and not a cohesive whole.

Particularly, cases of infringements solved through customary law are difficult to find in Latin American countries, as nearly no documentation on this specific issue exists. More time-intensive anthropological studies would be necessary, while this author's time window for field research was limited to a maximum of 20 days in a country.

I. Ownership and Rights of Use

In the point of view of the indigenous peoples talked to, the conception and content of "ownership" is closely linked to the "right" of use and its content, which is why these conceptions are dealt with jointly. This "does and does not" and "may and may not" by whom and whom not, also includes collective and individual ownerships and rights of use according to Western terms.

---

[777] Personal communication with J.M. of the Asháninka Indians of Peru on June 10, 2008, and with ethnologist Meiser on January 8, 2009.

[778] WIPO questionnaire: *see* Annex to WIPO/GRTKF/IC/7/INF/4. For details on the methods applied, proceedings, and practical experiences *see* the Introduction at Chapter I Section 3. above.

1. According to Wajãpi Indians in Brazil

"Ownership" from the perspective of the Brazilian Wajãpi, indigenous communities living in the western part of the Brazilian State Amapá,[779] implies two aspects:

(1) Everything and also everyone on this earth has an "owner", "the *I'jã*, or the *Janaijã*."[780]
(2) No human person can be the "owner" of their TCEs—the Wajãpi do not even consider themselves the "owners" of their TCEs: "[W]e are not the owners of the *kusiwa* [body] paintings, songs and festivals."[781]

The spiritual background for understanding these two principles is the following[782]:

The owner of everyone and everything, as Arantes tells, is the creator of the things and beings, and the connecting element, the reason why certain rules of behavior and use have to be observed. The chief, Matapi, explained, as Arantes cites[783]: "For example, usually, when someone kills a butterfly – which also has an owner – the person is punished, harmed by the owner. On the other hand, if the Wajãpi use a butterfly as inspiration for a traditional work of bodypainting art, a *kusiwa*, that is, when "we paint with *jenipapo*, we design the butterfly." "The owner becomes happy, nothing happens to the person, because he [the owner] sees that the person is painting and is pleased; ... because the design of the butterfly is truly traditional, it's not for anyone [to make,] ... it's just for us, because this knowledge came just for us [.... W]e learn this knowledge with the owner of the butterfly; he ... gave this knowledge to us and we discovered and practiced it." Therefore, if a non-indigenous person wants to see and to study this knowledge, "we will not authorize it."[784]

Translated into legal language, these are the customary concepts of guardianship and of possession, embracing commitment and punishment in cases of unauthorized appropriation.

According to Arantes, although the Wajãpi do not consider themselves as the "owners", they say, "this intangible knowledge remains for us, because we know and strengthen it until today."[785] Knowledge as a precondition for an authorized use thereby encompasses three aspects:

---

[779] IPHAN – Instituto do Patrimônio Histórico e Artístico Nacional (2008) 11. On the Wajãpi and their TCE *Arte Kusiwa*, *see* also at Chapter IV Section 2.C.III. below.

[780] Arantes (2009 I) 27. According to Arantes, a young Wajãpi Indian translated "*Janaijã*" as "Jesus.", *see ibid.* This way of translation might go back to the missionary influence in Brazil. On the latter *see* at Section 3.B.II.2.a. above.

[781] Arantes (2009 I) 27. The publication is partly based upon the publications from two workshops on "Ia ma'e kõ" (about the "owners") in 2006 and on "I'a" (about doubles and images) in 2008.

[782] *Id.* 26–29.

[783] As Arantes explains, the chief told about these concepts and his grandson further explained these tellings, *Id.* 28.

[784] *Ibid.*

[785] *Id.* 27.

(1) The technical knowledge, which is transmitted among the members of the same families in the local groups,
(2) With understanding of the meanings expressed by the motifs designed and that belong to the *Wajãpi* cosmology, and,
(3) With observance of the prohibitions established, from time immemorial, by the "owners" (*I'jã*) for the Wajãpi ancestors.[786]

Only if these preconditions and interdictions are observed, is the belief in the mystic strength of the *kusiwa* recognized and can be reinforced. Only those persons who observe these rules are regarded as the legitimate practitioners of the *kusiwa*—or "owners" in the Wajãpi sense.[787]

The belief behind the *kusiwa*, which are used as decoration and protection of the bodies, is the following, according to Arantes[788]:

At the beginning, there was nothing. "Within the passage of time," paintings and colours arose in the world. These coloured paintings came "from the belly of the dead *Cobra Grande* [Large Snake]". The animals, the birds and fish, took these colours to "paint themselves." This was the moment in time when "the 'origin' of the Wajãpi participated" and obtained the *kusiwa* paintings of the butterfly, *pacu* fish, *surubim* fish, macaws, monkeys, etc.", also "from the belly of the dead *Cobra Grande*". The animals, the birds and fish, "were like people and spoke a single language," and the Wajãpi "took advantage and learned the songs of birds and other animals and plants" and the *kusiwa* painting. For this reason, the Wajãpi say: "we are not the owners of the *kusiwa* paintings, songs, and festivals; but this intangible knowledge remains for our use, because we know and strengthen it until today."[789]

According to Arantes, with the participation of Brazilian non-indigenous anthropologists, the Wajãpi arrived at a phrase that could be used as a definition of the legal term "owner"—given that the reader knows about the greater socio-cultural and spiritual context of the language, as displayed above. This is: "I jarã omarã kuwa rupi te oinõ momae'ko".

"The owner is the one that makes things with knowledge, on the way to experience."[790]

The external experts having participated in the creation of this phrase and knowing about the discussions in the workshops, Arantes says, even interpret this statement as condensing basic areas of intellectual property law from the emic perspective, concretely: "(1) the moral foundation of ownership, (2) the relationship between ownership and effective practice; (3) commitment to socially codified and signified know-how as the legitimate basis of practice, and (4) experience in a changing context as a field where tradition can creatively meet with innovation."[791]

---

[786] *Id.* 29.

[787] *Ibid.*

[788] *Id.* 26 *et seq.*

[789] *Ibid.*

[790] *Id.* 37.

[791] *Ibid.*

The ownership is understood similarly—as regards the spiritual belief, although not in the concrete terms of use—when photos and film recordings of the TCEs and of the Wajãpi peoples "wearing" the body painting art or expressing other TCEs are made, Arantes tells.[792]

Major difficulties in understanding as well as in maintaining the continuity of the Wajãpi form of "possession" do not (only) lie in the rule of a prior informed consent, but in managing the deeper cultural issues. Such deeper cultural issues include the fact that the form of "possession" depends upon the "continuous and creative practice of this symbolic language as regulated by local custom, which includes the observance of cultural interdictions."[793] This, however, can only be found out in the continuous (oral) communication within the community as well as with outsiders—which again raises the question of whether to codify customary law at all.[794]

2. According to Kuna Indians in Panama

Similarly, there exists an origin and a spiritual background of the most famous TCE of the Kuna Indians in Panama, the textile *mola*. The "original" spiritual background of the *mola* was, in short, the following: *Nana Olonakekiryai*, or *Olonagegiryai*, one of the wise mothers and shamans of the tribe, travelled to a sacred place called *Kalu Dukbis*, or *Galu Dugbis*, where *Kalu* literary means "sacred place" and *Dukbis* "geometric figures," as Valiente López explains.[795] According to him, there, she found multi-colored trees tattooed with beautiful designs never seen before and acquired the knowledge about the aesthetics and geometric drawings of the *mola*. She brought back the art, the designs, and the technique of the *molas* and taught the Kuna women how to sew the *molas*, formerly using cotton and only geometric designs.[796]

Similarly, there exists a spiritual background for collective ownership: *Iberokun*, the "spiritual and ideological guide of the Kuna peoples and the brother of *Nana Olonakekiryai*", is told to have said that *Paba*, the great father or creator, "has not made us to live alone. He created us one needing the others, . . . like the stream the water, like the most resistant and strong tree the tender and moist earth. It is against the *Paba* to hoard everything for oneself. We need to share our little things and big things."[797]

[792] *Ibid.*

[793] *Id.* 38.

[794] On this *see* at Section 5.B.IV.2. above.

[795] Valiente López (2006) 41 *et seq.* with further references.

[796] *Ibid.*

[797] Aiban Wagua "Ibeorkun. El Gran Abuelo" in: "Así Habla Mi Gente," Kuna Yala, Panama (1986) 6, cited from *id.* 39 (2006).

This spiritual origin of both, the *mola*, and the conception of collective ownership, however, was not included in the registry of the "Rules of Use." It is also not the predominant factor for the modes of use in reality anymore. The designs of the *molas*, for example, are rather "inspired" by, or oriented towards, market requests. For example, a Kuna Indian I met creating *molas* in an art gallery in Panama City owned by a Spanish journalist, told me:

> Sometimes, I just create motifs that come to my mind, remembering the plants, animals, and colors of *Kuna Yala* [the land or territory of the Kuna Indians in the northern part of the country, along the Caribbean coast]. Sometimes, we are told to create particular designs, like the palm tree leaf, because they are more wanted by the tourists and Spanish ladies abroad.[798]

As regards the collective ownership, it should be mentioned that individual rights are not unknown, for example, rights of inheritance.[799] Moreover, also traditional ways of sharing situations, and with them, the practice of any customary rules, has partly changed: On a very small Kunan island, where the traditional lifestyle still is followed to a large extend, there is no fishing anymore, visits of tourists and the performance of "traditional dances" for them are organized by one Kuna lady who lives in the capital now, who is married to a non-indigenous man, and whose children have not even learned to speak the native Kuna language anymore.[800] In the cities, especially in the Capital, even more individualistic structures dominate, which directly affect the original concept of a collective ownership e.g. concerning the TCE *mola*.[801]

3. According to Ashа́ninka Indians in Peru

Within the Asháninka community, the traditional structures and allocation of responsibility or trusteeship are not as present now as they were decades ago. In general, the "holder of right" could be either the community or the creators and performers of the TCE in question. In order to make use of the work at the international level that had been done already, and to enhance it where possible, the author included in the interview the questions contained in WIPO's questionnaire, namely, whether the right should contain the exclusive right to give or deny free, prior, and informed consent (PIC) for and to define conditions of fixation in particular, as well as reproduction, publication, adaptation, broadcasting, public performance, communication to the public, distribution, rental, and making available to the public of the traditional cultural expressions. The answer of J.M. of the

---

[798] Personal communication with M.F. of the Kuna Indians in Panama City, February, 2009.

[799] Personal communication with Atencio López Martinez, lawyer and Kuna Indian in Panama City and other members of the Kuna tribe in Kuna Yala, Panama, February, 2009.

[800] Personal observations and communication with various members of the Kuna tribe in Kuna Yala, Panama, February, 2009.

[801] On details hereon *see* the Section on Panama at Chapter IV Sections 1.A. and D.II.3.a. below.

Asháninka was "yes."[802] Obviously, this answer is not representative for the real practice of customary law among the Asháninkas, and the situation perfectly illustrates that Western-shaped and prepared questionnaires might not always be too helpful in finding out about the content of customary law, or might at least require "translation" into the communal, social language.

4. According to COICA

An example of a more generalized concept of customary rules, elevated from the local to a regional level, is that of the common principles and understandings elaborated by COICA, the "Coordinator of the Indigenous Organizations of the Amazon Basin"[803] and probably the biggest and most important Latin American indigenous organization.[804]

This is thus rather a collection or sum of commonalities than the example of one concrete communal customary approach. Nonetheless, it should be remembered that even at a local level, research based upon interviews and communication is only able to reflect individual voices and only very rarely one "common understanding." Contradictions are a very part of the research and the topic as such.[805]

According to official statements of COICA, the ownership differs depending on the type of TCEs and knowledge. If the TCE, like handicrafts, spiritual health, leisure activities, music, dance, painting, attire, or a special celebration,[806] is based upon "collective knowledge," that is, "knowledge to which men and women have had access . . . through the education that the adult generations developed for new generations,"[807] then the owner is the collective.

If the concrete TCE is based upon "ancestral wisdoms," meaning "a type of highly specialized knowledge," which is of high importance and almost secret for most people, then only some members of the communities have access to it, namely "certain wise people of the new generations, which complied with certain personal and social requisites, . . . pre-determined conditions and traits." Due to essential link with the real world and the spiritual one, as demonstrated in details in the section on philosophy,[808] it requires mainly the demonstration of spiritual and physical strength, through ritual ceremonies and difficult tasks. For instance, specialized

[802] Personal communication with J.M. of the Asháninka Indians of Peru on June 10, 2008.

[803] "Coordinadora de las Organizaciones Indígenas de la Cuenca Amazónica".

[804] For further details on the organization *see* at Section 4.C.I. above.

[805] This is due, among other things, to the very nature of the traditional way of dealing with issues that in industrialized Western societies would be legal issues, as illustrated above, *see* at Sections 5.C.II. and A.I.1.(12) above and personal communication with J.M. of the Asháninka Indians of Peru on June 10, 2008, and with ethnologist Meiser on January 8, 2009.

[806] COICA (2005) 58, translation by COICA at http://www.coica.org.ec/ingles/aia_book/index.html.

[807] *Id.*

[808] *See* at Section 4. above.

wisdoms cannot be transmitted to "a person who is not capable of making long-term diets; of going to the forest in absolute solitude to live within it; of taking sacred plants and attaining the vision."[809] Therefore, in the case of this type of TCEs, "owners" or "guardians" can only be these special persons, not any member of the community or the whole community as collective. Accordingly, the right to use, execute, and create such TCEs is limited to certain individuals.

5. General Observations

In general, it is not possible to categorize and characterize rights on TCEs as being solely of a collective nature, or of either an individual or a collective nature. The definition depends to a great extent upon the understanding of each community and varies in relation to each particular TCE, and sometimes even in relation to the particular use of a TCE.

As expressed by COICA as well as in the international literature, there are "key individuals," wisemen, elders, or other persons, who "may bear particular responsibilities with respect to the use and management of certain objects, knowledge or resources." However, "their exercise of authority must be in accordance with the laws and customs of the people they belong to and must meet the interests of the group as a whole."[810]

This, of course, only describes an intact community system, or "customary law on paper." In general, one could say that in practice as well as according to the indigenous perception of their customary law, ownership is based upon a process of internal decision-making, which typically involves the whole community, and gives special weight to the elders of the group and has the overarching aim of respecting and implementing the common will of the group, responding to changing needs and priorities of the group. The functioning of these structures, the respect of these aims, and, finally, the concept of ownership depend for the most part upon the integrity of the social coexistence and the living conditions of each community, thus on whether the social structures are still intact. While formerly, sharing tasks, resources, and goods was part of the common socio-economic way of living, this "custom" is more and more dissolved in favor of individual thinking and the individual allocation and distribution of goods and cultural knowledge and skills.

Similar to the phenomenon of facing and being unified by the "common enemy," there exists a strong feeling within the communities for "our" collective culture in relation to outsiders, non-tribal members, or non-indigenous persons. In concrete, every-day practice, however, this feeling or custom is sacrificed or fading more and more.

This conclusion was also underlined by the Ecuadorian *sábia* or shaman Mama Rosario Pichamba in Quito. She reported that lately there was a lot of discussion

---

[809] *Id.* 58 (2005).

[810] Schillhorn (2000) 25, and Stoll and von Hahn (2008) 18.

between the communities and the shamans, as well as between the shamans themselves, on the mode of conducting cultural and spiritual rituals, especially for or with non-indigenous persons. The different points of view regarding the power to make such decisions as well as remuneration depended very much upon the living environment and degree of integration into the "national" urban life, mainly in the capital.[811]

II. Representation

In practice, representation is probably one of the most dynamic and problematic issues in the area of customary law on TCEs. At the same time, it is probably the most important one for protecting TCEs. In the following section, some examples of customary rules on representation among Latin American indigenous communities will be given, particularly difficult aspects highlighted, and practical experience and important measures indicated.

1. From Local to Global Representation: General Remarks on Organizational Structures of Representation

In the past decades, occidental notions have increasingly "shaped indigenous modes of activism," as well as modes of managing legal interests and rights,[812] as legal forms of representation according to customary law become increasingly relevant to the issue of political representation and vice versa, as Levi and Dean have observed. "Confronted with the need to construct political [or legal] subjects organized in terms of a perceived shared collective identity,"[813] indigenous peoples have established organizational structures other than the traditional, local society of collectives. As Levi and Dean describe it, a tendency "moving from local to global levels of representation" can be noted, for example among the Rarámuri (Tarahumara) Indians of northern Mexico.[814]

A consequence of this higher level of organization is that the "customary rules" on representation are becoming more and more adapted to Western political modes of representation, and transformed into structured, fixed, or even codified regulations. At the same time, "descriptions of 'tradition'" have often been "privileged over the evolving new or hybrid forms" of social action and of legal representation by "homogenizing discourses" in the political hemisphere.[815] This generates

[811] Personal communication with the *sábia* or shaman Mama Rosario Pichamba on March 12, 2009, in Quito, Ecuador.

[812] Levi and Dean (2003) 16.

[813] *Ibid.*

[814] *Id.* 23.

[815] *Id.* 24.

tension between (adapted) realities and (described) traditions, Levi and Dean observed. Precisely these tensions in turn reveal the dilemma inherent in the issue of "traditional" representation in particular and "customary law" in general in the topic of protecting TCEs.

In legal issues like TCEs, the occidental organizational structures at a supra-local level are used to represent the indigenous communities, in order to simplify the identification process for obtaining an authorization or for concluding agreements in issues relating to TCEs, or mostly traditional knowledge so far. In Brazil, for example, the regional organizations are the COIAB and the UNIAC,[816] in Ecuador, the CONAIE:

An example of such national representation according to an "advanced indigenous customary law" is the mode of organizational structures and representation of the CONAIE in Ecuador.

2. "Organized" Representation Within the Ecuadorian CONAIE

The CONAIE is the Confederation of the Indigenous Nationalities of Ecuador.[817] Today, the CONAIE is a "corporation" according to Ecuadorian private law.[818] Its legal structures on representation and organization are laid down in a fixed, complex body of rules. The codified statute ("Estatuto codificado") contains 47 articles, regulating (1) the constitution and aims of the confederation, (2) the members, (3) rights and obligations of the members, (4) the organs of executive bodies and directorate, (5) the goods of the organization, (6) sanctions, and (7) the dissolution.[819]

Three organs are in charge of other forms of representation and the execution of acts:

(1) The congress, as the highest authority, constituting the power of the CONAIE. It consists of 20 delegates from each of the indigenous peoples and nationalities of Ecuador and meets regularly every 3 years.[820]
(2) The council of the indigenous peoples and nationalities, as the organ of planning, evaluation, and control of the council of government of the CONAIE,[821]

[816] "Coordenação das Organizações Indígenas da Amazônia Brasileira" (Coordinator of Indigenous Organizations of the Brazilian Amazon). *See* http://www.coiab.com.br/, last visited January 10, 2010, and "União das Nações Indígenas do Acre e Sudoeste do Amazonas."

[817] "Confederación de Nacionalidades Indígenas del Ecuador".

[818] Article 2 of the Codified Statute.

[819] The author expresses her gratitude to Fausto R. Vargas, Director of Education, Science and Technology of CONAIE, for the valuable personal communication in March, 2009, in Quito, Ecuador, and for generously entrusting the author with very helpful documents, among others the Statute.

[820] Articles 11, 12 of the Codified Statute.

[821] Article 15 of the Codified Statute.

(3) The council of government, as the executive organ of the CONAIE, consisting of a president, a vice-president, and seven other heads ("*dirigentes*").

Legal representation is vested in the President of the CONAIE, who is democratically elected by the Congress of the CONAIE for a period of 3 years. The representation covers legal, judicial, and extra-judicial areas.[822]

Administrative and economic measures and procedures are defined by another regulatory body, the "Administrative and economic regulation of the CONAIE," issued by the Council of government of the CONAIE in accordance with Article 12 lit. a) of the Codified Statute, comprising another 55 provisions, regulating even details such as working conditions of the chauffeur.

From this example it becomes clear that "representation" according to the indigenous peoples' own rules might comprise very different techniques and "customs" at the different levels of action.

3. Partial Adaptations of the "Global" Structures: Representation in FICSHA in Ecuador and Among the Craô Indians in Brazil

The structures presented in the example of the CONAIE at the national level have impacts on those at local levels as well. For example, the Shuar Indians from the Ecuadorian Rainforest region (*El Oriente*) have established an organization that is supposed to politically and legally "represent" all Shuar communities: the FICSHA, the Interprovincial Federation of Shuar and Achuar Centers.[823] Similar to the structure of the CONAIE, the legal representative of the FICSHA is its "president."

A case is reported from the Shuar and Achuar communities, in which the Bavarian Broadcasting Service (Bayerischer Rundfunk) wanted to document the traditional lifestyle and cultural expressions among some of the communities as part of a major film and broadcasting project. The consent of the indigenous peoples was given in a two-step-process: First, the consent or general authorization for the project, defining the framework of its conditions, was given by the major organization FICSHA, under the precondition that the community concerned agreed, too, and then, additionally, each community that was to be filmed, had to additionally express its consent. This consent covered the concrete points of discussion, like what exactly could and should be shown (the indigenous persons had a strong interest in showing their efforts regarding bilingual education, for example), and what kind of remuneration should be paid, and was attained by one vote for each member of the community, except the small children.[824]

This latter aspect of the example underscores the importance given by indigenous persons to an active involvement in decisions and discussions on matters

[822] Articles 25, 26 of the Codified Statute.

[823] Federación Interprovincial de Centros de Shuars y Achuars.

[824] Personal communication with ethnologist Meiser on January 8, 2009.

touching their rights or interests: participation—in contractual negotiations as well as legislative processes[825]—is understood as a *sine qua non*.[826] Moreover, it also highlights the importance of the legitimacy and communal integration of organizational representatives, i.e. their contact with the "basis" by means of oral communication.[827]

A similar method of representation according to more or less adapted customary law can be found among the Craô Indians in Brazil. This group consists of 17 different Craô communities or "villages." According to customary rules, the representation of the Craô in external issues is carried out by the association of all Craô communities, the *Kapey*. One case in the area of traditional knowledge associated with biodiversity is known in which a contract with the Federal University of São Paolo (UNIFESP) and the laboratory Aché was signed, through the representation of the *Viti-Cati*. They were, however, alleged to be entitled to represent only 3 of the 17 Craô communities according to the customary rules, and the rest of the 17 communities claimed the knowledge to be of the collective nature of all Craô Indians. Consequently, the *Kapey* should have been in charge as legitimate representative of all Craô Indians.[828]

This example makes clear that the question of legitimate representation is not only of relevance for contracting parties or other interested outsiders, but very often of great importance for the communities and their members. The invalidity of the contract or authorization as a legal consequence might not always be in the interest of the persons involved—on both sides. An important follow-up question is then that of adequate and effective dispute resolution mechanisms—customary or otherwise.[829]

In Brazil in general, experts argue that the "internal organization of each group" should determine the legitimate representative.[830] This could be "a *cacique*, a *tuxuaua*, a *pajé*," but also "the president of an indigenous association, an indigenous professor, a leader (*liderança*)" or the like.[831]

---

[825] On this aspect in Brazil *see* Busch (2010) 220 *et seq.* and personal communication with Fernanda Kaingang, Indigenous lawyer from the Kaingang tribe on June 23, 2009, in São Paolo, Brazil.

[826] Personal communication with Indian Andrés Andrango, CONDENPE and member of the Advisory Board (*Consejo Consultivo*) of the Indigenous Peoples of the Andean Community, with Humberto Muenala, Ecuadorian Ministry of Culture, and with Patricio Sandoval, Instituto Iberoamericano del Patrimonio Natural y Cultural (IPANC), the Ibero-American Institute for the Natural and Cultural Patrimony, in March 2009 in Quito, Ecuador.

[827] *Ibid.*

[828] *See* Bucher (2008) 246 with further references to C. Bueno Wandscheer ("Patentes & Conhecimento Tradicional", 2004) and others. For the practical settlement of the dispute *see* at Section 5.D.VI. below.

[829] On this *see* also at Section 5.D.VI. below.

[830] Teixeira Coelho (2008) 61, 63.

[831] Baptista and Valle (2004) 23.

4. Representation Among the Kuna Indians in Panama

Not directly adapted from occidental political notions, but indirectly by means of a national legislative recognition of indigenous territorial rights is the following example: The legal representation of Kuna Indians, among other things with regard to their TCE *mola*, mainly corresponds to the legal division and political organization of the indigenous territories in Panama. There are three Kuna Indian territories and one protected area in Panama, the Comarca Kuna Yala, Comarca Kuna de Madungandi, Comarca Kuna de Wargandi, and a territorial part, called *Takarkunyala* in the Kuna language, which is located in the National Park of Darién.[832] Accordingly, the representation of the Kuna peoples in legal issues regarding their TCE *mola* is carried out by the four General Congresses of the Kuna Indians, the Congreso General Kuna or de Kuna Yala, Congreso General Kuna de Madungandi, Congreso General Kuna de Wargandi, and Congreso General Kuna de Takarkunyala.[833]

5. Challenge in Practice: Cohesion, Unification and Legitimacy

As mentioned before, in the topic of TCEs and particularly traditional knowledge so far, the occidental organizational structures at a supra-local level are used in order to simplify the identification process for obtaining an authorization or for concluding agreements.

While practical difficulties in determining the addressee of an authorization request, etc. appear to be decreasing, uncertainties in determining the legitimacy of the alleged representative in the concrete cases remain, as, parallel to the increasing level of abstractness, the risk of diverging political and cultural interests, internal disputes on allocation of power and competence, corruption, and missing links in the local identity grows.

A representation by means of the afore-mentioned intermediary CONAIE was held to be "difficult" in practice, as the current directorate is dominated by representatives of the *Sierra*, the Andean Region, and finds itself in a conflict with a great part of the Amazonian federations.[834] Jealousy also exists between CONAIE and other of the different indigenous organizations in the country, including those representing indigenous women, like FENOCIN and FEINE.[835]

Furthermore, the international intermediary COICA, the "Coordinator of the Indigenous Organizations of the Amazon Basin,"[836] was deemed by external

[832] Valiente López (2006) 38.

[833] Article 6 of the "Rules of Use of the Collective Right 'Mola Kuna Panama;'" on this *see* at Chapter IV Section 1.D.II. below.

[834] Wörrle (2008) 235.

[835] Personal communication with Diana Atemaint, indigenous professor and ex-deputy, in March, 2009, in Quito, Ecuador.

[836] For further details on the organization *see* at Section 4.C.I. above.

experts the "most capable" one for representation and negotiation matters on traditional knowledge of indigenous Amazon peoples. However, at the same time it is said to have suffered "a profound internal division in the last years, which culminated in the establishment of two 'parallel' directive councils, which are making war on each other."[837] The same is said to have happened to the CONFENAIE, the Confederation of the Indigenous Nationalities of the Ecuadorian Amazonia.[838]

The main reason for the organizational fragmentation as well as internal division is probably precisely the fact that these occidentally structured organizations are relatively new, and "diametrically opposed to the 'acephalic' structures of the old social organization."[839] Another great impact in practice is the interaction of external factors, as it is common policy of international oil companies to approach indigenous leaders and individuals and simply "buy" them out of the collective context.[840]

6. Challenge: Gender Inequality

Apart from these conflicts, creating a national or even regional representative network out of disparate local experiences faces other great challenges and contradictions. The latter are "particularly evident in indigenous women's challenges to 'tradition' when it is deployed in ways that constrain their autonomy," for example in the Mexican region of Chiapas, but especially in indigenous Amazonian federations.[841] These federations in Peruvian Amazonia, for example, are led only by men, and the gender inequality produced by thus excluding women from leadership is often justified "by appeal to 'tradition.'"[842] Exactly this fear of "tradition" being "strategically invoked to exclude certain groups while empowering others" was one reason against the application of "customary law" to TCE protection listed at the beginning of this chapter, and must be borne in mind when establishing legal provisions.[843]

Also in Panama, the General Congresses of the Kuna Indians consist only of men—according to "customary law."[844]

---

[837] Wörrle (2008) 234.

[838] *Ibid.*

[839] *Id.* 236.

[840] Ethnologist Philip Gondecki, who is researching conflicts and dispute settlements among indigenous peoples, mainly the Quichua and Huaoraní, in Ecuador, in March, 2009, in Quito, Ecuador.

[841] Levi and Dean (2003) 23.

[842] *Id.* 23 (2003).

[843] On this *see* at Section 5.A.III.1. above and Eisenstadt (no year) 11.

[844] On this *see* at Chapter IV Section 1.D.II. below.

7. Local Particularities: Diverging Customary Rules

At the local level, although a community might appear to have one traditional chief, the representative of one and the same community may vary according to the concrete situation. The form of representation or quantity of representatives may be different from one situation to another, though both involve questions on TCEs, and mostly depends upon the circumstances, object, or subject matter being dealt with. In Brazil, for example, some tribes are represented by only one elder in case of internal topics, while the full participation of three representatives is required in cases of external topics, e.g. negotiations with non-indigenous persons. There is not always just one representative for all issues in question.[845]

8. Challenge: Quick Changes Possible

A second peculiarity of representation norms is that both the individual representative as well as the rules and conditions of representation may change quickly. The first aspect may be illustrated by the fact that among some semi-nomadic tribes in Brazil, a common way for the members of a community to take the current leader out of office is just by moving on and leaving the "former" leader behind.[846] This quick change concerns the individual person of the representative.

Codification of such quick changes or of their concrete preconditions—which sometimes cannot even be concretized by the tribe members themselves—would probably be difficult. As regards the practicality of identifying the actual leader, it can only be mentioned that the possibility of quick changes should be borne in mind.

As regards the second aspect, conflicts over preconditions and the content of representation are notorious, especially at the structural level of authority and its exercise, to be observed e.g. in the *nahua* community Xilocuautla in the municipality of Huauchinango in Mexico with regard to a traditional celebration, *fiesta*, of the community.[847] According to customary law, as Sierra describes it, the principal authority of the community, the auxiliary president, had to fulfill tasks he was in charge of during the *fiesta*, like organizing dancers, providing a meal for the invited guests, and the further organization. One year, however, the president systematically refused to comply with those preconditions, as Sierra tells,—but at the same time saw himself obliged to fulfill his role as authority and was not able to stay apart from the celebration, as he would have liked to.[848] According to Sierra, instead of

[845] Personal communication with Hugo Meireles Heringer and other staff members of FUNAI in March, 2009, in Brasilia.

[846] Personal communication with Hugo Meireles Heringer and other staff members of FUNAI in March 2009 in Brasilia.

[847] Sierra 22, translation by the author.

[848] *See ibid.*

promoting traditional dances that included the members of the community or those of neighboring communities, he preferred to engage a professional dancing group, which performs at the traditional *fiesta* for reasons of money instead of for the reason of fulfilling a promise, as traditionally do the dancing members of the community. Thereby, the principal authority introduced a new practice in the celebrations, and also altered the preconditions of exercising authority according to the customary rules—which, of course, was the subject of great disputes within the community.[849]

9. Challenge in General: Intergenerational Conflicts—New Generations of Leaders

In former times, to be an accepted leader in a community, it was mainly necessary to have knowledge of the spiritual heritage, the ancestry and particularities of the local living environment as an integral part of the whole world, something that might be called "wisdom."

Today, other capacities seem to be more and more important, even at the local level. These are, Hernández and Calcagno say, communication skills in general, access to forums of communication and political and economic participation, knowledge of "Spanish as a second language," higher academic qualifications, access to "means of mass communication and new information technologies," and stimulation by "various forms of consumption through daily contact with the cultural offerings of the cities."[850] These advantages are especially fostered by living in an urban environment, Hernández and Calcagno observed, where access to work opportunities, training, political, and union experiences are more likely to exist. Some of the children of peasant origin who have enjoyed these opportunities are becoming the new generations of indigenous leaders. "They have the behaviours and values of a culture in which one finds both features of an autochthonous cosmovision and a modernizing social point of view that is sometimes expressed in proposals for self-management starting from the recuperation of one's ethnicity."[851]

In all areas of indigenous topics, Latin American scientists have therefore argued that "[t]he level of analysis should be focused on the internal dynamics of the indigenous society, in their communities and leadership."[852] They have observed that "(t)he conflicts between old and new leadership are numerous and make up a split that is comparable to that which the political parties or churches and religious sects have produced exogenously for decades."[853]

---

[849] *See ibid.*

[850] Hernández and Calcagno (no year) 6.

[851] *Id.* 4.

[852] *Ibid.*

[853] *Ibid.*

As a consequence, these conflicts also affect, sometimes even render useless, traditional customary rules on leadership. The irony in this situation is that at the same time, the role of leadership is becoming more and more important, because internal tensions are a critical aspect "for the process of indigenous involvement in the information society"[854] on the one hand, and for their very cultural survival on the other.

Therefore, in Brazil, even distinguished legal experts in the area of TCEs and other indigenous issues have left open the question of representation in publications particularly on indigenous peoples, copyright, and traditional cultures—due to the above-mentioned difficulties.

These legal experts state that there is no uniform answer to the question of who represents the collective. In addition, an answer to "such [a] general" question does "not fall into the ambit of the publication," as it affects the internal mechanisms of representation of each indigenous community, which, as should be noticed, are faced with current transformations in the course of contact with the surrounding society and the introduction of an institutionalistic logic that effects them.[855]

Notwithstanding these challenges in general, some Brazilian experts do also argue in favor of the application of customary law: The "internal organization of each group" should determine the legitimate representative.[856] However, as regards the topic of TCEs, the focus should be on the internal dynamics of the indigenous society, in their communities and leadership, in order to raise awareness of this problem.

10. Practical Problems of Identification and Proof

As the representative could be "a *cacique,* a *tuxuaua*, a *pajé*, the president of an indigenous association, an indigenous professor, a leader (*liderança*),"[857] who should be in charge of selecting and identifying the proper representatives in practice? Brazilian experts on TCE protection have argued that, in practice, the duty to find out who the correct representative is, and possibly even the burden of proving it, should lie upon the interested contracting party: "The answer lies within each collective and should be found out by the person interested in the use of the collective indigenous work of art."[858] Truly, identifying the relevant authorities is not always easy, as there are peoples with an extremely wide distribution and who do not have one person or institution representing the whole collective, or others, although living in a defined space, who are divided into communities or *aldeias*[859]

[854] *Id.* 7 (no year).

[855] Baptista and Valle (2004) 23.

[856] Teixeira Coelho (2008) 63.

[857] Baptista and Valle (2004) 23.

[858] *Id.* 23 (2004).

[859] Indigenous settlements in Brazil.

without even knowing who each other's leaders are. But all these possible situations only show once more that there is no way to set universally applicable rules, as the exceptions would be so numerous that they would invalidate the rules completely.[860]

A way out of these practical problems could be to contact a representative association of the community or peoples, either as a "door opener" or as a legitimate representative. In any case, as entities that have been created especially intermediate in the relations between indigenous communities and the non-indigenous world, "they should necessarily be consulted if they exist."[861] Moreover, as mentioned initially, in practice, various communities have begun to institute associations to manage their rights.[862]

As regards the substantive rules determining the representation, however, customs should be recognized, where existing. Similarly, an administrative regulation established by the Brazilian FUNAI provides for a two-step model that privileges a form of representation according to customary law over representation through legal persons or factual associations.[863]

11. Importance of Customary Representation

Case studies on traditional knowledge in the Andean Region are said to have revealed that the "recovery and revaluation of traditional authorities and their specific forms of organization are the best strategy for protecting traditional knowledge against misuse by third parties."[864] It has even been argued that in none of the analyzed cases a need had been identified for traditional knowledge to be protected or developed by means of intellectual property rights, "which incidentally are completely unknown to indigenous peoples."[865]

Although the author of this study does not regard the area of intellectual property rights as fully unimportant to the topic of protecting TCEs, in practice, this author has observed the functioning and estimation of traditional representation structures to be fundamental, too. In view of the challenges displayed above, recovery and revaluation from inside and outside the communities are an important precondition of such functioning.

[860] Baptista and Valle (2004) 24.

[861] *Id.* 24 (2004).

[862] For the situation in Brazil *see* also Teixeira Coelho (2008) 63.

[863] Article 15 of the administrative decree *Portaria* No. 177 of February 16, 2006, of the FUNAI, the Brazilian National Foundation of the Indian. On the Portaria *see* at Chapter IV Section 2.D.II. below.

[864] *See* de la Cruz I., (2006) 36.

[865] *Ibid.* As mentioned before, this might vary of course, *see* also at Chapter V Section 3. below.

COICA has also expressed as one essential element of protection of indigenous peoples' TCEs "to respect and guarantee their own institutions and organizations, including their original languages."[866]

III. Management of Rights and Benefits

1. Commercial or Non-commercial Value of TCEs?

With regard to the method of economic evaluation of TCEs, the customary understanding in a non assimilated form usually regards a decision of the receiver of the TCE as adequate and fair, similar to the understanding of "consideration" in the common law tradition.

J.M. of the Asháninkas of Peru said that according to the predominant understanding in their community, remuneration should be voluntary, to show estimation and honour of the performance, to save the pride of being indigenous people, and to give incentives to keep the tradition alive, even in a time in which other occupations are more urgent to ensure individual and community survival.

Among the indigenous population in Otavalo, Ecuador, a strong tendency away from "primitive communism" towards a "flourishing capitalism" can be noted: Traditional Otavaleñen textiles formerly have been sold only by the community or village *Quinchuqui*, who has worked as intermediary or seller. In the last 10–20 years, another community or village, Peguchi, has also moved from the simple creation of the textiles to selling them.[867]

Especially as regards the commercial or non-commercial value of rituals and expressions of *sábios*, wisemen, and shamans, divergent opinions exist among Ecuadorian indigenous peoples, as traditionally, these kind of cultural expressions or applications of wisdom were for the good of a human being and not for the exchange of money. Indian Miguel Guatemal, vice-president of CONAIE, said that there has even been a proposal for a law in this area, considering classifications and certifications of the "true" *sábios* according to customary law, made by CONAIE, as the problem of "false" *sábios,* who simply sell their "services" to tourists, is huge.[868] Besides an increasing mentality in which a monetary benefit is expected as an imperative exchange, the greatest concern still is their presentation by third parties and perception of their outwardly appearance and image, for example among the Shuar and Achuar peoples.[869]

---

[866] COICA (2005) 62, translation by COICA at http://www.coica.org.ec/ingles/aia_book/index.html.

[867] Personal communication with Indian Humberto Muenala, Ecuadorian Ministry of Culture, and with Patricio Sandoval, Instituto Iberoamericano del Patrimonio Natural y Cultural (IPANC), the Ibero-American Institute for the Natural and Cultural Patrimony, in March, 2009, in Quito, Ecuador.

[868] Personal communication with Indian Miguel Guatemal, vice-president of the CONAIE, in March, 2009, in Quito, Ecuador.

[869] Personal communication with ethnologist Meiser on January 8, 2009.

2. Distribution of Benefits

As regards the distribution of goods and/or remuneration, there exist various models of customary rules. Mostly, the "income" of whatever kind is either shared equally or stays with the individual person and his or her family.

Among the Kuna Indians in Panama, the original understanding of the allocation of goods followed the words of their spiritual father, saying that "[i]t is against the *Paba* to hoard everything for oneself. We need to share our little things and our big things"—as mentioned before.[870] As regards TCEs in particular, the indigenous peoples in Panama have even managed to include their customary understanding of sharing benefits, even between the different communities or peoples in the case of TCEs stemming from more than one community, into the legislative sui generis regime.[871] Whether this corresponds to the customary law in practice will be examined further below.[872]

The Gavião Parkatejê Indians living in the Brazilian Amazon State *Pará* in former times went hunting and collecting the harvest jointly, and shared their yields equally, Kayser argues.[873] This "rule" has been adapted to the current times regarding other "common" goods; as regards their crops, which the members of the community need for their daily sustenance, but also the remuneration for the part they sell, the benefit is shared equally by the members of the *Gavião*.[874]

Similar observations have been made among the Shuar and Achuar communities in Ecuador. However, in recent years, alongside the increasing interaction of the national and international economic system and lack of local natural resources, a more and more individualistic perception of the allocation of goods and benefits has taken place.[875]

J.M. of the Asháninkas of Peru could not indicate a general "custom," either. She said that especially in the case of TCEs, the beneficiaries should either be identified pursuant to the indigenous perspective, or pursuant to the wish of the donator. In the first option, depending upon the particular TCEs, this could be either the community as a whole, or, a group within the community (e.g. women who produce the TCEs) or, in very rare cases, an individual person. On the other hand, due to the underlying principle of reciprocity and free donation, it should be divided and determined according to the wish of the donator. If no assignation to a specified use of the donation is made, beneficiaries should be partly the performer, partly the community.[876]

---

[870] Aiban Wagua "Ibeorkun. El Gran Abuelo" in: "Así Habla Mi Gente", Kuna Yala, Panama, 6 (1986) cited from Valiente López (2006) 39.

[871] Article 5 *Parágrafo* of the Decree No. 12 of 2001; on this *see* at Section 1.D.II. below.

[872] On this *see* at Section 1 above.

[873] Kayser (2005) 103.

[874] *Ibid.*

[875] Personal communication with ethnologist Anna Meiser on January 8, 2009.

[876] Personal communication with J.M. of the Asháninka Indians of Peru on June 10, 2008.

As regards the technical method of distribution of the benefits and management of rights, usually the traditional authorities or representing organizations are regarded as the ones to be in charge of this task. This is the case among the Panamanian Kuna Indians, who entitle the General Congresses to do so, according to the customary law—on paper.[877] Most of the Shuar and Achuar peoples in Ecuador would probably also agree to a management of rights and distribution of benefits by the extended families or communities that have been created for the assertion of territorial requests on land rights, or, subsidiary, through FICSHA.[878] Nonetheless, as mentioned above, mistrust and concerns regarding the functionality of the high-level structures and integrity of the "functionaries" exist. Besides, due to the former family structures, there is still the desire to have a wide autonomy and to be involved in decision-making and distribution processes. Transparency within such processes would be elemental.[879]

J.M. of the Asháninkas in Peru said that in her community, despite the arising egoism outlined above, there is still confidence that the indigenous organizations would take care of fair distribution of the fees. The coordination should therefore be laid in their hands rather than done with the involvement of governmental institutions.[880]

IV. Registries and Databases

Of course, there are no registries or databases according to customary law. Nonetheless, in the view of the development of sui generis protections of TCEs, the question of registering expressions, knowledge, or even customary rules is discussed intensively. Therefore it is of interest to gain an impression of indigenous points of view, possibly indicating an adaptation or further development of their customary rules—or just to evaluate such a solution at the national level.

In Panama, indigenous peoples themselves, as consultants and drafters of the sui generis regime, included a registry for the TCEs and the customary rules governing the TCEs. The reason for that, however, was not the indigenous custom, but the fact that the drafters of the law, mostly indigenous peoples, believed that official registration was necessary for effective rights enforcement against non-indigenous peoples.[881]

---

[877] Articles 7 and 6 of the "Rules of Use of the Collective Right 'Mola Kuna Panama.'" For details hereon and on practical experiences *see* at Section 1.D.II. *et seq.* below.

[878] Personal communication with ethnologist Anna Meiser on January 8, 2009.

[879] Personal communication with ethnologist Anna Meiser on January 8, 2009.

[880] Personal communication with J.M. of the Asháninka Indians of Peru on June 10, 2008.

[881] Personal communication with Aresio Valiente, indigenous lawyer and one of the consultants of the deputies, on February 11, 2009, in Panama City. On details of the registration system and practical experiences *see* at Chapter IV Section 1.C.VI. *et. seq.* below.

J.M. of the Asháninka Indians in Peru expressed concern over the establishment of a registry, arguing that it would complicate the enforcement of rights too much. "Keep things simple," she said. Learning to understand and speak Spanish is already challenging for most of the members of the community, to read and write it even more so, particularly for a person coming from an oral background. Besides, a registry would probably be established in a public entity located in Peru's capital Lima, which would be too far away and too expensive to communicate and interact with.[882]

If registries or databases are used, databases must neither freeze the status quo and hinder new developments nor serve as a definition of "indigenous culture" and thus be legally understood as an exhaustive enumeration or inventory. This view dominated among the Shuar and Achuar Indians, where strong influences of Catholic rituals are mixed with other spiritualities, evolving from day to day. Whoever wishes to protect a culture must not disregard one essential part of the culture's nature, which is its steadily ongoing further development. New interpretation of old elements, creativity, and openness towards new elements are part of any culture, even one based on traditions, as the traditions are "only" the basis.[883]

V. Sanctions, Remedies, and Exercise of Rights

In one orally reported case from the Shuar and Achuar Indians in the Ecuadorian Rainforest, a *tsantsa*, a shrunken head, was stolen. The *tsantsa* represents material and immaterial cultural tradition, as it embodies certain spiritual beliefs of those indigenous communities. The theft was regarded as a major infringement of the material and immaterial good. Sanctions were the expulsion from the communal territory, which is equivalent to social exclusion, a fine, because the thieves had earned money by selling the *tsantsas,* the duty to reveal to whom the *tsantsas* were sold, and, the most important legal consequence from the perspective of the Shuars and Achuars, the duty to return the *tsantsa.*[884]

The Asháninka in Peru, in interviews on the subject, regarded the (immediate) expulsion of the infringer from the indigenous land as the most important sanction to serious infringements, for example in a case in which a non-indigenous person disregards the necessary distance and respect to indigenous women performing traditional dances—at least in their rural area. In cases of grievous infringements, it could also entail the refusal of access to land of other communities. In less serious

[882] Personal communication with J.M. of the Asháninka Indians of Peru on June 10, 2008.

[883] Personal communication with A.M. on January 8, 2009.

[884] Personal communication with A.M. on January 8, 2009. In contrast, as mentioned before, leaders of the Navajo Indians believe that by means of misappropriation, the cultural property become linked to evil spirits and therefore it is not in Navajo interest to have such cultural property back, *see* Moran (1998) 111 note 456.

cases, another important form of making amends is the personal apology in front of the woman concerned or even the whole community.[885]

Besides, other forms of sanctions were also held adequate, for example penalizing the infringer physically, e.g. with big spines ("*chalancas, espinas grandes*") as a means of castigation.[886] In light of the Western perception of respect for human physical integrity, tort law, and the punitive monopoly of the national state,[887] these customary practices appear questionable. Aside from the question of the scope of application of customary law which is limited according to elementary principles of national and international law, and which could be resolved within the framework of conflict-of-laws rules, this fieldwork reveals the necessity of implementing mediation procedures or other alternative dispute resolution in practice.

VI. Dispute Settlement

The statement made in international literature that "[a]n indigenous person is born into a group and becomes inseparable from it, the group forming an integral part of the identity of its members,"[888] might not be true for all current situations on the ground. Especially as a consequence of migration into the cities, but also simply as a consequence of integration into the public school system, learning Spanish or Portuguese as a second—or sometimes first—language, the individual indigenous people are becoming less and less "inseparable" from their place and community of birth. Similarly, their "identity" becomes rather a challenge than a naturally given fact,[889] as do communal communication, interaction, augmentation of conflicts, and, finally, dispute settlement.

Although traditional socio-cultural patterns and ways of dispute settlement are dissolving, the acceptance of public courts is increasing only slowly, particularly in TCE matters. *No* indigenous person talked to or communities researched here, be it in Panama, Ecuador, Peru, or Brazil, indicated that in TCE matters disputes were usually settled by means of the public court system. While in questions on land rights, the use of this system is increasing, this is not yet the case when internal conflicts on traditional culture are concerned. Contrary to the state system, dispute settlement among most of the still functioning indigenous communities is a form of communication or direct enforcement of interest, penalties, or the like, rather than a

---

[885] Personal communication with J.M. of the Asháninka Indians of Peru on June 10, 2008.

[886] Personal communication with J.M. of the Asháninka Indians of Peru on June 10, 2008.

[887] "Bestrafungsmonopol" or "Strafmonopol des Staates" and "Staatliches Gewaltmonopol" are essential principles in German criminal law that are based on the German Constitution, mainly Article 92, and prohibit punitive sanctions in Civil Law. The concrete content and scope of application of this principle are disputed, though. *See* Federal Constitutional Court, decision of January 14, 2004; BVerfGE 110,1,14, and Alexander (2010) 108.

[888] Stoll and von Hahn (2008) 18.

[889] On these aspects of "identity," and their role as a crucial precondition for obtaining and maintaining rights, *see* at Section 1.B.II.1. above.

decision upon substantive rules issued by an authority. More so than in a state system, "disputes are social processes embedded in social relations," and the "dimension of time is the essence of process,"[890] as the internal structures are horizontal and multi-relational. Although among the Kuna Indians in Panama, the General Congresses are increasingly taking over such a decisive role,[891] the situation is still in transition; the acceptance and practical implementation regarding disputes on TCEs will be examined further below.[892]

Among most of the Asháninkas in Peru, the Shuar and Achuar Indians in Ecuador, and also the Kuna Indians in Panama, the once-common custom of using physical force or even arms to "settle" or decide a dispute, even on rights or interests regarding TCEs, still exists.[893]

Usually, however, as regards conflicts in the local environment on TCEs and other issues, the whole community, the *Ahuta*, comes together and discusses until there is nothing left to discuss (which shows again that the dimension of time is the essence of process), and finally decides—among the Shuar and Achuar Indians for example—by one vote per each member of the community, with the exception of the small children—similar to the process of authorization or giving consent to the use of a TCE.[894]

This form of "alternative dispute resolution" is also used in cases involving more than one community, as regards the use and registration of a particular TCE, the Kuna hammock in Panama, for example—while in former times, armed "solutions" of such conflicts between different communities would have been more likely.

In the *tsantsa* case among the Shuar and Achuar Indians in the Ecuadorian Rainforest, the "process" was carried out involving the *jefes*, that means the chiefs of the formal, inter-communal organizations, as well as the members of all communities in local decision-making processes, as there exists a great culture of oral negotiation.[895]

Greater difficulties exist in inter-ethnic conflicts, as still regards most of the indigenous tribes in Ecuador. The most common way of settling disputes, for example between the Quichua and Huaraní Indians, but also elsewhere, is the physical use of the *machete*, the bush knife.[896] One reported inter-ethnic conflict

[890] Nader and Todd, Jr. (1978) 16, 24. For the different functions and cultural understandings of time in the disputing process *see id.* 24 *et seq.*

[891] *See* also Article 20 of the customary "Rules of Use of the Collective Right 'Mola Kuna Panama'" and below Chapter IV Section 1.D.II below.

[892] On this *see* at Chapter IV Sections 1.D.II.3.a.; E.II. and H.III. below.

[893] Personal communication with J.M. of the *Asháninka* Indians of Peru on June 10, 2008. On this *see* also above, personal communication with ethnologist Anna Meiser on January 8, 2009, who anthropological research in these communities in Ecuador since 2003, and on the situation of the Kuna, *see* De Obaldia (2005) 374 *seq.*

[894] Personal communication with A.M. on January 8, 2009.

[895] Personal communication with A.M. on January 8, 2009.

[896] Personal communication with Indian Miguel Guatemal, vice-president of the CONAIE, in March 2009 in Quito, Ecuador and ethnologist Philip Gondecki, who is researching conflicts and dispute settlements among *Quichua* and *Huaorani* Indians in Ecuador, in March 2009 in Quito, Ecuador.

even regarded a TCE: the *corona*, crown, of the Achuar Indians, which is a piece of jewelry, and at the same time represents the traditional Achuar leadership of the person wearing it. After the joint organization FICSHA was founded, the representative of the FICSHA, a Shuar Indian, used the *corona* to present himself as a being a good Achuar leader, too. However, the Achuar people interpreted this as a mis-use of the *corona*, as this person was a Shuar and not an Achuar leader and therefore not regarded as entitled to wear the *corona*.[897] This example reveals again aforementioned difficulties existing at higher levels of representation and organization of indigenous peoples due to their former family or tribal structures.

In the particular dispute of the Kunas over the hammock, the Department of Collective Rights and Folkloric Expressions within DIGERPI in Panama has been involved as a mediator.[898] Also, in disputes among Brazilian Indians, as regards questions of representation, authorization of use of TCEs, and other topics, administrative public entities—like the FUNAI[899] and the Ministry of the Public—and NGOs—like the Catholic CIMI in Brazil—are more and more often requested by the Indians to assist in settling disputes, especially when the dispute involves non indigenous persons as contracting or infringing parties.[900]

To illustrate this situation, one reported case should be described that concerned the dispute about the correct customary representation in a case on traditional knowledge among the Craô Indians in Brazil and has been mentioned before. The Craô consist of 17 different communities, or "villages," and according to customary rules, their representation in external issues takes place via the association of all Craô communities, the Kapey. According to Bucher,[901] a contract between these communities and the Federal University of São Paolo (*UNIFESP*) and the laboratory Aché was signed by the representation of the Viti-Cati, who were, however, alleged to be entitled to represent only 3 of the 17 Craô communities according to the customary rules. The other 14 communities claimed the knowledge involved to be the collective possession of all Craô Indians, meaning that the Kapey should have been in charge as the legitimate representative of all Craô Indians. This dispute, among the Craô themselves as well as between them and the non-indigenous third parties, was settled by means of a meeting of all persons involved in March, 2003. At this meeting, staff members of FUNAI[902] and the Ministry of the Public also participated, carrying out mediation functions.[903]

[897] Personal communication with ethnologist Anna Meiser on January 8, 2009.

[898] On details hereon *see* at Chapter IV Section 1.C.III.2.b.cc. below.

[899] *Fundação Nacional do Índio*, which is part of the Brazilian Ministry of Justice. *See* http://www.funai.gov.br/, last visited December 5, 2010, and for further details at Chapter IV Sections 2.A.I. and B.II. below.

[900] Busch (2010) 220 *seq.* and personal communication with Hugo Meireles Heringer and other staff members of FUNAI in March 2009 in Brasilia, and with Ana Cristina Bandeira Lins, *Procuradora da República* in the Ministry of the Public, on June 23, 2009 in São Paolo, Brazil.

[901] *See* Bucher (2008) 246 with further references.

[902] *Fundação Nacional do Índio*, for details *see* at Chapter IV Sections 2.A. and B.II. below.

[903] *See* Bucher (2008) 246 with further references to C. Bueno Wandscheer ("Patentes & Conhecimento Tradicional", 2004) and others. For the practical settlement of the dispute *see* at Section 5.E.II.3.d. below.

VII. Customary Rights: And Obligations?

Similar to the principle of reciprocity in sociology,[904] there exists a principle of reciprocity in law. According to this principle in the Western legal cultures, rights always also relate to duties, or, in other words: there are no rights without duties.[905]

In view of this principle, the following question arises: If specific rights were granted on TCEs according to customary law, would there also be—according to customary law—any kind of duties? In other words, as the principle of reciprocity generally constitutes an important principle among most indigenous communities as well,[906] does it also apply to the question of rights and duties on TCEs?

"In traditional societies," international authors have argued, "property ... (r) ights of use associated with this custodianship [as ownership] entail obligations. Failure to fulfil these obligations can lead to the loss of custodianship and a commensurate loss of access to the knowledge or resources concerned."[907] Is this confirmed by the results of the fieldwork in Latin America?

Among the Asháninkas of Peru it was felt that there was no obligation or responsibility to exercise traditional cultural practices.[908]

Among the Ecuadorian Shuar and Achuar Indians, the picture recorded was similar. The view dominated that there were only rights, no obligations, because: First, according to "customary law," the members of an indigenous community do not have any obligation or responsibility to keep the tradition alive, even if a member has received special training, e.g. as a dancer or a shaman, from one of the other community members. Second, one should leave space for the further development of the communities' culture, including new elements and the intercultural exchange that inevitably takes place, now more than ever, due to advanced mobility (the construction of many new (small) airports even in the Amazon, children much more often going to bigger schools or universities in the cities) and technological advancement, like the internet.[909] According to other voices in the community, there is or could be a responsibility, but there are still no means of enforcing it.[910]

---

904 The main " founders" of the principle of reciprocity in the early stage of the science of sociology were Georg Simmel, Richard Thurnwald, and Ferdinand Tönnies. On a comparative overview over their approaches *see* Adloff and Mau (2005) 21 *et seq.*

905 "Reziprozität von Rechten und Pflichten" in German Law, which corresponds to Alvin Gouldner's understanding of reciprocity, according to which a right of ego implies a duty of ego, or, in other words, that each party has rights *and* duties (in contrast to the concept of complementarity or the principle of *do-ut-des* in law): Gouldner (1960) 161–178.

906 *See, e.g.,* de la Cruz I. (2006) 26 *seq.*

907 Lettington and Manek (2001) 24.4.

908 Personal communication with J.M. of the *Asháninka* Indians of Peru on June 10, 2008.

909 Personal communication with ethnologist Anna Meiser on January 8, 2009.

910 Personal communication with ethnologist Anna Meiser on January 8, 2009.

By the way, this latter idea is in accordance with the principles of the rules on enforcement in German law, according to which personal duties cannot be enforced directly.[911]

E. Technical Ways of Applying Customary Law and Limits to Its Application

How can such customary rules then be applied from a technical legal perspective, and how can they be integrated into a legal protection of TCEs?

Similar to Lowies' initially cited observations of 1927,[912] more than 80 years later, the particular questions of whether at all, and if so, how to integrate indigenous customary law into a modern system of protecting TCEs still remain unsolved.

Yet, Latin American anthropologists criticize the legal terms describing possible ways of application like "exclusive or concurrent recognition" of customary law, or "their incorporation by reference or replication," as falsely implying that customary law consists of a set of legal categories and norms, a corpus similar to positive law.[913]

International legal experts observe that "relatively little attention has been given to the question of what legal mechanisms would be used to recognize and apply customary law" in the area of TCEs and traditional knowledge—not only in Latin America, but even at the international level.[914]

Especially in the area of TCEs, customary law appears as a quite new element, while in other, more general disciplines in the Americas—at least in North America—tribal law has been the subject of investigations for a long time already. Thus, in the view of the little experience with the recognition of customary law within a legal protection of TCEs, it might be helpful additionally to consider the treatment of customary law in other legal areas. This is also the recommendation made by the Intergovernmental Committee on Intellectual Property, Genetic Resources, Traditional Knowledge and Folklore at WIPO.[915]

Latin American countries can provide interesting examples in this regard, such as Venezuela. Moreover, on the continent, a growing interest in, discussion on and finally acknowledgement of customary law can be noted, which is, however, still at the very beginning—among other things, because of political concerns.

---

[911] Section 888 of the German Code of Civil Procedure, according to which the execution of a court order can only be enforced by means of a "Zwangsgeld" (fine) or "Zwangshaft" (coercive detention).

[912] On the "pigeonhole problem" *see* at Section 5.A.II.(1) above.

[913] Carneiro da Cunha (1990) 300, translation by the author.

[914] Taubman and Leistner (2008) 89. An example of such treatment of the issue is Cooter and Fikentscher (1998) 314.

[915] WIPO (2006).

As an inverse perspective on the application of customary law, the limits to such application will also be addressed.

I. Suggestions on Legal Mechanisms for Recognizing and Limiting the Application of Customary Law

1. Legal Mechanisms for Recognizing Customary Law

At the international level, several suggestions for such legal mechanisms have been made so far. Within the specific question of recognizing customary law in the area of TCEs, these are mainly the following ones, as stated by WIPO:

(1) Recognition as directly applicable law
(2) Recognition as a source of law
(3) Recognition as the factual background for interpreting and applying laws
(4) Constitutional recognition
(5) Statutory recognition
(6) Functional recognition
(7) Administrative recognition.[916]

A crucial element is the application of customary law to outsiders, either non-indigenous persons or those not residing in the indigenous territory. In this dimension, especially

(1) Conflict-of-laws rules are discussed, as well as the
(2) recognition of judgements issued by tribal courts, further the
(3) legal reference to customary law for specific issues, and, finally,
(4) the integration of customary law into the factual matrix of a case as happened in the famous Australian case *Bulun Bulun*.[917]

The option of applying conflict-of-laws rules was favored in combination with national tort law ("Deliktsrecht"), with parallel protection by means of intellectual property law.[918] This technical method has been proposed not only for the application of customary law, but as a means of providing for a solution to the question of appropriately protecting TCEs in general. Therefore, the main arguments supporting this approach were,

- First, no need of an international treaty or convention for the protection of TCEs at the international level;

[916] *Id.*, last visited March 15, 2010.

[917] *Bulun Bulun v R & T Textiles Pty Ltd.* (1998) 41 IPR 513. On the relevance of customary law *see* Janke (2002).

[918] Fikentscher (2005) 18.

- Second,—at least in theory—an easier handling of corresponding conflict-of-laws rules, as the applicable law is generally that of the *lex loci delicti commissi*, "the place of the wrong" or "the place where the offense was committed"[919];
- And third, a better consideration of the *emic* perspective through its culture-specific approach.[920]

Other legal scholars have in theory argued in favor of the mechanism of reference: "the best way of taking into account such customary law is the legal technique of reference."[921] Such references to customary law could be included in both, an international agreement (for the international application of customary law) as well as national legislations (for the application of customary law within the national legal system). Although it has to be admitted that there are disadvantages, in particular little legal certainty, "especially for outsiders who wish to use expressions of folklore," the advantages have been deemed to outweigh the disadvantages: The technique of reference would give "a certain flexibility" to the rules and honor "the dynamic nature of customary law."[922]

No common point of view has been developed or even agreed upon so far. This is due for one thing to the diverse situations in the various countries. Before having a look at the situation in Latin America, the second point limiting customary law will be called to mind.

2. Legal Mechanisms for Setting Necessary Limits to Customary Law

At the very beginning of this chapter, potential conflicts with other legal principles were mentioned as arguments against the very application of customary law. Considering this point, limits to the recognition of customary rules might be necessary, namely to avoid such conflicts with indispensable national regulations (*ius cogens*)[923] and principles or conventions of international standard, e.g. established by human rights, but also to avoid conflicts with concrete principles of intellectual property law.

In general, legal mechanisms for defining and implementing such limits are familiar from the principles of private international law or conflict-of-laws rules. These are mainly

(i) an explicit special *ordre public*, or "public policy," and

[919] *Id.* 6. A differentiation in some legal orders would still have to be made between the place of the tort and the place where the damaging result occurred.

[920] *Id.* 7.

[921] von Lewinski (2007) 220.

[922] *Ibid.*

[923] The *ius cogens* ("imperative law" or peremptory law) comprises such provisions, norms or principles in national or international law which are regarded as indispensable. On this *see* also Kropholler (2006) 245.

(ii) the indispensable principles of a national legislative system as a general *ordre public*.[924]

Codified examples of such an *ordre public* can be found in the Rome I Regulation, for instance.[925] Examples in the area of traditional knowledge or TCEs of a conflict with indispensable principles could be an indefinite protection of innovations, or "very unusual legal consequences" like communal social work in the case of an infringement of TCEs.[926]

In private international law, these principles apply in the relationship between the substantive law to be applied to the case (*lex causae*) and the law of the forum (*lex fori*). Subject to any explicit provisions at the national level, the idea of these principles could also be utilized for conflicts between customary law and the national law in an analogous mode, as the situation of conflict of "laws" is comparable to that in private international law.

Notwithstanding, in international private law, the precondition for the ordre public to apply is the one of sufficient connection to the country of the *lex fori*. This prerequisite does not seem to be an appropriate criterium for the situation of substantially conflicting customary law and national law.[927] A better criterium seems to be the international human rights standard, as they could be also the basis for an internationally homogen system of protection. As a consequence, national *ius cogens* should derogate customary law each time international human rights standards would be substantially violated by the customary law concerned.

II. Ways of Recognizing and Limiting the Application of Customary Law in Latin America

1. Historical Observations

In the time of colonization of Latin America, the very beginning of the question of how to define the relationship between indigenous customary or tribal law and "national law", the conquerors followed different approaches in the various parts of Latin America, although the main perception was the same, namely a general disregard of tribal law as regular "law."

The main difference in the legal treatment in general existed between the Spanish sovereignty (Western half of the "new world") and the Portuguese one (Eastern part of the "new world").[928] In the Spanish-reigned part, the Spanish

---

[924] *Id.* 244 *seq.* (2006).

[925] *See. e.g.* Art. 21 Rome-I Regulation (EC No. 593/2008), see also Art. 12 Rome-III Convention (EC No. 1259/2010).

[926] *See* Fikentscher (2005) 13.

[927] The author thanks Josef Drexl, who has made this important comment.

[928] The "distribution" of the continent was regulated by the Papal Bull *Inter ceterae* of 1493, the Treaty of Tordesillas of 1494, and the Treaty of Zaragoza of 1529. *See, e.g.*, http://www.uni-muenster.de/FNZ-Online/expansion/europ_expansion/unterpunkte/entdeckung.htm, last visited June 1, 2010.

monarchy, acting as a "supreme mediating institution," followed the reality of two distinct societies existing in the colonies, the Spanish and the "Indian," or indigenous, one, and introduced a separate system of laws.[929] That was the case in Guatemala, for example. The concept was the one "of the two Republics" and was implemented by a legal construction called the *encomienda* system.[930] In its beginnings, the *encomienda* system was intended to give the colonizers easy access to Indian taxes and labor.[931] Later, as a Spanish reaction to the growing power of the colonial great landowners, the *encomenderos*, the Spanish monarchy established a system of special indigenous rights (and duties), including special communities, jurisdictions, taxes, and services in favor of the Spanish settlers.[932] In Mexico, those constructions of collective land rights were the *ejidos*,[933] in Colombia, the *resguardos*—and these regulations are still in force.[934] Indigenous or tribal law was included in so far as legitimacy was given to the authority of traditional leaders by the introduction of so-called *cabildos*, a particular form of administration in which councils of the elders were given authority to exercise their own indigenous rights.[935]

This official (limited) acknowledgement of traditional authorities, jurisdiction, and rights, however, has been criticized as a special status that was *imposed* on the indigenous population by the dominant Spanish colonizers, and thus as being a rather paternalistic approach toward the indigenous population.[936]

Nonetheless, according to Torres, in certain periods of the colonial era, there existed forms of indigenous autonomy regarding among other things customs and

[929] Torres (1991) 131.

[930] Ibid. The *encomienda* was introduced by the first royal governor of Hispaniola, Nicolás de Ovando. *See* Elliot (1984) 163.

[931] *Ibid.* According to Elliot, as a consideration, the landowners had to provide the Indians with sufficient foodstuffs and ensure their assimilation to the Spanish culture and the Christian faith, *ibid.*

[932] For further references *see* Bucher (2008) 63 note 218.

[933] Article 27 of the 1917 Constitution of Mexico, http://www.diputados.gob.mx/LeyesBiblio/ref/dof/CPEUM_orig_05feb1917_ima.pdf, although no specific reference to the indigenous population was made. *See also* Article 231 of the Brazilian Constitution, which even recognizes land rights of the indigenous population as being natural "original rights to the lands they traditionally occupy." Because of this natural collective character, even the division of communal land is constitutionally prohibited, *see* Article 231(4) of the Brazilian Constitution. Bolivia, Colombia, Ecuador, and Venezuela also recognize this character of the lands of the indigenous peoples and communities. In Peru, a regressive process took place, where the Constitution of 1993 eliminated the "indefeasible and inalienable" character of indigenous territories. *See* COICA (2005) 31 note 15, translation by COICA at http://www.coica.org.ec/ingles/aia_book/index.html.

[934] *See* the Colombian Law No. 89/1890, and Semper (2008) 142.

[935] This form of indigenous administration is now recognized as special indigenous jurisdiction (*JEI, Jurisdicción Especial Indígena*) by Article 246 of the 1991 Colombian Constitution; on this *see* also at Chapter III Section 3.A.II. below and *id.* 142, 149.

[936] Grote (1999) 597, 501.

customary rules, either intentionally, established by law,[937] or, in some cases, even unintentionally—as in the case of the Miskito Indians in Nicaragua.[938]

2. Situation of TCEs Today

Today, there exist various levels of recognition of indigenous customary law in Latin America. In the majority of the cases, it is a rather formal recognition at the constitutional level.[939]

On the protection of TCEs in particular, there exist only few examples:

a. Application of Customary Law by Means of Reference and Registry

The application of customary law by means of a registry is mostly enabled in combination with a statutory reference. Then, to be precise, the registry is a precondition for the application provided for by the statute. One example of a sui generis system referring to customary law involving a registry is the Panamanian Special Intellectual Property Regime Governing the Collective Rights of Indigenous Peoples for the Protection and Defence of their Cultural Identity and Traditional Knowledge.[940] It integrates "customary rules" by means of Article 15, stipulating that "the rights of use and commercialization of [TCEs] must be governed by the regulation of each indigenous community, approved and registered in DIGERPI" (the administrative entity within the Ministry of Commerce and Industries in charge of registering patents, trademarks, and designs). This article has been rated "the core" and "most interesting part of the legislation."[941] It gives

[937] As mentioned at the beginning of this section, this was the case in Guatemala. There, the colonial power Spain created a *República de los Indios*, as Torres explains, "a communal village or region where indigenous peoples could live and follow many of their cultural traditions while remaining under the Crown's jurisdiction." Due to this dual-republic system, the Guatemalan Indians were able to preserve their cultural heritage and they currently form a majority of that state's population. As mentioned before, ironically, they are currently facing more aggravated problems than other indigenous minorities, due to, first, "their inability to articulate their needs effectively as a group because they are numerous and scattered throughout the country," and second, the fact that "the uniqueness of the Indians' situation is obscured even though their needs have a different context and require different policies", because "many of these problems – lack of education, unemployment, absence of adequate housing – are shared by all inhabitants of the country." Torres (1991) 130, 131 note 20.

[938] As also stated initially, the Miskito Indians were never conquered by the Spanish, but continued living in a state of *de facto* autonomy, which was then acknowledged as *de jure* by the Treaty of Managua in 1860. Therefore, the Miskitos were able to preserve their traditions, until the Sandinista attempted to incorporate them into Nicaragua's social and economic life in 1979, *see id.* 127, 131, 132 (1991).

[939] *See* at Chapter III Section 3.A. below.

[940] Law No. 20 of June 26, 2000 and its Executive Decree No. 12 of 2001, *see* at Chapter IV Section 1.B. *et seq.* below.

[941] Lucas-Schlötter (2008) 411.

binding effect to the customary law, which defines the means of use of the TCEs, provided that this law is written down, "approved" and registered, and thus made public.

This solution—on paper—is internationally rated an "original one."[942] Whether and how it works in practice will be subject to a detailed examination and analysis below.[943]

b. Application of Customary Law by Means of Collective Land Rights

In Venezuela, the application of customary law in areas that include issues of TCEs is technically enabled through collective territorial rights as traverse, bridging, or connecting rights. By means of land rights, the applicability of other indigenous rights concerning indigenous cultural heritage and knowledge including customary law is achieved.[944] In particular, the recognition of territorial rights constitutes the sphere of application and practice of customary law—also in the field of TCEs.[945] The scope of application, however, is limited: A differentiation must be made between disputes within indigenous territories, outside these territories involving exclusively indigenous people, and those involving third parties.[946]

c. Application of Customary Law by Factual Consideration

A third alternative is the simple factual recognition of customary law: In Brazil, for example, administrative entities consider customary rules and practices in cases regarding TCEs in their every-day practice.[947]

---

[942] *Id.* 412.

[943] *See* at Chapter IV Section 1.D. below.

[944] Article 124 of the Constitution of the Bolivarian Republic of Venezuela, Articles 101–104 of the Organization Act on Indigenous Peoples and Communities LOPCI), http://www.servindi.org/pdf/Ley_Indigena_Venezuela.pdf; Law on Demarcation and Guarantee of the Habitat and Lands of Indigenous Peoples http://www.leyesvenezolanas.com/ldghtpi.htm, last visited November 10, 2010. *See* also de la Cruz I. (2006) 10 *seq.*

[945] Which then again at the same time implies the restriction of the application of customary law to this geographical sphere. For further details and the legal situation outside this sphere *see* at Section 5.E. below.

[946] Article 133 of the Venezuelan Constitution.

[947] Personal communication with Ana Cristina Bandeira Lins, *Procuradora da República* in the Ministry of the Public, on June 23, 2009, in São Paolo, Brazil, *see* also Busch (2010) 220 *seq.* For the settlement of the dispute of the Craô mentioned before *see* at Section 5.E.II.3.d. below.

3. Means of Recognizing and Limiting the Application of Customary Law in Other Legal Areas

As there exists little experience with the recognition of customary law within a legal protection of TCEs, as mentioned at the beginning of this section, it is worth considering the treatment of customary law in other legal areas apart from TCEs.

a. Recognition by Means of Acknowledging Jurisdictional Competence

In Colombia, a certain form of indigenous administration is acknowledged, the *cabildo,* which has already been given the authority to exercise its own rights in the colonial area, and is now recognized as special indigenous jurisdiction (*JEI, Jurisdicción Especial Indígena*) by the 1991 Constitution.[948] Within the indigenous territories, the JEI is supposed to have the same level of legitimization or of authority as the system of ordinary courts. It includes the acknowledgement of formal and material norms (legal plurality). Nonetheless, the concrete content and scope of the JEI are unclear and disputed. The indigenous legal systems have been expressly protected by the Colombian Constitution since 1991. Their legal acts are nonetheless also subordinated under the juridical control of the regular national courts, i.e. the ordinary administrative and constitutional courts. Concerning this latter aspect, as Semper says, some of the indigenous spokesmen argue that the formal recognition of indigenous rights constituted a step backwards in the struggle to implement indigenous autonomy in the country.[949]

b. Recognition by Means of the Legal Instrument of (Limited) Reference

The Peruvian Law No. 27811 of July 24, 2002, introducing a Protection Regime for the Collective Knowledge of Indigenous Peoples Derived from Biological Resources[950] can serve as an advanced example in relation to the integration of customary law, on aspects that are also relevant for the treatment of TCEs. It refers to customary law by statute: it provides for the application of traditional forms of organization in its Articles 14 and 24, as well as for the application of customary alternative dispute resolution mechanisms in its Articles 39 and 46. These provisions contain explicit references to customary law.

Besides, the law considers traditional forms of representation, although not referring explicitly to corresponding customary rules, but by indirectly acknowledging these structures: it establishes a fund to enable at least the economic participation of those communities that also possess the traditional knowledge in question, but have not been involved as parties in existing licensing agreements on

---

[948] Article 246 of the 1991 Colombian Constitution, *see* also Semper (2008)142, 149.

[949] *Id.* 149.

[950] Available in English at http://world-intellectual-property-organization.com/wipolex/en/details.jsp?id=3420, last visited December 5, 2010.

said traditional knowledge. According to the Law, this fund must be managed exclusively by representatives of indigenous organizations.[951] Thereby, indirectly, the Law acknowledges inherently indigenous forms of representation. This acknowledgement also has an impact on the distribution of the benefits, which accordingly occurs corresponding to traditional distribution shares and mechanisms.

The Brazilian Indian Statute integrates customary law and regulates the limits of its application in the following ways: In the areas of "family relations, inheritance rules, property regime and acts and transactions between the Indians," uses, customs, and traditions of the indigenous communities and their effects are respected "unless they opt for the application of the common (national) law." To relations between "non-integrated Indians and persons from outside the indigenous community, the regulations of the common (national) law are applied, except those from less favourable regulations and diverging dispositions of this law."[952]

As regards penal law, the Statue provides that the application of "punitive or disciplinary sanctions against community members according to their own indigenous institutions is tolerated, as far as they do not have a cruel or debasing character. The death penalty is prohibited in any case."[953]

Limits to the application of customary law are thus:

(ii) Personal scope of application: aside from two exceptions, there is no application of customary law in cases involving "outside persons" and non-integrated Indians;
(iii) Differing choice of law: in cases between indigenous peoples themselves regarding particular matters similar to the area of "civil law" from a Western perspective, the application of the common (national) law can be chosen;
(iv) Special *ordre public*[954]: no "toleration" of death penalty and other customary rules in penal issues if they are regarded as cruel or debasing from a national Brazilian perspective.

c. *Application of Customary Law by Choice*

In Mexico, customary law in terms of *usos y costumbres*, "practices and customs," can be applied in election procedures at the local level. As mentioned formerly, that means that municipal leaders are selected through "customary law rather than secret votes and ballot boxes"—which is anthropologically and sociologically regarded as a "'choke point' between 'liberal' individualist and communitarian views."[955]

[951] Articles 37, 39 of the Peruvian Law No. 27811.

[952] Article 6 of the 1973 Brazilian Indian Statute.

[953] Article 57 of the 1973 Brazilian Indian Statute.

[954] The institution of the "ordre public" stems from private international law. *See* for example Article 21 Rome I Regulation (European Regulation No. 593/2008), and Article 26 Rome II Regulation (European Regulation No. 864/2007).

[955] Eisenstadt (no year) 1.

While elections seem to be a rather political issue at first glance, selection of leadership at the local level is closely related to the question of "representation" of a community according to customary law in TCEs matters.

The application of customary rules for the election procedures is governed by Book IV of the Electoral Law of the Mexican State of Oaxaca.[956] Article 131 stipulates that customary law is applicable in either those communities that have developed community assemblies or other collective forms of selecting local authorities, or in such communities that by their own choice decide to opt for such a system.[957] The second possibility provided by the Law of applying customary law thus constitutes an integration on the basis of "free choice" of the concerned local people themselves. It is even more: This mechanism of giving effect to "customary law" in the local election processes has been criticized as not requiring any existence of relevant traditions at all, neither as continuous practices nor as revitalized rules, and thus bears the risk of applying customary laws by means of "inventing" customs.[958]

d. Recognition by Factual Inclusion

As mentioned above, factual inclusion or consideration of customary law might occur in administrative interactions and alternative dispute settlements. This is often the case in Brazil. One example regarding traditional knowledge is a case of the Craô Indians in Brazil, which was mentioned above.[959] In the process of alternative dispute settlement in March, 2003, in which staff members of FUNAI[960] and the Ministry of the Public also participated, due consideration was given to the existing customary rules in regard to the question of representation.[961] Although not necessarily expressly, but by means of settling the dispute and involving all participants, as Bucher says, it was taken into consideration that the representation of the Craô in external issues has to be undertaken by the association of all Craô communities, the *Kapey*, and not the *Viti-Cati*.[962]

[956] "Código de Instituciones Políticas y Procedimientos Electorales de Oaxaca," Book IV is entitled "De la Renovación de Ayuntamientos en Municipios que Electoralmente se Rigen por Normas de Derecho Consuetudinario" and was amended in 1997 in response to a reform of Articles 25, 29 and 98 of the Local Political Constitution of the same year.

[957] Translation into English after Eisenstadt (no year) 15.

[958] On this *see* at Section 5.B.IV.1. above.

[959] On this *see* at Section 5.C.II.3. above.

[960] *Fundação Nacional do Índio,* for further details *see* at Chapter IV Sections 2.A. and B.II. below.

[961] *See* Bucher (2008) 246 with further references to C. Bueno Wandscheer ("Patentes & Conhecimento Tradicional", 2004) and others.

[962] *Ibid.*

4. Some Remarks on the Law on Paper and in Reality

To paint a more realistic picture, it might be interesting to mention some experiences regarding the application and non-application (*usos y desusos*) of customary law in practice.

a. Practices Regarding the Applicability of Customary Law

In some states of Mexico, for example, at local levels of jurisdiction, customary law is applicable, while at higher levels, the application of national law is imperative. According to Sierra, a recorded case regarding polygamy was to be decided at the superior instance—which theoretically was to apply only national laws.[963] It was observed that this formal obligation to apply exclusively national laws "does not, however, impede that in certain circumstances the judicial authorities accept customs or customary law as a defending argument even if it contradicts the law. . . . More than the governance of legality, what appears to dominate in these spaces is the money and the personal contacts. If one pays the judge, the agent of the *Ministerio Público*, or the lawyer, there are more possibilities to resolve the case in one's favor, including invoking custom" or customary law.[964]

b. Practices Regarding the Inapplicability of Customary Law

On the other hand, there are recorded cases in which the indigenous person concerned "opted" for the "inapplicability" of customary law, when he or she did not want formally applicable customary law to be applied in the particular case. This "opting out" was done, or better: attempted, by directly addressing the higher instance, invalidating thereby the local instances of conciliation. According to Sierra, this happened especially in cases of conflicts between neighbors or family members that could have been resolved by means of custom. Paradoxically, as Sierra tells, some of these cases had to be remitted by the superior authorities back to the local instances.[965]

5. Final General Remarks

The intensity of the (minor or major) presence of the dominant legality in the communities depends upon the ethnic vitality of each group and its degree of integration into the broader region. There is no "autonomy" of a customary law. According to Sierra, the juridical options at the individual as well as the collective level depend upon the range of structural possibilities of each ethnic group.[966]

---

[963] Sierra (no year) 20, translation by the author.

[964] *Ibid.*

[965] *Ibid.*

[966] *Id.* 21, translation by the author.

What stands at the center of the practice, maintenance, and evolution of customary law are disputes within the community on existing differences between customary norms and the "lived" practices. The modification or even non-use of customs and practices requires a re-assessment of their adequacy in specific situations, as some of the members continue to live the practices while others abandon them. Such disputes over continuity often have the character of a "generational court."[967] Sierra observed that the younger generations having had contact with "modernity" through a working place other than the traditional village, now question what they perceive as the apparent "atavisms" of their home clan. These conflicts are notorious, especially at the structural level of authority and its exercise, to be observed in the examples displayed above as well as, for instance, in the *nahua* community Xilocuautla in the municipality of Huauchinango in Mexico.[968]

These observations on customary law "in reality" reflect mainly two points that were initially stated as arguments against an application of customary law in the topic of TCEs:

First, that there exists—probably increasingly—legal uncertainty with regard to the actual authority of the customary rules. Second, being of a social nature, rather than abstract, codified legal rules, customary rules in their very essence are highly influenced and characterized by continuous social discussions and change.

Considering customary law for the topic of TCEs nonetheless, mainly in order to strengthen indigenous communities' will to maintain and further develop customs and practices and, thereby also TCEs, requires effective mechanisms of consideration at the international level as well.

F. Securing the Recognition of Customary Law at the International Level

For cases involving other than exclusively communal members or the local ambit, any application of customary law is effective only if it is secured at the international level. Various ways and mechanisms of such international consideration are theoretically possible, and in the end, the most important thing would be to secure its implementation. Any implementation, however, requires the creation of an international agreement on the technical legal means of allowing for customary law. Such options could be, among others, the following ones.

---

[967] *Id.* 22.

[968] *Ibid.*

I. Option 1: Recognizing Indigenous Jurisdiction and Decisions at a Procedural Level

One option would be to give due consideration to customary law by accepting indigenous jurisdiction over cases on TCEs.[969] According to private international law, that would mean the recognition, either formal or material, of a judgment issued under a foreign jurisdiction.[970]

Anthropologists have already argued in favor of a recognition of "the authority to develop" customary rules rather than of specific rules, which do not exist in most of the customary laws.[971]

Preconditions for the functioning of this option in practice, however, would be, first, an equivalent recognition at the national level, and, second, the existence of traditional authorities in practice. This latter aspect includes their successful recovery and re-evaluation, and ongoing respect and authority—a fact, or better: challenge, that is not to be underestimated in view of the internal and external threats discussed above, among them the strong tendency of emigration to urban areas.[972]

II. Option 2: Applying Customary Law as Part of the National Law by Means of Conflict-of-Law Rules of Private International Law

As mentioned in the context of general ways of recognizing customary law, another option would secure the application of customary law as part of the national tort law (or other area of law) by means of conflict-of-laws rules. This could be done in addition to a consideration by means of sui generis systems allowing for customary law.[973] Although this option would have the disadvantage of a potentially necessary execution of the sentence in the foreign country and the well-known associated difficulties, but similar difficulties would exist also in the case of an international treaty on TCEs. Out of the three advantages named,[974] the main argument in favor of this option is probably the dispensability of any international treaty or convention for considering customary law as a protection of TCEs at the international level.

---

[969] This option was favored by Wolfgang Fikentscher, in a personal communication in July, 2008, in Munich, to whom I express my gratefulness for all of the subsequent enriching conversations on the topic, as well. *See* also the fictive example of a case of a *Zuni* court: Fikentscher (2005) 12.

[970] On the recognition of foreign decisions in general in the German legal ambit *see* Schack (2010) § 17 – "Anerkennung ausländischer Entscheidungen".

[971] Carneiro da Cunha (1990) 301 *seq* translation by the author.

[972] Yet in Panama, for instance, 55% of the indigenous peoples do not live in "their territories" and context of their communities anymore. On this *see* at Chapter IV Section 1.A. below.

[973] Fikentscher (2005) 18 ("Doppelschutz mit grundsätzlicher Anspruchskonkurrenz").

[974] *Id.* 6 *seq.* First, no need of an international agreement, second, – at least in theory – an easier handling of corresponding conflict-of-laws rules, as the applicable law is generally the one of "the place of the wrong" (*lex loci delicti commissi*), and third, a better consideration of the *emic* perspective through its culture-specific approach. For further details *see* at Section 5.E.I. above.

However, especially in view of the Latin American legal and political realities, the problem remains of how customary law could be applied or acknowledged as *lex causae,* either as part of the tort law or of other areas of law, at the national level.

III. Option 3: One Single Conception of Customary Principles

Another option would be to codify (or seek to do so) numerous customary legal, social, and cultural practices into one single homogenized conception of protection of TCEs. With relation to such an option in the area of traditional knowledge, distinguished authors have stated that such a system "may radically miss the point – globalizing what is irreducibly, inherently and distinctively local."[975]

This is true for many aspects in TCEs, and to try to explicitly and substantively reproduce a system of customary laws has been criticized as "absurd," especially by anthropologists.[976]

Nonetheless, some common local principles can be identified, as shown above, and could be institutionalized as "backup," i.e. as principles of subsidiary legal application. Even in more general approaches, it has been discovered that although the content of legal rules is highly diverse, "an evolutionary perspective reveals common emotional and behavioral predispositions."[977] These predispositions do not constitute normative "rules." But according to a similar legal culture, general principles of what is considered to be fair and unfair, relating to each other or not, can be observed. Formulated from an indigenous, Western-trained point of view, the indigenous customary perspective on some of these principles in the area of protecting TCEs may be ambiguous and contradictory. But they represent an understanding of some basic legally relevant facts about TCEs: their generally collective character, their link to the cultural identity, territories, language, and biodiversity, the necessity of their intergenerational transmission, and their non-transferable and especially integral character. The latter especially means that they should not be divided thematically.[978]

IV. Option 4: Integrating Customary Law into a Sui Generis Protection

A third option would be what Taubman and Leistner have called a "*suorum genorum* protection", providing an international "network of mutual recognition"

[975] Taubman and Leistner (2008) 179.

[976] Carneiro da Cunha (1990) 303.

[977] Gruter and Masters called these common predispositions the "sense of justice," Gruter and Masters (1998) 93.

[978] Personal communication with Rodrigo de la Cruz, indigenous lawyer, staff member of the Ecuadorian Institute for Intellectual Property, IEPI, and consultant to WIPO, in March, 2009, in Quito, Ecuador.

of heterogeneous cultural traditions integrated with customary law in divergent national sui generis systems, "under the aegis of a general set of core legal principles."[979] As far as it concerns the aegis of common principles, supportive arguments have been expressed above. As far as the *"suorum genorum"* aspect is concerned, that would be useful especially if more and more (divergent) national sui generis systems on TCEs including customary law in their considered principles were established. The international processes then could concentrate on the "articulation and definition of general principles and legal norms, and building functional linkages between [those] divergent national systems."[980] While this is argued as an option in traditional knowledge,[981] in the area of TCEs—at least at the Latin American level—no more than one sui generis regime on TCEs exists so far, which could be "linked" to others.

G. Short Summary

Considering and applying customary law in the area of TCEs in Latin America can be described as a work still in progress. It is still at the very beginning of research, by both anthropologists and lawyers, as well as in the beginning of its political and legal acknowledgement in Latin America.[982] The main questions remaining, which have been addressed and, as far as possible, answered in the foregoing section, are:

When is customary law "customary"? Is there a precondition of authenticity in the rules? This term and criterion has, at least, been criticized in the related area of protecting immaterial cultural patrimony, including TCEs, in Brazil. Do re-defined, recovered rules belong to customary law? How can problems of leadership and representation be solved at the customary level, or at a subsidiary non-indigenous level? Should or may "customary rules" be written down or remain oral? If they should be written down, how can this be managed in practice? How can customary law technically be integrated into Western rules? What are the consequences of integrating customary law into a protection of TCEs, especially at a socio-cultural level within the indigenous communities? Should the special case of indigenous communities in voluntary isolation be treated differently?

In general, the fundamental difference between customary law and the positive law is that the latter is linked to state power, while the customary law belongs to societies which lack a state, or "simply operates without reference to the State."[983]

[979] Taubman and Leistner (2008) 179.

[980] *Id.* 179.

[981] *Id.* 179.

[982] This is different from the situation in Australia, and partly also in New Zealand, which is reflected by a well-developed case law in Australia, *see, e.g.*, Janke (2002).

[983] Stavenhagen (1990) 29 *seq.*, translation by the author.

Consequentially, customary law usually is embedded within the social structure.[984] These characteristics define also the main challenge in researching and applying customary law: the interface of law and anthropology, which requires expertise in both fields and raises the question of their compatibility and the modes of connecting them. The first aspect is also one of the main points of criticism raised at a national level in Latin America.[985] Other reasons are the lack of similar technical terms and the great intercultural, linguistic differences that exist, as well as the increasing adaptation, assimilation, and resettlement of indigenous communities, for example as a consequence of the construction of hydro-electric power plants in the Brazilian Amazon,[986] because the "vitality" of customary rules inseparably depends upon the vitality of the traditional way of life.

At the same time, the development by COICA shows that an increasing awareness of and action towards the revitalization of customs and the combination of customary and modern elements on the part of the indigenous peoples is evolving.[987] This aspect is crucial also for the effectiveness of applying customary law on TCEs: Depending upon how customary law becomes integrated into such a protection, an adapted application of it may bear the risk of parallel alterations of the social structures, moving towards the structures of complex societies, which might affect traditional socio-cultural patterns and even the viability of the very TCEs that were to be "protected" in the first place.

Among the plurality of different technical legal mechanisms of recognizing customary law disposed above, the option of considering customary law at a procedural level, by acknowledging decisions of tribal courts, is difficult in areas where such tribal courts do not exist, and is a politically delicate question, as it is closely linked to the ambit of rights of self-determination or autonomy.

In sum, it is an interdisciplinary question impossible to handle from a purely legal point of view alone. The future of the topic to a large extent depends upon scientific cooperation in the research and a common political will for (a) preserving circumstances, especially environmental and economic ones, that enable a traditional lifestyle to be upheld, and (b) for the legal application and implementation of customary rules—on all sides, expressly including the indigenous one.

---

[984] *Id.* 30.

[985] The criticism will be disposed in detail at Chapter IV Section 2.D.III. below.

[986] On this *see* at Chapter IV Section 2.C.III. below.

[987] As COICA explains, "Return to the *Maloca*" would mean to be open for a "balanced" exchange, to combine "elements of the occidental world" without abandoning the indigenous values and socio-cultural practices, *see* COICA (2005) 13, translation by COICA at http://www.coica.org.ec/ingles/aia_book/index.html.

Section 6. TCEs and Indigenous Land Rights

Although not an issue of great relevance at first glance, especially in the context of copyright law, land rights are worth having a look at when talking about an appropriate protection of TCEs.[988] In the early 1990s, experts even raised the opinion that "the most effective way" to protect the cultural heritage of indigenous peoples would be "to secure the recognition and protection of the right of indigenous peoples to the collective possession and use of their traditional territories, including the ability to control access by outsiders."[989]

This is even more important if the rightholders are defined only as the kind of communities still living in a traditional way, since the destruction of the communities is very often caused by the destruction of their livelihood and biospheres,[990] and thus, the preservation of indigenous peoples' habitats is a precondition of their qualification as rightholders—in other words: the loss of their habitats inevitably leads to the loss of the rights in their traditional culture.[991]

A. Factual Interdependence

The above-shown difficulties in defining the communities as bearers of TCEs[992] already evince that the question of protecting TCEs cannot be extracted from the social surroundings and living environment of the bearers of TCEs. There exists a strong factual interdependence.

In general, this was observed by Juan Martínez Cobo as early as the mid-1980s: "The expropriation, erosion, pillage, improper use and abuse of, and the damage inflicted on, indigenous lands are tantamount to destroying the cultural and spiritual legacy of indigenous populations. Forcing them to hand over such land is tantamount to allowing them to be exterminated. In a word it is ethnocide."[993]

This is especially true for the Amazon and other rainforest regions in Latin America, also from an emic perspective.[994] So the issue of land and land rights is

---

[988] For further details on indigenous land rights, *see, e.g.,* Grote (1999) 511 *seq.* For a focus on indigenous cultural rights and environment, *see* Schillhorn (2000) 45, 86.

[989] Daes (1993) 28.

[990] *Ibid.*

[991] *See, e.g.,* the insights gained from the project "Strengthening indigenous organisations in Latin America" supported by the GTZ ("Gesellschaft für technische Zusammenarbeit") (project No. 2006.2037.7).

[992] *See* at Section 1.B.II. above.

[993] Cobo (1986) Vol. IV p. 4.

[994] *See, e.g.,* Evaristo Nugkuag Ikanan (1992–1995 President of the Climate Alliance of European Cities with the Indigenous Rainforest Peoples): "Either we disappear or together with our peoples and the land, the rainforest, we will survive, because the rainforest is not one of many resources for us. It is life itself. For us, it is the only possible place to live. Migration means the death of the tribe,

central to the survival of the Latin American indigenous peoples and, with them, their traditional culture.

In concrete terms, the interdependence of the issue of protecting TCEs and that of indigenous land rights consists of three main aspects:

(1) The land provides the communities with the natural resources they need for their subsistence without dependence on the economic system of a global market, because the latter often requires assimilation to the economic and cultural rules of that market.[995] It also provides the communities with the resources needed for the mere creation of TCEs: The Brazilian *Wajãpi* Indians for example use the green fruits of the *jenipapo* tree, as Arantes tells, growing on their territory, to prepare the liquid for creating the traditional body painting art.[996]
(2) The land rights, if understood as effective, all-encompassing rights, would entail the right to and the actual feasibility of self-organization. Thereby, the communal structure of the indigenous communities, including forms of collective ownership and exploitation, could be upheld. This aspect is an essential one as well for the issue of protecting TCEs, as the collective act of creation and ownership is one of the main characteristics of TCEs. Therefore, the continuation of communal structures can be seen as a precondition for the survival and further development of TCEs.
(3) Territory is also a concept of the spiritual and cultural area. According to COICA, landscape functions as a localization of relationships with ancestors or spiritual figures.[997] Land is considered to be a "support of belief and social life".[998] It harbors the holistic view of life as rules for orientation and

because Amazonia is also the only heritage we can give to our children." http://www.gruenprojekt.de/html/adc.html.

[995] However, this first point might contain a demand for an unrealistic way of facing increasing globalization and might even be disproved by the example of the Kuna in Panama. The Kuna live on their own, somewhat isolated territory consisting of islands, but in a very lively exchange of goods (the *molas*) with the rest of the world. Thereby, they rather ensure their communal economic and cultural survival than lose it by assimilation.

[996] Arantes (2009 I) 27 and IPHAN – Instituto do Patrimônio Histórico e Artístico Nacional (2008). On the Wajãpi customs *see* at Section 5.D. above.

[997] COICA explains: While "(w)ithin the market" territories "acquire monetary importance and are negotiable", for the indigenous peoples of the Amazon region, territory is a widely integrated concept and a "collective good in interdependence with nature, the mountains and the waterfalls where our ancestors meditated", "inherited as sacred places and hold respect as sources of visionary and spiritual achievement." "Territory is understood by us as ... the unconditional freedom to manifest our spirituality, culture and ancestry". Therefore, the right to lands covers also the right to maintenance, or non-exploitation, "to precaution the ecological equilibrium and avoid environmental degradation." COICA (2005), 31, 59, translation by COICA at http://www.coica.org.ec/ingles/aia_book/index.html.

[998] This perception is illustrated *inter alia* on the homepage of the National Indigenous Representation of Brazil, FUNAI, available at http://www.funai.gov.br/funai.htm, last visited May 28, 2010.

> communal organization, as a source of acquiring knowledge and of inspiration for TCEs, and it provides the environs for the practice of those cultural expressions.[999] In Latin America and elsewhere, to indigenous peoples, land represents social space—social and cultural identity—and is therefore essential for these peoples' cultural survival.[1000]

Apart from that, indigenous customary understanding of sanctioning acts of misappropriation towards TCEs is also linked to the question of land rights. Besides from other forms of sanctions, the most important one—at least in rural areas—is the (immediate) expulsion of the infringer from the indigenous land.[1001]

For these and other reasons, demands for cultural protection are often closely linked to those for the recognition of indigenous land rights.[1002] Experts in the broader field of indigenous issues officially stated in the 1980s that "the preservation of the life and culture of the indigenous populations . . . [is] indissolubly linked to their land and resources."[1003]

From a specifically indigenous perspective, the question of land rights has first priority.[1004] Thus, at least in rural areas, the intensity of any indigenous engagement to protect TCEs, to get informed about the legal context, and to enforce rights in traditional culture depends upon the fulfilling of the prioritized need: the collective right to land.

B. Legal Embedding

Latin American constitutions,[1005] as well as their framework of international legal instruments,[1006] and especially their interpreters, have taken up this aspect of interdependence of TCEs and land rights. It has been underscored that, where indigenous groups are concerned, traditional land tenure is an aspect of the enjoyment of culture protected by Article 27 of the Covenant on Civil and Political

[999] *Ibid.*

[1000] *See* in general Barsh (1987) 761.

[1001] Personal communication with J.M. of the Asháninka Indians of Peru on June 10, 2008. In cases of grievous infringements, it could also be the refusal of access to land of other communities.

[1002] Torres (1991) 159.

[1003] U.N.-Subcommission on Prevention of Discrimination and Protection for Minorities (1984) 27.

[1004] Due to the simple question of survival, "we prioritize land over culture." Personal communication with J.M. of the Asháninka Indians of Peru on June 10, 2008, translation by the author.

[1005] *E.g.*, Article 2 of the Mexican Constitution.

[1006] *E.g.*, Article 27 of the International Covenant on Civil and Political Rights (ICCPR), which provides that "(i)n those States in which ethnic, religious or linguistic minorities exist, persons belonging to such minorities shall not be denied the right, in community with other members of their group, to enjoy their own culture, to profess and practice their own religion".

Rights.[1007] According to this understanding, securing indigenous land rights is part of securing indigenous cultural integrity and vice versa.

A more particular connection is the one between TCEs, especially traditional knowledge and cultural expressions of the holistic view of life, and environmentalism. This connection has also been legally recognized by now,[1008] by grounding the protection of TCEs, or traditional culture in general, in the protection of crucial elements for sustainable development.[1009] Certainly, where referred to in the legal instruments, cultural protection is not understood as an independent aim, but rather as a means to reach the envisaged target of sustainable environmental management, as Schillhorn points out correctly.[1010] Nonetheless, such reference reflects the growing appreciation of traditional culture as an especially valuable factor for a broader, even global objective.[1011] Furthermore, it shows the growing international awareness of the essential coherence of traditional culture and its living environment, and might lead to a greater awareness of the need for a holistic approach towards the protection of TCEs.

C. Parallels and Benefits

The need for said holistic approach was already discerned in 1993, when the Study of the Special Rapporteur of the U.N. Sub-Commission on Prevention of Discrimination and Protection of Minorities concluded that the most effective way to protect the cultural heritage of indigenous peoples would be to secure their right to collectively possess and control access to their lands.[1012]

[1007] General Comment adopted by the Human Rights Committee under Article 40, para. 4, of the ICCPR (Addendum); General comment No. 23(50) (Art. 27), CCPR/C/21/Rev.1/Add.5 of April 26, 1994: "One other aspect of the rights of individuals protected under that article [Article 27] – for example, to enjoy a particular culture – may consist in a way of life that is closely associated with territory and use of its resources. This may particularly be true of members of indigenous communities constituting a minority." Similarly, in *Ominayak, Chief of the Lubicon Lake Band v. Canada*, Communication No. 267/1984, U.N. Doc. A/45/40, Annex 9(A) (1990), the U.N. Human Rights Committee construed the cultural-rights guarantees of Article 27 of the International Covenant to extend to "economic and social activities" upon which the Lubicon Lake Band of Cree Indians relied as a group. Thus, the Committee found that Canada, a signatory to the International Covenant on Civil and Political Rights, had violated Article 27 by allowing the provincial government of Alberta to grant leases for oil and gas exploration and for timber development within the aboriginal territory of the Band. *Id.* at 27.

[1008] This connection is laid down for the first time in a universal legal instrument in Principle 22 of the Rio Declaration.

[1009] Suagee (1992) 677.

[1010] Still less, it does function as a cause of action, *see* Schillhorn (2000) 113 *et seq.*, translation by the author.

[1011] The use and appreciation of traditional knowledge and traditional cultural expressions for sustainable development has also been recognized in Latin America. *See* Andean Community (2005) "Elementos para la protección sui generis" 15.

[1012] Daes, (1993) 28; *see* also Suagee (1992) 671, 677.

However, indigenous land rights should not (only) be regarded as a precondition for an appropriate protection of TCEs, or even as an obstacle to it, as it adds greater complexity to the issue and probably complicates agreements on establishing such legal links. Besides, protecting indigenous land rights would only cover part of the problem.

But the issue of indigenous land rights can also serve as an example for certain questions arising in the issue of protecting TCEs. Experiences in the issue of indigenous land rights can not only benefit the understanding of the issue of protecting TCEs but also benefit the creation of an appropriate protection of TCEs in substantive and procedural matters, particularly in the following eight aspects:

(1) Collective character of the rights: From an indigenous point of view, the special relationship with the land excludes the acceptance of the individualistic concept of property rights,[1013] the reason why land is understood solely as a collective good. This understanding was recognized legally as early as 1917, when the Mexican Constitution conceded the right of collective property of communal or tribal lands (so-called *ejidos*).[1014] Similarly, in Colombia, the acknowledgement of a collective indigenous ownership of land (the so-called *resguardos*), dates back to the colonial era, and these regulations are still in force.[1015]
(2) Concept of "property" or "ownership": Regarding land as a location for keeping contact with ancestors generates the understanding of land as an object for ongoing relationships, and "land rights" as custodianships for the benefit of the community, rather than as property rights for commercial exploitation.
(3) Recognition and application of customary law: The consideration and recognition of indigenous customary law is essential for collective land rights[1016] and has been implemented legally for administrative and legal proceedings dealing with land rights for more than 15 years now.[1017]

[1013] Grote (1999) 497, 511.

[1014] Article 27 of the 1917 Constitution of Mexico, available at http://www.diputados.gob.mx/LeyesBiblio/ref/dof/CPEUM_orig_05feb1917_ima.pdf (last visited January 10, 2011), although no specific reference to the indigenous population was made. *See also* Article 231 of the Brazilian Constitution, which even recognizes land rights of the indigenous population as being natural "original rights to the lands they traditionally occupy." Because of this natural collective character, even the division of communal land is constitutionally prohibited: Article 231 para. 4 of the Brazilian Constitution. Bolivia, Colombia, Ecuador, and Venezuela also recognize this character of the lands of the indigenous peoples and communities. In Peru, a regressive process took place, where the Constitution of 1993 eliminated the words "inembargable and inalienable." *See* COICA (2005) 31, translation by COICA at http://www.coica.org.ec/ingles/aia_book/index.html.

[1015] Ley No. 89/1890. *See also* Semper (2008) 142.

[1016] Grote (1999) 512. Besides the question of individual or communal ownership, proving the ownership of land is regulated differently. Most legal systems require a registered title to prove ownership of land, whereas by customary law "ownership" was merely a question of ancestral or traditional occupation, *ibid.*

[1017] *See, e.g.,* Article 4 para. 1 of the 1992–2001 Constitution of Mexico, http://www.diputados.gob.mx/LeyesBiblio/ref/dof/CPEUM_ref_122_28ene92_ima.pdf, as well as Sec. V. b). of the Joint Proposals of the Federal Government of Mexico and the Zapatista National Liberation Army (EZLN) *id.* at 512 notes 87 *et seq.*

(4) Recognition as legal personality: As a consequence of the communal property rights, the indigenous community is, to the same extent, recognized as a legal personality and therefore as an entity itself entitled to claim or defend land rights in legal proceedings.[1018]
(5) Connecting right for the application of customary rights, including on TCEs: In some legislation, territorial rights even constitute the connecting or "traverse" right through which the applicability of other indigenous rights concerning their cultural heritage and knowledge, including customary law, is achieved.[1019] In particular, the recognition of territorial rights constitutes the sphere and scope of application and practice of customary law—in the field of TCEs as well.[1020]
(6) The right to be left alone or to non-commercialization: From an emic perspective, due to the spiritual meaning of land and the fact of a simple "inheritance" rather than an exclusive, all-embracing property right as in the Western concept, the right to lands also covers the right to "safeguard the ecological equilibrium and avoid environmental degradation."[1021] This idea of a right to maintenance or non-exploitation might serve as a way to better understand a right to be left alone or non-commercialization in the area of TCEs.
(7) Methods of managing collective rights: As within the *ejidos* or *resguardos* (see above) criteria have been established for collective rights to be managed, maybe practical experiences and lessons can be used for the design and implementation of an effective management of rights in TCEs.
(8) The change of the historical mindset and perception of illegal appropriation: While formerly it has been regarded as lawful to appropriate the land in which native communities lived as "the land did not belong to anyone," today, this "introduction of private property rights in land by the arriving European settlers and the expropriation of native community lands – often in conjunction with the forceful imposition of rules and regulations of the dominant society – has deprived these communities not only of the rights to their lands, but has also destroyed their traditional bonds to these territories and posed a serious threat to indigenous collective identity, their rights systems, and their understanding of ownership."[1022] A parallel development could take place in the issue of TCEs and their appropriation.

[1018] *E.g.* Article 75 No. 17 of the Argentinian Constitution; Article 171 para. 2 of the Bolivian Constitution; Article 286 of the Colombian Constitution; and Article 89 of the Constitution of Peru.

[1019] Article 124 of the Constitution of the Bolivarian Republic of Venezuela; Articles 101–104 of the Organization Act on Indigenous Peoples and Communities (LOPCI), available at http://www.servindi.org/pdf/Ley_Indigena_Venezuela.pdf; Law on Demarcation and Guarantee of the Habitat and Lands of Indigenous Peoples, available at http://www.leyesvenezolanas.com/ldghtpi.htm, last visited November 10, 2010.

[1020] For further details *see* at Section 5.E.II.2.b. above.

[1021] COICA (2005) 31, translation by COICA at http://www.coica.org.ec/ingles/aia_book/index.html.

[1022] Stoll and von Hahn (2008) 19. The U.N. Declaration addresses this issue in Articles 26 *et seq.*

In the light of these experiences, legal and fact-finding, on the protection of TCEs, first, the aforementioned holistic approach should be considered. Second, these aspects presented above should in the area of TCEs not be regarded as something new, alien, or even suspicious. Rather, they should be acknowledged as already established by law and practically approved. This means concretely: the understanding of TCEs as a collective good, the indigenous understanding of "property" rights when defining the content of the right, the recognition of customary law in substantive and procedural law, and finally, the enforcement of rights through a collective entity.

At the international human rights level, this interdependence has already been comprehended and officially acknowledged, lately by the 2007 U.N. Declaration on the Rights of Indigenous Peoples.[1023] At the level of the discussions at WIPO, a certain difficulty might be posed by the fact that the scope of competence of the World *Intellectual Property* Organization is limited to the area of intellectual property.

However, practical experiences beyond these organizations' scope of competence show that a purely immaterial approach towards the topic of TCEs rather constitutes an artificial separation of the factual situation and the needs of the peoples.

At the legal level in Latin America, several more comprehensive steps have been undertaken so far:

The Panama Sui Generis Regime of 2000, for example, also encompasses material goods, such as music instruments.[1024]

The Ecuadorian draft for a sui generis regime goes even further, including "respect for sacred places" as a general principle of the draft legislation, as well as listing the "security of the common lands" as a benefit for the use of TCEs.[1025]

In the same manner of bridging the gap of distinction between immaterial good and lands, in Brazil, a "sacred place" has been registered as part of the intangible cultural patrimony of the nation.[1026]

In sum, the relation between TCEs and indigenous land rights can be quite fruitful and should not be disregarded, not from an intellectual property point of view either.

[1023] On this, *see* at Chapter III Section 1.A. below, and Daes (1993).

[1024] On this point, *see* at Chapter IV Section 1.C.II. below.

[1025] Articles 6, lit e), and 25, lit h), of the Draft of the Ecuadorian Institute for Intellectual Property (IEPI), translation by the author.

[1026] For details, *see* at Chapter IV Section 2.C.III. below.

Chapter III. The Broader Legal Framework

The most relevant legal areas and instruments involved in the topic of protecting TCEs may be illustrated like this (see Fig. 1).

Section 1. International Framework: An Overview

Like in many other areas of law today, international law frames and influences the protection of TCEs in Latin America. However, even today, there exists no international treaty that covers the question of protecting TCEs in a specific and legally binding way, and no international customary law[1] that could establish a basis for the protection of TCEs.

Nonetheless, some instruments do touch on aspects of the topic. Here, only an overview of the most relevant parts bearing upon the protection of TCEs or setting up standards for a possible practical solution in Latin America will be given.

For a complete analysis of the international legal situation, including international instruments on human rights,[2] the existing studies and publications dealing specially with this international framework in the area of TCEs may be consulted.[3]

---

[1] On international customary law in general *see* Verdross and Simma (1984) §§ 567 *et seq.*; for the definition of the term, *see* especially p. 347.

[2] Those are, among others, Articles 7, 27 of the 1948 Universal Declaration of Human Rights, the International Covenant on Economic, Social and Cultural Rights (ICESCR), the International Covenant on Civil and Political Rights (ICCPR), and the ILO Convention No. 169.

[3] *See, e.g.*, Schlinkert (2007), and Lucas-Schlötter (2008) 339–506.

© Springer-Verlag Berlin Heidelberg 2015
A.F. Busch, *Protection of Traditional Cultural Expressions in Latin America*,
Munich Studies on Innovation and Competition 3, DOI 10.1007/978-3-662-46770-1_3

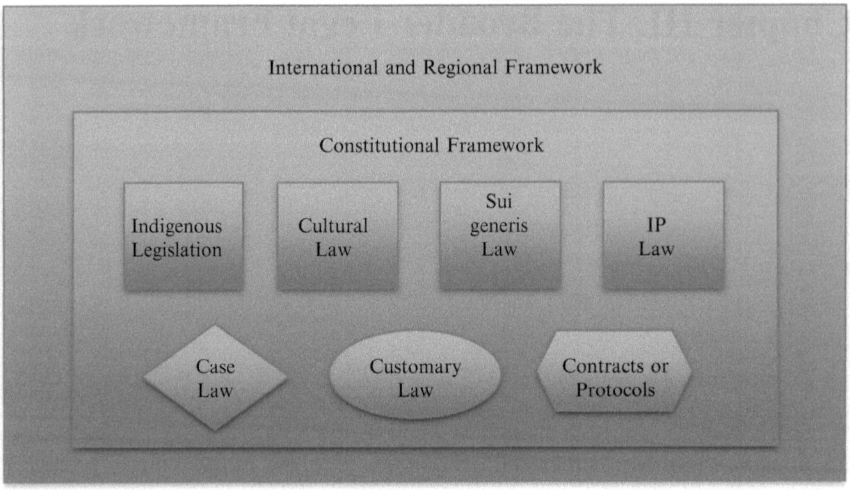

Fig. 1 Legal framework and instruments

A. The UN Declaration on the Rights of Indigenous Peoples (2007)

The most recent relevant instrument is the UN Declaration on the Rights of Indigenous Peoples, which was adopted by the General Assembly of the United Nations on September 13, 2007. Drafted by the Working Group on Indigenous Populations (WGIP) and issued on August 24, 1994, the Declaration was the subject of negotiations for over 13 years and was finally adopted just before the end of the 61st session of the General Assembly in September of 2007.[4] Of the Latin American States, the great majority voted in favor of the adoption of the Declaration, and only Colombia abstained from voting.[5]

[4] It was adopted by a vote of 143 in favor to 4 against (Australia, Canada, New Zealand and the United States), with 11 abstentions. *See* UN Department of Public Information (non official report), available at http://www.un.org/News/Press/docs//2007/ga10612.doc.htm, last visited January 10, 2011.

[5] The representative of Colombia is reported to have referred to "legal incompatibilities" of the text as the reason for that country's abstention: provisions of Articles 30, 19, and 32 "were in direct contradiction with Colombia's internal system," as the UN Press Release states. However, he pointed to the Colombian Constitution "as one of the most advanced with regard to recognizing the collective rights of indigenous peoples" – particularly regarding the recognition of traditional territories – and he stressed that the abstention would not affect Colombia's commitment to carry out internal provisions aimed at preserving Colombia's multiethnic nature and diversity. UN Department of Public Information (non-official report), available at http://www.un.org/News/Press/docs//2007/ga10612.doc.htm, last visited January 10, 2011.

I. Content of the Declaration

Provisions of major relevance for the protection of TCEs are the following five Articles:

(i) Article 11, granting the indigenous peoples the right to practice and revitalize their cultural traditions and customs,[6]
(ii) Article 12, on the right to manifest, practice, develop, and teach their spiritual and religious traditions, customs, and ceremonies,
(iii) Article 13, laying down the right to revitalize, use, develop, and transmit to future generations their histories, languages, oral traditions, philosophies, writing systems, and literatures, and to designate and retain their own names for communities, places, and persons,
(iv) Article 15, granting the right to the dignity and diversity of their cultures, traditions, histories, and aspirations, which shall be appropriately reflected in education and public information,[7] and finally, most important,
(v) Article 31 of the Declaration, granting the right to maintain, control, protect, and develop their cultural heritage, traditional knowledge, and *traditional cultural expressions*.[8]

II. Relevance of the Declaration

1. General Aspects

As the power of the UN General Assembly is limited to making non-binding recommendations,[9] the Declaration as such is merely a non-binding instrument of international law. Nevertheless, single provisions can become binding either

---

[6] This includes the right to "maintain, protect and develop the past, present and future manifestations of their cultures, such as ... artefacts, designs, ceremonies, technologies and visual and performing arts and literature." Paragraph 2 reads: "States shall provide redress through effective mechanisms, which may include restitution, developed in conjunction with indigenous peoples, with respect to their cultural, intellectual, religious and spiritual property taken without their free, prior and informed consent or in violation of their laws, traditions and customs."

[7] Paragraph 2 of Article 13 reads: "States shall take effective measures to ensure that this right is protected and also to ensure that indigenous peoples can understand and be understood in political, legal and administrative proceedings, where necessary through the provision of interpretation or by other appropriate means."

[8] Emphasis added by the author. Article 31 then continues: "1. ... as well as the manifestations of their sciences, technologies and cultures, including human and genetic resources, seeds, medicines, knowledge of the properties of fauna and flora, oral traditions, literatures, designs, sports and traditional games and visual and performing arts. They also have the right to maintain, control, protect and develop their intellectual property over such cultural heritage, traditional knowledge, and traditional cultural expressions. 2. In conjunction with indigenous peoples, States shall take effective measures to recognize and protect the exercise of these rights."

[9] *See* Articles 10 and 11 of the Charter of the United Nations.

through the development of international customary law or through their incorporation into a newly created legally binding agreement.[10] Until now, these options have not been developed and critics promptly argued that the Declaration itself "could not be cited as evidence of the evolution of customary international law," as the Declaration did "not describe current State practice or actions that States considered themselves obliged to take as a matter of law."[11]

Nonetheless, the Declaration is not only attributed to have a "strong symbolic value" and "moral force behind it."[12] It has also been rated a measure for national legislation[13] and been subject to practical application already—only 10 weeks after having been adopted.[14]

2. Relevance in the Latin American Ambit

a. Practical Relevance in Court Decisions

The practical application of the 2007 UN Declaration just mentioned is of special interest for the protection of TCEs in Latin America: First, the Inter-American Court of Human Rights referred to the Declaration in a ruling, and second, the Court even drew a parallel between property (i.e. land) rights and the right to culture of an indigenous population[15] (although referring only to Article 32 of the Declaration[16]).[17] Furthermore, the Court explicitly pointed to the statement of the

[10] Verdross and Simma (1984) §1234; Stoll and von Hahn (2008) 27.

[11] Representative Hill of Australia, UN Department of Public Information, http://www.un.org/News/Press/docs//2007/ga10612.doc.htm.

[12] Lucas-Schlötter (2008) 339–506. Torres has also argued in general that "noncompulsory mechanisms are the best suited to encourage states to adopt the norm in the long run," as formally acknowledging indigenous claims would render states "vulnerable to international intervention in what are usually considered domestic concerns." Torres (1991) 127, 128.

[13] Reputable legal scholar Wolfgang Fikentscher in a personal communication on July 2, 2008.

[14] *See, e.g.*, the Ruling of the Inter-American Court of Human Rights in the case of Saramaka People vs. Suriname Inter-American Court of Human Rights, *Saramaka People v. Suriname* (Judgment of November 28, 2007, Series C No. 172).

[15] Article 27 of the ICCPR, applied in an earlier decision by the Human Rights Committee (*Apirana Mahuika et al. v. New Zealand*). Communication No. 547/1993, U.N. Doc. CCPR/C/70/D/547/1993 (2000).

[16] Article 32 states: "1. Indigenous peoples have the right to determine and develop priorities and strategies for the development or use of their lands or territories and other resources.
2. States shall consult and cooperate in good faith with the indigenous peoples concerned through their own representative institutions in order to obtain their free and informed consent prior to the approval of any project affecting their lands or territories and other resources, particularly in connection with the development, utilization or exploitation of mineral, water or other resources.
3. States shall provide effective mechanisms for just and fair redress for any such activities, and appropriate measures shall be taken to mitigate adverse environmental, economic, social, cultural or spiritual impact."

[17] Inter-American Court of Human Rights, *Saramaka People v. Suriname* (Judgment of November 28, 2007, Series C No. 172).

Defendant (Suriname) made at the session of the General Assembly on September 13, 2007 on the UN Declaration. As Suriname had then argued in favor of the UN Declaration, the Court implicitly urge the country to hold itself bound by its own manifested statement.[18]

In view of this court decision, it is worth having a closer look at some relevant statements issued by Latin American countries.

b. Comments and Political Positions of Latin American Countries on the Declaration

Most of the representatives are reported to have welcomed the Declaration as "a significant step" (Chile), "a step forward" (Bolivia), "a tool" (Ecuador); alternatively "the first instrument" (Guatemala) for the promotion and protection of indigenous people's rights.[19] It was valued as "a balanced, useful instrument that would serve as a genuine guide for improving the living conditions of indigenous peoples" (Guatemala) and that "would serve to strengthen such national efforts" as the internal legal system of Chile, aiming to develop and protect indigenous rights.[20] At the same time, concerns were raised in both ways: While some Latin American representatives expressed reservations as to the legality of the Declaration,[21] others did so as to the reach of it.[22]

c. Other Voices

Latin American experts in indigenous policies and laws have rated the Declaration an "ambivalent and 'bittersweet' sensation."[23] Representatives of indigenous peoples at the international level have expressed their "most profound emotion about the adoption.... The true legacy of the Declaration will be the way in which the indigenous peoples ..., in cooperation with the States, give life to these words. The true test is thus if they have an impact on the every day life of the indigenous peoples."[24]

---

[18] *Ibid.*

[19] UN Department of Public Information (non-official report), available at http://www.un.org/News/Press/docs//2007/ga10612.doc.htm, last visited January 10, 2011.

[20] *Ibid.*

[21] The representative of Argentina (indirectly) alluded to incompatibilities with the principle of territorial integrity and national unity. Mexico, Paraguay, and Brazil interpreted the reference to self-determination in a similar way, *supra*.

[22] It would "not solve the problems of the planet," the representative of Bolivia is reported to have said, *supra*.

[23] "Una sensación ambivalente y 'agridulce'", *see* Barié (2008) 33, translation by the author.

[24] Declaración de representantes indígenas reunidos en el Caucus de los Pueblos Indígenas en 2006 al aprobarse el proyecto de la Declaración Universal de Derechos de los Pueblos Indígenas en el Consejo de Derechos Humanos de las Naciones Unidas, 29 junio 2006, *see* http://www.aulaintercultural.org/article.php3?id_article=1836.

d. Impacts on the National and Regional Legal Situation in Latin America

A Latin American country was the first country in the world to grant the Declaration legal status: Only a few weeks after the adoption of the Declaration by the UN General Assembly, Bolivia adopted Act No. 3760 of November 7, 2007, granting legally binding form to the Declaration.[25] In the spring of 2008, Bolivia decided to include it in its Constitution, as approved by the Constituent Assembly.[26] Ecuador gave due consideration to the Declaration in its process of reforming the new 2008 Constitution.

Moreover, the UN Declaration had been the impulse and reason for revising the topic of establishing an indigenous entity within the Andean Community and has indeed led to the establishment of new legislation on such an indigenous council.[27]

e. Political Impact on Indigenous Peoples

In the every-day life of indigenous peoples, the political impact of the Declaration is great, especially in areas where it has been published in a booklet and distributed among indigenous communities, as for example in Mexico and Ecuador. Among the Shuar and Achuar communities in Ecuador, for example, a growing consciousness about their own legal *status* was observed.[28]

III. Conclusion

To conclude, three main points can be made about the 2007 UN Declaration on the Rights of Indigenous Peoples in relation to TCEs:

(1) It contains several provisions which can be used as inspiration for establishing a system of protection of TCEs.
(2) The Declaration itself does not have legally binding effect and is thus no adequate instrument for legally protecting TCEs.
(3) It has practical impacts in Latin America though, in various dimensions:

- it has become binding law at the national level in Bolivia,
- it has been applied in a decision of the Inter-American Court of Human Rights, and
- it raises socio-political awareness within the every-day life in indigenous communities.

[25] U.N. Doc. E/C.19/2008/5/Add.3.

[26] U.N. Doc. E/C.19/2008/L.7.

[27] *See* at Section 2.B.IV. below.

[28] Personal communication with ethnologist Anna Meiser on January 8, 2009.

B. Other Relevant International Instruments

Other relevant international instruments stem from the area of (1) intellectual property and (2) cultural law.

Most of the Latin American countries are state parties to international treaties relating to Intellectual Property Rights, like the Revised Berne Convention, the Paris Convention, the WIPO Performances and Phonograms Treaty (WPPT),[29] and the WTO Trade-Related Aspects of Intellectual Property Rights (TRIPS) Agreement.[30] WIPO has also done a lot of work in the area of TCEs already.[31]

Latin American countries mainly have a stronger cultural-law approach though. Thus, the most relevant instruments influencing the national cultural laws will be highlighted in the following.

All of the cultural legislative instruments have two main disadvantages:

- They do not apply to infringements by individuals, but rather address member states.
- Though they address the member states, they do not bind them legally.

Nevertheless, the existing legislation reflects the states' increasing valuation of cultural diversity and increasing awareness of the need to protect their cultural wealth.

I. The 2005 Convention on the Protection and Promotion of the Diversity of Cultural Expressions

One important international cultural agreement relating to TCEs is the Convention on the Protection and Promotion of the Diversity of Cultural Expressions.[32] It was signed on October 20, 2005, and entered into force on March 18, 2007, in accordance with its Article 29.[33] This Convention and the 2003 Convention for the Safeguarding of the Intangible Heritage are the two most relevant texts for cultural-law approaches to protecting TCEs, as they specifically refer to the immaterial aspects of culture. Such positive effects and incentives can be observed at Latin American national levels also, for example in Brazil.[34]

---

[29] *See* the table giving a complete overview of all Latin American countries in Roffe (2007) 147. All treaties are available at http://www.wipo.int/treaties/en/, last visited January 10, 2011.

[30] Available at http://www.wto.org/english/docs_e/legal_e/27-trips_01_e.htm, last visited January 10, 2011.

[31] *See, e.g.*, the gap analysis on the protection of TCEs commissioned by the WIPO Intergovernmental Committee on Intellectual Property and Genetic Resources, Traditional Knowledge and Folklore (IGC), WIPO/GRTKF/IC/13/4(b) Rev. (2008), available at http://www.wipo.int/edocs/mdocs/tk/en/wipo_grtkf_ic_13/wipo_grtkf_ic_13_4_b_rev.pdf, last visited October 28, 2010.

[32] http://www.unesco.de/155.html?&L=0, last visited July 5, 2010.

[33] *See* http://portal.unesco.org/en/ev.php-URL_ID=31038&URL_DO=DO_TOPIC&URL_SECTION=201.html#ENTRY, last visited July 5, 2010.

[34] On legislative and especially practical impacts, *see* at Chapter IV Section 2.II.1. below.

As regards the adoption of the Convention, it is worth mentioning that Chile has issued a declaration,[35] and Mexico a reservation,[36] on this Convention. Experts of the Andean Community have made reference to this Convention in the preparatory work on a sui generis protection of traditional knowledge and TCEs.[37]

It is interesting to note that Mexico said it made the reservation to the Convention "due to pressure made by the North-American government."[38] This fact indicates, that the existing, economically influenced legal system prevails.

Contentwise, the 2005 Convention contains many relevant aspects for discussion in the area of protecting TCEs. However, it addresses only states, is non-binding, and therefore only serves as soft law. In this dimension, however, it has had influence on the promotion and "protection" (in a non-technical sense) of TCEs and other cultural expressions in various Latin American states, as will be shown later.[39]

II. The 2003 Convention for the Safeguarding of the Intangible Cultural Heritage

The Convention that comes closest to the issue of protecting folklore is at the same time one of the latest Conventions of the UNESCO: the Convention for the Safeguarding of the Intangible Cultural Heritage, adopted in Paris on October 17, 2003.[40] In accordance with its Article 34, it entered into force on April 20, 2006.[41] With regard to TCEs, the most interesting aspects are the following ones:

---

[35] The declaration reads as follows: "La República de Chile formula reserva a lo previsto en el N° 3 del Artículo 25, sobre Solución de Controversias y al Anexo a la Convención, por lo cual declara no reconocer el Procedimiento de Conciliación allí establecido, el que considera inaplicable a su respecto, de acuerdo a lo señalado en el N° 4 del Artículo 25." *See* http://portal.unesco.org/en/ev.php-URL_ID=31038&URL_DO=DO_TOPIC&URL_SECTION=201.html, last visited July 5, 2010.

[36] The reservation reads: "The United Mexican States wishes to enter the following reservation to the application and interpretation of Article 20 of the Convention: (a) This Convention shall be implemented in a manner that is in harmony and compatible with other international treaties, especially the Marrakesh Agreement Establishing the World Trade Organization and other international trade treaties. (b) With regard to paragraph 1, Mexico recognizes that this Convention is not subordinate to any other treaties and that other treaties shall not be subordinate to this Convention. (c) With regard to paragraph 1 (b), Mexico does not prejudge its position in future international treaty negotiations." Original: Spanish, *see* http://portal.unesco.org/en/ev.php-URL_ID=31038&URL_DO=DO_TOPIC&URL_SECTION=201.html, last visited July 5, 2010.

[37] *See* at Section 2.B.V. below.

[38] Larrea Richerand (2008) Chapter SEGUNDO. translation by the author.

[39] *See e.g.* at Chapter IV Section 2.II.1. and Section 2.B.V. below.

[40] Available at http://www.unesco.org/culture/ich/index.php?pg=00006, last visited July 5, 2010.

[41] *See* http://portal.unesco.org/en/ev.php-URL_ID=17716&URL_DO=DO_TOPIC&URL_SECTION=201.html#ENTRY, last visited July 5, 2010.

1. Progressive Approach Towards TCEs

This Convention does not only deal directly with the subject of TCEs and folklore. It also has a very progressive approach, aiming at "protection" as such, along with the "documentation, ... promotion, enhancement, transmission," and even "revitalisation of the various aspects of such heritage,",[42] rather than only tending to the conservation of intangible heritage—as its counterpart, the 1972 Convention Concerning the Protection of the World Cultural and Natural Heritage, still does.

2. Active Involvement of Traditional Communities

"Safeguarding" in the sense of the 2003 Convention encompasses "measures aimed at ensuring the viability of the intangible cultural heritage."[43] In this sense, it does not only address state parties, but aims at the active involvement and participation of communities and groups who are the bearers of the traditions, especially with regard to TCEs.[44]

At the Latin American national level, this is one aspect of great relevance, for example in the Brazilian practice: The Institute of National Historic and Artistic Patrimony, the IPHAN,[45] regards and respects the free consent of the group, especially in cases of indigenous communities as tradition bearers, as an imperative precondition for documenting and registering cultural expressions as intangible cultural heritage, or, more precisely, immaterial cultural patrimony—at any stage of the process.[46]

3. Reference to Customary Law

Interestingly enough, the Convention itself makes reference to customary rules, by stipulating that the state parties respect customary practices governing access to specific aspects of their populations' intangible cultural heritage.[47]

---

[42] Article 2.3 of the 2003 Convention.

[43] Article 2.3 of the 2003 Convention.

[44] Articles 11 and 15 of the Convention.

[45] "Instituto do Patrimômino Histórico e Artístico Nacional", Article 3(1) of the Brazilian Decree 3551 of 2000. On this *see* at Chapter IV Section 2.C. below.

[46] Personal communication with Ana Gita de Oliveira, Department for the Immaterial Patrimony of the IPHAN, in March 2009 in Brasilia. For details on the Brazilian situation *see* at Chapter IV Section 2.C. below.

[47] Article 13(d) of the 2003 Convention.

4. Protection Through Registration as Intangible Cultural Heritage

Finally, the Convention's aspect of safeguarding intangible cultural heritage by means of documentation and registration, is made use of by Latin American countries with the aim, among others, of "protecting" expressions by the state against unauthorized copies. This is true for the registration as intangible cultural heritage at the national as well as (according to the relevant legal instruments and procedures) the international level, at UNESCO.

One of the latest cases was the declaration of five traditional dances ("Morenada," "Caporales," "Llamerada," "Kullawada," and "Saya Afroboliviana") as "immaterial and cultural patrimony of the plurinational State of Bolivia" by means of five acts of legislation that also make the dances applicable for the declaration as UNESCO intangible cultural heritage.[48] Aside from the identification of these as national cultural patrimony, one of the reasons for the declaration was the fact that elements of the traditional clothes worn in the dances "have been unprotected and find themselves subject to the arbitrariness of globalization processes."[49] While this background information reveals the desire of an effective legal instrument on the protection of such TCEs against unauthorized commercial use and exploitation it should be clarified that neither by means of the Convention itself, nor by the public registry in any Latin American country, are legal consequences at the level of private law established as effective measures against unauthorized use or imitations of TCEs.

This fact is often misunderstood, even where cultural law instruments have been established already. This is among the reasons why also indigenous communities in Brazil, for instance, have sought the registration of certain TCEs and other aspects of indigenous culture as "immaterial cultural patrimony" within the respective national legal instrument.[50]

III. The UNESCO Convention Concerning the Protection of the World Cultural and Natural Heritage

Established in 1972, the UNESCO Convention Concerning the Protection of the World Cultural and Natural Heritage[51] was an important step forward towards a more integrated and encompassing protection of cultural heritage at the international level, giving encouragement and incentives for the protection of cultural

---

[48] El Diario (of Bolivia) (August 27, 2010), available at http://www.eldiario.net/noticias/2010/2010_08/nt100827/6_01clt.php, last visited November 10, 2010.

[49] *Ibid.*

[50] *See* at Chapter IV Section 2.C.III. below.

[51] Available at http://portal.unesco.org/en/ev.php-URL_ID=13055&URL_DO=DO_TOPIC&URL_SECTION=201.html, last visited July 5, 2010.

heritage at the national level, especially in developing countries, like those in Latin America.[52]

The Convention does not provide for any particular, direct protection of TCEs, though, by means of legal instruments to settle conflicts of interests on TCEs. Even if parts of TCEs are understood as being part of the (tangible) "cultural heritage," the concept and content of the "protection" is directed and defined by the aim of the Convention: "the establishment of a system of international *co-operation and assistance* designed to support *States Parties* to the Convention in their efforts to *conserve and identify* that heritage."[53] Accordingly, the Convention rather provides a political and indirect protection.[54] The only material protection to be granted by the member states is the submission of an "inventory of property forming part of the cultural . . . heritage," as Article 11 stipulates.[55]

This is not astonishing in view of the historical background and context of the Convention—as only in 1973, 1 year after the establishment of this Convention, the Bolivian government approached the Director General of UNESCO asking for the elaboration of a better system of protection for TCEs, formerly "expressions of folklore."[56]

In many Latin American countries, apart from some states with indigenous roots including Guatemala, which elaborated legal instruments for the protection of their national cultural heritage at a very early stage, the 1972 Convention established the basis for the ways of "protecting" tangible and intangible cultural expressions as heritage or national patrimony existing today.

IV. The Universal Declaration on Cultural Diversity

In view of the increasing relevance of cultural diversity as a common value worldwide, it is worth mentioning one last document, the UNESCO Universal Declaration on Cultural Diversity,[57] adopted on November 2, 2001. This Declaration emphasizes that cultural diversity, "as a source of exchange, innovation and creativity, . . . is as necessary for humankind as biodiversity is for nature. In this sense, it is the common heritage of humanity and should be recognized and affirmed for the benefit of present and future generations."[58]

Moreover, "[t]he defense of cultural diversity is an ethical imperative, inseparable from respect for human dignity. It implies a commitment to human rights and

---

[52] Article 7 of the Convention. Emphasis added by the author.

[53] Article 7 of the Convention. Emphasis added by the author.

[54] Lucas-Schlötter (2008) 420.

[55] *Ibid.*

[56] Lipszyc (1993) 96.

[57] Available at http://unesdoc.unesco.org/images/0012/001271/127160m.pdf, last visited November 10, 2010.

[58] Article 1 of the Declaration.

fundamental freedoms, in particular the rights of persons belonging to minorities and those of indigenous peoples."[59]

The Declaration, however, has no legally binding effect, especially not in regard of protecting TCEs. It is notable, though, that in this first decade of the millennium, even Latin American countries recognized or esteemed the cultural diversity that exists within their national society, sometimes mentioning the multicultural character of the state or introducing the principle of multi-culturality at the constitutional level.[60] This opening up towards a multicultural society constitutes an about-face from the centuries-long policy of integration and assimilation. It can be regarded as an essential precondition for politically and legally considering TCEs as objects of specific rights—given that such an approach in the end does not lead to "reverse discrimination."

Section 2. Regional Framework

Apart from the international legal instruments, there are also special regional instruments that shape the topic of protecting TCEs in Latin America. Most of them do not cover TCEs as particular objects of a concrete type of protection, though. Therefore, only a short overview completing the picture of the broader legal framework will be given here. The Andean Community plays a kind of special role in this respect: It has developed some binding decisions and a concrete policy with regard to TCEs in the region. These instruments and the political development will be looked at more closely below.

A. *Latin America in General*

I. Intellectual Property Rights and Regulations on TCEs

1. Free-Trade Agreements

To a growing extent, free-trade agreements contain clauses dealing with intellectual property, and sometimes even specifically with TCEs or folklore.[61] With regard to the consideration of intellectual property aspects in general, these agreements can be divided into two groups: those addressing intellectual property rights merely in

[59] Article 4 of the Declaration.

[60] *See* for details at Section 3.A. below.

[61] On the consideration of intellectual property in free-trade agreements in general, *see* Drexl (2010) paras 106 *et seq.*

general terms, on the one hand, and those containing concrete duties as regards the acknowledgement and respect of intellectual property rights, on the other hand.[62]

a. NAFTA

The North American Free Trade Agreement (NAFTA), negotiated between Mexico, Canada, and the United States, contains provisions on intellectual property rights that do not cover TCEs as such, but might be of relevance for certain aspects in the area of protecting TCEs.[63]

It might be mentioned here that, according to Article 19 of the Paris Convention, Article 20 of the Revised Berne Convention, and Article 21 of the Rome Convention, bilateral or (as in this case) multilateral agreements are given priority in relation to the other international conventions, as far as no contradiction ensues.[64]

b. EC–CARIFORUM EPA

One of the latest examples of a free-trade agreement in the Latin American region that addresses TCEs (although termed "folklore") among other things is that negotiated between the European Union and the CARIFORUM countries, the EC–CARIFORUM Economic Partnership Agreement (EPA) of 2008.[65]

The most relevant provision on TCEs, Article 150, is entitled "Genetic resources, traditional knowledge and folklore" and addresses mainly genetic resources and traditional knowledge on biodiversity.[66] With regard to "folklore," only the regular exchange of "views and information on relevant multilateral discussions" in WIPO is laid down.[67]

c. Free-Trade Agreements in Other Latin American Countries

As Panama is one of the few countries in the world having established a sui generis protection of TCEs, some free-trade agreements concluded by the countries

---

[62] The division into two groups is inspired by the observation of two phases of negotiation of free-trade agreements by the European Union with "remoter trading partners" ("weiter entfernt liegende Handelspartner") made by *id.* para 115.

[63] Relevant provisions are Article 1705 on copyright, including the protection of databases, Article 1706 on the rights of the producer of a sound recording, Article 1708 on trademarks, Article 1711 on trade secrets, Article 1712 on geographical indications, and Article 1713 on industrial designs. The full text is available at http://www.nafta-sec-alena.org/en/view.aspx?conID=590, last visited October 28, 2010.

[64] On this *see* Drexl (2010) para 106.

[65] Economic Partnership Agreement between the CARIFORUM States, of the one part, and the European Community and its Member States, of the other part, Official Journal of the European Union No. L 289/I/52, 53 of October 30, 2008.

[66] Article 150(1)–(4) of the Agreement.

[67] Article 150(5) lit a) and 150(6) of the Agreement.

ensuring this protection at the international level are of special interest here. Of major relevance is the free-trade agreement of Panama with Taiwan, which establishes concrete regulations on the treatment of specific TCEs, like handicrafts. All relevant agreements will be dealt with in detail in the context of the Panamanian system of protecting TCEs below.[68]

The FTA between Colombia and the United States was first negotiated at the level of the Andean Community, also including Ecuador and Peru. Although there had been a proposal elaborated by the Andean Countries of Colombia, Ecuador, and Peru on the issue of traditional knowledge and TCEs, the topic was not included in the articles in any way.[69]

d. Draft Agreement on a Free-Trade Area of the Americas

In 1994, at the Summit of the Americas in Miami, the idea arose to "unite the economies of the continents of the Americas" within a free-trade area.[70] A process preparing such an agreement involving the 34 national states of the broader American region, including the United States of America and Canada, began.[71] The latest version of the Draft Agreement on a Free Trade Area of the Americas (FTAA) was amended in November 2003.[72] It contains an enormous chapter on intellectual property rights, which even explicitly addresses TCEs, although under the term "expressions of folklore."

Although the targeted deadline of the agreement was set for 2005, the last summit held at Mar del Plata, Argentina, in November of 2005, failed to reach an agreement on the free-trade area of the Americas or any other comprehensive agenda to keep the FTAA alive.[73] Negotiations have not actively developed since, and at this stage, it is unlikely that the Draft Agreement or any similar agreement will be signed in the foreseeable future.[74]

Notwithstanding the fact that the Draft Agreement is (currently) of no practical importance, for purposes of illustration, it is worth having a look at how it handles TCEs.

The Draft sets up a definition of "expressions of folklore" in the Subsection on Copyright and Related Rights, and includes this category in the definition of performers.[75] As regards the content of protection, three versions of a regulation

[68] *See* at Chapter IV Section 1.E. below.

[69] Monroy Rodríguez (2006) no pagination.

[70] http://www.ftaa-alca.org/alca_e.asp, last visited November 2, 2010.

[71] *Ibid.*

[72] Chapter XX Intellectual Property Rights, Draft Agreement, FTAA – Free Trade Area of the Americas, FTAA.TNC/w/133/Rev. 3 (November 21, 2003), available at www.ftaa-alca.org/ftaadraft03/ChapterXX_e.asp, last visited November 2, 2010.

[73] *See* http://www.ftaa-alca.org/alca_e.asp, last visited November 2, 2010.

[74] Current developments can be found at *ibid.*

[75] Article 1 of the Draft Agreement.

have remained in discussion, none of which goes into detail: First, "[1.1. Each Party shall ensure effective protection of all expressions of folklore and artistic expressions, of the traditional and folk culture.]", second, "[1.1. Each Party shall ensure effective protection of all expressions of folklore, particularly those forms that are the product of the traditional and folk culture of indigenous people and communities, Afro-American and local communities.]", and third, "[1.1. Each Party shall protect traditional and popular culture manifested in any kind of folklore expression and production, as well as creations of popular art or craftwork.]"[76]

These three versions reveal the difficulties remaining at the regional level even at the very first steps, namely, the difficulties in merely defining or determining the subject matter of protection.[77]

One aspect of the content had been laid down in the Draft Agreement, though: the indication of the source of the TCEs. "[1.2. Each Party shall provide that any fixation, representation or publication, communication or use in any form of a literary, artistic, folk art or craft work, shall identify the community or ethnic group to which it belongs.]"

The Draft Agreement contains provisions on traditional knowledge and biodiversity which are by far more detailed and carefully developed than those on TCEs[78]—a finding that also reflects the general situation in the Latin American countries.

In total, the Draft Agreement reveals the "state of art" of the official discussion and public measures regarding an adequate protection of TCEs in Latin America: It is still at the beginning.

2. IP Harmonization in MERCOSUR

Within MERCOSUR ("Mercado Común del Sur"), consisting of the countries of Argentina, Brazil, Paraguay and Uruguay,[79] some steps have been taken to harmonize intellectual property law, especially regarding industrial property.[80]

With relation to TCEs, the "Protocol for the Harmonization of Intellectual Property Norms in MERCOSUR with respect to Trademarks and Indications of Source or Denominations of Origin," issued as a decision by the Mercosur Council in 1995 and in force since August 6, 2000, can be of some relevance in practice.[81]

---

[76] [Subsection B.2.d. Protection of [Expressions of] Folklore][Article 1. Protection of [Expressions of] Folklore] of the Draft Agreement.

[77] On this issue *see* at Chapter II Section 1. above.

[78] Chapter XX Intellectual Property Rights, [Subsection B.2.f. Traditional Knowledge and Access to Genetic Resources under the Intellectual Property Framework] of the Draft Agreement.

[79] Venezuela signed a membership agreement on June 17, 2006, to become the fifth full member of MERCOSUR, but its incorporation has not yet been ratified by the Brazilian and Paraguayan parliaments, *see* http://www.mercosur.int, last visited November 1, 2010.

[80] *See* for details Martinez Medrano and Soucasse (no year).

[81] Available at http://www.mercosur.int/msweb/Normas/normas_web/Decisiones/ES/Dec_008_095_.PDF, last visited October 29, 2010.

The Protocol does not treat TCEs in particular. But its provisions on collective and certification trademarks[82] as well as on indications of source and appellations of origin[83] might be of use for certain aspects in protecting TCEs by means of the regular intellectual property system.

Similarly, another MERCOSUR Protocol might be of practical relevance in the area of TCEs, that is, the one on the Harmonization of Provisions in the Field of Industrial Designs of 1998,[84] if the design is original and has an industrial application.[85] Titleholders can be natural or legal persons; communities or collectives are not mentioned.[86]

3. The Central American Convention on the Protection of Industrial Property

This 1968 Convention, signed by Guatemala, El Salvador, Nicaragua, and Costa Rica, deals, *inter alia* with collective trademarks, unfair competition, indications of source, and appellations of origin.[87] However, it was repealed in 1999 and has no longer been in force since January 1, 2000.[88]

II. Cultural Law

1. The Convention of San Salvador

Only 3 years after the Bolivian government had appealed to the Director General of UNESCO for international action to protect traditional cultural expressions like the traditional Andean folk song "El condor pasa,"[89] in 1976, the Organization of American States (OAS) elaborated a "Convention on the Protection of the Archaeological, Historical and Artistic Heritage of the American Nations," known as the Convention of San Salvador.[90] State parties are Argentina, Bolivia, Chile, Costa Rica, Ecuador, El Salvador, Guatemala, Haiti, Honduras, Nicaragua, Panama, Paraguay, and Peru; of these, Argentina and Paraguay ratified the Convention

---

[82] Article 5, para. 3, of the 1995 Protocol.

[83] Article 19 of the 1995 Protocol.

[84] Decision No. 16/98 of the MERCOSUR Council, available at http://www.mercosur.int/msweb/Normas/normas_web/Decisiones/ES/Dec_016_098_Prot-Armonización_Normas_Mat-Diseños_Indust_Acta%202_98.PDF. An English version is available at http://untreaty.un.org/unts/144078_158780/12/10/5009.pdf, last visited October 29, 2010.

[85] Article 8 of the 1998 Protocol.

[86] Article 7, para. 2, of the 1998 Protocol.

[87] Lucas-Schlötter (2008) 364.

[88] *Ibid.*

[89] Lipszyc (1993) 96.

[90] http://www.oas.org/juridico/english/treaties/c-16.html, last visited December 7, 2010.

only in 2002 and 2005, respectively.[91] This latter fact actually shows that the Convention is not just a historic ornament but still vital and—at least—of political relevance. At the same time, the big time gap between adoption and ongoing ratification in recent years indicates that even the protection of archaeological, historical, and artistic heritage as cultural objects of long-term worldwide recognition is a topic of very slow advance.

The Convention aims at the identification, registration, protection, and safeguarding of the property making up the cultural heritage of the American nations in order to prevent illegal exportation or importation of cultural property and to promote cooperation among the American states for mutual awareness and appreciation of their cultural property.[92]

This means that the addressees of the Convention are the states themselves. No particular rights are granted. The objects covered by the Convention explicitly include indigenous objects, i.e. objects "belonging to American cultures existing prior to contact with European culture,"[93] and also all cultural property that any of the states parties specifically declares to be included within the scope of the Convention.[94] However, from the structure and organization of the Convention it becomes clear that material property is meant, like monuments, objects, fragments of ruined buildings, and archaeological materials, as well as culture-related remains of human beings, fauna, and flora.

The effectiveness of this protection thus is somewhat limited—similar to the UNESCO Convention on the Means of Prohibiting the Illicit Import, Export, and Transfer of the Ownership of Cultural Property of 1970.[95]

Interesting to note is that the United States of America is also a member of the OAS, but has not ratified the Convention. The OAS—in contrast to the Andean Community, for example[96]—does not have the power to issue directly binding legislative instruments.[97] The political position implied by the non-ratification corresponds to the situation of the current negotiations on an international agreement on the protection of TCEs at WIPO.

---

[91] *Ibid.*

[92] Article 1 of the Convention.

[93] Article 2, lit. a), of the Convention. Lucas-Schlötter (2008) note 429 refers to the colonial era and following periods in Article 2, lit. b).

[94] Article 2, lit. e), of the Convention.

[95] http://portal.unesco.org/en/ev.php-URL_ID=13039&URL_DO=DO_TOPIC&URL_SECTION=201.html, last visited December 7, 2010. For further details on this Convention with regard to the protection of TCEs *see* Lucas-Schlötter (2008) 422 *et seq.*

[96] *See* at Section 2.B. below.

[97] For details on the OAS *see* the Charter of the Organization of American States, http://www.oas.org/dil/treaties_A-41_Charter_of_the_Organization_of_American_States.htm#ch9, last visited December 6, 2010.

2. Other Treaties or Protocols

A document worth noting is the "Protocol on Cultural Integration in MERCOSUR",[98] which aims at the promotion of the cooperation and exchanges between the respective cultural institutions and individuals involved in culture of the member states Argentina, Brazil, Paraguay, and Uruguay and thereby "enriching and disseminating the cultural and artistic expression of MERCOSUR."[99] Although the Protocol does not mention TCEs in particular, and refers only to the "individuals," all aspects of the national cultures are covered, including TCEs—while at the same time, no special treatment for TCEs is stipulated either.

Two aspects are notable:

- First, the preservation and dissemination of culture is to be promoted and harmonized through a common registry of the historical and cultural heritage of the member countries[100] and a common database that the Protocol recommends be established.[101] With regard to the documentation and dissemination of culture, including TCEs, for research or publication purposes, there exist various "ethics codes" at the national levels of MERCOSUR countries. In Brazil, for example, those are the Codes of Conduct of the Max Planck Institute and the DoBeS Program, the Code of Ethics and Discipline of the Brazilian Bar Association, Codes of Ethics of the Brazilian Anthropological Association, Codes of Ethics of ethno-biologists, Codes of Ethics of linguists, and the Codes of Ethics for museums/ICOMOS.[102]
- Second, the Protocol even expressly addresses intellectual property aspects, including a (limited) principle of reciprocity, whereby the member countries acknowledge each others' intellectual property rights in the works "in accordance with" the relevant national legislation.[103]

---

[98] For the original version in Spanish *see* http://www.mercosur.int/msweb/Normas/normas_web/Decisiones/ES/Dec_011_096_.PDF, last visited October 29, 2010.

[99] Article 1, para. 1, of the Protocol, available in English at http://untreaty.un.org/unts/144078_158780/18/3/8544.pdf, last visited October 29, 2010.

[100] Article 6 reads: "The States Parties shall encourage cooperation among their respective historical archives, libraries, museums and institutions responsible for preserving their cultural heritage in order to harmonize the criteria used in classification, cataloguing and preservation and to establish a register of the historical and cultural heritage of the countries members of MERCOSUR."

[101] "[T]he use of a common computerized databank established within the Cultural Information System in Latin America and the Caribbean (SICLAC)," Article 7 of the Protocol.

[102] Arantes (2009 II) 351 *seq.*

[103] Article 8 stipulates that: "Each State Party shall protect within its territory the intellectual property rights attached to works originating in the other States Parties, in accordance with its domestic legislation and with any international treaties to which it has acceded, or to which it may accede in the future, and which are in force in each State Party." Translation according to the UN

Finally, another Treaty may be of some relevance for certain tangible objects of TCEs in the region: the "Treaty of Cooperation between the United States of America and the United Mexican States Providing for the Recovery and Return of Stolen Archaeological, Historical and Cultural Properties". It addresses only these two states, however, and is limited to the aims of recovery and return of particular stolen objects, as the title already indicates.[104]

III. Human and Indigenous Rights Legislation

Although even human and indigenous rights legislation can serve as a basis for the protection of TCEs—as in the case of the UN Declaration on the Rights of Indigenous Peoples[105]—specific legislation in Latin America exists only with regard to the American Convention on Human Rights[106] and the Proposed American Declaration on the Rights of Indigenous Peoples.[107]

The American Convention on Human Rights contains a Chapter on economic, social, and cultural rights (Chapter III), but only stipulates a progressive implementation of the standards set forth in the 1967 Protocol of Buenos Aires—which do not make any particular reference to the protection of TCEs.[108]

The Proposed American Declaration on the Rights of Indigenous Peoples was drafted by the Inter-American Commission on Human Rights of the Organization of America States (OAS)[109] and approved at its 133rd meeting on February 26, 1997. It still has not been adopted by the General Assembly of the OAS. After 11 "Meetings of Negotiations," the current reference text for the Working Group's deliberations reflects a still ongoing process of trying to achieve a consensus—it is called the "Record of the Current Status of the Draft American Declaration on the Rights of Indigenous Peoples."[110] Notwithstanding, the different steps of this process indicate a certain direction of development including the protection of TCEs—like

- collective ownership of rights,
- indigenous communities as legal persons,
- appreciation of cultural identity and its maintenance,

version in English, available at http://untreaty.un.org/unts/144078_158780/18/3/8544.pdf, last visited October 29, 2010.

[104] *See* also Article 1 of the Treaty. The full text is available at http://exchanges.state.gov/heritage/culprop/laws/pdfs/treaty01.pdf, last visited October 29, 2010.

[105] *See* at Section 1.A. above.

[106] http://www.oas.org/Juridico/english/treaties/b-32.html, last visited December 4, 2010. The Convention was adopted on November 22, 1969 and entered into force on July 18, 1978, *see ibid.*

[107] http://www.cidh.oas.org/Indigenas/chap.2g.htm, last visited December 4, 2009.

[108] Article 26 of the Convention. For the Protocol of Buenos Aires *see* http://www.oas.org/dil/treaties_B-31_Protocol_of_Buenos_Aires_sign.htm, last visited December 4, 2010.

[109] For details on the OAS *see* at Section 2.A.II. above.

[110] It is dated November 19, 2009 and available at http://www.oas.org/dil/GT-DADIN_doc_334-08_rev4_eng.pdf, last visited December 4, 2010.

- acknowledgement of traditional structures and organization, as well as of the interdependence between one's own world view and life in a healthy environment.

Certainly, these "rights" will be difficult to implement. Even if adopted, the Declaration would not be binding on the member states. With regard to TCEs in particular, concrete rights are not even provided for.

B. Specific Focus: The Andean Community

With regard to the regional framework of protecting TCEs, it is interesting to have a more detailed look at the Andean Community. This is for mainly four reasons:

- First, at the factual level, the geographic area of the Community covers a very high indigenous and traditional population and thus a very high variety of still vital TCEs.
- Second, the Community has the legal competence to issue binding legislative instruments and thus the power to create effective legal answers to the question of TCE protection.
- Third, it is actively involved in doing so, or, to put it in more realistic words, a least slowly moving toward this goal.
- Fourth,—at least on paper—the Community generally follows a policy promoting a broader South American integration[111] and thus could serve as a starting point for a common regional South American instrument on the protection of TCEs.[112]

I. General Aspects[113]

As of 2011, Member States of the Andean Community are Bolivia, Colombia, Ecuador, and Peru.[114]

[111] *E.g.*, policies and aims of the Andean Community at http://www.comunidadandina.org/ingles/who.htm, last visited December 8, 2010.

[112] For further details hereon and on a possible regional Latin American solution *see* at Section 2. C. below.

[113] For more details on general aspects of the Andean Community *see, e.g.*, Unterguggenberger (1999) 17–38 and Markowski (2004) 23-33.

[114] Initially, the Cartagena Agreement of 1969 also included Chile as a member state, and in 1973 Venezuela joined the "Andean Pact," as it was then called. Chile left the Integration System in 1976, Venezuela on April 22, 2006. Associated members, which might be invited to participate in meetings of Andean Integration System organs and institutions, are Argentina, Brazil, Paraguay, and Uruguay: *see* Article 2 para. 1 of Decision 613; and Chile: *see* Decision 645 and http://www.comunidadandina.org/ingles/Exterior/chile.htm, last visited December 7, 2010.

Despite all current political developments,[115] from a theoretical legal perspective, the Andean Community is a sub-regional organization with an "international legal capacity or status," according to Article 48 of the Cartagena Agreement.[116] Similar to the European Union, it has the competence to issue binding legislative measures. The relevant competent organs are the Andean Commission and the Andean Council of Foreign Affairs.[117] The Commission constitutes the main policy-making body of the Andean Integration System[118] and is competent to issue legally binding decisions.[119] The Council of Foreign Affairs is regarded as the political leadership body, consisting of the Ministers of Foreign Affairs of the member countries. It may release non-binding statements called "Declarations" as well as legally binding "Decisions."[120]

The decisions of both organs are in principle directly applicable in member countries.[121] Only when their text so stipulates, the decisions have to be incorporated into national law through an express act determining the date they will enter into effect in each member country.[122] Equivalent to the principle of prevalence of the European Community law governing the legal system of the European Union,[123] the Community law established by these decisions has primacy over national legislations.[124]

The existing legal regime of the Andean Community does not contain any particular protection of TCEs so far. It has relevance to the topic in the area of

[115] On this *see* at Section 2.C.II. below.

[116] The Cartagena Agreement (CA) is available at http://www.comunidadandina.org/ingles/normativa/ande_trie1.htm, last visited December 7, 2010.

[117] Besides, the General Secretariat, being the executive body of the Andean Community, may also issue measures that are directly applicable in the member countries, so-called Resolutions, *see* Article 29 CA and Article 3 para. 1 of the Treaty Creating the Court of Justice of the Cartagena Agreement (amended by the Cochabamba Protocol), http://www.comunidadandina.org/ingles/normativa/ande_trie2.htm, last visited December 7, 2010.

[118] Article 22 of the Cartagena Agreement (CA). *See also* http://www.comunidadandina.org/ingles/sai/estructura_3.html, last visited December 7, 2010.

[119] Article 21, Sentence 2, CA.

[120] Articles 16 and 17 CA. *See also* http://www.comunidadandina.org/ingles/sai/estructura_2.html, last visited December 7, 2010.

[121] Article 3, para. 1, of the Treaty Creating the Court of Justice of the Cartagena Agreement (amended by the Cochabamba Protocol), http://www.comunidadandina.org/ingles/normativa/ande_trie2.htm, last visited December 7, 2010.

[122] Article 3, para. 2, of the Treaty Creating the Court of Justice of the Cartagena Agreement (amended by the Cochabamba Protocol), http://www.comunidadandina.org/ingles/normativa/ande_trie2.htm, last visited December 7, 2010.

[123] "(Anwendungs-) Vorrang". *See* the Decision of the European Court of Justice 6/64, [1964] ECR 585 – *Costa v ENEL* stating that the application of Community law takes precedence over the member states' own domestic law.

[124] *Preeminencia*, *prevalencia*, or *primacía* are the originally used Spanish terms, *see* Pachón Muñoz, "El Régimen Común sobre Derecho de Autor y Derechos Conexos al Derecho de Autor," presentation held at the "Seminario de Formación Para Profesores de Derecho Privado", Popayán August 30 – September 2, 1994, cited from Unterguggenberger (1999) 43, note 17.

intellectual property rights (below II.), cultural law (below III.), and legislation on indigenous peoples in general (below IV).

II. Intellectual Property Rights

1. Decision 351 on a Common Copyright and Neighboring Rights System

Decision 351 of 1993 sets up a common regime on copyright and neighboring rights in the member states of the Andean Community.[125] It is directly applicable[126] and even entitles the holder of rights directly to the status of copyright or neighboring right.[127] Thus, it could be very effective indeed—if it included TCEs as subject matter of protection.

However, TCEs[128] are not dealt with in Decision 351 at all. They are neither mentioned explicitly nor implied. Thus, and according to the principle of primacy of Community law,[129] Decision 351 only designs the framework of a protection of TCEs according to the areas covered by the Decision. The content of a particular system of protection is defined by the national laws of the member states, as Unterguggenberger has already stated.[130] The framing principles of Decision 351 simply rule that if the expressions and creations fulfil the requirement of originality, they deserve protection as anonymous works under Decision 351 in all member states of the Andean Community.[131]

With regard to a future establishment of protection of TCEs, the silence of Decision 351 on TCEs does not contain a statement in favor of or against protection, either. There are no recitals or similar official introductory explanations in Decision 351 regarding its content and limitations. However, the drafting background indicates that the reasons for leaving aside TCEs might have been as follows:

One aim of creating Decision 351 was to bring the copyright protection in the member countries in line with the international standard, in particular with the Revised Berne Convention.[132] However, the international standard did not (and still does not) include adequate protection of TCEs: The 1982 WIPO–UNESCO Model

---

[125] For details on the Decision and a comparison to the situation in Europe at that time, *see* von Lewinski (1994) 470–472.

[126] *Argumentum e contrario* to Article 3 para 2 of the Treaty Creating the Court of Justice of the Cartagena Agreement (amended by the Cochabamba Protocol), http://www.comunidadandina.org/ingles/normativa/ande_trie2.htm, last visited December 9, 2010.

[127] Unterguggenberger (1999) 63.

[128] Or "folklore"; the analysis refers to the content rather than to the wording.

[129] *See* at Section 2.B.I. above.

[130] Unterguggenberger (1999) 97.

[131] *Ibid.*

[132] *Id.* 45 and 47 *et seq.*

Provisions[133] had not become part of the "international standard" by, e.g., inclusion into the Berne Convention, nor had the inclusion of a reference to TCEs (formerly "folklore")[134] within the Berne Convention led to broader international resonance.

Moreover, as the intention was to establish a copyright legislation, this might have seemed not to be the proper means for protecting TCEs. Bolivia, for example, had instead proposed to attach a protocol on the preservation, promotion, and commercialization of TCEs to an international convention on copyright at the international level,[135] and established special provisions on TCEs in the copyright system at the national level.[136]

The latter fact indicates, at the same time, that the political positions with regard to protecting TCEs diverged strongly between the different member countries. Colombia, for example, rather insisted on (and still maintains) a very low level of "protection" under cultural law.[137]

Finally, other motivating factors for drafting Decision 351 had been socio-political elements at the national level, and economic reasons at the international level: According to Unterguggenberger, the member states wanted to promote a movement away from a rather agrarian society towards a more progressive, culture-orientated democracy and market economy.[138] At the international, especially bilateral level, industrialized countries, namely the United States of America, had strong economic interests in stemming cultural piracy and establishing a copyright system in *lato sensu* to ensure adequate protection for worldwide investments of the US-American copyright industry, as Unterguggenberger argues.[139] These factors, however, are not conducive to the protection of traditional national phenomena like TCEs.

In conclusion, these background details might still present challenges,[140] but do not necessarily constitute legal obstacles to an elaboration of a regime to protect TCEs more than 10 years later. Decision 351 itself does definitely not contain such limitations.

---

[133] WIPO-UNESCO Model Provisions for National Laws on the Protection of Expressions of Folklore Against Illicit Exploitation and other Prejudicial Actions, available at http://www.wipo.int/export/sites/www/tk/en/documents/pdf/1982-folklore-model-provisions.pdf, last visited December 10, 2010.

[134] Article 15(4) as amended by the Stockholm (1967) and Paris (1971) Acts of the Berne Convention.

[135] Lipszyc (1993) 96.

[136] *See* Article 1 para. 3 and Articles 58, 60, 62 of the Bolivian Copyright Law of 1992.

[137] Personal and electronic communication with Fernando Zapata Lopez, General Director of the National Copyright Directorate of Colombia, in October, 2008 and February, 2009.

[138] Unterguggenberger (1999) 51 *et seq.*

[139] *Id.* 55 *et seq.*

[140] On the state of the political "patchwork" within the Andean Community today as a possible obstacle to the successful elaboration of a system of protection of TCEs, *see* at Section 2.B.V.3. below.

2. Decision 486 on Industrial Property

In force since December 1, 2000, Decision 486 of the Andean Community replaced Decision 344 of 1993, and has the heading "Common Industrial Property System."[141] It is specifically meant to bring the Andean countries' intellectual property rights systems in line with the WTO's TRIPS Agreement and at the same time to comply with the demands and principles of the Convention on Biological Diversity (CBD), as Bucher argues.[142]

In accordance with these objectives, TCEs are only considered in terms of "traditional knowledge," and only as far as patent law is concerned.[143] A further indirect protection of TCEs can be found in Article 136, lit. g), of Decision 486. It excludes those signs from being registered as trademarks that consist of names of indigenous, African-American, or local communities, or names, words, letters, characters, or signs used to distinguish their products or services or the manner in which they are processed, or that constitute an expression of their culture or practice.[144] The registration of these signs as trademarks requires an application filed by the community itself or its express consent to an application made by third parties. Thereby, the provision ensures an exclusive right of the indigenous and local communities to apply for the registration of folkloristic signs and symbols as trademarks.[145]

Without any judgement on the policy of the Decision, it does not grant direct or further protection for TCEs, especially not for choreographic, literary, or musical

---

[141] *Decisión 486 sobre el Régimen Común Andino sobre Propiedad Industrial* of September 14, 2000, http://www.comunidadandina.org/normativa/dec/d486.htm (Spanish), http://www.comunidadandina.org/ingles/normativa/D486e.htm (unofficial English translation).

[142] Bucher (2008) 148.

[143] Article 3, para. 13, provides: "The Member Countries shall ensure that the protection granted to intellectual property elements shall be accorded while safeguarding and respecting their biological and genetic heritage together with the traditional knowledge of their indigenous, African American, or local communities. As a result, the granting of patents on inventions that have been developed on the basis of material obtained from that heritage or that knowledge shall be subordinated to the acquisition of that material in accordance with international, Andean Community, and national law. The Member Countries recognize the right and the authority of indigenous, African American, and local communities in respect of their collective knowledge."

[144] Article 136, lit. g), stipulates that "those signs the use of which in commerce may constitute an impediment to the rights of third parties may likewise not be registered as trademarks, in particular where [they]: . . . g) consist of the name of indigenous, African American, or local communities, or of such denominations, words, letters, characters, or signs as are used to distinguish their products, services or methods of processing, or that constitute an expression of their culture or practice, unless the application is filed by the community itself or with its express consent." http://www.comunidadandina.org/ingles/normativa/D486e.htm, last visited December 7, 2010.

[145] Group of Countries of Latin America and the Caribbean (GRULAC) (2001) Annex I, 6. Some authors therefore consider the decision to be progressive (*see* Bucher (2008) 159 *et seq.*, while critics argue that it unnecessarily goes "beyond TRIPS" by declaring microorganisms patentable without providing practically efficient provisions on community rights, access, and traditional knowledge with the same weight as IP rights, *see* GRAIN (October 5, 2000).

expressions. Within its limited scope of considering aspects of TCEs in a broad sense, the provision can be seen as progressive, providing at least negative protection for signs of a traditional cultural background.[146]

3. Decision 391 on Genetic Resources

Traditional practices are covered by the complementary regional instrument Decision 391 of 1996, setting up a Common Regime on Access to Genetic Resources, but only as far as they are associated with genetic resources and their by-products.[147]

Despite this limited value for TCEs as regards the direct scope of application, there are some lessons learned that also can serve for TCEs: According to Ruiz Muller, during the drafting, but especially in relation to the implementation of Decision 391, a lack of consideration of regional interests or even the communication of national authorities with those of other member states of the Andean Community was criticized.[148] This practical experience and criticism emphasizes that even within an existing legal entity at the regional level, cooperation and coordination between the different countries involved is an important aspect, and is not easy to achieve. "Regulations based on careful and participatory planning, which takes into account some of these points and undertakes this comprehensive multi-disciplinary analysis, will probably result in more effective laws," local experts argue. "In all cases, the national interest should be assessed in the light of practical considerations."[149]

III. Cultural Law: Decision 588 on Tangible Cultural Heritage

Another instrument worth mentioning is Decision 588, adopted by the Andean Council of Foreign Ministers in July 2004. It created new Community mechanisms to protect and recover goods belonging to the member countries' cultural heritage.[150] However, the scope of application of the Decision is limited to tangible

---

[146] *See* Bucher (2008) 149, 150, note 221, also for further details and critique of the Decision 486.

[147] Article 7 of Decision 391. Decision 391 is titled the "Common Regime on Access to Genetic Resources" and is available at http://www.comunidadandina.org/ingles/normativa/d391e.htm, last visited December 7, 2010.

[148] Ruiz Muller (2004) 247.

[149] *Id.* 256.

[150] Article 3 lit. l), deals with traditional cultural expressions, but expressly applies only to objects, documents and other vehicles that are related to such immaterial cultural expressions: "Objetos, documentos y cualquier soporte relacionados con el patrimonio inmaterial: poesía, ritos, folklore, modos de vida, medicina tradicional, religiosidad popular y tecnologías tradicionales, lenguas, modismos regionales y locales, música, danzas religiosas y bailes festivos, mitos y leyendas y otros que tengan interés para la identidad cultural de cada país." Andean Community (2004) Decision 588.

cultural heritage and therefore of limited value for the protection of TCEs.[151] Moreover, it categorizes TCEs as being part of the cultural heritage of the respective country, rather than of a certain traditional community.

This categorization, however, does not contain a general statement against a particular protection of TCEs granting collective ownership to the traditional communities. The background of Decision 588 is simply the aim of an improved fight against the illicit traffic and transfer of cultural goods, an aim also supported by UNESCO.[152]

The current policy of the Andean Community on TCEs does indeed contain steps towards an establishment of a particular means of protection.[153]

IV. Legislation and Policy on the Rights of Indigenous Peoples in General

As the topic of TCEs to a large extent relates to indigenous issues, especially in view of the draft of future instruments to protect TCEs, it is worth having a look at the legislation and policy on the rights of indigenous peoples of the Andean Community.

1. Machu Picchu Declaration

The starting point and the basic document of the Community's policy on indigenous peoples is the Machu Picchu "Declaration on Democracy, the Rights of Indigenous Peoples and the War against Poverty" issued by the Andean Presidential Council in July 2001.[154] On TCEs and indigenous peoples, the main statement therein is that the Andean Community "firmly supports all efforts that are geared towards promoting and protecting the basic rights and freedoms of the indigenous peoples," including

> their individual and collective right to their spiritual, cultural, linguistic, social, political, and economic identity and traditions, their right as peoples to retain control of their historic cultural heritage; their right to their systems, know-how and practice of traditional medicine, including the right to the protection of their ritual and sacred places.[155]

To implement this indigenous policy, in particular to ensure the "active participation" of indigenous peoples "in all spheres of national life," this Declaration, among other things, instructs the Andean Council of Foreign Ministers to establish

[151] Article 3 of the Decision 588 and Andean Community (no year) Culture.

[152] *See* Recital 4 of the Decision.

[153] *See* at Section 2.B.V.1. below.

[154] Available at http://www.comunidadandina.org/ingles/documentos/documents/machu_picchu28-7-01.htm, last visited December 10, 2010.

[155] Point 7 of the Machu Picchu Declaration.

a working group on the rights of indigenous peoples, with the participation of indigenous organizations, human rights organizations, and others.[156]

2. Working Group and Consultative Council

The then so-called Working Group on the Rights of Indigenous Peoples[157] was established by Decision 524 of July 7, 2002. The Working Group was intended to constitute a consultative entity within the Andean Integration System with the aim to promote the "active participation" of indigenous peoples in the "economic, social, cultural and political spheres of subregional integration."[158] However, Decision 524 has never been implemented.

More than 5 years later, on September 27, 2007, Decision 674 was issued,[159] repealing the former one and creating in place of the Working Group the "Consultative Council of the Andean Community Indigenous Peoples," with similar aims and tasks and only a slightly different composition of the Members of the Council.[160] Only 2 weeks earlier, the General Assembly of the United Nations had adopted the UN Declaration on the Rights of Indigenous Peoples.[161] This close timely connection is not a coincidence: While the First Forum of Indigenous Intellectuals and Researchers of the CAN had already urged work on that issue,[162] it was the UN Declaration that became the main reason for returning to the goal of establishing an indigenous entity within the Andean Community. The corresponding Decision 674 that then followed was even signed in the City of New York.[163] On September 8, 2008, the Consultative Council was indeed installed.[164]

3. Conclusion

Two points are remarkable in this context with regard to the political direction of the Community:

First, the delicate task of the Working Group, or Consultative Council, is to combine integration and indigenous identity—as its purpose is to "incorporate" the indigenous peoples "fully" into the economic, social, and political life of their home

[156] *Supra.*

[157] Mesa de Trabajo sobre Derechos de los Pueblos Indígenas.

[158] *See* Article 1 of Decision 524, Andean Community (2002) Decision 524.

[159] Andean Community (2007) Decision 674.

[160] El Consejo Consultivo de Pueblos Indígenas de la Comunidad Andina.

[161] On September 13, 2007; for further details on the UN Declaration, *see* at Section 1.A. above.

[162] *See* Andean Community (2007) Conclusions of the Indigenous Forum.

[163] *See* recitals to and end of Decision 674, Andean Community (2007) Decision 674.

[164] Andean Community (CAN) (2008).

states while "at the same time respecting and promoting their cultural diversity."[165] This task reflects one of the main challenges in appropriately protecting TCEs (second most important to the special situation of indigenous peoples in voluntary isolation).

Second, the "safeguarding" of the above-mentioned indigenous rights should occur "within our public order" and "in compliance with existing constitutional and legal provisions."[166] This could be interpreted as an expression of a common will *not* to establish new rights in this area.

V. Sui Generis Approach of the Andean Community

Of special interest is the current work of the Andean Community on a sui generis protection of subject matter that includes TCEs.

1. General Aspects: The Cultural Policy of the Andean Community

According to its own official statement, the cultural policy of the Andean Community includes strengthening and promoting cultural diversity. In concrete, the Andean Community designated the following areas as of political focus:

- The "preservation of the Andean cultural identity",
- "safeguarding of the different cultural and artistic expressions",
- promotion of an intercultural dialogue as "a means for deepening the understanding among Andean peoples", and
- the "protection of indigenous cultures".[167]

In view of these major aims, the General Secretariat of the Andean Community has designed a concrete working program in three basic areas, namely:

- Development of "cultural industries",
- "preservation and protection of the tangible and intangible cultural heritage", and,
- "strengthening and promotion of cultural diversity".[168]

While these topics had also been aspects of discussion at the higher presidential level,[169] the indigenous peoples themselves have indicated that they were "disposed

[165] Point 9 Sentence 3 of the Machu Picchu Declaration.

[166] Point 7, Sentence 2 of the Machu Picchu Declaration.

[167] Andean Community (no year) Culture.

[168] *Ibid.*

[169] At their Lima Summit in July, 2004, for example, the presidents of the member states emphasized the development of a culture of integration. With regard to cultural diversity, the countries were also entrusted with promoting the adoption of the proposed Convention on the

to share their TCEs and the underlying knowledge", provided that they can determine "when, where, and how" the TCEs and knowledge would be used.[170] The basis for such a use should be "respect for their ways of life, for cultural diversity, and the indigenous cosmovision."[171]

Under a new approach towards a development that "integrates environmental, social, and economic criteria," it has been regarded necessary to recover the ancestral knowledge and practices of indigenous communities "to conserve the resources for the coming generations."[172]

Input has also been provided by the First Forum of Indigenous Intellectuals and Researchers, which in their "Conclusions and Recommendations" formulated "Strategies to follow up on the 'Community of the Knowledge, Wisdom and Art of the Indigenous-Native Peoples.'"[173]

2. Proposed Elements for a Future Decision Establishing a Sui Generis Protection

Given this position, the Andean Community has started to work on research and recommendations for a sui generis protection of collective and integral traditional knowledge as the basis for the adaptation of a future decision of the Community on this issue.[174] Such a decision would then establish the supranational standard of protection and, according to the law-making power of the Community, be binding for all member states.[175]

The main document within this preparatory process is a proposal of elements for a sui generis protection of collective and integral traditional knowledge made by representatives of indigenous organizations of the Community's region.

It is essential to note that the document does neither represent an official position of the Community nor "compromise" it.[176] The responsibility for the content and the opinions expressed lays with the Group of Indigenous Experts, and more precisely, their Regional Coordinator, and with other indigenous experts of the region, as the preface reads.[177]

Protection and Promotion of the Diversity of Cultural Expressions at the Thirty-third Session of UNESCO's General Conference in Paris in October, 2005. *See ibid.*

[170] Andean Community (2005) Elementos para la protección sui generis 22, translation by the author.

[171] *Ibid.*, translation by the author.

[172] *Id.* 15, translation by the author.

[173] Andean Community (2007) Conclusions of the Indigenous Forum.

[174] Andean Community (2005) Elementos para la protección sui generis (2005) preface.

[175] *See* at Section 2.B.I. above.

[176] Andean Community (2005) Elementos para la protección sui generis (2005) preface. The Regional Coordinator is Rodrigo de la Cruz, Ecuador.

[177] *Ibid.*

a. Reasons for Favoring a Sui Generis Approach

The proposal emphasizes that, from the indigenous perspective, traditional knowledge and TCEs in their entirety constitute the collective intellectual patrimony of the indigenous peoples.[178] This approach is no matter of course; it is even contrary to some of the legislations of Community members, which regard indigenous art including its intangible bases as patrimony of the respective national state.[179]

According to the proposal, as TCEs are regarded to constitute the collective intellectual patrimony of the indigenous peoples in their entirety, the protection should be designed to cover it all, namely, traditional knowledge in general, especially concerning cultural aspects and TCEs,[180] ancestral knowledge, innovations, and practices.[181] The most appropriate way to protect this entirety was to design a sui generis regime, the proposal argues; industrial property and copyright law could serve as complementing models.[182]

b. Aims of Protection

Out of seven general and concrete aims mentioned, the following ones are most relevant for the protection of TCEs in particular. According to the proposal, these are to

(1) Promote respect, protection, preservation, a broader application, and the development of the collective knowledge and TCEs of the indigenous peoples;
(2) Guarantee the survival of the indigenous peoples and the consolidation of their cultural identity, considering that their ancestral knowledge and expressions form part of the indigenous cosmovision;
(3) Strengthen the exchange of ancestral wisdom and knowledge and increase their use within the own indigenous communities;
(4) Guarantee that the use of collective knowledge and expressions is made only with prior informed consent of the communities;
(5) Guarantee and establish guidelines for a just and equal distribution of the benefits deriving from collective knowledge and expressions, aiming at the strengthening of a sustainable development of the indigenous peoples and countries of the region;

---

[178] *Id.* 11.

[179] In Colombia, for example, indigenous arts, including dances, singing, handicraft, drawings, and sculptures are qualified as cultural patrimony (*patrimonio cultural*). *See* Article 189 of the Copyright Act, Ley 23 de 1982 – Ley de derecho de autor y derechos conexos. Folkloristic and traditional works of unknown authors (*las obras folclóricas y tradicionales de autores desconocidos*) are allocated within the public domain (*dominio público*); Article 187, No. 2, of the same law. *See* at Section 3.B.IV. below.

[180] Andean Community (2005) Elementos para la protección sui generis (2005) preface and 7.

[181] *Id.* 11.

[182] *Id.* 8.

(6) Prevent intellectual property rights from being conceded in ancestral knowledge and expressions if they are not obtained adequately.[183]

c. Subject Matter of Protection

While special research focused on traditional knowledge on biodiversity in 2003, as the preface tells, the final proposal deals with traditional knowledge in general, especially that concerning cultural aspects and TCEs.[184] Traditional knowledge, innovations, and practices are understood as "any knowledge of indigenous peoples about relationships and practices with their environment and which is transmitted from generation to generation, habitually in an oral manner."[185] According to this definition, the knowledge is related to a wide range of practices and sciences, among others, to those resembling categories of copyright, like songs, rituals, dances and rhythms, literary creations, legends, and myths. Insofar, the reach and scope of the proposal makes reference to the "necessity of establishing an Andean regime protecting the entirety of said ancestral knowledge, innovations, and practices."[186]

d. Beneficiaries of Protection

Beneficiaries of an economic use should be the "indigenous peoples themselves".[187]

e. Contents and Scope of Protection

According to the proposal, the principle of prior informed consent should be upheld. The terms of use should be mutually beneficial.[188] Particularities like "collective property, intergenerational character, exchange of knowledge between communities, an indissoluble link with land and territories", and "traditional forms of organization" should be considered.[189]

f. Management of Rights

Proceedings should be established to guarantee a fair and just distribution of the benefits derived from the use.[190]

---

[183] *Id.* 22, translation by the author.

[184] *Id.* preface and 7, translation by the author.

[185] *Id.* 11, translation by the author.

[186] *Ibid.*

[187] *Id.* preface and 11, translation by the author.

[188] *Ibid.*

[189] *Id.* 23, translation by the author.

[190] *Id.* preface and 11.

g. (No) Formalities

According to the proposal, registers and databases could serve as practical support for the protection of traditional cultural expressions and traditional knowledge, but should not be a precondition for protection.[191] Registers might bear the risk of, first, being interpreted as containing data belonging to the public domain and thus free for use by anyone, and, second, facilitating access to data by external entities and thereby making the data more vulnerable to unauthorized use, the proposal argues. Therefore, registers should only function as defensive mechanisms against unauthorized use but not limit the scope of protection to the registered expressions and thereby either hinder further development of them, or promote or favor the application of IP legislation, the proposal suggests.[192]

h. General Principles to Be Observed

In general, in a sub-regional system of protection within the Andean Community, some principles should be observed. According to the proposal, these are the following ones:

(1) Traditional knowledge is collective property.
(2) There is an indispensable link between the traditional knowledge and expressions, territoriality and cultural identity.
(3) The intercultural principle aiming at the dialogue of culture and knowledge is fundamental for any development of a sui generis regime.[193]
(4) The collective and integral traditional knowledge as a whole constitutes one system of ancestral knowledge.[194]
(5) The conservation, revitalization, and use of traditional knowledge and expressions should be a component of the independent determination of the indigenous peoples.[195]

3. Evaluation of the Proposed Elements

The proposal reflects many aspects contained also in the above-presented examples of Latin American indigenous philosophies.[196] It therefore supports and is shaped by an emic perspective—not disregarding that a "general" emic indigenous perspective does not exist,—rather than by a Western classic approach of intellectual

[191] *Id.* 24, in agreement with the position of the FIIB, in the GT about "Article 8j y Disposiciones Conexas," Montreal – Canada, December 2003.
[192] *Id.* 23.
[193] *Id.* 29, translation by the author.
[194] *Id.* 29, *see also* the evaluation at Section 2.B.V.3. just below.
[195] *Ibid.*
[196] *See* at Chapter II Section 4.G. above.

property experts. Such an approach probably best addresses expressed "indigenous" needs and understandings.

At the same time, it is also the reason why the known tensions would probably arise when trying to agree upon this kind of protection in the Andean Region. One difficulty in establishing a legal framework that respects the formulated principles is, first of all, compatibility with the Western legal systems that also dominate the national legislations of the Andean Countries.

In addition, following an integral approach faces two other difficulties, namely that there are many differences and particularities even within the Andean Community, and that regulations already exist in the special sector of particular traditional knowledge, *e.g.* Decision 486 of the Andean Community at the regional level, and the CBD at the international one.

As regards the broader perspective, the position that an integral protection of TCEs should be "a component of the independent determination of the indigenous peoples" bears further challenges: First, the more general demands are made, the more difficult it is to fulfill them. Concrete questions can enable precise answers more easily, especially in the technical ambit of legal instruments. Second, general demands are even more difficult to fulfill when they have a strong political content. Independent determination by indigenous peoples in general might provoke tensions with the national member states of the Andean Community, which do not favor a pluri-national conception (except Bolivia).[197]

Similarly, the "imperative" or "indispensable link" with territory absolutely reflects the content of the examples of indigenous cosmovision displayed above as well as the concrete suggestions for a protection formulated by COICA.[198] At the same time, it is difficult to implement, as the understanding according to the dominant national society in the member states is a very distinct one, the economic importance of territorial demands is extremely high, and at the legal level, there exist special rules on the issue of territory in some legislations.[199]

Finally, considering the policies of the Andean Community on paper and in reality, it is questionable whether the sui generis approach proposed by the Group of Indigenous Experts of the Andean Community constitutes a realistic course. Different positions of the Member States regarding FTAs with the United States as well as the European Union are another reason for (political and legal) difficulties in advancing a common system of protection of TCEs and traditional knowledge in general at the level of the Andean Community and limitations for the protection at the national level in Colombia and Peru. While Peru and Colombia follow a rather liberal approach, Ecuador and Bolivia have expressed major concerns, and negotiations with Ecuador have drawn to a halt, with Bolivia likewise.[200]

---

[197] On the relevant aspects of the constitutions, *see* at Section 3.A. below.

[198] *See* at Chapter II Section 4.G. above.

[199] Especially on constitutional aspects hereof *see* at Section 3.A. below.

[200] Personal and electronic communication with Fernando Zapata Lopez, General Director of the National Copyright Direction of Colombia, in October 2008 and February 2009, who was in

In general, politically, the Andean Community would currently be "faced with its self-dissolution," Mols argues.[201] Despite the precisely elaborated content and high quality of the proposal, the topic of highly political relevance involving demands of self-determination of indigenous peoples like an integral protection of TCEs and traditional collective knowledge is not an issue of great potential success in the Andean Community these days.

C. Outlook: A Regional Latin American Agreement—A Realistic Future Scenario?

With regard to the protection of TCEs in Latin America in general, and due to the existing conflict of interests at the international level, namely, at the ongoing negotiations at WIPO, the question arises whether it is a wiser and more realistic step to work out a regional legal instrument in the Latin American region.

I. What Kind of Instrument Should That Be?

Such an agreement could be of two different legal types: First, a model law—like the Model Law 2002 for the Pacific Islands—or, second, a binding agreement, a treaty. Although the first option would not require as strong efforts to be agreed upon as the second one, and would leave room for national or even local adjustments, the convincing advantage of the latter is its—theoretically—secure enforcement even at the national level once the state parties have signed the treaty.[202]

In case of diverging positions on particular questions or of existing varieties of preconditions and consequences of a protection of TCEs, the respective questions could be left open, with a mere reference to the national situation. An example of such an approach is the regional approach combined with a case-by-case determination under national law set up by the FTAA Draft Agreement. There, for instance, the determination and definition of potential right holders, i.e. indigenous peoples

charge of negotiating the intellectual property aspects in the FTA between Colombia and the European Union, for instance. Ecuador has elaborated studies on the direct impacts on traditional knowledge and practices and on biodiversity in the case of a potential signing of the FTA with the United States, *see* "Impactos directos en la biodiversidad y los conocimientos tradicionales por la posible firma del TLC con los EE.UU" available at http://www.wipo.int/tk/en/consultations/customary_law/index.html, last visited December 29, 2010. On this aspect *see also* at Section 2. B.V.3. and C. above.

[201] Mols (2009) 57, translation by the author.

[202] The problems of the "final" implementation of the Model Law 2002 for the Pacific Community should be a sufficient example to learn from. Von Lewinski expressed that "it is even somewhat disturbing to learn that the individual Pacific islands still seem to be somewhat reluctant to implement the Model Law 2002 into local law," von Lewinski (2007) 230.

and other local or cultural communities, is left to each state party, which "shall provide for a definition of local communities in its national legislation."[203]

II. Is There a Realistic Chance for a Regional Agreement?

To avoid drafting another paper tiger,[204] the starting point for a regional agreement would have to be at least the common political will to provide for adequate protection of TCEs.

The protection of TCEs as a part of Latin American cultural diversity might be a promising field for regional integration, for mainly two reasons:

- First, it unifies similar interests of the Latin American countries due to their common cultural, historical and socio-economic background. As illustrated within the context of the "setting" at the beginning,[205] the different Latin American countries have a similar colonial background, each with historical ties to a certain European nation, and the later struggle for independence as a common (and somewhat misleading) point of reference for the topic of TCEs.
- Second, as it is mostly firms from industrialized countries that will be alleged to infringe TCEs at the international level, there is the effect of a "common enemy to fight," especially considering that the interests of the developed countries—at least those with little to no vital tradition—are to a great degree contrary to those of developing countries when the protection of TCEs is concerned.

Furthermore, to a certain extent, there exists cooperation at the international level, in the form of the Group of Countries of Latin America and the Caribbean (GRULAC). GRULAC has expressed its members' common points of view in relation to a legal system of further multinational protection, such as: taking advantage of the existing intellectual property rights and developing them further towards a new sui generis regime,[206] considering the "appropriateness and feasibility of recognizing" these rights, as well as specific legal instruments, such as licenses of right, regimes "comparable to the domaine public payant" and systems for the "collective management of the exploitation" of TCEs, "including the creation of funds in which the proceeds from economic exploitation would be deposited for subsequent distribution."[207]

---

[203] Chapter XX Intellectual Property Rights, SubSec. B.2.f, Art. 1.1. of the Draft Agreement, FTAA – Free Trade Area of the Americas, FTAA.TNC/w/133/Rev. 3 (November 21, 2003).

[204] *See* the "somewhat disturbing" practical experiences with the WIPO Pacific Model Law as just mentioned, *supra* note 93.

[205] *See* at Chapter II Section 3. above.

[206] Group of Countries of Latin America and the Caribbean (GRULAC) (2001) Annex II 4.

[207] *Id.* 5.

A concrete step towards regional regulations regarding TCEs is contained in the above-mentioned FTAA Draft Agreement, containing an explicit provision on TCEs.[208]

However, the common points set up by GRULAC must be interpreted as an expression of diffuse negotiating positions at the international level, rather than as a positive statement on a common regional position in favor of adequate protection of TCEs. Although the author was not allowed to participate in the consultations of GRULAC in the 13th session of the IGC, some opinions voiced outside the sessions give the impression that the political positions are too distinct one from another to agree upon a legally binding instrument even at the regional Latin American level only. Most of the countries are more interested in a solution to the issue of protecting traditional knowledge, as is Mexico.[209]

Similarly, the analysis of the FTAA Draft Agreement, aside from this apparently positive sign of its existence, leads to two rather disappointing conclusions.

- First, the fact that the reference is contained in a (draft) free-trade agreement indicates a strong connection to economic issues. The dominating economic policies and systems, however, diverge greatly in the various Latin American countries, and are therefore difficult to unify, even if only in an agreement over how to protect TCEs in the region.
- Second, the fact that the Draft has yet to come to a conclusion and is no longer in development reveals a lack of dynamics towards regional integration, at least as regards economic cooperation, and particularly free-trade aspects.

In more general political terms, a long-term aim of the Latin American countries is to create a union of South American nations, "Unasur." A step that has been taken towards this so-called integration is Decision 613 of the Andean Community on the Association of the Republic of Argentina, the Federative Republic of Brazil, the Republic of Paraguay and the Eastern Republic of Uruguay, States Parties of MERCOSUR, with the Andean Community.[210]

In 2005, the Andean Community stated:

> Latin American integration is incorporated into the Andean agenda as a priority objective in order to make the Andean Community a space that links up South America, Central America and the Caribbean. . . . We have planned to move ahead in deepening an integral integration process that will contribute effectively to sustainable and equitable human development, in order to live well, with respect for the diversity and asymmetries that agglutinate the different visions, models and approaches and that will converge in the formation of the Union of South American Nations (Unasur).[211]

[208] Chapter XX Intellectual Property Rights, [Subsection B.2.d. Protection of [Expressions of] Folklore] of the Draft Agreement, FTAA – Free Trade Area of the Americas, FTAA.TNC/w/133/ Rev. 3 (November 21, 2003), available at www.ftaa-alca.org/ftaadraft03/ChapterXX_e.asp, last visited November 2, 2010. For the details *see* at Section 2.A.I.1.d. above.

[209] Personal Communication with members of the Mexican Delegation at the XIII. Session of the IGC of WIPO in October 2008 in Geneva.

[210] Andean Community (2005) Decision 613.

[211] http://www.comunidadandina.org/ingles/who.htm, last visited December 27, 2010.

The process of Latin American integration, which has begun in the 1950s and 1960s, enjoys only a rudimentary existence these days. While in 1991 a "new regional dynamic," was felt, even a "new climate of integration,"[212] today "we are rather faced with the 'ruins' of that process", Mols argues.[213] Beside many other factors,[214] it became clear that the Bolivarism that formed the former historical and ideological basis, and the ideology of import substitution that was the economic basis of Latin American regionalism could not persist against an ever-advancing orientation towards worldwide exportation, market economy, and privatization. Additionally, diverging national political goals obstruct the building and maintenance of the "common concerns and interests" necessary for any regional integration, Mols argues.[215]

The cause of these diverging national interests is, according to many experts on Latin America,[216] closely connected to the geographical, political, and cultural diversity within the countries concerned. Other scholars, however, argue that diversity *per se* is no obstacle to a regional integration, but that common strategic interests are of much greater importance—as a comparison of Latin American to the ASEAN[217] countries would show.[218]

In Latin America, such dominating strategic interests are rather substituted by pressing basic needs. "Rhetorically, many are in favor of 'unity' in Latin America. In case of conflict, however, [it is] every man for himself."[219] The political experience[220] shows that often, national problems turn regional cooperation into competition, especially when urgent and basic needs as are at stake.[221]

With regard to the concrete topic of protecting TCEs, a consensus on a Decision establishing protection of TCEs can not be found even in the small group of the

[212] Expressions of highly respected Venezuelan analyst Andrés Serbin, cited from Mols (2009) 56, translation by the author.

[213] *Ibid.*

[214] For a more detailed analysis of this political failure, which cannot be laid out here, *see id.* 57 *et seq.*

[215] *Ibid.*, translation by the author.

[216] *See, e.g.*, Grabendorff (2003) 163 *et seq.*

[217] Association of South East Asian Nations.

[218] Mols (2009) 57.

[219] *See* Frankfurter Allgemeine Zeitung, March 5, 2008: At the small summit of different presidents of the region, the representatives of the Latin American countries "again and again conjure up the importance of regional coalescence or integration; . . . however, these are merely crisis talks, because everyone looks for the help of the other with urgent problems, especially concerning the adequate energy and alimentary supply." Translation by the author.

[220] Remember for instance the crisis between Venezuela, Ecuador, and Colombia in February/ March 2008 when the Colombian military attacked a *guerrilla* camp on Ecuadorian ground and Raúl Reyes, the second most important leader of the Farc, died. Hugo Chavez threatened to not attend the following meeting of the Unasur at the end of March 2008.

[221] *Ibid.*

members of the Andean Community.[222] A consensus in the big round of all countries of the Latin American continent is even less likely.

Concerns about protection at the regional level also exist from a legal perspective, and have been formulated by Latin American experts. Distinguished scholar Ricardo Antequera Parilli argues that a regional system of protection, as well as a supranational system of protection (*protección comunitaria*) like that within the European Union or the Andean Community, would have the deficiency of limited scope of application, in two dimensions: first, that its application is limited to the member states and does not have binding effect on other countries; and second, that cross-border tribes or TCEs are not covered in the part of their territory lying within the non-member states.[223]

However, recent exchange on the topic of protecting TCEs, especially based upon practical experiences in the different Latin American countries, shows that a regional agreement would make sense, as well as "simple" regional cooperation and exchange of experiences.[224] The illicit or improper exploitation of TCEs by individuals or companies located in third countries is only one kind of threat out of many. A lot of others can well be dealt with by means of a regional agreement.

Moreover, in comparison to the existing legal standard of protection in several Latin American countries, where TCEs in total are qualified as cultural heritage, patrimony of the state, and/or belonging to the public domain,[225] an ambitious or at least seriously elaborated system of protection at the regional level would provide a perceptible improvement of the protection of TCEs for many individuals and indigenous and national entities dealing with the issue within several Latin American countries.

As desirable as a regional agreement would be in view of the above arguments, at the same time, the latter aspect reveals another obstacle: In legal terms, national protection of TCEs in Latin America presents a very heterogeneous picture, at the constitutional as well as the simple legislative level.[226] Some countries provide no protection of TCEs at all, like Mexico and Colombia, where TCEs are regarded as belonging to the public domain, while others, like Panama, have even established a sui generis regime to protect TCEs. As a consequence, the "technical" obstacle of

---

[222] *See* at Section 2.B.V.3. above.

[223] Antequera Parilli (2007) 542, translation by the author.

[224] Personal communication with Ana Cristina Bandeira Lins, *Procuradora da República* (equivalent of a state prosecutor or district attorney) in the Ministry of the Public (*Ministerio Público*), on June 23, 2009 in São Paolo, Brazil, *see* also Busch (2010) 220 *et seq*. For details, especially on the situation in Brazil (and Argentina), *see* at Chapter IV Section 2.C.III. and E. below.

[225] In Colombia, for instance, indigenous arts, including dances, singing, handicraft, drawings and sculptures are qualified as cultural patrimony (*patrimonio cultural*), *see* Article 189 of the Copyright Act, Ley 23 de 1982. Apart from that, folkloristic and traditional works of unknown authors ("las obras folclóricas y tradicionales de autores desconocidos") are allocated within the public domain (*dominio público*): Article 187, No. 2, of the same law. This is also the situation in Mexico.

[226] A survey of the national situations will be displayed in the following. *See* at Section 3. below.

drafting a regional agreement based upon at least a minimum consensus within the Latin American region is high, and the step towards a common political position even bigger.

In sum, it is very unlikely that a common instrument of protection of TCEs will be established in the Latin American region in the near future.

Section 3. National Frameworks

Existing legal instruments can—to a certain extent—grant protection of TCEs.[227] Further protection can be provided by new laws, sui generis systems, or the extension of the scope of either the application or the function of existing rights.[228]

According to the principle of hierarchy of norms,[229] any provision on a lower legal level has to be measured by the provisions and values laid down at a higher level, first of all, the constitutional framework.

A. Constitutions

I. General Remarks

Although naturally there exist variations from country to country, some common characteristics of Latin American constitutions can be observed.

First, there is a tendency to change constitutions quickly—similar to the situation of political leaderships. This is especially true of the 1990s and onwards. The most impressive example thereof might be the situation in Ecuador, where new constitutions were adopted in 1996, 1998, and 2008. Sometimes, these constitutional revisions contain radical changes, in these days especially as regards the indigenous population. The slogan in Ecuador, for instance, is "Un año más de Revolución con la Nueva Constitución"[230]—"Another Year of Revolution with the New Constitution." Amending constitutions is a relatively common instrument used for various political aims, lately, e.g., in the case of the Correa government in Ecuador—to move elections ahead to a point of time that appears advantageous for the current leadership.

[227] For details *see* Nordmann (2001) and the gap analysis on the protection of TCEs commissioned by WIPO (2008).

[228] Kur (2001) 23 *et seq.* and Ramsauer (2005) 6 *et seq.*

[229] Principle of the "Supremácia de la Constitución" laid down in Article 424 para 2 of the Ecuadorian Constitution of 2008, "Princípio da supremacia da constituição" in the Brazilian Law, or "Grundsatz des Vorrangs der Verfassung" in German law, laid down in Article 20 para 3 of the German Constitution. *See* at Chapter IV Section 2.B.I. and III. below.

[230] *See* http://www.presidencia.gov.ec, last visited September 1, 2010.

In some other Latin American countries, however, the situation is different, and not as unstable, for example in Brazil, which instated its last new Constitution in 1988, and before that had decades of "constitutional stability." The situation in sum, however, is relatively mutable, in comparison, say, to Western Europe.

The second important point is a frequently observed discrepancy between the constitutional law in the books and constitutional reality.[231] This regards the direct implementation of provisions on the one hand, and by means of national laws on the other, in different areas, especially indigenous issues. While in Mexico, discussions on a new constitution tend to lead to the demand for the mere implementation of the existing one,[232] in Ecuador, a new constitution has been established before concrete actions provided for in the former one had ever been implemented—concretely, on the enhancement, use, and development of the collective intellectual property of indigenous ancestral knowledge.[233]

With regard to the legal nature and interpretation of constitutional provisions, no generalizations can be made.[234]

In relation to the content, some aspects of Latin American constitutions with regard to TCEs will be pointed out to provide a survey of the constitutional situation in the region. One of the most recent constitutions, and one that is extremely far-reaching regarding indigenous issues, is the Bolivian Constitution of 2009.[235] This constitution will therefore be given closer consideration here.

II. Constitutional Rules with TCE Relevance

1. Acknowledgement of "Pluri-Culturality" or Even "Pluri-Nationality"

In the "Latin American constitutional history," the first step towards a new legally anchored policy regarding the indigenous peoples was the acknowledgement of the state as being "pluri-cultural." This was the case e.g. in the 1993 Constitution of

---

[231] *See, e.g.*, the recent discussions on a new constitution in Mexico, which overwhelmingly come to the result that not a new constitution is needed, but the implementation of the existing one, *see* El País (of Mexico) (February 1, 2010).

[232] *Ibid.*

[233] *Ibid.*, and Article 191 of the (former) Ecuadorian Constitution of 1998, which provided that the enhancement, use, and development of the collective intellectual property of indigenous ancestral knowledge should occur in accordance "with the law" – a law which never was implemented. The new Constitution was adopted in 2008. *See* for details at Section 3.A.II.1. below.

[234] One interesting interpretation has been released by the Constitutional Court of Colombia, which is the most active and progressive juridical body in the Latin American region regarding indigenous rights. The decision particularly deals with the relations between public domain, cultural patrimony, collective, and individual ownership, Corte Suprema de Justicia, Sala Plena. Sentencia de abril 2 de 1987. Magistrado Ponente Jairo Duque Pérez, cited from Monroy Rodríguez (2006) no pagination. On details hereon *see* at Section 3.B.IV.1. below.

[235] Available at http://www.presidencia.gob.bo/download/constitution.pdf, last visited September 1, 2010.

Peru, whose Article 2 No. 19 recognizes and protects the "ethnic and cultural plurality of the Nation."

Ecuador and Bolivia were the first countries to lay down the principle of "pluri-nationality" in their Constitutions of 2008 and 2009, respectively.[236] Theoretically, this step could be regarded as a very big one, constitutionally acknowledging the existence of different "nations" within the country, which is of special importance in indigenous issues, as it is particularly the indigenous peoples who have fought for the worldwide acknowledgement as "nations."[237] However, while in both of these countries the legal terminology "indigenous nations and peoples" is used,[238] clear limitations are set, both in theory as well as especially in practice. In Bolivia, the pluri-national conception of the law and the culture is limited by the common, larger, and all-encompassing aim of the "integrative process of the country."[239] In Ecuador, the all-embracing instrument is that of "citizenship;" disregarding the affiliation with an indigenous "nationality," the legal and political link of the individuals to the state is the Ecuadorian nationality.[240] In practice, as a consequence of the principle of the unifying political concept of the "citizen" (*ciudadano*), no special rights should be granted to particular groups in the country, be it indigenous "nationalities," Afro-Ecuadorians or any others.[241]

2. Reference to Indigenous Culture

Many constitutions make reference to indigenous culture. The Peruvian Constitution provides that "the State shall respect the cultural identity of rural and native communities."[242] The Brazilian Constitution, for example, contains a specific concept of culture[243] and explicitly includes indigenous cultures, establishing a public mission of protecting, among other things, indigenous cultural expressions:

---

[236] Art. 1 of the 2008 Constitution of the Republic of Ecuador and Art. 1 of the 2009 Constitution of the Bolivian Republic.

[237] On this aspect of the terminology with regard to TCEs, *see* at Chapter II Section 1.A. above.

[238] *See* for example Article 3 of the Bolivian Constitution and Article 56 of the Ecuadorian Constitution.

[239] Article 1 of the Bolivian Constitution: "dentro del proceso integrador del país."

[240] Article 6 of the 2008 Ecuadorian Constitution: "Sin perjuicio de su pertenencia a alguna de las nacionalidades indígenas que coexisten en el Ecuador plurinacional."

[241] Personal communication on the political reality in Ecuador with Professor Fernando García Serrano, longtime professor and researcher in the Anthropology Department at FLACSO University (Facultad Latinoamericana de Ciencia Sociales) in Quito, Ecuador, in March 2009, in Quito, and *see* the concept of the equalizing "Consejo de Participación Ciudadana y Control Social" in Articles 207 *et seq.* of the 2008 Constitution of Ecuador.

[242] Article 89 at the end.

[243] Articles 215 and 216 of the 1988 Brazilian Constitution. For details related to TCEs, *see* at Chapter IV Section 2.B.I.2. below.

> The state shall ensure all the full exercise of the cultural rights and access to the sources of national culture and shall support and foster the appreciation and diffusion of cultural expressions.
>
> Paragraph 1 – The State shall protect the expressions of popular, Indian and Afro-Brazilian cultures, as well as those of other groups participating in the national civilization process.[244]

The Guatemaltecan Constitution even stipulates that "national artistic expressions, popular art, folklore, and handicraft and autochthonous industries is to be the subject matter of special protection by the state, with the aim of preserving their authenticity". The state propitiates the opening of national and international markets for the free commercialization of the work of the handicraftsmen, promoting their production and adequate mechanization.[245]

3. Acknowledgement of "Collective Rights," Including "Intellectual Rights" and the Recognition as "Legal Entity"

References to collective rights of indigenous peoples in Latin American constitutions are particularly insightful when looking at any draft of future sui generis instruments on the protection of TCEs.

The most advanced existing instrument as regards collective intellectual property rights of indigenous peoples, although mainly referring to traditional knowledge *stricto sensu*,[246] is the 1999 Venezuelan Constitution. Its Article 124 provides:

> The collective intellectual property of indigenous knowledge, technology, and innovations is guaranteed and protected. Any work on genetic resources and the knowledge associated therewith shall be for the collective good. The registration of patents in those resources and ancestral knowledge is prohibited.

The Venezuelan Constitution thereby not only acknowledges collective rights of indigenous peoples, but even regulates specific questions like distribution of benefits and patentability.[247]

The Peruvian Constitution, when providing that "the State shall respect the cultural identity of rural and native communities," includes herein the recognition of the intellectual rights of indigenous peoples.[248] This Constitution even recognizes the status of rural and native communities as "legal identities" and "legal entities."[249] These communities are granted autonomy in their organization, communal work, and the use and free disposal of their lands, as well as in economic and

[244] Article 215 of the 1988 Brazilian Constitution.

[245] Article 62 of the Guatemalan Constitution.

[246] On the terminology *see* at Chapter II Section 1.A. above.

[247] For questions of compatibility of such prohibitions or sui generis provisions with the international framework on intellectual property rights, namely, TRIPS, *see* Straus (2008) 229–295.

[248] Article 89 at the end.

[249] Article 89 of the 1993 Constitution of Peru.

administrative terms, within the framework established by the law. Ownership of their land is not subject to prescription, apart from the case of abandonment provided for in the previous article.

Although the Colombian Constitution does not acknowledge specific collective rights of indigenous peoples, it makes reference to the consideration of collective indigenous interests as regards the exploitation of natural resources in indigenous territories. In this area, the government is urged to "promote the participation of the representatives of the respective communities," without explicitly granting procedural rights of participation, however.[250]

The former, 1998 Constitution of Ecuador acknowledged the collective intellectual property of indigenous ancestral knowledge, stipulating among other things that the enhancement, use and development should occur in accordance "with the law"[251]—though no such national law has been implemented so far.

The current, 2008 Constitution of Ecuador establishes the principle of the "prior consultation"—which is, however, not of the same legally substantive quality as the "prior informed consent" often dealt with in the area of TCEs and traditional knowledge.[252]

4. Reference to Customary Law, Including Jurisdiction, Political Organization, and Other Forms of Autonomy

Particularly when it comes to the consideration of customary law in the drafting of instruments to protect TCEs, references to rights of self-determination, in concrete, indigenous or ancestral jurisdiction and customary law contained in Latin American constitutions, are of special interest here.

Only the Constitution of Paraguay explicitly uses the term "customary law" (*normas consuetudinarias*).[253]

The 1993 Constitution of Peru in its Article 149 considers customary law of native and rural communities, stipulating that, within their territories, the authorities of such communities may exercise jurisdictional functions according to their

[250] "The exploitation of natural resources in indigenous territories shall be done without prejudice to the cultural, social and economic integrity of indigenous communities. The government shall promote the participation of the representatives of the respective communities." *See* Article 330 of the 1991 Colombian Constitution, translation by de la Cruz I. (2006) 14.

[251] Article 191 of the former Ecuadorian Constitution.

[252] Article 57, No. 17, of the 2008 Ecuadorian Constitution states: "The following collective rights of the indigenous communes, communities, peoples, and nationalities are recognized and guaranteed in conformity with the Constitution and international pacts, treaties, conventions, declarations and other instruments of human rights: ... 17. To be consulted before the adoption of a legislative measure that could effect any of their collective rights." For a good overview and details on the principle of prior consultation, *see* http://www.codenpe.gov.ec/images/descargables/consulta2.jpg, last visited October 28, 2010.

[253] Article 63 of the Constitution of Paraguay.

customary law, with the support of rural councils and provided that they do not infringe the fundamental rights of individuals.

The 1998 Constitution of Brazil stipulates: "The Indians shall be accorded recognition of their social organisation, customs, languages, and traditions, and the original rights in the lands that they occupy by tradition, it being the responsibility of the Union to demarcate them, protect them and ensure respect for all their property."[254]

The "protection of the cultures, uses, and customs" is laid down in the Mexican Constitution.[255] The Guatemalan Constitution decrees "respect to the forms of life, customs, traditions"[256] of native communities.

The 1991 Constitution of Colombia provides for the right of indigenous peoples to their own jurisdiction: Article 246 stipulates that "the authorities of indigenous peoples may exercise jurisdictional functions within the indigenous territories, in accordance with their own rules and procedures, provided that they do not contradict the Colombian Constitution and national laws".[257]

As regards political organization and representation, the Colombian Constitution also lays down that indigenous territorial entities are granted autonomy as regards the management of their interests and, within the limitations of the Constitution and the law, may be governed by specific authorities and exercise the corresponding powers.

The recognition of the political organization, cultures, and customs is also contained in the 1999 Constitution of Venezuela: "The State shall recognize the existence of indigenous peoples and communities, their social, political and economic organization, their cultures, usages and customs, their languages and religions."[258] It goes even further and gives an encouraging example for a concrete regulation: "The legitimized authorities of the indigenous peoples may apply juridical instances in their territory which are based in their ancestral traditions, according to their own norms and proceedings."[259]

The former, 1998 Constitution of Ecuador acknowledged the administration of justice in accordance with indigenous customary law and human rights standards.[260] It also provided that the traditional forms of coexistence and social organization and of the generation and exercise of authority should be conserved and developed.[261]

The 2009 Bolivian Constitution stipulates that, within the scope of State unity and in accordance with the Constitution, the indigenous peoples and nations of

254 Article 231 of the 1998 Constitution. For details *see* at Chapter IV Section 2.B.I. below.

255 Article 4 of the Mexican Constitution.

256 Article 66 of the Constitution of Guatemala.

257 Translation by de la Cruz I. (2006) 13.

258 Article 119 of the 1999 Constitution of Venezuela.

259 Article 260 of the 1999 Constitution of Venezuela.

260 *See* Article 191 of the former Ecuadorian Constitution.

261 *See* Article 191 of the former Ecuadorian Constitution.

peasant origin enjoy the right, among others, to exercise their political, economic, and juridical systems according to their cosmovision.[262]

This overview shows that there are many different, but likewise progressive approaches.

5. No Reference to Traditional Cultures or Indigenous Peoples at All

In contrast to those rather progressive provisions displayed above, there also exist Latin American constitutions that completely disregard the particular topic of traditional cultures and indigenous peoples.

No explicit reference to the status of indigenous peoples can be found, for example, in the constitutions of Chile, Uruguay, El Salvador, and Costa Rica. While Uruguay has no special legal treatment of the marginal indigenous population at all, Costa Rica and Chile, on a secondary level, have adopted special legislation on the rights of indigenous peoples,[263] and Costa Rica has even established a special regime on biodiversity covering related traditional knowledge of indigenous peoples and local communities.[264]

Thus, in the latter two cases, at first glance, the lack of specific constitutional provisions does not signify the absence or even negation of indigenous rights. However, it might raise the question of how effective the protection granted solely through ordinary legislation can be. Concerns brought forward regard particularly the conformity of this legislation with "traditional principles of constitutional law ... [like] the concept of the homogenous nation state, most notably national unity and equality before the law."[265] Nonetheless, an ordinary law providing specific measures to be applied in this difficult issue of indigenous and traditional culture can have a much bigger impact on the status of TCEs than a slightly abstract and general principle laid down in a constitution.

Especially in Latin American countries, the effectiveness of any law, either ordinary or constitutional, is determined by its mode of application more than anything else, particularly more than by constitutional parameters—which sometimes are rather political concessions established to calm the waves of current, oftentimes resurfacing, political debates.[266]

---

[262] "En el marco de la unidad del Estado y de acuerdo con esta Constitución las naciones y pueblos indígena originario campesinos gozan de los siguientes derechos: ... 13. ... Al ejercicio de sus sistemas políticos, jurídicos y económicos acorde a su cosmovisión," Article 30, para. 2, of the 2009 Constitution of Bolivia.

[263] Costa Rica: Indigenous Law No. 6172, which grants the indigenous peoples the right to organize themselves as traditionally structured communities within their territory. Chile: The Indian Law, *Ley Indígena* 19.253, for details *see* Heise (2000).

[264] Costa Rican Law No. 7788 on Biodiversity (*Ley de Biodiversidad*); for more details *see* Bucher (2008) 251 *et seq.*

[265] *See* Grote (1999) 507 *et seq.*

[266] On a comprehensive analysis of the difference between indigenous rights on paper and in reality, particularly as regards the afore-mentioned Indian Law in Chile, *see* Heise (2000).

B. Intellectual Property Rights

Returning to the international level, the analysis on gaps in the protection of TCEs that was commissioned by the WIPO Intergovernmental Committee on Intellectual Property and Genetic Resources, Traditional Knowledge and Folklore (IGC) has shown that the conventional IP instruments are not the appropriate answer to the question of how adequately to protect TCEs.[267] Comments issued lately by Latin American countries, despite being only two of them, Brazil and Mexico, reflect the same general perception.[268]

To the same extent, it has become clear that, partly, conventional IP rights can be of use in the protection of TCEs when (only) specific aspects of legal problems in protecting TCEs are addressed. Since most of the Latin American countries are member states to the main WIPO Treaties and TRIPS,[269] the content of the national IP legislation is harmonized along these international lines to a certain extent, to which the result of the WIPO gap analysis then also widely applies. The leeway left in the international treaties for certain national flexibilities, however, leads to certain variations in the national IP systems, including the Latin American countries.

As a consequence, this study gives a general survey of relevant aspects and highlights some special IP regulations, cases, practical examples of the application of IP rights and particularities actually treating TCEs in the region rather than displaying all national "classical" IP systems.

I. Special Regulations

In this respect, a special highlight to be mentioned is the Guatemalan Legislative Decree No. 426 of September 1947, issued in the National Interest of Protecting the Production of Indigenous Textiles.[270] With the aim of avoiding the counterfeiting of autochthonous or authentic textiles, the Decree directs the National Indian Institute to organize in each municipality or indigenous community a mixed committee, called "Committee for the Control of Indigenous Textiles," consisting of three persons, one representative each of the municipality, the National

---

[267] WIPO (2008).

[268] The comments of Brazil are available at http://www.wipo.int/export/sites/www/tk/en/igc/gap_analyses_pdf/tce_tk_brazil_general.pdf, and http://www.wipo.int/export/sites/www/tk/en/igc/gap_analyses_pdf/tce_brazil.pdf; those of Mexico at http://www.wipo.int/export/sites/www/tk/en/igc/gap_analyses_pdf/tce_tk_mexico_general.pdf, http://www.wipo.int/export/sites/www/tk/en/igc/gap_analyses_pdf/tce_mexico_1.pdf, and http://www.wipo.int/export/sites/www/tk/en/igc/gap_analyses_pdf/tce_mexico_2.pdf, last visited October 28, 2010.

[269] On this *see* at Section 1. above.

[270] Guatemalan Legislative Decree No. 426 of 1947, as printed in Valiente López (2006) 83 *et seq*.

Indigenous Institute, and the textile makers.[271] Each committee is to register the designs and embroidery patterns of the textiles of a municipality or community with the Trademark and Patent Office, in order to acquire the exclusive ownership of their use. Both the Indigenous Institute and the Trademark and Patent Office are to establish a special registry for this purpose. All administrative measures for obtaining the registration are taken without any fees.[272] In case the same drawing or design is or has been used traditionally in various municipalities or indigenous communities, all of them can obtain the registration of ownership.[273] Only the Guatemalan nationals who traditionally produce indigenous textiles, and the members of the indigenous communities and populations, may dedicate themselves to the elaboration of textiles belonging to especially established categories of "indigenous autochthonous textiles" and "authentic indigenous textiles."[274]

In turn, those manufacturers or industrialists dedicated to the production of "Guatemalan Textiles," which do not comply with the requirements of the categories of "indigenous autochthonous textiles" or "authentic indigenous textiles," are not allowed to use registered designs, drawings, or embroidery patterns. In case of infringement, the sanctions of the Trademark and Patent Law apply. Nonetheless, any manufacturer or industrialist may register drawings of designs himself, provided they are not part of any such designs classified as "autochthonous" or "authentic," even if the latter are not registered yet.[275]

This Guatemalan legislation of 1947 is utterly advanced for its time. It can be considered as progressive even 60 years later. It combines diverse, interdisciplinary elements relevant for the protection of these kinds of handicrafts, and thus can be qualified as sui generis protection. It is the biggest source of inspiration for and reveals evident parallels to the current sui generis protection in Panama, which will be subject to a detailed analysis in this study.[276] Unfortunately, as Valiente López argues, the biggest problem of the Guatemalan legislation would be its lack of implementation in practice.[277]

II. Trademarks

Apart from this legal highlight, it is also interesting to note that some TCEs, again mainly handicrafts,[278] have been protected under existing, non-specialized intellectual property statues in other Latin American countries.

---

[271] *Ibid.* and Articles 1 et seq. of the Guatemalan Legislative Decree No. 426 of 1947.

[272] Article 7 of the Decree.

[273] Article 8 of the Decree.

[274] Articles 2 and 9 of the Decree.

[275] Article 9 of the Decree.

[276] *See* at Chapter IV Section 1. below.

[277] Valiente López (2006) 85.

[278] For the inclusion of handicrafts in the concept of TCEs *see* at Chapter II Section 1.B.I.1.b. above.

In Mexico, the *Arte Seri* was registered as a trademark in 1994 and 1995 in five different classes, by the Cooperative Society "Artesanos Los Seris" as a study by WIPO shows.[279] The Seri people is made up of a number of communities organized as clans in the Sonora desert. In creating their art, the Seri apply culturally specific skills and use "five local plants" as material.[280] In Panama, the *mola*, a traditional textile of the Kuna Indians,[281] was intended to be registered as a collective trademark, which was regarded as insufficient, however, and finally rendered unnecessary when the Panamanian sui generis regime was established in 2000.[282]

Although they have not necessarily been registered as trademarks yet, some names and ideas for protection by means of collective trademarks also have been developed at the International Workshop "Protecting the Intellectual Property of the Indigenous Design" in November 27 and 28, 2006, in Lima (Peru).[283] The TCEs referred to were mainly traditional indigenous handicrafts like textiles, jewelry, stone and woodworks, and other designs. Names, associations and ideas for trademarks developed were for example "Llamak'ac Mak'e" (Peru), "GUAPECUA" (Guatemala, Peru, Ecuador), "QORY CCAYTO (Hilo de oro)" (Peru).[284]

From another indigenous perspective of a community living in the Peruvian Rainforest, the Asháninkas, trademarks granted by the existing IP system are not a realistic form of protection, as their precondition of registration can hardly be fulfilled by indigenous peoples faced with pressing challenges in their every-day life.[285]

---

[279] WIPO Secretariat (2005) 7.

[280] *Id.*

[281] On this *see* at Chapter IV Section 1.A. *et seq.* below.

[282] *See* at Chapter IV Section 1.B. below. Collective trademarks have been used for protecting TCEs elsewhere, though, e.g. in Portugal. There, the Arraiolos carpets, having been produced by local artisans since the 13th century, as well as "handkerchiefs of the fiancées," embroidery manufactured in a few villages in Minho with origins in the 17th century, have been registered as trademarks. *See* WIPO Secretariat (2005) 8 *et seq.* On design and trademark law and TCEs in general, especially regarding the use of certification marks and the experience with them in Australia and Canada, *see* Lucas-Schlötter (2008) 399 *et seq.*

[283] *See* CHIRAPAQ/Rivera Zea (ed.) (2007): The original title of the workshop was "Taller Internacional 'Protegiendo la Propiedad Intelectual del Diseño Indígena.'"

[284] *Id.* 32–34.

[285] Personal communication with J.M. of the Asháninka Indians of Peru on June 10, 2008: The system of trademarks and their administrative entities situated in the Peruvian Capital Lima would require steps which are too difficult, too intricate, too labor-intensive for the members of their community living in the Amazon rainforest.

III. Geographical Indications

In Mexico, the geographical indication *Olinalá* is used to protect handicrafts made by the Olinalá Indians, as a WIPO study shows.[286] This indigenous tribe from the Sonora Desert creates various articles applying special traditional techniques and skills, using the wood from the aloe tree, which is native to the region.[287]

Mexico has been particularly supportive of the idea of using geographical indications as a means of protection of TCEs at the international level at the negotiations within the IGC at WIPO, especially favoring the use of geographical indications over trademarks.[288] Especially because "both marks and collective marks, if not registered on behalf of all accredited craftspeople, permit the registered owners to exclude other local craftspeople from using the same signs," the delegation of Mexico favored the use of geographical indications.[289]

Notwithstanding, not much use has been made of this legal instrument in Latin American countries. In the biggest country, Brazil, for instance, not even one registration of either a trademark or geographical indication on a TCE has been made so far.[290]

IV. Copyright

1. General Aspects

Some copyright laws of Latin American countries contain provisions on TCEs, mainly using the terms "folklore," "handicraft," or "popular culture."[291] In Bolivia, there are—in theory—even quite detailed provisions on TCEs, or folklore and cultural heritage, worth looking at more closely. The Bolivian Copyright Act, for example, has introduced three articles on the protection of folklore and handicrafts since 1992.[292] The protection of the cultural patrimony is laid down as a guiding principle of the copyright law.[293]

---

[286] WIPO Secretariat (2005) 10.

[287] *Ibid.*

[288] *Ibid.*

[289] Other arguments against the use of trademarks are that "distinctive signs do not permit the craftspeople to prohibit others to manufacture the crafts; they only give the right to prevent others from using similar signs in the course of trade to designate similar or identical handicrafts," *id.* 13. However, geographical indications do not provide for protection against imitations, either. The author thanks Josef Drexl for this valuable hint.

[290] Personal communication with Lucia Regina Fernandes, Official for Geographic Indications at the National Institute of Industrial Property, "Instituto Nacional de Propiedade Industrial (INPI)" in March 2009 in Rio de Janeiro, Brazil.

[291] On the different terms and their meanings *see* at Chapter II Section 1. above.

[292] Articles 21–23 of the Bolivian Copyright Law, Act No. 1322 of April 13, 1992.

[293] Article 1, para. 3, of the Bolivian Copyright Law.

The Mexican Federal Copyright Law contains a specific chapter of regulations on "popular culture."[294] It protects popular culture in its moral aspects similar to integrity in so far as the "literary, artistic works and those of popular or handicraft art, developed and perpetuated in a community or ethnicity which is original to or rooted in the Mexican Republic," are protected against their deformation done with the purpose of causing harm to the community, or prejudice to the reputation or image of the community or ethnicity to which the works belong."[295] Reference to the "authorship" of these works, which do not have an identifiable author, as Article 157 stipulates,[296] is granted in so far as the community, ethnicity, or region has to be mentioned in any fixation, representation, publication, communication, or use of such a work of popular culture.[297] Apart from that, the use of these works is free.[298] Finally, it resides with the Institute of Copyright to monitor the fulfillment of these provisions and to contribute to the protection of the works covered by them.[299]

In sum, the provisions are not specifically designed for TCEs and only provide for limited protection, as they do not grant economic or moral property rights in the manner in which the classic copyright does.

A specific provision of the Mexican law deals with participation in any remuneration for creators of plastic art (*artes plásticas*), excepting works of applied art.[300] Moreover, fixation is a requirement under Mexican copyright law,[301] so that this legislation provides an example of how very little protection for TCEs at the national level in Latin America is granted by copyright.

Similar to the Mexican provision on referring to the source as comparable to an author, the Copyright Law of Nicaragua establishes that if an "expression of

---

[294] "Capítulo III – De las Culturas Populares", Articles 157–161 of the Mexican Copyright Law, "Ley Federal del Derecho de Autor" of 1996, as amended in 2003.

[295] *See* Article 158: "Las obras literarias, artística, de arte popular o artesanal; desarrolladas y perpetuadas en una comunidad o etnia originaria o arraigada en la República Mexicana, estarán protegidas por la presente Ley contra su deformación, hecha con objeto de causar demérito a la misma o perjuicio a la reputación o imagen de la comunidad o etnia a la cual pertenecen."

[296] *See* Article 157: "La presente Ley protege las obras literarias, artísticas, de arte popular o artesanal, así como todas las manifestaciones primigenias en sus propias lenguas, y los usos, costumbres y tradiciones de la composición pluricultural que conforman al Estado Mexicano, que no cuenten con autor identificable."

[297] *See* Article 160: "En toda fijación, representación, publicación, comunicación o utilización en cualquier forma, de una obra literaria, artística, de arte popular o artesanal; protegida conforme al presente capítulo, deberá mencionarse la comunidad o etnia, o en su caso la región de la República Mexicana de la que es propia."

[298] Article 159 stipulates: "Es libre la utilización de las obras literarias, artísticas, de arte popular o artesanal; protegidas por el presente capítulo, siempre que no se contravengan las disposiciones del mismo."

[299] Article 161 provides that "Corresponde al Instituto vigilar el cumplimiento de las disposiciones del presente capítulo y coadyuvar en la protección de las obras amparadas por el mismo."

[300] Article 92bis para. 3 of the Mexican Copyright Law.

[301] Article 5 of the Mexican Copyright Law. *See also* the optional requirement of fixation laid down in Article 2 para. 2 of the Revised Berne Convention.

folklore"[302] serves as a basis of an original work, this fact, as well as the place or region where the expression comes from and its appellation, if it has one, have to be indicated by the author of said work, or by the person who publishes or disseminates it by means of whatever medium or process.[303]

The Cuban Copyright Law protects "expressions of folklore, which have been transmitted from generation to generation, contributing to shaping the national cultural identity in an anonymous or collective or other manner" in an indirect way, by means of protecting compilations of TCEs, more precisely, by granting copyright to those persons who collect and compile manifestations of national folklore, providing that they constitute authentic works.[304]

Finally, the Colombian situation is of interest, as the Colombian Copyright stipulates, first, that "indigenous art in all its manifestations, including dances, songs, handicraft, drawings, and sculptures, belongs to the cultural patrimony,"[305] and, second, that "folkloric and traditional works of unknown authors" belong to the public domain.[306] Particularly, the Colombian Supreme Court had to decide on the question of whether the classification of indigenous art within the cultural patrimony deprived the indigenous peoples of a copyright and therefore contradicted the former Article 35 of the Colombian Constitution.[307]

The Supreme Court decided that there was no violation of the right to literary and artistic property, as the statement in Article 189 of the Copyright Law, namely, that indigenous art belongs to the cultural patrimony, does not contain any statement on the (individual) copyright of any indigenous person according to the general provisions of the Copyright Law. In the Court's reasoning, the "allocation" of indigenous art to the cultural patrimony, rather, is "superfluous," as any art of the relevant human society can be and is part of the cultural patrimony. The "cultural patrimony" does not constitute a legal person, which can acquire rights and accept

---

[302] On the terminology *see* at Chapter II Section 1. above.

[303] Article 96 of the Copyright Law of Nicaragua, Law No. 312 of 1999, which stipulates: "Cuando la expresión del folklore sirva como base de una obra, deberá indicarse por el autor y por quien lo divulgue o lo difunda por cualquier medio o procedimiento esta circunstancia, así como el departamento o región de donde proviniere esa expresión y su título, si lo tuviere."

[304] Articles 26 and 27 of the Cuban Copyright Law, Ley 14 de 1977, which are entitled Chapter IV – On National Folklore. Article 26 reads: "Se protegen por esta Ley todas aquellas obras folklóricas que han venido siendo transmitidas de generación en generación, contribuyendo a conformar la identidad cultural nacional de manera anónima y colectiva o en cualquier otra forma." Article 27 stipulates that "Quienes recojan y compilen bailes, canciones, melodías, proverbios, fábulas, cuentos y otras manifestaciones del folklore nacional, disfrutan del derecho de autor sobre sus obras, siempre que las mismas, por la selección o la disposición de los materiales que incluyan, lleguen a constituir obras auténticas y rigurosas."

[305] Article 189 of the Colombian Copyright Law, Law No. 23 of 1982.

[306] Article 187 No. 3 of the Law.

[307] Corte Suprema de Justicia, Sala Plena. Sentencia de abril 2 de 1987. Magistrado Ponente Jairo Duque Pérez, cited from Monroy Rodríguez (2006) no pagination. The former Article 35 of the Colombian Constitution protected literary and artistic property.

obligations. Therefore, if there are known indigenous authors of "works" protected by the Copyright Law, this protection can also be obtained by such authors.[308]

The decision is of special interest in view of the current discussions in Brazil whether qualifying TCEs as part of the immaterial cultural patrimony at the same time constitutes their allocation within the public domain in the ambit of copyright.[309]

2. Legislations Establishing the Paying Public Domain

One of the most important attempts to establish adequate protection of TCEs in copyright legislation is the institution of a paying public domain. At the international level, UNESCO and WIPO in the 1970s and 1980s promoted the paying public domain as an instrument for the protection of TCEs, which at the time was called "folklore."[310] Through the paying public domain, a user of works or objects that legally are located within the public domain is required to pay for a compulsory license.

A system of paying public domain was instituted in Bolivia, namely, in Articles 58 and 60 of the Bolivian Copyright Law[311] and, for a time, in Brazil.[312]

In Bolivia, works of folklore (*obras del folklore*)[313] are qualified as part of the regime of the National Patrimony (*Patrimonio Nacional*),[314] equalizing them with works whose duration of protection has expired or whose authors have died without

[308] Corte Suprema de Justicia, Sala Plena. Sentencia de abril 2 de 1987. Magistrado Ponente Jairo Duque Pérez, cited from *id.*

[309] On this discussion *see* at Section 3.B.IV.4. below.

[310] *See* the 1976 Tunis Model Law, dealing with folklore among other copyright legislation, especially Article 17 establishing the paying public domain, and the 1982, "Model Provisions for National Laws on the Protection of Expressions of Folklore Against Illicit Exploitation and Other Prejudicial Actions," and the "Draft Treaty for the Protection of Expressions of Folklore Against Illicit Exploitation and Other Prejudicial Actions". On a discussion on Article 17 of the Tunis Model Law *see* Lucas-Schlötter (2008) 447.

[311] Bolivian Copyright Act of April 29, 1992.

[312] On this *see* at Chapter IV Section 2.B.IV.1. below.

[313] Article 21 defines "folklore in the strict sense" as "the sum of literary and artistic works created in the national territory by unknown or unidentifiable authors, who are presumed to be nationals or the ethnic communities of the country, and which [works] are transmitted from generation to generation, constituting one of the fundamental elements of the traditional cultural patrimony of the Nation". It reads fully: "Se consideran protegidas por esta Ley todas aquellas obras consideradas como folklore, entendiéndose por folklore en sentido estricto: el conjunto de obras literarias y artísticas creadas en el territorio nacional por autores no conocidos o que no se identifiquen y que se presuman nacionales del país o de sus comunidades étnicas y se trasmitan de generación en generación, constituyendo uno de los elementos fundamentales del patrimonio cultural tradicional de la nación."

[314] Article 22 provides: "Las obras del folklore de acuerdo con la definición anterior, para los efectos de su utilización como obras literarias y artísticas, serán consideradas como obras pertenecientes al patrimonio nacional de conformidad con las normas contenidas en el título XI

leaving heirs.[315] This might astonish, as the basis of TCEs, the tradition, only survives when heirs exist and maintain the tradition.

The consequence of the legal qualification as belonging to the national patrimony is the special system of a paying public domain: The non-commercial use of these works is free; for commercial use, a culture tax (*participación*) must be paid to the Bolivian state.[316] This can be between 10 and 50 % of what would be paid to authors for the use of comparable works subjected to the private regime of protection.[317] The concrete amount is determined by the Executive Decree, which was released only 3 years after the entry into force of the Copyright Act. Depending upon the type of use, this is between 10 % of the regular fee for copying and publishing as a book and 50 % for broadcasting or transmitting the work to the public.[318]

A share of 10 % of the paying-public-domain fee are to be given to the compiler of the works, and another 10 % to the communities where the expressions come from, if they can be identified.[319] As for the rest, it goes to finance cultural programs and institutions.[320] They are collected and distributed by the authors' collective rights management organization authors' collecting society in cooperation with the National Copyright Directorate.[321]

Apart from the obligation to pay a fee, moral rights on the "works of folklore" have to be respected, independent of the aim of use. Instead of the individual author

de la presente Ley, sin perjuicio de las normas de protección que puedan ser adoptadas por otras instituciones del Estado o por acuerdos internacionales."

[315] Article 23 establishes: "Las artesanías y el diseño artesanal serán protegidos por las normas generales de la presente Ley y especialmente por aquéllas referidas a las artes plásticas y al patrimonio nacional." Article 58 lit. a) stiuplates: "Patrimonio Nacional es el régimen al que pasan las obras de autor boliviano que salen de la protección del derecho patrimonial privado, por cualquier causa; pertenecen al Patrimonio Nacional: a) Las obras folklóricas y de cultura tradicional de autor no conocido."

[316] *See* Article 60 of the Copyright Law: "La utilización bajo cualquier forma o procedimiento de obras del Patrimonio Nacional y del dominio público será libre, pero quien lo haga comercialmente, pagará al Estado, de acuerdo con lo establecido en los reglamentos, una participación cuyo monto no será menor del diez por ciento (10%) y no mayor del cincuenta por ciento (50%) que el que se pague a los autores o sus causahabientes por utilización de obras similares sujetas al régimen privado de protección."

Article 61 reads: "Los montos recaudados por concepto de utilización de obras del Patrimonio Nacional, se aplicarán únicamente al fomento y difusión de los valores culturales del país."

[317] Article 60 of the Copyright Law.

[318] Article 25, para 2, of the Executive Decree.

[319] Article 62 of the Copyright Law, which provides: "El Estado a través de la Dirección Nacional de Derechos de Autor reconocerá del porcentaje recaudado por obras de Patrimonio Nacional, un diez por ciento (10%) al recopilador y un diez por ciento (10%) a la comunidad de origen en caso de ser identificados."

[320] Article 25, para. 1, of the Executive Decree.

[321] Article 62 of the Copyright Law ("Dirección Nacional de Derechos de Autor") and Article 25 of the Executive Decree.

of the work, the community that is the source of the folklore has to be indicated as the author.[322]

The law aims at the combination of moral and economic approaches: to keep "folklore" alive through its free non-commercial use, on the one hand, and to control commercial use and share the remuneration for this use directly with the communities. The law even introduced an international aspect: It provided the ministry of culture with the competence to preserve of the integrity of Bolivian "folklore" abroad.[323]

3. Practical Experiences and Current Legislative Situation

Neither in Brazil nor in Bolivia did the paying-public-domain approach work out in practice. In Brazil, the instrument of the paying public domain was abolished from the copyright law again, and in Bolivia, already in 1999, the implementation of the provisions, especially regarding the control of the integrity of the works and the correct allocation of the remuneration was questioned by authors,[324] and the WIPO fact-finding missions determined that "it is clearly understood by Bolivian authorities, however, that copyright protection for traditional knowledge is not sufficient."[325] Moreover, as regards the international approach of the Bolivian Executive Decree to the Copyright Act, it remained unclear whether the country concerned would respect the "cross-border" competence of the Bolivian Ministry of Culture or how the Ministry would enact relevant measures outside the country. As of 2010, the introduction of a sui generis system on the protection of TCEs, inspired by the one in Panama, is being discussed in Bolivia.[326]

Worth mentioning in this context is the sui generis law on traditional knowledge in Peru.[327] As one of the first legislations of its kind worldwide,[328] it establishes a system similar to the paying public domain with regard to traditional knowledge that "has been made accessible to persons other than the indigenous peoples by mass communication media such as publication or, when the properties, uses or characteristics of a biological resource are concerned, where it has become extensively known outside the confines of the indigenous peoples and communities."[329]

[322] Article 7 of the Executive Decree.

[323] Article 7 para 2, 2nd sentence, of the Executive Decree.

[324] Unterguggenberger (1999) 111.

[325] WIPO (2001), *see* especially the Fact Finding Mission to Bolivia, p. 5.

[326] Information of the Panamanian DIGERPI on a respective Bolivian request, personal communication with Luz Celeste Ríos de Davis, General Director of the Industrial Property Registry, in February, 2009, Panama City.

[327] Law on the Protection of Indigenous Peoples' Collective Knowledge Associated with Biological Resources No. 27811. For details *see* at Chapter II Section 1.A.IV. above.

[328] Bucher (2008) 185.

[329] Article 13 of the Peruvian Law No. 27811.

When this traditional knowledge is used within 20 years after its falling into the public domain, the law provides that—similar to the paying public domain in the situation of a retrospective extension of copyright—"a percentage of the value, before tax, of the gross sales resulting from the marketing of the goods developed on the basis of that knowledge shall be set aside for the Fund for the Development of Indigenous Peoples."[330]

While some authors highlight the progressive and balanced character of the regulation,[331] others, however, have criticized it as retroactively "legalizing former misappropriations" of traditional knowledge.[332]

4. Current Discussion

Inspired in part by the new law of Peru in the parallel situation of protecting traditional knowledge, discussions on protecting TCEs by means of a system of the paying public domain have re-emerged, at the international as well as the Latin American level.[333] Although Brazil was one of the countries that introduced the paying public domain and then abolished it again, there are growing arguments in Latin American countries in favor of an approach that applies the instrument of the paying public domain. Brazilian authors especially argue in favor of an "updated version" of the paying public domain.[334]

a. Arguments in Favor of an "Updated Version" of the Paying Public Domain

aa. The Idea

The proposal is called "Community Intellectual Rights" and its basic idea is that "traditional knowledge should stay in the public domain for anyone to use, but that originators should share in the benefits when it is used for commercial purposes. Furthermore, these rights should not be subject to time limits."[335] This is exactly what the instrument of a paying public domain could implement. The idea of such "Community Intellectual Rights" would be "in stark contrast to contemporary practice of IPRs, which requires exclusivity and a limited timeframe. In other words, the expectations of the two systems are reversed: free access and public domain versus monopoly and secrecy; unlimited time frame for intellectual rights versus loss of intellectual rights after a certain time."[336]

---

[330] Article 13 of the Peruvian Law No. 27811.

[331] Bucher (2008) 194.

[332] Tobin (2002) 386, 387.

[333] Taubman and Leistner (2008) 147.

[334] Carneiro da Cunha (no year) no pagination.

[335] *Ibid.*

[336] *Ibid.*

bb. The Points of Criticism

(i) The International Scope of Application: Principle of Reciprocity

A successful use of the paying public domain as a legal instrument for the dealing with TCEs, however, would depend upon appropriate international circumstances. These circumstances are not given at the moment, due to the limited principle of reciprocity.[337] TRIPS does not oblige the member states within their boundaries to respect the allocation of immaterial goods within the public domain according to the member states' legislations. Thus, the authors in favor of an "updated version of a paying public domain" argue that:

> knowledge that has been in the public domain for generations in one country might be privatized and enjoy IPRs in another country. The original country is not only excluded from benefits but also ironically obliged by the TRIPS Agreement to honor such an intellectual right. What was originally in the public domain in the country could come back, thanks to these regulations, as private property. No country on its own can ensure that other countries will respect its internal regulations unless an International Convention is subscribed to.[338]

As a consequence of this criticism, Carneiro da Cunha appeals to UNESCO and WIPO to develop an international agreement "under which countries could make traditional knowledge publicly available, with the provisions that: it would not be privatized in other countries, local and Indigenous communities would share in the benefits of commercial initiatives or products that derive from their knowledge," for example, through an "updated version" of the paying public domain.[339]

(ii) Practicability

Carneiro da Cunha acknowledges that "much could be argued in relation to the states being the recipients of the domaine public payant fees and there being no necessary provisions for channeling them to the local people."[340]

One solution could be the one established in the Executive Decree in Bolivia—a solution that the authors in favor of the "updated version of a paying public domain" do not see. This solution on paper, however, did not work out in Bolivia in practice. Nevertheless, "the fact remains that this is an important attempt at dealing with the intangible heritage," according to the cited discussions.[341] One could also argue that the times and modes of organization of collecting societies and indigenous representations might have changed during the last 10 years, so that a new attempt could be worthwhile. However, an overarching study of collective rights management organizations in Latin America and their practices does not support such an

[337] Articles 2 and 3 of the TRIPS Agreement.

[338] Carneiro da Cunha (no year).

[339] *Ibid.*

[340] *Ibid.*

[341] *Id.*

assumption,[342] and neither does the Bolivian approach, favoring a sui generis regime instead of relaunching the country's own paying public domain.[343]

(iii) Political Realities

Why should a paying public domain or an "updated version" of it be a good and politically realistic solution, if the attempt to enforce such a model in relation to "folklore" failed in the 1980s for lack of political support? Considering "the unprecedented mobilization of traditional people and some governments around the issue of local and Indigenous knowledge after the Convention for Biological Diversity of 1992," the author in favor of an "updated version of the paying public domain" argues, "this is a totally new situation that would permit UNESCO to launch a successful initiative."[344] Whether UNESCO would be the right entity to do so remains questionable, as negotiations at WIPO, and specifically on the topics of TCEs, are extremely difficult already.

b. Arguments Against a Paying Public Domain

The official position of Brazil, communicated by the Permanent Mission of the country in Geneva, is against the protection of TCEs by means of a public domain, be it a paying one or not. The statement officially communicated in 2008 makes clear that:

> TCEs are not in the public domain, as they belong to a specific group, which should be compensated by their use by non-members of the group in question as a benefit-sharing mechanism. An international instrument should, inter alia, clearly ensure communities the entitlement of collective rights, moral and economic, related to their TCEs/EoFs.[345]

At the international level, similar discussions are known, as well, regarding the approach of WIPO or even former ones like the Tunis Model Law.[346] The paying public domain established in Article 17 of the 1976 Tunis Model Law has been criticized with regard to TCEs, mainly because the protection of TCEs or "folklore" established by the Model Law on the one hand appears to be equivalent to the classic, exclusive and time-limited copyright ("works of national folklore", Article 6), and on the other hand allocates it to the paying public domain (Article 17),

---

[342] *See* the encompassing study of Alich (2010).

[343] On this *see* at Section 3.B.IV.3. above.

[344] Carneiro da Cunha (no year).

[345] EoFs stands for Expressions of Folkore, and was used interchangeably with "TCEs" at WIPO at that stage. The citation constitutes the specific comment of Brazil on Paragraph 89 of the gap analysis on the protection of Traditional Cultural Expressions (TCE)/Expressions of Folklore (EF) of the IGC of WIPO, and is available at http://www.wipo.int/export/sites/www/tk/en/igc/gap_analyses_pdf/tce_brazil.pdf, last visited October 28, 2010.

[346] For a discussion on the public domain and the WIPO approach, *see* De Roman Pérez (2007) 66–110.

which is unlimited in time, "and it is consequently difficult to identify the time at which the paying public domain replaces the principle of the exclusive right."[347]

An "updated version" of the paying public domain therefore does not seem to be a realistic scenario in the near future in either the Latin American region or the international ambit.

C. Culture-Law Aspects

Especially as a consequence of the work of UNESCO, but also before that time, some Latin American countries approached the issue of TCEs and "folklore" from a point of view of the public law, mainly cultural law.

First, only cultural heritage or patrimony in general was dealt with. For instance, the Peruvian General Act for the Protection of the Nation's Cultural Heritage provides for general "protection" of TCEs as part of the cultural heritage. It lays down that "the nation's cultural heritage is made up of the cultural assets which are testimony to human creation, tangible or intangible, declared expressly as such by virtue of its artistic, scientific, historical or technical importance"[348] and provides for the identification, protection, research, maintenance, restoration, and dissemination of the cultural heritage,[349] in a system implemented by the Council of the National Cultural Heritage.[350]

A quite early and interesting approach explicitly addressing and containing intangible expressions as part of the national cultural heritage is the Guatemalan Cultural Heritage Law.[351] The intangible cultural heritage is defined as "constituted by institutions, traditions, and customs like oral, musical, medical, culinary, handicraft, religious tradition, and that of dances and theatre."[352] These cultural expressions, provided that they are included in the Culture Goods Registry,[353] are under the protection of the state and cannot be disposed of by means of contractual agreements without authorization by the Directorate-General of the Cultural and Natural Patrimony,[354] a quite remarkable legal consequence.

---

[347] Lucas-Schlötter (2008) 447.

[348] Article 1, para. 2, of Law No. 24047, of January 5, 1985.

[349] Article 3 of Law No. 24047.

[350] Article 9 of Law No. 24047, translation inspired by Lucas-Schlötter (2008) 429.

[351] *See* the definition of cultural patrimony in Article 1 and of the intangible cultural heritage in Article 3 para. 2 of the Law "Ley para la Proteccion del Patrimonio Cultural de la Nación", No. 26–97 of April 25, 1997, contained in the Decree of the Congress of the same date, available at http://www.mcd.gob.gt/, last visited November 2, 2010.

[352] "Es el constituído por instituciones, tradiciones y costumbres tales como: la tradición oral, musical, medicinal, culinaria, artesanal, religiosa, de danza y teatro," Article 3 para. 2 of the Law.

[353] Lucas-Schlötter (2008) 430 *et seq.*

[354] *See* for details Articles 9 and 10 of the Law.

In Brazil, for instance, a complex system of a cultural registry and promotion policy was implemented as a consequence of an international seminar on intangible cultural heritage conducted by UNESCO at Fortaleza, and of the 2003 Convention for the Safeguarding of the Intangible Cultural Heritage.[355]

Another good example of a very recent introduction of a special concept of protection of immaterial cultural heritage or patrimony including TCEs is the new Article 11-1 of the Colombian General Law of Culture, added in 2008.[356] Before, it was unclear whether TCEs were covered by the definition and understanding of the "cultural patrimony of the Nation" contained in Article 4 of the same Law.[357] The terms "the cultural goods and values which are expressions of the Colombian nationality" are interpreted widely and thus also encompass tangible and intangible expressions, including TCEs.[358] The content of protection of the cultural patrimony including TCEs is regulated by Article 5, namely, that the state policy regarding the cultural patrimony has the principal aims of "protection, conservation, rehabilitation, and dissemination of said patrimony with the purpose of serving as a testimony to the national cultural identity in the present as well as in the future".

In comparison to this rather broad and imprecise concept of protection, the new Article 11-1 constitutes a major step forward. The immaterial cultural patrimony is understood as consisting of, among other things, "the manifestations, practices, uses, performances, expressions, knowledge, techniques, and cultural spaces that the communities and groups recognize as an integral part of their cultural patrimony."[359] The concept of a "representative list" resembles the concept of the "Registry" of the immaterial cultural patrimony in the Brazilian system of cultural law, which will be subjected to a detailed examination and analysis below.[360]

---

[355] *See* at Chapter IV Section 2.C.II.1. below.

[356] The Article was inserted by means of Article 8 of Law No. 1185 of 2008 as new Article 11-1 of the Colombian "Ley General de Cultura," Law 397 of 1997.

[357] Monroy Rodríguez (2006) no pagination, translation by the author.

[358] *Id.*

[359] "Artículo 11-1. Patrimonio Cultural Inmaterial. El patrimonio cultural inmaterial está constituido, entre otros, por las manifestaciones, prácticas, usos, representaciones, expresiones, conocimientos, técnicas y espacios culturales, que las comunidades y los grupos reconocen como parte integrante de su patrimonio cultural. Este patrimonio genera sentimientos de identidad y establece vínculos con la memoria colectiva. Es transmitido y recreado a lo largo del tiempo en función de su entorno, su interacción con la naturaleza y su historia y contribuye a promover el respeto de la diversidad cultural y la creatividad humana."

[360] No. 1. of Article 11-1: "Lista Representativa de Patrimonio Cultural Inmaterial. Las manifestaciones del patrimonio cultural inmaterial podrán ser incluidas en la Lista Representativa de Patrimonio Cultural Inmaterial.
Cualquier declaratoria anterior como bien de interés cultural del ámbito nacional respecto de las manifestaciones a las que se refiere este artículo quedará incorporada a la Lista Representativa de Patrimonio Cultural Inmaterial a partir de la promulgación de esta ley.
2. Plan de Salvaguardia. Con la inclusión de una manifestación cultural en la Lista Representativa de Patrimonio Cultural Inmaterial se aprobará un Plan Especial de Salvaguardia orientado al fortalecimiento, revitalización, sostenibilidad y promoción de la respectiva manifestación.

Of special interest for the relationship between culture and copyright law in the ambit of TCEs is another provision contained in the Colombian General Law of Culture, which deals with "Rights of Ethnic Groups," and provides that "with the aim of protecting languages, traditions, uses, and customs, and knowledge, the State *guarantees the collective rights of authorship of the ethnic groups*, supports the processes of ethno-education, and stimulates the diffusion of their patrimony by means of communication."[361]

In light of this article, Colombian experts have called for the creation of a collective copyright that recognizes the intellectual property of the indigenous communities. Monroy Rodríguez argues that it is an urgent obligation of the national government to immediately comply with the order of the Cultural Law and establish said collective copyright.[362]

D. Other Legislative Measures of Relevance

A provision worth mentioning is the very early approach towards a minimum protection of TCEs, more precisely, handicraft, by means of a prohibition of importation contained in a special Guatemalan law called "Decree in Defense of Indigenous Industries of May 4, 1936."[363] Article 1 of the Decree prohibits the importation of textiles and woven fabrics with typical indigenous characteristics and dyes or similar ones to those that are produced in the country.

This Decree inspired a corresponding Panamanian law, Law 26 of 1984 of the Mola, as Valiente López tells, which was part of the "preparatory work" enabling

---

El Ministerio de Cultura reglamentará para todo el territorio nacional el contenido y alcance de los Planes Especiales de Salvaguardia.
3. Identificación. Como componente fundamental para el conocimiento, salvaguardia y manejo del patrimonio cultural inmaterial, corresponde al Ministerio de Cultura, en coordinación con el Instituto Colombiano de Antropología e Historia, definir las herramientas para la identificación de las manifestaciones. La identificación de las manifestaciones a que se refiere este artículo se hará con la participación activa de las comunidades.
4. Competencias. La competencia y manejo de la Lista Representativa de Patrimonio Cultural Inmaterial corresponde al Ministerio de Cultura en coordinación con el Instituto Colombiano de Antropología e Historia, y a las entidades territoriales según lo previsto en el artículo 8o de este Título.
En todo caso, la inclusión de manifestaciones en la Lista Representativa de Patrimonio Cultural Inmaterial, deberá contar, según el caso, con el concepto previo favorable del Consejo Nacional de Patrimonio Cultural, o de los respectivos Consejos Departamentales o Distritales de Patrimonio Cultural."

[361] Article 13 stipulates: "Derechos de Grupos Etnicos. … Con el fin de proteger lenguas, tradiciones, usos y costumbres y saberes, el Estado garantizará los derechos de autoría colectiva de los grupos étnicos, apoyará los procesos de etnoeducación, y estimulará la difusión de su patrimonio a través de los medios de comunicación." Emphasis in the English translation added by the author.

[362] Monroy Rodríguez (2006) no pagination.

[363] "Decreto en Defensa de las Industrias Indígenas del día 4 de mayo de 1936."

the establishment of the current sui generis regime on TCEs of the country and even influencing the actual content of the Panamanian sui generis law.[364]

E. Alternative or Additional Protection Through Contracts and Protocols

Protection apart from national legislative measures or the acknowledgement of solutions according to customary law can be granted through contracts or protocols.

In Latin America, there is no special reference to such instruments in any legislative body on TCEs so far. Unfortunately, there neither exist general databases or collections and publications of examples of such contracts or protocols so far, as, for instance, WIPO is trying to establish at the international level.[365]

Nonetheless, there are some institutions, mainly universities or non-governmental organizations, that provide legal aid and have designed or contributed to the design of various clauses, contracts, or ethical guidelines that are available online. Two such institutions are the Socio-Environmental Institute[366] and the "Conselho Indigenista Missionário (CIMI)"[367] in Brazil.

I. Relevance: Useful Modes of Protection?

At the international level, this sort of protection through contracts or protocols has been rated no "real" alternative:

> Given the asymmetry of the power relationship between the two parties, there can be little doubt about what the inevitable outcome would be. However carefully any model contract is drafted, however ardently such contracts try to correct the huge imbalance between the provider and the user, such an approach simply cannot lead to anything even remotely resembling a fair and equitable regime. Law regulating private contractual relationships, combined with carefully crafted model contracts, cannot therefore be the solution. A solution can only be found in a legally binding universal instrument which balances the rights of intellectual property holders against a concomitant obligation on their part to submit to clearly defined, mandatory requirements relating to genetic resources and associated traditional knowledge.[368]

---

[364] Valiente López (2006) 81.

[365] Some international examples of contracts and licensing agreements at WIPO can be found under http://www.wipo.int/tk/en/folklore/creative_heritage/agreements/, as well as on the database prepared by the Intergovernmental Committee of WIPO at http://www.wipo.int/tk/en/databases/contracts/index.html, last visited October 25, 2010.

[366] *See* www.socioambiental.org/, last visited October 27, 2010.

[367] *See* www.cimi.org.br/, last visited October 27, 2010.

[368] Report of the Seventh Session of the WIPO IGC, WIPO/GRTKF/IC/7/15, para. 175.

Notwithstanding those negotiating and informational asymmetries, some positive practical experiences have been gained already, for example in Brazil.[369] Admittedly, the contracting parties on the non-indigenous side in those cases were public or scientific organizations with previous experience in intercultural interactions with indigenous peoples.[370]

In sum, if regulations set up at the national level or through agreements at the international level do not suffice or do not even exist, this kind of alternative protection might be quite helpful. Especially in Latin America, these alternatives to a lacking regulated protection are of importance. Some aspects of these legal instruments are worth pointing out.

II. Contracts

Contracts can be concluded between two or more persons and contain agreements about all aspects of treating TCEs, for example to omit commercial photography at a festival or to establish and respect a collective copyright.

1. Model Contract of the Association of Multi-Sector Handicraftsmen Aymara CAMACANI, Peru

a. The Model Contract

In Peru, a cooperation of Peruvian women and the Centre for Rights and Democracy of Canada designed a quite detailed Model Contract, which aims at "the defense of the intellectual property of the designs of the indigenous women in the market."[371] The design of the Model Contract is integrated into a 2002 pilot project on the Model Contract and its practical application, as part of other activities developed by the Intellectual Property and Biodiversity Commission of the Continental Liaison Group of Indigenous Women of the Americas.[372]

The Model Contract was adapted for use by the Association of the Multi-Sector Handicraftsmen Aymara CAMACANI–AAMAC, Peru, for licensing "the use of the indigenous designs" of this Association.[373] The Association is composed of 65 handicraft members of the Aymara peoples and is based in the peasant

[369] *See* at Section 3.E.II. below. On the other hand, such negotiations or contracts have also resulted in legal problems afterwards – which, however, were not always due to negotiating asymmetries, but rather to internal problems like representation. See the experiences made by FUNAI in Brazil, see at Chapter IV Section 2.D.II. below.

[370] Like the *Museu do Índio* in Rio de Janeiro, Brazil; on this *see* at Chapter IV Section 2. below.

[371] CHIRAPAQ/Rivera Zea (ed.) (2007) 35, translation by the author. Legal support for drafting the contract was given by Milagritos Chía López, *ibid.*

[372] *Id.* 35, translation by the author.

[373] *Id.* 137–140, translation by the author.

community of Camacani, in the district of Puno.[374] They mainly produce handicrafts, particularly clothes made of Alpaca wool, decorated with their own design, which they distribute through the *Central Interregional de Artesanos del Perú – CIAP*.[375]

The contract stipulates that "the indigenous peoples have the right to possession, control, and protection of their cultural patrimony, in particular, their designs. This property is of a collective character, inalienable and unlimited in time."[376] The holder of this collective right is the Association.[377] Benefits arising from these rights are distributed according to internal rules.[378]

The object of the contract is to license the collective right to use the design in a non-exclusive way. Although the wording of the Contract refers to the licensing of "the use," intellectual property rights on theses designs are established and licensed in the Model Contract. The license covers the use for exhibition, reproduction, and other purposes.[379] Although these "other" types of use are not determined concretely, "any other kind of use" as well as sub-licensing without express authorization is excluded.[380] Non-authorized use causes the termination of the contract, giving the licensor the right to damage compensation.[381]

It is also remarkable that the contract entitles the Association to suspend the contract without obligation to give a financial compensation if it believes—considering the opinion of the competent indigenous authority—that the integrity of the cultural patrimony is threatened by the respective use.[382]

b. Practical Experiences

Considering other results gathered together in this context, it is not astonishing that the practical result of the pilot program "Application of the Model Contract" is, unfortunately, quite disappointing.

According to Rivera Zea, the Association tried to "make a contracting company sign the Model Contract, but that was very difficult. At the end, we did not manage it."[383] Then they applied another "method" of "protecting" their designs and intellectual property, which is the following one: To avoid copying in Peru, they

---

[374] *Id.* 37.

[375] *Id.* 38.

[376] Clause 1 para. 1 of the Contract. *Id.* 137.

[377] Clause 1 para. 4 of the Contract. *Ibid.*

[378] Clause 1 para. 5 of the Contract. *Ibid.*

[379] Clauses 2 and 1 para 6 of the Contract. Exclusive rights of use for a certain period of time may be licensed in addition: clause 3 para 1 point 3. *Ibid.*

[380] Clause 3 para. 2 point 2 and clause 8 of the Contract. *Ibid.*

[381] Clause 3 para. 2 of the Contract. *Ibid.*

[382] Clause 5 of the Contract. *Ibid.*

[383] Hermelinda Nina, president of the Association at that time, cited from *id.* 38, translation by the author.

only reproduce their most well-known designs, while the newest ones they earmark for exportation. "But, of course, we don't have the security that they do not copy us outside the country."[384]

From this example it becomes clear that indigenous initiatives in the legal ambit as well are able and suited to strengthen cooperation among indigenous persons, in this case women, and contribute to maintaining the vitality of TCEs. Apart from that, it is also clear that, first, model contracts have to be designed in a somewhat balanced manner, second, that negotiation skills or strong market positions are needed to apply such a model, not to mention potential implementation and litigation or dispute resolution difficulties, and third, that an international instrument is needed to provide effective protection for TCEs.

2. Contract Clause of the Indigenous Peoples of the Alto-Xingu Region, Brazil

Another, more successful example, at least as regards the negotiation of a clause, is the following one: a contractual regulation negotiated by indigenous peoples on the one hand and non indigenous ones on the other, although under more modest circumstances. This is the clause on collective indigenous copyright contained in the publication "Ikú Ügühütu Higei – Arte Gráfica dos Povos Kari do Alto Xingu," organized by Bruna Franchetto, with texts and illustrations by Mestres Karib of the Alto Xingu, and published by the Museu do Índio—FUNAI in Rio de Janeiro in 2003.[385]

The clause deals with the copyright on the designs and drawings (*desenhos*) of indigenous authorship (*autoria*). It might be regarded as a bit ambiguous, as on the one hand, it mentions that the copyright is with the indigenous associations Kuikuro, Kalawao, Nahukwá and Manipur, and on the other hand, the clause itself then stipulates that the copyright is "of a collective nature and possessed by (all) the peoples (*povos*) of the Alto-Xingu Region, *represented* by their associations."[386]

As regards the question of reproduction, the clause stipulates that: "Total or partial reproduction of the illustrations contained in the book without previous, express and written authorization of the Alto-Xingu peoples granted by the associations and representatives is prohibited."

The clause also treats the issue of distribution and even determines the intended use of benefits: "The remuneration generated by the selling of this publication will be reverted in its entirety to the educative activities of these peoples."[387]

---

[384] *Ibid.*

[385] Fausto and Franchetto (eds.) (2008).

[386] *Ibid.* Translation, insertions (all) and emphasis added by the author.

[387] The clause reads: "Copyright 2003 Associações Kuikuro, Kalapalo, Nahukwá e Matipu para os desenhos de autoria indígena. Os direitos autorais sobre os desenhos constantes da presente obra são de natureza coletiva e pertencem aos povos alto-xinguanos, representados por suas

What is remarkable, however, is that not the "traditional leaders" have been chosen as representatives, but legally created institutions like "associations."[388] It should be mentioned, further, that the publication had institutional support by the Volkswagen Foundation and the Brazilian Socio-Environmental Institute, the Instituto Socioambiental (ISA). The latter is specialized, competent, and advanced in the treatment of indigenous issues like traditional knowledge and TCEs.[389]

In general, it can be observed once more, that it is of great help to involve institutions or individuals who are competent and experienced in the specific area to be negotiated—in Brazil, e.g., the ISA. These remarks are also applicable to the situation in Latin America in general, while naturally national particularities might have to be considered.

III. Protocols

Protocols in the area of TCEs are described as means of documenting and communicating "the requested appropriate ways of respecting traditional cultural expressions in behavior and in recording them."[390] As regards their legal nature, they are universally considered as a non-binding legal instrument, because these protocols rely on the good will of participants.[391] A binding effect can be added through their combination with contracts, by which means the binding contractual relation includes the content of the protocols.

Although not understood as a protocol, such requested appropriate ways of respecting and treating TCEs are communicated for example in the "Elements for an Alternative System of Protection" of the COICA, the Coordinator of the Indigenous Organizations in the Amazon Basin.[392]

Sometimes, there are more general principles and recommendations for the treatment and valorization of TCEs laid down and communicated. Those communications can thus be considered as a political agenda, rather than what is understood by the term "protocol" as used above. Nonetheless, they might contain the above-cited "requested appropriate ways of respecting traditional cultural expressions in behavior and in recording them."

---

associações. Fica proibida a reoridzção total ou parcial das ilustrações contidas nesta obra sema prévia e expressa autorização, por escrito, dos povos alto-xinguanos, através de suas associações e representantes. A renda proveniente da venda desta publicação reverterá integralmente para as atividades educacionais desses povos," *ibid.*

[388] On anthropological thoughts on the difference between associations and social structures and communities and its impact on the broader topic of TCEs *see* the challenges in representation according to customary law, at Chapter II Section 5.D.II. above.

[389] For details on and publications of ISA *see* http://www.socioambiental.org, last visited December 29, 2010.

[390] *See* Janke (no year) 16 *et seq.*

[391] *Ibid.*

[392] For details *see* at Chapter II Section 4.E. above and COICA (2005) 62 *et seq.*

Although addressing not only TCEs, but "popular culture" in general, an example of such requests can be found in the "Principles, parameters and recommendations for the valorization of popular cultures" documented as an outcome of the Brazilian "National Seminar of Public Policies for the Popular Cultures," understood as a "basis for cultural policies of public entities as well as other organizations and persons dedicated to and dealing with the valorization of the popular cultures."[393]

F. Case Law

There exists very little case law on TCEs in particular. Latin American experts, like the Argentinian Delia Lipszyc, the Venezuelan Ricardo Antequera Parilli, or the Colombian Juan Carlos Monroy Rodríguez, either do not refer to case law at all,[394] or only mention it as regards derivative works in copyright,[395] or in citing Australian cases on TCEs.[396]

Still, probably the most active and progressive court in the field of indigenous rights in general is the Colombian High Court.[397] Among others, it has issued a historic decision on the "free, prior informed consent" in a mining case, thus not specifically on TCEs, but with a larger impact on the topic of prior informed consent in general—at least according to Latin American critics.[398]

Besides this decision, it has also ruled on the interesting question about the relationship between cultural patrimony and public domain, precisely, whether indigenous art, including TCEs, being part of the cultural patrimony, can be subject to intellectual property rights like copyright at the same time, which has been disposed above.[399]

[393] Ministério da Cultura – Secretaria de Identidade e da Diversidade Cultural (2006) 161–163, translation by the author. The principles are entitled in the original: "Princípios, parâmetros e recomendações para valorizar as culturas populares.", *ibid.*

[394] Lipszyc (1993).

[395] Antequera Parilli (2007) 518.

[396] Monroy Rodríguez (2006) at section 6.

[397] For decisions of Brazilian courts in the area of indigenous rights and aspects thereof relevant to the topic of TCEs, *see* at Chapter IV Section 2.D.V. below.

[398] Decision T–769 of October 29, 2009: "Acción de tutela instaurada por Álvaro Bailarín y otros, contra los Ministerios del Interior y de Justicia; de Ambiente, Vivienda y Desarrollo Territorial; de Defensa; de Protección Social; y de Minas y Energía". *See* http://ccr6.pgr.mpf.gov.br/destaques-do-site/corte-constitucional-colombiana-dicta-sentencia-historica-sobre-consulta-previa-a-pueb los-indigenas-y-comunidades-negras, last visited May 31, 2010.

[399] On this decision and further details on the discussion, *see* Corte Suprema de Justicia, Sala Plena, Sentencia de abril 2 de 1987. Magistrado Ponente Jairo Duque Pérez, cited from Monroy Rodríguez (2006) no pagination and *see* at Section 3.B.IV.1. above.

G. Practical Approaches: Documenting and Digitizing TCEs

Besides theses legal aspects, practical approaches to protecting TCEs are also undertaken in various Latin American countries. "Protection" in this regard mainly encompasses documentation and digitalization of TCEs, in order to preserve the expressions and facilitate their being passed on to coming generations. At a quite early stage in the late 1990s, as WIPO reports, in Bolivia, a

> huge effort by some organizations, such as the *Taller de Historia Oral Andina (THOA)*, was made to document, preserve, and disseminate cultural traditions through radio broadcasts, video tapes, and publications. Preservation of the cultural heritage of Bolivian indigenous communities encompasses a process that THOA has designated as "reconstitution of the *ayllus*", which means the assumption of a cultural identity and a work of administrative organization at the local level. The work concerning organization has relied mainly on the establishment of titles to the lands occupied by the communities. However, it is not forgotten that a relevant portion of the cultural heritage of communities consists of traditional knowledge.[400]

As a consequence of the experiences of such "reconstitution of the ayllus", it became clear that

> the adoption, both at the national and international levels, of mechanisms of intellectual property protection of such knowledge, (. . .) is seen as a relevant tool for the conservation of the cultural heritage of indigenous communities.[401]

Two other institutions that are very active in documenting, presenting, and digitizing TCEs and indigenous culture in general, including capacity-building measures as regards the use of technical support, are the Museum of the Indian in Rio de Janeiro, Brazil,[402] and the Brazilian Ministry of Culture.[403]

H. Consequences of This Diverse Picture of the Legal Status Quo

Such a heterogeneous status quo of the national protection of TCEs in Latin America has the following consequences:

First, not all of the countries can be looked at more closely in this thesis. Therefore, the focus will be placed on two different examples to provide a deeper insight into the topic: a sui generis system and the broader situation of protecting

---

[400] WIPO (2001) *see* in particular Fact Finding Mission to Bolivia, p. 4 *et seq.*

[401] WIPO (2001) *see* in particular Fact Finding Mission to Bolivia, p. 4 *et seq.*

[402] *See, e.g.*, Fausto and Franchetto (eds.) (2008). On other activities and publications of the "Museu do Índio" *see* at Chapter IV Section 2.D.IV. below and http://www.museudoindio.org.br/, last visited December 29, 2010.

[403] *See, e.g.*, IPHAN – Instituto do Patrimônio Histórico e Artístico Nacional (2008) and at Chapter IV Section 2.D.IV. below.

TCEs in Panama (below Chapter IV Section 1.), and a cultural-law approach and further discussions at the national level of Brazil (below Chapter IV Section 2.).

Second, the question arises whether at least a minimum consensus within the Latin American region can be found in order to establish a common instrument of protection of TCEs in the near future—a question which has been dealt with above.[404]

[404] *See* at Section 2.C. above.

Chapter IV. Selected Countries

Section 1. Panama: A Sui Generis System

Panama does not in fact belong to those Latin American countries with the highest percentage of an indigenous population[1]—approximately 10 % of the population are indigenous peoples.[2] Notwithstanding, Panama is the first and so far the only country in Latin America and in the world to have established a complete body of law dealing with the protection of TCEs.[3] This body of law is the "Special Regime of Intellectual Property Rights on the Collective Rights of the Indigenous Peoples for the Protection and Defense of their Cultural Identity and Traditional Knowledge."

Within just the last couple of years, the law was noted as being an "interesting" first attempt ever, but it was held that "(i)t is still too early to assess the system established by the Panamanian law."[4]

This assessment notwithstanding, nearly 10 years after the entry into force of the law and 8 years after the first registration of a TCE in Panama, it is worth having a more detailed look at the regulations, their implementation, and experience gained in practice, which can also serve as lessons learned for the protection of TCEs at other national levels and even the international one, as the protection of TCEs is still a work in progress.

To provide an adequate, i.e. realistic and comprehensive insight into the Panamanian approach towards protecting TCEs,

---

[1] These are Bolivia, Guatemala, Ecuador, and Peru.

[2] *See* Contraloría General de la República de Panamá, Dirección de Estadística y Censo (2000). According to the census of 2000, there are 285,231 indigenous peoples in Panama, *ibid.*

[3] Presentación de Experiencias Nacionales con Sistemas Normativos de Protección Jurídica de las Expresiones Culturales Tradicionales (Las Expresiones del Folclore) de 2002 (available only in Spanish), Annex II of WIPO/GRTKF/IC/4/INF/4.

[4] Lucas-Schlötter (2008) 413.

© Springer-Verlag Berlin Heidelberg 2015
A.F. Busch, *Protection of Traditional Cultural Expressions in Latin America*,
Munich Studies on Innovation and Competition 3, DOI 10.1007/978-3-662-46770-1_4

(1) both bodies of regulations, i.e. Law No. 20 of 2000 and the Executive Decree No. 12 of 2001,
(2) an example of the customary law being integrated into the Sui generis Regime, which defines the rules of use of the respective TCE and the rights therein, here, the "Rules of Use of the Collective Right 'Mola Kuna Panama'", and,
(3) practical experience

will be considered jointly.

Before we go into detail, some relevant facts on Panama are intended to give an impression of the relevant circumstances of the protection of TCE in the country.

A. Some Relevant, TCE-Related Facts from Panama

Panama, with a population of approximately 3.4 million peoples and approximately 30,000 miles^2 (77,400 km^2) is one of the smallest countries in Latin America.[5] It gained national independence only in 1903.[6] Until the return of the Panama Canal to the country in December 1999, there was a factual economic and cultural predominance of US Americans in the country. Only in 1977, with president Omar Torrijos Herreras' "fight against the foreign dominance over the Panama Canal", as nationals call it, did the search for a national identity begin.[7] And only after 1999, after the return of the Canal and the withdrawal of the North American managers, workers, and population, did the country begin to develop its own national cultural identity.[8]

Due to this "weak" national background in combination with a successful revolution of the indigenous *Kuna* Indians in Panama in 1925, the position of the *Kuna* Indians in the country is relatively strong. The successful revolution ensured them territorial rights and several autonomous rights, and they have become actively involved in national political representation.[9] As a consequence, the status of the *Kuna* as bearers and creators of TCEs is likewise special: they are proud of their culture and have a certain degree of political power due to their autonomous representation and administration.

---

[5] The official data of the census of 2010 is 3,405,813, *see* http://www.censos2010.gob.pa/, for the size *see* http://www.nationsencyclopedia.com/economies/Americas/Panama.html, last visited January 29, 2011.

[6] *See* http://www.britannica.com/EBchecked/topic/440722/Panama, last visited November 20, 2010.

[7] *See* http://www.britannica.com/EBchecked/topic/440722/Panama, (for general data on Panama's history) and on the dates and treaties on the Panama Canal, *see* http://www.britannica.com/EBchecked/topic/440784/Panama-Canal?anchor=ref466153, last visited November 20, 2010.

[8] Personal Communication with Edmundo de la Cruz, Chief of the Department of Folklore of the INAC, the National Institute of Culture in Panama City on February 13, 2009.

[9] Valiente López (2008) 207 *et seq.*

In total, according to the census of 2000, eight different ethnic groups of indigenous peoples still live in Panama: the Ngöbe, Kuna, Emberá, Wounaan, Buglé, Naso, Bri-Bri and Bokotas, which all together make up approximately 10 % of the whole population.[10]

There are five indigenous territories, or *comarcas*,[11] which all have different legal status, regarding, for example, autonomy in indigenous jurisdiction, which is a highly disputed issue.[12] According to an indigenous perspective, a *comarca* is "a special political division of the Panamanian territory, governed in accordance with the law which constitutes it and with the norms, customs, and cosmovision of the indigenous people or peoples inhabiting it, based on the traditional indigenous institutions which have been created in accordance with their spiritual, social, economic, cultural, juridical, and political values. Its highest authority is the General Indigenous Congress or the Indigenous Council or a traditional authority elected according to the tradition."[13] The oldest and most "famous" one, established in 1938, in the earliest wake of the 1925 Revolution, is the Comarca Kuna Yala.[14]

The *comarcas* are among "the last ecological refuges of the biosphere". Nevertheless, the situation of the indigenous groups is "far from idyllic",[15] as most of them live in absolute poverty, without fresh running water, sanitary systems, or electricity.[16] Additionally, one of the most serious environmental problems, as De Obaldia states, is the accelerated destruction of forests in Panama, which has been approached by establishing special protected areas—mostly in the environmentally best conserved *comarcas*—and in theses areas, hunting, fishing, plant growing and the traditional use of natural resources is (partially) prohibited, which, of course, affects the traditional communities most.[17]

Not surprisingly, in the last years, a strong migration towards urban and semi-urban regions, in particular the capital, has taken place. Today, only less than half of the indigenous population (around 45 %) continues living in the *comarcas*,[18] i.e. in traditional communal structures and socio-cultural patterns.

As regards the understanding of TCEs, a certain "common sense" exists at the national level as regarding them to be those traditional expressions that are created

[10] *See* Contraloría General de la República de Panamá, Dirección de Estadística y Censo (2000).

[11] Ngöbe-Buglé, Kuna Yala, Kuna de Madungandi, Kuna de Wargandi and Emberá-Wounaan.

[12] For details on the (disputed) legal and political situation regarding the scope of autonomy, *see* Valiente López (2008) 203–237, translation by the author.

[13] *Id.* 205, translation by the author.

[14] *See* Law No. 2 of September 16, 1938, originally creating the *Comarca San Blas*, which was organized according to Law No. 16 of February 19, 1953. The change of the name to *Comarca Kuna Yala* took place by means of Law No. 99 of December 23, 1998. For details *see* at Section 1. D.I. below.

[15] *See* De Obaldia (2005) 352, with further references.

[16] Personal research in the Comarca Kuna Yala.

[17] De Obaldia (2005) 352, with further references.

[18] Valiente López (2008) 205.

within the traditional environment and thus enjoy a connotation of "authenticity", whereas "folklore" is used for any kind of traditional art that is not necessarily created by indigenous peoples and is performed in a non-traditional environment.[19] Legal definitions, however, do not exist

B. Historical Development: The Birth of the Sui Generis Regime

The Panamanian Law No. 20 of 2000 goes back to an initiative of the indigenous peoples themselves, which then was supported by the Panamanian government.[20]

The "muse" or inspiration for the Law was the *mola*, a special part, or even type, of traditional women's blouses. The regulations themselves describe the *mola* as "a women's blouse; application of a small decorative piece to a larger piece of fabric with working on the back; a combination of fabrics of many different, striking colors. The technique used is derived from the craft of embroidery (appliqué). They are hand-made by native Kuna women, and consist of one or more layers of fabric, cut and sewn together in such a way that the color of each of the lower layers shows through. The designs of the *molas* are based on the cosmovision, while others merely use a geometric shape."[21] *Mola* refers also to the traditional dress of Kuna women, called "dule mor".[22]

The *mola* art goes back to inspirations by different cultures: According to De Obaldia, in the seventeenth century, Kuna women did not wear any cloth at all, but used body paintings for decorating their bodies, painting the upper part of their bodies with intricate designs. During the eighteenth century, French Huguenots settled among the Kunas and introduced the European art of appliqué, sewing layers of cloth one on top of the other. The French were expelled or murdered, as De Obaldia tells, but the Kuna women kept the appliqué art, which the evolved into the *molas*.[23]

The spiritual origin as told by Panamanian indigenous authors is the story of *Olonagegiryai*, "one of the wise mothers of the tribe", who travelled to a sacred place called *Galu Dugbis*, "a place where all the designs and colours of the *molas* dwell".[24] She was taught the art, designs and techniques of the *molas* there and later

[19] Personal communications with staff members of Direction of the Registry of Industrial Property (DIGERPI) and Aresio Valiente, Kuna Indian and lawyer, in February, 2009, in Panama.

[20] Annex II of WIPO/GRTKF/IC/4/INF/4.

[21] Article 3(14) of Decree No. 12, which regulates Law No. 20. *See* at Section 1.C. below. The translation is based on WIPO Secretariat (2005) 18.

[22] Article 2 of the Rules of Use of the Collective Right "Mola Kuna Panama." On this *see* at Section 1.D.II. below, and Article 3(1) of Law No. 20.

[23] *See* De Obaldia (2005) 357 with further references.

[24] Valiente López (2006) 41 *et seq.* and De Obaldia (2005) 357 with further references.

instructed the rest of the Kuna women in sewing them using cotton.[25] Due to this believed sacred origin, Kuna women expressed and sometimes still express their religious relationship with mother Earth when creating *molas*.

The *mola*, or *morra* in the native language,[26] became very popular especially among tourists as early as the 1970s. Along with its growing popularity, the non-indigenous commercial reproduction increased.

The first step of protecting the *mola* was taken in 1984, when Panama established the Importation Law,[27] which was inspired by a Guatemaltecan law from 1932.[28] This law prohibited the import of *mola* fabrics, embroideries, and imitations into Panama.[29]

However, this law afforded very little protection: First, the law only prohibited the import of copies entering the Panamanian country, and not those illegal copies being produced in the national territory itself.[30] Second, the indigenous peoples criticized the fact that the law did not establish collective property of the Kuna Indians over their *molas*.[31]

According to Valiente López, therefore, starting in 1991, the authorities of the ethnic group of the Kuna long sought a way to legally protect the *mola*, their principal cultural manifestation, through the existing system of industrial property. However, the use of this system did not succeed for various reasons, *inter alia*, the inadequacy of the existing instruments.[32] These difficulties revealed the need for developing new mechanisms of legal protection.

Indigenous lawyers prepared a draft containing indigenous needs with regard to intellectual property rights, one of which was to receive the benefits gained from the economic exploitation of their expressions and knowledge and thereby attain a fair and adequate remuneration.[33] According to Valiente López, after years of debate,[34] in 1999 the time had come for formal support by the Panamanian legislative assembly due to the fact that for the first time in Panamanian history, the president of the General Assembly stemmed from an indigenous community and was thus

[25] *See id.* 357, with further references.

[26] Article 3(14) of Decree No. 12.

[27] Ley Por la Cual se Prohibe la Importación de Copias de Molas y se Dictan otras Disposiciones, Ley 26 of October 22, 1984, published in the Gaceta Oficial No. 20,174 of October 31, 1984.

[28] Personal communication with Aresio Valiente López in Panama City in February 2009, and *see* Valiente López (2006) 112 *et seq.*

[29] Law No. 26 of 22nd of October 1984: "It is prohibited to import copies of Molas."

[30] *See* Article 1 of Law No. 26 of 1984.

[31] Valiente López (2006) 113.

[32] For a comprehensive analysis, *see id.* 101 *et seq.*

[33] *Ibid.*

[34] During this period of discussions, the first step was to set up a law that was to "establish the protection, the promotion and the development of traditional handicraft". However, in effect, it only enlarged the former prohibition of the import of copies of *molas* to also cover handicraft products that imitate autochthonous and traditional pieces and cloths. *See* Chapter VIII of Law No. 27 of July 24, 1997.

equipped with the necessary cultural background and personal involvement to fully support the political demand to discuss these demands in the legislative body.[35] The preliminary draft was then also presented at WIPO, with a request for comments and observations. The subsequent national legislative debates also involved traditional authorities, indigenous NGOs, handicraftsmen, national indigenous experts and governmental representatives of the General Direction of the Registry of Industrial Property,[36] of the Ministry of Commerce and Industries,[37] of Education, and many others.[38] The involvement of such a variety of specialists and professionals reveals the interdisciplinary character of the topic.

Finally, after being accepted by the Commission for Indigenous Affairs,[39] the law was adopted by the legislative plenary.

C. Content of the Sui Generis Regime on Paper and in Practice

Law No. 20 is regulated by the related Executive Decree No. 12 of March 20, 2001. Both regulations will be considered jointly for the reason of their closely linked context.

However, it has to be noted that the legal nature of the Decree is different from that of the Law. The Decree is an administrative regulation set up by an administrative, not a legislative, body, and can be changed simply by establishing a later, contrary regulation in the same modus. This aspect has to be borne in mind, for example, whenever the Decree appears to have a distinct scope of application.[40]

Any such divergences have their origin in the different points of time and circumstances of the adoption of the two legal instruments. While at the time of the adoption of Law No. 20, concessions had to be made by the indigenous politicians and consultants to get the Law passed through the General Assembly,[41] the Decree was "adopted" 9 months later, in March 2001, and the process of hard negotiations had become much smoother during these months,[42] enabling the inclusion of some further aspects not covered by the Law.

---

[35] President Enrique Garrido, whose mandate began in that year.

[36] La Dirección General del Registro de la Propiedad Industrial (DIGERPI).

[37] Ministerio de Comercio e Industrias.

[38] Dirección Nacional de Política Indigenista del Ministerio de Gobierno y Justicia; Ministerio de Economía y Finanzas Instituto Nacional de Cultura.

[39] Comisión de Asuntos Indígenas.

[40] For example, it also considers traditional medical knowledge, Article 2 No. 3 of the Decree.

[41] Personal communication with Aresio Valiente, indigenous lawyer and one of the consultants of the deputies, in Panama City on February 11, 2009.

[42] Personal communication with Aresio Valiente, indigenous lawyer and one of the consultants of the deputies in Panama City on February 11, 2009.

I. Political Objectives of the Sui Generis Regime

The main objective of Law No. 20 is "to give prominence to the socio-cultural values of the indigenous cultures and to bring them social justice".[43] A strong socio-political emphasis can be noticed in the Law, which has to be read in light of decades-long struggles for protection of the symbol and embodiment of the socio-cultural and economic situation of the Kuna Indians, the *mola*. In accordance with this greater objective, the collective intellectual-property rights and traditional knowledge of indigenous communities are to be protected through the registration, promotion, commercialisation and marketing of their rights.[44] Another key objective is the protection of the originality and authenticity of crafts and other traditional artistic expressions.[45]

II. Subject Matter of Protection

The subject matter of protection seems to follow easily from Articles 1 and 2 of Law No. 20. However, not even Panamanian legal experts themselves see a clear interpretation.[46]

1. An Apparently Broad and Holistic Approach

At first glance, Law No. 20 follows a very broad approach. The protected subject matter includes "creations, like inventions, models, drawings and designs, innovations contained in the pictures, figures, symbols,"[47] as well as "customs, traditions, beliefs, spirituality, religiosity, cosmovision, folkloric expressions, artistic manifestations, traditional knowledge, and any other type of traditional expressions of indigenous communities"[48] which are part of their cultural heritage.[49] It includes tangible[50] and intangible goods.[51] Special provisions are set up for, first, traditional

---

[43] Article 1 of Law No. 20.

[44] Article 1 and Preamble of Law No. 20 and Preamble of the Executive Decree No. 12.

[45] Article 6 of Law No. 20.

[46] De Obaldia (2005) 368, says: "It is also unclear from the language of Law No. 20 what exactly is covered by the indigenous 'expression' used in Articles 2 and 4." She addresses this unclarity when asking which rights are conceded by Law No. 20.

[47] Article 1 of Law No. 20.

[48] Article 2 of Law No. 20. Ambiguous WIPO/GRTKF/IC/9/INF 4 Annex II, page 2.

[49] There is no definition or classification of cultural heritage in Panama. It is regarded to be more important to create the organizational structure than to set up a definition, "esas palabritas se puede arreglar", personal communication with Edmundo de la Cruz, Chief of the Department of Folklore ("Departamento de Folklore") of the National Institute of Culture (INAC) on February 13, 2009 in Panama City.

[50] Such as musical instruments, Art. 4 of Law No. 20, and traditional tools, Art. 5 of Law No. 20.

[51] *Supra*.

dresses[52]; second, music, musical instruments, dances, and oral or written expressions[53]; and third, traditional work and art instruments and technique[54]—without differentiating content-wise between these special forms and provisions.

In the literature, this apparently broad approach regarding the subject matter has led authors to the somewhat misleading conclusion that Law No. 20 follows a "holistic scope of application".[55] Indeed, Law No. 20 does not distinguish between the different technical and creative categories of intellectual property law, and it even includes ideas, and the "cosmovision". However, it does not follow a "holistic" approach, neither in the narrower sense, i.e. including all kinds of TCEs and traditional knowledge, nor in the wider sense, i.e. including even land rights and organization rights.[56] There are not only restrictions within the broad approach, but also subjects not covered by Law No. 20. This will be shown in the following.

2. Restricting Criteria and Subjects Not Covered

a. Restricting Requirements

The apparently broad approach of Law No. 20 is limited by mainly four criteria:

(1) The subject matter must be "based upon tradition", although it does not need to be "old"[57];
(2) It must be "collective", i.e. the subject matter must have "no known author or owner and no date of origin" and constitute the heritage of an entire indigenous people[58] or must be regarded as belonging to one or more of the indigenous communities of Panama[59];
(3) The subject matter must be capable of commercial use[60]; and
(4) It must fit within the classification system established by Article 3 of the Decree.

[52] Article 3 of Law No. 20.

[53] Article 4 of Law No. 20.

[54] Article 5 of Law No. 20.

[55] *E.g.*, Ramsauer (2005) 100.

[56] This kind of holistic approach here called the holistic approach in a wider sense is reflected in Article 31 of the UN-Declaration on the Rights of Indigenous Peoples and favoured e.g. by the INBRAPI in Brazil or the COICA in the Amazon region, *see* at Chapter II Section 4.E. and Chapter III Section 1.A. above.

[57] *See* Annex II p. 5 of WIPO/GRTKF/IC/4/INF/4 – Presentación de Experiencias Nacionales con Sistemas Normativos de Protección Jurídica de las Expresiones Culturales Tradicionales (Las Expresiones del Folclore) de 2002 (available only in Spanish), and Article 5 of Law No. 20.

[58] Article 2 of the Decree.

[59] Articles 5 and 6 of the Decree.

[60] Article 1 of Law No. 20.

b. "Traditional"

The first criterion of being "based upon tradition" includes both the requirement of being "based upon" and "tradition". The term "traditional" is used without further definition or interpretation aid. This provokes the question: when may a cultural expression, having an indigenous background, be regarded as traditional and therefore as falling under the scope of Law No. 20?

The situation in Panama can be depicted as follows:

In Panamanian practice, there seems to be no problem in understanding which TCEs belong to the subject matter of Law No. 20, and consequently, it is not questioned which cases fulfill the requirement of tradition. The Decree lists around 80 examples of the most relevant TCEs in Panama and thus covers many possible registrations—maybe all of the TCEs that will ever be registered in Panama.[61]

Moreover, the Decree, as well as DIGERPI practice,[62] understand tradition as "history". The Decree stipulates, in the rules of use of the collective right, that the "history (tradition) of the collective right" has to be indicated and attached.[63] That means that in each application for the registration of a TCE, the indigenous peoples themselves have the right and duty to display the connection of the TCE to their tradition. The final decision over the registration and thus the fulfilment of the requirement of "tradition" or "history", lies with DIGERPI.[64] So far, the tradition has not been questioned in any case of registration yet. It could be argued that, in a case of dispute, according to the right and duty to display their tradition, the indigenous communities would have the burden of proof for said criteria. Court decisions or academic statements have not been issued on this question so far.

This status quo reveals the whole practical approach towards the topic of TCEs in Panama: it is rather a process of discussion and mediation than of official legal disputes on the question of "tradition", but also, e.g., on the relationship between the bearers of rights and DIGERPI.[65]

It should be mentioned, however, that the criterion "history" itself does not establish any reference to the aspects of actual vitality or viability, traditional continuance or authenticity of the TCE.

Therefore, and in light of lacking precedents, it remains unclear how the aforementioned aspects should be treated according to the sui generis regime, especially to what extent the tradition still has to be alive.

---

[61] So far, eight TCEs have been registered in the past more than eight years of existence of the law. Taking this as the basis for a prognosis, it would take 80 years to register all TCEs contained in Article 3 of the Decree.

[62] La Dirección General del Registro de la Propiedad Industrial (DIGERPI).

[63] Article 7 No. 7 of the Decree.

[64] Article 15 of Law No. 20, "approved" by DIGERPI.

[65] Personal communication with Yahelys Arenas of the Department of Collective Rights and Folkloric Expressions within DIGERPI, with Aresio Valiente, indigenous lawyer and one of the consultants of the deputies, with staff members of the General Kuna Congress, with Luis Touar, General Cacique Dagar Kunyala, translation by Flaviano Iglesias in Panama in February, 2009.

In international literature, "tradition" in the meaning of "the special cultural importance" of the TCE has been regarded as the essential precondition and delimiting criterion[66] of the protection of the TCE. Reason for that has been seen in the reason for the protection itself.[67]

However, the situation in Panama is a slightly different one. As mentioned before, the main object of protection is not only to save the preservation of culture. Rather, it is to "give prominence to the socio-cultural values of the indigenous cultures and to bring them social justice."[68] In this regard, it might not even be necessary to establish such a precondition of special cultural importance or enduring traditional vitality of the TCE. Or, to be more precise, it might appear to be unnecessary to establish general criteria, as in practice, solutions are sought in every single case of registration.

Nonetheless, in practice, discussions do exist, in particular in a third dimension regarding the interest of non-indigenous persons. This is especially the case when modifications and new forms of the TCE are also covered by a registration of a "traditional" cultural expression.[69] Non-indigenous peoples have felt that from their perspective, the regulation is not balanced enough.[70] The intensity of this conflict might even increase in the future, as the collective indigenous rights are not limited by any timely termination of the rights.[71] However, as mentioned before, even these concerns have not provoked legal disputes at court so far.

c. Commercial Use and Classification System

Comparisons of Law No. 20 to other systems of protection of TCEs, such as the 2002 WIPO Pacific Model Law, have evaluated especially the criteria of fitting within the classification system established by Article 3 of the Decree and of being capable of commercial use[72] as limiting criteria, and indeed these appear as such *on paper*.

In light of the experiences in the Panamanian reality, however, these criteria do not effectively limit the subject matter of protection of Law No. 20.[73] This can be explained as follows:

First, as regards inclusion in the classification system, the examples of objects capable of protection listed in the classification of the Decree already cover all known or at least all of the so-far relevant TCEs existing in the country and thus all

---

[66] Ramsauer (2005) 102.

[67] *Ibid.*

[68] Article 1 of Law No. 20. *See* at Section 1.C.I. above.

[69] *See* Articles 4 and 27 of Rules of Use of the Mola and at Section 1.D.II. below.

[70] De Obaldia (2005) 375 has noticed the criticism of a "lack of balance."

[71] *See* "Term of protection" at Section 1.C.VII. below.

[72] Article 1 of Law No. 20.

[73] Similarly, De Obaldia (2005) 367: "The existence of this requirement does not imply that heritage that cannot be sold cannot be protected."

potential objects of rights under Law No. 20.[74] Thus, at least so far, no TCEs other than those contained in the exemplifying classification established by the Decree have been applied for registration.

Second, the requirement of being capable of commercial use has not brought along any disputes so far, either. This requirement was even in line with the indigenous desires when establishing the Law: the reason to include the criterion of being "capable of commercial use" was the political objective of Law No. 20 to "apply social justice."[75]

Moreover, in practice, the commercial use criterion will be fulfilled in nearly every case. This is true from a perspective in line with the political objective of applying social justice, thus from a teleological and systematic perspective, as well as from a "Western" factual point of view, because nearly everything is capable of commercial use today.[76]

This interpretation does not contradict a corresponding analysis according to the emic approach, because at least in the case of the eight indigenous peoples in Panama, the assimilation of those peoples is so strong that market interactions are part of the indigenous culture already.

Today, there do not exist indigenous communities in (voluntary) isolation in Panama anymore. All of the communities have at least a minimum degree of exchange with the national society, be it only for integration into the national school system, or police vigilance, for example along the border with Colombia. Simply by virtue of their integration in the primary education system,[77] or a journey to the capital once or twice a year for the meeting of the General Kuna Congress, indigenous families and communities are in touch with the national monetary system.[78]

With regard to TCEs, market interactions especially take place with those objects that are registered already or that are intended to be registered—as the economic need of those indigenous communities and the possible economic exploitation of the relevant TCE by third parties usually prevails and has thus to be addressed first. Thus, indigenous peoples themselves would regard at least those TCEs that they want to have registered as capable of commercial use.

Those TCEs that are not capable of commercial use according to indigenous spiritual values from a customary law perspective, will as a rule also not be registered and made public.

---

[74] Article 3 of the Decree, Articles 3–5 of Law No. 20.

[75] Article 1 of Law No. 20. *See* Ríos de Davis (2002) Anexo II, 5, translation by the author.

[76] Even waste: In this manner, the European Court of Justice (ECJ) ruled that waste was a "good" covered by the principle of free movement of goods, *see* Case C-2/90 Commission v Belgium [1992] ECR I-[4431].

[77] Bonilla (2004 I) no pagination.

[78] Personal investigation in Kuna Yala and personal communication with Luis Touar, General Cacique Dagar Kunyala, translation by Flaviano Iglesias, in February, 2009, in Panama.

An example of this Panamanian reality will help to illustrate the situation: Kuna Indians thought about registering a special type of traditional Kuna hammock, hand-made of cotton and dyed in seven distinct natural colors. Kuna communities still living in a more traditional way, in a remote area in the rainforest close to the Colombian border, faced, among other things, two points of conflict within the internal, communal discussions on whether to protect, i.e. register, the hammock or not. These two points referred, first, to the spiritual meaning and function of the hammock, and second, to the traditional knowledge on producing the dyes used for the creation of the hammock.[79]

As regards the first point: The hammock has not only a practical function of relaxation and decoration, but also another, immaterial meaning: It is the throne of the *Cacique* (traditional leader) in reunions. Similarly, the different figures and colors have spiritual and social meanings reflecting the community's spiritual beliefs.[80]

These aspects, naturally, would lose their existence and functions in a different socio-cultural environment after being sold to non community members. This is one reason why some members of the community argued against the sale of the hammocks at all, as they feared losing the "third dimension" besides those of practicality and visual beauty, an immaterial dimension, which was immanent to the material "piece" of hammock according to the community's worldview and way of life. The "masters" of the cultural values explained this to the rest of the community, and intense discussions took place within the community on whether the hammock was capable of commercial use and whether it *should be* used commercially.[81]

As regards the second point: an intrinsic part of this TCE is the special knowledge of how to produce the natural dyes for the cotton, in particular which plants or animals to use for which dye, and how it is technically managed that the different dyes do not mix. As a registration according to the Sui generis Regime requires the disclosure of the traditional techniques of creation, a great fear exists among the Kuna community of revealing this knowledge in the registration process.[82]

Thus, there seem to exist two gaps in the envisaged protection: the first is based in the objective of the law and the scope of protection—only against unauthorized commercial use. The second arises in the case of spiritually sensitive or sacred TCEs, which are not meant to be disclosed and thus registered. This second gap is therefore due to the registration system—which will be dealt with later—rather than to the requirement of being capable of commercial use.[83]

---

[79] *Supra.*

[80] *Supra.*

[81] Personal communication with Luis Touar, General Cacique Dagar Kunyala, translation by Flaviano Iglesias, in February 2009 in Panama.

[82] *Supra.*

[83] On aspects and critics on the registration system *see* at Section 1.G. below.

In regard to the criteria of being capable of commercial use, the question is rather whether this criteria is interpreted as "shall not be commercially used" from a customary-law perspective, or as not being capable of commercial use according to Western market criteria.

Under the latter interpretation, probably no TCE would be excluded, and under the former interpretation, the indigenous community will probably not apply for registration in the relevant cases anyway.

If TCEs should be protected *per se* by means of a right of authorization in case of (non-commercial) use by third parties, it is questionable whether this aspect is covered by Law No. 20. Although this is also a question of the content of rights conferred, it is related to the requirement of commercial use of the subject matter and thus addressed in this context already. One could argue that no distinction should be made between commercially usable or non-usable objects of protection, because the other, equally important objective of the Law is "to give prominence the socio-cultural values of the indigenous cultures" and "to promote their culture." However, "promotion" in this regard is argued to only cover commercial promotion. This direction of the Law might be explained by the "muse" and initial reason for establishing the Law: the very focus on an adequate treatment of the commercially used and endangered Kuna *mola*.

However, this question also remains unclear in light of Article 15, which stipulates that the rights of "use" and "commercialization" be governed by the rules of use of every indigenous tribe. This distinction between "use" on the one hand and "commercialization" on the other could be used as an argument in favor of the inclusion of non-commercially used TCEs in the scope of application.[84]

Finally, notwithstanding the clear wording, the Panamanian literature just states that the "existence of this requirement [of being capable of commercial use] does not imply that heritage that cannot be sold cannot be protected."[85] Rather, De Obaldia argues, the requirement simply reflected the purpose of the law to promote "social justice."[86]

d. Subjects Not Covered

aa. Traditional Knowledge on Biodiversity and Genetic Resources

Although in the international literature it has been stated continually that Law No. 20 also covers traditional knowledge regarding biodiversity,[87] and while even the Decree defines "traditional knowledge" as expressions that "cover sciences . . ., including genetic resources, medicine,"[88] and others, Law No. 20 does not cover such traditional knowledge *in lato sensu*.

---

[84] On this problem, *see* at Section 1.C.IV. below.

[85] De Obaldia (2005) 368.

[86] *Ibid.*

[87] Ramsauer (2005) 99; Taubman and Leistner (2008) 136 note 236.

[88] Article 2, No. 3, of the Decree.

A grammatical interpretation of the Decree reveals that according to its own wording, the Decree limits the application of its definition: "for the effects of the Decree."[89] Moreover, Law No. 20 does not use the express terms of "genetic resources" and "medicine." Rather, it refers to "traditional knowledge" only as part of "traditional expressions," with the wording "traditional knowledge and *any other type* of traditional expressions of indigenous communities."[90]

This interpretation is also due to the legislative history of the law. It shows that the delicate topic of traditional knowledge on genetic resources and biodiversity in the area of traditional medicine as well as alimentary products[91] was not to be touched by this law.[92] According to Valiente López, one reason was that even the representatives of the indigenous peoples in the General Assembly felt that there were still some fundamental principles and conceptual elements to be worked out beforehand.[93] The other reason was that the opposition of political interests of the pharmaceutical industries had been too strong. Fearing that the legislative initiative would fail completely, this topic was excluded from the final discussions and left aside for later ones.[94] And indeed, 1 year later, when the Decree to the Law was elaborated, the public attention was not as great as it had been during the discussions of the law. Furthermore, the Decree is only of an administrative nature, which means that neither the General Assembly was involved as the competent authority, nor was the weight of the provisions that great, because they can be changed easily, by only enforcing new administrative rules. Against this background, indigenous representatives took the chance to push forward the inclusion of traditional knowledge associated with genetic resources and biodiversity at least by means of the Decree—knowing that this aspect was not intended to be covered by Law No. 20.

Even DIGERPI has to a certain extent moved a step forward to respect the indigenous position, and issued information brochures defining the subject matter of TCEs and traditional knowledge as including "practices which embrace traditional styles of life and of the cultural identity [of the indigenous peoples], relevant for the conservation and sustainable use of biological diversity."[95]

Nonetheless, the critical topic of genetic resources and specific traditional *knowledge* in *stricto sensu*[96] is not explicitly mentioned.

---

[89] *See* the beginning of Article 2 of the Decree: "Para los efectos de este Decreto se aplicarán las definiciones siguientes."

[90] Article 2 of Law No. 20. Emphasis added by the author.

[91] Valiente López (2006) 124, 114.

[92] Personal communication with *Kuna* Indian and Lawyer Aresio Valiente López in February 2009 in Panama City. *See* also Congreso General Kuna (2006) 23 and Valiente López (2006) 114.

[93] Valiente López (2006) 124.

[94] Personal communication with *Kuna* Indian and Lawyer Aresio Valiente López in Panama City in February 2009.

[95] Ministerio de Comercio e Industrias – DIGERPI (no year) 3 *et seq.*

[96] On the terms, *see* at Chapter II Section 1.C.I. above.

In this regard, even the Kuna Indians themselves felt that for the use of biodiversity and the related traditional knowledge, a special regime was needed to conserve nature, which, according to the understanding of the Kuna, implies the conservation of historical memory, Valiente López says. As mentioned before, it was still necessary to "unify some fundamental principles and conceptual elements."[97]

Finally, the Panamanian reality today confirms this conclusion in *ex post* interpretation: At the moment, a new legislation on traditional knowledge of indigenous peoples regarding genetic resources and biodiversity is in preparation.[98]

So far, there has been neither a case of an application for the registration of traditional knowledge concerning biology, biodiversity, or genetic resources, nor any court decision on this subject.

bb. Ideas and Motifs

What remains unclear from Law No. 20 is to what extent motifs may also be protected, and consequently, how derivative works are treated legally, i.e., as De Obaldia puts it, when or how the use of "an indigenous motif becomes a violation of a derivative right."[99] It has been criticized that "Law No. 20 does not mention whether the monopoly on an indigenous expression or invention includes the 'idea' behind it." It does mention "beliefs" as well as "inventions" and "innovations contained in the images, figures, symbols [and] graphics" separately, though.[100]

cc. Material Aspects

As regards material and immaterial aspects, it has been stated initially that material objects are covered,[101] but what about the prime material? This does not seem to be a classic question in intellectual property law, or even relevant in the topic of subject matters of TCE protection. However, this aspect seems to raise questions in the broader practical area of handicrafts: According to De Obaldia, "it is clear that there are property rights on the processes" by which the indigenous peoples convert the natural products, but there is no presumption in the law that indigenous communities own the natural products of the environment.[102] "Whether that means that no one else can carve a *tagua* seed, even if for different purposes than those of the Emberá, is a question not answered by the text of the law."[103]

[97] Valiente López (2006) 125 and Congreso General Kuna (2006) 23, translation by the author.

[98] This is the state of the art as of 2009. Personal communication with Yahelys Arenas of the Department of Collective Rights and Folkloric Expressions within DIGERPI in Panama City in February 2009.

[99] De Obaldia (2005) 368.

[100] Articles 2 and 1 of the Law.

[101] Musical instruments and working tools, for example. *See* Articles 4 and 5 of the Law.

[102] De Obaldia (2005) 368.

[103] De Obaldia (2005) 368.

3. Conclusion

In effect, the subject matter of protection in Panama so far covers any kind of tangible or intangible cultural expression that is regarded to be part of the tradition, i.e. cultural history, of the indigenous peoples, except for traditional knowledge on medicine, biodiversity, genetic resources, and alimentary products. "Traditional" cultural expressions are not understood as static, meaning that when these are registered, their protection might also be extended to modifications and new forms of the TCE. Notwithstanding the clear wording of being "capable of commercial use," this requirement of protection is not very clear. Finally, in practice, the element of registration is also a crucial one for the subject matter of protection.

III. Holders of Rights and Beneficiaries of Protection

1. General Aspects: Who Is the Holder of Rights?

Law No. 20 does not contain any provision explicitly determining the holders of rights.

Publications on Law No. 20 postulate that the law clearly provides for collectivity in rightholding.[104] Nonetheless, disagreements hereon exist in practice, as well as uncertainties within the comprehensive legal framework. The voices raised in the literature are rather based upon an interpretation than an explicit statement of the law.

De Obaldia, for example, refers to Article 4 of the Law as being the main provision that "expressly establishes [that] collectivity is at the center of the law."[105] Article 4 indeed contains the wording "collective rights of the indigenous peoples" ("derechos colectivos de los pueblos indígenas")—but so do many others (like Articles 1, 5, 6). Moreover, following a literal and systematic interpretation, Article 4 rather deals with particular types of TCEs like musical instruments, music, dances, or other forms of written or oral expressions[106]—in contrast to the prevailing Article 3, dealing with "traditional cloths" as a certain type of TCE and the following Article 5, dealing with those TCEs like tools for work and instruments of traditional art or handicraft. Thus, it is not convincing to argue that Article 4 contains the core provision expressly establishing collectivity as the main principle of the law or the concrete right holder.

Ramsauer, on the other hand, refers to Article 6 as the relevant provision, which "explicitly states collective ownership."[107] However, Article 6 rather simply *defines* the expression "collective rights," as the provision states:

[104] *See*, for example, De Obaldia (2005) 367 and Ramsauer (2005) 104.

[105] De Obaldia (2005) 367.

[106] "(I)nstrumentos musicales, música, danzas, o forma de ejecución, expresiones orales y escritas".

[107] Ramsauer (2005) 104.

> The objects capable of protection which can be registered in accordance with the determinations of this Law, with the aim of protecting their originality and authenticity, are called collective rights of the indigenous peoples.[108]

Article 15 is also relevant for comprehending this topic, as it refers to the rules of use of each particular TCE, regulating the terms of use according to the understanding of the relevant indigenous community. Such rules also mention or even define holders of rights. Therefore, in particular the diverging terms in these different sets of provisions—Law No. 20, the Decree, and the particular rules of use—are reasons for uncertainty regarding the proper determination of the holder (s) of rights. The rules of use, however, only treat one single TCE—in the example given here, the *mola*—and thus the different rules of use may vary from TCE to TCE. Therefore, the example of the "Rules of Use of the Mola" will be treated separately below. At this point, it is essential to mention the need for a full comprehension of the complexity and interaction of the three different bodies of rules in each case of TCE. Therefore, when discussing the Law and Decree as the general framework here, it is necessary to bear in mind the existence of rules of use, possibly with their own regulations on the question of right holders.

As regards the Law and the Decree, many Articles in the Law do in fact speak of the "collective rights of the indigenous peoples."[109] Thus, it could be deduced that the holder of rights is a collective—the indigenous collective, the people, or the community—as a whole. Yet, even this deduction reveals ambiguity, and there are other good reasons to question whether the community is regarded to be the one and only[110] holder of rights under Law No. 20. Even if affirmed, other, more detailed questions on the beneficiaries of protection arise for which Law No. 20 does not provide concrete answers.

So far, there has been no jurisprudence on any of these questions in Panama.[111] In general, there exist the following possibilities of right holders in the area of protection of TCEs, which will be discussed below: Most likely, it could be the collective, i.e. either a "people" or a "community", and either *all* members of the entity or *some* of them, or the entity as such. But the state and the individual also play important roles giving rise to the question of who holds the rights.[112]

It must be underscored that this is not only a dispute on paper, but especially of practical relevance.[113]

---

[108] "Se *denominan* derechos colectivos de los pueblos indígenas *los objetos susceptibles de protección que pueden ser registrados*, conforme lo determina esta Ley, a fin de proteger su originalidad y autenticidad."

[109] "Derechos colectivos de los pueblos indígenas". *See* Articles 1, 4, 5, 6 of the Law.

[110] De Obaldia (2005) 367.

[111] The fact that there have not been any legal proceedings on this issue, although disputes arose, reveals a certain legal culture as well as circumstances at the socio-economic level, which have an important impact on the effectiveness of the protection of TCEs and differ a lot from the situation in the "Western" legal society. *See* at Section 5.G.II.2.c. below.

[112] Details hereof will be discussed below at a.–c.

[113] *See* at Chapter II Section 5.D.II.3.a. below.

Interesting to note are also two aspects from the international discussion and negotiations. First, the state parties at WIPO especially avoided using the term "owners".[114] While in Panama, Law No. 20 as well as the Decree follow this policy, the "Rules of Use of the Collective Right 'Mola Kuna Panama'"—as one example of a rule of use set up by the indigenous peoples themselves—explicitly speak of the "owners" of rights.[115]

Second, although in the international literature it has been held that "the establishment of the concept of collective ownership of the rights relating to folklore" or TCEs is one of the main points of difference in indigenous customary law in comparison to intellectual property rights in their Western interpretation,[116] even the 2002 WIPO Pacific Model Law acknowledges the alternative of an "individual who is recognized by the group, clan or community" as being the right holder "in accordance with customary law and practices."[117]

Finally, what also must be remembered here is that one must differentiate between the collective holdership of rights and the right or authority to claim the rights in their substantive and procedural dimension. The latter is the question of representation of the community, which will be dealt with further below.[118]

a. Collective as Right Holder

The most likely right holder is the, or rather *a*, collective, as the law speaks of "*collective* intellectual property rights."[119]

However, first, it is not quite clear what kind of collective is meant: is it the indigenous "people", "tribe", and/or "ethnicity" as a whole, thus one of the eight ethnicities existing in Panama, or is it the indigenous "community"? Second, is the right holder then the entity as such—whether as a legal entity or not—or the sum of its members?

As regards the first question, neither the Law nor the Decree established general definitions of the collectives. It could be the rules of use on the specific TCE—and thus the indigenous community itself to set up the particular holder of rights in the TCE—maybe even including its relevant legal quality. It could also be regarded to be DIGERPI, by approving the rules of use when registering the right.

---

[114] WIPO/UNESCO Model Provisions, foreword to Article 10, WIPO/UNESCO, Commentary on the Model Provisions Part III, marginal number 72, 1985.

[115] "El titular del Derecho Colectivo . . .", Article 6 of the Rules of Use of the Mola, "The owner of the . . . Collective Right . . ." in the unofficial English translation provided by a Kuna lawyer himself, *see* Valiente López (2002).

[116] Lucas-Schlötter (2008) 415.

[117] This more differentiated solution is laid down in Articles 4 and 6 of the 2002 Model Law for the Pacific. For more details *see* Ramsauer (2005) 105.

[118] *See* at Chapter II Section 1.D.III., E.II., and G.II.2. below.

[119] *See, e.g.*, Article 1 of Law No. 20.

In determining a community, tribe, or people, the lack of a definition might be due to a "common understanding" in the country, where only eight different ethnic groups or peoples live. Moreover, in practice, it is more a "hands-on-approach", as the communities usually appear as such—by self-definition, one could say—in front of DIGERPI, indicating their "scope of community" and their traditional representative. The question of determining a community, however, is of special relevance in cases in which more than one community considers itself as the source of the TCE in question and consequently as the right holder.[120]

Whether it is the "community" or the "people/tribe/ethnicity", the second, follow-up question displayed above then embraces the following, more detailed issue: For the purpose of this "new" collective right, is the right holder the entity itself? Or is it the sum of the members in a loose connection? If it is the entity itself, is it considered as a legal person or a different legal type of collective?

Law No. 20, the Decree, or the example of the "Rules of Use of the Mola" do not provide explicit answers. The Decree differs from the terminology used in the Law. While the Law only speaks of the collective rights of the indigenous people,[121] Article 5 *Parágrafo* of the Decree introduces the term "members" ("miembros") of a community as possible sources or holders of TCE—without further clarification.[122]

Moreover, at the common level of the (non-customary) Law No. 20 and the Decree, the wording "collective rights of indigenous peoples" seems to argue in favour of the tribe itself, as does their reference to the official representatives and the strict, Western-like organizations of these peoples, namely the General Congresses.[123]

The particular rules of use differ from the terms employed in the law, and even *within* this set of rules of use, the terminology varies, as will be shown in the example of the "Rules of Use of the Collective Right 'Mola Kuna Panama.'"[124]

Moreover, not only the terms of the "Rules of Use of the Mola" vary in the example of the registration of the *mola*, but the registration even lists the population of the community,[125] which might be an indication for the members as right holders—or at least as beneficiaries. Moreover, the institutionalized representation through General Congresses does not exist in all cases of TCEs. There might be (only) traditional authorities, as the Decree itself considers.[126]

---

[120] On this *see* at Section 1.C.III.2. below.

[121] Either "pueblo indígena" or "pueblos indígenas". See, *e.g.*, Articles 1, 15 of the Law.

[122] It states that in case TCEs are of more than one community ("de los pueblos indígenas"), these creations are "shared between the *members* of the different communities" ("son creaciones compartidas entre los miembros de varias communidades"). Emphasis added by the author.

[123] *See, e.g.*, Articles 2 No. 10 and 7 No. 2 of the Decree.

[124] On this *see* at Section 1.D.II. below.

[125] "Población (cantidad) y Comunidad Beneficiada – Titulares", *Boletín del Registro Oficial de Propiedad Industrial* No. 123 of November 18, 2002, available at http://mici.gob.pa, last visited November 19, 2010.

[126] Article 2 No. 10 of the Decree.

It becomes clear that it is not always as easy to determine the correct holder(s) of rights as it might seem at first glance. When looking more closely at the whole system of the sui generis regime, it is actually important to consider each relevant TCE's rules of use to determine the concrete holders of rights. For the case of the *molas*, this will be done by way of an example below.[127]

In sum, no court decision exists on these aspects so far, and the publications on Law No. 20 do not touch the topics, either.[128]

With regard to the question of qualifying the community or tribe as a legal person, the issue is a different one, from this author's perspective. The question and potential answers touch on areas of civil law that go far beyond the question of how to protect TCEs. Therefore, this question should be governed by civil law provisions. Or, in case of special regulations on indigenous aspects in Panama, answers to this question would have to be found in the Laws on the *comarcas*, the indigenous territories. Law No. 20 and Decree No. 12 are tacit on this particular aspect, and the rules of use are not the appropriate legal ambits to govern this question, because they are intended solely to govern the traditional way of use of the particular TCE, as Article 15 of Law No. 20 stipulates.

b. State Authorities as Right Holders?

The general concept of Law No. 20 is based upon the idea of collective IP rights of the indigenous peoples,[129] i.e. on the idea of (exclusive) positions of rights within the area of private law. Hence, the state as right holder seems to be no possible interpretative conclusion.

However, it should not be disregarded that even the Panamanian state has certain kind of competences or rights: Besides its procedural involvement in the act of registration, it is the decisive act of DIGERPI to approve or disapprove the rules of use set up by the indigenous communities that is the core of protection.[130] By means of registration, the state concedes the collective intellectual property right to the indigenous communities. That makes it clear, on the one hand, that the state, i.e. DIGERPI, is the entity competent to decide over the concession of the collective rights.[131] On the other hand, it also clarifies that holders of the collective

[127] *See* at Section 5.D. below.

[128] Especially the question of recognizing Panamanian indigenous tribes as legal persons has rarely been discussed, *see, e.g.*, De Obaldia (2005), Ramsauer (2005), or Lucas-Schlötter (2008).

[129] *See* Article 1 of the Law.

[130] "reglamento de uso …, aprobado y registrado en la DIGERPI…", Article 15 of the Law. Ramsauer (2005) 104 refers to the relevant uses and the consent of the indigenous peoples that would have to be registered with DIGERPI ("fraglichen Nutzungen zusammen mit der Einwilligung der Gemeinschaft bei der Aufsichtsbehörde anzuzeigen ('aprobado y registrado en la DIGERPI')").

[131] Article 2, No. 9, of the Decree defines the "collective register of intellectual property" as an "exclusive right conceded by the state by means of an administrative act to exclude third parties

intellectual property rights are rather the communities, a fact that has also been underscored by the General Director of the Registry of Industrial Property.[132]

c. The Individual

Beside the above-shown involvement of the state authority, it is questionable to what extent individuals are regarded as right holders. The Law itself does not give rise to such a question, as it only uses the terms "collective intellectual property rights of the indigenous peoples".[133]

In practice, however, often individual decisions on the use of TCEs are taken, rather than a collective rights management. During my field research, I met two Kuna women who earned a living by creating *molas* for a Spanish lady who owns a traditional art gallery in the capital of Panama, Panama City, and was prepared an export business to sell the *molas* on the Spanish market. The Kuna women produced *molas* according to the "traditional", inventive style, as well as according to the "market" suggestions of the Spanish lady, and they also taught her the knowledge and technique of creating the *molas*—without prior consent of their traditional communities' *cacique* or the Kuna General Congress. Most of the time, they lived in the capital city anyway.[134] In conversations with staff members of the General Congress about the issue, they were not even surprised about the case—apparently not the first and probably not the last one illustrating difficulties in the implementation of collective ownership.

As regards the legal treatment of the case, which I discussed with different people involved in the area of TCEs in Panama, even indigenous peoples themselves, aware of the socio-economic needs of Kuna women, argue that the *benefits* should be received by the (individual) person who creates the TCE, in particular the *mola*.[135]

However, consequently, if part of the right is to receive benefits arising from the use of a TCE, should not this person, who is regarded as the appropriate recipient of the benefit, also be regarded as the appropriate holder of the right? Or do we need to distinguish between the benefit arising from the use of the concrete piece of TCE (belonging to the "producer") and immaterial knowledge about the creation of the TCE (belonging to the collective)?[136] Would this distinction be enforceable at all?

from the exploitation of a collective right being a product of traditional knowledge or folkloristic expression and whose effects and limitations are regulated by Law No. 20."

[132] Personal communication with Luz Celeste Ríos de Davis, General Director of the Industrial Property Registry, in February, 2009, in Panama City, and Ríos de Davis (2002) 10.

[133] Article 1 of the Law.

[134] Personal communications with the two Kuna women and the Spanish owner of the gallery (who wished to stay anonymous) in February, 2009, in Panama City.

[135] Personal communication with Aresio Valiente, Kuna Indian and lawyer on February 11, 2009, in Panama City.

[136] For problems regarding the differentiation between the material and immaterial good *see* at Section 1.G.I.2. below.

These questions have not been posed, much less answered properly, in Panama so far.

At the legal level, the principle idea of the source of the TCE or holders of the "collective intellectual property rights" are the "indigenous peoples".[137] In the whole system of the sui generis regime, however, including the example of the "Rules of Use of the Mola", there can indeed be found references to individuals as well as to a partial collective within the community as possible right holders in the regulations, too.[138]

What is worth being mentioned here is that in view of 55 % of the indigenous population in Panama now living in urban or semi-urban environments, and not in the indigenous territories,[139] the concept of collective ownership or collective rights management is challenged in practice. There is a strong tendency towards more individual mentalities and behavior even among the indigenous population, and this has a great impact on the idea and implementation of a collective intellectual property right as well as on the transmission from generation to generation in a collective way of living, which once was the reason and justification for collective ownership, even if it was individuals who were creating the TCEs.

While the question of right holders or "owners" is a highly political and emotional one, a "smoother" solution for the problem could be found at the level of defining the use, i.e. to include a *fair use* exception or an equivalent for Kuna women, allowing them to create and sell or teach *molas* and the techniques individually, if they obtain the approval of a Special Kuna Women's Committee, which will be discussed further below.[140]

2. More than One Community or People as Source of the TCE

a. Legal Regulation of the Case

If more than one community considers itself to be the traditional owner of a certain cultural expression, both communities may be—but do not have to be—registered collectively as holders of rights.[141] However, the registration is assigned (only) to those representatives of congresses or traditional authorities that apply for a registration and fulfill the application requirements.[142] Besides, it is expressly stated that the TCEs constitute "creations shared between the members of the different

[137] Article 1 of Law No. 20.

[138] *See* at Section D II.3.a. below.

[139] Valiente López (2008) 205

[140] *See* also De Obaldia (2005) 374.

[141] Article 5 of the Decree. Even if this instrument seems to contain an equalized compromise, the enforcement of the rule provoke problems. *See* at cc. below.

[142] Article 5 of the Decree and Ríos de Davis (2002) 8.

communities",[143] while no further rights, procedures, or concepts are laid down.[144] Besides, benefits are received collectively in favor of all of the communities.[145]

It is also explicitly stated that the registration should not affect the traditional exchange of the traditional object or knowledge between the indigenous peoples themselves.[146]

b. Resulting Questions and Reflections on This Legal Status Quo

When reflecting on the legal situation just displayed, three main questions arise:

(1) As there is no clear definition of a "community," especially no explicit distinction between "community" and "people(s)": When does the provision apply at all (hereunder aa.)?
(2) If on the one hand the registration is assigned only to those representatives who apply for a registration and fulfill the application requirements, and on the other hand the TCEs nonetheless are regarded as creations of all communities concerned and the benefits to be shared between all of them—what difference does a registration or non-registration make (hereunder bb.)?
(3) What are the experiences on the ground, how is the result of a collective registration of different communities and benefit-sharing among all of them achieved in practice (hereunder cc.)?

aa. Different "Communities"

If there is no clear definition of and distinction between different "communities" and one "people", when does the provision apply at all? Official documents vary in the use of terms "pueblo" and "pueblos"—singular and plural.[147] An example of different ethnic groups, but the same people, is the people of Ngöbe-Buglé. They filed registrations[148] of "Kra" or "Chácara", which are purses or bags woven with threads made of various fibers, decorated with traditional designs and patterns and used in various ways by the Ngöbe and Bugle people,[149] and the "Chaquira",[150] a necklace of two or more rows produced by threading small colored beads to

[143] *Parágrafo* of Art. 5 of the Decree: "Son creaciones compartidas entre los miembros de varias comunidades."

[144] According to this concept, the entitled groups can only decide jointly over the commercialization of the work, especially as regards licensing agreement with third parties. *See, e.g.*, § 8 para. 2 of the German Copyright Law.

[145] *Parágrafo* of Article 5 of the Decree: "Concebidos a favor de todos ellos colectivamente."

[146] Article 11 of the Decree.

[147] *See, e.g.*, the leaflet of the Ministerio de Comercio e Industrias – DIGERPI (no year).

[148] Registered on November 23, 2003, published in the *Boletín del Registro Oficial de Propiedad Industrial* No. 145 of May 7, 2004, available at http://mici.gob.pa, last visited September 17, 2010.

[149] *See* also Article 3, No. 8, of the Decree.

[150] Muñon-Kus (in Ngöbe), Crade (in Buglé)

produce abstract designs used by Ngöbe and Buglé natives.[151] Another example is the "Taaudau Waum" (of the Wounaan peoples) and the "Áta Neo" (of the Embera peoples), which are wood carvings of the *tagua*, which is a vegetal seed of a dense consistency similar to vegetable ivory.[152]

The *mola* is registered in favor of all Kuna peoples, consisting of different communities, which are represented according to the subdivision of the Kunas and their different representation through four general congresses.[153]

The system seems to work in practice, so is a differentiation and thus the lack of definition of communities of any practical relevance at all? This is not the case if the legal result is the same. Therefore, the important question is rather the following one, namely, what exactly is the nature of the act of registration and, accordingly, what rights exist for the communities whose General Congresses or traditional authorities have applied and for those which have not.

bb. Registration of Traditional Authorities of Only One Community

In the view of Article 5 of the Decree, does it make a difference whether the General Congresses or traditional authorities of one community are registered or those of all of the communities concerned? Given that the assigned representatives only represent their own communities, it would make a difference if the registration were considered to be of a constitutive nature for the right, meaning a precondition for the existence of the right.[154] Then, the right could come into existence only for those communities represented by those traditional authorities that have been registered.

In copyright in general, the author's right automatically comes into existence at the point in time at which the work is created. Here, it is different, as Article 2 No. 9 of the Decree defines the "collective registration of intellectual property" as an "exclusive right conceded by the state by means of an administrative act to exclude third parties from the exploitation of a collective right, being a product of traditional knowledge or folkloristic expression and whose effects and limitations are regulated by Law No. 20". In light of this definition, the registration would have to be considered as a constitutive act, bringing the collective intellectual property right into existence.

---

[151] *See* also Article 3, No. 5, of the Decree.

[152] Registered on December 12, 2005, published in the *Boletín del Registro Oficial de Propiedad Industrial* No. 195 of August 30, 2006, available at http://mici.gob.pa, last visited November 10, 2010.

[153] The General Congress of the Kuna, the General Congress of the Kuna of Madungandi, that of the Kuna of Wargandi and that of the Kuna of Tarkarkunyala. *See* Art. 6 of the Rules of Use of the Mola.

[154] The contrary would be a solely declaratory registration or even a formless coming into existence *ex lege*. The latter is the case in copyright law. *See* Article 5(2), first sentence, of the Revised Berne Convention. De Obaldia (2005) 366 argues in favor of a conditional precedent for protection, referring to Articles 4 to 6, although these articles rather only state to which public entity the application for registration has to be addressed and by whom it has to be done.

In practice, this issue has not been subject to discussions or even decisions yet. This might be due to the fact that most of the communities are located within the *comarcas*, the indigenous territories,[155] and are thus represented by the general congresses, the highest traditional representation level, anyway. Only few communities live outside these territories, and are thus more likely to have to face the problem.

But there do also exist cases in which the different communities do not unanimously support a (common) registration though their highest-level representation, the General Congresses. Then, theoretically, the traditional authorities at the local, communal level could apply or not for a registration. However, Article 4 of the Decree stipulates that the registration can be applied for by the traditional authority (only) in those cases, in which the indigenous community does not have a General Congress—thereby establishing a subsidiary rule of representation as admitted applicants. Thus, it appears to be rather a question of achieving consensus between the different communities at the practical level.

cc. Practical Experience with the Process of Collective Registration and Benefit Sharing

No procedure is set up to achieve the result of a collective registration and the distribution of the benefits in practice. As regards the latter aspect, there are simply no experiences of benefit sharing so far.[156]

With regard to the first aspect, the process of joint registration, there do exist positive results from such registrations: the registrations of TCEs of the Nböge and Buglé tribes, the "Kra o Chácara,"[157] and the "Krade o Chaquira,"[158] which were registered on November 28, 2003.[159]

However, conflicts and difficulties in the processes have also become known. The experience with the implementation unveils three main areas of relevance here:

(1) The simple need for preparatory communication between the different communities for a joint application if they are all in favor of registering the TCE
(2) negotiations on a consensus or dispute resolution, if the different communities do not agree, and,
(3) the treatment of cross-border TCEs.

---

[155] Valiente López (2008) 204 *et seq.*

[156] Personal communication with Aresio Valiente, Kuna Indian and lawyer on February 11, 2009 in Panama City and Yahelys Arenas of the Department of Collective Rights and Folkloric Expressions within DIGERPI, on this *see* also the management of rights below at Section 1.C.VI.

[157] Purses or bags woven with threads made of various fibers, decorated with traditional designs and patterns and used in various ways by the Ngöbe and Buglé people. *See* also Art. 3 No. 8 of the Decree.

[158] Muñon-Kus (in Ngöbe), Crade (in Buglé): necklace of two or more rows produced by threading small colored beads to produce abstract designs used by Ngöbe and Buglé natives. *See* also Article 3, No. 5, of the Decree.

[159] Ministerio de Comercio e Industrias – DIGERPI (no year) 7.

On the first point, experiences on the ground show that solely the *process* of a joint registration even within one people might be difficult. In the case of *mola* registration, for example, various communities of Kuna origin all over the country were involved, with very limited resources. Therefore, the communication between the different groups was not very easy, as Ríos de Davis reported.[160] In order to accelerate the communication process, DIGERPI visited some Kuna communities and supported the registration process by providing capacity-building measures, specifically regarding the application.[161] However, although the interest in registering the *mola* existed even before the entry into force of the law in 2000, and was a strong driving force for establishing the law at all, the registration of the *mola* was not completed until November 25, 2002.

After all, as time is changing, the process and culture of communication between the Kuna communities is also changing. Starting in 2006, more and more mobile phone antennas have been installed throughout the whole Kuna *comarca* now.[162] As far as the economic situation of the relevant communities allows, the communication process will probably modify and overcome at least physical distances more quickly.

However, in 2009, the process of registering the Kuna hammock still faced similar external challenges like long distances not easy to overcome in the north-eastern Panamanian jungle area.[163]

Besides these "external" aspects, practical experience has also brought to light internal challenges indicating the need for adequate mechanisms of conflict resolution. This situation shows again that the creation of new rights, and thus monopolies in the "Western" system, also might create new conflicts in an environment that assimilates to the "Western" lifestyle as regards the specialization in law as well as social individualistic behaviour. But also the traditional, socio-cultural background of the people concerned is an important factor in the case of the Kuna hammock: Used to small family structures, the different communities, but especially different tribes, have displayed rather hostile behavior in their interrelationships, and some of the tribes have had belligerent attitudes. The overarching concept of the indigenous Kuna territories, the *comarcas*, is relatively young. To a certain extent, even today, Panamanian indigenous groups "are not shy about taking up arms when having to defend their rights."[164]

Even in diplomatic ambits, they are allies based rather upon common interests than on the mere fact of belonging to "the indigenous population." Thus, when common political aims are reached or dissolve, the cooperation fades likewise—

[160] Ríos de Davis (2002) 6, translation according to the author.

[161] *Ibid.*

[162] Personal communication with staff members of the Kuna General Congress in February, 2009, in Panama City.

[163] Personal communication with Luis Touar, General Cacique Dagar Kunyala, translation by Flaviano Iglesias, in February, 2009, in Panama.

[164] De Obaldia (2005) 374 *seq.*

reaffirming observations made by anthropologists at international levels.[165] For example, in order to unify the voices of all indigenous tribes and peoples in the country for better representation on environmental, cultural, and other indigenous issues, particularly also the protection of handicrafts like the *mola*, a special cooperation was founded, the *Coordinadora Nacional De Los Pueblos Indígenas De Panama* (COONAPIP).[166] A few years after the entry into force of the Law, COONAPIP no longer actively operated on TCEs at the national level and was not even reachable in Panama.[167] It was said that, at least for issues dealing with Law No. 20, activities of the organization hat been replaced by another organization.[168] Indigenous alliances—as any others—apparently work at the moment when fighting for a common political aim, but besides this, no further, unifying commonalities exist. Wherever a new political aim arises, common interests and activities can be re-established.[169]

When it comes to disputes over existing rights or even "fights" for new rights, like those evolving through the registration system established by Law No. 20, indigenous peoples are also "no angels".[170] As they are also human beings, this is hardly surprising. Sometimes, however, a rather one-sided image of "the indigenous peoples" is painted, especially where abstractions are needed, as in legal terms. Generalizations, however, do not help to solve the problem.

In the case of the registration of a TCE of the Ngöbe and Buglé Indians, according to DIGERPI, a dispute between the General Congress and a *Cacique*, the traditional leader at a community level, arose, because the *Cacique* did not recognize the competence of the Congress. To solve the problem, DIGERPI took on, or had to take on, a dispute-settling role, even deciding to whom to "grant" the intellectual property right by means of the registration of the TCEs in favor of only one.[171]

The process of registering the Kuna hammock is also an example of all three aspects mentioned above: difficulties in the communication as well as the negotiation process, and in the territorial question of "cross-border tribes".

As detailed above,[172] Kuna Indians considered registering a special type of traditional Kuna hammock, hand-made of cotton and dyed in seven distinct natural colors. Several different Kuna communities are involved in this handicraft,

---

[165] On this point *see* at Chapter II Section 1.B.II.1.c. above.

[166] It was founded in 1991; for further details *see* http://www.cicaregional.org/leer.php/570046, last visited November 20, 2010.

[167] Result of the personal fieldwork mission to Panama in February, 2009.

[168] *Mundo Dugbis*, personal communication with Aresio Valiente López, Kuna Indian and lawyer, in February, 2009, in Panama City.

[169] Along this line, a new aim was e.g. the cooperation with the UN-REDD Program. *See* http://www.fao.org/climatechange/unredd/53078/en/pan/, last visited November 20, 2010.

[170] Personal communication with staff members of the Department of Collective Rights and Folkloric Expressions within DIGERPI in February, 2009, Panama City.

[171] *Supra*.

[172] *See* at Section 1.C.III.3. below.

including those who still live in a more traditional way, in a remote area in the rainforest close to the Colombian border.[173]

The negotiations between the three "greater" different Kuna communities within the Panamanian territory are first of all characterized by challenging distances between the different communities, in a landscape of rainforest and rivers that flanks the Caribbean Sea.

Second, communication habits and customs are also lacking, as Kuna Indians are used to communal structures and discussions rather than inter-communal ones, a fact that is mainly influenced by the (former) family structures of the indigenous life. There also was no common sentiment or desire to register the hammock jointly. An important argument for the Kuna peoples living in the remoter areas of the tropical rainforest close to the Colombian border was that the necessary material and resources for traditionally creating the hammock do not exist in all parts of the indigenous territories of the Kuna Indians. Raw material like cotton and certain plants and animals for producing the natural dyes for the hammocks existed only in their territory—which would facilitate the production within their territory and ensure the preservation of the tradition and authenticity.[174] From an external point of view, this argumentation makes very much sense.

However, all Kuna groups wanted to be bearers of the tradition and legitimate creators and users of the hammock. According to Yahelys Arenas, four groups had been negotiating over the application for registering the Kuna hammock. Conflict resolution according to customary law was difficult to implement, as the whole registration process is not part of the customary law, but rather a non-traditional procedure. Thus, especially the smaller communities from the remoter areas preferred to seek help and support from DIGERPI. Moreover, DIGERPI was regarded to be neutral, or at least more neutral than other Kuna entities, and equipped with sufficient knowledge, and, finally, competence to decide over the dispute—or at least over the registration.[175]

Finally, the third difficulty was that there are also two Kuna communities in the rainforest across the Panamanian–Colombian border on Colombian national territory, and for this reason the question arose *whether*, and if so, *how*, these two communities, should be considered in the registration process as well. These communities in the Colombian part of the rainforest still possess the resources and material—in contrast to some of the communities in Panama itself. However, the legal question of treating non-citizens by means of Law No. 20 and a need for bilateral agreements on a national level arose. As if this weren't enough, there was another difficulty in solving the problem: the instability and insecurity of the region,

---

[173] Personal communication with Luis Touar, General Cacique Dagar Kunyala, translation by Flaviano Iglesias, in February, 2009, in Panama.

[174] *Supra.*

[175] Personal communication with Yahelys Arenas of the Department of Collective Rights and Folkloric Expressions within DIGERPI and Luis Touar, General Cacique Dagar Kunyala, translation by Flaviano Iglesias in February 2009, Panama City.

as Bonilla says, where mainly paramilitaries "reign" over every-day life, oppressing, and even killing members of the indigenous communities.[176] Thus, how could, under these circumstances, negotiations be held?

These examples from the fieldwork show that, while positive outcomes can be recorded, the procedure of getting to that outcome so far mainly depended upon the role of DIGERPI. The role of DIGERPI, more specifically its Department of Collective Rights and Folkloric Expressions, thereby embraces the following qualities: being a "neutral" and competent entity, with some financial and especially very capable human resources, i.e. people in charge of the Department who show a high personal dedication to the cause, and have great intercultural empathy and facility. Nonetheless, suggestions for improvement of the system have been made.[177]

3. Exercise of Right and Representation

A distinctive question is that of the administration of rights or the right or authority to claim the rights in their substantive and procedural dimension. This is the question of representation.

Although international authors argue that the Law and the Decree entitle the official authorities of the communities concerned to administer the rights,[178] the Law and the Decree only determine the representatives concerning the *application for the registration* of a right.[179] These are the general congresses and, in case of lack of such, the traditional indigenous authorities, under Article 7 of the Law and Article 4 of the Decree.

The use and commercialization themselves, and the modes of representation related to these aspects, are determined by the regulation of use or rules of use particularly set up for each and every TCE, according to Article 15 of the Law. In the case of the *mola*, for example, the "Rules of Use of the Mola" determine that the General Congresses, represented through their *Sahilas*,[180] administer the rights and corresponding actions. The registration, however, mentions the names of these four individuals,[181] but also names a diverging "legal representative," including his concrete contact data.

---

[176] Bonilla (2004 I) no pagination.

[177] On this *see* at Section 1.H.III. below.

[178] Ramsauer (2005) 107 arguing that the Panamanian Regime in principle empowers the official authorities of the particular community.

[179] *See* wording of Art. 7 of the Law, Art. 4 of the Decree, *id.*, 104, refers to representation in general.

[180] Or *saila dummagan*, which means traditional representative; Art. 7 of the Rules of Use of the Mola.

[181] And the numbers of their identification document, *Boletín del Registro Oficial de Propiedad Industrial* No. 123 of November 18, 2002, available at http://mici.gob.pa, last visited May 23, 2010.

By the way, this organization in the rather Western-shaped concept of "General Congresses" might even be identified as an example of the change of traditions, as it is not very closely connected to "traditional family structures" anymore. The practicability of an easy identification of the representatives has been given priority over the acknowledgement of rather traditional, local structures and representation models—a decision that is comprehensible in view of the Panamanian reality of the indigenous territories and organizational structures of the *comarcas*.[182] In practice, however, this allocation of representation has provoked conflicts so far[183]—while, at the same time, probably no solution on paper would have absolutely dispute-free consequences in practice.

4. Conclusion

As depicted above, Law No. 20 in various articles mentions the "collective rights of the indigenous peoples," without clearly defining the holders of rights. Contrary to many voices in the literature, the whole system including the rules of use, as well as the experiences on the ground, show that a strict interpretation of the collective as the right holder is neither unambiguous nor does it provide for answers to subsequent questions. Solutions have been searched for solely at the factual level so far.[184] A clarification would be desirable, especially as regards the rights of use established by the specific rules of use, like the "Rules of Use of the Collective Right 'Mola Kuna Panama.'" Nonetheless, a clarification of Law No. 20 alone would probably not solve the problems—especially the socio-economic ones—hampering its effective implementation in practice.

IV. Contents and Scope of Protection: Rights Conferred

The Law provides for indigenous collective (IP) rights, defined as "rights in indigenous cultural and intellectual property, which refer to arts, music, literature, . . . and other aspects and expressions."[185] What aspects do these sui generis rights particularly comprise?

1. Direction of Protection and Nature of Rights

The Law grants negative as well as positive protection; negative, in that registrations of other, "classical" intellectual property rights in TCEs in favor of third

[182] *See* in general at Section 1.A. above; for details at Section 1.D.I. below.

[183] *E.g.* discussions on the registration of a Kuna hammock at Section 1.D.III.2.b.cc. above.

[184] *E.g.* the establishment of a special Congress of Kuna Women, *see* at Section 1.H.III.

[185] Article 2 No. 5 of the Decree.

parties are prohibited. TCEs "cannot be subject to any form of non-authorized exclusivity of third parties within the intellectual property system," "except that the application was formulated by the indigenous peoples."[186] Although this Article 2 is located in the Chapter entitled "Objectives" of the Law, the wording as well as the historical background of Law No. 20 (to "save" the *mola* from being registered as trademark in favor of non-indigenous companies) argue in favor of such a negative scope of protection.

The protection is positive in the sense that it establishes several active rights, as well as prohibitions and penalty provisions, to be discussed all together below.

The rights are partly of a substantive nature—for example, the right to determine the use of the TCE (Article 15)—and partly procedural, which is, however, disputed in detail.[187]

2. Rights Conferred

As the flip side of the negative scope mentioned above, a collective right to apply for conventional intellectual property rights in the protected subject matter as well as to authorize third parties to use or prevent them from acquiring exclusive IP rights in the protected subject matter can be regarded as granted by Article 2.[188]

As its core provision, Article 15 establishes the right of the indigenous peoples to autonomously determine the use of the TCE by means of setting up rules of use—which however then have to be approved and registered by DIGERPI.[189] It is thus the "rules of use" or "regulation of use" of each community that has to be "approved and registered" by DIGERPI, and not the intended uses together with the consent of the respective community.[190] The right is granted to authorize or prevent the use and commercialization of TCEs.[191]

Apart from that, a right to "prior and express consent" of the indigenous General Congresses in the case of industrial reproduction is granted, in combination with the authorization by the Ministry of Commerce and Industries.[192] This "right" is formulated as a public prohibition, though: "The total or partial industrial

[186] Second half sentence of the first sentence of Article 2 of the Law: "...no pueden ser objeto de ninguna forma de exclusividad por terceros no autorizados a través del sistema de propiedad intelectual, tales como derecho de autor, modelos industriales, marcas, indicaciones geográficas y otros, salvo que la solicitud sea formulada por los pueblos indígenas."

[187] On the question of the nature of the authorization of industrial reproduction *see* at Section 1.C. III.1.b. above.

[188] *See* at Section 1.C.IV.1. above and Article 2 of the Law.

[189] Different view: Ramsauer (2005) 111 note 406.

[190] Different view: *Id.* 104: "Allerdings sind *die fraglichen Nutzungen* zusammen mit der Einwilligung der Gemeinschaft bei der Aufsichtsbehörde *anzuzeigen* ('apropado y registrado en la DIGERPI')"; emphasis added by the author.

[191] Article 15 of the Law.

[192] Article 20 of the Law.

reproduction of the traditional textiles and other collective rights recognized in this Law is prohibited, unless it is authorized by the Ministry of Commerce and Industries, with the prior and express consent of the indigenous General Congresses and Councils, and unless it does not contravene the dispositions of this Law."[193] According to the drafters of the law, "authorization" should not be interpreted as an extra formal procedural requirement, but is rather included in the participation of the DIGERPI within the Ministry of Commerce and Industries in the registration process, i.e. the act of registering and thereby confirming the accordance of the registration with the law.[194] This, however, is controversial, as is the resultant question of the nature of the act of authorization by DIGERPI.[195]

Industrial reproduction is defined by the Decree as "the reproduction of goods derived from the utilization of a collective right registered and/or granted (amparado) by the Law; as well as the proceedings developed from (a partir del) a collective right of one or more indigenous communities."[196] Apart from that, definitions or explanations of what exactly "personal use" and "commercial use" mean, especially in differentiation to "industrial reproduction," cannot be found in the Law. As the case of industrial reproduction requires different preconditions to be fulfilled—at least according to the text of the law, i.e. prior, express consent and additional authorization by the ministry of commerce[197]—it could be deduced that, because of these different requirements for the types of "use", one must differentiate between those types at the level of use, too. However, the (co-)drafters of the law argue that there was no difference intended between commercial use and industrial reproduction.[198] In practice, there has been no need to clarify the question, as there has not been even one request for an authorization of an industrial reproduction of a TCE so far.[199]

According to the explanations given by DIGERPI, the following four principles exist to determine which actions require authorization:

(1) The use has a lucrative aim,
(2) the use takes place outside of the traditional or customary context,
(3) the use distorts the socio-cultural values of the indigenous cultures, and
(4) it entails a "piracy of traditions" (a term not further explained).[200]

[193] Article 20 of the Law. Not quite clear De Obaldia (2005) 368.

[194] Personal communication with Aresio Valiente, Kuna Indian, lawyer, and consultant in the legislative process, on February 11, 2009, in Panama City.

[195] On the question of the nature of the authorization of industrial reproduction, *see* at Section 1.C. III.1.b. above.

[196] Article 2, No. 17, of the Decree.

[197] Article 20 of the Law, Article 17 of the Decree.

[198] Personal communication with Aresio Valiente, Kuna Indian and lawyer, on February 11, 2009, in Panama City.

[199] Personal communication with Luz Celeste Ríos de Davis, General Director of the Industrial Property Registry, and Aresio Valiente, Kuna Indian and lawyer in February, 2009 in Panama City.

[200] Ríos de Davis (2002) 7.

Further, DIGERPI has stated that there exists another action requiring authorization, that is, "access to traditional knowledge with commercial or industrial intents."[201] This kind of use has not been laid down in the law, though.

With regard to the other aspects of the rights of "use" and "commercialization", a differentiation also seems to be needed, as "personal use" is "free" and commercial use requires a licensing contract. According to Article 15, this differentiation is determined by the specific regulation on each TCE set up by each indigenous community.

In cases of indirect use—when, for example, a traditional music group has been engaged to play music and wears *molas* while playing the traditional music—the lucrative aim of the "direct" use of one object—here, playing the traditional music—should not automatically include the use of the other object—here, wearing the *mola* for this commercial occasion, Aresio Valiente suggests.[202] This case could be arguable, of course.

Another right conferred is the right to consent to a certification of TCEs as works of indigenous traditional art or handicraft and handmade by natives.[203] This certification is free and granted by either the National Direction of the Historic Patrimony of the National Institute of Culture (INAC)[204] or by the Direction of National Handicrafts (DGAN) of the Ministry of Commerce and Industries[205] if a work protected by industrial property rights is concerned.[206]

V. Exemptions

All these rights just displayed are not granted for every expression. Several exemptions are made. The exemptions contained in Law No. 20 have to do with different aspects like the way an object is used, subjects of protection, and objects of protection, and are partly full exemptions and partly limited ones.

1. Educational Use

Similar to exemptions in copyright, the "Schranken" in German Copyright law, for example, Law No. 20 provides for exemptions in cases of use of TCEs in educational activities by public institutions—in accordance with the traditional

[201] *Ibid.* Although not explicitly stated in the Law or the Decree, this aspect can be deduced from the spirit and objective of the Law, she argues. *See* also the objectives in Arts. 2 and 1 of the Law.

[202] Suggestion by Aresio Valiente, Kuna Indian and lawyer on February 11, 2009, in Panama City.

[203] Article 10, para. 2, of Law No. 20, Article 15 of the Decree.

[204] La Dirección Nacional de Patrimonio Histórico del Instituto Nacional de Cultura, Article 15, para. 1, of the Decree.

[205] La Dirección General de Artesanías Nacionales del Ministerio de Comercio e Industrias.

[206] Article 15, para. 2, of the Decree.

indigenous authorities, and use of TCEs in school expositions and fairs promoted by students for the benefit of their school.[207]

2. Folkloric Dances

Exemptions are made for folkloric dance groups performing in a national or international setting.[208] The special regulation on folkloric dances can only be understood properly when it is considered that the indigenous peoples themselves, being the driving force of the drafting and establishment of the law, do not regard their own (traditional) culture or their cultural patrimony as "folklore". "Folklore" is rather regarded as that kind of culture, i.e. dance, that is not performed in a traditional context but rather as some kind of public presentation.[209]

Traditional dances *in general* are among the objects capable of protection[210] and thus can be objects of registration.[211] *Folkloric* dances, however, are exempted from being subject to collective rights. Nonetheless, in order to promote partially or integrally indigenous culture, the persons organizing the dancing performances must include members of said communities in the performance. In case no such members can be recruited for the dance, an authorization expressed by the respective general congress or traditional indigenous authority is necessary to preserve the authenticity of the dance. The National Institute of Culture (INAC) is designated to supervise the fulfillment of this obligation.[212]

This regulation reflects the second objective of the Law: apart from establishing economic rights, it also aims to protect the authenticity of the traditional expressions.[213]

In practice, no dances including members of indigenous communities have been organized so far. The stated reason for this was that without funding, the indigenous peoples performing traditional dances are not able to come to the capital or bigger cities where such performances normally take place, as the journey would be too long and expensive. Two days of folkloric dances including the Afro-Panamanians have been planned, however.[214]

---

207 Article 14 of the Law.

208 Article 16 of the Law.

209 On the terminology *see* also at Chapter II Section 1.A.II. above.

210 On this *see* at Section 1.C.II. above and Article 4 of the Law.

211 For example, the K'ari chipar dance of the Wounaan community and the Jegui dance of the Ngöbe and Buglé peoples. *See* Article 2, Nos. 52, 60 of the Decree.

212 Article 16 of the Law.

213 Article 6 of the Law.

214 Personal Communication with Edmundo de la Cruz, Chief of the Department of Folklore of the INAC, the National Institute of Culture on February 13, 2009, in Panama City.

3. Small Non Indigenous Artisans

There exist two special regulations with regard to certain non-indigenous artisans.

a. Handicraftsmen from Chiquirí

First, there is a special exemption for certain small non indigenous artisans producing specific TCEs in the style of the Ngöbe-Buglé Indians.[215] This exemption is rooted in the following circumstances[216]: A small non-indigenous community living in the village of Tolé at the outside border of the Chiquirí Province, and thus close neighbours of the Ngöbe, have observed their neighbours and adapted their way of sewing and decorating cloths that are sold at the side of the road to the Chiriquí Province. When negotiating the Law, no consensus could be reached on leaving aside this economically attractive cultural "expression," or rather, production.

Thus, although only imitating the Ngöbe culture, the people from Tolé[217] are (still) allowed to manufacture and market reproductions. However, they are not able to claim the collective rights recognized by Law No. 20.[218]

In effect, this regulation respects and integrates the factual status quo. It could thus be qualified as a special type of transitional arrangement.[219]

b. Registered Panamanian Non-indigenous Handicraftsmen

The second special provision in the Chapter with "Final dispositions" constitutes a transitional rule for those non-indigenous handicraftsmen who at the date of entry into force of Law No. 20 were dedicated to the creation and selling of replicas of traditional indigenous art and were registered with the General Directorate of National Crafts. These persons are allowed to continue their activities with the announcement of the indigenous traditional authorities and respective authorizations issued by the Ministry of Commerce and Industries. These Panamanian handicraftsmen, however, have to indicate in an easily visible manner that the product constitutes a replica, as well as its origin.[220]

---

[215] Article 23 of the Law.

[216] Personal communication with Enrique Montezuma, Ngäbe Indian, ex-deputy, and legislator, on February 13, 2009, in Panama City.

[217] As well as the peoples from the other villages mentioned in that same Article.

[218] Articles 23, 24 of the Law and Articles 26, 27 of the Decree. These provisions also apply to the similar situation of the other villages in that *Comarca*: Remedios, San Félix, and San Lorenzo, Art. 23.

[219] For transitional arrangements in general *see* at Section 1.C.VIII. below.

[220] Article 24 of the Law.

4. Traditional Exchange Between Indigenous Communities

The traditional exchange of a cultural object or the traditional knowledge between indigenous peoples is covered by the protection insofar as it is not to be affected by the registration of any collective right.[221]

VI. Registration and Management of Rights, Sanctions, and Enforcement Procedures

1. Registration Proceedings and Competent Authorities

As mentioned before, the sui generis protection of Law No. 20 regarding the use and commercialization of TCEs is not without formalities; rather, it is granted by means of a special registration system.[222] The "collective registration of intellectual property" is defined as an "exclusive right conceded by the state by means of an administrative act to exclude third parties from the exploitation of a collective right, being a product of traditional knowledge or folkloristic expression and which effects and limitations are regulated by Law No. 20."[223]

a. Why a Registry?

The reason for establishing a system of protection on the basis of a registration requirement was that the drafters of the law, mostly indigenous peoples, believed that official registration was necessary for the effective enforcement of rights vis-á-vis non indigenous peoples.[224] Especially before the enactment of Law No. 20, the Panamanian society rather considered indigenous culture as a part of the national cultural heritage belonging to "everyone": According to De Obaldia, the register was intended to give notice to the non-indigenous public, as well as serve as "a *property deed* of sorts for the monopoly."[225]

b. What Is the Nature of the Act of Registration?

While there is some dispute over whether the registration is considered to be of a constitutive nature for the rights, meaning a precondition for the existence of the

[221] Article 11 of the Decree.

[222] Article 1 of the Law.

[223] Article 2 No. 9 of the Decree.

[224] Personal communication with Aresio Valiente, indigenous lawyer and one of the consultants of the deputies, on February 11, 2009, in Panama City.

[225] De Obaldia (2005) 366.

right,[226] at least according to the wording of the special registration system, the material right comes into existence only if it meets the formal requirement of registration.

This is different from copyright in general, where the author's right automatically comes into existence when the work is created. Here, it is different, as Article 2 No. 9 of the Decree defines the "collective register of intellectual property" as an "exclusive right conceded by the state by means of an administrative act to exclude third parties from the exploitation of a collective right, being a product of traditional knowledge or folkloristic expression and whose effects and limitations are regulated by Law No. 20." In light of this definition, registration would have to be considered as a constitutive act.

c. Is the Registry Public?

Access to the Registry of the Collective Rights is public, except for the experiences and cognitive processes developed by the indigenous peoples, techniques and methods of traditional elaboration.[227]

This limited publicity appeared to be an obstacle for the registration in practice, as there exists mistrust among the indigenous peoples concerning a non-public, safe treatment of the sensitive information on the creation methods of their TCEs. These concerns were expressed, for example, by a *Cacique,* a traditional leader of the Kuna Indians when they were considering registering a Kuna hammock. An intrinsic part of this TCE is the special knowledge of how to produce the natural dyes for the cotton, in particular which plants or animals to use for which color, and the technique for keeping the different dyes from bleeding. Although the Decree provided for a limitation of the publicity of the registry in this case, the obligatory disclosure of the traditional techniques of creation provoked great fear among the Kuna community and doubts of whether to register the hammock at all.[228]

d. Who Is the Competent Authority?

In theory, applications for registration are to be made either to the Industrial Property Office or to the National Copyright Office, depending on which "it corresponds" to.[229] This differentiation apparently corresponds to the distinction in the classic intellectual property system.

---

[226] The contrary would be a solely declaratory registration or even a formless coming into existence *ex lege*. The latter is the case in copyright law. *See* Article 5(2), first sentence of the Revised Berne Convention. As explained above, De Obaldia (2005) 366, argues in favor of a condition for protection and refers to Articles 4 to 6. However, these articles only state to which public entity the application for registration has to be addressed and by whom it is effectuated. *See* also at Section 1.C.III.1.b. above.

[227] Article 12 of the Decree.

[228] Personal communication with Luis Touar, General Cacique Dagar Kunyala, translation by Flaviano Iglesias, in February, 2009, in Panama.

[229] Articles 4 and 5 of the Law.

In practice, there exists no case in which applications have been addressed to the National Copyright Office.[230] This may be due to the fact that only handicrafts have been registered so far. Nevertheless, in fact, what the experiences in Panama have shown is that what is needed more than anything else is competence in and dedication to the special aspect of interacting with indigenous communities, taking into account their habits and needs. This specific focus and dedication is housed within DIGERPI's Department of Collective Rights and Folkloric Expressions.[231] Thus, the provision dividing the competences between the Industrial Property Office and the National Copyright Office reveals a too strong inspiration by and adaptation to the Western system and categories of intellectual property law, whereas the specific needs in the area of TCEs are dominated by other factors, as just demonstrated.

The sense of this division is even more questionable in light of Article 7 of the Law. This Article provides for the creation of a special Department of Collective Rights and Folkloric Expressions within DIGERPI, by means of which, among other things, the registration of the collective rights of the indigenous peoples is conceded.

e. Who May Apply?

Applications for registration are to be made by the General Congress of the indigenous community, and, in case such an institution does not exist, by the traditional indigenous authorities.[232] General Congresses or traditional authorities are defined as those acknowledged by the Panamanian state—through an administrative act—as organs of the highest expression, decision, consultation and administration established by the indigenous community in accordance with their traditions and with the relevant national laws.[233]

Besides the action of the General Congresses or traditional authorities, in theory, no involvement of a lawyer is required.[234]

f. How to Proceed ?—Application

The registration process is divided into the steps of application, formal examination, appeals, and, finally, the act of registration itself.

---

[230] Personal communication with Marcos Polano, Head of the National Copyright Office, (Dirección del derecho de Autor del Ministério de Educación), in February, 2009, Panama City.

[231] Personal research in Kuna Yala, personal communication with Marcos Polano, Head of the National Copyright Office, (Dirección del derecho de Autor del Ministério de Educación), Yahelys Arenas, and other staff members of the Department of Collective Rights and Folkloric Expressions within DIGERPI in February, 2009, Panama City.

[232] Article 4 of the Decree.

[233] The Law that creates the indigenous *comarcas* and their *Carta Orgánica*, in accordance with the Constitution and other laws of the Panamanian Republic; Article 2, No. 10, of the Decree.

[234] Article 7 of the Law.

The application is to indicate (a) that it deals with a collective right; (b) that it belongs to one of the indigenous peoples of the country; (c) the applied technique (if is an object); and (d) its history (tradition) and a short description, including the rules of use of the collective indigenous right.[235]

The rules of use thereby should comprise: (a) the identification of the indigenous peoples concerned; (b) the representative bodies; (c) the request (in the native language and in Spanish); (d) the description of the object (techniques, materials, patters, etc); (e) the history (tradition); (f) the communities and population benefited; (g) a sample of the object.[236]

The application, as well as the whole process of applying, is free of charge.[237]

g. Further Proceedings

Within 30 days of receiving the application, the competent authorities must approve the fulfillment of the application requirements.[238]

Once the registration has taken place and been published in the Official Bulletin of Industrial Property (BORPI), appeals against it have to be made known to the representatives of the collective rights personally.[239]

2. Process of Certification

With the announcement of the local indigenous authorities and an application by any interested party, the special certification of a traditional work is granted by the General Direction of National Handicrafts (DGAN) within the Ministry of Commerce and Industries and must indicate that the specific TCE is a traditional indigenous art or handicraft and hand-made by members of the indigenous population.[240]

The process and grant of the certification is completely free of charge.[241]

3. Prior Consent to and Authorization of Industrial Reproduction

In case of an intended industrial reproduction of a TCE, an authorization has to be obtained through the General Direction of the National Handicrafts (DGAN) within the Ministry of Commerce and Industries. In reality, no such case exists so far.[242] In

[235] Article 6 of the Decree.

[236] Article 7 of the Decree.

[237] Article 7 of the Law.

[238] Article 8 of the Decree, with further details.

[239] Articles 7 of the Law and 10 of the Decree.

[240] Articles 10 of the Law and 15 of the Decree.

[241] Articles 10 of the Law and 15 of the Decree.

[242] Personal communication with Luz Celeste Ríos de Davis, General Director of the Industrial Property Registry, in February, 2009, Panama City.

theory, the application for this authorization would have to encompass (a) the document proving the express consent or authorization of the relevant General Congress or traditional authority, in which the cession of the registered collective right by means of a licensing agreement in favor of third parties is specified; (b) a copy of the licensing agreement; (c) the identification of the indigenous representatives as well as of the other parties and representatives signing the contract; and (d) the concrete use which is intended to be made of the TCE.[243]

The licensing contract has to fulfill the requirements laid down in Article 18 of the Decree.

4. Prohibitions, Sanctions, and Enforcement

Aside from the rights displayed above,[244] Law No. 20 at the same time establishes specific prohibitions and sanctions, thereby amending the Panamanian Fiscal Code and customs law. In this manner, the import of non original products imitating traditional cloths, musical instruments, and traditional artworks of indigenous peoples is prohibited,[245] as is the non-declared, non-authorized possession of such products.[246]

Fifty percent of the fines are to be given to the National Treasury (Tesoro Nacional), and the other 50 % to the indigenous people or *comarca*. The amount of the sanction may vary between 1,000 and 5,000 Panamanian dollars.[247]

So far, no case of implementation of these provisions and sanctions has been documented, which is one reason among others why the effectiveness of the distribution mechanisms cannot be evaluated.[248]

Apart from these sanctions to be implemented by the national authorities, also indigenous peoples themselves are granted competence with regard to the enforcement of the law. In particular, the governor of the *comarcas*, of the indigenous territories, and, in case the former does not exist, of the province, as well as the General Congress of the corresponding *comarca* are granted competence to apprehend infringers of the Law, take preventive actions on the respective products and articles, and hand them over to the corresponding public entities.[249]

---

[243] Articles 20 of the Law and 17 of the Decree.

[244] *See* at Section 1.C.VI. above.

[245] Article 17 of the Law, amending Article 439 of the Fiscal Code.

[246] Article 18 of the Law, amending Article 16 of Law No. 30 of 1984.

[247] Articles 19 and 21 of the Law.

[248] Personal communication with staff members of the Direction of the National Handicrafts (DGAN), of the Department of Collective Rights and Folkloric Expressions within DIGERPI, and Aresio Valiente López, Kuna Indian and lawyer, in Panama City in February 2009.

[249] Article 22 of Law No. 20, *see* De Obaldia (2005) 366 (though referring to Article 23).

In practice, however, indigenous peoples have doubted the effectiveness of this provision. For them it is difficult to make use of this competence due to the lack of economic possibilities, and as a counter-effect, it was alleged that state entities relied on this provision as an excuse for not intervening actively (enough) themselves.[250]

5. Conclusion

The registration system, originally based upon a "good idea," faces various difficulties in practice, as showed above, like the obligatory disclosure of the traditional creation methods. Besides these challenges, other problems in practice are institutional in nature, mainly the different allocation of competences for the various tasks. More particularly, within the General Direction of the National Handicrafts, the staff members rotate to a new department every 4 years, and as a consequence, experience gained or information obtained in one 4-year period of work mostly gets lost. Thus, there is a noticeable lack of documentation. Another difficulty lies in the division of competence, and the communication and exchange of experiences between the DGAN and the DIGERPI Department of Collective Rights and Folkloric Expressions that this division necessitates.[251]

VII. Term of Protection

No term of protection exists, as first, the collective rights themselves are not submitted to any temporal limitation, and second, it is stated that the registrations themselves are regarded to be indefinite, or, in other words, as not having a limit in duration.[252]

The reason for this was, according to De Obaldia, the unanimous consensus during the negotiations of the law that the cultural traditions of nations could not be subject to expiration.[253]

Although there might be a broad consensus for the perpetuation of cultures or artistic expressions,[254] there are also transformation processes that might lead to a complete disappearance of a culture or even a nation.

---

[250] Personal communication with members of the Kuna tribe on February 14, 2009, in Panama City.

[251] Personal communication with staff members of the Direction of the National Handicrafts (DGAN) and the Department of Collective Rights and Folkloric Expressions within DIGERPI in February 2009, Panama City.

[252] Art. 7, para. 3, sentence 1 of the Law: "Los registros (...) no caducarán ni tendrán término de duración."

[253] De Obaldia (2005) 368.

[254] On a more abstract level, Hippocrates in his Aphorims Sect. I, No. 1. said: "Vita brevis, ars longa", "Live is short, Art long".

Moreover, distinctions might have to be made between the question of the persistence of a culture and the duration of the rights granted for cultural expressions, as rights determine relationships between people and express concrete thoughts and valuations of justice. Introducing monopolies for collective ownership of traditional cultural expressions can only be justified if both the kind of collective and the concrete tradition protected continue to exist as such.

These general considerations are of concrete practical relevance in the case of the use of TCEs on the basis of Law No. 20. The problems arising are even more complicated, as the question of duration of protection is closely linked with another one—that of incorporating newly evolving forms or styles of the TCEs in the protection.[255] This is the case regarding the protection of the *mola,* for example.[256]

The "possibility for perpetual monopolies", which Law No. 20 opens up, without establishing a requirement of a TCE's still "being a reflection of indigenous culture"—whatever exactly this might be in legal terms—has also been criticized by Panamanian authors.[257] While it will be recalled that one precondition of the protection is the characteristic of being "traditional,"[258] it will be interesting to see how this is considered in practice and whether envisaged reforms of the Law would deal with this conflict of interests.

VIII. Interaction with Other Existing Laws

Several interactions are dealt with, including transitional arrangements. Rights accorded previously under the relevant legislation are to be respected and not affected by Law No. 20.[259] However, the Panamanian Copyright Act of 1984 does not provide for copyright protection of objective expressions of folklore.[260]

Besides, the Law supplements the Fiscal Code and the Penal Law,[261] establishing new import regulations and offenses ("delitos").[262]

[255] *See* the remarks on the criteria "traditional" at Chapter II Section 1.B.I.1.d. above.

[256] On this *see* at Section 1.D.II.3. below.

[257] De Obaldia (2005) 376.

[258] On this *see* at Section 1.C.II.2.b. above.

[259] Sentence 2 of Article 2 of the Law.

[260] Article 9 of the Copyright Act.

[261] Law No. 30 of November 8, 1984.

[262] Articles 27, 17–23 of the Law.

IX. Reference to Customary Law

1. The Legal Situation

The Panamanian Sui generis solution also includes the application of customary law. This is perhaps the most interesting aspect and the core of the regulation. It gives binding effect to customary law, which defines the means of use of the TCE, provided that the TCE is written down and registered, i.e. made public. In concrete terms, "the rights of use and commercialization of . . . [TCEs] must be governed by the regulation of each indigenous community, approved and registered" with DIGERPI.[263] This solution—on paper—is internationally rated an "original one."[264]

The legal technique of considering customary law used here is that of reference, in combination with the requirement of fixation and registration of the rules of use. Specifically, the requirements for applying customary law are the following:

There must be a fixation of the "regulation," or rules on the use of a specific TCE of an indigenous community, which have to be approved by the Industrial Property Office (formal examination) and registered, i.e. made available to the public.[265] It is thus the "rules of use" or "regulation of use" of each community that has to be "approved and registered" by DIGERPI, and not the intended uses together with the consent of the respective community, as some international interpreters of the law state.[266]

The rules of use or regulations of use are defined in the Decree as "specifying the common characteristics of the traditional knowledge and objects capable of being registered as intellectual property. They represent the support of the tradition of the Collective Right and its application in the indigenous communities."[267]

According to Article 7 of the Decree, these rules should provide information about, among others, the specific use and "collective right" itself.[268]

2. Some Further Reflections on This Regulation

In general, within the topic of protecting TCEs, the application of indigenous customary law is a big issue. It is understood that TCEs are part of the living heritage and culture of special communities. The vitality and further existence of the expressions are ensured best within these communities' own socio-cultural

263 Article 15 of the Law.

264 Lucas-Schlötter (2008) 413.

265 Article 15 of the Law.

266 Differently Ramsauer (2005) 104.

267 Article 2, No. 12, of Decree No. 12. This article establishes definitions to be applied "for the effects of this Decree." Thus, the definitions have a limited scope of application.

268 Article 7 of the Decree.

environment, and thus by giving effect to their own legal treatment of these creations.

This idea is similar to the main approach in international private law in the attempt to find a solution for legal disputes with connections to different national legal systems. There, the main principle for the most adequate treatment of the case is to find and apply the legal system that has the closest connection to the factual problem.

In light of the international discussions on an adequate protection of TCEs, one absolutely crucial question is whether customary rules must be or might be written down, a topic that has been addressed generally above.[269]

In Panama, this question is even more particular, i.e. whether approved and registered rules can indeed be qualified as "customary law". Besides the definition of the rules of use indicated above, no further discussions on this question are known in the country.

The requirement of laying down in writing and registering the rules was introduced by the indigenous drafters of the law themselves. Their reason for introducing it was that they deemed official registration necessary for the effective enforcement of rights against non-indigenous peoples by giving notice on the sui generis Collective Right and its traditional form of use.[270]

Having gathered some initial experiences in the last years of implementing the law, the practicability of this requirement, however, has been questioned in Panama by both sides, the indigenous and state one.[271]

X. Promotion of TCEs

In line with the objective of giving "social justice" to the indigenous communities, Law No. 20 contains a whole Chapter on the promotion of indigenous art and cultural expressions.[272] It embraces the afore-mentioned grant of a certification on a particular TCE (Article 10), and several promotional measures as the obligatory exhibition of traditional textiles, dances and other TCEs within national and international presentations of Panamanian indigenous culture,[273] the inclusion of such TCEs in other fairs where possible, and the introduction of a "Day of Indigenous Handicraft" organized by the Ministry of Commerce and Industries.[274]

[269] *See* at Chapter II Section 5.B.IV.2. above.

[270] Personal communication with Aresio Valiente, indigenous lawyer and one of the consultants of the deputies, on February 11, 2009, in Panama City.

[271] Personal communications with Aresio Valiente, indigenous lawyer and one of the consultants of the deputies, Luis Touar, General Cacique Dagar Kunyala, translation by Flaviano Iglesias, and staff members of DIGERPI in February, 2009, in Panama.

[272] Chapter IV "Promoting indigenous art and cultural expressions", translation by WIPO. The Chapter covers Articles 10–14 of the Law.

[273] Article 12 of the Law.

[274] Article 11 of the Law. For further details *see* at Section 1.F. below.

Revealing its interdisciplinary, holistic, namely sui generis nature, the Law even charges the Ministry of Education to "include content in the school curriculum referring to indigenous artistic expressions as an integral part of national culture."[275]

XI. International Protection

The principle of territoriality governing intellectual property rights in general also dominates this sui generis regime, i.e. the application of the Law is limited to the national territory of Panama. However, a rule providing for the principle of reciprocity has been set up. It stipulates that, as regards the effects of protection, use, and commercialization of the collective rights established by Law No. 20, artistic and traditional expressions of other countries will have the same benefits of the law if these benefits are given effect by means of reciprocal international agreements.[276] This national-treatment clause, by the way, was introduced through the initiative and advice of WIPO's Intergovernmental Committee on Intellectual Property and Genetic Resources, Traditional Knowledge and Folklore (IGC),[277] which indicates the importance of the excellent work of the ICG even at the national level of protection of TCEs.

D. Example of Applied Customary Law: "Rules of Use of the Collective Right 'Mola Kuna Panama'"

After having presented and reflected on the content of the Sui generis Regime, some particularly interesting aspects will be made the subjects of a more detailed examination in the following. These aspects are, first, the rules of use as an example of how customary law is considered and applied within the framework of the Sui generis Regime (below D.), second, ways of and difficulties in securing the Sui generis protection at the international level (below E.), and, third, some observations and short remarks on the promotional aspect of the law and the promotion of the commercialization of TCEs in Panama (below F.).

As regards the use and commercialization of the TCEs in Panama, the sui generis regime can only be fully understood and evaluated when considering at least one example of rules of use. This is due to the fact that the rules concretely govern important questions of content and management of the rights for each particular

---

[275] Article 13 of the Law, translation by WIPO.

[276] Article 25 of the Law.

[277] According to Valiente López, the background of this assistance was the visit of the – indigenous – then president of the Panamanian General Assembly, Enrique Garrido, at WIPO's IGC in 1999 to present the draft of the Law and ask for advice, Valiente López (2006) 132 and 120.

TCE. Moreover, the rules and their practical dimension are of special interest and can contribute valuable insights to the discussion of how to consider customary law in the area of protecting TCEs at a regional or the international level as well.

I. Legal Framework

1. Integration of Customary Law into the Sui Generis System: Connecting Provisions

As demonstrated before, Article 15 of Law No. 20 integrates the particular rules of use into the sui generis protection by stipulating that "the rights of use and commercialization of [TCEs] must be governed by the regulation of each indigenous community, approved and registered with DIGERPI." This is also the technical method of giving effect to the particular "Rules of Use of the Collective Right 'Mola Kuna Panama.'"

2. Legal Framework at the Tribal Level: Tribal Code Law

The broader question of legal pluralism and its particular issue of indigenous jurisdiction, which is a legally and politically highly disputed one in Panama (and beyond), will not be addressed here fully.[278] What will be mentioned—in addition to the introduction into the factual situation in Panama at the very beginning of the chapter[279]—are some relevant aspects framing the "Rules of Use of the Collective Right 'Mola Kuna Panama.'"

The Kuna Indians creating the *molas* traditionally inhabit three different indigenous territories or *comarcas*, the *Comarca Kuna Yala*,[280] the *Comarca Kuna de Madungandi*[281] and the *Comarca Kuna de Wargandi*,[282] legally created in 1938, 1996, and 2000, respectively.

According to an indigenous perspective, a *comarca* is "a special political division of the Panamanian territory, governed in accordance with the law which constitutes it and with the norms, customs, and cosmovision of the indigenous

---

[278] Valiente López (2008) 203–237, portraying the situation from an engaged indigenous perspective.

[279] Especially on the five *comarcas*, *see* at Section 1.A. above.

[280] This *comarca* was established by Law No. 2 of September 16, 1938, originally creating the *Comarca San Blas*, which was organized according to Law No. 16 of February 19, 1953. The change of the name to *Comarca Kuna Yala* took place by means of Law No. 99 of December 23, 1998.

[281] It was created by Law No. 24 of January 12, 1996, Valiente López (2008) 203, 207 on all of them.

[282] This was the last indigenous territory to be demarcated or "legalised" in Panama, and was created by Law No. 34 of July 25, 2000.

people or peoples inhabiting it, based on the traditional indigenous institutions which have been created in accordance with their spiritual, social, economic, cultural, juridical and political values. Its highest authority is the General Indigenous Congress or the Indigenous Council or a traditional authority elected according to the tradition."[283]

As regards the customary law, it is noted that the indigenous peoples have their own "norms of social control," which do not necessarily have to be written down. In recent years, however, the indigenous *comarcas* and communities without legalized territory have started to codify their "indigenous law."[284]

In this manner, the *Comarca Kuna Yala*, for example, has elaborated a "fundamental law," the *Ley Fundamental de la Comarca Kuna Yala*, which in its Article 38 also addresses the topic of Kuna Indian culture. As a whole, the Kuna Indians regard the Fundamental Law as a proposal for a reform of Law No. 16 of 1953, the national law that currently governs the *comarca*. Moreover, it has a statute, the *Estatuto Comarca*, which is a proposal for a *Carta Orgánica*.[285]

While "in reality," these are the "legal instruments that are applied in the communities in the *comarca*," as Valiente López tells,[286] the Panamanian state does not acknowledge this codified customary law, namely, the Fundamental Law of the Comarca Kuna Yala.[287]

In any case, the indigenous customary law, as "codified," i.e. written down and registered, binding law governing the use and commercialization of TCEs, like the "Rules of Use of the Collective Right 'Mola Kuna Panama'", is acknowledged by the Panamanian state by means of the Sui generis Regime.[288]

II. Reglamento de Uso: "Rules of Use of the Collective Right 'Mola Kuna Panama'"

1. Proceedings

In 2002, the Kuna Indians, together with DIGERPI, developed the regulation of use of the "Mola Kuna Panama", the "Rules of Use of the Collective Right 'Mola Kuna Panama'". In the same year, the "Mola Kuna Panama" was registered as a collective right of the Kuna Indians. The history of this registration as described by DIGERPI reads as follows: On October 25, 2002, the four General Kuna Congresses applied

---

[283] Valiente López (2008) 205, translation by to the author.

[284] *Id.* 211.

[285] *Ibid.*

[286] *Ibid.*

[287] *See* http://www.digerpi.gob.pa/pls/portal/docs/PAGE/NOTICIAS/CONGRESO_DERECHO_COLECTIVO/HERACLIO%20HERRERA%2C%20PANAMÁ-KUNA.PDF, last visited November 12, 2010.

[288] Article 15, *see* at Section 1.C.IV.2. above.

for the registration of a regulation of use of the *mola* Kuna Panama, the first application in Panama ever. On November 22, 2002, the application was approved and registered by DIGERPI. On November 28, 2002, the registration was published in the Official Bulletin.[289]

2. Structure and Overview of the Content

The "Rules of Use of the Collective Right 'Mola Kuna Panama'" (in the following: "Rules of Use of the Mola") consist of 27 Articles, which are divided into ten Chapters, each of which has been provided with a different title. The Chapters treat the following issues: I: Objective of regulation, II: Definition, III: Emblem, IV: Innovations, V: Use of *mola* by indigenous communities, VI: Holders of right, VII: Use of the collective right, VIII: Licensing, IX: Sanctions, X: Final dispositions.[290]

The document recognizes the rights of the Kuna Indians in their *molas* as cultural right and "intellectual property," as stated in Article 1.

3. Particular Aspects of the "Rules of Use of the Mola"

a. Holders of Rights

According to Article 6 of the "Rules of Use of the Mola", the holder ("titular") of the collective right "Mola Kuna Panama" is the Kuna tribe ("Pueblo Kuna") organized by its General Congresses. "Collective rights" is also the terminology used in Law No. 20.

The concept of collective ownership in customary law is no apodictic, absolute, and clear cut principle, but rather depends upon the current social circumstances and conceptions of the particular TCE in question.[291] For this very reason, it is challenged more and more every day in practice. Even the 2002 Pacific Model Law acknowledges the alternative of an "individual who is recognized by the group, clan or community" as being the right holder "in accordance with customary law and practices."[292]

---

[289] Ministerio de Comercio e Industrias – DIGERPI (no year) 7.

[290] Translation by the author.

[291] On the specialty of customary law as a social and therefore very flexible phenomena rather than an abstract, separated juridical sphere *see* at Chapter II Section 5.B.III.2.b. above. As a consequence of the lack of a separated, highly specialized juridical sphere, there is also no precise definition of who makes up any given collective. This lack of definition (and of its implementation) might also contribute to the mentioned vagueness of the concept of collective ownership here.

[292] This more differentiated solution is laid down in Articles 4 and 6 of the 2002 Model Law for the Pacific. For general aspects of Law No. 20 and Decree No. 12 in this regard *see* at Section 1.C.III.1. above.

The "Rules of Use of the Mola" are not as clear on this aspect as it might seem at first sight. Even according to the Rules, the holders of rights could be the individuals, i.e. the women, who produce the *mola*, or those women in their collective, i.e. some members of a community, or all members of the Kuna peoples or the Kuna tribe as such.

aa. Collective Entity as Right Holder

As stated before, Article 6 of the "Rules of Use of the Mola", the holder ("titular") of the collective right "Mola Kuna Panama" is the Kuna tribe ("Pueblo Kuna"), organized by its General Congresses. However, the *Parágrafo* of the same Article 6 states that the "holders" ("titulares") of the collective right are the "members" ("miembros") of the Kuna peoples. Moreover, the registration itself specifies the population (61,707 persons) and beneficiary community as holders of rights.[293]

bb. The Individual as Possible Holder of Rights

Besides the "Kuna tribe" and the "members," the same initially mentioned Article 6 of the "Rules of Use of the Mola" states that the "owners" of the collective right Mola Kuna Panama are "*especially* the Kuna *women* who produce the Mola."[294] Similarly, the persons entitled to use the right are the "members" of the collectivity of the Kuna tribe, and "especially the Kuna women who produce the Mola" in the Panamanian Republic.[295] Consequently, the right holder in the case of the TCE *mola* could be each Kuna woman who produces the *mola*—or all such women in their collectivity.

On the other hand, the "Rules of Use of the Mola" also describe the *mola* as "an art, a traditional knowledge, which belongs to the indigenous peoples of the Kuna. Therefore, it is collective property and *not of determined individuals* which form a part of said peoples. It has been transmitted from generation to generation and is thus the intellectual property of the Kuna peoples."[296]

In light of the afore-mentioned rule stipulating that persons entitled to use the right are the "members" of the collectivity of the Kuna tribe, and "especially the Kuna women who produce the Mola"[297] the "determined individuals" can be

---

[293] "Población (cantidad) y Comunidad Beneficiada – Titulares", *Boletín del Registro Oficial de Propiedad Industrial* No. 123 of November 18, 2002.

[294] *Parágrafo* of Article 6 of the Rules of Use. Emphasis added by the author. In Spanish it reads "Los titulares (...) son (...), de manera especial las mujeres kunas productoras de la mola", available at http://mici.gob.pa, last visited September 21, 2010.

[295] Article 9 of the Rules of Use, available at http://mici.gob.pa, last visited September 21, 2010.

[296] *See* Article 1 of the Rules of Use, which stipulates that the Mola is "...un arte, un conocimiento tradicional que pertence al pueblo indígena Kuna; por ende, es propiedad colectiva y *no de individuos* determinados que forman parte de dicho pueblo. Se ha transmitido de generación en generación, por lo tanto, es propiedad intellectual del pueblo Kuna," emphasis added by the author.

[297] Article 9 of the Rules of Use, available at http://mici.gob.pa, last visited September 21, 2010.

understood as other individuals than Kuna women, leaving some leeway for an individual interpretation in favor of each Kuna woman. However, in view of the collective spirit of the law, it is more likely that this wording is meant to underline the fact that the Mola is subject to a collective right of the whole Kuna tribe, or, at least, the entirety of the Kuna women and not one single woman.

While thus, on paper, the wording "collective right" itself seems to leave no leeway for an interpretation in favor of the individual woman, the experiences on the ground show that, as a result of the implementation of the Law so far, it is indeed each individual woman producing the *mola* who decides over both the piece itself, and the right of use, of disclosing the knowledge concerning the creation of the *mola*.

This observation, however, should not tempt the reader to jump to a simple conclusion, from the factual *status quo* to the legal target state, in disrespect of David Hume's dichotomy of the "is" and the "ought." This dualism advises that no simple deduction from the "is" to the "ought" should be made, as the latter is "entirely different from [the former]."[298]

Nonetheless, this observation could serve as an argument in favor of an interpretation leading to the widest possible effectiveness of the regulation. This principle of interpretation, known in European Law as *effet utile*, has been developed by the European Court of Justice (ECJ). It is directed to the interpretation of a national norm in the light of the European Law, and states that the national norm should be interpreted in the manner that gives greatest effect to the meaning and purpose of the European Law—even if such interpretation contradicts the explicit wording of the national provision.

Here, at the Panamanian level of national and customary law, there is no such specialty of a supranational integration policy.

However, there are no other regulations in either the Law or the Decree treating the question of how to interpret the concrete rules of use, especially in cases of contradicting expressions and provisions, either. Thus, several questions arise: First, how should the rules of use—as a regulation set up by indigenous peoples themselves—be interpreted? Second, if those rules differ from the national law on protection of TCEs—here, Law No. 20—are they considered either as solely filling the broader legal framework or as independently interpreting the Law? If they even contradict the law, which regulation should prevail?

According to the principle of the hierarchy of norms, in the case of contradiction, the superior law prevails over the lower-level norms. Article 15 of the Law may support the application of this principle, as it provides for DIGERPI, competent for the registration of national industrial property, to "approve" the Rules of Use. Moreover, Article 14, lit. (d), of the Decree stipulates that among other things,

[298] The idea of the imperative distinction between the "is, and is not" and the "ought, and ought not" goes back to the philosophy of Hume (1739) Book III, Part 1, (I). Immanuel Kant and Hans Kelsen further developed this concept in the area of European philosophy and law in the 18th to 20th century.

one task of the Department of Collective Rights and Folkloric Expressions within DIGERPI is to oversee the fulfillment of the existing laws, which refer to the protection of the collective intellectual property rights in TCEs. Also, Article 27 of the "Rules of Use of the Mola" themselves could be regarded as supporting the prevalence of Law No. 20, as it provides that any modifications of the "Rules of Use of the Mola" not complying with Law No. 20 would be disregarded.[299]

In this manner, "collective rights" as established in Law No. 20 would not leave room for an interpretation in favor of an individual person as a holder of rights in the *mola*.

On the other hand, paper tigers are not of very much use in the matter of protecting TCEs, and Article 15 of Law No. 20 is explicitly intended to give effect to the customary rules of use. The idea *behind* the afore-demonstrated principle of the *effet utile*, to give a norm the best effect through an adequate interpretation, may be of use. This idea also exists, for example, as a principle of interpretation at the German national level of law.

However, what would then be the maximal effectiveness of protection according to both, the "superior" Law No. 20 and the concrete rules of use?

According to the aim of Law No. 20 as the basic legal framework, it could be the protection of the collective heritage of the Kuna tribe, on the one hand, and "social justice", i.e. its commercial promotion and use, on the other.[300] With regard to individuals, it is only stated that the TCEs form part of the cultural patrimony of the indigenous peoples and can therefore not be subjected to any unauthorized exclusivity of "third persons."[301]

According to the "Rules of Use of the Mola," "effectiveness" could relate to the preservation of the collectivity of the intellectual property rights on the Mola, as "it is *collective property* and *not that of certain individuals* who form part of said peoples. It has been transmitted from generation to generation and is thus the intellectual property *of the Kuna peoples*."[302] "Effectiveness" of the Rules could also mean the preservation of the cultural heritage as such, as it has been "transmitted from generation to generation".[303]

Against the backdrop of a social reality in which currently around 55 % of the indigenous population in Panama live in urban or semi-urban environments and not in indigenous territories,[304] isn't it rather the Kuna women who maintain the *molas* and thus the cultural heritage? Isn't the preservation and transmission of the *mola*

---

299 Article 27 of the Rules of Use of the Mola. *See* at Section 1.D.II.3.f. below.

300 *See* Articles 1, 2 of the Law.

301 Article 2 of the Law.

302 *See* Article 1 of the Rules of Use, which stipulates that the Mola is "…un arte, un conocimiento tradicional que pertence al pueblo indígena Kuna; por ende, es propiedad colectiva y *no de individuos* determinados que forman parte de dicho pueblo. Se ha transmitido de generación en generación, por lo tanto, es propiedad intellectual del pueblo Kuna"; emphasis added by the author.

303 *See* Article 1 of the Rules of Use.

304 Valiente López (2008) 205.

better ensured, or at least practiced, by the individual woman creating and selling the *molas* in view of the actual social realities?

If implementing "social justice" in an economic dimension is the point of reference for determining the criteria of "effectiveness," this would rather aim at excluding other, non-indigenous parties from obtaining commercial rights in the *molas*, as socio-economic justice could imply both a fair remuneration for the Kuna women or for the Kuna tribe as such.

Any line of argument seems to end up in the common and well-known conflict between collective and individual interests, which also determines the life in a traditional community.

A final remark should be made on this subject: If a provision should be interpreted in such a manner as to achieve the greatest effectiveness of its meaning, the flipside of this principle at the same time provokes the question of whether a regulation should be interpreted in a manner that is hardly enforceable in practice. Applied to the situation in Panama, that means that, although the wording seems to clearly argue in favour of collective ownership by the tribe, the effective promotion and management of rights on the *molas* in practice is difficult for the Kuna tribe and General Congress to implement.[305]

However, this aspect could also be addressed and solved at a different level, as discussed in the area of Law No. 20 above: In view of the clearly expressed customary understanding that the *mola* "is *collective property* and *not that of certain individuals* who form part of said peoples,"[306] the formulation "especially the Kuna women" can solely be regarded as declaratory, as a political expression. A "smoother" solution for the problem could be found at the level of defining the use, for example to include a *fair use* exception or an equivalent for Kuna women, allowing them to create and sell or teach *molas* and the techniques individually, if they obtain approval from a Special Kuna Women's Committee, as De Obaldia suggests.[307] This solution would answer the question of a (more) effective implementation of the "Rules of Use of the Mola" and the Law.

The field work also shows that this issue in particular is one of the crucial points in implementing the Law. Furthermore, the discussion above also reveals that even applying customary law is sometimes not able to ensure an adequate solution—neither on paper nor in practice.

[305] On specific problems in this regard, *see* at Section 1.E.II. and G.II.2.e. below.

[306] *See* Article 1 of the Rules of Use, which stipulates that the Mola is "...un arte, un conocimiento tradicional que pertence al pueblo indígena Kuna; por ende, es propiedad colectiva y *no de individuos* determinados que forman parte de dicho pueblo. Se ha transmitido de generación en generación, por lo tanto, es propiedad intellectual del pueblo Kuna;" emphasis added by the author.

[307] The latter suggestion was made by De Obaldia (2005) 374.

b. Exercise of Right and Representation

A different question is that of representation, which is answered as follows: The "Rules of Use of the Mola" determine that the three general congresses of the Kuna comarcas and one of the whole tribe, defined in Article 6, and represented through their *Sahilas,*[308] administer the rights and corresponding actions.

It is interesting to note that the *registration* as a whole, however, which contains the "Rules of Use of the Mola", mentions the names of the four concrete persons,[309] but also a different "legal representative" including concrete contact data.[310] The latter aspect reflects, first, the complexity of the sui generis regime, especially the registration part, and second, as a consequence thereof, a certain progress in the assimilation process: traditional authorities hand over the legal issues to specialists acting in a separate "sphere" of law. This separate "sphere" and activity of specialists are, however, characteristics rather of complex societies (with states) than of traditional ones governed by customary law.[311]

With regard to this observation, it is interesting to note that—although solely with reference to the aspect of economic remuneration—it has been stated that Law No. 20 "also helps [the indigenous peoples] live more like westerners", which would "seem counterintuitive."[312]

c. Content and Management of the "Collective Right"

Authorized users of the *mola* collective right are the "members of the Kuna people, and in a special manner the Kuna women producing the *Mola* in the Republic of Panama."[313] The right holders have the right to "negate the authorization of their use to third parties in the case that it would be against the spirituality and cultural identification" of the Kuna tribe.[314]

The right to license the use of the collective right is defined more precisely in Articles 12 to 19. The licensing agreement requires express authorization of the traditional authorities, the four General Congresses represented by their *Sahilas*, it has to indicate the places of use of authorized persons, and the other requirements laid down in Article 18 of the Decree No. 12, and it has to be registered by DIGERPI then.[315] The Kuna women and organizations producing the *molas* must

---

[308] Or *Saila Dummagan*, which means traditional representative; Article 7 of the Rules.

[309] And the numbers of their identification document; *Boletín del Registro Oficial de Propiedad Industrial* No. 123 of November 18, 2002.

[310] This is the Kuna Indian and lawyer Aresio Valiente López. For details on this question, *see* at Section 1.C.III.3. above.

[311] On this *see* Stavenhagen (1990) 30 and at Chapter II Section 5.B.III.2.b. above.

[312] De Obaldia (2005) 379.

[313] Article 9 of the Rules of Use of the Mola.

[314] Article 11 of the Rules of Use of the Mola. The scope of this right remains unclear, especially read in the context of the preceding and following articles and in view of its spirit as an exclusive right.

[315] Articles 12–14 of the Rules of Use of the Mola.

be consulted previously.[316] The right to license may not interrupt the traditional transmission of knowledge from one generation to the other.[317]

While WIPO argues that the "Rules of Use of the Mola" "establish a collective mark and a certification mark (nominative and figurative),"[318] this is, however, at least questionable. Law No. 20 indeed stipulates that for the registration or process of registering, the provisions on collective trademarks and guarantee marks apply, if they do not jeopardize the rights contained in Law No. 20.[319] However, the "Rules of Use of the Mola" as "codified" customary rules are not the legal instrument competent for establishing a collective mark or certification mark. They can just lay down the rules of use according to the customs and traditions of the Kuna communities. This is also what Article 15 of the Law provides for: to determine the use and commercialization of the TCE. Besides, Law No. 20 was drafted precisely because collective trademarks and certification marks did not suffice, and thus to establish a different, a sui generis right. The content of Law No. 20 also shows that the new right established does not coincide with a collective trademark and certification mark. The certification, which can be obtained according to Article 10 of Law No. 20, is issued by the General Direction of National Handicrafts, and thus does not comply with the preconditions of a regular certification mark. To have the TCE registered as a collective trademark, an association would have to be established, while the indigenous peoples of the Kuna as such are denominated holders of rights in the "Rules of Use of the Mola."

d. Modalities of Use

The modalities of use include the duty to fix or print the emblem *kalu ducbis* on each piece of *mola* (Article 8), a note stating that this piece of *mola* has been elaborated according to traditional proceedings and handmade by Kuna Indians, and giving its place of origin. All *mola*-producing organizations must be registered with the respective General Congress (Article 10).

This author's personal fieldwork experience has shown that most of those *molas* sold at the Handicraft Market in Panama City possessed such indications. In the remoter areas on the small islands in Kuna Yala, in contrast, such indication was absolutely rare.[320]

In fact, at the same time, the probability of selling or buying non-Kunan *molas* in a personal exchange situation with the indigenous creator of the *mola* in such remote areas in Kuna Yala is by far not as great as it is in bigger, "commodified" (extra-cultural), and rather anonymous places like market areas or airports in the capital.

---

[316] Article 12 in combination with Articles 6 and 7 of the Rules of Use of the Mola.

[317] Article 17 of the Rules of Use of the Mola.

[318] WIPO Secretariat (2005) 19.

[319] Article 8 of Law No. 20.

[320] The research and fieldwork took place in both Panama City and Kuna Yala in February, 2009.

e. Violation of Customary Rules by Kuna Indians Themselves

What happens if a member of the Kuna tribe itself does not comply or conflicts with the "customary" rules laid down in the "Rules of Use of the Mola"?

The Rules provide for the following measures: the "Administration [or management] of the Collective Right" is empowered to sanction unlawful use by Kuna Indians themselves, and the content or consequence of this sanction may be the revocation of the authorization of use, according to Article 20.[321] The Administration is regulated in Articles 7 and 8, as displayed above.

Whether this provision has been made use of and/or worked in practice will be addressed below.[322]

f. Dynamic Nature of the Molas*—And the Rights?*

The "Rules of Use of the Mola" acknowledge that the *molas* "are in constant evolution" (Article 4 of the Rules). Apart from being used as women's cloths, they are used as glasses cases, pillow cases, covers for kitchen tools, Christmas decorations, cloths for babies, hats, bags, and other accessories.[323]

At the Handicraft Market in Panama City, I was offered *molas* in the form of small bags for mobile phones.

It is important to remember that the art of the *mola* goes back to inspirations by different cultures: Around 300 years ago, Kuna women did not wear any clothes at all. They covered and decorated their bodies with body paintings, painting the upper part of their bodies with intricate designs. During the eighteenth century, according to De Obaldia, French Huguenots settled among the Kunas and introduced the European art of *appliqué*, sewing layers of cloth one on top of the other. While the French were expelled or murdered later on, as De Obaldia tells, the Kuna women kept the appliqué art, which then evolved into the *molas*.[324]

Until now, the "intricate and particular style" had inspired a range of artistic expressions, from a distinctive style of decoration, to the inspiration behind paintings, trademarks, and logos, De Obaldia observed, reason why the Mola was a living, "breathing" art, always evolving.[325]

Then, a logical question is how the customary law, once fixed, approved, and registered, can or may react to such "evolution" of the tradition—or whether and how the customary rules themselves may "evolve." The "Rules of Use of the Mola" answer these questions as follows: they acknowledge future modifications of regulation, which are to be notified to DIGERPI, in as far as they are in accordance

---

[321] "El incumplimiento del Reglamento de Uso [. . .] por parte de cualquier miembro del pueblo Kuna titular del derecho, podrá ser sancionado por la Administración del Derecho Colectivo, con la revocación de la autorización para utilizar el Derecho Colectivo."

[322] *See* at Section 1.E.II. and G.II.2.e. below.

[323] Article 4 of the Rules of Use.

[324] *See* De Obaldia (2005) 357, with further references.

[325] *See id.*, 359, with further references.

with Law No. 20. The "requirements established by Law No. 20" probably embrace procedural as well as substantive requirements, although this is aspect is not explicitly addressed.[326]

III. Conclusion

The example of the "Rules of Use of the Mola" and of experiences in practice therewith reveals several interesting points in the particular ambit of the protection of TCEs in Panama and in the topic of considering customary law in general.

The involvement of the indigenous peoples themselves in the process of protecting TCEs has led to a very positive echo. The communication and interaction between the indigenous leaders and DIGERPI with regard to, among other things, the rules of use is probably the most essential and successful factor within the whole system of the Sui generis solution in Panama. The act of registering the "Rules of Use of the Mola" in view of practical and inter-cultural challenges can be rated as a great achievement from this point of view.

The related question of an obligatory registration or "codification" of such rules, however, remains crucial, as it has a strong impact on traditional socio-cultural patterns, as well as representation structures—as the additional involvement of a lawyer and denomination of a "legal representative" reveals, although Law No. 20 explicitly states that no lawyer is required for the application and registration process.[327]

One particular "hot topic" of the "Rules of Use of the Mola" on paper as well as in practice is the collective holdership and management of rights, namely, the tension between the individual Kuna women who create *molas*, all these women as a whole, and the whole community. It has been revealed that, even where applied, customary law itself is sometimes not able to provide for a solution. Alternative solutions for practical problems, as well as for legal disputes arising out of the application of these customary rules, may be needed, as, at least in the case of the "Rules of Use of the Mola," the regulation in Article 20 does not suffice.

Moreover, the "codified customary law" sometimes lays down desired outcomes rather than reflections of the customs in reality. For example, the modalities of use laid down in Article 8 of the "Rules of Use of the Mola" on the obligatory use of the emblem may be a very desired outcome, but they do not reflect the social custom—at least in the remoter areas of the Kuna territories. Of course, when "designing" customary rules, space may and should be given to further adaptations and developments of customs—be it such customs of socio-legal behavior or of the creation of traditional art. This is also an aspect reflected by the dynamic approach of the

[326] Article 27 reads: "El titular del Derecho Colectivo presentará a la DIGERPI toda modificaión del reglamento de uso. Se desestimaran las modificaciones que no cumplan los requisitos establecidos en la Ley 20 de 2000."

[327] Article 7 of the Law.

"Rules of Use of the Mola" as regards both the TCE, in Article 4, and the Rules of Use, in Article 27. The only question that remains is whether such rules can be considered as based upon tradition anymore, and in how far a better balancing of interests is needed; such balance might be needed especially when the right holders define their own rights.

Finally, the codification of the "Rules of Use of the Mola" on paper on the one hand, and the socio-cultural and socio-economic realities on the other reveal the existence of different legal cultures, habits, and the prevalence of economic needs.

E. Securing Sui Generis Protection at the International Level

How can such sui generis protection at the national level, then, also be ensured at the international level?

An alternative to the still difficult negotiations at the multinational level at WIPO[328] is to negotiate the recognition of to the sui generis regime by means of bilateral agreements. As mentioned before, in its Article 25 Law No. 20 provides for such a possibility on a reciprocal basis.[329]

Indeed, to a certain extent, Panama has already made use of this option. These steps might provide interesting insights and could act as an example and provide encouragement for other countries to enhance their own protection of TCEs.

At the same time, factual situations and negotiations have revealed certain challenges to the national protection of TCEs in Panama. To display a complete picture of the situation of the sui generis protection of TCEs in Panama, and to give an example of how the protection can be secured at the international level, apart from the very difficult negotiations at WIPO—e.g. in a bilateral way,—particularities of the protection at the international level will be outlined in the following.

Since the most famous and economically important TCE in Panama consists of the Kuna Indian textile *mola*, provisions dealing with handicrafts like certain industrial property rights or import prohibitions can be of relevance. At the international level, those provisions are sometimes also contained in bilateral agreements aiming at free trade between the countries concerned.[330]

Out of the seven bilateral free-trade agreements currently in force in Panama,[331] two of them relate to the trade aspect of the issue of protection of TCEs: the free-trade agreement (in the following FTA) with Chile and that with Taiwan. The 2006

[328] The World Intellectual Property Organization

[329] On this provision *see at* Section 1.C.X. above.

[330] For details on the consideration of TCEs and folklore in free-trade agreements in general, *see* Drexl (2010) paras 106 *et seq.*

[331] So far, Panama has signed free-trade agreements with Chile, El Salvador, Taiwan, Singapore, Honduras, Costa Rica, and Nicaragua, available at http://www.mici.gob.pa/TLC_nueva.php, last visited August 10, 2010. The free-trade agreement with the United States has yet to be approved by the North-American Congress to enter into force. Other free-trade negotiations with Canada,

FTA between the Republic of Singapore and Panama[332] does not contain provisions on TCE at all.

Apart from the existing agreements regulating aspects of TCEs, another interesting situation at the international level in Panama worth having a look at is how TCEs are dealt with in practice in the relationship between Panama and its neighboring countries Costa Rica and Colombia.

These two points will be outlined in the following (I. and II. below). Afterwards, it will be seen whether these examples can be of value for a general recommendation (below III.).

I. Free-Trade Agreements Covering TCEs in Panama

1. Free-Trade Agreement with Taiwan

The free-trade agreement (FTA) between Panama and Taiwan[333] was signed on August 21, 2003 and entered in force on January 1, 2004.[334] In this FTA, the parties agree to protect *inter alia* collective intellectual property rights, traditional knowledge, and cultural expressions of indigenous and local communities.[335]

Under the title "Protection of Traditional Knowledge," the treaty provides for protection of "the collective intellectual property rights and the traditional knowledge of the indigenous peoples regarding their creations that are used commercially" by means of a special registration system, "promotion and commercialization of their rights."[336] Both parties acknowledge further that the "customs, traditions, beliefs, spirituality, religiosity, cosmovision, folkloristic expressions, artistic manifestations, traditional dexterities and any other form of

Mexico, and other Latin American countries are ongoing. *See* http://www.state.gov/r/pa/ei/bgn/2030.htm, last visited August 10, 2010.

332 http://www.sice.oas.org/Trade/PAN_SGP/PAN_SGP_e/Text_e.pdf, last visited October 29, 2010.

333 In the agreement, the wording is "la República de China (Taiwán)" – "the Republic of China (Taiwan)", available at http://www.mici.gob.pa/TLC_nueva.php, last visited February 18, 2010.

334 In Panama, it was approved through Law No. 62 of October 18, 2003. *See* Gacetas Oficiales No. 24,915 of October 23, 2003; No. 24,916 of October 24, 2003; No. 24,917 of October 27, 2003, No. 24,918 of October 28, 2003, No 24,919 of October 29, 2003, No 24,919-A of October 29, 2003 and http://www.mici.gob.pa/tratados/informes/informe-taiwan.pdf, last visited February 18, 2010.

335 Articles 16.05, 16.06, 16.07 of the FTA.

336 The FTA also regulates access to genetic resources, "vegetal obtainings" and the respective traditional knowledge. *See* Articles 16.07 and 16.08 of the FTA. However, with regard to the topic of this thesis, those aspects will not be considered in more detail here.

traditional expression of the indigenous peoples and local communities" form part of their cultural patrimony.[337]

According to the treaty, this cultural patrimony may not be subject to any form of exclusivity by non-authorized third parties that apply the intellectual property system, unless the application is made by the indigenous peoples and local communities or by third parties that have been authorized by these peoples or communities.[338]

Additionally, under the title "Protection of Folklore," it is agreed that both parties ensure "the effective protection of all folkloristic expressions and manifestations and of the artistic manifestations of the traditional and popular culture of the indigenous and local communities."[339]

With regard to the application of the afore-mentioned protection, i.e. to suspend or forestall the free circulation of concerned merchandise, the parties also agree to adopt legislation on means of border control to allow customs authorities to inspect or detain such products.[340]

Especially with regard to the first provisions, on a special registration system, promotion and commercialization of "the collective intellectual property rights and the traditional knowledge of the indigenous peoples regarding their creations that are used commercially,"[341] the system of protection established by the Panamanian Law No. 20 is secured at the bilateral level. The provision even contains the terms and wording used in the sui generis regime.

It is also interesting to note that the parties even agree to give a TCE protection a farther reach, going beyond the bilateral scope of application of the agreement: They underline the "increasing importance" of such protection, especially for "sustainable economic development," and confirm that any of the two parties, which is not a member state to other relevant international treaties on intellectual property rights, like TRIPS and the WIPO-treaties yet, compromises its greatest efforts signing those treaties.[342]

These treaties, however, do not contain any special protection of TCEs so far, which is why the clause could be understood in one of two ways: either as limiting the scope of protection to the framework of those treaties, or, more likely, as aiming at a minimum protection of TCEs in the area of intellectual property rights existing at the level of those treaties.

[337] Article 16.05, para. 2 of the FTA.

[338] Article 16.05, para. 3 of the FTA.

[339] Article 16.06 of the FTA.

[340] Article 16.11 of the FTA.

[341] The FTA also regulates access to genetic resources, "vegetal obtainings" and the respective traditional knowledge, *see* Articles 16.07 and 16.08 of the FTA.

[342] Article 16.09 of the FTA.

2. Free-Trade Agreement with Chile

The FTA between Panama and Chile was signed on June 27, 2006 and entered in force on March 7, 2008.[343]

In this agreement, no general regulations on the protection of TCEs have been established. However, in Chapter Three, reference is made to the particular TCE of the Panamanian *mola*: Chile legally acknowledges the *mola* as a distinctive product from Panama. Moreover, Chile obliges itself to prohibit the import, fabrication, or sale of any product similar to the *molas* except those produced in Panama in accordance with the laws and regulations that govern the production of *molas*.[344]

Thus, in relation to Chile, no "collective intellectual property rights" are acknowledged, but a protection at the level of import of goods is established.

3. Free-Trade Agreement with the United States

A free-trade agreement with the United States has been negotiated, similar to the existing North American Free Trade Agreement (NAFTA) with Mexico, but it still has to be approved by the U.S. Senate to enter into force.[345]

Within the negotiations between the United States and Panama on the FTA, one issue was trade with the *molas*. According to Panamanian sources, the United States were interested in commerce with *molas* in their territory.[346] However, to enjoy the privileged status provided by the FTA and to be permitted to enter the North American market in accordance with the rules of origin, the United States requested the *mola* to be made of cloth originating from either the United States or Panama.[347] The Kuna women, however, use cloth of Asiatic origin, arguing that it is of better quality.[348] According to Valiente López, the Kuna General Congress solicited the Panamanian government to not give in, and Panama successfully negotiated in favor of the Kuna women, preventing the inclusion of a limiting clause to this effect in the free-trade agreement.[349]

---

[343] In Panama, it was approved through Law No. 7 of January 12, 2007. *See* Gaceta Oficial No 25,714 of January 19, 2007 and http://www.mici.gob.pa/tratados/informes/informe-chile.pdf, last visited February 18, 2010.

[344] *See* Chapter 3, Article 3.12, of the FTA: "Chile reconocerá las Molas como productos distintivos de Panamá. Por consiguiente, Chile no permitirá la importación, fabricación o venta de ningún producto como Molas, a menos que éstas hayan sido producidas en Panamá de acuerdo con las leyes y regulaciones de Panamá que rijan la producción de Molas. Lo anterior se entenderá sin perjuicio del reconocimiento que Chile pueda otorgar y que legítimamente pertenezca a un país no Parte con relación a las Molas," available at http://www.mici.gob.pa/TLC_nueva.php, last visited February 18, 2010.

[345] *See* http://www.state.gov/r/pa/ei/bgn/2030.htm, last visited July 31, 2010.

[346] La Prensa, Panama, January 12, 2005, as cited in Valiente López (2006) 143.

[347] *Ibid.*

[348] *Ibid.*

[349] *Ibid.*

II. The Situation Between Panama and Its Neighboring States Costa Rica and Colombia

The FTA between Panama and its westerly neighbor Costa Rica does not contain provisions regulating the protection of TCEs. Also, there is no other bilateral agreement nor the intention to negotiate one.[350]

However, in fact, the biggest problem for the effective protection of TCEs, especially of the *mola*, or for a full implementation of the protection contained in Law No. 20 in Panama appears to be in Costa Rica. In Costa Rica, Panamanian *molas* are sold as "Made by Kuna indigenous peoples in Costa Rica."[351] However, there do not any Kuna people live in Costa Rica,[352] nor are these *molas* made in Costa Rica. But they are sold at a much lower price in Costa Rica,[353] where tourism flourishes, and pretending to be authentic Kuna *mola* handicrafts, as Jordán argues, they thus affect the *mola*'s authenticity, its factual indication of origin, and perception in the market, and finally its economic value in the Panamanian market.

Observing this situation, one could think of a solution: to negotiate a bilateral agreement. When asked about it, the Ministry of Commerce did not provide much of an answer, and a bit more research seemed to be needed. The "curious" and quite "simple" aspect about the situation was that the problem was rather to be found within the Kuna tribes themselves.

Kuna women created the *molas* and sold—and still sell—them to Costa Rican traders sailing between the more than 360 different San Blas Islands within the Kuna territory in Panama and the Caribbean cost of Costa Rica.[354] It is stated that in 2004, some women even travelled to Costa Rica themselves and produced *molas* directly for a Costa Rican company.[355]

While the costs for producing a *mola* lay around 20 $, Bonilla argues, the *molas* were offered in Costa Rica for 10 $ only.[356]

Of course, knowing about the false labelling and the commercial conduct in Costa Rica, the Kuna women themselves act(ed) against the spirit of Law No. 20, against the "Rules of Use of the Collective Right 'Mola Kuna

[350] Personal communication with Luz Celeste Ríos de Davis, General Director of the Industrial Property Registry, in February, 2009, Panama City. Superseded: De Obaldia (2005) 372.

[351] *Ibid.* and personal communication with Aresio Valiente, Kuna Indian and lawyer on February 11, 2009, in Panama City. *See* also the Panamanian newspaper article: Jordán V. (2004) no pagination.

[352] Bonilla (2004 I) no pagination. The (only) indigenous tribes living on both sides of the Costa Rican–Panamanian border are the Ngöbe-Buglés.

[353] Jordán V. (2004) no pagination.

[354] Personal communication with Aresio Valiente, Kuna Indian and lawyer on February 11, 2009 in Panama City.

[355] Jordán V. (2004) no pagination.

[356] Bonilla (2004 I) no pagination, translation by the author.

Panama'"[357]—for basic economic needs, e.g. to finance the primary education of their children.[358] As mentioned above, the production and trading of *molas* is regarded as the main source of income of the Kuna women.[359] The problem was not only the false advertising on the labels, but also the effective cheapening of the labor of the Kuna women.

A similar problem appeared with the other neighboring country, Colombia. According to the Panamanian press, Colombian sailors have bartered with Kuna communities for several decades now, mostly as regards staples like rice, salt, hammocks, *machetes* (bushwhackers), or gas in exchange for coconuts.[360] Lately, however, more and more Kuna women, mostly after having been abandoned by their husbands and due to pressing financial needs, Bonialla states, have sold their *molas* in exchange—although only receiving one or two dollars per piece.[361] In Cartagena, Colombia, these *molas*, packed in bundles, were then sold for 200 $ each.[362] The General Kuna Congress regarded the buying of the *molas* for such a low and injust price not only as exploitation, but also as leading to the disruption of Kuna family values and the decreasing the value of the *mola* itself.[363]

Even the particular "Rules of Use of the Mola" displayed above provide for a solution on paper: according to Article 20 of the "Rules of Use of the Mola," the administrative entities, i.e. General Kuna Congresses, have the right to sanction the unlawful use by Kuna Indians themselves, e.g. by revoking the authorization of use.[364]

How did the Kuna Indians try to settle the dispute over their collective right?

As regards the bartering situation with the Colombian sailors, the General Kuna Congress approved a resolution to prohibit the Colombian marines from exchanging goods for *molas*.[365]

---

[357] Although the nature of Law No. 20 is regarded to be an intellectual property legislation, due to its title, "special intellectual property regime," and its aim to protect "collective intellectual property rights and traditional knowledge", it does not only cover the intangible aspect of the TCEs, i.e. the transmission or licensing of the knowledge of how to produce a *mola*. For details on this interpretation, *see* at Section 1.G.I.2. below and at C.II.1. above. In the context detailed here, the "Rules of Use of the 'Mola Kuna Panama' collective right" themselves establish the obligation of each Kuna producer of the *mola* to write, fix, or stamp "Mola Kuna Panama" and the emblem (*kalu ducbis*) on each product; Articles 8 and 10 of the Rules of Use. For further details on the Rules, *see* at Section 1.D. below.

[358] Bonilla (2004 I) no pagination, translation by the author.

[359] *Ibid.*

[360] *Ibid.*

[361] *Ibid.*

[362] *Ibid.*

[363] *Ibid.*

[364] "El incumplimiento del Reglamento de Uso ... por parte de cualquier miembro del pueblo Kuna titular del derecho, podrá ser sancionado por la Administración del Derecho Colectivo, con la revocación de la autorización para utilizar el Derecho Colectivo."

[365] "'Prohibir *a los marinos* de las embarcaciones colombianas el intercambio de mercancía por molas', detalla parte de la resolución aprobada por el CGK", *see* Bonilla (2004 II) no pagination. Erroneously translated as "(i)n July 2004, the Kuna General Congress forbade *Kuna women* from bartering with Colombian sailors" by De Obaldia (2005) 372. Emphasis added by the author.

As regards the trade situation with Costa Rica, the General Kuna Congress issued a prohibition against the women,[366] but that did not help, as the Kuna women simply "disobeyed." Part of the problem seemed to be that, according to their own customary law, the Kuna peoples are organized by General Kuna Congresses, consisting only of men, while the individuals producing the *molas* are strictly Kuna women. Thus, the idea came up to establish another General Congress consisting of women representing the *mola* creators, a Special Congress of Kuna Women,[367] to settle the dispute, giving Kuna women the opportunity to address the problem of the *molas,* their commercialization, and relating intellectual property issues.[368] As far as insights are possible, the general problem, however, remains.

What one can also see from this case is that applying customary law may not always be the perfect solution; it may even lead to gender issues, or, more generally, new rights may provoke new conflicts, and tensions between the individual and the collective are part of the very nature of humans, in any society or community.

The suggestion was made to establish a permanent Special Committee comprised of Kuna women issuing the permissions of use, as such a committee is likely to be "more sensitive to the interests of the tribe, and thus better able to strike a fair balance."[369]

Other voices, Kuna male ones, suggested creating a permanent commission to legally train the Kuna women, supervise the use of the emblem "*kalu tucbis*," and address questions and applications for licensing contracts on the collective right "Mola Kuna Panama."[370]

III. Conclusion and Evaluation of the Examples at the International Level

With regard to the protection of TCEs, the FTA between Panama and Taiwan is the most extensive agreement—at least on paper.

The treaty seems to implement bilaterally the sui generis regime in Panama established shortly before. The latter entered into force in 2000, the decree to the law in 2001, only 2 years before the FTA was signed. Beside this close timely connection, the explicit aim of the protection as well as the formulations used in the treaty resemble those contained in Law No. 20. The aim of the protection established in the FTA is to emphasize the cultural and sociological autochthonous

---

366 When aware of this situation, the Kuna General Congress released such a prohibition; for further details and resulting problems, *see* at Section 1.G.III.1. (7) *et seq*. and 2 below.

367 Personal communication with staff members of the General Congress in February, 2009, in Panama.

368 Bonilla (2004 I) no pagination.

369 De Obaldia (2005) 374.

370 *See also* Valiente López (2006) 150.

values of the indigenous peoples and local communities and to bring them "social justice"—like in Law No. 20.[371] Then, the wording "the collective intellectual property rights and the traditional knowledge"—without clear distinction between the object of protection and the rights conferred[372]—as well the precondition of commercial use shows the parallel construction to Law No. 20.[373] Moreover, the "negative approach" of the protection, excluding the establishment of exclusive intellectual property rights regarding TCEs by third parties, is exactly the same approach followed in Law No. 20 and reflects the starting point of that law—to avoid existing attempts of non-indigenous companies to register trademarks on the Kuna *mola* in Panama.[374] Finally, the technical system of a special registry corresponds to Law No. 20.

To some extent, the protection in the treaty goes even beyond the scope of protection, i.e. the subject of protection, of the Law: Apart from the traditional knowledge and cultural expressions of indigenous communities, it also covers those of local communities.[375]

Apart from the outlined situation on paper, it would have been interesting to know to what extent these provisions have—successfully—been implemented. However, data e.g. on the detainment of products or other concrete information on the implementation could not be obtained.[376]

Furthermore, when assessing whether this regulation in the FTA could be an effective and realistic model for bilateral protection in general, it is worth having a look at the factual circumstances and background of the FTA. Taiwan and Panama have a very special political and economic relationship. Taiwan is one of the major investors in, or even "sponsors" of, Panama.

Thus, it becomes clear that the actual legal situation is also influenced by the financial weight of the actors involved. Consequently, neither can this situation be transferred to any other international relationship, nor can the content of the FTA deriving thereof be taken as a realistic example for other possible bilateral agreements in Latin America.

Even the situation in Panama itself reveals this conclusion: The later FTA with Chile, agreed upon in 2006, does not contain any protection of TCEs in general, but rather only deals with one special "product" out of the TCEs. Also, the mode of protection is not constructed by a sui generis system establishing intellectual

[371] Article 1 of Law No. 20.

[372] For details *see* the parallel problem in Law No. 20, Section 1.C.III. and G.I.1.

[373] The commercial use is a specialty of the Panamanian Law No. 20. The WIPO Model provisions do not provide for this requirement.

[374] Article 2 of Law No. 20, and *see* at Section 1.B. above.

[375] Articles 16.05, 16.06, and 16.07 of the FTA.

[376] Personal communication with staff members of the Direction of the National Handicrafts (DGAN) and the Department of Collective Rights and Folkloric Expressions within DIGERPI in February, 2009, Panama City.

property rights, but the protection is rather integrated into the free circulation of products.

It can be noticed that the specific forms of TCE are included in the protection by means of an FTA for mainly two reasons: (a) their economic importance or (b) their close connection to the (economically important) classic fields of law—like trade marks or geographical indications in intellectual property law. This differentiation, however, contravenes the national concept of implementation of an adequate, general and all-encompassing protection of TCEs. It rather promotes the transformation of certain TCEs into simple, two-dimensional products in the sense of "Western" markets and societies. An international, especially multilateral protection following such an all-encompassing approach should thus be promoted and finally be put into practice to secure such a national path.

Finally, the situation presented above between Costa Rica, respectively Colombia, and Panama shows that despite the statement just made, sometimes it is not even a question of negotiating and establishing rights at the bilateral or multilateral level. Instead, it is rather a socio-economic problem at the local level that has to be dealt with.[377]

F. Harnessing TCEs for Development and Trade: Promoting Commercialization and Innovation of TCEs

In line with the objective of giving "social justice" to the indigenous communities, several promotional measures are provided for in Law No. 20 contained in its proper Chapter IV on the promotion of indigenous art and cultural expressions, which has been disposed above.[378]

Another concrete example of promotion is the prize awarded to the Ngöbe Indians for a traditionally manufactured type of coffee by the Ministry of Commerce and Industries in the national Handicrafts Fair.[379]

An effective implementation regarding the object of "social justice" and economic development of the indigenous peoples is also regarded to include capacity-building measures concerning business strategies—not necessarily according to a purely Western style.

Therefore, the Panamanian government is giving an impulse for the inclusion of indigenous products and companies as direct beneficiaries of the *Programa de Desarrollo Empresarial Indígena de Panamá* (PRODEI) and *Impulso Panamá*, part of the Panamanian Ministry of Commerce and Industries. The idea is to

---

[377] For further aspects of and conclusions *see* at Section G.III.1. below.

[378] *See* at Section 1.C.X. above.

[379] Personal communication with Yahelys Arenas of the Department of Collective Rights and Folkloric Expressions within DIGERPI in February, 2009, Panama City.

"make business people out of indigenous peoples,"[380] and to strengthen their export competitivity and competence. While some of the indigenous products are not necessarily regarded as TCEs protected under Law No. 20, the program also encompasses TCEs like the *mola*. With regard to the *mola*, one idea and project that PRODEI worked out with the indigenous peoples was to establish a company for international protection, taking over the same name of the emblem "*kalu tukbis*," and to prepare a cooperation with "great Spanish designers" or other export projects.[381] The company supported by the program is the Association of Women Producing the Mola Kalu Dugbis Kuna Yala.[382]

The experiences in practice made clear that a different world view and mentality still dominate among the indigenous people, and that "doing business" is still a strange and unknown habit within most of those traditional communities.[383]

In light of preserving the "authenticity" of the TCEs and their socio-cultural environment, this fact finding of a still traditional manner of behavior may be regarded as a kind of "positive" signal. Especially establishing commercial structures and associations, excluding non-integrated members of the community, leads to the disappearance or assimilation of traditional cultures. It runs the risk of contravening important indigenous customary principles of exchange and reciprocity. At the same time, socio-economic problems, if not solved by other means like funding and public support, probably remain unsolved without any promotion of entrepreneurship.

Moreover, it is at least questionable whether market-oriented "productions" of the *mola*, i.e. creating motifs, styles, and functions of the *mola* adapted to market desires, for example bags for mobile phones, can still be considered as authentic, or whether the effect might even contravene the object of protecting authenticity, as Article 6 of the Law stipulates.

The dilemma, which runs through the whole topic of "protecting TCEs," is exposed at its best here. The final questions that pop up every once in a while on this issue are legal and political ones:

As to the political dimension, how much good can commercial promotion, any legal system of protection, and the necessary equivalent "education" do? In view of the unneeded mass, the overproduction, and consumption that dominates the greater part of the global community, is it really the right direction to change the mentality of an old *salidugman* living in the life-circle of the Panamanian rainforest, in what is probably a much more balanced and integrated way than regular "business men" in any big city in this world, saying that he would be very grateful—once they had registered their Kuna hammock—if I bought *one* for my home in Germany?

[380] Personal communication with Kathia Arjona and Maria Teresa Muñoz of the PRODEI, which is integrated in the Ministry of Commerce and Industries, February, 2009, Panama City.

[381] Article 11 of the Law.

[382] Asociación de mujeres productoras de Mola Kalu Dugbis Kuna Yala.

[383] Personal communication with Kathia Arjona and Maria Teresa Muñoz of the PRODEI, which is integrated in the Ministry of Commerce and Industries, February, 2009, Panama City.

In the legal dimension, should there be a reference to "authenticity" anymore, or what should it encompass, when cultural expressions turn into market-oriented productions? When are (indigenous) expressions and creations still "traditional" and worth protecting?

G. Evaluation of the Panamanian Approach

Although it has been held in international literature that "it is still too early to assess the system established by the Panamanian law,"[384] some evaluative remarks can be made already.

Before going into details, it should be mentioned that according to the official statement of Panama and of Panamanian indigenous peoples, the Law No. 20 signifies a big advance in the protection of TCEs.[385]

Considering other national and international situations in this area, this statement generally can be supported.

I. Evaluation of the Law on Paper

Whenever evaluating the Law more closely, it should be borne in mind that the Law was mostly drafted by indigenous peoples themselves, at a time when they had the historical chance of pushing through the National Congress a legal protection of their *molas*. It has a strong emotional background and draw, and is rather focused on the objective and matter of protection than on the creation of a formally clear law balancing diverging interests, according to the general task of a legislature.

1. On the Structure

The sui generis law, as well as the executive Decree, possess common external structures: They are both divided into articles and chapters, entitled and dealing with the subjects of (1) "aim" of the law/decree, (2) "objects capable of protection," (3) "registration of collective rights," (4) "promotion of indigenous arts and cultural expressions," (5) "rights on use and commercialization," (6) "prohibitions and sanctions," and (7) "final dispositions."[386]

Although an internal structure exists insofar as most of the provisions within one chapter deal with the issue of the respective chapter, the concrete allocation of the

[384] Lucas-Schlötter (2008) 413.

[385] "La Ley N° 20 representa la vía legal utilizada por los indígenas panameños para proteger sus derechos intelectuales en el plano nacional y ellos mismos reconocen que significa un gran avance en este tema", Annex II of WIPO/GRTKF/IC/4/INF/4.

[386] There are seven chapters containing in sum 28 articles ("artículos").

different provisions is not easy to understand. Articles 1 and 2 of the Law, which are allocated within the "aim of protection" are often referred to as indicating the content and scope of the collective rights as well as the definition and content of the subject matter of protection—although the next chapter is supposed to deal with "objects capable of protection." This second chapter then, however, also contains the definition of "collective rights" (Article 6), which leads some of the interpreters of the law to the conclusion that Article 6 expressly lays down the collective ownership—although allocated to the chapter "objects capable of protection."[387] Apart from the first chapter, on the aims of protection, another aim can be found in the chapter just mentioned, on objects capable of protection: the protection of originality and authenticity of the TCEs, which can easily be overlooked and is not clear in its dimension either.[388]

Moreover, no clear differentiation between procedural and substantive matters is discernible. The second sentence of both Articles 4 and 5 of the Decree determines the relevant applicant as well as the competent entity for applying for the registration and is thus a procedural provision concerning the process of registration, although the articles are allocated in the chapter "objects capable of registration" and procedural matters seem to be governed by Chapter III the "Registry of Collective Rights." Similarly, the differentiation between the procedure and content of the "rights of use and commercialization" (Chapter V) and the procedure in case of "industrial reproduction" as a "prohibition" (Chapter VI) is not very clear.

2. On the Content

One of the most challenging aspects of the content of Law No. 20 is its heterogeneous use of terminology. Especially the differentiations between legal and factual aspects, as well as tangible and intangible ones, are not easy to understand. The terms "collective rights" and the factual subject matter or objects of protection are often used with varying references, sometimes interchangeably. On the one hand, the term of "collective right" is even equated with the objects capable of protection,[389] on the other, there are considered to be collective rights *on* ("sobre") factual objects of protection.[390]

No differentiation is made between the tangible and the intangible, *e.g.* musical instruments and music itself,[391] although the rights are mostly termed "collective intellectual property rights" and the Law is entitled "Special Intellectual Property Regime". Sometimes, however, the rights (or objects) are only called "collective property rights" of the indigenous peoples.

[387] Ramsauer (2005) 104.

[388] Article 6 of the Law.

[389] Article 6 of the Law.

[390] Articles 4 and 5 of the Law.

[391] *See* at Section 1. above and Article 4 of the Law.

While the Decree defines "collective indigenous rights" as rights of cultural and intellectual indigenous property that refer to art, music, literature, etc., it has been shown before that—also according to the indigenous peoples themselves—especially this provision does not coincide with the scope of Law No. 20, also as regards the traditional knowledge on medical and biological aspects.

Regardless of these terminological aspects, the scopes of rights with regard to the "intellectual" and "cultural" or material aspects of the collective rights are unclear—which indeed is an important aspect for the implementation of the Law in practice. The Law was intended to overcome the limits set by classic intellectual property rights, like trademarks or designs, which protect only partial aspects of a *mola*, for example, which is a very positive approach. The result besides the misleading terminology and titles, however, is that the concrete scope of protection is blurred and its practical implementation faces difficulties.

While the Law respects and gives room to the "codified" customary rules, in the case of the "Rules of Use of the Mola," the aspects of "intellectual" and "cultural" rights rather lead to confusions than to legal certainty. For example, it does not clearly distinguish between the right to sell a piece of craft, a *mola* for example, and the right to teach the design or hand over the knowledge of its creation—although differences are noted from a customary perspective.

Apart from that, especially interests of non-indigenous persons are disregarded.[392] Does the use of indigenous motifs constitute an infringement already? Where are the limits of "inspiration"?

Likewise, no statement is contained in the regime on how to deal with derivative works. If a derivative work is created, is it also covered by the collective intellectual property right, or does the intellectual property in the work vest in the creator, as provided for by the intellectual property law? The 2002 WIPO Pacific Model Law provides for the latter option, for example, while the scope of Law No. 20 in this regard is unclear, or according to other point of views, even tacit.[393]

Notwithstanding these weaknesses, the difficulties in implementing the law have rather come from other aspects, as for example the management and exercise of the collective rights.

II. Panamanian Experiences in Practice

Besides this rather theoretical analysis of the regulations on paper, some observations can also be made and first résumés be drawn based on the practical experiences in Panama in the past nearly 10 years since the Law entered into force.

The general concern about sui generis legislations is that they seem "to exist only on paper."[394] According to von Lewinski, this is due to, in short, three main

[392] On this aspect *see* also De Obaldia (2005) 376 *et seq.*

[393] *Ibid.*

[394] *See* von Lewinski (2007) 214, Wendland (2002) 115.

factors: first, in many developing countries much more basic and urgent problems have to be tackled; second, the appreciation of TCEs there is often low; and, third, indigenous communities may not have the power to fight for the enforcement of such protection (especially due to tensions between them and non-indigenous governments).[395] At least in Panama, on the one hand, this general concern—in its first aspect (only)—can be confirmed, and on the other hand, it overlooks other essential aspects. In particular, additionally, such regulations sometimes produce unexpected outcomes, even new realities.

The legislation is thus only comprehensively appraisable when considering—as far as possible—factual implications and effects and trying to analyze the reasons behind them.

1. Implementation So Far

In this manner, the observed *status quo* reveals the following: First and foremost, the *mola* was saved from being registered as trademark or design by national or international non-indigenous companies. The initial aim of the law to provide for "defensive protection"[396] has thus been reached.

Besides, it is interesting to note that another registration as a trademark has been denied. This trademark was intended for the product of an industrially produced coffee of a non-indigenous coffee company, and contained a picture of a Ngöbe woman. The Ngöbes themselves traditionally manufacture Ngöbe coffee. While it was disputed whether the traditionally manufactured coffee constituted a TCE according to Law No. 20, and thus Article 2 of the Law would have applied, the denial of the registration was based upon Article 91 No. 19 of the Panamanian Industrial Property Law, which prohibits the registration of "words, letters, characters or symbols which use the indigenous communities" as trademarks.[397]

In its positive dimension of protection, Law No. 20 has enabled eight registrations of TCEs in total so far. The first was the *Mola Kuna Panamá*, which was registered for the Kuna Indians as holder of the rights in 2002.[398] Then, in 2003, four different types of handicrafts of the Ngöbe[399] and Buglé Indians were

---

[395] von Lewinski (2007) 214.

[396] On the legislative history, *see* at Section 1.B. and C.I. above.

[397] Article 91, No. 19, of Law No. 35 of May 10, 1996, the Panamanian Industrial Property Law, stipulates: "Article 91. The following can not be registered as trademarks or elements thereof: 18. The words, letters, characters, or symbols which are used by the Indian or religious communities or nonprofit organizations to distinguish the manner of processing the product, the finished products or services, as well as those which constitute the expression of their cult or custom, idiosyncrasy or religious practice, except when the application be made for the benefit of one of the communities or associations to which this numeral refers." Translation by WIPO.

[398] The emblem is *kalus tucbis*. *See* Ministerio de Comercio e Industrias – DIGERPI (no year) Chapter "Conocimientos Tradicionales".

[399] In the DIGERPI *Catálogo*, the spelling "Ngöbe" is still used. However, the Ministry of Education has indicated that the official spelling now is Ngäbe. Talk with Enrique Montezuma,

registered,[400] and in 2005, three different types of handicrafts of the Emberá and Wounaan Indians followed.[401]

No licensing agreement has been signed so far, and no use has been made of the special authorization procedure in case of requested industrial reproduction.[402]

Apart from that, no court decision exists. No fairs have been organized, and no dances.[403] No concrete information could be obtained concerning the number of handicraftsmen having applied for a certification.[404]

Thus, in total, in the first 10 years of existence, eight TCEs of three different indigenous peoples were registered, while the Decree alone lists 80 TCEs as examples.[405] At this rate, it would take 100 years to register only the 80 examples contained in the Decree.

Why does the implementation of the Law take so long?

2. Reasons for Slow Implementation

The experience in Panama shows that it is not always a question of the (non-) existence of laws or agreements but rather of dealing with social and economic problems. More particularly, some reasons for the slow implementation of the sui generis protection are:

(1) Pressing factual needs like lack of raw material
(2) Difficulties and mistrust in the registration process
(3) Long physical and financial distances
(4) Little legal knowledge or—in contrast—a strong acculturation
(5) Administrative difficulties like blocked flow of information
(6) Internal socio-cultural challenges
(7) Different legal culture

---

ex-deputy and legislator from the community of the Ngäbe, on February 13, 2009, in Panama City. Both forms of spelling are used interchangeably here.

[400] Different De Obaldia (2005) 370, stating that until 2005, "with the exception of the Kunas, the indigenous groups have not started the registration of their rights;" and that "The Emberás-Wounnaán and the Ngöbes-Buglés have not shown much interest in registering their rights" (note 210). In 2003, the Ngöbe-Buglés registered four different TCEs, and in 2005, the Emberá-Wounaan had been preparing and finishing the registration of three different TCEs. *See* the foregoing and following footnotes.

[401] For details *see* Chapter "Conocimientos Tradicionales" in the Catálogo de Propiedad Industrial Panamá of the Ministerio de Comercio e Industrias.

[402] Personal communication with Luz Celeste Ríos de Davis, General Director of the Industrial Property Registry, and Aresio Valiente, Kuna Indian and lawyer in February, 2009, in Panama City.

[403] Personal communication with Aresio Valiente, *supra*.

[404] Personal communication with staff members of the Direction of the National Handicrafts (DGAN) and the Department of Collective Rights and Folkloric Expressions within DIGERPI in February, 2009, Panama City.

[405] On this *see* at Section 1.C.II. above.

Some of these aspects will be addressed below.

a. Lack of Raw Material

It has become clear that one of the most urgent problems was not the legal protection and/or procedure itself, but rather the lack or disappearance of the raw material necessary for the creation or production of the handicraft, like specific plants for the production of *chácaras*—hand-woven bags made of the wild pineapple plant. The Department for Collective Rights and Folkloristic Expressions became aware of the problem, elaborated a "rescue plan," and initiated a huge planting project in the territory of the tribe of the Ngöbes. However, the financial resources provided by the state were limited, which limited the planting project.

Nonetheless, it became clear that the disposability of the raw material and ways of securing it is an absolutely essential factor, as it not only provides for economic income of the members of the tribes concerned but factually enables the survival of the traditional handicraft. The Department for Collective Rights and Folkloristic Expressions shared this experience by producing official documentation of the project on a CD and by publishing this way of factually protecting TCEs on the DIGERPI's news ticker.[406]

b. Difficulties in the Registration Process

The general observation that registration of traditional knowledge for legal purposes "remains controversial and problematic"[407] finds support in the situation of TCEs in Panama. The registration itself appeared to be rather an obstacle for the right holders for legal and factual reasons. At the factual level, the reality of the Panamanian jungle and Caribbean Sea, with little infrastructure and scarce financial resources, enlarge real distances and slow down any communication process.

Although the traditional exchange of a cultural object or the traditional knowledge between indigenous peoples explicitly is not supposed to be affected by the registration of any collective right,[408] in reality it is, at least as far as concerns natural recourses for the cultural object. Especially when initiating the registration process in the case of more then one community claiming to be the "original" and thus one and only "owner" of the cultural object or traditional knowledge, difficulties in agreeing upon the ownership arise which as a consequence sometimes have an impact on the exchange of goods and knowledge.[409] Certainly, according to the spirit of this regulation, this might not be the kind of situation Article 11 of the Decree was intended to deal with. The effects in reality thus show, on the one hand,

[406] "Crop garanties disposability of raw material for art handicraft," news of October 21, 2009 on http://www.mici.gob.pa/index2.php, last visited November 2, 2009.

[407] Taubman and Leistner (2008) 148.

[408] Article 11 of the Decree. *See* at Section 1.C.V.4. above.

[409] *See e.g.* the case of a hammock of the Kunas as displayed at Section 1.C.III.3. above.

that sometimes difficulties occur where not expected, and on the other hand, that a successful implementation of the Law to a great extent also depends upon the indigenous communities actively taking part in and adapting to internal and external negotiating processes—whether one regards this as a positive or negative consequence of establishing positions of rights.

Another obstacle was the mistrust in the limited publicity of the registry, and it might be at least questionable whether the disclosure requirement should be upheld.

c. Little Legal Knowledge, Different Legal Culture—And Legal Acculturation

On the one hand, among most of the indigenous peoples in Panama there exists little knowledge of Western legal systems, including the "codification" and registration of the customary rules on the use and commercialization of the TCEs. This is one of the reasons why the idea of indigenous peoples themselves applying for a registration of their rights, without compulsory representation by a lawyer,[410] is not implemented in practice.

Moreover, Panamanian indigenous communities have a different legal culture in general, also in dispute settling. They "have a long tradition of defending and exercising their rights by their own hand" and "traditionally do not solve their problems through the Panamanian judiciary."[411] This is the main reason why no precedent cases have been decided by Panamanian courts so far, which would clarify interpretation problems of Law No. 20 and the entire sui generis system.

On the other hand, one area where the indigenous population shows noticeable tendencies toward acculturation is in matters of law. Traditional authorities hand over legal issues to specialists acting in a separate "sphere" of law. This separate realm and the involvement of specialists are, however, rather characteristics of complex societies (with a state structure) than of traditional ones governed by customary law.[412] The "Rules of Use of the Mola," for example, establish a "legal representative" competent for all legal aspects for "external" questions, i.e. those related to non-indigenous persons, of the legal treatment of the *mola*.[413] The latter aspects reflect, first, the complexity of the sui generis regime, especially the registration part, and, second, and consequentially, progress in the assimilation process.

d. Administrative Difficulties

Administrative difficulties appear at both levels, within the national public entities as regards the flow of information, documentation, and passing along of

[410] Article 7 of the Law.

[411] De Obaldia (2005) 375.

[412] On this *see* Stavenhagen (1990) 30 and above Chapter II Section 5.B.III.2.b.

[413] Kuna lawyer Aresio Valiente López, *see* at Section 1.C.III.3. above.

experiences and information between the different public entities, as well as at the level of indigenous entities like the General Congresses.

At the indigenous level, one reason for these administrative difficulties lies within the customary law itself: General Congresses consisting exclusively of men try to administer the rights on creations invented and produced exclusively by women, as in the case of the *molas*, and this may provoke gender conflicts.

e. Socio-Economic Problems Within Tribes

The issues and problems within the tribes might be existing ones—like the difficult economic situation of the tribes. Or they might even be provoked by the creation of a sui generis legislation—like the gender issue—and lead to unforeseen impacts on the social structure within the traditional culture that was supposed to be protected in the first place. Third, even in native communities traditionally based on the principle of collectivity, a collective mentality when executing the collective rights cannot be taken for granted (anymore). The reference to and application of customary law might neither be the wish of all members of the communities, e.g. the women in the case of the *molas,* nor always be in accordance with national principles of law (for equal rights for men and women).

These gender issues, as well as the increasing tensions between the individual creators and the collectivity of the indigenous tribe, reflect implementation difficulties within the ambit of the tribes. The background of most of these difficulties are economic needs.

f. International Protection

The principle of territoriality also limits the effectiveness of the sui generis regime. This regards the protection of cross-border TCEs, like the Kunan hammocks, as well as an effective implementation of the Law. However, the biggest problems at the international level appear to have been the conflict with the neighboring states Costa Rica and Colombia, and the negotiation of bilateral agreements was not regarded as an effective solution, as the root of these difficulties was socio-economic problems of the Panamanian indigenous peoples, rather than questions of legal implementation.[414]

[414] Personal communication with Enrique Montezuma, ex-deputy and legislator who comes from the community of the Ngöbe, on February 13, 2009, in Panama City.

H. Conclusion and Outlook: The Panamanian Sui Generis Approach—A Model Law?

As Law No. 20 is one of the first sui generis approaches to protecting TCEs worldwide, and constitutes a big step forward in the challenging topic of protecting TCEs, especially in comparison to the situation in other countries without any similar measures at all, one could think of relying on it as a model law for other countries, especially Latin American ones.

I. A Model Law for Other Latin American Countries?

Could the Panamanian regime be recommended as a model law for other Latin American countries or even a Regional Agreement, and, in particular, would any such recommendation be practicable and of realistic value?

Aside from the legal and practical remarks and evaluations regarding the Panamanian approach already made in this chapter, there are some further points to be considered in addressing this question.

First, is the factual and legal situation concerning TCEs in Panama comparable to that in other Latin American countries? At the legal level, strong inspirations for the preparatory work on Law No. 20 have come from the progressive legislation on handicrafts in Guatemala, as displayed above in the genesis of the Law. Apart from these preparatory works, the existence of the special territories and acknowledgement of the traditional organizations of the indigenous peoples living in the *comarcas* enabled the sui generis design of Law No. 20. Similarities to these two aspects can partially be found in other Latin American countries, too. Nonetheless, with the possible exception of Bolivia, the situation of the indigenous peoples in Panama is somewhat different from that in other Latin American countries. Due to their revolutionary history and decade-long support of the United States, the *Kuna* peoples have a very special, strong position, and proud mentality regarding their culture, as was mentioned at the very beginning of this chapter. Moreover, the political power for passing through Law No. 20 is an important circumstance that is unlikely to be found in most of the other Latin American countries.

Second, does the law contain sufficient answers to the needs of other Latin American countries—also in view of the further development of other possible model laws?

There might be concerns about reaching a consensus on the content of the law in its current version. In Panama itself, first suggestions have been made for improving the regulations, as showed above.

Statements from other Latin American countries have revealed that there is either no knowledge on the Panamanian solution, or that—regardless of any consideration of the legal approach—a solution valuable for the very small country of Panama would be regarded as probably not fitting in the case of a giant like

Brazil.[415] From a Peruvian perspective, two important limitations have been criticized: first, that the Law is only applicable in Panama, and, second, the commercial focus of the regime.[416] The first point, however, is the very consequence of a national legislation, especially with relation to intellectual property aspects, where the principle of territoriality governs. This aspect should rather be a motivation to negotiate regional agreements for enlarging the scope of application of sui generis measures.

II. Actual Tendencies and Impact of Law No. 20

In Panama itself, Law No. 20 has also set an example and inspired further legal projects in that field, concerning not only indigenous but also local and other communities.

First, on the basis of Law No. 20, a preliminary draft has been designed to set up a special intellectual-property regime for the protection and promotion of collective rights on traditional knowledge, traditional cultural expressions, and folklore of local communities and other formations.[417] However, this draft has been set aside again already.[418]

Second, it has inspired the legal project of establishing sui generis regulations on the protection of traditional knowledge on biodiversity, genetic resources, and especially regarding traditional medicine.[419] These were, by the way, the aspects formerly left aside during negotiations of Law No. 20 in 1999.[420]

Also, at the international level, Law No. 20 has had an impact already. Bolivia, for example, has requested information from DIGERPI on the Law and the Panamanian experience in order to possibly use the Law as an example and an inspiration for its own sui generis solution.[421] Even in Brazil, some voices showed interest in the experiences gained in Panama—although it was doubted that a small country

[415] Personal communication with staff members of IPHAN, the General Coordination of Copyright, Ministry of Culture, in March 2009 in Brasilia, Brazil.

[416] Ruiz, Lapeña and Clark (2004) 767.

[417] "Del Régimen Especial de Propiedad Intelectual para la Protección, Salvaguardia y Fomento de los Derechos Colectivos sobre Conocimientos Tradicionales y/o Manifestaciones Culturales, Expresiones Folklóricas o Tradicionales Folklóricas de las Comunidades Locales y Otras Disposiciones". *See* Celeste de Davis (2006) no pagination.

[418] The main problem was the lack of similar socio-cultural patterns, organizational structures, and identifiable traditional representatives of the local communities; Personal Communication with Edmundo de la Cruz, Chief of the Department of Folklore of the INAC, the National Institute of Culture in Panama City on February 13, 2009.

[419] Personal Communication with Aresio Valiente López in Panama City on February 11, 2009.

[420] *See* at Section 1.C.II.2.d.aa. above.

[421] Personal communication with staff members from the Department of Collective Rights and Folkloric Expressions within DIGERPI in Panama City in February 2009.

like Panama would truly fit the situation in such a huge country displaying a great diversity of TCEs and indigenous tribes (220 in Brazil, 8 in Panama).[422]

III. Lessons Learned from Panama for the Protection of TCEs in General

There are lessons learned from Panama that can be of use for advancing the protection of TCEs in general.

(1) First and foremost, it has become clear that efficient and successful protection of TCEs depends on the respective attitude, i.e. the will and action, of each and *all* persons involved. This includes the individuals "producing" the cultural expressions, the other members of the community, and the members of the major national society, as well as the individuals working in the different state authorities dealing with the subject of protection of TCEs and possible users of TCEs.
(2) Second, efficient and successful protection requires a common understanding of all these persons of the meaning of "protection".
(3) Third, and finally, respective measures at the factual and legal level have to be agreed upon *and* put into practice.

1. At the Factual Level

If "protection" is understood as conservation, promotion, and legal monopolization, as is the case in Panama, essential measures are to be taken first of all at the factual level. These measures might seem obvious, but are quite difficult to put into practice and fundamental at the same time. Important points are:

(1) Necessary immediate rescue needs should be identified and addressed, so as to conserve or re-cultivate raw material to prevent TCEs from disappearing or being unintentionally transformed due to the lack of the traditional raw material. In Panama, DIGERPI set up a huge planting program—which had great success where conducted and found its limits in the limited economic resources provided for by the government.
(2) While in the case of the Kuna Indians and Panamanian Indians in general, the estimation of the culture within the general society and in the communities themselves is relatively high, this is not the case in other Latin American countries. This estimation, however, was identified as a precondition for maintaining the TCEs and even for advancing their legal protection.
(3) Economic pressures should be averted in a different way so that they do not provoke a lack of self-fulfilment of the requirements and compliance with the rules.

[422] There are indeed essential differences, which especially appear in questions of effective implementation of a new law. For the situation in Brazil *see* at Section 2.A. below.

(4) Any kind of legal protection, whether positive or negative, should be communicated to the indigenous communities affected by such protection, as well as to the public, including non-indigenous companies and other possible infringers.
(5) When thinking about the creation of such a complex system as the sui generis regime in Panama, it should be borne in mind that any implementation and necessary capacity-building measure at the legal as well as the economic level does have an impact on the socio-cultural way of life of the communities. Law No. 20 has been criticised as "helping" the indigenous peoples to "live more like Westerners," which would "seem counterintuitive."[423] However, cultures have always evolved and influenced each other. The essential thing is to consider this aspect when defining the political aim of the law and drafting the legal concepts accordingly. Besides, potential new conflicts, provoked by the juridification of social relationships, should be taken into consideration.
(6) In most of the cases of handicrafts being TCEs, indigenous women are the traditional creators. Moreover, traditional male tasks like fishing and hunting are becoming less important or—due to the loss of indigenous territory or the quantity of animals on the territory and in the waters—less effective. As a consequence of men's losing their social role and function in the community, social problems like increasing consumption of alcohol rise, affecting even more questions of gender issues. Such conflicts should be taken into consideration.
(7) If a law is established, especially the competent indigenous as well as public entities should supervise and control the effective implementation and fulfilment of any legislative sui generis regime, even or especially when it embraces customary rules. In the case of Panama, that would be the supervision of the implementation of the "Rules of Use of the Mola," through the various public institutions addressed by Law No. 20 as well as the General Kuna Congresses. Indigenous peoples themselves have suggested such an approach.[424]
(8) Special entities should be created in case the creators or producers of the TCEs are not part of the official representatives of the indigenous communities according to the customary law to provide capacity building measures as well as to supervise and control the correct use of the collective rights. In the case of the Kuna Indians, as Valiente López suggests, that could be a permanent commission to legally train the Kuna women, supervise the use of the emblem "Kalu Tucbis," and address questions and applications for licensing contracts on the collective right "Mola Kuna Panama."[425]
(9) The actual legal culture as well as the economic situation of the traditional communities usually does not include a preparedness to take action in national courts. As a consequence, it is conceivable to either empower local tribunals to

[423] De Obaldia (2005) 375.
[424] Valiente López (2006) 149.
[425] *See* also *id.*, 150.

deal with disputes or to set up alternative dispute resolution mechanisms, e.g., facilitated by public administrative bodies, or to implement factual measures to improve the willingness and readiness of the communities and their members concerned to employ the existing national court structures. In the latter case, however, it should be taken into account that this might have a strong impact on the traditional culture and in the end likely lead to an effect contrary to the intention of the law of protecting the expressions of a traditional culture. In the special case of Panama, Valiente López says, an assisting organ consisting of representatives of DIGERPI, the National Direction of Handicraft, the representatives of the indigenous Congresses, and of the producers of indigenous art, could be created within the Ministry of Commerce and Industries.[426] Thereby, disputes could be settled more easily, and a better flow of information could be achieved between the different entities—also within the public ambit—involved.

(10) For TCEs to be sold as market products, a standard price could be established to avoid unfair competition between the indigenous persons themselves, but especially between indigenous and non-indigenous persons, natural or legal ones. In Panama, Valiente López has observed, the lack of such a standard price has affected the economic value of the *molas* and thus the income of Kuna families.[427]

(11) While it is desirable that the distribution of benefits primarily be organized by means of the traditional indigenous structures themselves, e.g. representative entities like the General Congresses, this is of special difficulty when such entities do not include at least some representatives of the group of indigenous persons creating the TCEs or maintaining the necessary traditional knowledge for such creation. Classic collective rights management organizations—at least in the Latin American reality—would not be able to successfully fulfill such a task of distribution of benefits among the indigenous communities. Still, a similar entity consisting of representatives of the public and indigenous entities, as Valiente López suggest, which are in charge of the implementation of the sui generis regime and familiar with the specific indigenous needs, behaviors and social structures, could—and should be created.[428]

(12) At the regional or international level, factual cooperation is a first, probably less complicated step towards a protection of TCEs beyond national borders. This refers to such cases in which the relevant TCEs are based on traditions of a tribe living in a border region like the Kuna communities on the Panamanian and the Colombian side of the border. It also can address concrete situations affecting TCEs, like the false labelling and pricing policy in relation to the *molas* in Costa Rica.

---

[426] *Id.*, 149.

[427] *Id.*, 150.

[428] Valiente López regards this to be necessary in Panama, *see ibid.*

2. At the Legal Level

At the legal level, the main lessons learned from the situation in Panama are these:

(1) Even if apparently clear regulations of a sui generis regime are specifically set up for the protection of TCEs, uncertainty might arise in practice, for example as regards the holders and scope of rights. As clarifying court decisions are very unlikely due to the particular indigenous legal culture and economic resources, it would be good to simplify and clarify the provisions as far as possible, by neutralizing the highly disputed topic, leaving aside strong political aspirations and emotional involvements as much as possible.
(2) Simplifying a system of protection as far as possible could also help to avoid strong acculturation effects provoked by the juridification of the internal social relationships.
(3) A distinction between material and immaterial goods or TCEs is not practical. However, the holdership of rights regarding immaterial and material rights should be clarified in the legal regime, which is lacking in the case of the Panamanian regime.
(4) Similar to patent law, both directions of a negative and a positive protection should be covered. That means that a protection of TCEs against the establishment of individual or collective rights in favor of third, non-traditional parties should be granted as well as the original right of "self-determination" over the use of the TCEs in favor of the traditional owners.
(5) An essential question is in how far new forms or designs of TCEs should also be covered by protection. Responding to the need not only to protect a museum culture, it would be favorable if they were covered. However, a good balance is needed between new forms or designs of TCEs covered by the protection, and such a balance could maybe consist of a limit of duration—which is not the case in Panama.
(6) An obligatory registration system, which is of a constitutive nature for the rights, acted to rather complicate and to decelerate the protection of TCEs. The cooperation necessary for the process of registration between a specialized public entity like the Department of Collective Rights and Folkloric Expressions within DIGERPI and the indigenous communities turned out to be fruitful, though. Such cooperation for supportive measures at the legal as well as factual level should be integrated into a legal protection of TCEs—as long as it is based upon mutual respect and does not provoke relationships of dependency. This seemed to be the case with the staff members of the Department of Collective Rights and Folkloric Expressions within DIGERPI.
(7) References to customary law should be examined carefully, especially under the point of effective right management, gender issues, and effective distribution of benefits.
(8) Subsidiary measures should be integrated into the protection, like organs competent for alternative dispute measures; see above.

(9) At the international level, e.g. in bilateral agreements such as in Panama, a splitting of the protection of the specific forms of TCEs according to their different economic importance or their closeness to classic fields of law is very likely. A distinction between protection and non-protection of the different TCEs based on these elements, however, does not reflect an adequate protection of TCEs. Thus, to avoid this splitting, a multilateral agreement covering TCE in general in a sui generis manner covering—as far as possible—the whole content of the expressions is of great importance. Accordingly, the important role of WIPO should be emphasized.

(10) The effectiveness of any regime, finally, depends upon the capacity, economic resources and personal engagement of the right holders and staff of the competent national authority involved.

Section 2. Brazil: A Cultural-Law Approach and Further Discussions

Another interesting example of dealing with TCEs at the national level is the situation in Brazil, as regards both the factual and the legal level.

At the factual level, Brazil represents diversity *par excellence*: it is a huge country and home to a wide variety of different cultural backgrounds and traditional communities. Brazil has a unique position among the Latin American countries, as this amount of socio-cultural diversity is found nowhere else. At the legal level, Brazil follows a cultural approach (so far), which even international experts describe as a new legislation that "opens ways which could be useful as an inspiration for the whole international community," especially in order to safeguard a vital diversity.[429]

The latter aspect—cultural legislation aiming at the safeguarding of cultural diversity as a whole—is at the same time the crux of question of protecting TCEs in particular, as we will see below.[430] To adequately illustrate the situation of TCE protection in Brazil and its international effects, the following section describes cultural legislation, focussing on the aspects relevant to TCEs, on the one hand. On the other hand, the section addresses the legal framework of a future protection of TCEs and intensive Brazilian discussion on TCEs beyond this area of cultural law.

This broader picture of a special Latin American national situation regarding the protection of TCEs is also very useful for better understanding the dynamics and

[429] Laurent Lévi-Strauss (2006) 81, translation by the author. Laurent Lévi-Strauss is Deputy Director for the Division of Cultural Heritage, Chief of Section for Tangible Heritage at UNESCO, Paris, and supported the preparation of the respective Brazilian Decree No. 3.551 by, among other things, participating in the international seminar elaborating the *Carta de Fortaleza* in Brazil in 1997, which is regarded to be one of the initiating factors of Decree 3.551, *see* at Section 2.C.II.1. below.

[430] *See* at Section 2.C. below.

negotiating positions at the international level, be it at WIPO or at WTO. Brazil, in this case, is an interesting and—in the international dimension—important example.

At the Brazilian national level, there also exist active discussions and even specific regulations on a decree-level, particularly on collective personality rights (*direito do imagem indígena*), which address aspects of the holistic approach in protecting TCEs. At the same time, they also cover other aspects besides what is concretely understood by TCEs ("expressions") and will therefore not be treated in detail here.[431]

A. *Some General Facts*

I. "Sociodiversity"

According to official data of UNEP, Brazil is one of the 17 megadiverse countries in the world.[432] It possesses a similarly high level of "sociodiversity," i.e. diversity in culture and different ethnic groups in the society.[433] Although the indigenous population in comparison to the whole population of Brazil is quite low, the communities are very diverse. There exist around 220 different tribes,[434] speaking around 180 different languages—which is by far the highest degree of linguistic diversity in Latin America.[435]

The socio-cultural realities of the identified ethnies vary extremely, as Kayser shows,[436] mainly with regard to three different aspects:

- the amount of the ethnies' members—which varies between only 200 (in case of the Zóé) and 35,000 (in case of the Guaraní)[437];

[431] For the discussions *see* Busch (2010) 215 *et seq.*, and for general comments and further reading *see* at Section 2.D.II. below.

[432] *See* http://www.unep.org/geo/geo4/media/fact_sheets/Fact_Sheet_11_LAC.pdf, last visited November 2, 2010. For further aspects in relation to biodiversity and environment in Latin America *see* at Chapter II Section 3.B.I. above.

[433] Studies by ISA, the "Instituto Socioambiental", http://www.socioambiental.org/prg/pib.shtm#enciclop, last visited November 2, 2010.

[434] Although official numbers are very difficult to obtain, serious sources of reference are the studies conducted by ISA, the "Instituto Socioambiental". A study in 2000 documented 216 ethnies with a total number of 345,000 to 500,000 members, *see* Kayser (2005) 36, while the encyclopedia itself even documents 227 different ethnies. *See* http://www.socioambiental.org/prg/pib.shtm#enciclop, last visited November 2, 2010.

[435] Kayser (2005) 61 note 46.

[436] *Id.* 36.

[437] *Ibid.*

- the stage of acculturation and the extension of the settlements[438]—there are communities having only first contacts with the national "civilization" and others completely "integrated,"[439] and
- the geographic situation, having a fundamental impact on daily living conditions and socio-cultural structures—there are tribes widely spread over the Amazon forests and riversides and others living in villages (*aldeias*), or even in urban areas.[440]

Within these differences, there are some commonalities at the national level. The indigenous communities have own organizations, particular policies, and activities (as for example the *Premio Culturas Indígenas*),[441] as well as special legislation.[442] Besides, the public National Indian Foundation (FUNAI), plays an important role.[443] Therefore, whenever particularities appear beyond general regulations and policies including all groupings, the focus here will be placed on indigenous populations.

Another Brazilian specialty compared to most of the other Latin American countries is the existence of the *quilombolas*, particular traditional communities of African descent, who—at least for the purposes of demarcation law—are determined by means of self-identification.[444] Although there are Afro-Latin-Americans in several other countries, especially in Colombia and Ecuador, the situation of the *quilombolas* in Brazil can be considered as somewhat particular, due *inter alia* to historically communal forms of living. As a consequence, in the issue of TCEs, the *Fundação Cultural Palmares*, promoting the *quilombolan* and Afro-Brazilian culture in general,[445] plays an important role in the Brazilian discussion on the topic of TCEs.

---

[438] *Ibid.*

[439] *Id.* 37.

[440] *Ibid.*

[441] Ministério da Cultura and SESC SP (2007), Ministério da Cultura and SESC SP (2008).

[442] On the history of the indigenous population and the historical development of the legal status, *see* Kayser (2005) 111-198.

[443] *Fundação Nacional do Índio,* which is part of the Brazilian Ministry of Justice. For details *see* http://www.funai.gov.br/, last visited December 5, 2010 and on the particular role of FUNAI *see* at Section 2.B.II. below.

[444] Article 2 of the Decree No. 4,887 of November 20, 2003 stipulates: "Consideram-se remanescentes das comunidades dos quilombos, para os fins deste Decreto, os grupos étnico-raciais, segundo critérios de auto-atribuição, com trajetória histórica própria, dotados de relações territoriais específicas, com presunção de ancestralidade negra relacionada com a resistência à opressão histórica sofrida. § 1° Para os fins deste Decreto, a caracterização dos remanescentes das comunidades dos quilombos será atestada mediante autodefinição da própria comunidade." For further details on the criteria of self-determination and case law thereon, *see* http://www.cpisp.org.br/acoes/html/jurisprudencia.aspx?LinkID=64, last visited November 2, 2010.

[445] As a consequence of Article 215 of the 1988 Brazilian Constitution (on this *see* the following paragraphs of this Section), the foundation formulates and implements public policies that have the objective of enabling the participation of the Brazilian Afro-population within the cultural development process, considering their historical and cultural background. It is a public entity

II. Economy and Environment

Besides its natural beauty and socio-cultural richness, Brazil is also described as "a place of misery where 17% of homes do not have running water," and "a place of environmental devastation that government is powerless to stop," as a special feature in the Economist states.[446] Oil spills and elevated oil pollution from refineries off the coast of Brazil are a serious problem.[447] Ironically, Petrobras, the biggest national oil company, is the one of the major sponsors and patrons, financially supporting official and non-governmental cultural activities in Brazil, as a patron of the "National Indigenous Cultures Award."[448] According to UNEP, the country also continues to face (halting) deforestation.[449] As mentioned above, the road just constructed across the Amazon region, starting/ending in Manaus, also affects a great part of the Brazilian rainforest.[450]

These two aspects, poverty and environmental devastation, are the biggest threats to TCEs and to indigenous peoples in Brazil in general, apart from persistent racial discrimination. While the Brazilian government supports exploitive projects on hydroelectric energy, and agriculture like soy plantations, other entities, mainly NGOs or private persons, move in more protectionist directions.[451] As regards the economic situation of indigenous peoples, similar facts can be found to those in other Latin American countries, although, again, the situations vary from community to community. This variation is mainly due to different intensities of acculturation policies and missionary work in former times.[452]

---

linked to the Ministry of Culture and instituted by the Federal Law No. 7,688 of August 22, 1988, having approved its Statute by Decree No. 418 of January 10, 1992. *See* http://www.palmares.gov.br/, last visited November 2, 2010.

[446] The Economist (Nov 14-20, 2009) 18.

[447] *See* http://www.unep.org/geo/geo4/media/fact_sheets/Fact_Sheet_11_LAC.pdf, last visited November 2, 2010.

[448] Patronage of Petrobras for the annual "Indigenous Cultures Award", *see* Ministério da Cultura and SESC SP, "Prêmio Culturas Indígenas" (2007) and Ministério da Cultura and SESC SP, "Prêmio Culturas Indígenas, Edição Xincão Xukuru" (2008). Financial support was given *e.g.* for the publication of the book Iepé – Instituto de Pesquisa e Formação em Educação Indígena/ Dominique Tilkin Gallois (org.), "Patrimôno Cultural Imaterial e Povos Indígenas – Exemplos no Amapá e norte do Pará" (2006). This financial support is also due to the cultural fee, constituting a certain percentage of the income of Brazilian companies; personal communication with Marcelo Manzatti, Secretariat for Cultural Identity and Diversity within the Ministry of Culture, on March 25, 2009 in Brasilia. *See* also Article 216, para. 6, of the Brazilian Constitution, which stipulates that "the States and the Federal District may allocate up to five tenths percent of their net tax proceedings to a State fund for fomenting culture, it being prohibited the use of these funds to pay for: I – expenses with salaries and social duties; II – interests of debts; III – any other current expense not directly linked to the investments or activities supported."

[449] UNEP – United Nations Environment Programme (2010) 1.

[450] On the construction project, *see* at Chapter II Section 3.B.I. above.

[451] For example, Erwin Kräutler, internationally respected bishop, was awarded the "Alternative Nobel Prize" in 2010, *see* Süddeutsche Zeitung (December 7, 2010).

[452] On these aspects *see* at Chapter II Section 3.B.II.2. above.

B. General Legal Framework

The protection of TCEs in Brazil is framed by constitutional and other provisions touching on the topic of TCEs, particularly of indigenous peoples.

I. Constitutional Framework

The current Brazilian Constitution was enacted in 1988.[453] At that time, it was rated a big step, Kayser argues, as regards

- the constitutional acknowledgement of the country's cultural diversity and
- the constitutionally anchored obligations of the state to protect the "different" indigenous cultures and thereby to establish special rights based upon a certain ethnic status.[454]

The 1988 Brazilian Constitution marked a constitutional change from an integrationist policy of the foregoing decades, even centuries, anchored in Article 8 para. 18 of the 1967 Constitution to a (formal) recognition of indigenous peoples' rights to their own culture. The 1967 Constitution still regarded the indigenous population as "wildes" and ruled on the "integration of the savages into the national society."[455]

One important reason for this change was, according to Kayser, the new anthropological theory of cultural relativity, provoking a national demand for permanent legal recognition and respect of indigenous cultures.[456]

There was a general movement towards constitutional acknowledgements of indigenous rights in the constitutions drafted in the 1980s in several Latin American countries.[457] However, no other constitution contained provisions as far-reaching as those in Brazil with regard to indigenous cultures, Kayser argues.[458] Later, even more progressive and detailed rights were contained in the 1992 Constitution of the neighboring country Paraguay.[459]

---

[453] Constitution of the Federative Republic of Brazil of 1998.

[454] Kayser (2005) 249.

[455] Article 8, para. 18, of the 1967 Constitution.

[456] Kayser (2005) 241. According to *ibid*, early proponents of this theory were the French Anthropologist Claude Lévi-Strauss, who did the majority of his research in Brazil, and the Brazilian Anthropologists and brothers Orlando and Cláudio Villas Bôas, who have been nominated for the Nobel Peace Prize in 1961 for having established the first Indigenous National Park (Xingu) in Brazil.

[457] *See* at Chapter III Section 3.A. above.

[458] Kayser (2005) 250, 254.

[459] The Paraguayan Constitution even declared the country *expressis verbis* as a pluri-cultural state at the very early stage in 1992 already, *see* Article 140, para. 1. It also contains very detailed Articles acknowledging the ethnic identity, indigenous habits, political, social, economic, cultural, and religious organizations, as well as the application of customary law in internal disputes, and

In Brazil, a more detailed conception on the diversity of Brazilian cultures and the cultural patrimony was then added to the Constitution in this new millennium.[460]

Concretely, the Constitution contains several provisions of relevance for the topic of TCEs, dealing with both traditional communities and cultural patrimony.

1. Indigenous Rights and Policies Relevant to TCEs

The general conception of the treatment of indigenous communities includes reference to and (limited) acknowledgement of customs, traditions, and property rights: "The Indians shall be accorded recognition of their social organisation, *customs*, languages and *traditions,* and the original rights in the lands that they occupy by tradition, it being the responsibility of the Union to demarcate them, protect them, and ensure respect for *all their property*."[461]

2. Cultural Rights and Policies Relevant to TCEs

a. The Concept of Cultural Patrimony

The constitutional concept of the Brazilian cultural patrimony is defined by the interaction of the two Articles 215 and 216.[462] According to this concept, the cultural patrimony covers material and immaterial goods,[463] and expressly includes

---

the consideration of indigenous customary law in regular legal actions, Article 63 of the Constitution. For other aspects *see* Articles 62–67, 77 of the Paraguayan Constitution. Besides, the later Venezuelan Constitution of 1999 embraces a wide-range of indigenous cultural rights in a directly applicable form, *see* Articles 119–126, and at Chapter III Section 3.A. above.

[460] *See* at Section 2.B.I.2.a. below.

[461] Article 231 of the Constitution. Emphasis added by the author. The translation is according to WIPO DOC WIPO/GRTKF/IC/1/5.

[462] Translation by http://www.v-brazil.com/government/laws/titleVIII.html, last visited January 27, 2010.

[463] Article 216 of the Constitution. The complete provision and concept read as follows: "The Brazilian cultural heritage consists of the assets of a material and immaterial nature, taken individually or as a whole, which bear reference to the identity, action and memory of the various groups that form the Brazilian society, therein included: I – forms of expression; II – ways of creating, making and living; III – scientific, artistic and technological creations; IV – works, objects, documents, buildings and other spaces intended for artistic and cultural expressions; V – urban complexes and sites of historical, natural, artistic, archaeological, paleontological, ecological and scientific value. *Paragraph 1* – The Government shall, with the cooperation of the community, promote and protect the Brazilian cultural heritage, by means of inventories, registers, vigilance, monument protection decrees, expropriation and other forms of precaution and preservation. *Paragraph 2* – It is incumbent upon the Government, in accordance with the law, to manage the keeping of the governmental documents and to make them available for consultation to whomever may need to do so. *Paragraph 3* – The law shall establish incentives for the production and knowledge of cultural assets and values. *Paragraph 4* – Damages and threats to

TCEs: "The State shall protect the *expressions of popular, Indian, and Afro-Brazilian cultures*, as well as those of other groups participating in the national civilization process."[464]

"Protection" thereby encompasses the fostering of "appreciation and diffusion of cultural expressions," promotion and protection "by means of inventories, registers," and "other forms of precaution and preservation," and the mandate to establish a detailed "National Plan of Culture" which is intended to lead to the "valorization of ethnical and regional diversity," including a concrete type of funding.[465]

This concept of cultural patrimony and its protection laid down in Articles 215 and 216 is rooted in a developing acknowledgement of the important role cultural expressions play in the socio-cultural identity in Brazil. This recognition began in the 1930s and resurged in the 1970s.[466] Despite the long history constituting the background of the main concept, some relevant paragraphs have been introduced or revised only within the last couple of years.[467]

b. Connection Between the Constitutional Concept and National Cultural Law

The connection between the constitutional provisions on the one hand and simple cultural legislation linked with factual action dealing with cultural patrimony on the

---

the cultural heritage shall be punished in accordance with the law. *Paragraph 5* – All documents and sites bearing historical reminiscence to the ancient communities of runaway slaves are protected as national heritage. *Paragraph 6* – The States and the Federal District may allocate up to five tenths percent of their net tax proceedings to a State fund for fomenting culture, it being prohibited the use of these funds to pay for: I – expenses with salaries and social duties; II – interests of debts; III – any other current expense not directly linked to the investments or activities supported." Paragraph 6 was added by CA 19, December 19, 2003. Translation according to http://www.v-brazil.com/government/laws/titleVIII.html, last visited January 27, 2010.

[464] Para. 1 of Article 215 of the 1988 Constitution. Emphasis added by the author. The article fully stipulates: "The state shall ensure to all the full exercise of the cultural rights and access to the sources of national culture and shall support and foster the appreciation and diffusion of cultural expressions. *Paragraph 1* – The State shall protect the expressions of popular, Indian and Afro-Brazilian cultures, as well as those of other groups participating in the national civilization process. *Paragraph 2* – The law shall provide for the establishment of commemorative dates of high significance for the various national ethnic segments. *Paragraph 3* – The state shall establish the National Plan of Culture, with a plurianual duration, aiming at the cultural development of the Country and at the integration of the actions by the Public Power which lead to: I – defense and valorization of the Brazilian Cultural Heritage; II – production, promotion and diffusion of culture; III – formation of qualified personnel for the management of Culture in their multiple dimensions; IV – democratization of access to culture; V – valorization of ethnical and regional diversity." Paragraph 3 was added by CA 48, August 10, 2005. Translation according to http://www.v-brazil.com/government/laws/titleVIII.html, last visited January 27, 2010.

[465] Articles 215 and 216 of the Constitution. *See* the foregoing two footnotes.

[466] Sant' Anna (2006 II) 15; for details *see* at Section 2.C.I. below.

[467] They were inserted by the 42nd and 48th amendments of the Constitution in 2003 and 2005, respectively. *See* http://www.planalto.gov.br/ccivil_03/Constituicao/Constitui%E7ao.htm, last visited January 27, 2010.

other, is characterized by a mutual influence. At the legal level, the principle of hierarchy of norms[468] is also acknowledged in the Brazilian legal system, where it is called the *princípio da supremacia da constituição.*[469]

The definition of "Brazilian cultural patrimony" contained in Article 216 was in the end also the one chosen as the *terminus technicus* used in the most important legislative institution here, the Decree No. 3551.[470] In view of the principle of constitutional supremacy just mentioned, it might come as a surprise that there has been heated discussion about taking over the constitutional definition, and that it was not simply understood as an imperative. In the end, however, the definition of Article 216 was adopted at the lower level of the Decree, which is why the problem has not gained practical relevance.

c. Predispositions for and Influence on a Future Regulation on TCEs

With regard to a future protection of TCEs, but also to the current factual treatment of TCEs, analysis of the constitutional provisions allows some guiding observations. These are:

(1) The concept of protection is elaborated in a quite detailed manner at the constitutional level and thereby reveals an incipient, active development in the area of cultural law—at least on paper.
(2) TCEs understood as "expressions of popular, Indian, and Afro-Brazilian cultures" are regarded as belonging to the Brazilian cultural patrimony. This, however, does not necessarily imply an allocation of TCEs within the "public domain" in the area of private law, i.e. copyright law.[471]

---

[468] This principle of "Normenhierachie" is also predominant in German law, for instance.

[469] For the "Princípio da supremacia da constiutição" in special relation to indigenous law, i.e. the 1973 Indian Statute in Brazil, *see* Kayser (2005) 250. It stipulates that constitutional provisions are superior to all other legislative or administrative acts. The latter must therefore be in accordance with the constitutional provisions. In case of contradicting or diverging legal concepts, the constitutional provisions prevail over differing regular laws, i.e. the latter norms are void. Expressed as a rule, it states "lex superior derogat legi inferiori" – the higher-ranking law repeals the lower-ranking law. Consequently, as regards the discussions on a concept and definition of cultural patrimony within the preparatory work on Decree 3.551, one would assume that the legislature, or, in this case, administrative entity would not knowingly bear the risk of provoking a case of normative conflict, but rather directly take over the constitutional definition of the concept of cultural patrimony. It remains unclear whether preparatory entities thought of this aspect when entering into the detailed discussions on a definition, or defined the normative relationship somewhat differently.

[470] Article 1 of the Decree 3551. On the foregoing intensive discussions, *see*: Sant' Anna (2006 II) 17. On the Decree in general, *see* at Section 2.C. below.

[471] *See* at Section 2.B.IV.2. below. Similarly, traditional knowledge on genetic resources is regarded to be part of the "Brazilian cultural patrimony" and at the same time object to specific rights of indigenous and local communities to a "prior informed consent," *see* Article 8 of the MP 2186-16.

(3) The addressee of protection by means of cultural law within the constitutional framework is the Brazilian state, rather than any subjects of private law.
(4) Due to the late implementation of the concept of the intangible cultural patrimony in administrative legal instruments,[472] practical experiences with the framework on cultural legislation are relatively new.
(5) In view of the "progressive" constitutional concept of promoting cultural diversity, derogating the former integrationist policy, the protection of indigenous cultural expressions and acknowledgement of indigenous "customary" law in the existing indigenous legislation has been regarded as insufficient. Negotiations on these aspects within the broader framework of a new law on indigenous communities are taking place—in a very slow mode, however.

II. The Former Article 6 of the Civil Code, Legal and Jurisdictional Representation

Until only recently, in 2003, the "Savages", as the indigenous peoples were called even legally,[473] were considered legally incompetent in relation to certain acts[474] or the method of conducting them,[475] according to the Brazilian Civil Code.[476]

This legal finding raises the question: how can indigenous peoples in Brazil legally be able to give prior informed consent if they are not legally competent? As the relevant Article was only reformed in 2003, this was an important question indeed—though barely considered—in international discussions. While today, this legal aspect need not be discussed anymore, at least for the situation in Brazil, it is still interesting to note, and of practical influence today, that the guardianship required for non-integrated Indians[477] and executed by the FUNAI is still contained in Articles 7 *et seq.* of the current *Estatuto do Índio*, the Indian Statute. Thus, this background knowledge on the former Article 6 of the Civil Code is necessary to understand the regulations contained in the Brazilian Indian Statute, as well as the practical effect of the relationship between FUNAI and the indigenous communities.

In general, according to Stavenhagen, FUNAI played a contentious role in the history of the Brazilian Indians in the second half of the twentieth century.[478] FUNAI is not a representative of indigenous interests set up by indigenous peoples

[472] On this *see* at Section 2.B.I.2. above and C.I. *et seq.* below.

[473] On the terminology *see* at Chapter II Section 1.B.II.1.a. above.

[474] These acts were defined further in Article 147, para. 1, of the Civil Code.

[475] Article 6, No. III, of the former Brazilian Civil Code, printed in Portuguese *e.g.* in Kayser (2005) 601. On details of the background and genesis of the provision *see* Kayser (2005) 317 *seq.*

[476] Law No. 3.071 of January 1, 1916.

[477] On the different categories contained also in the Indian Statute *see* at Chapter II Section 3.B. II.2.b. above.

[478] Stavenhagen (1988) 254 *seq.*

themselves, but institutionalized by the State. In accordance with Article 8, para. 18, of the 1967 Constitution, its former task was to socio-culturally integrate the "wild" peoples. Today, it serves as a supportive institution. It is still not elected or established by indigenous communities themselves to represent indigenous interests, policies, or rights. Apart from the question of a legitimate representation, also the role of a supporter might have downsides: it bears the risk of creating dependencies, as over the past decades, the indigenous people have become used to external support.

Another Brazilian particularity of practical relevance is worth noting: According to Article 129 para. 5 of the Brazilian Constitution, the indigenous peoples shall still be represented by, and their rights defended before court by the Ministry of the Public.

It becomes evident that both, FUNAI and the Ministry of the Public, especially the sixth Chamber, play an important role in the development of indigenous rights in the country.

III. Indigenous Legal Framework: The Indian Statute and Proposals on a Reform with Relation to TCEs

1. General Aspects

As regards a future protection of TCEs, there are some framing provisions of relevance contained in the Brazilian Indian Statute.[479] Those are particularly such on cultural rights and customary law.

Due to the rights and concepts laid down in the 1988 Constitution, parts of the Indian Statute are no longer in line with the constitutional conceptions. It "was felt necessary"—as the officials formulate it—that the Indian Statute should be revised in order to make it compatible with the new Constitution, as mentioned before.[480] Currently, as a consequence of the afore-mentioned principle of hierarchy of norms,[481] various articles of the Indian Statute are regarded as invalid by different Brazilian authors. The concrete extent to which the Statutes' articles are now invalid is disputed. Here, only the aspects touching TCEs will be dealt with, within the context of the corresponding regulation.

---

[479] Law No. 6001 of December 19, 1973, the *Estatuto do Índio*, available at http://www.funai.gov.br/quem/legislacao/estatuto_indio.html, last visited January 28, 2010.

[480] Presidência da República Federativa do Brasil (1996).

[481] On the *princípio da supremacia da constituição, see* at Section 2.B.I.2.b. above.

2. The Current Indian Statute on TCEs

a. Cultural Rights

In general, "respect" is "ensured" by the Statute for the cultural heritage, artistic values, and expressions of the indigenous peoples.[482]

More particularly, although not located in the section on culture but in the one on sanctions, Article 58 of the Statute defines certain actions that offend indigenous culture as crimes against "the Indians and the indigenous culture." These are, first, mocking indigenous cultural ceremonies, rituals, uses, customs, or indigenous cultural traditions,[483] disparaging them or disturbing, in whatever way, their practice; second, the use of Indians or the indigenous community as objects of touristic advertising or in exhibitions for commercial aims. The first action is punishable with imprisonment from 1 to 3 months, the second with imprisonment from 2 to 6 months.

This provision seems to be very helpful at least on paper, indeed at least answering some of the indigenous needs and claims. In the Brazilian practice, however, the mere existence of Article 58 has not brought along great changes, as the official indigenous policy reveals. Moreover, in light of the new constitutional Articles 231 and 216, Article 58 has been argued to contradict the Constitution and thus to be invalid.[484]

Another interesting aspect of the Indian Statute regarding indigenous culture is the legally anchored promotion of indigenous handicrafts, an aspect that will be taken up again in the context of harnessing TCEs for development and trade below.[485]

b. Customary Law

Similar to Article 231 of the Constitution, the Indian Statute of 1973 already legally "respects" the uses, customs, and traditions of indigenous communities and their effectiveness within family and inheritance affairs, the property regime, and dealings between indigenous peoples.[486]

Article 57 of the Indian Statute stipulates that the application of penal or disciplinary sanctions by the tribal groups, in accordance with their own

[482] Article 47 of the 1973 Indian Statute.

[483] "Article 58. Constituem crimes contra os índios e a cultura indígena: I – escarnecer de cerimônia, rito, uso, costumes ou tradição culturais indígenas, vilipendiá-los ou perturbar, de qualquer modo, a sua prática. Pena – detenção de um a três meses; II – utilizar o índio ou comunidade indígena como objeto de propaganda turística ou de exibição para fins lucrativos. Pena – detenção de dois a seis meses..."

[484] Kayser (2005) 368.

[485] *See* at Section 2.D.IV. below.

[486] Article 6 of Law No. 6001. On the relevance of this provision for the recognition of customary law as regards protecting TCEs *see* at Chapter II Section 5.E.II.3.b. above.

institutions, "is tolerated," as long as they are not of a cruel or discreditable nature. The death penalty is prohibited in any case.[487]

The provision does not apply to cases involving people not belonging to the indigenous community.

Article 57 of the Indian Statute might seem progressive at first glance. However, it may be criticized in two regards:

- Its main aim is still the integration of the indigenous peoples into the national community: The spirit of the 1973 Law in general as well as the political direction aims at a "progressive and harmonious integration" of indigenous peoples into the "national community."[488] Their cultural values, traditions, uses, and customs should (only) be respected "within this process of integration of the Indian into the national community."[489] This clearly contradicts the new Article 231 of the Constitution, which substituted the political aim of integration with the permanent recognition of different indigenous cultures.
- "Respect" for the cultural values, traditions, uses, and customs might be too vage to effectively implement a protection of the different cultures according to Article 231 of the Constitution.

Kayser even goes further[490] and argues the application of customary law should not only be respected or "tolerated," as Article 57 of the Indian Statute states, but must be "acknowledged as indigenous law" due to Article 231 of the Constitution.[491] Indigenous customary law would constitute an integral part of the indigenous culture—therefore, Article 231 of the Constitution would also cover the acknowledgment of the "legal system" of the indigenous peoples.

This latter point of view, however, might currently not constitute the prevalent opinion in the country.

c. Collective Property

The Indian Statute of 1973 recognizes collective holding of property rights of indigenous peoples. In particular, it stipulates that the owners of indigenous goods, property, and income is the indigenous population of the country, without differentiating between any individuals or tribal groups. As regards the usufruct of territory belonging to or occupied exclusively by one tribal group or determined indigenous community, the property belongs to them. Finally, with relation to acquired titles on certain immovable or movable goods, the holder of the collective right is the tribal group or indigenous community named in the property title.[492]

[487] Article 57 of the Indian Statute/Law No. 6001.

[488] Article 1 of Law No. 6001.

[489] Article 2 para 6 of Law No. 6001.

[490] Kayser (2005) 333.

[491] *Id.* 335, translation by the author.

[492] Article 40 of the Indian Statute.

Certain goods like personal belongings, an individual's house, and goods for living, are excluded from this type of "indigenous property."[493]

What is remarkable about this provision is that the administration of the indigenous property falls to the FUNAI. In the case of goods owned by certain Indians or indigenous communities, their participation shall be endorsed. Only in the case that these Indians have shown their effective capability of administering their goods themselves, will they be entrusted to do so.[494]

3. Discussions on a Reformed Indian Statute on TCEs

Since the adoption of the "new" Constitution in 1988, there was a "need to revise the Indian Statute in order to make it compatible with the new Constitution".[495] With this intent, three draft laws had been introduced in the Chamber of Deputies *(Câmera de Deputados)* since the beginning of the legislative procedure, in 1992.[496] So far, no new legislation has been passed. Currently, the process stands at the stage of awaiting approval by the National Congress and negotiations seem to be at a crunch, although no quick solution is to be expected.[497] According to Kayser, the most crucial point of discussion concerns the scope of rights of third parties regarding the exploitation of natural resources within indigenous territories.[498]

With regard to TCEs, it is interesting to note that the first draft from 1991 not only aims at a better adaptation to the new Constitution,[499] but goes even further: While neither the Constitution nor the 1973 Indian Statute addresses the intellectual property rights of indigenous peoples, the 1991 draft contains one entire chapter dealing with the intellectual property of indigenous peoples, guided by the main idea that "the indigenous knowledge and utility or industrial models should only be used commercially or industrially with the consent of the indigenous communities and for their benefit."[500] The project also addresses the issue of cultural diversity and patrimony, following the idea that the Indians should be attributed their own patrimony, recognized as the "exclusive good of each community, so that their earnings can guarantee the sustainability and development of the indigenous economy, in conformity with their own cultural patterns."[501] These ideas are laid down

[493] For details *see* Article 41 of the Indian Statute.

[494] Article 42 of the Indian Statute.

[495] Presidência da República Federativa do Brasil (1996).

[496] *Ibid.*

[497] Personal communication with José Carlos Levinho, Director of the *Museu do Índio*, Indigenous Museum, and member of the commission on elaborating a legislative proposal of a new law, on March 16, 2009, in Rio de Janeiro. The current version of the proposal is not for official use yet.

[498] Kayser (2005) 369.

[499] *Projeto de Lei* No. 2057 of 1991, *see* De Hollanda Sheldrick (2009) 98.

[500] *Supra.*

[501] *Supra.*

in Articles 12 to 19 of the 1991 draft, and if adopted in this manner, they would constitute a real innovation in this area in Brazil.[502]

Currently, both proposals in discussion for a new Statute of Indigenous Communities, the *Estatuto das Sociedades Indígenas*, *inter alia* provide for copyright, protection of traditional knowledge, and the particular question of representation according to indigenous uses and customs.[503]

Whether these rights or even the law project will become reality at all cannot be predicted.[504] Even so, it is questionable whether a single solution with sole focus on indigenous cultural rights would be a good, i.e. durable, one, considering the socio-cultural realities in Brazil. Unlike the project to draft a new indigenous law, the existing legislation on traditional knowledge related to genetic resources and biodiversity also includes local communities,[505] and the constitutional provisions on culture also refer to expressions of popular, Indian, and Afro-Brazilian cultures.[506] Thus, the topic of protecting TCEs has been taken up by organizations representing interests of the Afro-Brazilian community, and has made up the object of discussions at a broader level.[507] Moreover, the legal connection to copyright and the discussion on a copyright reform in Brazil complicate things further.

IV. Relevant Aspects of the Copyright Legislation

To fully display the legal situation and actual discussion framing the current legal situation of TCEs in Brazil, some aspects of the Brazilian copyright law are worth mentioning.

1. The Former Paying Public Domain

During a period of 10 years, from 1973 to 1983, the concept of a paying public domain existed in the Brazilian copyright system.[508] According to De Hollanda

---

[502] With relation to TCEs, the most important provision is Article 19, stipulating that: "the indigenous communities are title holders of copyright over their intellectual works and creations which have been produced in a collective spirit, especially their music, tales and legends."

[503] IPHAN – Instituto do Patrimônio Histórico e Artístico Nacional (2008) 105.

[504] Personal communication with José Carlos Levinho, Director of the *Museu do Índio*, Indigenous Museum, and member of the commission on elaborating a legislative proposal of a new law, on March 16, 2009, in Rio de Janeiro. The current version of the proposal has not been made officially public. For details on the process since 1992 *see* Kayser (2005) 357 *seq.*

[505] Article 8 of the MP 2186-16.

[506] Article 215, para. 1, of the Constitution.

[507] On this *see* at Section 2.D. below.

[508] That was the former Article 93 of Law No. 5988/73, which was revoked by Law 7123 of September 12, 1983 then. It stated: "A utilização, por qualquer forma ou processo que não seja livre, das obras intelectuais pertencentes ao domínio público depende de autorização do Conselho

Sheldrick, it aimed at the "protection of culture" through financial promotion of cultural activities in the country, i.e. by means of a fund which was collected in case of use of a work contained in the public domain.[509] As this concept at the same time limited the free use of the work, the real value of the concept was disputed among scholars.[510] The main point of criticism was, as De Hollanda Sheldrick says, that the Brazilian paying public domain was merely pecuniary in nature and intention, although the legislative policy had the pretext of encompassingly promoting cultural activities in the country.[511]

2. Current Situation

The current Brazilian Copyright Law[512] does not deal with the situation of TCEs explicitly. It indirectly touches TCEs in three ways: in the context of, first, unknown authors, second, "folklore," and third, "traditional knowledge" (below a.– c.). All three aspects are disputed as regards their value in terms of protecting TCEs. But interesting suggestions have also been made in this context in the Brazilian literature on the differentiation between individual and collective holders of rights (below d.).

a. Unknown Authors

Regarding the first point, the copyright law stipulates that if the author of a work cannot exactly be identified, the author would be considered unknown and the work as anonymous; Article 5 para. 7 lit. b). Consequently, the work falls into the public domain until the purported author appears. In the case of the collective authorship of TCEs, Baptista and Valle argue, a thus legitimized individual author will hardly come forward to claim individual authorship, and the work will remain "anonymous" and therefore unprotected by copyright.[513]

b. Folklore

Some voices in Brazil tend to regard TCEs or indigenous art as being "works of folklore" and therefore as part of the public domain. According to this point of

---

Nacional de Direito Autoral. – Parágrafo único. Se a utilização visar a lucro, deverá ser recolhida ao Conselho Nacional de Direito Autoral importância correspondente a cinqüenta por cento da que caberia ao autor da obra, salvo se se destinar a fins didáticos, caso em que essa percentagem se reduzirá a dez por cento." Article 120 then stipulated: "Integrarão o Fundo de Direito Autoral: I – o produto da autorização para a utilização de obras pertenecentes ao domínio público."

509 De Hollanda Sheldrick (2009) 74 with further references, translation by the author.

510 *See id.* 74 *seq.* for details on diverging views.

511 *Id.* 78.

512 Law No. 9610 of February 19, 1998.

513 Baptista and Valle (2004) 19.

view, folklore should be understood as "the sum of traditions, knowledge, and beliefs of a popular character, expressions in proverbs, tales, or songs" whose source is unknown.[514]

This conclusion has been rejected by others, for mainly four reasons:

The first reason is similar to an internationally known argument, namely, that there is a difference between the works of folklore as described above and TCEs: Contrary to the works of folklore, the "derivative works"[515] from the indigenous artistic heritage do have an identifiable source, which is however simply not individual, but collective.[516]

Second, this view would result in what one could describe as an "unbearable practical outcome."[517] Baptista and Valle argue that it would not be "legally reasonable" to claim that indigenous peoples do not have rights in their artistic creations, or that these creations should remain unprotected. If the indigenous patrimony could be appropriated liberally, without any kind of authorization, its significance could be unduly altered and its holiness disrespected.[518]

The third reason relates to the principle of interpreting statutes in accordance with constitutional precepts and values,[519] an idea that is derived from the principle of the supremacy of the constitution, as introduced above. Baptista and Valle argue that the Brazilian Constitution guarantees the indigenous peoples rights in their material and immaterial patrimony, and that a simple copyright law provision could not impede this constitutional protection.[520] According to Articles 215, 231, the Brazilian state is obliged to protect goods of a collective nature and of the indigenous artistic patrimony as part of the indigenous customs and traditions.[521] Thus, also copyright law would have to be interpreted as enabling this constitutional protection.[522]

Fourth, and finally, Article 45 para. 2 of the copyright law itself expressly exempts ethnic and traditional knowledge from belonging to the public domain.

---

[514] Lisboa (2001) 58, translation by the author.

[515] "(O)bras derivadas" – The scholars do not differentiate between the legal category of works and derivative works here. On this distinction with relation to TCEs in Latin America in general, especially in distinction to works merely "inspired" by TCEs or folklore, *see* Antequera Parilli (2007) 516 *seq.*

[516] Baptista and Valle (2004) 20.

[517] *Id.* 19, translation by the author.

[518] *Id.* 19, translation by the author.

[519] "Verfassungskonforme Auslegung" in German law.

[520] Baptista and Valle (2004) 19, translation by the author.

[521] Article 231 states "(t)he Indians shall be accorded recognition of their social organisation, customs, languages and traditions and the original rights in the lands that they occupy by tradition, it being the responsibility of the Union to demarcate them, protect them and ensure respect for all their property," translation according to WIPO DOC WIPO/GRTKF/IC/1/5, and para 1 of Article 215: "(t)he State shall protect the expressions of popular, Indian and Afro-Brazilian cultures, as well as those of other groups participating in the national civilization process."

[522] *Id.* 20.

This knowledge thus falls within the scope of copyright protection. With regard to TCEs, Baptista and Valle therefore argue that "the indigenous peoples can rely on the provisions of this law to protect their works of a collective character."[523]

c. Traditional Knowledge, Article 45 Para. 2

Article 45 para. 2 reads:

> In addition to the works in respect of which the protection of the economic rights has expired, the following shall pass into the public domain: (...)
> II. the works of unknown authors, subject to the legal protection of ethnic and traditional knowledge.[524]

Some commentators interpret the wording "traditional knowledge" in the Law to mean that the Law also protects TCEs, or at least employ it to plead in favor of some form of protection.[525] Contrary opinions in Brazil argue that Article 45 para. 2 is rather erroneous and does not contain a statement one way or the other. It was inserted when the Provisional Act No. 2186-16 of 2001 on traditional knowledge associated with genetic resources and biodiversity, which will be presented below,[526] was adopted in order to avoid potential conflicts between the Copyright Law and the Provisional Act. However, traditional knowledge does not constitute a "work" at all and is thus not even covered by copyright to begin with, so a conflict in this respect would not occur.[527]

d. Protection by Copyright: Differentiation of Individual Authorship from Collectivity

Regardless of whether the copyright legislation, and mainly the three points of discussion shown above, is interpreted in one way or the other, it does not expressly entail protection of TCEs.

Nonetheless, the differentiation between individual and collective authorship is of interest as concerns TCEs. The dichotomy of individual and collective status is not as strict as it might appear at first glance.

First of all, there might be artists belonging to an indigenous community which are individual authors of individual works, which then are protected by copyright. Brazilian authors require, however, that the works of such individuals should have "no direct or immediate causal connection with the culture of their community."[528] Such strict legal differentiation may constitute a challenge in practice. In turn, there

---

[523] *Ibid.*, translation by the author.

[524] Translation by WIPO.

[525] *Id.* 20 (2004).

[526] *See* at Section 2.D.I. below.

[527] Personal communication with Marcos Alves de Souza, Head of the Brazilian General Coordination of Copyright, Ministry of Culture, in March 2009, in Brasilia.

[528] Baptista and Valle (2004) 21.

may also be situations, in which "the collective appropriates an originally individual creation", Brazilian authors admit: the group starts to use the individual creation as a collective cultural expression, and the individual author recognizes the collective ownership.[529] Baptista and Valle say examples are some songs of the Xavante Indians: An individual would invent a song or a melody, present it to the group, and then it is sung by the whole group or community in a genuine collective performance.[530]

The overall legal question is how to determine the parameters for identifying collective ownership. Based upon the use of anthropological experiences, Brazilian voices tend to argue in favor of what could be characterized as (1) customary law, (2) local law, or (3) a similarly emic approach.[531]

Following any such approach, Baptista and Valle have suggested the following guiding criterion for identifying the collective nature of a work:

- The works "original conception" derives from a collective artistic creation, which "is characterized by generally uniform or similar aesthetic parameters acknowledged by the indigenous collective", and
- it "has not suffered a relevant alteration in its aesthetic aspects when being concretized by an individual."[532]

It becomes clear that the differentiation between collective or individual ownership in practice might be quite difficult and pretty much depend upon the particularities of each single case. Moreover, even when a work is characterized as collective expression, the answer of what special legal protection this work may enjoy in the area of copyright or beyond has not been found in Brazil yet.

3. Reform of the Brazilian Copyright Law

Currently, there are national discussions on a reform of the Brazilian Copyright legislation. In how far such a reform would concretely effect the topic of TCEs cannot be predicted at this stage. Considering the position of the General Coordination of Copyright expressed in the Technical Note of 2007,[533] there could be a great change in the copyright treatment of TCEs, in the end, depending upon the relations of political power. Another issue of scholarly debate is the question of a

---

529 *Id.* 22.

530 *Ibid.*

531 *Id.* 22: "[T]entando aferir se aquela determinada obra, não obstante o grau de inovação individual que uma obra abarque, *é compreendida pelos membros daquela etnia* como algo pertenecente ao patrimônio imaterial coletivo." Emphasis added by the author.

532 *Id.* 22.

533 On the technical note in detail *see* at Section 2.D.II. below.

re-launch of the instrument of the paying public domain, which was previously part of the Brazilian copyright system.[534]

C. Special Focus: Cultural Law on TCEs

So far, particular aspects of Brazilian cultural law are of theoretical but sometimes also practical relevance for the protection of TCEs.

I. Relevant Legal Instruments: An Overview

There exist various pieces of legislation on material and immaterial cultural goods in Brazil.[535] The most recent statutes are inspired by the work of UNESCO: Decree No. 6177 of 2007, for instance, stipulates the execution and implementation of the entire 2005 UNESCO Convention on the Protection and Promotion of the Diversity of Cultural Expressions,[536] approved by the Brazilian National Congress by means of Legislative Decree No. 485 of 2006.[537] Similarly, Decree No. 5.753 of 2006 ratified the 2003 UNESCO Convention for the Safeguarding of the Intangible Cultural Heritage.[538]

These specific Conventions indeed had a strong impact on the further development and implementation of the legal protection of cultural expressions and immaterial heritage. The special section on immaterial cultural patrimony within the respective cultural institution, the IPHAN, for example, was only implemented as a reaction to the adoption of said UNESCO Convention for the Safeguarding of the Intangible Cultural Heritage in 2003.[539]

Nevertheless, the legal bases most relevant for the topic of protecting TCEs by means of cultural law are earlier regulations: Decree Law No. 25 and Decree No. 3551.

As early as 1937, Decree Law No. 25 on the "Protection of the National Historic and Artistic Patrimony" was issued—and still functions today as the basis for the current Brazilian protection of TCEs.[540] This Decree Law provides for the material

---

[534] On the different arguments *see* at Chapter III Section 3.B.IV.4. above. For the progress of the discussions *see* http://www.reformadireitoautoral.org/, last visited January 14, 2011.

[535] For an overview over the different instruments *see* http://www.cultura.gov.br/site/categoria/legislacao/, last visited February 4, 2010.

[536] Available at http://portal.unesco.org/en/ev.php-URL_ID=31038&URL_DO=DO_TOPIC&URL_SECTION=201.html, last visited February 4, 2010.

[537] Decree No. 6177 of August 1, 2007, available at http://www.planalto.gov.br/ccivil_03/_Ato2007-2010/2007/Decreto/D6177.htm, last visited February 4, 2010.

[538] Available at http://www.unesco.org/culture/ich/index.php?pg=00006, last visited November 2, 2010. For details hereon *see* at Chapter III Section 1.B.II. above.

[539] Personal communication with Ana Gita de Oliveira, Department of Immaterial Patrimony of IPHAN, in March 2009 in Brasilia.

[540] Decreto-Lei No. 25 (1937).

area and institutional framework of the national historic and artistic patrimony. It regulates the former cultural institution "Serviço do Patrimônio Histórico e Artístico Nacional", SPHAN, the direct predecessor of today's Institute of National Historic and Artistic Patrimony, or IPHAN.[541] While in its Article 1, Decree Law No. 25 defines the "national historic and artistic patrimony" as "the entirety of all movable and immovable goods existing in the country," which are, among other things, of exceptional "artistic value," in its scope of subject matter, it only covers the *material* portion of these goods.

The mere theoretical understanding of cultural patrimony as also including immaterial values developed in Brazil later, as Sant' Anna says, i.e. in the 1970s.[542] This new, wider conception of cultural patrimony and the legal protection of it was codified in the Constitution in 1988.[543] However, it was only in 2000, that Decree No. 3551 of 2000 was adopted that provides for concrete protection of the immaterial cultural patrimony.[544]

Interestingly enough, in July 2000, shortly before the enactment of Decree 3551 in August, the President of FUNAI issued a *Portaria*, an administrative decree, establishing the Special Registry (*Cadastro*) on Indigenous Cultural Heritage[545] based upon Articles 215, para. 1, and 231 of the Brazilian Constitution. The concept is quite similar to that of Decree No. 3551, as it also establishes a special catalog or database registering the indigenous cultural patrimony (though in this case not restricted to immaterial goods) as well as a special commission, the *Comissão Deliberativa*, though the latter is not competent for deciding on the registry, but for allaying doubts or solving conflicts resulting from the *Cadastro*.[546] The competent authority administering the *Cadastro* is the *Museu do Índio*, the Indian Museum, located in Rio de Janeiro, or more concretely the Head of the Museum.[547] The scope of application is, in accordance with the limited competence of the FUNAI, limited to administrative acts regarding the indigenous cultural patrimony, and has no influence on property aspects.[548]

II. Main Body of Law on Immaterial Patrimony: Decree No. 3551 of 2000

The special focus here lies on the legislation on immaterial cultural patrimony.

---

541 "Instituto do Patrimômino Histórico e Artístico Nacional", Article 3 para 1 of the Decree.

542 Sant' Anna (2006 I) 9.

543 Article 215 *seq.* of the 1988 Constitution, on this *see* at Section 2.B.I. above.

544 Available at http://www.cultura.gov.br/site/wp-content/uploads/2007/10/decreto-3551.pdf, last visited February 4, 2010.

545 FUNAI Portaria No. 693 of July 19, 2000.

546 Article 7 of the Portaria.

547 Articles 2 and 4 of the Portaria.

548 *See* the Decree No. 564 of June 8, 1992 for the competence, and Article 2, *Parágrafo Único*, of the *Portaria* No. 693, as well as details on FUNAI, *Portarias*, and the question of competence at Section 2.D.II.3. below.

1. Overview and Background of the Decree with Specific Regard to TCEs

a. Main Structure

In accordance with Article 216 of the Constitution, the Decree institutes two pillars of protection:

- first, a registry, the "Registry of Cultural Goods of Immaterial Nature,"[549] and
- second, a "National Program of Immaterial Patrimony" aiming at the valorization of said patrimony.[550]

Before going into details on these two pillars, it is worth having a look at the context of the Decree and the specific role of TCEs in this regard.

b. Role of TCEs and General Development of the Decree

It is necessary to emphasize that Decree No. 3551 is not and has never ben intended to be a specific instrument on the protection of TCEs in particular. It rather was aimed at the recognition and valorization of the Brazilian "immaterial patrimony" as a whole.[551] This being said, TCEs indeed played a specific role in the genesis of the Decree, as TCEs were, at first, a driving force in preparing the ground for a rising awareness of the importance of cultural patrimony in Brazil in general, then particular objects of discussion during the process of designing the Decree, and finally,—to a certain extent—a reason for choosing the type of regulation that was chosen in the end.

According to Sant' Anna, in the 1930s a common understanding arose that "popular expressions"—as they were still called at that time in Brazil—were an important factor for the formation of a national Brazilian cultural identity. Even a legislative project on the institution of a registry of those expressions was initiated in 1936—which, however, failed.[552]

In the 1970s, the idea of protecting particularly folklore and TCEs, re-emerged—as a reaction to then recent adoption of the UNESCO Convention on the Safeguarding of the World Natural and Cultural Heritage and the quest for a protection of TCEs, still called "folklore" then, initiated by Brazil's neighbor Bolivia. Studies of UNESCO on this topic resulted in 1989 in the "Recommendations on the Safeguarding of Traditional and Popular Culture," which ushered in a change in terminology, with the terms "intangible" or "immaterial cultural patrimony."[553]

---

549 "Registro de Bens Culturais de Natureza Imaterial", Articles 1–7 of the Decree.

550 "Programa Nacional do Patrimônio Imaterial", Article 8 of Decree No. 3551.

551 Sant' Anna (2006 II) 15, 19.

552 *See id.* 15.

553 It is also one of the three principle documents that have inspired Decree 3551, *see* at Section 2. C.II.1.d. below.

The international demand for a specific method of protecting TCEs, namely in Bolivia, re-animated the discussions on protection with specific regard to popular and traditional cultural expressions in Brazil, Sant' Anna argues: The legislative project on an institution of a "Special Registry" was renewed, proposing a registry be an instrument for protection of immaterial cultural goods and adopting a rather anthropological approach.[554] This interdisciplinary approach, involving anthropologists in legal questions on folklore, immaterial cultural goods or TCEs, is a special attribute that still characterizes the situation in Brazil today.[555]

Finally, in November 1997, an international seminar on ways of protecting immaterial patrimony took place in Fortaleza, which constituted the renewal of a "historic discussion", Sant' Anna argues, and followed a "new vision": the understanding that the participation of the communities in defining and implementing preservationist acts was essential.[556]

In March, 1998,[557] the Ministry of Culture created a commission[558] to elaborate proposals for regulations on the safeguarding of the cultural patrimony and, for technical support, a Working Group on Immaterial Patrimony,[559] which conducted extensive, 17 months-long "research on the Brazilian experience and international recommendations, experiences and legislations"[560] regarding immaterial patrimony, including TCEs.[561]

As an outcome specifically on TCEs, principal problems to the continuity and maintenance of TCEs were identified:

- "predatory tourism"
- "inadequate coverage or appropriation by the media"
- "uniformization of products as a result of the economic globalization process"
- "industrial appropriation", and
- "inadequate commercialization of the underlying knowledge on a national and international scale".[562]

---

[554] Sant' Anna (2006 I) 9, translation by the author.

[555] On this *see* at Section 2.C.III. and D.II.3.b., and D.V. below.

[556] Sant' Anna (2006 I) 9, translation by the author.

[557] International Seminar on Strategies and Forms of Protection of Immaterial Patrimony in Fortaleza, Brazil, November 1997

[558] "Comissão," consisting of Joaquim Falcão, Marcos Vilaça and Thomas Farkas, members of the Conselho do Patrimônio Cultural, the Council on Cultural Patrimony, and Eduardo Portella, President of the National Library, *see* Sant' Anna (2006 II) 16 note 1.

[559] "Grupo de Trabalho Patrimônio Imaterial (GTPI)", as Sant' Anna displays, which is consisting of eight members of different cultural and administrative entities like IPHAN, FUNARTE, and the Secretariat of Patrimony, Museums and Plastic Arts, and, additionally, one juridical consultant, *see id.* (2006 II) 16 note 2.

[560] *Id.* 16, translation by the author.

[561] The outcome and information on the research is summed up in two documents, *see* Sant' Anna: "A experiência brasileira no trato das questões relativas à proteção do patrimônio cultural imaterial" and "Propostas, experiências e regulamentos internacionais sobre a proteção do patrimônio cultural imaterial", *see id.* 15–17.

[562] *Id.* 18.

The latter problems were found especially detrimental when mass (re-) production of traditional objects took place, inappropriate or inadequate materials were introduced, and original patterns or traditional techniques were appropriated gratuitously.[563]

As regulatory answers to these problems faced by TCEs, the following options were discussed according to Sant' Anna[564]:

(1) defining traditional culture as a "specific area of intellectual property, including its industrial aspect,"
(2) creating a sui generis right that would entitle the traditional communities to authorize or refuse the use of their cultural expressions and knowledge by third parties,
(3) including intellectual-property provisions on TCEs[565] in the proposal for regulating immaterial patrimony, and
(4) combining the acknowledgement of TCEs and traditional knowledge as cultural patrimony of Brazil with the legal possibility of patent registration at the National Institute of Industrial Property[566]—though with no concrete details.[567]

Following the reports, this was one of the longest debates in the Commission and Working Group on Immaterial Patrimony.[568] In the end, the Group found it to be too early to decide conclusively on the issue and held it more important to "start identifying, taking inventory of, registering, and appreciating immaterial patrimony of national relevance"[569] and to discuss the topic within the Inter-ministerial Group for Intellectual Property on a larger context.[570] Only in a second step, provisions on specific questions as the use and commercialization of TCEs and related products, should be established.[571]

---

[563] *Id.* 15–17.

[564] *Ibid.*

[565] The literal translation of said idea would be "provisions relating to the protection of intellectual property" ("disposições relativas à propriedade intelectual", *ibid.*). That, however, might be misleading, as it would presuppose TCEs to be recognized as "intellectual property" in the sense of IP law, which was not the case at that time and still is not at the present stage of discussion in Brazil. Therefore, the translation chosen here slightly modifies the wording of the option expressed by the Working Group on Immaterial Patrimony without intending to change the idea behind it. The documents, however, convey the impression that the connection to legal areas other than that of cultural patrimony defied an accurate use of legal technical terms in the discussions.

[566] "Instituto Nacional de Propiedade Industrial (INPI)".

[567] Sant' Anna: "Cogitou-se, inclusive, a possibilidade de que o reconhecimento do saber tradicional como patrimônio cultural do Brasil ensejasse o registro de sua patente no Instituto Nacional de Propiedade Industrial – INPI.", Sant' Anna (2006 II) 18. What exactly should be registered "as a patent" and how, i.e. under what kind of intellectual-property instruments and how to keep it in conformity with the international legal framework of IP, i.e. the TRIPS Agreement, remains unclear.

[568] Sant' Anna (2006 II) 18.

[569] Sant' Anna (2006 II) 18, translation by the author.

[570] "Grupo Interministerial de Propiedade Intelectual (GIPI)".

[571] *Id.* 18.

Consequently, when proposals were being drafted for Decree No. 3551 in the late 1990s, the idea was to create a legal instrument based upon two main principles, Sant' Anna argues:

(1) First, aim for "more documentation and accompaniment, and less intervention," and,
(2) second, as a consequence, require a mere "historic continuity" rather than a "notion of authenticity."[572] This would allow the transformative dynamics of the immaterial good to be acknowledged, and enable the legal instrument to rather "accompany" the good and give it some permanency in the registry.[573]

Various consequences were drawn from these two principles for the shape and content of the legal protection.[574] One of them was the decision to establish a registry as first pillar of protection, with a limited duration.[575] This decision was then implemented by adopting Decree No. 3551 in 2000.

2. Details on the Content of the Decree: "Protection" via the Registry

As such first pillar of protection, the Decree No. 3551 sets up a "Registry of Cultural Goods of Immaterial Nature which constitute Brazilian cultural patrimony."[576] According to the legislator, the main function of the registry is to identify the cultural good, raise awareness of it and demonstrate appreciation for it, rather than to legally "protect" it in the sense of granting a right or title to the holder of the patrimony.[577]

a. Overview Over the Content

The Registry is divided into four "books:"

(1) The "Book of Knowledge", in which knowledge and "ways of makings," rooted in the everyday life of the communities, including handicraft methods, are registered,
(2) the "Book of Celebrations", in which rituals and festivities are recorded,

---

[572] *Ibid.*

[573] *Id.* 19.

[574] Another consequence of the principle of public accompaniment, through which the state neither "intervenes" nor purely passively observes, is the establishment of the second part of the Decree: the "National Program of Immaterial Patrimony", a supportive public policy, which will be dealt with below at Section 2.C.II.3.

[575] *See* the letter from 1999: Vilaça, Portella, Falção and Farkas (2006) 73.

[576] Article 1 of the Decree.

[577] Sant' Anna (2006 II) 18.
Id. 19.

(3) the "Book of Forms of Expression", in which literary, musical, plastic, scenic, and ludic manifestations are registered, and finally,
(4) the "Book of Localities", in which markets, fairs, sanctuaries, and other places where collective cultural practices are held or performed are recorded.[578]

Further books can be created for other immaterial cultural goods not matching the four existing ones.[579]

The relevant criteria for recording an item are the historical continuity of the good and its "national relevance to the memory, identity and formation of the Brazilian society."[580]

The Advisory Council on Cultural Patrimony then decides whether an item will be recorded.[581] In case of a positive decision, the good will be registered in the corresponding book and receive the title of "Cultural Patrimony of Brazil."[582]

The Ministry of Culture then has to assure, first, that the registered good is documented by all technical means, while it is up to the IPHAN to maintain a database containing all material that has been produced since the initiation of the registration procedure. Second, the Ministry of Culture has to ensure an ample divulgation and promotion of the good.[583]

b. Competent Authorities and Parties Involved

The competent entities differ according to three different tasks, which are:

- Initiating the registration process,
- supervising it, and finally,
- deciding over the act of registration.

aa. Parties Authorized to Initiate the Registration Process

The parties that are authorized to initiate the registration procedure are (1) the Ministry of Culture, (2) institutions linked to the Ministry of Culture, (3) Secretariats of the State, Municipalities, and Federal Districts, and (4) civil societies or associations.[584]

---

[578] "Livro de Registro dos Saberes," "das Celebrações," "das Formas de Expressão," "dos Lugares," Article 1, para. 1, of the Decree.

[579] Article 1, para. 3, of the Decree. A new book is likely to be opened for languages, as a way of acknowledging the Brazilian linguistic plurality, *see* http://www.telesurtv.net/noticias/secciones/nota/index.php?ckl=29260-NN, last visited May 10, 2010.

[580] Article 2, § 2, of the Decree.

[581] "Conselho Consultivo do Patrimônio Cultural," Article 4 of the Decree.

[582] Article 5 of the Decree.

[583] Article 6 of the Decree.

[584] Article 2 of the Decree.

The question of who may propose a cultural good for entry in the registry has been the most controversial one within the legislative process, as Sant' Anna tells.[585] According to her documentations, many of its participants favored the idea that any citizen should be able to apply for the registering of an immaterial cultural good. Others preferred to widen the circle of institutions listed in the proposal in order to include municipal institutions, to avoid obliging cultural entities to enact regional or national representation, and—something that would have been most relevant for TCEs—to include ethnic groups as authorized parties.[586] According to Sant' Anna, these suggestions were then rejected because of the worry that the Consultative Council would be flooded with applications, a prospect that did not comply with the obligatory requirement that a good have "national relevance" in order to be registered.[587] Therefore, it was preferred that proposals should always be made collectively by the entities that were in the end enumerated in Article 2 para. 5 of the Decree, as indicated above.[588]

bb. Supervising the Registration Process and Executing the Documentation

The competent entity for the task of supervising the initiation of the registration process is the Institute for National Historic and Artistic Patrimony, or IPHAN.[589] The IPHAN is also the principal entity to execute the proceedings of registering.[590]

cc. Authority Deciding on Registration

The competent authority for deciding whether the immaterial good in question will be registered as Immaterial Patrimony of Brazil is the Advisory Council on Cultural Patrimony.[591] This entity was chosen, Vilaça and others explain, to avoid the creation of another new institution within the Ministry of Culture. Instead, the lawmakers wanted to give "value and prestige to the existing Council by equipping it with decision-making and regulating competence."[592]

585 Sant' Anna (2006 II) 21.

586 *Ibid.*

587 *Ibid.*

588 *Ibid.*

589 "Instituto do Patrimômino Histórico e Artístico Nacional", Article 3, para 1, of the Decree.

590 The decision to make the IPHAN the principal (although not only) entity to execute the process of documentation was made in order to "give value and prestige to the IPHAN"; Vilaça, Portella, Falção and Farkas (2006) 74.

591 "Conselho Consultivo do Patrimônio Cultural", Article 3 of the Decree.

592 Vilaça, Portella, Falção and Farkas (2006) 73, translation by the author.

c. Procedure

At first, any of the authorized parties indicated above has to make a proposal. Any such proposal, including its technical documentation, must be directed to the President of the IPHAN, who in turn submits it to the Advisory Council on Cultural Patrimony.[593] The IPHAN comments on the proposal and sends the comments to the Council. These comments are also to be published in the *Diário Oficial da União,* the Official Brazilian Gazette, to give all persons interested in the case the opportunity to express pros or contras concerning the intended registration within a period of 30 days after the publication.[594] Apart from providing transparent information, this concept is intended to "stimulate civic participation in the selection and registration process of the national immaterial patrimony – a tribute to democracy, as the creators called it, of which transparency and participation are indispensable principles."[595] After considering potential objections, the final decision on registration is then made by the Advisory Council.[596]

d. Substantive Law: Legal Requirements for Registration as Brazilian Immaterial Patrimony

The Decree requires the good to possess "historical continuity" and "national relevance for the memory, identity, and formation of the Brazilian society."[597] According to the wording of the regulation, these two elements constitute a mere "reference," not a "precondition," for the decision on entering a good in the registry—however, the preparing Commission regarded it as an "indispensable" reference.[598]

The background for requiring a higher level of importance, i.e. "national relevance" in contrast to mere importance at municipal or state level,[599] is the idea that this regulation should set an example at the federal level and thereby initiate a whole national system of protecting the immaterial patrimony. Similar to the events that occurred after Decree Law No. 25 was established,[600] it is probable that "Decree No. 3551 will inspire different municipalities and states within the country of Brazil to create their own proceedings to regulate local immaterial patrimony."[601]

---

[593] "Conselho Consultivo do Patrimônio Cultural", Article 3 of the Decree.

[594] § 5 of Article 2 of the Decree.

[595] Vilaça, Portella, Falção and Farkas (2006) 74, translation by the author.

[596] Article 4 of the Decree.

[597] Article 1, para. 2, of the Decree.

[598] Article 1, para. 2, of the Decree and Vilaça, Portella, Falção and Farkas (2006) 74.

[599] The Federal Republic of Brazil is divided into 26 States and one Federal District.

[600] On this *see* at Section 2.C.I. above.

[601] Vilaça, Portella, Falção and Farkas (2006) 74, translation by the author.

What exactly is meant by "historical continuity" is not defined in the Decree. According to the Commission, it should be understood as "a better and more *actualized* sense than *tradition*."[602]

With regard to TCEs, however, the concept of TCEs literally and conceptually embraces "tradition". Did the Commission intend to exclude TCEs from the scope of application of the protection provided by the registry? No, it did not:

- First, "historical continuity" was not meant as contrasting with tradition, but simply as emphasizing the aspect of enduring vitality of the expression or immaterial good.[603] This vitality is required in the case of protecting TCEs, as well: an ongoing, living connection shall exists between the expression and the cultural practice or social reality of the respective traditional or local community.[604]
- Second, TCEs are included within the concept of Articles 215 and 216 of the Constitution. The Decree was created in order to realize this constitutional concept. Its scope of protection should correspond to the constitutional scope of subject matter of protection, i.e. including cultural expressions laid down in Article 215.
- Third, the decree-makers intentionally left open a more specific definition of "historic continuity" up to the competent Advisory Council, which "could then define the concrete elements in each case in response to the concrete needs of the society."[605] Meanwhile, two TCEs have already been registered.[606]

In order to facilitate the task of defining "historic continuity" and "national relevance" in practice and of evaluating whether the good is worth registering, four different categories of goods ("books", see above) were established.[607] These four categories take up the concept and generic parameters set up in the Constitution (Articles 215, 216). The preparing Commission preferred the system of exemplifying categories rather than an abstract and dogmatic definition which could have provoked controversy over the arising gaps.[608] Although a conceptual competence ("jurisprudência conceitual") does not avoid controversies either, as the Commission admitted, it held the chosen path to be more productive and convenient to

[602] *Id.* (2006) 74, emphasis added by the author.

[603] Sant' Anna (2006 II) 18.

[604] On the content of the term TCEs and particularly the dynamic aspect of it *see* at Chapter II Section 1.B.I.1.d. above.

[605] Vilaça, Portella, Falção and Farkas (2006) 74. The competence is called "jurisprudência conceitual", which will be discussed just below.

[606] On this *see* at Section 2.C.III. and E. below.

[607] Article 1, para. 1, of the Decree.

[608] Vilaça, Portella, Falção and Farkas (2006) 74, translation by the author.

handle in practice.[609] At the same time, it instituted the possibility for all interested parties to oppose to the registration before the Advisory Council.[610]

In this context, it is astonishing that the Advisory Council, being the organ to apply the Decree, should at the same time be the entity that defines what the legal criteria of this application are.[611] Legally, this situation raises questions: As the Advisory Council is part of a public administrative entity, and not one concerned with jurisprudence, where is the legal basis for intentionally equipping it with the competence of a "jurisprudência conceitual," considering that, generally, the principle of separation of powers requires a division of executive, legislative and jurisprudential powers? Or is the term "jurisprudência" not meant in the sense of the legal technical term but simply as room for interpretation when applying a legal instrument? The Decree and accompanying documents neither pose nor answer these questions. Probably, in view of the legal nature of the Decree as an administrative instrument, this concept is just understood as matter of (administratively) interpreting the norm during the act of its implementation.

e. Duration of Protection

At least 10 years after the registration, the IPHAN is to undertake a re-evaluation of the registered goods and direct its findings to the Advisory Council so that the latter may decide upon the revalidation of the title "Cultural Patrimony of Brazil."[612] In case the Council declines to revalidate a good—e.g. in case of complete transformation or disappearance of its essential elements[613]—the good nonetheless will be maintained within the register, but only as "a cultural reference of its time."[614]

This limited duration of the registration as cultural patrimony reflects the fact that, as Lévi-Strauss puts it, "more than anything else, the immaterial patrimony is born, lives and dies. (. . .) Tastes, necessities, ways of life, values and performances have always evolved and will continue to do so."[615] As the immaterial patrimony—and this is particularly true for TCEs—is "intimately associated with the daily life of the people, one cannot freeze or perpetuate it by a decree."[616]

Moreover, this provision also reflects a general principle in law stipulating that a claim, entitlement, or right is forfeited if the constituting requirements cease to

[609] Article 3, para 5, of the Decree, for details of the procedure *see* at Section 2.C.II.2.c. below and for details of the teleological background *see ibid.*

[610] Article 3, para 5, of the Decree, for details of the procedure *see* at Section 2.C.II.2.c. below and for details of the teleological background *see ibid.*

[611] *Id.* 74: "A definição concreta do que seja continuidade histórica deverá ser construída pelo Conselho através da jurisprudência conceitual a partir das demandas da sociedade."

[612] Article 7 of the Decree.

[613] Vilaça, Portella, Falção and Farkas (2006) 73.

[614] Para. 1 of Article 7 of the Decree.

[615] Lévi-Strauss (2006) 81, translation by the author.

[616] Lévi-Strauss (2006) 81, translation by the author.

exist: As "historical continuity" is a requirement,[617] the duration of "protection", i.e. how long a cultural expression or good keeps its place on the list of cultural patrimony, depends upon maintaining this historical continuity.[618] The legal consequences, however, are not as severe, because the good remains in the registry, it only loses the title "Cultural Patrimony of Brazil."

Similarly, when Laurent Lévi-Strauss refers to the "historic content" as *not* being the object of safeguarding,[619] he presumably means historic in the sense of past, or bygone, rather than said historical *continuity.* With respect to cultural patrimony as a whole and its function as a comparative element for any society to understand its own culture, Lévi-Strauss underlines that diversity and its continuing vitality should be safeguarded—in contrast to the sole historic content.[620]

This is also the direction the official statement of the preparatory Commission follows: the limited duration of the registration as "Cultural Patrimony of Brazil" is intended to "emphasize the essentially dynamic character of the good and should encourage people, namely the bearers of the immaterial good, to follow its evolution."[621]

f. Is There a Duty to Maintain TCEs Qualified as Immaterial Cultural Patrimony?

Once an immaterial good or expression has been registered as "Brazilian Cultural Patrimony," are the bearers of the good obliged to maintain the good as such?

The idea of an obligation to maintain TCEs in particular has arisen in a more general context before.[622] Here, the Decree itself does not explicitly address this question. The situation differs from the initial general discussion about whether rights on TCEs should at the same time establish any kinds of duties for the traditional community. Here, besides the indigenous communities as main addressees, a second level becomes (much more) relevant: the national society.

Qualifying goods and expressions as "Brazilian Cultural Patrimony" requires them to be of "national relevance for the memory, identity, and formation of the Brazilian society."[623] As a consequence, one could argue that this qualification in turn implies a national and nationwide responsibility of maintaining the patrimony in favor of the Brazilian society.

However, a closer look at the regulations reveals at least three arguments against such view:

---

617 *See* at Section 2 C.II.2.d. below.

618 Sant' Anna (2006 II) 19.

619 Lévi-Strauss (2006) 82.

620 *Ibid.*

621 Vilaça, Portella, Falção and Farkas (2006) 73, translation by the author.

622 On this *see* at Chapter II Section 5.D.VII. above.

623 Article 2 § 2 of the Decree, *see* at Section 2.C.II.d. above.

- a lack of "rights,"
- consent as a permanent precondition of the procedure, and
- the genesis of the Decree.

First of all, by "simply" establishing a system to identify, document, and register the patrimony and a promoting policy, the decree does not create any rights for the holders of the goods. Thus, in view of the principle of reciprocity, no positive legal instrument corresponding to such duty exists.

Second, the procedure of identifying, documenting, and registering the good requires the agreement of the holder(s) at every stage of the process.[624] If the holders can withdraw from the procedure of "establishing" a cultural patrimony, they keep full autonomy over their expression or immaterial good. This is also the underlying idea of the Decree. Even after the moment of registering, neither this concept nor the nature of the legal institution changes. Immaterial cultural patrimony understood as a vital good in its historical continuation embraces the understanding of a voluntarily upheld cultural expression.

This legal concept corresponds to the third argument against the assumption of a duty to maintain a certain cultural patrimony: the history of the Decree's origins. The preparatory discussions on the regulations reveal the dominating opinion that

> if a community abandons a social practice, there is no way how to oppose it. What can be done – and the Decree attends to that – is to inventory, study, and preserve on the one hand, and to offer social acknowledgement to the holder of the patrimony on the other hand, in order to underline the importance of the patrimony, and thereby stimulating the holders to maintain it and transmit it to the new generations, which, in turn, can raise the awareness of its value.[625]

Consequently, the registration of an immaterial good or expression as "Brazilian Cultural Patrimony" does not bring along any obligation to maintain the good/expression.

3. "Protection" by Means of the National Program of Immaterial Patrimony

As a second pillar, the Decree institutes a "National Program of Immaterial Patrimony."[626] Although the Working Group on Immaterial Patrimony itself indirectly describes the policy as an "effect of the registry,"[627] the Decree institutes the Program as a second, separate aspect, even with different competences.[628]

The program's principal objective is to implement specific policies on inventory, referencing, and valuation of this patrimony.[629] The knowledge on the cultural

[624] *See* at Section 2.C.II.c. above.

[625] Lévi-Strauss (2006) 81.

[626] Article 8 of the Decree.

[627] Sant' Anna (2006 II) 20, translation by the author.

[628] Article 8 of the Decree.

[629] Article 8 of the Decree.

expressions gained during the process of identification and registering may serve to determine the most adequate form of statal support for its continuation. Such forms can be very different in their nature: According to the preparatory discussions, they could range "from financial aid for the holders of the specific expressions aiming at their ongoing transmission, to the divulgation or facilitation of access to raw materials," and so forth.[630]

Although legally referring to cultural "goods," the policy on safeguarding the immaterial patrimony aims at supporting their sources: material and personal ones. According to Sant' Anna, the policy is intended to strengthen the cultural references of the social groups in their heterogeneity and complexity, and to promote sustainable use of patrimonial resources as "economic, social and cultural development." That would inclusively mean "sharing responsibilities and duties of this preservation and promoting the access of all social groups concerned to the rights and benefits the preservation generates."[631]

The competence for this is allocated in the Ministry of Culture in general, without specific reference to the IPHAN[632]—unlike the case of the registry.[633]

III. Practical Experiences and Evaluation of the Cultural Law Approach

When establishing the Decree, the preparative Commission named four positive effects that the registry was expected, or hoped, to have, as Sant' Anna displays:

(1) A public obligation to "document and accompany the dynamic of the registered cultural expressions";
(2) "promotion of the acknowledgement of the importance of those goods" by the concession of the title "Cultural Patrimony of Brazil" and promotion activities;
(3) establishment of a "database on the registered goods that is open to the public"; and,
(4) "facilitated transmission and continuity of the expressions through supportive activities within the National Program of the Immaterial Patrimony".[634]

How does the practice look like now? During the first 6 years after establishment of the Decree in 2000 alone, nine goods were registered, more than 30 projects of allocation and inventory were implemented in the country, around 18 publications were supported, a new institution was established,[635] and new legal instruments

[630] Sant' Anna (2006 II) 20.

[631] Sant' Anna (2006 I) 9, translation by the author.

[632] Article 8 of the Decree.

[633] *See, e.g.*, Article 3 and 7 of the Decree.

[634] *See* Sant' Anna (2006 II) 21, translation by the author. According to its own analysis, this latter aspect constitutes an effect of the Program rather than the Registry, *see ibid.* How the substantial details of these two principles were implemented will be examined below.

[635] "Câmara do Patrimônio Imaterial", side by side with the "Conselho Consultivo do Patrimônio Cultural," the Advisory Council on Cultural Patrimony.

were issued, e.g. Resolution No. 001/2006, which regulates details on the installation, instruction, and transmission of procedures of the registry.[636] Currently, in 2010, 10 years after the Decree was established, there are even 22 goods registered as immaterial cultural patrimony of Brazil.[637]

As the registration requires the consent and cooperation of the bearers of the culture at any stage of the registration and documentation process, the documentation and registration of the cultural expressions have been experienced as successful projects so far.[638]

At the international level, Brazil has provided for technical assistance including presentations of know-how and experiences gained by IPHAN, and advanced to the vanguard of the field, becoming a reference for other countries, especially in Latin America. It also played an important role in creating the Regional Center for Safeguarding Immaterial Cultural Patrimony of Latin America, CRESPIAL, in Cuzco, Peru.[639] A "Protocol of Intentions" of the Brazilian and Ecuadorian Ministries of Culture was signed on the cultural co-operation and exchange of experiences and technical support in April 2010, including the special valorization of cultural expressions as part of the Immaterial Cultural Patrimony in co-operation with CRESPIAL and capacity-building measures of indigenous communities in the area of audio-visual documentations and activities.[640] Moreover, the Brazilian "public law model" facilitated cooperation with the Argentinean Ministry of Culture. A joint project, supported in part by FUNAI and a special team of anthropologists, was initiated regarding the protection of the traditional culture of the tribe of the Huaraní, or Guaraní, the members of which live on both sides of the countries' common border.[641]

At the national level, with regard to TCEs in particular, there are currently four "goods" registered as immaterial cultural patrimony, stemming from indigenous peoples: the "Arte Kusiwa," bodypainting and graphic art of the Wajãpi Indians, the

---

[636] *See* Sant' Anna (2006 I) 9 *et seq.* (for an overview over the first six years of practice). For current activities and details *see* http://portal.iphan.gov.br/portal/montarPaginaSecao.do?id=10852&retorno=paginalphan, last visited April 29, 2010.

[637] http://portal.iphan.gov.br/portal/montarPaginaSecao.do?id=12456&retorno=paginalphan, last visited January 15, 2011.

[638] Personal communication with Ana Gita de Oliveira, Department of Immaterial Patrimony of IPHAN, in March 2009 in Brasilia, and with Francisco Avelino Batista, president of the Coordination of Indigenous Organizations of the Brazilian Amazon (COIAB), in March 2009 in Quito, Ecuador.

[639] Sant' Anna (2006 I) 9, 10. For the legal basis of the creation, competence, and tasks of CRESPIAL (Centro Regional para la Salvaguardia del Patrimonio Cultural Inmaterial de Améria Latina) *see* CRESPIAL (2007).

[640] "Protocolo de Intenciones entre el Ministerio de Cultura de la República Federativa de Brasil y el Ministerio de la Cultura de la República del Ecuador para el Desarrollo de Acciones Conjuntas en el Marco de la Cultura" of April 14, 2010 (Spanish version), and *see* the note of IPHAN "Brasil e Equador assinam protocolo de intenções sobre patrimônio cultural" of April 16, 2010.

[641] Personal communication with Ana Gita de Oliveira, Department of Immaterial Patrimony of IPHAN, in March 2009 in Brasilia, and *see* the note of IPHAN "Iphan realiza encontro de Comunidades Mbyá-Guarani do Brasil e da Argentina" of December 4, 2006.

"Cachoeira de Iauaretê," waterfall of *Iuauaretê*, sacred place of the indigenous peoples of the Uaupés and Papuri rivers; furthermore, a special, 7-month-long ritual of the Enawene Nawe Indians called the "Ritual Yaokwa do Povo Indígena Enawene Nawe," and a traditional indigenous agricultural system relating to the *manioc*, which determines the social organization of the indigenous, and even allows a mapping of their languages and customs, the "Sistema Agrícola Tradicional do Rio Negro."[642]

The bodypainting and graphic art "Arte Kusiwa – Pintura Corporal e Arte Gráfica Wajãpi" was registered quite early, in 2002, as the second immaterial good registered in Brazil.[643] A year later, it was even proclaimed by the UNESCO "Masterpiece of the Oral and Intangible Heritage of Humanity" in 2003 and is now inscribed in UNESCO's Representative List of the Intangible Cultural Heritage of Humanity.[644]

The waterfall area "Cachoeira de Iauaretê – Lugar sagrado dos povos indígenas dos Rios Uaupés e Papuri," was the eighth good registered.[645] The registration might surprise at first glance, as it constitutes a place, a material, immovable good rather than an immaterial one. According to IPHAN, the push to register it was initiated by the indigenous peoples who live there because the Brazilian air force was planning to enlarge a small runway for military actions in the area, and the attendant migration of settlers into the area turned the traditional living environment into a regular, commercially oriented city.[646] Thus, although it does have a bearing on the sacred aspect, the source of inspiration, myths, and legends as "immaterial goods," the desire for the registration and intended "protection" in concrete is for the living conditions and geographic region. Similarly, there are current attempts initiated by indigenous communities to register other regions in the Amazon part of Brazil, especially where the Belo Monte Dam is to be constructed.[647] This fact is at the same time the reason for the registration sought, as the indigenous peoples hope to obtain protection of their territory by means of the registration as Brazilian immaterial cultural patrimony.[648]

---

[642] *See* the official documentary books edited by IPHAN – Instituto do Patrimônio Histórico e Artístico Nacional, "Arte Kusiwa: Pintura Corporal e Arte Gráfica Wajãpi" (2008), and IPHAN - Instituto do Patrimônio Histórico e Artístico Nacional, "Cachoeira de Iauaretê – Lugar sagrado dos povos indígenas dos Rios Uaupés e Papura (AM)" (2007) and http://portal.iphan.gov.br/portal/montarPaginaSecao.do?id=12456&retorno=paginaIphan, last visited January 15, 2011.

[643] *See* http://portal.iphan.gov.br/portal/montarPaginaSecao.do?retorno=paginaIphan&sigla=Institucional&id=12456, last visited February 10, 2010.

[644] http://www.unesco.org/culture/ich/index.php?RL=00049, last visited April 29, 2010.

[645] *See* http://portal.iphan.gov.br/portal/montarPaginaSecao.do?retorno=paginaIphan&sigla=Institucional&id=12456, last visited February 10, 2010.

[646] IPHAN – Instituto do Patrimônio Histórico e Artístico Nacional (2007) 102 *et seq*.

[647] A good overview over the project, its history, advantages, and disadvantages can be found at http://www.oneworld.at/stArticleasp?ID=231997, and another one in English: http://www.amazonwatch.org/amazon/BR/bmd/, last visited May 31, 2010.

[648] Personal communication with Ana Cristina Bandeira Lins, *Procuradora da República* in the *Ministerio Público*, on June 23, 2009 in São Paolo, Brazil, *see* also Busch (2010) 220 *et seq*.

However, the legal consequence of being registered as immaterial cultural patrimony does not include any prohibiting function. Such consequences or legal positions are neither provided for by Decree No. 3551 itself nor by any other regulation, on land rights for instance. This is also the reason why the protest against the construction of the Belo Monte Dam did not even refer to the fact that the region is culturally "protected," i.e. registered as immaterial cultural patrimony of Brazil. There were rather three injunctions based upon other legal arguments.[649] One of the things criticized by experts involved in the topic therefore is that the system of registration according to Decree No. 3551 does not provide for any legal title or effective legal measures, something that is often not understood by the indigenous communities seeking a registration.[650]

The documentations and publications are impressive awareness-raising measures, of immeasurable value for the expansion and dissemination of knowledge on these cultural "treasures." They provide extremely helpful insights for generally dealing with the intercultural and interdisciplinary issue of TCEs in other legal procedures as well, and, together with the process of identifying, documenting, registering, and publishing the goods, they pay extraordinary attention and express great appreciation and respect to the indigenous communities involved. Therefore, it is of extraordinary value for the maintenance of the vitality of the TCEs dealt with as well as the development and implementation of further protection of TCEs.

Nonetheless, this kind of public "protection" of TCEs does not supersede the discussion of a sui generis regime granting collective intellectual property rights. Two examples of recent cases show why protection by means of public law is insufficient: First, there is a case of recordings of a traditional song by MTV International without proper authorization from the tribe; second, the case of commercialization of traditional indigenous body painting art in Japan, "exported" by a Japanese company in cooperation with one member of an indigenous tribe without proper consent of the tribe.[651]

For such concrete infringements of TCEs, Decree 3551 does not constitute an adequate instrument of protection. In the daily work in Brazil, alternative and additional forms of legal protection have been developed and applied, mainly through contracts and protocols, as for instance in exhibitions and accompanying documentations and publications of the Museu do Índio, the Indian Museum, in Rio de Janeiro, another public institution dealing with documentation of indigenous cultural expressions.[652]

---

[649] *See* http://www.amazonwatch.org/amazon/BR/bmd/index.php?page_number=9, last visited May 31, 2010.

[650] Personal communication with Ana Cristina Bandeira Lins, *Procuradora da República* in the *Ministerio Público*, on June 23, 2009 in São Paolo, Brazil, *see* also Busch (2010) 220 *et seq.*

[651] Personal communication with Hugo Meireles Heringer and other staff members of the General Coordinating Office for Indigenous Rights (CGDDI) within FUNAI, in March 2009 in Brasilia.

[652] On the details of these instruments and clauses *see* at Chapter III Section 3.E. above.

Moreover, the Museum implements a policy of "active involvement of the indigenous peoples in their documentations and exhibitions", teaching them to document their TCEs themselves using modern technology, as Frausto and Franchetto tell, for instance in the project of linguistic and cultural documentation and exhibition "Tisakisü" involving the Kuikuro community of the region of the Upper Xingu.[653] This documentation includes "around 90 hours of vocal songs and instrumental pieces, without repetition, intended to be transmitted to the next generations."[654] The project of the *Tiskisü* was only possible due to "a deep engagement between a group of people united by a common aim, the record of a dialogue bringing together anthropologists and Indians, indigenous filmmakers and linguists, indigenous researchers and film directors, master singers and ethnomusicologists, in the name of a shared adventure in defence of a unique culture."[655] Similar to the projects facilitated by Decree 3551, these factual rather than legal solutions promote and support the vitality of TCEs and tackle the ongoing discrimination against indigenous peoples in the Latin American countries—and thus are effective soft-law measures.

Aside from all positive signals mentioned before, and despite the long history of discussion on immaterial patrimony in Brazil,[656] it can be noted that the legal instrument and applied measures are relatively new. The Working Group itself calls it a "public policy in construction"—which is not only due to the little time and novelty of methodology and procedures.[657] As regards the most important institution for implementing the Decree, the Department for Immaterial Patrimony within IPHAN, the people in charge realized that material and personal resources are lacking.[658] In effect, both the special Department for Immaterial Patrimony within IPHAN as well as the Indian Museum, officially part of FUNAI, but actively involved in the protection of TCEs, have very limited economic and human resources.[659]

All in all, in addition to all dedicated activities and considerable achievements in the area of cultural protection and promotion, within the country of Brazil as well it has become clear that for concrete infringements, a different legal protection is needed or should at least be discussed. Currently, national and regional discussions on improved protection of TCEs are taking place.[660]

---

[653] Fausto and Franchetto (2008) 11.

[654] *Id.* 11, translation by the author.

[655] José Carlos Levinho, Director of the Indian Museum in Rio de Janeiro, in: *id.* 10, translation by the author.

[656] On this *see* at Section 2.C.I. *et seq.* above.

[657] Sant' Anna (2006 I) 9 translation by the author.

[658] Personal communication with Ana Gita de Oliveira, Department of Immaterial Patrimony of IPHAN, in March 2009 in Brasilia.

[659] Personal communication with Ana Gita de Oliveira, Department of Immaterial Patrimony of IPHAN, in March 2009 in Brasilia, and José Carlos Levinho, Director of the *Museu do Índio*, Indigenous Museum, and member of the commission elaborating a legislative proposal of a new law, on March 16, 2009, in Rio de Janeiro.

[660] For discussions at the Latin American level hosted by Brazil, *see, e.g.*, Busch (2010) 215 *et seq.*

D. Other Approaches and Current Tendencies

Apart from the cultural law approach contained in Decree No. 3551, there are other provisions already existing and new proposals currently discussed in Brazil, which are of relevance for the topic of protecting TCEs. The most important points are the following ones:

I. Provisional Act No. 2186-16 of 2001

Against its background of being a mega-diverse country, Brazil is one of the few countries worldwide having established a sui generis protection on genetic resources, biodiversity and associated traditional knowledge.[661] Although it does not specifically cover TCEs (below 1.), this legislation is noteworthy in the context of protecting TCEs in Brazil from a—though limited—direct as well as an indirect perspective (below 2.).

1. Scope of Application

Act No. 2186-16 directly covers the kind of TCEs that are associated with genetic resources, and regulates direct access to such TCEs: According to its Article 1, para. 2, Act No. 2186-16 regulates the "access" to "traditional knowledge associated with genetic heritage, relevant for the conservation of the biological diversity, the integrity of the genetic patrimony of the country and for the use of its components." This associated traditional knowledge is legally defined as the "individual or collective information *or practice* of an indigenous or local community which is of real or potential value and associated with the genetic heritage."[662] Consequently, any traditional practice that is regarded as both cultural expression and linked to genetic heritage is covered by Act No. 2186-16—as far as its access is concerned.[663] Obviously, this would be only a small part of what is generally understood as TCEs, and a new, specific regime on TCEs probably would—or at least should—contain useful forms of differentiating between the scope of application of such a regime and that of Act No. 2186-16.

[661] Act No. 2186-16 (2001), available at http://www.planalto.gov.br/ccivil_03/mpv/2186-16.htm. For details *see* Bucher (2008) 199 *et seq.* and Straus (2008) 229–295.

[662] Article 7 para. 2 of Act 2186-16. Emphasis added by the author.

[663] The question under which circumstances the knowledge and practices are sufficiently "associated" with the genetic heritage of course remains unanswered by this definition. For further details on the discussions *see* Bucher (2008) 199 *et seq.*, especially 209 note 62.

2. Further Value for the Issue of Protecting TCEs

Indirectly, Act No. 2186-16 is of value for the issue of protecting TCEs with regard to at least three aspects:

- First, consequences can be drawn for the relationship between TCEs, cultural patrimony, and the public domain.
- Second, practical experiences that have been gained so far can serve as lessons learned for other collective rights of indigenous peoples.
- Third, discussions about a new legislation on TCEs at the national as well as international level are deeply interwoven with Act No. 2186-16.

a. Relationship Between TCEs, Cultural Patrimony, and the Public Domain

Regarding the first point, it can be observed that Act No. 2186-16 explicitly includes traditional knowledge on genetic resources within the "Brazilian cultural patrimony."[664] At the same time, the same legislation legally qualifies it as subject to specific rights of indigenous and local communities based on "prior informed consent."[665]

Drawing the parallel to the topic of TCEs, one can deduce that the mere inclusion of TCEs within the Brazilian cultural patrimony in Article 215, para. 1, of the Constitution does not contain any statement on the allocation of TCEs within the civil material or intellectual property system, particularly not an allocation within the public domain in copyright law.

b. Lessons Learned

As regards the second point, in practice, critics have brought forward several arguments questioning a successful implementation of Act No. 2186-16. Relevant criticism for the topic at hand relates to the process of obtaining a prior informed consent by indigenous communities and to a fair consideration to be received by the communities in exchange.[666] For obtaining the prior informed consent, the *Conselho de Gestão do Patrimônio Genético* (CGEN)[667] is the institution involved in the process. Thereby, a lacking appropriate representation of indigenous or local communities within this essential institution, and its mode of decision-making, has been criticized. Moreover, indigenous peoples have argued that as consideration at least a copy of the study could be given to the community, which so far they claimed was not the case in practice.[668]

---

[664] Article 8, para 2, of Act No. 2186-16 states: "O conhecimento tradicional associado ao patrimônio genético de que trata esta Medida Provisória integra o patrimônio cultural brasileiro e poderá ser objeto de cadastro, conforme dispuser o Conselho de Gestão ou legislação específica."

[665] Article 8 of Act No. 2186-16.

[666] On this *see* Busch (2010) 215 *et seq.*

[667] Managing Council of the Genetic Patrimony, Articles 10 *et seq.* of Act No. 2186-16.

[668] On this *see* Busch (2010) 215 *et seq.*

c. Impact on Discussions on a New TCE Legislation

With regard to the third aspect, it becomes clear that Act No. 2186-16 has not only an impact on the discussions about a new legislation on TCEs with respect to a possible content of such legislation. The even more important aspect is the institutional allocation of competences regarding traditional knowledge on genetic resources as regulated by Act No. 2186-16, which differ from the actors and potential competent institutions within the area of TCEs. The access to the respective knowledge covered by Act No. 2186-16 is mainly administered by the CGEN, which is integrated into the Ministry of Environment. In contrast, TCEs are rather dealt with at the IPHAN or other entities of the Ministry of Culture like the General Coordination of Copyright.[669] Discussions at the national as well as international level are deeply interwoven with the authorities dealing with the different aspects involved in the topic. This is an obstacle or at least challenge for a further development of a protection of TCEs.[670]

The situation gets more complicated as, within the scope of application of Act No. 2186-16, i.e. the field of access to genetic resources, biodiversity, and associated traditional knowledge, powers and competences, and even legal opinions and political positions are divided, sometimes even opposing. Besides the potentially contracting parties and representatives of the Brazilian cultural patrimony, which are also involved in the discussions on TCEs, additionally, other authorities are involved. The Ministry of Environment, the Ministry of Science and Technology, the Ministry of Development, the Ministry of Agriculture, and even the Ministry of Defense if resources from Brazilian waters are taken and thus the navy is involved.[671] These entities, however, do not have single positions, but again encompass diverging interests and point of views within the different ministries.[672]

Notwithstanding the existence of these practical difficulties, there seems to be no other way out of the dilemma than to solve these problems: The interdependence of TCEs and traditional knowledge on genetic resources and biodiversity is given at both the legal level and the factual level: The common categorization of both TCEs and the said traditional knowledge as constituting "Brazilian cultural patrimony" requires a minimum consensus and cooperation on a jointly coordinated and equal treatment of the cultural patrimony as one and the same legal category. At the factual level, it has become clear that the remaining biodiversity is also a result of the socio-cultural behavior of the diverse Brazilian indigenous communities, i.e. biodiversity no longer constitutes a "mere natural phenomenon, but exists within and depends upon a cultural context."[673] Consequently, it is essential to consider this interdependence, and to direct national policies on biodiversity and

[669] On this *see* at Section 2.D.III. below.

[670] On the clear words of the General Coordination of Copyright on exactly this aspect *see* below *ibid.*

[671] Decree 96.000/88 of May 2, 1988, for further details *see* Bucher (2008) 209 *et seq.*

[672] *Id.* 247 *et seq.*

[673] Santilli (2003) 55, translation by the author.

related traditional knowledge on the one hand, and on TCEs on the other, towards a maintenance of the (necessary) balance between cultural and biological diversity.[674]

Finally, also with regard to the content of Act No. 2186-16, there are further similarities: Practical experiences with Act No. 2186-16 have revealed that the protection of traditional knowledge is insufficient so far. Which further protection could be provided? In view of Article 8, para. 2, of the Act, stipulating that the traditional knowledge associated with genetic resources is part of the Brazilian cultural patrimony,[675] an application of the legislation on the protection of the immaterial cultural patrimony—Decree No. 3551—has been suggested.[676]

II. The *Portaria* No. 177 of 2006 of FUNAI on Access to Indigenous Territories in Relation to Copyright and Right of Personal Portrayal

1. Background of the *Portaria* and Relevance for the Topic of TCEs

The discussion on rights of the indigenous peoples in relation to copyright and right of personal portrayal in Brazil started only in 2004 approximately. One of the earliest major publications particularly addresses both these aspects.[677]

The *Portaria* No. 177 of 2006 does so as well. This common treatment of such collective indigenous copyrights and rights of personal portrayal by the *Portaria* No. 177 reveals the high relevance of the latter topic as well as its close connection to the issue of TCEs in practice in Brazil.[678] The practical need for answers to the question of collective personality rights of indigenous communities is particularly high in Brazil, where the entertainment industry is strong and the mentality in this sector as well as in other media, like newspapers, yellow press, etc. in general, still likes to convey a certain type of "lazy, dirty, stupid Indian."[679] The topic of "dano moral colectivo," rather understood as a collective moral *tort* than collective moral *rights*, is also a legal instrument used by the Brazilian public ministry, e.g. in order to defend indigenous or *quilombolan* land rights.[680]

---

[674] Bucher (2008) 22, as regards this aspect of the policy on biodiversity.

[675] For this provision *see supra* note 536.

[676] Azevedo, Lavratti and Moreira (2005) 132.

[677] Baptista and Valle, "Os povos indígenas frente ao direito autoral e de imagem" (2004). The publication stems from two lawyers belonging to the active circle of the "Instituto Socioambiental", and was published in 2004, two years before the establishment of the *Portaria* No. 177. For the main questions in the discussion *see* Baptista and Valle (2004) 9.

[678] On this question in general *see* the more detailed discussion in Taubman (2006) 485–492.

[679] Busch (2010) 220 and personal communication with Eurico L. Sena Baniwa of the *Instituto das Tradições Indígenas*, Institute of Indigenous Traditions, on June 23, 2009 in São Paolo.

[680] *See* http://ccr6.pgr.mpf.gov.br/classificacao-tematica/dano-moral-coletivo, last visited May 31, 2010.

This finding also indicates the idea and function of the *Portaria* No. 177, namely, to answer practical needs in the every day work at FUNAI—which deals with several problems of indigenous peoples, not only as regards the protection of TCEs.

Although discrimination is a great threat to TCEs from a broader perspective, the *legal* focus in this study lies on TCEs in the stricter sense, i.e. on the topic of protecting "traditional cultural *expressions*" rather than the question of a collective right of personal portrayal. The latter aspect thus will be considered only when and as far as it is of direct relevance for the topic of TCEs.

2. Relevant Aspects of Content

a. Aim, Competence, and Main Aspects

The *Portaria* No. 177 envisages the "respect for the indigenous peoples, the protection of their material and immaterial patrimony related to their portrayal as well as cultural and artistic creations." For its competence, FUNAI refers to the "attributions which it has been conferred by the State," approved by the Decree No. 4645 of March 25, 2003.[681]

As FUNAI's competence is limited to administrative acts, Article 1 of the *Portaria* ensures that its provisions are (only) intended to serve as guidelines for the administrative process of authorization by FUNAI, which is a condition for any entry into indigenous territories of persons who "are interested in the use, acquisition, or licensing of indigenous copyrights or rights of personal portrayal." The guiding principle is to respect the values, artistic creations, and other aspects of indigenous cultural expressions, as well as to protect their social organization, customs, languages, beliefs, and traditions.[682] The concrete condition for obtaining an administrative authorization by FUNAI for the entry into the territories and realization of use and exploration of indigenous expressions, works, images, and the like are quite detailed.[683]

Aside from the important linking provision of Article 1, the *Portaria* addresses four aspects:

(1) Indigenous copyrights (*Direitos Autorais Indígenas*),[684]
(2) indigenous right of personal portrayal (*Direito de Imagem Indígena*),[685]
(3) research (*Pesquisas*),[686] and,
(4) administrative Proceedings (*Procedimientos Administrativos*).[687]

---

[681] *Portaria* No. 177 of 2006 of FUNAI on Access to Indigenous Territories in Relation to Copyright and Right of Personal Portrayal ("Entrada em Terra Indígena em Relação ao Direito Autoral e de Imagem").

[682] Article 1 of the *Portaria*.

[683] Article 12 of the *Portaria*.

[684] Articles 2 to 4 of the *Portaria*.

[685] Articles 5 to 10 of the *Portaria*.

[686] Articles 11 to 16 of the *Portaria*.

[687] Articles 17 to 23 of the *Portaria*.

b. Indigenous Copyrights

Indigenous copyrights, or copyrights of the indigenous peoples, are defined as "the moral and economic rights on the aesthetic, artistic, literary, and scientific manifestations, reproductions, and creations; above all the interpretations, graphics, and phonograms of indigenous collective or individual, material, and immaterial character."[688]

The rights conferred are: holdership of the copyright, decision over the use of the work, protection against abuse by third parties, and the right to always be recognized as creator. In case of an "individual indigenous right," the holder is the author, in case of a collective right, it is the "collective."[689]

In accordance with the Federal Copyright Law, the economic rights are understood as referring to the economic use of the creations, and can be "licensed or authorized for free or by means of remuneration or other conditions." The moral rights are understood as being "inalienable, non-renounceable and independent of the economic rights in their subsistence."[690]

The use of the indigenous creations covered by this "indigenous copyright" is permitted, for cultural dissemination or other activities, including those with commercial aims, if the following criteria are fulfilled:

(i) Indication of the rightholders,
(ii) respect for the voluntary permission of the rightholders regarding the authorization, veto, or limitations of use,
(iii) fair consideration, especially if the use is commercial, and
(iv) conclusion of a civil contract between the rightholder (in case of an individual work: the author according to the Federal Copyright Law) or representative of the rightholders and the interested party.[691]

If solicited, FUNAI participates in the contractual negotiations and authorizations of use and licensings within its ambit of competence and by supporting the indigenous interests. According to its Article 4, it is also recommended that the material and immaterial indigenous patrimony should be registered by the national institution competent for the registry of the patrimony before any authorization of use or licensing, which, however, does not impede the full exercise of the copyright at any time.[692]

---

[688] Article 2 of the *Portaria*.

[689] Article 1 para. 1 of the *Portaria*.

[690] Article 1 para. 2 and 3 of the *Portaria*.

[691] Article 3 and para. Único of the *Portaria*.

[692] Article 4 of the *Portaria*.

c. Indigenous Right of Personal Portrayal ("Direito de Imagem Indígena")

The *direito de imagem indígena* is understood as "constituting moral and economic rights of the individual or collective displayed in photographs, films, printings, paintings, drawings, sculptures, and other forms of reproduction of images which display aspects and particularities of the indigenous culture," which is absolutely personal, inalienable, and non-transferable.[693]

The regulations on the *direito de imagem indígena* are similar to those on copyright as far as the use is concerned. The use for public information, however, is free of authorization and remuneration, but has to respect limitations dictated by privacy, honor, and intimacy.[694]

d. Interesting Aspects: Individual—Collective Distinction and Representation

Of special interest for the area of TCEs are also the criteria set up for the distinction between an individual and a collective right. The rights are collective when

(i) The image is based on collective cultural and social manifestations (then the right belongs to the represented indigenous collective, group or ethnicity),
(ii) The use of the image of persons affects the moral, customary, social, or economic order of the collective, exceeding the individual sphere.[695]

Worth noting is also the treatment of the question of representation, which the *Portaria* regulates by means of what one could call a three-step model:

(i) As a general rule, the representation of the indigenous community as collective rightholder should be made "in accordance with its customs and traditions".
(ii) If (only) the "clear identification of the traditional representatives is lacking", other forms of representation that may exist should be given due consideration.
(iii) If such traditional representation is lacking (completely), the representation through "legal persons or through factual associations" (*associações de fato*) is admitted.[696]

e. Special Provisions on Isolated Indigenous Peoples

It is also remarkable that special administrative proceedings are provided for in the case of "indigenous groups considered isolated or of little contact with non indigenous persons," requiring the additional analysis of the authorization request by the General Coordinating Agency of the Isolated Indians.[697]

---

[693] Article 5 and 5, para. 1, of the *Portaria*.

[694] Article 10 of the *Portaria*.

[695] Article 5, para. 2 and 3, of the *Portaria*.

[696] Articles 15 and 15 §§ 1, 2 of the *Portaria*, translation by the author.

[697] Article 20 of the *Portaria*. On the topic of voluntarily isolated indigenous peoples *see* also at Chapter II Section 3.B.I.2. above.

f. Legal Consequences

Due to the initially mentioned limited competence of FUNAI addressed in Article 1 of the *Portaria*, the legal consequences are linked to the administrative act of authorization of the entry into indigenous territories.

In the case that such prior authorization by FUNAI has not been obtained, contracts between indigenous communities and the other party are not necessarily void, but considered valid anyhow if the indigenous persons involved had full consciousness and knowledge about the practiced actions and the extension of their effects, and if they were not prejudicial.[698]

Moreover, FUNAI may suspend the authorization granted to enter the indigenous territories for any use of indigenous images, sounds, graphics, creations, and indigenous works. This is the case e.g. (1) if the indigenous community concerned solicits the cancellation of the authorized activities, (2), the activities provoke conflicts, affect the environment, or cause harms or threaten to harm the moral or economic rights in the indigenous territories.[699]

3. Legal and Practical Evaluation and Experiences

a. Legitimacy of the Portaria

aa. Positions in the Brazilian Discussion

Probably the most crucial aspect of the *Portaria* No. 177 is the question of its legitimacy, which is highly disputed in Brazil. The criticism is directed towards the content, but also the competence of FUNAI to enact such a regulative instrument.

Voices supporting the validity of the *Portaria* argue that it only "reiterates" what is explicitly or implicitly contained in the Brazilian Copyright Law interpreted in the light of the 1988 Constitution, precisely, in the light of the constitutional concept of cultural patrimony.[700] According to this interpretation, the Copyright Law includes collective ownership in copyrights. Those collective rights of indigenous peoples, as Teixeira Coelho argues, would imply in concrete (1) the right to the prior and express authorization, free or paid, of the community's representative or the author with mention of each of the intended uses, or (2) the right to sign a free or paid contract on the licensing of the economic rights, excepting the moral ones.[701]

Others argue that such an "interpretation" does not reveal the current status quo of the Brazilian legislative instruments.[702] The provisions established in the

---

[698] Article 14 of the *Portaria*.

[699] The third criteria is the observation of epidemic situations, Article 22 of the *Portaria*.

[700] Teixeira Coelho (2008) 63, *see* also at Section 2.B.IV.2. above.

[701] *Ibid*.

[702] Personal communication with Marcos Alves de Souza, Head of the Brazilian General Coordination of Copyright, Ministry of Culture, in March 2009, in Brasilia.

Portaria thus would go far beyond the current national legislative framework and would be therefore void. Moreover, FUNAI would exceed its limits of competence as a simple administrative institution.[703]

The opposing positions are not limited to an academic or practitioner's area, but can be found especially at the public, ministerial level. The Ministry of Culture, in particular the General Coordination of Copyright, regards the *Portaria* to be unlawful and therefore not any solution for the problem of protecting TCEs at all. FUNAI, part of the Ministry of Justice, applies the *Portaria*, notwithstanding the criticism. This controversy also reveals the diverging points of views and conflicts of competences within the Brazilian ministerial area, complicating the draft and implementation of a common legislative solution on the protection of TCEs.[704]

A court decision on the lawfulness of the *Portaria* has not been issued yet.

bb. Evaluation

While it could be argued that the application of the *Portaria* as simple, non-binding guidelines within the administrative process of FUNAI might be covered by its sphere of competence, the content, in particular the establishment of collective rights and their consequences, indeed goes beyond the current Brazilian legislative framework. Such an "interpretation" of the Copyright Law might be the desirable outcome of a discussion on an appropriate protection of TCEs, or even doubts on how far the constitutional concept of the cultural patrimony conforms with the current concept of (individual) copyright.

However, first, the actual conception of cultural patrimony laid down in the Brazilian Constitution primarily implements the ideas of the promotion and safeguarding of the national cultural diversity and multi-culturality, but does not contain any statement on the design or content of subjective rights, much less in the sphere of private law. Second, the question of collective copyrights for indigenous or other communities is of greater impact and thus importance than that it can simply be answered on the basis of a constitutional interpretation of the current copyright legislation. Different from the concept of cultural patrimony in public law, which regulates only a bi-polar relationship (between the state or public and the creator of the cultural patrimony), regarding the question of collective copyrights, belonging to the sphere of private law, the tripolarity of interests has to be balanced. That means a balance has to be found between indigenous interests, those of third parties, and state policies. Such an important balancing of different interests—even if the outcome may be tremendously desirable or even predictable by some lawyers—should be left to the legislative power, respecting the political system of democracy and the principle of division of powers.

---

703 *Supra.*

704 On this *see* the Technical Note of the General Coordination of Copyright at Section 2 D.III. below as well as parallel difficulties in regard to the implementation of the protection of traditional knowledge and genetic resources at Section 2.D.I. above.

b. Practical Experiences

aa. Experiences of FUNAI

Though the *Portaria's* scope of application is limited to cases of access to indigenous territories (Article 1, see above), the "procedural guidelines" are also considered in other cases of every-day administrative support and actions.

FUNAI has established a special department for legal issues of indigenous peoples, the "Coordenação-Geral de Defesa dos Direitos Indígenas da FUNAI" (CGDDI), the General Coordinating Office for Indigenous Rights within FUNAI. A common scenario is that indigenous peoples or representatives approach FUNAI in Brasilia and ask for support in cases of alleged infringement of cultural property "rights" or perceived unfair behavior in disputes about use of TCEs, cultural skills, photographs, images, or the like.[705]

Sometimes, these cases are brought to court, by means of the intervention of the Ministry of the Public. Most of the time, however, especially in relation with TCEs, no such alleged "rights" exist, according to the Brazilian legislations, that could support the position of the indigenous peoples. Moreover, aside from interim injunctions, in general, court procedures often take a long time.[706] Alternative solutions, one may even say "alternative dispute resolutions" are sought, mainly by "simply" trying to reach agreements between the parties or persons involved—if they can ever be identified and allocated. In practice, this is also one of the main challenges: to identify the infringing persons.

It is also remarkable that in the majority of the cases, as FUNAI staff reports, not only two parts are involved, i.e. the indigenous community and the interacting party or person. Often, the dispute would arise also within the community, between the group and one member or between the group and the leader—or, if the customary rules provide for plurality of leaders, one of the—(former) traditional representatives.[707] Actually, in many of the cases of "external threats" against the traditional use of TCEs, members of the tribes rather seek help of the FUNAI, regarding the relationship to the infringing person as well as the internal problem of representation and leadership.[708]

From these examples it becomes clear that beside the question of proper representation of the tribe, the problem often is the collective consent to the relevant use

[705] Personal communication with Hugo Meireles Heringer, Claudio Romero, Paolo Pankararu, Melissa Curi, and other staff members of FUNAI, especially of the General Coordinating Office for Indigenous Rights (CGDDI), in March 2009 in Brasilia.

[706] Kayser (2005) 533.

[707] Personal communication with Hugo Meireles Heringer, Paolo Pankararu, Celso de Oliveira, Claudio Romero, Melissa Curi, and other staff members of FUNAI, especially the General Coordination for the Defense of Indigenous Rights (CGDD), in March 2009 in Brasilia.

[708] Personal communication with Hugo Meireles Heringer, Paolo Pankararu, Celso de Oliveira, Claudio Romero, Melissa Curi, and other staff members of FUNAI, especially the General Coordination for the Defense of Indigenous Rights (CGDD), in March 2009 in Brasilia.

of TCEs—the crucial aspect of the tension between the individual and the collective.

While most of the—progressive—academics might see the solution for both problems in the application of customary law, the situation in Brazil also raises questions concerning the efficiency and adequacy of a consideration of customary law. In these cases dealt with at FUNAI, it became clear that internal customary rules or dispute-resolution mechanisms do not function anymore. A possible juridical reaction to this scenario could be the incorporation of provisions of mediation or other instruments of alternative dispute resolution into a future *sui generis* regime, providing FUNAI with the competence for such cases. Besides this conclusion, it definitely makes it clear that an effective solution at the level of private law is needed. However, in reality, such solution seems highly improbably in the near future either at the national Brazilian or at the international level.

bb. Comparison with a Customary-Law Approach: The Wajãpi Point of View

Last but not least, it is remarkable that in its procedural provisions for obtaining authorization and on content requirements of the agreements, the *Portaria* corresponds to one indigenous (emic) perspective on how to treat questions dealing with the issue of research and production of audio-visual documentations of TCEs or indigenous peoples themselves, namely, that of the Wajãpi Indians.[709] The content has been displayed in details in the context of "customary law" already.[710] Rules and expectations corresponding to regulations contained in the *Portaria* are mainly the following ones:

(i) Request for authorization,
(ii) involvement of (at least guiding statements of) FUNAI and other official entities (like the CGEN of the CNPq) in the process of authorizing documentations or similar planned activities,
(iii) approval of the request for authorization by the indigenous communities according to their own decision-making processes,
(iv) representation by indigenous entities, in this case, the Council of the Wajãpi Villages (*Apina*) and the Association of the Wajãpi Indigenous Peoples of the Amapari Triangle (APIWATA)—which corresponds to the subsidiary form of representation according to the *Portaria*,[711]
(v) agreement upon the moral and economic terms of use and upon penalties for non-compliance,[712]
(vi) deposition of integral copies of the documentations.[713]

[709] For the respective Wajãpi perspective *see* Arantes (2009 I) 35 *et seq.* (2009).

[710] *See* at Chapter II Section 5.D. above.

[711] *See* at Section 2.D.II. above.

[712] Article 14 para. Único of the *Portaria*.

[713] Article 4 para. 2 of the *Portaria*.

It cannot be said whether these "customary rules" are influenced by the *Portaria*—as customary law is not understood as something old, static, and non-adaptable—or vice-versa, i.e. that the *Portaria* has taken up ideas and expectations of indigenous peoples. This might even not be the point. What becomes clear and what is of relevance is that there can be noted a mutual influence, understanding, and moving towards each other—although, of course, differences remain.

III. Position of the Ministry of Culture: General Coordination of Copyright on TCEs

Apart from FUNAI, another entity plays an important role in the discussion on an adequate protection of TCEs in Brazil: The Brazilian General Coordination of Copyright (CGDA).[714] It is collocated within the Ministry of Culture. It deals with all kind of copyright topics and related issues, and is also actively involved in the current discussions on an adequate protection of TCEs in the country and beyond.

A technical note issued by the Coordination, or Coordinating Agency in 2007, although without legally binding character of any kind, provides instructive and revealing insights into the national situation regarding TCEs from the perspective of a public entity involved.[715]

1. Status Quo as Observed by the Brazilian General Coordination of Copyright

As a consequence of the afore-mentioned discussions in the country, according to the CGDA, several segments of the civil society and other public entities have approached the different sectors of the Ministry of Culture with respect to a definition of a policy on TCEs, especially regarding their relation to intellectual property.[716] An increasing necessity to protect TCEs from illegal use and appropriation had been noted. From the CGDA's point of view, this increasing demand results from the rise of a market for sustainably manufactured products and those

[714] "Coordenação-Geral de Direito Autoral (CGDA)".

[715] Author expresses her deepest gratitude to Marcos Alves de Souza, Head of the Brazilian General Coordination of Copyright, Ministry of Culture, for sharing the document and experiences in March 2009, in Brasilia.

[716] Ministério da Cultura – Coordenação-Geral de Direito Autoral (2007) 1, translation by the author.

related to ethnic cultures—an environment that facilitates different forms of illegal appropriation like the unauthorized reproduction of graphics, wickerwork, handicrafts and other cultural goods.[717]

While Decree 3551/2000 stipulates the acknowledgement, safeguarding, and promotion of TCEs in their dimension as immaterial cultural patrimony, the questions concerning intellectual property are still unanswered to a very large extent. To answer those questions through an adequate legal framework, therefore, is a major challenge, the CGDA argues.[718]

Regarding the development of designing the relationship between intellectual property and TCEs and traditional knowledge, within the Ministry of Culture, "very little has been done so far."[719] The principal activity was regarded to be the participation in the meetings of the CGEN, the *Conselho de Gestão do Patrimônio Genético,* dealing with traditional knowledge on biodiversity and genetic resources.[720] This participation, the CDGA argues however, was rather formal and thus not satisfactory, and moreover, it only covered traditional knowledge related to biodiversity.[721] In total, since the mere creation of the CGEN, "the role of the Ministry of Culture was that of an assistant, without greater propositions regarding the cultural interface of the topic."[722]

Another activity with regard to the CGEN was the elaboration of a new draft law[723] on access to genetic resources and associated traditional knowledge in the country, which is intended to substitute the afore-mentioned (provisional) Act No. 2186-16.[724] According to the note, the CGDA[725] worked out opinions[726] on at least three versions of these draft laws, the last one of which even provoked objections on the part of the Foundation Palmares[727] and the IPHAN themselves. Moreover, the last version of the draft law stipulated "the transfer of competences in the Brazilian cultural patrimony away from the system of the Ministry of Culture towards the CGEN and the Ministry of Environment." However, "within the Ministry of Culture, only the CGDA opposed this last version of the draft law."[728]

---

[717] *Id.* 1.

[718] *Id.* 1.

[719] *Id.* 1, translation by the author.

[720] Managing Council of the Genetic Patrimony, Articles 10 *et seq.* of Act No. 2186-16, *see* at Section 2.D.I. above.

[721] Ministério da Cultura – Coordenação-Geral de Direito Autoral (2007) 2.

[722] *Id.*, translation by the author. On the division of tasks and competences and relationship between the different public entities in this area *see* at Section 2.D.I. above.

[723] "Anteprojeto de Lei (API)".

[724] On this *see* at Section 2.D.I. above.

[725] "Coordenação-Geral de Direito Autoral", the Brazilian General Coordination of Copyright.

[726] "Pareceres".

[727] "Fundação Palmares", an institution promoting the Afro-Brazilian and *quilombolan* culture in general, *see* at Section 2.A.I. and footnote 320 above.

[728] Information according to the legal advisors of the Ministry of Culture, the "Consultoria Jurídica (CONJUR/MinC)."

According to the note, the Ministry of Culture itself made another attempt in 2004 and 2005 to elaborate a working directive on the issue of TCEs and traditional knowledge. A working group was established to deal with this issue, including the Secretary of Cultural Identity and Diversity[729] and the Foundation Palmares, the chair under the responsibility of the IPHAN, and the Secretary of Cultural Policies.[730] However, according to the CGDA, no concrete results were presented. The main reason for the poor result was "the lack of knowledge of most of the group members on the field of intellectual property."[731]

Another action of the Ministry of Culture regarding the issue of TCEs and traditional knowledge was the creation of a "Working Group on Cultural Policies for Indigenous Peoples."[732] Still, according to the note, only one discussion took place on the relevant issue, and it was prepared and coordinated by the CGDA. No practical result on the issue was presented, the CGDA criticized, but simply the creation of a specific sector within the Ministry was recommended, to deal with the topic and to be responsible for the definition of a specific policy for this area of operation and its legal framework. Besides, a "National Seminary on Copyright and the Role of the State," organized by the CGDA, involved a panel on collective intellectual property rights of traditional populations. As a result, it became clear that "the development of a specific line of work for said segment is necessary within the Ministry of Culture."[733]

In conclusion, "there was little progress in defining positions or policies on the topic of protecting TCEs," as the treatment of this issue would require knowledge in all three areas, namely, the traditional populations of the country of Brazil, popular culture, *and* intellectual property law.[734]

2. Recommendations of the General Coordination of Copyright for Adequate Future Work on TCEs in Brazil

As the topic of protecting TCEs would require expertise or at least knowledge in all three areas of traditional populations of the country, popular culture, and intellectual property, the CGDA argues that only the creation of an entity specialized in the dealing with TCEs and traditional knowledge would allow an adequate treatment

[729] "Secretaria da Identidade e da Diversidade Cultural (SID)", http://www.cultura.gov.br/site/2007/09/25/quem-somos-2/, last visited April 8, 2010.

[730] "Secretaria de Políticas Culturais (SPC)" of the Ministry of Culture.

[731] Except from the Secretariat for Cultural Policies of the Ministry of Culture as at that time it was represented by the General Coordination of Copyright, Ministério da Cultura – Coordenação-Geral de Direito Autoral (2007) 3, translation by the author.

[732] "Grupo de Trabalho sobre Políticas Culturais para Povos Indígenas", created by the Secretariat of Cultural Identity and Diversity, "Secretaria da Identidade e da Diversidade Cultural (SID)."

[733] Ministério da Cultura – Coordenação-Geral de Direito Autoral (2007) 3, translation by the author.

[734] *Ibid*, translation by the author.

thereof, combining the expertise in all three topics.[735] Therefore, the CGDA suggests implementing a special competent entity within the CGDA particularly dealing with this issue.[736] The "mission" of this entity would be "to guarantee the protection the traditional knowledge and cultural expressions of the country against their unauthorized use and appropriation." To fulfil this mission, the following activities should be involved, according to the CGDA[737]:

(1) The "definition of a structured and transversal policy" within the Ministry of Culture on the protection of traditional knowledge and TCEs in Brazil;
(2) Promotion of "reflection on collective rights and on the protection of TCEs to support the creation of a legal instrument for the protection of TCEs and collective rights of the traditional populations of the country"—drafting such legal system would be of fundamental importance;
(3) Promotion of the use of existing instruments for the protection of intellectual property, like collective trademarks, certification marks, geographical indications, patents, and copyright by the traditional populations of the country—better stimulation for and visualization of the use of those legal instruments should be worked out;
(4) The Ministry of Culture should be the Brazilian institution to represent the country in intergovernmental fora (such at WIPO, WTO and UNESCO) along with the CGEN[738] and the Inter-ministerial Group for Intellectual Property.[739] At the moment, these positions were rather solely defined by the Ministry of Foreign Affairs and not by the Ministry that at the national level is, and also at the international level should be, as the CGDA says, responsible for the issue of TCEs—the Ministry of Culture.[740]
(5) Communication with the IPHAN "to create a connection between the protection of TCEs and that of the immaterial cultural patrimony". According to the CGDA, in most of the cases, the object of the policies on a protection of TCEs and traditional knowledge and on a protection of the immaterial cultural patrimony is or will be the same. Nonetheless, the legislation on the immaterial cultural patrimony would not cover questions of illegitimate appropriation, abusive or unauthorized use. These questions would refer to the area of intellectual property. It is essential to note, the CGDA emphasises, that patrimony "does not equate with property – the latter being a monopolistic right. In

[735] *Id.* 3 (2007).

[736] Concretely, the CGDA argues, that would involve the establishment of three new positions, occupied by experts in the area of traditional populations, popular culture and intellectual property, whose work would be coordinated and supervised by the deputy Coordinator-General of copyright, *id.* 3 (2007).

[737] *Id.* 3–5 (2007).

[738] Managing Council of the Genetic Patrimony, Articles 10 *et seq.* of Act No. 2186-16, *see* at Section 2.D.I. above.

[739] "Grupo interministerial de Propriedade Intelectual (GIPI)."

[740] *Id.* 4, 5, translation by the author.

cases of unauthorized use and illegitimate appropriation, the legislation on intellectual property should be the one to treat those questions in communication with the policy on Immaterial Cultural Patrimony of the IPHAN, making use of the path already travelled by the IPHAN."[741]

3. Conclusion and Evaluation of the Position of the General Coordination of Copyright

The technical note of the General Coordination of Copyright within the Ministry of Culture contains a political statement of this unity dealing with TCEs in the current national treatment of TCEs as well as on a possible further development of the topic. Aside from this apparently rather descriptive character, it also makes visible different political and legal aspects regarding the protection of TCEs in Brazil, which are worth taking into account when dealing with the question of protecting TCEs.

It has become clear that the protection of TCEs is an issue of great importance and awareness in the different ministries, entities within the ministries, and other representations of interests. At the same time, very little progress in protecting TCEs, or even defining a common Brazilian policy on it, has been made so far. Crucial points are material and procedural ones: on the one hand, the lack of knowledge on TCEs, traditional populations and intellectual property law, and on the other hand the division—or unclear allocation—of competences regarding the larger topic in general (including traditional knowledge related to biodiversity and genetic resources), i.e. divided competences between the different ministries, as well as regarding TCEs in concrete, i.e. divided competences within the Ministry of Culture itself.

Thus, beside the need for substantial anthropological and legal qualifications, there is a strong tendency to absorb resources by focusing on the rather political question of allocating competences to deal with the issue. This latter aspect appears to have amounted to a certain deadlock preventing the development of an adequate protection of TCEs in the country and beyond.

In its effect, this scenario indeed calls to mind a miniature replica of the situation at the international level: competences, especially of WIPO and WTO, but also of UNESCO, are not clearly defined or consistently "respected" in the negotiations on protecting TCEs, traditional knowledge, and cultural heritage. This "struggle for competence"—whether intentionally provoked by some member states themselves or not[742]—constitutes one factor among others that obstruct the progress of a (successful) substantial outcome of the negotiations.

---

[741] *Id.* 5, translation by the author.

[742] One source states that especially Brazil itself employed a "tactic" of questioning competences in one forum or the other, mainly at WIPO, to strengthen its negotiating position on traditional knowledge at WTO. The informant wishes to remain anonymous, though.

Thus, it is not surprising, though it complicates the situation even more, that the Ministry of Culture, in particular the General Coordination of Copyright, argues a "fundamental importance" of Brazilian positions at WIPO, WTO, and UNESCO based upon the policy defined by the Ministry of Culture—and to be visualized by the team proposed above. It is clear: The topic of protecting TCEs is in part an intra-national and international political struggle for competences.

IV. Harnessing TCEs for Development and Trade: Promoting Commercialization and Innovation of TCEs

Not just as a consequence of WIPO's policy on harnessing TCEs for development and trade, but at a very early stage, the idea of promoting TCEs, or, at that time rather parts of them like indigenous handicrafts, was even anchored legally in the 1973 Indian Statute in Brazil. Article 53 of the Statute stipulates: "The handicraft and rural trade shall be promoted in order to elevate the standard of living of the Indians, adapting it adequately to modern technical conditions."

It is disputed, however, whether this provision contradicts the "new" Article 231 of the 1988 Constitution and is thus void. Some authors argue that Article 53 is intended to serve the former integrationist policy and therefore does not correspond to the new permanent recognition of indigenous cultures set up by Article 231 of the Constitution.[743]

Nonetheless, Article 53 of the Indian Statute, alongside Article 231 of the Constitution, is still employed as a legal basis for argumentation in current juridical processes regarding indigenous handicraft and its commercialization.[744]

Whether the provision has led to any significant changes in the indigenous reality regarding their handicraft, is not noted.

Currently, a special entity within FUNAI, the Coordenação Geral de Artesanato (CGART), General Handicrafts Directorate, works on using opportunities for and ways of commercializing TCEs, TCEs-based products, and services in an appropriate surrounding, as well as the promotion of entrepreneurship. The CGART has established a special program on the commercial promotion of culture (PPA), which is set to be launched during the period of 2008–2011.[745] The main idea is a different form of "sale," characterized by a contextualization of the indigenous handicraft and other artistic products, consisting of an appropriate setting to display the goods—a loggia close to a museum for instance—and offering a wide range of

[743] Kayser (2005) 333 *et seq.*

[744] On details of this interesting argumentation and its connection with the promotion policy of FUNAI *see* at Section 2.D.V. below and *Parecer* of the *Procurador Regional da República* of the 4. Region, the Regional Public Prosecutor (including actions in civil and public law) Paulo Gilberto Gogo Leivas, of September 14, 2007, appealing against the Decision 2007.72.08.000014-0, in which the judge had not followed this view.

[745] Personal communication with Pedro Mortale, General Director of the Handicraft Section/Head of the General Direction of Handicrafts (CGART) of FUNAI on March 25, 2009 in Brasilia.

information and knowledge on the goods, their mode of production, traditional meaning, and spiritual basis to make visible the difference from ordinary products sold on the global market. Further, the sale is to involve the participation of the indigenous handicraftsmen themselves, and raise awareness of particularities and interdependences of the traditional cultural goods, e.g. the connection to the environment for growing the raw material.[746]

Besides, the use of indicative signs like self-certifications, stating, for example, "this is a product of the indigenous community of the Rio Negro region," or even of geographic indications for "the cultural art of the Xingu National Park," for instance, is planned.[747]

Recalling the legal criticism on Article 53 of the 1973 Indian Statute, particularly that the promotion of indigenous handicraft might contradict the permanent recognition of indigenous culture as such, one could think of a risk involved in this progressive project: this promotion and commercialization might contravene indigenous principles of exchange and reciprocity. However, this is the permanent dilemma plaguing the topic of TCEs, and for this reason it should be at the discretion of the particular indigenous person or community itself to decide in how far it wants to participate in the project or not. Besides, especially the approach of raising awareness, providing information, and producing knowledge, might facilitate the attempt to uphold these principles and even pass them on, thus the "sale" of particular TCEs could help contribute to intercultural communication.

V. Case Law

So far, no court decisions on TCEs are known in Brazil. The main reason for this is that neither indigenous peoples themselves nor the public entities involved expect adequate or helpful dispute resolution from decisions issued by the courts.[748] Here, in addition, there is a Brazilian particularity at work, namely the jurisdictional representation of indigenous peoples and defense of their rights by the Ministry of the Public as provided by Article 129 para. 5 of the Brazilian Constitution. Having experience in the Brazilian juridical system, the experts and staff members of the Ministry of the Public prefer to settle such disputes at the administrative level, and avoid bring cases to the regular courts.[749] While this approach might be useful in every-day practice to settle disputes quickly, it disables the establishment of precedences and guidelines by the Brazilian Judicature, although every new decision

---

[746] *Supra.*

[747] *Supra.*

[748] Personal communication with Ana Cristina Bandeira Lins, *Procuradora da República* in the *Ministerio Público*, on June 23, 2009 in São Paolo, Brazil, *see* also Busch (2010) 220 *et seq.*

[749] Personal communication with Ana Cristina Bandeira Lins, *Procuradora da República* in the Ministry of Public (Ministerio Público), which is similar to a prosecutor/Staatsanwältin, on June 23, 2009 in São Paolo, Brazil, *see* also *id.* 220 *et seq.*

issued could increase legal certainty and might even promote the adoption of new legislation on the topic.

Research has revealed that on the topic of "indigenous culture" in the broader sense, three interesting cases have been published in the last few years.[750] At first glance, the facts of the cases seem to have nothing whatsoever to do with protecting TCEs. Still, a closer look at the legal argumentation within and circumstances of the cases reveals interesting statements and/or aspects that can be of value for this topic as well.

(1) All three statements of claim of the *Ministério Público* and decisions provide practical examples of the connection between case law and anthropology, as does even the official recognition of anthropological expert opinions, which unfortunately have not been attached to the publications.
(2) In a case regarding the Kaingang community, the *Ministério Público* as defendor of the indigenous rights argued that the "the production and commercialization of handicrafts constitutes an expression of indigenous cultural identity," as well as of social relations, and goes beyond the usual commerce from a capitalistic perspective.[751] The places where commercialization of indigenous handicraft takes place should not be understood merely as space needed for the economic sustainability of the indigenous communities, but "also as an important point of encounter for intercultural and interethnic communication, maintaining the culture as well as mutual respect between societies, which is essential for maintaining cultural diversity in the country."[752]
(3) There exists a collective right to one own's picture, a right held by an indigenous community, and this had been infringed, the *Ministério Público* argued in a case regarding the Tupinikins and Guarani communities. The court decision supported this opinion, ruling in favor of "collective moral damages."[753]

---

[750] Cases 2006.50.04.000458-0 6001 – ACAO CIVIL PUBLICA; ACP – ES – 2006.50.04.000458.0 – contra Aracruz Celulose; 2003.42.00.001505-0; 2007.72.08.000014-0. The author expresses her greatest thanks to Carla Daniela Leite Negócio, Legal Coordinator at the 6. Chamber of Coordination and Appeal, competent for indigenous and minority issues, at the *Ministério Público Federal* (Federal Public Ministry), for sharing the documents and for the personal communication on March 27, 2009, in Brasilia.

[751] *Parecer* of the *Procurador Regional da República* of the 4. Region, the Regional Public Prosecutor (including actions in civil and public law) Paulo Gilberto Gogo Leivas, of September 14, 2007, appealing against the Decision 2007.72.08.000014-0, in which the judge had not followed this view. Whether the court followed this argument was unfortunately not known. Translation by the author.

[752] *Parecer* of the *Procurador Regional da República* of the 4. Region, the Regional Public Prosecutor (including actions in civil and public law) Paulo Gilberto Gogo Leivas, of September 14, 2007, appealing against the Decision 2007.72.08.000014-0, in which the judge had not followed this view. Whether the court followed this argument was unfortunately not known. Translation by the author.

[753] *See* the case *Ministério Público Federal v. Aracruz Celulose S.A.*, especially the statement of the *Procurador* and *Procuradora da República* of October 20, 2006, and the according Interim Decision 2006.50.04.000456-0 6001.

(4) There exists a right to self-identification as an indigenous person (Article 3, para 1, and Article 1, No. 2, of ILO Convention 169, which is applicable in Brazil through the Decree No. 5.051/2004), as well as a right to cultural identity, as argued in the same case.[754]

(5) The fundamental rights are also applicable in private relations, as the fundamental norms have horizontal effects if there is a "manifest inequality" between the parties involved.[755] For example, between the weak ("hiposuficiente") indigenous community and a multinational company which is dominant in the cellulose market, there exists such inequality.[756]

E. Concluding Evaluation and Outlook on the Situation in Brazil

Different legal approaches and practical experiences have been made by the different Brazilian public entities involved in the broader topic of protecting TCEs, mainly IPHAN, FUNAI, and NGOs allocated in the country, as laid out in detail above.

In general, some voices argue that, within its legal limits, the system in Brazil functions well. When the president of the national indigenous organization, the COIAB, was queried, for instance, he answered that the protection of TCEs in Brazil works well, that the government implements many different projects with different tribes all over the country and that the relationship between the government and the indigenous peoples is a good one.[757] This point of view might be an expression of a functionary attitude. Nonetheless, indeed, many different projects of the various entities have been launched, like the annual "Indigenous Cultures Award" of the Secretariat of Cultural Identity and Diversity within the Ministry of the Public,[758] documentations and exhibitions of the Indian Museum, commercial promotion of TCEs by FUNAI, and the currently quickly increasing documentations and registrations of goods as immaterial cultural patrimony in accordance with Decree No. 3551, administered by IPHAN. The existing instrument of cultural

---

754 *See* the case *Ministério Público Federal v. Aracruz Celulose S.A.*, especially the statement of the *Procurador* and *Procuradora da República* of October 20, 2006, and the according Interim Decision 2006.50.04.000456-0 6001.

755 *See* the similar principle of Fundamental Rights having a binding effect on third parties at a private level under certain circumstances in European law ("Horizontale Drittwirkung von Grundrechten").

756 *See* the case Ministério Público Federal vs. Aracruz Celulose S.A., especially the statement of the *Procurador* and *Procuradora da República* of October 20, 2006, and the according Interim Decision 2006.50.04.000456-0 6001.

757 Personal communication with Francisco Avelino Batista, president of the Coordination of Indigenous Organizations of the Brazilian Amazon (COIAB), in March 2009 in Quito, Ecuador.

758 *See* the official publications: Ministério da Cultura and SESC SP (2007) and Ministério da Cultura and SESC SP (2008).

law, namely Decree No. 3551, is an effective measure for documenting and promoting TCEs—in its limited capacity of financial and human resources. However, it does not provide for individual rights and therefore does not answer the needs in cases of infringements. The reaction of FUNAI, to establish its own *Portaria* No. 177 of 2006 with relation to collective copyright and right of personal portrayal, reveals the practical need of more concrete legal solutions.

The discussion of a sui generis protection within the country is as complicated as the complexity of the factual issue itself, especially when considering the diversity of the different traditional minority groups in Brazil. Furthermore, economic and political powers are rather interested in the exploitation of natural resources within the indigenous territories than in strengthening the rights of those peoples to the benefit of cultural diversity, sustainable development, or "social justice"—as was the driving force behind the sui generis regime in Panama.[759] While especially experts with an intellectual property background, as well as the practical experience of FUNAI, argue in favor of a sui generis regime—of whatever kind—Brazilian anthropologists express concerns in view of unforeseeable impacts on the traditional socio-cultural structures that will go hand in hand with a juridification of social relations within indigenous communities, and these anthropologists have started a long-term research project on exactly this question, whose outcome will be extremely interesting to follow.[760]

In total, the legal aspects of the topic of TCEs in their concrete dimension of infringements have rarely been discussed so far. As the insights provided by the Technical Note of the CGDA expose, the discussion is still at the beginning, and one of the biggest problem is the lack of expertise in the relevant areas of this interdisciplinary topic.

Similarly, this is also the impression obtained during the registration and promotion of certain TCEs as Brazilian immaterial cultural patrimony under the regime of Decree 3551: Notwithstanding the legal system existing in the country, "very little had been done in practice to assure the respect for the different cultures. Worse still is the lack of capacity building enabling the functionaries of the official organs dealing with the indigenous policy to know, respect, and valorize the continuity of the transmission of the different oral wisdoms of the indigenous peoples in Brazil. There continues to exist a considerable difference between the excellent legal dispositions and the immense difficulties encountered by the local agents in understanding and implementing these instruments of protection and valorization."[761] Among the majority of the agents, the idea still dominates that

[759] On this *see* at Section 1.B. above.

[760] Personal communication with Marcela Stockler Coelho de Souza, Professor of Anthropology at the University of Brasilia, on March 27, 2009 in Brasilia, who is conducting the research project, together with a team of other anthropological experts including Professor Manuela Carneiro da Cunha and others.

[761] IPHAN – Instituto do Patrimônio Histórico e Artístico Nacional (2008) 106.

the indigenous ways of life and thoughts are transitory and have to be "modernized" urgently.[762]

Even distinguished Brazilian legal experts in publications entitled "Intangible heritage and collective intellectual rights"[763] refer to Articles 215 and 216 of the Constitution, and focus on traditional knowledge on biodiversity.

As regards the discussion on collective rights in the ambit of copyright law, Brazilian authors argue that "in a globalized world like the current one, the principle of individuality seems to be not adequate anymore as a precondition for the soul of copyright. Today, the utilitarian and easily reproducible works also deserve protection by copyright, following the North-American maxim, according to which 'everything that is worth copying is worth protecting.'"[764] Whether such a collective copyright as established by the Portaria of FUNAI will be taken up either in the reform of the Copyright Law or the ongoing one of the Indian Statute cannot be predicted at this stage.

Meanwhile, court decisions could provide for a bit more legal certainty, at least as interim solutions. Still, they are lacking so far. Also, the jurisdictional path seems to be not the appropriate one, as, first, the competence for appropriately dealing with the interdisciplinary issue of TCEs and finding practical solutions is lacking, and second, court proceedings are usually characterized by lengthiness in Brazil.[765]

Finally, the situation in Brazil displays once more that a crucial aspect of protecting TCEs as part of the indigenous culture goes back to the question of land rights, exploitation of natural resources, and the invasion of "Western" socio-cultural habits in the indigenous territories. Beside the experience gained in the processes of registering immaterial cultural patrimony, for instance in the case of the waterfall region *Cachoeira de Iauaretê*,[766] disputes on land rights and the situation of indigenous rights in general also reveal that the survival of the habits and cultures of indigenous peoples in Brazil are not ensured permanently by the current legislative provisions in the country. In this regard, the deficiency particularly relates to the core issue of indigenous territory and access privileges to all kind of natural resources, including water, by third parties,[767] because in most of the cases, the collective territory is one of the best and most important preconditions for ensuring the continued existence of the indigenous traditional culture. Besides, contradictions between the progressive constitutional, and obsolete administrative provisions exist, impeding a major step towards an improved legal treatment of questions relating to the indigenous culture, especially as regards the persisting

[762] IPHAN – Instituto do Patrimônio Histórico e Artístico Nacional (2008) 106.

[763] Santilli (2006) 81-98.

[764] De Hollanda Sheldrick (2009) 68, translation by the author.

[765] Kayser (2005) 533 *et seq.* argues that in indigenous issues, this would be true particularly for demarcation questions.

[766] IPHAN – Instituto do Patrimônio Histórico e Artístico Nacional (2007) 102 *et seq.*

[767] On practical experiences and legal processes dealing with indigenous land rights in Brazil *see* Kayser (2005) 431 *et seq.*

provisions on the guardianship in Articles 7 *et seq.* of the current Indian Statute.[768] The anthropological progress made by the development of the theory of relativity of cultures[769] has not been implemented juridically so far—although precisely this is an essential precondition for the adequate protection of TCEs. To a certain extent, however, adequate practical solutions are found in the every-day approach, mainly due to the personal engagement and anthropological involvement pushed forward by some individuals within the public entities in charge.[770] Correspondingly, it is also the proper engagement and dedication of the indigenous peoples themselves in maintaining and transmitting their TCEs to the next generation—a challenge within the communities themselves—that has been addressed in some projects with the support of national entities and personal involvement, as the documented experiences on measures taken to assure the transmission of the *Arte Kusiwa* show.[771] While there is a need for an international solution in some cases, as for example in the bodypainting case involving Japanese citizens,[772] the Brazilian experience shows that in the issue of protecting TCEs, much can be enhanced at the local and national level.

---

768 *Id.* 428.

769 On this *see* at Section 2.B.I. above.

770 Personal communication with Ana Cristina Bandeira Lins, *Procuradora da República* in the *Ministerio Público*, on June 23, 2009 in São Paolo, Brazil, *see* also Busch (2010) 220 *et seq.*

771 IPHAN – Instituto do Patrimônio Histórico e Artístico Nacional (2008) 106 *et seq.*

772 On this *see* at Section 2.C.III. above.

Chapter V. Conclusion and Outlook

Based upon the study conducted and experiences gathered in Latin American countries final remarks will provide an overview over the topic and draw general conclusions.

In particular, this last chapter will shortly summarize the current situation on the legal protection of TCEs at the regional level of Latin America (below Section 1.). It will then highlight theoretical approaches discussed at the international level and formulate an own, holistic approach based upon the specific Latin American experiences (below Section 2.). Both, arguments in favor of the approach as well as specific elements of this approach are discussed. In line with the holistic approach, related recommendations of indigenous persons themselves will be summarized (below Section 3). The study concludes with summarizing remarks and an outlook on the topic.

Section 1. Summary of the Regional Situation of TCEs in Latin America

Currently, the legal situation regarding the protection of TCEs in Latin America looks like this:

(1) No common regional agreement or uniform national legislation on TCEs exists so far.

(2) At the supra-national level, the Andean Community has issued some decisions that touch the topic, and has elaborated preparatory work on a sui generis regime on TCEs. Currently, however, the process has not moved forward since a corresponding common political will among the member states is lacking.

© Springer-Verlag Berlin Heidelberg 2015

A.F. Busch, *Protection of Traditional Cultural Expressions in Latin America*,
Munich Studies on Innovation and Competition 3, DOI 10.1007/978-3-662-46770-1_5

(3) Unlike the situation in the United States of America, for instance, in Latin America, there exists no uniform indigenous legislation framing the legal treatment of TCEs and related issues like recognition of customary law.

(4) Similarly, there is no common political direction towards reforms or the implementation of new regimes on the topic. The establishment of a regional law similar to the WIPO Model Law of the Pacific seems to be very unlikely at the moment. Factual cooperation is more likely. The Brazilian "public law model," for instance, facilitated a cooperation with the Argentinean Ministry of Culture, initiating a project regarding the protection of TCEs of the Huaraní tribe, whose members are living on both sides of the common border.

(5) At the national level, similarly, the crucial precondition for the implementation of an adequate system of TCE protection is the corresponding political will and power. The situation in Panama was quite special due to the allocation of political power and the existence of a concrete driving force to pass the sui generis regime: The muse to the creators of this law was the country's most famous TCE, at the same time a source of cultural identity and the most important source of income of the Kuna Indians, the *mola*. The *mola* was in actual danger of being registered as trademark or design by non-indigenous companies *and* at the time an indigenous person was the president of the Panamanian Parliament. He was able to unify enough various votes to make the law pass. Such a situation is not the general case in most of the Latin American countries.

(6) Even theoretically, due to the legal, political, but also factual differences regarding the geographic and economic situation of the countries, the quantity and diversity of their ethnic groups (220 different indigenous peoples living in Brazil in contrast to 7 in Panama for instance), the local and national organization of these groups, administrative and local representation, and internal distribution rules, the content of an adequate future regional agreement is hard to predict.

(7) Case law on TCEs, which could serve as guiding lines, is highly underdeveloped in Latin American countries.

Section 2. Approaches to and Recommendations for Protection of TCEs

A. Theories Developed at the International Level

At the international level, different theories and approaches towards a protection of TCEs have been discussed:

(1) "No Protection" approach: No legal protection should be granted, especially, no further legal instrument should be established. TCEs must be interchangeable material and immaterial goods and remain within the "free flow of cultural

evolution" and interaction. Thus, "respect" would be the most appropriate means of addressing TCEs.[1]

(2) "IP approach": TCEs should obtain protection as far as they fit within the existing system of intellectual property rights by means of subsumption and interpretation of these instruments. In addition, international guidelines, individual agreements, protocols and other "soft law" may be applied.[2]

(3) Sui generis approach: A new agreement or system of its own kind should be established. Examples could be the 2002 WIPO Pacific Model Law or the Panamanian Sui Generis Regime of 2000.[3]

(4) Recognition and Enforcement of Judgements of Tribal Courts: Decisions taken by indigenous "courts" on TCE-related cases should be recognized and enforceable within the country as well as abroad. Recognizing and enforcing such decisions would be the most appropriate way of giving effect to the traditional legal handling of TCEs, i.e. customary law, and thereby of protecting TCEs themselves.[4]

B. Individual Approach of Protection: A Combined Approach

Based upon the results of this study in the Latin American ambit,[5] the author suggests a combined, holistic approach of protecting TCEs.

In order to be both, effective in the long run, and implementable within a rather narrow time frame, the combined approach includes both, "hard law" and "soft law".

In detail, the arguments for and elements of such combined approach are as follows:

I. Legal Protection Is Needed

The "No"-approach is not convincing. "Respect" and soft law turned out to be important modes of implementing protection and promoting the vitality of TCEs, as it stimulates the appreciation of TCEs by the indigenous communities themselves,

---

[1] *See* also at Chapter II Section 2.A. above.

[2] *See* also at Chapter II Section 2.A. and Chapter III Section 3. above.

[3] *See* also at Chapter II Section 2.F.IV., Chapter III Section 2.B. and C., and Chapter IV Section 1. above.

[4] For details hereon *see* at Chapter II Section 2.F.I. and E. above. For ways of recognizing and enforcing judgements issued by foreign courts *see* for instance the "Brussles I" Regulation, Council Regulation (EC) 44/2001 of December 22, 2000 on jurisdiction and the recognition and enforcement of judgments in civil and commercial matters.

[5] *See* also the focus and aim of the study defined in accordance with the experiences made at the international level at Chapter I Section 1. above.

which have passed through decades of discrimination; but "respect" is not an exclusive solution in itself when concrete infringements occurred. In the latter cases, a concrete legal instrument would be of value.

II. A Legal Instrument Is of Value—And Bears Certain Risks

New rights may provoke new conflicts, as experiences in Panama have shown. Such conflicts may arise with regard to the allocation of social roles, of power, with regard to organization, and gender issues. It may have an unforeseen impact on the social structure within the traditional culture that was supposed to be protected. Such long-term effects of a juridification of social relationships are an important and very interesting aspect to be examined more carefully before establishing new legal systems on paper—and currently it is indeed subject of a major anthropological research project currently under way in Brazil. At this stage, the new conflicts should, however, be no reason for neglecting to create a law at all, but should instead be a point for consideration, more intensive study, and adequate treatment in the designing and implementation of a system of protection.

III. A Legal Instrument Alone Is Not Sufficient

(1) A holistic approach is needed. Although generalizations are critical in view of the diverse indigenous realities, the probably most pressing problem of the traditional communities in their every-day life is that of safeguarding resources and the traditional living environment. This is crucial for a continued existence of their collective and the different social functions within it, which, in turn, is an essential precondition for maintaining TCEs. For instance, the registration as Brazilian immaterial cultural patrimony of the indigenous sacred place "Cachoeira de Iuararetê", an inspiring source for traditional indigenous rituals, was initiated by the indigenous peoples because the Brazilian air force planned to enlarge a small runway for military activity in the area, and new settlement turned the traditional living environment into a regular city with a commercial face. Besides maintaining the collective way of life, the problem more specifically concerns resources used to create or produce certain TCEs themselves: as observed in Panama, the most urgent problem was not the legal protection or procedure, but rather the lack or steady disappearance of specific raw materials necessary for producing the handicraft, like the wild pineapple plant used to make the hand-woven bags called *chácaras*. The Department for Collective Rights and Folkloristic Expressions set up a "rescue plan" and initiated a huge planting project in the territory of the Ngöbe tribe. However, limited financial resources also limited this project. Such factual problems would not be solved by an IP-related legal instrument alone.

(2) At the international level, it turned out to not always be a question of the (non-) existence of laws or agreements, but of dealing with socio-economic problems

of the "right holders" within existing legislations, as the conflict on the *mola* in Panama and Costa Rica revealed. At the same time, this finding indicates the need for an economic aspect of legal protection, i.e. the establishment of economic rights or an exclusive legal status—even if traditional indigenous worldviews in Latin America refer to the exchange of goods as a specific characteristic of reciprocity. Without disregarding the particularities, a balance between theoretical fundaments and practical realities and needs has to be found, providing economic rights for those communities that would like to make use of them.

(3) Promotion by public entities is an important and—to a certain extent—successful "second pillar," in both a cultural law and a sui generis system, as experiences in Panama and Brazil have shown. Thus, if implemented successfully,[6] it is important to promote the estimation of TCEs as a means of furthering their vitality, but this as well is not adequate as an exclusive solution.

IV. Recognizing Tribal Court Decisions Faces Practical Challenges

The idea of acknowledging and recognizing decisions of traditional authorities on the basis of customary law seems very appealing.

At the same time, realities in Latin America have revealed that an approach of recognizing and enforcing indigenous court decisions faces major practical challenges.

(1) Considering legal and political current realities, such an approach is hardly realizable in the near future.[7] To some extent, jurisdictional competence of indigenous authorities is acknowledged, as e.g. of the Cabildos in Colombia. However, this competence is mostly subordinated under the juridical control of the regular national courts.[8] Political concerns against a further recognition derive from the particular history of most of the Latin American nations, as well as new tendencies towards uniform citizenships, and the topic's embedding in the major issue of legal plurality and indigenous autonomy in general. As regards the future development, the political potential towards a greater or smaller scope of application of customary law in general varies in the different Latin American countries. Regional workshops and seminars are held on the issue, but no common political position exists with regard to legal pluralism, much less on the specific situation of TCEs.

(2) Different from the situation of the Pueblo Indians in the United States of America, for instance, the "traditional courts" in Latin America do not issue "decisions" but mostly enact the settlement of conflicts as social processes embedded in social relations. Orality is still dominating (except the Codes of

[6] On aspects on the implementation *see* at Chapter VIII Section 6. below.

[7] For details hereon *see* at Chapter II Section 2.F. above.

[8] *See* at Chapter II Section 2.E.3.a. above.

the Kuna Indians in Panama, for instance). The recognition and enforcement of such dispute settlement by a foreign court would be difficult or, alternatively, require the altering of the traditional form of treating TCE-related cases.

(3) More and more, traditional authorities are changing rather quickly and are lacking legitimacy within the community.

V. Customary Law in General Is an Important and: From a Western Point—Challenging Element of Protection

Applying customary law has increasingly been rated the best qualified and most capable answer to various questions in TCEs, especially regarding holders of rights, representation, and distribution of benefits.

Giving effect to customary law might indeed reflect and maintain better, or even best, the socio-cultural peculiarities and diversity of the communities concerned. This has been confirmed by the Panamanian experiences with customary law on the one hand and regulations inspired strongly by the intellectual property system on the other.

The examination and analysis of concrete examples of customary law dealing with TCEs and its idiomatic and spiritual particularities is also imperative to understand and further develop the topic properly. Examples have been disposed here from indigenous persons and communities from Ecuador, Peru, Panama, and Brazil.

At the same time, from a Western legal perspective, the topic of customary law in protecting TCEs is complex:

(1) Research on it is only at the beginning in the Latin American region. This is due to the afore mentioned political concerns and to challenges in the research of customary law in this particular area:

 a. Rather than "decisions", the whole process of dispute settling has to be analyzed. The dimension of time as well as the involvement of the community are essential to these processes, which makes research activities time-consuming.
 b. The still dominating orality as well as impacts of a fast changing environment favor a quick alteration of customary in practice.
 c. Communities in their traditional living environment are hard to approach in remote areas like the Amazon region. Additionally,
 d. The issue is characterized by a high degree of diversity on the factual basis. In Brazil alone, there exist over 220 different indigenous peoples.
 e. In the broader area of customary law, rather family and criminal law, land rights, and administration of justice had been subjects to research in the past, and, in addition, the topic of TCEs in its IP- and interdisciplinary dimension bears a challenging complexitiy.

(2) Also the legal treatment of customary law in general and on TCEs in particular varies a lot in the different Latin American countries. First of all, the Spanish,

Portuguese, and Native terminology is very heterogenous and thus not clear, what is understood by "customary law", especially by lawyers. Second, legal provisions that refer to customary law vary widely. Interesting examples are Venezuela, where the application of customary law in general is provided by constitutional provisions and linked to collective land rights, and, with regard to TCEs, Panama. The latter is also the only country to have officially acknowledged and implemented the application of customary law in the topic of TCEs in a sui generis regime.

(3) Also critical points to be considered: There is not always a common will favoring the application of customary law. This regards for instance the traditional role and rights of women. Therefore, the implementation of customary law in the concrete case of protecting TCEs in Panama provoked gender issues, and, as a consequence, the question of "reforming" or re-structuring the traditional rules, with regard to organization and representation in issues of a certain TCE, the *mola*.

(4) In practice, customary rules are not always capable of settling TCEs-related disputes between different tribes or even within one community. This problem depends upon different factors, e.g. the legal culture, in particular traditional forms of (physical) conflict settlement, the current legitimacy of the traditional leader within the community, the status of integration of a community into the national society, the complexity of the issue, or "simply" factual obstacles like finding the infringing persons. The establishment of new administrative bodies or advisory councils might be inevitable for an effective functioning of the application of customary rules in practice. In practice, inter-culturally experienced staff members of public entities like the Brazilian Ministry of the Public, the FUNAI, or the Panamanian DIGERPI have mediated in such cases. Thus, besides customary rules, applicable alternative dispute resolution should be incorporated as a subsidiary measure in a system of protection, with provisions of mediation or arbitration allocating competences in interdisciplinary, i.e. inter-culturally, legally, and anthropologically trained entities. Whether such instruments are effectively implemented, and what effect they have, however, depends upon the very engagement and personal skill of the one person in charge.

(5) In the Latin American legal ambit, there are various possibilities of giving binding effect to customary law. These are, among others, the application of customary law (1) by means of reference and registry, (2) by means of collective land rights, (3) by factual consideration, (4) by acknowledging jurisdictional competence, (5) by the legal instrument of (limited) reference, (6) or by choice. Two options discussed intensively at the international level i.e. by acknowledgement either at the material or at the procedural level, are legal reference and using collective land rights to acknowledge (tribal) court decisions. In those places where an effective tribal or local court system exists (e.g. in the United States), the latter option would be favorable. This turned out to not be true for most of the situations in Latin America.

(6) Another crucial question is whether customary law might include or even should require formalities. Should it be written down or even registered, as provided for by Law No. 20 in Panama? The typical element of customary law is the fact that, due to its oral nature and the underlying philosophical concept that is in opposition to Western formalities, it is intended to and capable of being adapted easily to changing circumstances. This element would be lost in codification. Moreover, the rules consist rather of dispute-settlement procedures than of static material conceptions to be laid down as substantive provisions.

(7) Similar to general political observations, there exists a great difference between the (theoretical) reference to customary law, especially in the constitutions, and its application or implementation in practice by Latin American public entities.

(8) A similar divergency regards the community's practice. Although an important legal principle based on David Hume's dichotomy of the "is" and the "ought" stipulates that no simple deduction from the "is" to the "ought" should be made, as the two differ entirely,[9] considering the social and customary legal is necessary in order to avoid difficulties in the later application. The concrete examples given here have revealed that the most crucial points within the communities, i.e. as regards a common understanding and implementation of their "customary law", are the questions of representation, holders and managements of rights. The question of representation is linked to the emerging adaptation of Westerly organized structures in political representation at the global, national, and local level, and to *inter alia* intergenerational conflicts at the local level. As regards the every-day implementation of the *collective* rights, even in native communities traditionally based on the principle of collectivity, a "collective mentality" when executing the collective rights cannot be taken for granted, and this becomes less and less the case with a growing acculturation to the individualistic lifestyle in the national society. Especially in view of the analysis conducted of the Panamanian system, the implementation of collective rights requires first, clear rules on paper which respond to the peoples' needs and real socio-cultural conditions, and, second, it requires subsidiary, appropriate dispute-solution measures.

(9) In its legal dimension, the application of customary law might not always be in accordance with national or even international principles of law, for instance equal rights of men and women, but also as regards common physical castigation, even the persisting application of death penalty (mostly in family or criminal cases). A minimum standard of common values within the national society and international legal frameworks, even if they are not binding, is

[9] The idea of the imperative distinction between the "is, and is not" and the "ought, and ought not" goes back to the philosophy of Hume (1739) Book III, Part 1, (I), *see* at Chapter II Section 5.A. III.2. above.

needed for peaceful cohabitation. A solution to the conflict even at the national level could be similar to the *ordre public* in private international law.

(10) The application of customary law necessarily finds its limits in the principle of *good faith*. It is important to understand deep resentments and a corresponding strong political movement towards more self-determination, as emotionally expressed in different workshops and congresses in Ecuador and Brazil that the author was allowed to attend. The application of customary rules in the field of TCEs, however, should not be understood or misused as an instrument for "fighting back," but as a balance of different interests and positions when answering concrete juridical questions. In a less radical way, this aspect also touches the phenomenon of "inventing traditions" by Hobsbawm, here dealt with as inventing customary law. A legal parameter for determining the limit in each concrete case could be the principle of good faith.

VI. The Holistic Approach Begins with Adequate Elaboration of Protection

(1) As international publications have stressed that "a key development in the work of the IGC has been incremental steps to ensure that the voices of indigenous and local communities" have been "central to the work,"[10] it is essential to question whose voices they are. In official procedures and the negotiations in the formally intergovernmental process, the intermediaries are rarely representatives of the respective community, and there seldom exists "one indigenous position," as the chapter of this study on indigenous philosophies has revealed. Likewise, there were also varied reactions and criticism on the legislative process establishing the parallel system of protecting certain traditional knowledge in Peru and in Brazil.[11]

(2) Another lesson learned from particularly these two cases is the importance of involving the potential bearers of TCEs in the process of drafting a protection at the earliest stage possible—taking the disadvantage of a more time-consuming procedure. This would facilitate the legitimacy and acceptance of a legal instrument and thereby support its implementation.

(3) Another important aspect is the permanent awareness of the intercultural character of the dialog on protecting TCEs in official or non-official environments, including different modes of thoughts, concepts of words and conceptions of the means of communicating, conceptions of interaction, (collective) decision-making, and time. This encompasses especially the intergenerational perspective and a sense of responsibility, different socio-cultural settings, and concepts of decision-making. Moreover, particularities of non-literate societies in the use of language and forms of communication are to be considered, like

[10] Taubman and Leistner (2008) 68.

[11] On these aspects *see* at Chapter I Section 1. above.

the importance (and, in the international negotiations mostly lack) of the relationship between symbol and referent, vocal inflections and physical gestures, and constant change in the meaning of words according to the social process of memory and forgetting, as the chapter on indigenous philosophies has revealed.

(4) In the ambit of "external" experts and public staff members dedicated to the topic, mainly at the national level, an interdisciplinary exchange of experts is also essential, as for instance the technical note of the Brazilian General Coordination of Copyright has shown.

(5) Exchange of experiences at the regional level would be of great value, too, i.e. an exchange between the different Latin American countries directly at the level of national entities in charge, apart from the representative delegations at WIPO. This need is in part made clear by a result of my personal fieldwork on the ground: When I asked the three different main entities involved in the field of protecting TCEs in Brazil what they thought about the Panamanian solution as another Latin American model, they either did not even know about the existence of the Panamanian regime or argued that the situation in their huge country was too different for a comparison or a lessons-learned approach anyway. Nonetheless, the experience gained by the special entity within DIGERPI, the Department for Collective Rights and Folkloristic Expressions, could be of great value for other national entities, as examined in the chapter on the national situation in Panama.

VII. Further Recommendations with Regard to the Content of Protection

Designing a system of protecting TCEs in line with the combined approach should consider certain aspects vis-a-vis the content of such protection:

(1) Above all, the particular goals of protection are crucial, and is still controversial at the regional or international level so far. The Latin American examples regulating or at least touching TCEs vary as regards the objectives of legal treatment. The only sui generis system in existence, Law No. 20 in Panama, aims to preserve the indigenous cultural heritage and to "apply social justice"—a strong political, social and, finally, economic focus selected by one group of the historically most oppressed people of the world. In contrast, a legislation or policy aiming at freezing any status quo would address neither the needs of the subjects of protection nor the nature of the objects of protection, as Panamanian realities show. The traditional cultures where the expressions stem from constitute developing, vital processes or "paths" rather than exhibition pieces, and the creators are evolving social beings. This is the setting on the one hand. On the other, the factual specialty justifying the design of a new legal regime is the traditional aspect of the objects of protection and the collective as the subject of protection. A protection should thus both, aim at stamping out concrete infringements of concrete TCEs as objects of protection, and aspire to be effective and sustainable by supporting

the ongoing vitality of the environments in which TCEs are created in the long run. The Brazilian legal solution on immaterial cultural patrimony including TCEs, could serve as inspiration, since it aims less at "authenticity," than at "historical continuity" and thereby an ongoing vitality of the immaterial cultural good.

(2) As regards the nature of the instrument, the cultural law approach particularly like the one in Brazil is extremely useful as regards documentation, appreciation, and awareness-raising measures. However, it provides neither an answer nor an appropriate legal instrument to repel a concrete infringement of the TCEs by third parties, as it does not establish individual or collective private rights. Those rights are however needed in practice, as the public indigenous authority FUNAI as well as the Ministry of the Public experience in their daily practice. Besides, large-scale discussions are going on in Brazil on an adequate protection of TCEs, indicating that the cultural-law approach is not the final word. The legal categorization as "immaterial cultural patrimony" could be designed to provide a legal position providing for sanctions, e.g. in cases of infringements to be impaired by public entities. But that is not the case in the current legislation in Brazil. Procedural rights—as the right to participation and the right to be heard—have been acknowledged by the Brazilian court lately in disputes that take place in the area of *Lugares* of the cultural patrimony. However, those rights were not based on "immaterial cultural patrimony" as a legal status.

(3) The establishment of a collective copyright, a collective right of personal portrayal, as well as the revival of a paying public domain are topics intensively discussed especially in the Brazilian ambit. These discussions are useful for drafting a protection of TCEs, which, however, should not be limited to those concepts.

(4) In this regard, especially provisions and solutions contained in the Portaria No. 177 of 2006 of the Brazilian FUNAI could serve as examples, particularly the link to the access to and integrity of indigenous territories. This is a three-step-model for considering customary law legal in representation, special provisions for isolated indigenous peoples, and legal consequences of the incompliance with the provisions. The legitimacy of this administrative instrument is hardly disputed though. Another similar, even more detailed, comprehensive, and TCE-related solution in theory has been elaborated by the Ecuadorian Institute of Intellectual Property (IEPI). An enactment of this draft in the near future is doubtful, though.

(5) Interestingly enough, most of the provisions of said Portaria No. 177 correspond to customary law and/or needs and expectations expressed by indigenous communities, here e.g. the Brazilian Wajãpi Indians. These are:

   a. Request for authorization
   b. Involvement of appropriate public entities
   c. Approval of the request for authorization by the indigenous communities according to their own decision-making process

d. Representation by local and regional indigenous entities
e. Agreement upon the "moral and economic terms of use" and upon penalties for non-compliance
f. Deposition of "integral copies" of any documentations or agreements.[12]

(6) The interaction and compatibility of any TCE-protection with other legal areas has to be examined. A precondition for giving the authorization or a prior informed consent by the indigenous person or community is its legal capability to do so, for instance—a requirement which is not necessarily fulfilled according to the national legislations. This was the case according to the former Article 6 of the Brazilian Civil Code, for example, and is still disputed under the current Brazilian Indian Statute. Likewise, the procedural capacity of an indigenous person, community, or bearer of TCEs in general would have to be examined, since a representation by means of particular public entities might be required. This is the case of the Ministry of Public as provided by the Brazilian Indian Statute.

(7) Classic distinctions according to intellectual property law, e.g. between copyright and industrial property rights, do not provide proper answers to real needs. As experiences in Panama have shown, even within a sui generis regime, a differentiation between modes of TCEs according to the intellectual property categories of copyright on the one hand and industrial property on the other is not helpful, since it does not address the prime concerns of the communities. The legislative allocation of competences according to the intellectual property differentiation at either the Copyright Office or the entity in charge of the registration of industrial property (DIGERPI), is not implemented, as, rather than IP expertise, intercultural competences were and are of need. Within the scope allowed by existing international treaties, chiefly the TRIPS Agreement, a sui generis approach should give consideration to the particularities of the topic of TCEs rather than being oriented too much towards the system of intellectual property rights.

(8) At the same time, intellectual property rules should be included and adapted in so far as the "negative scope" of protection is concerned, namely, to avoid the establishment of IP rights of third parties. This aim of a defensive protection was the driving force for the establishment of the sui generis system in Panama, for instance, and was also achieved in practice.

(9) While integrating such negative IP-protection, the classic distinction between material and immaterial goods should be avoided as far as possible. It contradicts the background of still vivid indigenous world views and the practical handling of TCEs, as observed in the case of the *mola* in Panama and that of the *Cachoeira de Iauaretê* in Brazil. The legal solutions in both countries take note of this particularity and cover both aspects, taking the loss of legal precision as a consequence.

[12] For details and references *see* at Chapter IV Section 2.D.II. above, especially the Portaria itself, and Arantes (2009 I) 35 *et seq.*

(10) As regards the subject matter of protection as well as its duration, a crucial point is whether to include new elements of TCEs or recovered "traditional" cultural expressions, and how to theoretically define and practically distinguish them, not least with regard to the copyright distinction concerning arrangements. These questions are legally answered differently in Latin American countries. The *Reglamento de Uso* of the *mola* for example explicitly also embraces new forms of use. In the cultural-law solution of Brazil, the determining criteria set up in the provisions are "historical continuity" and an ongoing vitality of the immaterial cultural good. In Mexico, not even arrangements of TCEs are protected by the intellectual property rules.

(11) In view of a high factual diversity on the one hand and the need for a minimum of legal certainty, it is questionable whether concrete legal definitions of legislative terms, namely, constituent elements should be laid down in the legislation. This question again reflects an overlap between anthropology and law: Generalizations are hardly possible, while at the same time abstract definitions are needed—thus, it requires a minimum consensus in this dilemma. A practical solution could be the one opted for in the Brazilian Decree 3.551 on the immaterial cultural patrimony, where room has been left for reactions from case to case. Another option would be an indicating list, for example as the Executive Decree to Law No. 20 in Panama provides for, listing more than 80 TCEs known in Panama in an exemplifying, not exclusive manner. However, with already more than 220 different indigenous peoples existing in Brazil alone, this might be a challenging solution for other countries. As regards the definition of the bearers of TCEs and rights therein, a solution involving reference to the respective national situation is contained in the Draft Agreement on a Free Trade Area of the Americas.

(12) The principles of reciprocity and sustainability, in relation to nature, but also as regards the continuous exchange of goods and services between persons, constituting a compulsory social mechanism are essential elements for an appropriate use and means of protection of TCEs. In line with the examples of Latin American indigenous philosophies presented above, besides, the principles of balance and duality are essential as regards the social and legal relationship with (1) the other members of the community, (2) the environment and its spiritual meaning, and (3) the sacred world. Legally, capacities, needs, and efforts therefore must be subject to the criteria of proportionality.

(13) Other crucial questions are those of representation and distribution. International scholars argue increasingly in favor of customary law as regulating solutions. In Latin America, adequate answers to these questions depend pretty much upon the particular situations in the different countries, *inter alia* on the factual and legal organization of the communities as well as on the competence and functioning of public entities involved. In Brazil, for example, the Indian Statute provides that a department within the Ministry of Public is the legal representative of indigenous communities in legal disputes at court. Collective indigenous goods are administered by the FUNAI, as the

Indian Statute regulates. The validity of these provisions, however, is highly questionable in view of the current Brazilian Constitution.

(14) The shape of rights and modes of procedures should reflect the different situations of the communities. At least one important difference should legally be considered: the differentiation between isolated and non-isolated communities with regard to the general aspect of a right to be left alone, and concrete inalienable rights in their TCEs, as provided for by the proposal for a sui generis protection elaborated by the Ecuadorian Intellectual Property Institute. The differentiation conducted in the 1973 Brazilian Indian Statute, in turn, due to the contradictions with the current Brazilian Constitution, may only be useful for a categorization of different needs of the communities.

(15) Regulations on dispute resolution should provide for procedures free of charge, as far as possible, and involve anthropologists as mediators or experts in the case, as to a certain extent it is practiced in Brazil. The reasons why case law is rarely developed in Latin American countries are, on the one hand, that the indigenous peoples themselves lack the mentality, i.e. the legal culture of persecuting infringements, and the economic resources on the other hand. Moreover, the legal tradition in settling disputes does not include the involvement of the public court system, and due to the ongoing discrimination against the indigenous population, this population places little trust in public courts. Sometimes, as in the case of a European store and gallery in Panama, indigenous individuals cooperate and thereby "contribute" to infringements by working with the supposed "infringers," rather than going to court—due to the pressing need for income. On the other hand, public entities in charge of representing the peoples prefer alternative dispute-resolution measures, i.e. to settle the dispute by administrative means, as even they do not expect an adequate or practically workable decision. As a consequence, the disadvantage is that no precedents, no directions for future legislation and, no legal certainty are created. In the long run, court decisions could be helpful for the development of an adequate protection of TCEs, provided that they give consideration to the specific setting of the case, namely, the intercultural dimension and anthropological particularities. This aim could be achieved by a legal instrument on the protection of TCEs which provides for the involvement of anthropologists as mediators or experts in the case, as to a certain extent is practiced in Brazil. In line with the terminology used in competition law, this could be characterized as "a more anthropological approach in intellectual property issues."

(16) At the same time, in favor of practical solutions, legislation on TCEs should provide alternative dispute resolution measures instead of giving jurisdiction to regular courts, irrespective of any prior or alternative application of customary law.

(17) Avoiding technical complexity in general is important. At both sides, of the bearers as well as the public entities involved, a great lack of expertise has been recognized, e.g. by the Technical Note of the Brazilian General Coordination of Copyright. Moreover, as observed in Latin American reality, new,

culturally differently shaped rights are likely to introduce new complexity, lead to the phenomenon of juridification of social relationships, and acculturation, or at least provoke new socio-cultural conflicts. A protection might thus even turn out to be counterproductive, and contravene the intention of the law when artificially interfering with the "traditional culture." That does not mean that the intention of the type of legal protection favored here would be to freeze any status quo. It means that possible socio-cultural impacts should be considered in such manner, that new rights, procedures, and competences are to be designed as simple as possible in order to minimize the need of creating a special juridical expertise among the bearers of TCEs and the public entities in charge. Another option for determining the concrete technical shape of the instrument could be to consider the outcome of anthropological studies on especially this phenomenon, as the afore-mentioned study of the Brazilian team of anthropologists.

(18) Any sui generis system should be guaranteed at the international level, whereby bilateral agreements could be a practical alternative to the ongoing international negotiations at WIPO. An example hereof is the FTA between Panama and Taiwan. However, the unbalanced political power of the negotiating countries would set certain limits in practice.

VIII. Further Recommendations with Regard to Implementing Protection of TCEs

An adequate protection of TCEs based upon a holistic approach would also rely on certain experiences made in respect of implementing protection:

(1) In both areas of promotion and protection, seemingly trivial aspects are eminently essential in practice, though they cannot be taken as given—especially as regards certain structures and mentalities in developing countries. These aspects are: first, a well-functioning communication, second, flow of information, third, coordination, and fourth, cooperation in the intra- and inter-administrative dimension, that means within the competent entity as well as between different entities. These principles are of prior importance in order to avoid dissipations, energy loss, conflicts of competences, and diverging methods of support.

(2) Disputes on competences should be avoided by minimizing the actors involved, focussing on the subject, and de-politicing the topic in the every-day practice. To illustrate this challenge, the entities involved in Brazil alone will be indicated: the IPHAN, the General Coordination of Copyright, the Secretariat for Cultural Identity and Diversity within the Ministry of the Public, the FUNAI, the Ministry of the Public, and, additionally, to deal with traditional knowledge on biodiversity, more than five other different public entities, including the National Institute of Industrial Property, the Ministry of Environment. The Technical Note of the General Coordination of Copyright reveals exactly this challenge of overlapping competences.

(3) Another content-related challenge is the inter-disciplinarity of the topic. To address this challenge, it would be helpful first, to enact administrative positions lasting longer than 4 years, and, second, to entrust officials or specialists with particular competences for the topic, or/and to provide capacity building measures not only for bearers of TCEs, but also public staff members involved.

(4) Hereby, the appropriate "mindset" or attitude is of importance—a challenging balance between strengthening the communities' situation and respecting the differences. Part of a continuing considerable difference between the progressive legal dispositions and "immense difficulties encountered by the local agents in understanding and implementing these instruments of protection and valorization" in Brazil is the fact, that most of the agents are still convinced that the indigenous ways of life and thoughts "are transitory and are in urgent need to be 'modernized'."[13]

(5) Similarly, the implementation of promotion and supportive measures by public entities and NGOs should at the same time support the competence and activity of the bearers themselves or at least not hinder the development of such. Otherwise, new dependencies and weakness would be created—an effect of the past decades, which in general has been criticized by indigenous persons especially in Ecuador.

(6) Another great issue for the competent entities in concrete areas, either regarding the cultural-law approach in Brazil or the sui generis regime in Panama, is to ensure sufficient financial and human resources for the implementation of the rules, particularly for the documentation, the preparation and execution of the registration processes and for the planning projects. Interestingly, a study on the Brazilian forestry law on paper and in practice, precisely on the question of whether law can save the forest in Brazil, has revealed similar reasons for the poor implementation of the forestry law in the country, which were in the main: (i) "lack of personnel and training, (ii) lack of sustainability of governmental institutions, (iii) lack of institutional coordination, and (iv) lack of financial resources."[14]

(7) Finally, similar to the current movement in environmental policies and legislations, the success of implementing new legislation depends crucially upon the personal engagement of the people concerned with the topic. This is true for the third parties, public officials, as well as bearers.

   a. Third parties as well as officials could involve experts of qualified NGOs as the Environmental Institute in Brazil (ISA), or dedicated individuals, anthropologists for instance, as the Brazilian Indian Museum has done in publication projects.[15]

---

[13] IPHAN – Instituto do Patrimônio Histórico e Artístico Nacional (2008) 106, translation by the author.

[14] Hirakuri (2003) 37 *et seq.*

[15] *See, e.g.*, Fausto, C. and B. Franchetto as editors of the publication "Tisakisü: tradição e novas tecnologias da memória: Kuikuro do Alto Xingu", Museu do Índio, (2008).

b. Both, the theory of Psychological Ownership,[16] as well as the Social Identity theory[17] can be of use in this regard: Strengthening the communal feeling of self-identity would support the inner cohesion of the community and thus the legal concept of collective ownership on the one hand, as well as the appreciation of the own traditional culture and corresponding attitude of protectiveness towards it on the other—and thereby strengthen the vitality of the TCEs. To promote the estimation of TCEs as well as to encourage this personal engagement, the indigenous self-conception as inner phenomenon could be supported, as well as external motives (in psychological terms) and incentives (in economic terms) or "nudges"[18] be offered. Successful Latin American examples are the "National Indigenous Cultures Award," as issued and organized by the Secretariat for Cultural Identity and Diversity within the Brazilian Ministry of the Public, exhibitions, publications, and capacity-building measures organized by the Brazilian Indian Museum, and awards granted by the Panamanian Department for Collective Rights and Folkloristic Expressions. These activities are, however, only select projects, which are not able to address the major challenges indirectly affecting the maintenance and persisting vitality of TCEs, like economic needs, environmental exploitation, alcohol, and need of formal education.

C. Recommendations Made by Latin American Indigenous Persons Involved in the Field

Since the effectiveness of TCE protection also depends upon the engagement, will, and actions of the individual indigenous persons themselves in maintaining the vitality of their TCEs, the final words will be given to bearers concerned. In this manner, recommendations have been made by indigenous persons who have had practical experience in the area of TCEs. According to *Rivera Zea*,[19] these are:

(1) To "create mechanisms to transmit the cultural appreciation and values necessary for a successful preservation of the peoples' philosophy, culture, knowledge, and resources to future generations";
(2) To "raise awareness and sensibility in indigenous communities, families, and schools about their artistic heritage and the quality of their own handicraft products";

[16] Pierce, J. L., T. Kostova, et al. (2003).

[17] Tajfel, H., and J. Turner, "An Integrative Theory of Intergroup Conflict", in: W. G. Austin and S. Worchel (eds.), "The Social Psychology of Intergroup Relations", 33–47 (1979).

[18] On the term and concept of "nudges" in general *see* Thaler and Sunstein (2009).

[19] CHIRAPAQ/Rivera Zea (ed.) (2007) 56.

(3) To "elaborate strategies for the recovery of the ancestral traditions and knowledge that can enrich the creativity of the indigenous craftspeople";
(4) To "establish or strengthen indigenous organizations as a basis for the legal defence of the intellectual property";
(5) To "know the legal instruments used to protect intellectual property and elaborate legislative initiatives to guarantee an effective protection of the creativity of the indigenous craftspeople";
(6) Finally, and probably most important, not to be "seduced by the monetary system that contradicts the traditional philosophy and sell out one's own 'treasures'."[20]

Section 3. Closing Words and Outlook

In sum, the study revealed that similarly to the general legal and political situation on the South American continent, there exist various contradictions within the issue of protecting TCEs in Latin America. It would be too easy and, indeed unrewarding to simply hide or try to smooth out these contradictions on paper. This is even more the case as also in the broader area of TCEs, one of the biggest internal contradiction is the fact that, normatively, Latin America seems to stand at a highly developed level, but regarding implementation, the majority of these countries reveal "vast segments of underdevelopment."[21] Apart from the question of reaching an agreement on the protection of TCEs at all, to overcome this discrepancy would be one, maybe even *the* crucial element deciding over the effectiveness of a system of protection of TCEs. The fact that the ILO Convention No. 169 has been ratified by some of the major Latin American countries only recently—Brazil on 25 July 2002, Chile in September 2008—reveals that the political acceptance, as well as the social estimation, of indigenous minorities is just in its inception. It could be a great opportunity for Latin America to take hold of the topic of TCEs and their protection, which reveals so much of the continent's richness and creative, intellectual, and diverse potential. However, whether it indeed is willing and able to embrace that opportunity, is unfortunately rather doubtful. Some things are for sure: Protecting TCEs is not only a national, but an international issue, not only a legal problem, but also a political, socio-economical, and environmental topic.

[20] Rivera-Zea (2006) 3, translation by the author.

[21] This outcome confirms the initially cited observation made on the political situation in general *see* the Introduction and Mols (2009) 67, translation by the author.

Bibliography

Adloff, F. and S. Mau (2005). "Zur Theorie der Gabe und Reziprozität", in: F. Adloff and S. Mau, "Vom Geben und Nehmen – Zur Soziologie der Reziprozität", Frankfurt a.M., 9–60.
Albó, X. (2004). "Ethnic Identity and Politics in the Central Andes – The Cases of Bolivia, Ecuador, and Peru", in: J.-M. Burt, and P. Mauceri (eds.), "Politics in the Andes – Identity, Conflict, Reform", Pittsburgh, 1–37.
Alexander, C. (2010). "Schadensersatz und Abschöpfung im Lauterkeits- und Kartellrecht", Tübingen.
Alich, S. (2010). "Das Recht der Verwertungsgesellschaften in Lateinamerika", Baden-Baden.
Andean Community (2000). Decisión 486 sobre el Régimen Común Andino sobre Propiedad Industrial of September 14th, 2000, from http://www.comunidadandina.org/normativa/dec/d486.htm (Spanish), http://www.comunidadandina.org/ingles/normativa/D486e.htm (non-official translation into English) (cited as Andean Community (2000) Decisión 486).
Andean Community (CAN) (2002). Decision 524 of July 7, 2002 on the Working Group on the Rights of Indigenous Peoples, from http://www.comunidadandina.org/ingles/normativa/D524e.htm (cited as Andean Community (2002) Decision 524)
Andean Community (2004). Decisión 588 – Sustitución de la Decisión 460 sobre la protección y recuperación de bienes del patrimonio cultural de los Países Miembros de la Comunidad Andina of July 10, 2004, from http://www.comunidadandina.org/normativa/dec/D588.htm (cited as Andean Community (2004) Decision 588).
Andean Community (2004). Decision 601 – Integral Plan for Social Development of September 21, 2004, from http://www.comunidadandina.org/ingles/normativa/Decision601e.pdf (cited as Andean Community (2004) Decision 601).
Andean Community (2005). Decision 613 – Association of the Republic of Argentina, the Federative Republic of Brazil, the Republic of Paraguay and the Eastern Republic of Uruguay, States Parties of MERCOSUR, with the Andean Community of July 7, 2005, from http://www.comunidadandina.org/ingles/normativa/D613e.htm (non-official translation into English) (cited as Andean Community (2005) Decision 613).
Andean Community (2005). "Elementos para la protección sui generis de los conocimientos tradicionales colectivos e integrales desde la perspectiva indígena", from http://www.comunidadandina.org/public/libro_perspectiva_indigena.pdf (cited as Andean Community (2005) Elementos para la protección sui generis).
Andean Community (2007). Conclusions and recommendations of the First Forum of Indigenous Intellectuals and Researchers of July 7, 2007, from http://www.comunidadandina.org/ingles/documentos/documents/Indigenous_conclusions.htm (cited as Andean Community (2007) Conclusions of the Indigenous Forum).

© Springer-Verlag Berlin Heidelberg 2015

A.F. Busch, *Protection of Traditional Cultural Expressions in Latin America*,
Munich Studies on Innovation and Competition 3, DOI 10.1007/978-3-662-46770-1

Andean Community (2007). First Forum of Indigenous Intellectuals and Researchers MANIFESTO of July 7, 2007, from http://www.comunidadandina.org/ingles/documentos/documents/Indigenous_manifesto.htm (cited as Andean Community (2007) Manifesto).

Andean Community (2007). Decision 674 – Consultative Council of the Andean Community Indigenous Peoples of September 26, 2007, from http://www.comunidadandina.org/ingles/normativa/D674e.htm (cited as Andean Community (2007) Decision 674).

Andean Community (2007). "Los Pueblos Indígenas y la Integración Andína", from http://www.comunidadandina.org/public/libro_indigenas.pdf (cited as Andean Community (2007) Integración Andína).

Andean Community (CAN) (2008). En reunión calificada de "histórica" – Instalan Consejo Consultivo que permitirá participación de pueblos indígenas en proceso andino de integración, from http://www.comunidadandina.org/prensa/notas/np8-9-08a.htm.

Andean Community (2009). "Philosopher Edgar Morin asserts that integration does not mean doing away with diversity", Press Release of August 29, from http://www.comunidadandina.org/ingles/press/press/np27-8-09.htm.

Andean Community (no year). Culture, from http://www.comunidadandina.org/ingles/culture.htm.

Andean Community (no year) http://www.comunidadandina.org/ingles/who.htm, last visited December 8, 2010.

Antequera Parilli, R. (1991). "El derecho de autor y el derecho a la cultura en el marco de los derechos humanos", in: "I Congreso Iberoamericano de Propiedad Intelectual: Derecho de autor y derechos conexos en los umbrales del año 2000", Madrid, 65–78 (cited as Antequera Parilli, R. (1991 I)).

Antequera Parilli, R. (1991). "Tendencias legislativas autorales en América Latina", in: "I Congreso Iberoamericano de Propiedad Intelectual: Derecho de autor y derechos conexos en los umbrales del año 2000", Madrid, 311–318 (cited as Antequera Parilli, R. (1991 II)).

Antequera Parilli, R. (2007). "La tutela del folklore en el marco de los derechos intelectuales", in: "Estudios de derecho de autor y derechos afines" 504–548, Madrid.

Antweiler, C. (2009). "Was ist den Menschen gemeinsam? Über Kultur und Kulturen", Darmstadt.

Arantes, A. (for WIPO) (2009). "Documenting and Disseminating Traditional Knowledge and Cultural Expressions in Brazil – Volume I – Survey". (cited as Arantes for WIPO (2009 I)).

Arantes, A. (for WIPO) (2009). "Documenting and Disseminating Traditional Knowledge and Cultural Expressions in Brazil – Volume II – Brazil Intellectual Property and Heritage Legislation, Institutional Guidelines and Instruments", from http://www.wipo.int/export/sites/www/tk/en/culturalheritage/casestudies/arantes_report_vol2.pdf. (cited as Arantes for WIPO (2009 II)).

Aylwin, J. (2002). "El Acceso de los indígenas a la Tierra en los Ordenamientos Jurídicos de América Latina: Un Estudio de Casos", vol. I and II, Santiago de Chile.

Azevedo, C. d. A., P. C. Lavratti, et al. (2005). "Convenção sobre Diversidade Biológica no Brasil: considerações sobre sua implementação no que tange ao acesso ao patrimômio genético, conhecimentos tradicionais associados e repartição de beneficios", 37 Revista de Direito Ambiental 113–143.

Baptista, F. M. and R. S. T. d. Valle (2004). "Os povos indígenas frente ao direito autoral e de imagem", São Paolo.

Barié, C. G. (2003). "Pueblos Indígenas y derechos constitucionales en América Latina: un panorama", La Paz.

Barié, C. G. (2008). "El debate acutal sobre autonomías en la legislación internacional: experiencias prácticas", in: R. Sevilla and J. Ströbele-Gregor, "Pueblos indígenas: Derechos, estrategias económicas y desarollo con identidad", Bad Honnef, 32–56.

Barsh, R. L. (1987). "Revision of ILO Convention No. 107", 71 American Journal of International Law 756–762.

Becker, L. C. (1990). "Reciprocity", Chicago, London.

Berryman, C. A. (1994). "Toward More Universal Protection of Intangible Cultural Property", 1 J. Intell. Prop. L. 293–334.
Bolivia U.N. Doc. E/C.19/2008/5/Add.3.
Bonilla, A. "Especial para La Prensa", La Prensa, December 16, 2004, http://biblioteca.prensa.com/contenido/2004/12/16/16-10a-nota1.html, last visited January 10, 2010 (cited as Bonilla (2004 I)).
Bonilla, A. "Prohíben a Kunas el intercambio por molas", La Prensa, July 5, 2004, http://biblioteca.prensa.com/contenido/2004/07/05/5-10a-nota1.html, last visited November 10, 2010 (cited as Bonilla (2004 II)).
Boytha, G. (1968). "Reciprocity in International Copyright Law", in: Hungarian Branch of the International Law Association, "Questions of International Law", Budapest, 37–63.
Brundtland Commission (1987). "Report of the World Commission on Environment and Development: Our Common Future" – The Brundtland Report, from http://www.un-documents.net/wced-ocf.htm.
Bucher, S. (2008). "Der Schutz von genetischen Ressourcen und indigenem Wissen in Lateinamerika", Baden-Baden.
Busch, F. (2010). "Amazonien – Diversität und Integration in das Recht des geistigen Eigentums" – Internationaler Kongress zum geistigen Eigentum in São Paolo, 21. bis 23. Juni 2009, und einige Gedanken dazu, GRUR Int. 215–221.
Carneiro da Cunha, M. (no year). "The Role of UNESCO in the Defense of Traditional Knowledge", from http://www.folklife.si.edu/resources/unesco/dacunha.htm, last visited October 16, 2010.
Carneiro da Cunha, M. (1990). "El concepto de derecho consuetudinario y los derechos indígenas en la nueva Constitución de Brasil", in: R. Stavenhagen and D. Iturralde (eds.), "Entre la ley y la costumbre – El derecho consuetudinario indígena en América Latina", México, 299–313.
Carneiro da Cunha, M. (1991). "Custom is not a Thing, it is a Path: Reflections on the Brazilian Indian Case.", in: A. An'naim, "Human Rights in Cross-Cultural Perspectives.", Philadelphia, 276–294.
Carter, L. E. (2008). "Achieving Holistic Sacred Sites Conservation for Indigenous Communities in Ecuador", Fall 2008 Perspectives 4.
Celeste de Davis, L. (2006). "Desarrollo, Logros y Perspectivas de la Propiedad Industrial en Panamá", en: Legislación & Economía, Edición Julio 2006, La Pluma Invitada, from http://www.riveboca.com/ediciones.asp?iProd=203&iCat=43&hierarchy=0.
CHIRAPAQ/Rivera Zea (ed.), (2007). "Protegiendo la Propiedad Intelectual del Diseño Indígena – Memoria del Taller Internacional", Lima.
Clavero, B. (2008). "Carta de Bartolomé Clavero", from http://www.mapuexpress.net/?act=news&id=3303&PHPSESSID=ad11781211ea2769317e3092c36d45ef.
Clifford, J. (1988). "The Predicament of Culture: Twentieth-Century Ethnography, Literature, and Art", Cambridge et. al.
Cobo, J. M. (1983). "Study of the Problem of Discrimination Against Indigenous Populations" ("Cobo Report"), U.N. Doc. E/CN.4/Sub.2/1983/21/Add.8.
Cobo, J. M. (1986). "Study of the Problem of Discrimination Against Indigenous Populations" ("Cobo Report"), U.N. Doc. E/CN.4/Sub.2/1986/7.
Cohen, R. (1978). "Ethnicity: Problem and Focus in Anthropology", 7 Annual Review of Anthropology 379–403.
COICA (2005). "Agenda Indígena Amazónica – Volviendo a la Maloca", Quito. English version: "Returning to the 'Maloca' – Amazon Indigenous Agenda" from http://www.coica.org.ec/ingles/aia_book/index.html.
Collier, J. F. (1987). "Legal Processes", 4 Annual Review of Anthropology 121–144.
Colombia U.N. Doc. E/C.19/2008/5/Add.5.
Congreso General Kuna, Congreso General de la Cultura Kuna (2006). "Conocimiento Kuna, Biodiversidad y Propiedad Intelectual", Panama.

Contraloría General de la República de Panamá, Dirección de Estadística y Censo (2000). "Censos", http://190.34.178.20/dec/cgi-bin/RpWebEngine.exe/PortalAction?&MODE=MAIN&BASE=LP2000&MAIN=WebServerMain_censos.inl, last visited November 10, 2010.

Cooter, R. D. and W. Fikentscher (1998). "Indian Common Law: The Role of Custom in American Indian Tribal Courts", 46 American Journal of Comparative Law 287–330, 509–580.

Cooter, R. D. and W. Fikentscher (2008). "American Indian Law Codes: Pragmatic Law and Tribal Identity", 56 American Journal of Comparative Law 29–74.

CRESPIAL (2007). "CRESPIAL – Centro Regional para la Salvaguardia del Patrimonio Cultural Inmaterial de América Latina", Cusco.

Daes, E.-I., Special Rapporteur of the U.N.-Sub-Commission on Prevention of Discrimination and Protection of Minorities and Chairperson of the U.N.-Working Group on Indigenous Peoples (1993). "Study on the protection of the cultural and intellectual property of indigenous peoples", E/CN.4/Sub.2/1993/28.

Daes, E.-I. (2000). "Defending Indigenous Peoples' Heritage", Keynote Address at the Conference on Protecting Knowledge: Traditional Resource Rights in the New Millennium, Union of British Columbian Indian Chiefs, from http://www.ubcic.bc.ca/files/PDF/Keynote.pdf.

de la Cruz I., R. (2006). "Regional Study in the Andean Countries: 'Customary Law in the Protection of Traditional Knowledge'", from http://www.wipo.int/export/sites/www/tk/en/consultations/customary_law/study_cruz_en.pdf.

de la Cruz I., R. (2008). "Conocimientos propios y patentes desde la visión indígena", in: R. Sevilla and J. Ströbele-Gregor (eds.), "Pueblos indígenas: Derechos, estrategias económicas y desarollo con identidad", Bad Honnef, 206–220 (cited as de la Cruz I. (2008 I)).

de la Cruz, R. (2008). "Conocimiento tradicional en el Ecuador: valoración, protección y legislación", in: M. Rios, R. de la Cruz, and A. Mora, "Conocimiento tradicional y plantas útiles del Ecuador: saberes y prácticas", Quito, 33–50 (cited as de la Cruz I. (2008 II)).

De Obaldia, I. (2005). "Western Intellectual Property and Indigenous Cultures: The Case of the Panamanian Indigenous Intellectual Property Law", 23 Boston University Int'l Law Journal 337–394.

De Roman Pérez, R. (2007). "Comparison between the public domain system and the model of the WIPO draft provisions for the protection of traditional cultural expressions/expressions of folklore", 212 AIDA 66–110.

Dietz, A. (1981). "Urheberrecht und Entwicklungsländer", München.

Die Zeit, January 26, 2006, "Die Achse des Guten".

Draft Agreement on a Free Trade Area of the Americas (FTAA) (2003). http://www.ftaa-alca.org/alca_e.asp, last visited November 2, 2010.

Drexl, J. (1994). "Dienstleistungen und Geistiges Eigentum: Die Bedeutung der neuen Welthandelsorganisation für Entwicklungsländer", in: W. v. Urff and J. Drexl, "GATT und die Folgen – Ein Kolloquium", München, 25–61.

Drexl, J., (1994). "Nach "GATT und WIPO": Das TRIPS-Abkommen und seine Anwendung in der Europäischen Gemeinschaft", 1994 Journal 777–788.

Drexl, J., (1999). "Urheberrecht und Handelspolitik: Zweckehe oder Mesalliance? – Zugleich eine Besprechung von "Maximilian Wilhelm Haedicke: Urheberrecht und die Handelspolitik der Vereinigten Staaten von Amerika", 1999 Journal 1–13.

Drexl, J. and A. Kur (2005). "Preface" in: Drexl, J. and A. Kur, (eds.), "Intellectual Property and Private International Law", Oxford, vii–viii.

Drexl, J. (2010). "Internationales Immaterialgüterrecht", in: R. Rixecker and F. J. Säcker (eds.), "Münchener Kommentar zum Bürgerlichen Gesetzbuch", vol. 11, 5th ed., München, 1344–1491.

Eisenstadt, T. A. (no year). "Elections by Customary Law in Oaxaca, Mexico: Expression of Cultural Rights or Violations of Democratic Electoral Norms?", from http://www1.american.edu/ia/cdem/pdfs/1_OaxacaCaseStudy.pdf.

El Diario (of Bolivia) (August 27, 2010). "Con finalidad de evitar plagios: Diputados declaran patrimonio cultural e inmaterial a cinco danzas folklóricas", available at http://www.eldiario.net/noticias/2010/2010_08/nt100827/6_01clt.php, last visited November 10, 2010.

Elliot, J. H. (1984). "The Spanish Conquest and Settlement of America", in: L. Bethell (ed.), "The Cambridge History of Latin America, vol. I, Colonial Latin America", Cambridge, 149–206.

El País (of Mexico) (February 1, 2010). "¿Una nueva Constitución para México?", available at http://internacional.elpais.com/internacional/2010/02/01/actualidad/1264978804_850215.html, last visited March 1, 2010.

Espino R., B. (2004). "Protection of Traditional Artisanal Crafts in Panama", in: S. Twarog and P. Kapoor, "Protecting and Promoting Traditional Knowledge: Systems, National Experiences and International Dimensions", New York/Geneva, 181–183.

Esser, J. (1972). "Vorverständnis und Methodenwahl", Frankfurt.

Fausto, C. and B. Franchetto (eds.), (2008). "Tisakisü: tradição e novas tecnologias da memória: Kuikuro do Alto Xingu", Museu do Índio, Rio de Janeiro.

Ferreira de Pragmácio Telles, M. and R. Vieira Costa (2007). "Direitos Culturais: Aspectos Jurídicos do Registro de que Trata o Decreto 3551/2000", from http://www.cult.ufba.br/enecult2007/MarioFerreiradePragmacioTelles_RodrigoVieiraCosta.pdf.

Feser, H. (2008). "Die Huaorani am Anfang des neuen Jahrtausends. Eine kleine Amazonasethnie gibt Vollgas", in: M. Amelung, C. Uzcátegui, N. O. Wallowski and M. Zander, (eds.), "INDIEGEGENWART – Indigene Realitäten im südamerikanischen Tiefland", Berlin, 175–183.

Fikentscher, W. (1983). "Wirtschaftsrecht I", München.

Fikentscher, W. (1997). "Wirtschaftliche Gerechtigkeit und kulturelle Gerechtigkeit – Vom Sinn der Kulturvergleichung in Anthropologie, Wirtschaft und Recht, Abschiedsvorlesung an der Juristischen Fakultät der Universität München vom 14. Juni 1996, Heidelberg.

Fikentscher, W. (2004). "Culture, Law and Economics: Three Berkeley Lectures", Bern and Durham, NC. (cited as: Fikentscher (2004 I))

Fikentscher, W. (2004). "Modes of Thought: A Study in the Anthropology of Law and Religion", 2nd ed. (1st ed. 1995), Tübingen. (cited as: Fikentscher (2004 II))

Fikentscher, W. (2005). "Geistiges Gemeineigentum – am Beispiel der Afrikanischen Philosophie –", in: A. Ohly, et. al., "Perspektiven des Geistigen Eigentums und Wettbewerbsrechts", München, 3–18.

Fikentscher, W. (2006). "The Whole is More Than the Sum of the Parts, Therefore I have Individual Rights: African Philosophy and the Anthropology of Developing Economies and Laws", in: M. O. Hinz and H. K. Patemann (eds.): "The Shade of New Leaves: Governance in Traditional Authority, A Southern African Perspective, International Conference on Traditional Government and Customary Law, Windhoek, 26–29 July 2004", Münster, 295–328.

Fikentscher, W. (2009). "Law and Anthropology – Outlines, Issues, and Suggestions", München.

Fikentscher, W. and T. Ramsauer (2001). "Traditionswissen – Tummelplatz immaterialgüterrechtlicher Prinzipien", in: P. Ganea, C. Heath, and G. Schricker, "Urheberrecht, Gestern – Heute – Morgen, Festschrift für Adolf Dietz zum 65. Geburtstag", München, 25–41.

Fitschen, T. (1998). "Protecting Indigenous Peoples and Communities in the Philippines: The Indigenous Peoples Rights Act of 1997", 7 No. 2 International Journal of Cultural Property 526–537.

Frankfurter Allgemeine Zeitung, March 5, 2008, "Die Not zwingt sie zusammen".

Frankfurter Allgemeine Zeitung, November 28, 2008, "Ein Zivilist in der Fremde – Zum 100. Geburtstag von Claude Lévi-Strauss".

Freeman, M. D. A. (1994). "Lloyd's Introduction to Jurisprudence".

Frieden, M. (2000). "Indigene Gesellschaften und geistige Eigentumsrechte – Der potentielle Beitrag geistiger Eigentumsrechte zum Schutz indigenen Wissens", Bern.

Gadamer, H.-G. (1965). "Wahrheit und Methode", Tübingen.

Gálvez Krüger, M. A. (2000). "Más allá de las fronteras – Estudio comparativo de la legislación sobre la actividad artesanal", Lima.

Gehr, R. (1990). "The Lambada Craze", SPIN April 1990, 128.

George, N. (2008). "Feldforschung bei den Huaorani Ecuadors", in: M. Amelung, C. Uzcátegui, N. O. Wallowski and M. Zander, (eds.), "INDIEGEGENWART – Indigene Realitäten im südamerikanischen Tiefland", Berlin, 185–195.

Gierke, O. v. (1943 (orig. Berlin 1889)). "Die soziale Aufgabe des Privatrechts", Frankfurt/M.

Gil, R. (2006). "The Law of the Sé: Linking the Spiritual and Material", in: B. T. Hoffman, "Art and Cultural Heritage – Law, Policy and Practice", Cambridge, New York, Melbourne, Madrid, Cape Town, Singapore, São Paolo, 21–27.

Giraudo, L., Ed. (2007). "Ciudadanía y derechos indígenas en América Latina: poblaciones, estados y orden internacional", Madrid.

Gluckman, M. (1969). "Concepts in the Comparative Study of Tribal Law", in: L. Nader, "Law in Culture and Society", Chicago, 349–373.

Goody, J. and I. Watt (1968). "The Consequences of Literacy", in: J. Goody, "Literacy in Traditional Societies", Cambridge, 27–68.

Gouldner, A. W. (1960). "The Norm of Reciprocity: A Preliminary Statement.", 25 American Sociological Review 161–178.

Grabendorff, W. (2003). "Globalisierungserfahrungen in Lateinamerika", in: M. Mols and R. Ölschläger (eds.), "Lateinamerika in der Globalisierung", Frankfurt a. M., 163–172.

GRAIN (October 5, 2000). "Andean Community Adopts New IPR Law".

Grosheide, W. a. B., J. (ed.), Ed. (2002). "Intellectual property law 2002 – Articles on Cultural Expressions and Indigenous Knowledge", Antwerp.

Grote, R. (1999). "The Status and Rights of Indigenous Peoples in Latin America", 59 ZaöRV 497–528.

Group of Countries of Latin America and the Caribbean (GRULAC) (2001). "Traditional Knowledge and the Need to Give it Adequate Intellectual Property Protection" WIPO/GRTKF/IC/1/5 Annex I.

Group of Countries of Latin America and the Caribbean (GRULAC) (2001). "WIPO Committee on the Relationship Between Intellectual Property, Genetic Resources and Traditional Knowledge", WIPO/GRTKF/IC/1/5 Annex II.

Gruter, M. and R. D. Masters (1998). "Compassion, Common Sense, and Deception: Social Skills and the Evolution of Law", in: B. Großfeld, R. Sack, T. M. J. Möllers, J. Drexl and A. Heinemann, "Festschrift für Wolfgang Fikentscher zum 70. Geburtstag", Tübingen, 91–113.

Gulliver, P. H. (1969). "Case Studies of Law in Non-Western Societies", in: L. Nader, "Law in Culture and Society", Chicago, 11–23.

Hahn, A. v. (2004). "Traditionelles Wissen indigener Gemeinschaften zwischen geistigen Eigentumsrechten und der 'public domain'", Berlin/Heidelberg/New York.

Hann, C. M. (1998). "Introduction: the embeddedness of property", in: C. M. Hann, "Property relations – Renewing the anthropological tradition", Cambridge, 1–47.

Hassemer, M. (2000). "Gewerbliche Schutzrechte im Mercosur – Patent-, Muster-, Sorten- und Kennzeichenschutz in Argentinien, Brasilien, Paraguay und Uruguay", Baden-Baden.

Hassemer, M. (2009). "Biodiversidade e Bem Imaterial – Desafio para o Direito da Propriedade Intelectual", in: K. d. I. Grau-Kuntz and D. Borges Barbosa (eds.), "Ensaios sobre o Direito Imaterial – Estudos Dedicados a Newton Silveira", Rio de Janeiro, 153–167.

Heckenberger et al., M. J. (2008). "Pre-Columbian Urbanism, Anthropogenic Landscapes, and the Future of the Amazon", Science 321, 1214–1217.

Heise, W. (2000). "Die Rechtssituation indigener Völker in Chile: Eine rechtsethnologische Analyse der chilenischen Indianergesetzgebung (No. 19.253) von 1993 vor dem Hintergrund der Schutzbestimmungen im Völkerrecht", Kassel.

Hernández, I. and S. Calcagno (no year). "Indigenous Peoples and the information society in Latin America and the Caribbean: a framework for action", from http://www.unige.ch/iued/wsis/DOC/437EN.PDF.

Hinz, M. O. (2006). "Jurisprudence and Anthropology", in: M. O. Hinz, "The Shade of New Leaves: Governance in Traditional Authority – A Southern African Perspective", Berlin, 459–469.

Hippocrates Aphorisms.

Hirakuri, S. R. (2003). "Can Law Save the Forest? Lessons from Finland and Brazil", Jakarta.

Hobsbawm, E. (1983). "Introduction: Inventing Tradition", in: E. Hobsbawm and T. E. Ranger, "The Invention of Tradition", Cambridge, 1–14.

De Hollanda Sheldrick, C. (2009). "Das Criações Intelectuais Tradicionais Oruindas do Espírito Colectivo Indígena e sua Proteção Jurídica", Revista Criação, Ano I – Número II, 59–101.

Huber, R., J. C. Martínez, et al., Eds. (2008). "Hacia sistemas jurídicos plurales – Reflexiones y experencias de coordinación entre el derecho estatal y el derecho indígena", Bogotá.

Hume, D. (1739). "A Treatise of Human Nature – Being an Attempt to introduce the experimental Method of Reasoning into Moral Subjects".

Ibarra, M. (2004). "Statement by the International Indian Treaty Council", in: S. Twarog and P. Kapoor, "Protecting and Promoting Traditional Knowledge: Systems, National Experiences and International Dimensions", 347–348.

Iepé – Instituto de Pesquisa e Formação em Educação Indígena/Dominique Tilkin Gallois (org.), Ed. (2006). "Patrimôno Cultural Imaterial e Povos Indígenas – Exemplos no Amapá e norte do Pará", São Paolo.

IEPI – Instituto Ecuatoriano de la Propiedad Intelectual (February 2009) "Proyecto de Ley: Protección de los Conocimientos Colectivos, los Saberes Ancestrales y las Expresiones Culturales Tradicionales de las Nacionalidades y Pueblos Indígenas, Pueblo Montucio, Afroecuatoriano, y de las Comunas y Comunidades Ancestrales del Ecuador" (not published, shared by Rodrigo de la Cruz of the IEPI).

Inter-American Court of Human Rights (2007). Saramaka People v. Suriname (Judgment of November 28, 2007 Series C No. 172), from http://www.corteidh.or.cr/bus_fechas_result.cfm?buscarPorFechas=Search&fechaDeInicio=26%2F9%2F2007&fechaDeFin=12%2F31%2F2007&id%5FPais=11&chkCasos=true&chkOPiniones=true&chkMedidas=true&chkSupervisiones=true.

InWEnt and GTZ, Ed. (2005). "Indigene Völker in Lateinamerika: Hintergründe – Fakten", Bochum.

IPHAN – Instituto do Patrimônio Histórico e Artístico Nacional (2007). "Cachoeira de Iauaretê – Lugar sagrado dos povos indígenas dos Rios Uaupés e Papura (AM)", Brasilia.

IPHAN – Instituto do Patrimônio Histórico e Artístico Nacional (2008). "Arte Kusiwa: Pintura Corporal e Arte Gráfica Wajãpi", Brasília.

Irwin, L. (2000). "Introduction", in: L. Irwin, "Native American Spirituality – A Critical Reader", Nebraska, 1–8.

Isaacs, H. (1975). "Idols of the Tribe: Group Identity and Political Change", New York.

Iturralde, D. (1990). "Movimiento indio, costumbre jurídica y usos de la ley", in: R. Stavenhagen and D. Iturralde (eds.), "Entre la ley y la costumbre – El derecho consuetudinario indígena en América Latina", México, 47–63.

Janke (for WIPO), T. (2002). "Minding Culture: Case Studies on Intellectual Property and Traditional Cultural Expressions" Study No. 1, Geneva.

Janke, T. & Company (no year), http://www.wipo.int/export/sites/www/tk/en/folklore/culturalheritage/pdf/janke.pdf, last visited October 20, 2010.

Janke, T. (1998). "Our Culture Our Future. Report on Australian Indigenous Culture and Intellectual Property Rights", from http://www.icip.lawnet.com.au.

Jhering, R. v. (1877). "Der Zweck im Recht", Leipzig.

Jonas, H. (1979). "The Imperative of Responsibility: In Search of Ethics for the Technological Age" (trans. of "Das Prinzip Verantwortung"), Chicago.

Jordán V., G. "Ticos compran molas no autorizadas", La Prensa, July 26, 2004, http://bibliotea.presa.com/contenido/2004/07/26/26-8a-nota1.html, last visited January 10, 2010.

Kayser, H.-E. (2005). "Die Rechte der indigenen Völker Brasiliens – historische Entwicklung und gegenwärtiger Stand", Aachen.

Kloosterman, J. (1997). "Identidad indígena: 'Entre romanticismo y realidad'", Amsterdam.

Kropholler, J. (2006). "Internationales Privatrecht", Tübingen.

Kummels, I. (2008). "Rarámuri (tarahumara): comercio y exportación de plantas medicinales y artesanías en Chihuahua, México", in: R. Sevilla and J. Ströbele-Gregor (eds.), "Pueblos indígenas: Derechos, estrategias económicas y desarollo con identidad", Bad Honnef, 240–248.

Kur, A. (2001). "Funktionswandel von Schutzrechten", in: G. Schricker, Dreier and A. Kur (eds.), "Geistiges Eigentum im Dienst der Innovation", Baden-Baden, 23 *et seq.*

Lao Tsu (1997). "Tao Te Ching", New York.

Larenz, K. and C.-W. Canaris (1995). "Methodenlehre der Rechtswissenschaft", Berlin.

Larrea Richerand, G. E. (2008). "Convención Sobre la Protección y Promoción de la Diversidad de las Expresiones Culturales".

Leibholz, G. (1933). "Die Auflösung der liberalen Demokratie in Deutschland und das autoritäre Staatsbild", München.

Lettington, R. and M. Manek (2001). "Indigenous Knowledge Rights: Recognizing Alternative Worldviews", from http://www.culturalsurvival.org/publications/csq/csq-article.cfm?id=1332.

Levi, J. M. and B. Dean (2003). "Introduction", in: J. M. Levi and B. Dean (eds.), "At the risk of being heard: Identity, indigenous rights, and postcolonial states", Michigan, 1–44.

Lévi-Strauss, C. (1961). "Tristes Tropiques" (translated by John Russell), New York.

Lévi-Strauss, L. (2006). "Patrimônio Imaterial e Diversidade Cultural: o Novo Decreto para a Proteção dos Bens Imateriais", in: Ministério da Cultura/Instituto do Patrimônio Histórico e Artístico Nacional, "O Registro do Patrimônio Imaterial", Brasília, 79–82.

Lipszyc, D. (1993). "Derecho de autor y derechos conexos", Paris/Bogota/Buenos Aires.

Lipszyc, D. (2004). "Nuevos temas de derecho de autor y derecho conexos", Paris/Bogotá/Buenos Aires.

Lisboa, R. S. (2001). "A obra de folclore e sua proteção", in: S. J. Chinelato et al., "Estudos de direito de autor, direito da personalidade, direito do consumidor e danos morais", São Paolo, 57–58.

Llewellyn, K. N. and E. A. Hoebel (1941). "The Cheyenne Way. Conflict and Case Law in the Primitive Jurisprudence", Oklahoma.

López Martinez, A. (2000). "Sistemas Sui Generis para la protección del Conocimiento Tradicional", prepared for the UNCTAD Expert Meeting on Systems and National Experiences for Protecting Traditional Knowledge, Innovations and Practices, 2000, from http://www.unctad.org/trade_env/docs/lopez.pdf.

Lucas-Schlötter, A. (2008). "Folklore", in: S. von Lewinski, "Indigenous Heritage and Intellectual Property – Genetic Resources, Traditional Knowledge and Folklore", Alphen aan den Rijn, 339–506.

Macaulay, T. B. (1997). "Parlamentsrede vor dem englischen Unterhaus, Parlamentsprotokoll vom 5. Februar 1841", 135 UFITA 243–261.

Mader, E. (no year). "Kultur und Globalisierung – Beispiel Kuna (Panama): Molas, Kultur und Globalisierung", in: Mader, "Kultur- und Sozialanthropologie Lateinamerikas, Eine Einführung", from http://www.lateinamerika-studien.at/content/kultur/ethnologie/ethnologie-1213.html, Chapter 7.3.

Mader, E. (no year). "Kultur, Macht, Identität", in: Mader, "Kultur- und Sozialanthropologie Lateinamerikas, Eine Einführung", from http://www.lateinamerika-studien.at/content/kultur/ethnologie/ethnologie-237.html, Chapter 5.1.2.

Maffi, L. (2000). "Toward the Integrated Protection of Language and Knowledge as a Part of Indigenous Peoples' Cultural Heritage", Cultural Survival Quarterly 24 (4), Special Issue "Culture as Commodity: Intellectual Property Rights", M. Riley and Katy Moran (guest eds.) 32–36.

Mann, C. C. (2008). "Ancient Earthmovers of the Amazon", Science 321, 1148–1152.
Manners, R. A. and D. Kaplan, Eds. (1968). "Theory in Anthropology – A Source Book", London.
Markowski, A. (2004). "Der gewerbliche Rechtschutz in den Ländern der Andengemeinschaft", Baden-Baden.
Martinez Medrano, G. and G. Soucasse (no year). "Armonización de la Propiedad Industrial en el MERCOSUR", from http://www.derecho-comercial.com/Doctrina/armoniza.pdf, last visited October 28, 2010.
Meentzen, A. (2007). "Staatliche Indigena-Politik in Lateinamerika im Vergleich – Mexiko, Guatemala, Ekuador, Peru und Bolivien", Lima.
Mercosur (no year), http://www.mercosur.int, last visited November 1, 2010.
Mexico (2008). U.N. Doc. E/C.19/2008/5/Add.2.
Ministério da Cultura and SESC SP (2007). "Prêmio Culturas Indígenas", São Paolo.
Ministério da Cultura and SESC SP (2008). "Prêmio Culturas Indígenas, Edição Xincão Xukuru", São Paolo.
Ministério da Cultura – Coordenação-Geral de Direito Autoral (2007). Nota Técnica/CGDA/SPO No. 002/07.
Ministério da Cultura – Secretaria de Identidade e da Diversidade Cultural (2006). "Seminário Nacional de Políticas Públicas para as Culturas Populares", Brasília.
Ministério da Cultura/Instituto do Patrimônio Histórico e Artístico Nacional (2006). "Patrimônio Imaterial: O Registro do Patrimônio Imaterial – Dossiê final das atividades da Comissão e do Grupo de Trabalho Patrimônio Imaterial", Brasília.
Ministerio de Comercio e Industrias – DIGERPI (1991) "Nota dirigida al Congreso General Kuna".
Ministerio de Comercio e Industrias – DIGERPI (2002). "Población (cantidad) y Comunidad Beneficiada – Titulares", *Boletín del Registro Oficial de Propiedad Industrial* No. 123 of November 18, 2002, available at http://mici.gob.pa, last visited September 23, 2010.
Ministerio de Comercio e Industrias – DIGERPI (2009). "Crop garanties disposability of raw material for art handicraft," news of October 21, 2009 on http://www.mici.gob.pa/index2.php, last visited November 2, 2009.
Ministerio de Comercio e Industrias – DIGERPI (no year). "Catálogo de Propiedad Industrial Panamá", Panama City.
Mohawk (Irokesen) (1992). "Spruch der Mohawk (Irokesen)", in: K. Recheis and G. Bydlinski, "Weißt du, dass die Bäume reden? – Weisheit der Indianer", Wien.
Mols, M. (2009). "Lateinamerikas internationale Zukunft. Der Subkontinent zwischen 'Dependencia' und Globalisierung", in: S. Scheuzger and P. Fleer (eds.), "Die Moderne in Lateinamerika – Zentren und Peripherien des Wandels", Frankfurt a. M., 51–69.
Monroy Rodríguez, J. C. (2006). "Las Expresiones Artísticas de las Culturas Tradicionales y Populares Frente al Derecho de Autor", 11 "El Derecho de Autor – Estudios" (edited by CECOLDA, Colombia) no pages.
Moran, L. M. (1998). "Intellectual Property Law Protection for Traditional and Sacred 'Folklife Expressions' – Will Remedies Become Available to Cultural Authors and Communities?", 6 U. Balt. Intell. Prop. J., 109–116.
Müller-Plantenberg, C. (2008). "Territorios y Ccooperación – Pueblos indígenas en el Brasil", in: R. Sevilla and J. Ströbele-Gregor (eds.), "Pueblos indígenas: Derechos, estrategias económicas y desarollo con identidad", Bad Honnef, 173–190.
Nader, L. (1969). "Introduction", in: L. Nader, "Law in Culture and Society", Chicago, 1–10.
Nader, L. (1990). "Harmony Ideology – Justice and Control in a Zapotec Mountain Village", Stanford.
Nader, L. (1996). "Preface", in: L. Nader, "Naked Science", New York, London, xi–xv.
Nader, L. (1996). "Anthropological Inquiry into Boundaries, Power, and Knowledge", in: L. Nader, "Naked Science", New York, London, 1–25.
Nader, L. (1996). "The Three-Cornered Constellation – Magic, Science, and Religion Revisited", in: L. Nader, "Naked Science", New York, London, 259–275.

Nader, L. (2002). "The Life of the Law – Anthropological Projects", Berkeley, Los Angeles, London.
Nader, L. and H. F. Todd Jr. (1978). "Introduction", in: L. Nader and H. F. Todd Jr. (eds.), "The Disputing Process – Law in Ten Societies", New York, 1–40.
Nordmann, M. (2001). "Rechtsschutz von Folkloreformen", Baden-Baden.
Ochoa García, C. (2002). "Derecho Consuetudinario y Pluralismo Jurídico", Guatemala.
Ohly, A. (2003). "Geistiges Eigentum?", Juristen Zeitung (JZ) 545–554.
Organization of American States (OAS) (2004). Declaration of Mexico.
Otero Lastres, J. M. (2002). "Los diseños industriales en la Decisión 486 del Acuerdo de Cartagena", Medellín.
Pacón, A. M. (2004). "The Peruvian Proposal for Protecting Traditional Knowledge", in: S. Twarog and P. Kapoor, "Protecting and Promoting Traditional Knowledge: Systems, National Experiences and International Dimensions", New York/Geneva, 175–180.
Pahud, E. (2000). "Die Sozialbindung des Urheberrechts", Bern.
Parnell, P. (1978). "Village or State? Competitive Legal Systems in a Mexican Judicial District", in: L. Nader and H. F. Todd Jr. (eds.), "The Disputing Process – Law in Ten Societies", New York, 315–350.
Peru – Government of Peru (2008). U.N. Doc. E/C.19/2008/5/Add.4.
Peterson Royce, A. (1982). "Ethnic Identity: Strategies of Diversity", Bloomington.
Peterson Royce, A. (1982). "The Phenomenon of Ethnicity", 216 Science 48–49.
Pflüg, M. A. (2000). "Pimadaziwin – Contemporary Rituals in Odawa Community", in: L. Irwin, "Native American Spirituality – A Critical Reader", Nebraska, 121–144.
Phaedrus (no year) "Plato in Twelve Volumes", Vol. 9, translated by Harold N. Fowler (Cambridge, MA, Harvard University Press 1925), available at http://www.perseus.tufts.edu, last visited December 6, 2010.
Pierce, J. L., T. Kostova, et al. (2003). "The State of Psychological Ownership: Integrating and Extending a Century of Research", 7 Review of General Psychology, 84–107.
Plattner, H., C. Meinel, et al. (2009). "Design Thinking – Innovation lernen, Ideenwelten öffnen", München.
Posey, D. A. (1994). "International Agreements and Intellectual Property Right Protection for Indigenous Peoples", in: T. Greaves, "Intellectual Property Rights for Indigenous Peoples", 223–251.
Posey, D. A. and G. Dutfield (eds.) (1996). "Beyond Intellectual Property. Toward Traditional Resource Rights for Indigenous Peoples and Local Communities", Ottawa.
Posey, D. A. and K. Plenderleith (eds.) (2004). "Indigenous Knowledge and Ethics – A Darrell Posey Reader", New York and London.
Pospíšil, L. (1969). "Structural Change and Primitive Law: Consequences of a Papuan Legal Case", in: L. Nader, "Law in Culture and Society", Chicago, 208–229.
Presidência da República Federativa do Brasil (1996). "Sociedades Indígenas e a Ação do Governo – Aspectos Legais", from http://www.planalto.gov.br/publi_04/COLECAO/INDIO4.HTM.
Prieto, E. (1990). "Derecho consuetudinario indígena en la legislación paraguaya (siglo XX)", in: R. Stavenhagen and D. Iturralde (eds.), "Entre la ley y la costumbre – El derecho consuetudinario indígena en América Latina", México, 315–331.
Puri, K. (1993). "Copyright Protection for Australian Aborigines in the Light of Mabo", in: M. A. Stephenson and S. Ratnapala, "Mabo: A Judicial Revolution. The Aboriginal Land Rights Decision and Its Impact on Australian Law", Brisbane, 132–164.
Purnell, J. (1995). "Popular Resistance to the Privatization of Communal Lands in 19th Century Michoacán".
Ramsauer, T. (2005). "Geistiges Eigentum und kulturelle Identität", München.
Rehbinder, M. (1967). "Die Begründung der Rechtssoziologie durch Eugen Ehrlich", Berlin.
Rehbinder, M. (1998). "Universalität im Zeitalter der Globalisierung? Eine Auseinandersetzung mit dem anthropologischen Rechtsbegriff von Leopold Pospíšil", in: B. Großfeld, R. Sack,

T. M. J. Möllers, J. Drexl and A. Heinemann, "Festschrift für Wolfgang Fikentscher zum 70. Geburtstag", Tübingen, 200–214.

Ricketson, S. (1987). "The Berne Convention for the Protection of Literary and Artistic Works: 1886–1986", London.

Ríos de Davis, L. C. (2002). "Cuestionario sobre experencias nacionales en la protección jurídica de las expresiones del folclore – Respuesta de Panamá", from http://www.wipo.int/export/sites/www/tk/en/consultations/questionnaires/ic-2-7/panama.pdf.

Rivera-Zea, T. (2006). "El Conocimiento Tradicional en la Visión Indígena", from http://www.wipo.int/export/sites/www/tk/en/ngoparticipation/ind_loc_com/pdf/rivera-zea.pdf.

Roffe, P. (2007). "América Latina y la Nueva Arquitectura Internacional de la Propiedad Intelectual: de los ADPIC–TRIPS a los Nuevos Tratados de Libre Comercio", Buenos Aires.

Röhl, K. F. (1974). "Das Dilemma der Rechtstatsachenforschung", Tübingen.

Ruiz, M., I. Lapeña, et al. (2004). "The Protection of Traditional Knowledge in Peru: A Comparative Perspective", 3 Wash. U. Global Stud. L. Rev. 755–797.

Ruiz Muller, M. (2004). "Regulating Bioprospecting and Protecting Indigenous Peoples' Knowledge in the Andean Community: Decision 391 and Its Overall Impacts in the Region", in: S. Twarog and P. Kapoor, "Protecting and Promoting Traditional Knowledge: Systems, National Experiences and International Dimensions", New York, Geneva, 241–262.

Ruiz Muller, M. (2006). "La protección jurídica de los conocimientos tradicionales: Algunos Avances Políticos y Normativos en América Latina", Lima.

Rüthers, B. (1986). "Rechtsordnung und Wertordnung – Zur Ethik und Ideologie im Recht", Konstanz.

Rüthers, B. (2009). "Das Ungerechte an der Gerechtigkeit", Tübingen.

Ryffel, H. (1974). "Rechtssoziologie", Neuwied.

Sant' Anna, M. (2006). "Avanços da Política de Salvaguarda do Patrimônio Cultural Imaterial", in: Ministério da Cultura/Instituto do Patrimônio Histórico e Artístico Nacional, "Patrimônio Imaterial: O Registro do Patrimônio Imaterial – Dossiê final das atividades da Comissão e do Grupo de Trabalho Patrimônio Imaterial", Brasília, 9–11. (cited as Sant' Anna (2006 I)).

Sant' Anna, M. (2006). "Relatório Final das Atividades da Comissão e do Grupo de Trabalho Patrimônio Imaterial", in: Ministério da Cultura/Instituto do Patrimônio Histórico e Artístico Nacional, "Patrimônio Imaterial: O Registro do Patrimônio Imaterial – Dossiê final das atividades da Comissão e do Grupo de Trabalho Patrimônio Imaterial", Brasília, 15–21. (cited as Sant' Anna (2006 II)).

Santilli, J. (2003). "Biodiversidade e conhecimentos tradicionais associados: novos avanços e impasses na criação de regimes legais de proteção", in: A. Lima and N. Bensusan (eds.), "Quem cala consente? Subsídios para a proteção aos conhecimentos tradicionais", São Paolo, 53–74.

Santilli, J. (2006). "Intangible heritage and collective intellectual rights", in: F. Mathias and H. de Novion, "The Crossroads of Modernities – Debates on Biodiversity, Technoscience and Culture", São Paolo, 81–98.

Schack, H. (2007). "Urheber- und Urhebervertragsrecht", Tübingen.

Schack, H. (2010). "Internationales Zivilverfahrensrecht", München.

Scheuzger, S. (2009). "Mestizierung und Moderne in Mexiko", in: S. Scheuzger and P. Fleer (eds.), "Die Moderne in Lateinamerika – Zentren und Peripherien des Wandels", Frankfurt a. M., 101–137.

Schillhorn, K. (2000). "Kulturelle Rechte indigener Völker und Umweltvölkerrecht – Verhältnis und Vereinbarkeit", Berlin.

Schlinkert, J. C. (2007). "Lebendige folkloristische Ausdrucksweisen traditioneller Gemeinschaften – Rechtliche Behandlungsmöglichkeiten auf internationaler Ebene", Berlin.

Schneider, A. (1992). "Traditional, Entlehnung, Werkbegriff: Anmerkungen zu den Entscheidungen 'Brown Girl I'/'Brown Girl II' des BGH", 2 GRUR 82–85.

Schweitzer, A. (1966). "Die Ehrfurcht vor dem Leben – Grundtexte aus fünf Jahrzehnten", München.

Semper, F. (2008). "Die Rechte der indigenen Völker in Kolumbien", in: M. Amelung, C. Uzcátegui, N. O. Wallowski and M. Zander, (eds.), "INDIEGEGENWART – Indigene Realitäten im südamerikanischen Tiefland", Berlin, 141–155.

Shrestha, R. (2006). "Celestial Gallery", San Rafael (California) (cited as Shrestha (2006 I)).

Shrestha, R. (2006). "Goddesses of the Celestial Gallery", San Rafael (California) (cited as Shrestha (2006 II)).

Sierra, M. T. (1990). "Lenguaje, prácticas jurídicas y derecho consuetudinario indígena", in: R. Stavenhagen and D. Iturralde (eds.), "Entre la ley y la costumbre – El derecho consuetudinario indígena en América Latina", México, 231–258.

Sierra, M. T. (no year). "Usos y desusos del derecho consuetudinario indígena", from http://www.juridicas.unam.mx/publica/librev/rev/nuant/cont/44/pr/pr2.pdf.

Solomon, T. (2000). "Dueling Landscapes: Singing Places and Identities in Highland Bolivia", 44 Ethnomusicology 257–280.

South-American Nations (2008). "Tratado Constitutivo de la Unión de Naciones Suramericanas of May 23, 2008", http://www.comunidadandina.org/unasur/tratado_constitutivo.htm.

Special Rapporteur on the situation of human rights and fundamental freedoms of indigenous people, R. S. (25 November to 7 December 2007). U.N. Doc. A/HRC/6/15/Add.2.

Starr, J. and J. F. Collier (1987). "Historical Studies of Legal Change", 28 Current Anthropology 367–372.

Stavenhagen, R. (1988). "Derecho Indígena y Derechos Humanos en América Latina", Mexico City.

Stavenhagen, R. (1990). "Derecho consuetudinario indígena en América Latina", in: R. Stavenhagen and D. Iturralde (eds.), "Entre la ley y la costumbre – El derecho consuetudinario indígena en América Latina", México, 27–46.

Stavenhagen, R. (1992). "La situación y los derechos de los pueblos indígenas de América", Comisión Interamericana de Derechos Humanos, Washington.

Stavenhagen, R. and D. Iturralde (1990). "Introducción", in: R. Stavenhagen and D. Iturralde (eds.), "Entre la ley y la costumbre – El derecho consuetudinario indígena en América Latina", México, 15–25.

Stoll, P.-T. and A. von Hahn (2008). "Indigenous Peoples, Indigenous Knowledge and Indigenous Resources in International Law", in: S. von Lewinski (ed.), "Indigenous Heritage and Intellectual Property – Genetic Resources, Traditional Knowledge and Folklore", Alphen aan den Rijn, 7–57.

Straus, J. (2008). "How to Break the Deadlock Preventing a Fair and Rational use of Biodiversity", 11 The Journal of World Intellectual Property, No. 4, 229–295.

Suagee, D. B. (1992). "Self-Determination for Indigenous Peoples at the Dawn of the Solar Age", 25 University of Michigan Journal of Law Reform 671–749.

Suagee, D. B. (1994). "Human Rights and Cultural Heritage: Developments in the United Nations Working Group on Indigenous Populations", in: T. Greaves (ed.), "Intellectual Property Rights for Indigenous Peoples", Oklahoma City, 191–208.

Süddeutsche Zeitung, December 7, 2010, "Alternativer Nobelpreis: Erwin Kräutler – Ein Bischof gegen das Kartell".

Tajfel, H., and J. Turner (1979). "An Integrative Theory of Intergroup Conflict", in: W. G. Austin and S. Worchel (eds.), "The Social Psychology of Intergroup Relations". Monterey, CA, 33–47.

Taubman, A. (2006). "Is there a right of collective personality?", 28 European Intellectual Property Review, no 9, 485–492.

Taubman, A. and M. Leistner (2008). "Analysis of Different Areas of Indigenous Resources – Traditional Knowledge", in: S. von Lewinski, "Indigenous Heritage and Intellectual Property – Genetic Resources, Traditional Knowledge and Folklore", Alphen aan den Rijn, 59–179.

Teixeira Coelho, D. M. (2008). "As Comunidades Tradicionais Indígenas Brasileiras têm Direitos Autorais Colectivos?", 92 Revista da ABPI 61–63.

Thaler, R. H. and C. R. Sunstein (2009). "Nudge - Wie man kluge Entscheidungen anstößt", Berlin.
The Economist (Nov 14–20, 2009). "Brazil takes off – A special report on business and finance in Brazil".
Tobin, B. (2002). "Protecting Collective Intellectual Property Rights of Indigenous Peoples Related to Biodiversity in Peru", in: S. Laird (ed.), "Biodiversity and Traditional Knowledge – Equitable Partnerships in Practice", London, 386–388.
Torremans, P. (2008). "Copyright (and other intellectual property rights) as a Human Right", in: Torremans, P. "Intellectual Property and Human Right", Alphen aan den Rijn, 195–215.
Torres, R. (1991). "The Rights of Indigenous Populations: The Emerging International Norm", 16 Yale Journal of International Law 127–175.
Twarog, S. and P. Kapoor, Eds. (2004). "Protecting and Promoting Traditional Knowledge: Systems, National Experiences and International Dimensions", New York and Geneva.
U.N. Department of Public Information (2007). "General Assembly adopts Declaration on Rights of Indigenous Peoples", from http://www.un.org/News/Press/docs//2007/ga10612.doc.htm.
U.N. Doc. A/61/L.67.
U.N. Doc. E/C.19/2008/L.7 (2008). Recommendations on Implementation of UN Declaration of Indigenous Rights made by the Permanent Forum on Indigenous Issues.
U.N.-Subcommission on Prevention of Discrimination and Protection for Minorities (1984) "Study of the Problem of Discrimination Against Indigenous Populations, Report of the Working Group on Indigenous Populations on Its Third Session".
U.S. Department of State (no year). "Background Notes", from http://www.state.gov/r/pa/ei/bgn/.
UNEP – United Nations Environment Programme (2010). "State of Biodiversity in Latin America and the Caribbean", from http://new.unep.org/dec/PDF/LatinAmerica_StateofBiodiv.pdf.
Union of South American Nations (UNASUR) (2008). South American Union of Nations Constitutive Treaty of May 23, 2008, from http://www.comunidadandina.org/ingles/csn/treaty.htm.
Unterguggenberger, T. (1999). "Das Urheberrecht in der Andengemeinschaft", Baden-Baden.
Valiente López, A. (2002). "Panama's Indigenous Intellectual Property Law", from http://www.dd-rd.ca/site/publications/index.php?id=1346&subsection=catalogue.
Valiente López, A. (2006). "Régimen jurídico de protección a la Mola como manifestación cultural", Panama City.
Valiente López, A. (2008). "La jurisdicción indígena en la legislación panameña", in: R. Huber, J. C. Martínez, C. Lachenal and R. Ariza, (with the Foundation Konrad Adenauer), "Hacia sistemas jurídicos plurales – Reflexiones y experencias de coordinación entre el derecho estatal y el derecho indígena", Bogotá, 203–237.
Venezuela (2008), U.N. Doc. E/C.19/2008/5/Add.7.
Verdross, A. and B. Simma (1984). "Universelles Völkerrecht – Theorie und Praxis", Berlin.
Vilaça, M., E. Portella, et al. (2006). "Carta da Comissão do Patrimônio Imaterial Brasileiro" (1999), in: Ministério da Cultura/Instituto do Patrimônio Histórico e Artístico Nacional, "Patrimônio Imaterial: O Registro do Patrimônio Imaterial – Dossiê final das atividades da Comissão e do Grupo de Trabalho Patrimônio Imaterial", Brasília.
von Lewinski, S. (1994). "Urheberrechtsharmonisierung im Andenpakt – interessant auch für Europa?", 6 GRUR Int. 470–472.
von Lewinski, S. (2007). "Adequate protection of folklore – a work in progress", in: P. Torremans (ed.), "Copyright Law – A Handbook of Contemporary Research", Cheltenham/Northampton, 207–231.
von Lewinski, S. (2008). "Final Considerations", in: S. von Lewinski, "Indigenous Heritage and Intellectual Property – Genetic Resources, Traditional Knowledge and Folklore", Alphen aan den Rijn, 507–529.
Weber, M. (1978 (1922)). "Economy and Society" (Roth, G. and C. Wittich, eds.), Berkeley.
Weber, M. (1976). "Wirtschaft und Gesellschaft", Tübingen.

Wendland, W. B. (2002). "Intellectual Property, Traditional Knowledge and Folklore: WIPO's Exploratory Program", 4 IIC 485–504 and 606–621. (cited as Wendland 2002 I).

Wendland, W. B. (2002). "Intellectual Property and the Protection of Cultural Expressions: The Work of the World Intellectual Property Organization (WIPO)", in: W. a. B. Grosheide, J. (eds.), "Cultural Expressions and Indigenous Knowledge", Antwerp, 101–138. (cited as Wendland 2002 II).

WIPO (2001). "Intellectual Property Needs and Expectations of Traditional Knowledge Holders – Report on Fact Finding Missions (1998–1999)", Geneva.

WIPO (2006). "Draft Document: Customary Law & the Intellectual Property System in the Protection of Traditional Cultural Expressions and Traditional Knowledge: Issues Paper – version 3.0", from http://www.wipo.int/export/sites/www/tk/en/consultations/customary_law/issues-revised.pdf, last visited March 15, 2010.

WIPO (2008). "The Protection of Traditional Cultural Expressions: Draft Gap Analysis", WIPO/GRTKF/IC/13/4(b) Rev., available at http://www.wipo.int/edocs/mdocs/tk/en/wipo_grtkf_ic_13/wipo_grtkf_ic_13_4_b_rev.pdf, last visited October 28, 2010.

WIPO (2010). "The Protection of Traditional Cultural Expressions/Expressions of Folklore: Revised Objectives and Principles", WIPO/GRTKF/17/4 Prov.

WIPO Secretariat (2005). "International Experiences in the Sui Generis Protection of Handicrafts", WIPO National Seminar on Omani Traditional Values in a Globalized World, Muscat, February 13 and 14, 2005.

WIPO/UNESCO (1985). Commentary on the Model Provisions.

Wörrle, B. (2008). "Hacia un modelo cooperativo para el uso comercial de plantas medicinales, y conocimientos tradicionales en la Amazonía ecuatoriana", in: R. Sevilla and J. Ströbele-Gregor (eds.), "Pueblos indígenas: Derechos, estrategias económicas y desarollo con identidad", Bad Honnef, 231–239.

Zweigert, K. and H. Kötz (1992). "An Introduction to Comparative Law", Oxford.

MIX
Papier aus verantwortungsvollen Quellen
Paper from responsible sources
FSC® C105338

FSC
www.fsc.org

If you have any concerns about our products,
you can contact us on
ProductSafety@springernature.com

In case Publisher is established outside the EU,
the EU authorized representative is:
Springer Nature Customer Service Center GmbH
Europaplatz 3, 69115 Heidelberg, Germany

Printed by Libri Plureos GmbH
in Hamburg, Germany